GLOBAL ECONOMIC STUDIES

GLOBALIZATION DYNAMICS

PSYCHOLOGICAL, ECONOMIC, TECHNOLOGICAL, AND CULTURAL INTERCOURSES

GLOBAL ECONOMIC STUDIES

Additional books in this series can be found on Nova's website
under the Series tab.

Additional E-books in this series can be found on Nova's website
under the e-books tab.

GLOBAL ECONOMIC STUDIES

GLOBALIZATION DYNAMICS

PSYCHOLOGICAL, ECONOMIC, TECHNOLOGICAL, AND CULTURAL INTERCOURSES

KUANG-MING WU
EDITOR

Nova Science Publishers, Inc.
New York

Copyright © 2012 by Nova Science Publishers, Inc.

All rights reserved. No part of this book may be reproduced, stored in a retrieval system or transmitted in any form or by any means: electronic, electrostatic, magnetic, tape, mechanical photocopying, recording or otherwise without the written permission of the Publisher.

For permission to use material from this book please contact us:
Telephone 631-231-7269; Fax 631-231-8175
Web Site: http://www.novapublishers.com

NOTICE TO THE READER

The Publisher has taken reasonable care in the preparation of this book, but makes no expressed or implied warranty of any kind and assumes no responsibility for any errors or omissions. No liability is assumed for incidental or consequential damages in connection with or arising out of information contained in this book. The Publisher shall not be liable for any special, consequential, or exemplary damages resulting, in whole or in part, from the readers' use of, or reliance upon, this material. Any parts of this book based on government reports are so indicated and copyright is claimed for those parts to the extent applicable to compilations of such works.

Independent verification should be sought for any data, advice or recommendations contained in this book. In addition, no responsibility is assumed by the publisher for any injury and/or damage to persons or property arising from any methods, products, instructions, ideas or otherwise contained in this publication.

This publication is designed to provide accurate and authoritative information with regard to the subject matter covered herein. It is sold with the clear understanding that the Publisher is not engaged in rendering legal or any other professional services. If legal or any other expert assistance is required, the services of a competent person should be sought. FROM A DECLARATION OF PARTICIPANTS JOINTLY ADOPTED BY A COMMITTEE OF THE AMERICAN BAR ASSOCIATION AND A COMMITTEE OF PUBLISHERS.

Additional color graphics may be available in the e-book version of this book.

Library of Congress Cataloging-in-Publication Data

ISBN: 978-1-62100-750-0
ISSN: 2163-3940

Published by Nova Science Publishers, Inc. † New York

CONTENTS

Introduction: Globalization: Its Necessity, Its Difficulties, Its Essentials		vii
A. Problems and Prospects		1
Chapter 1	Debt Cancellation: A Global Solution and Win-Win Task *John Wu*	3
Chapter 2	Unfulfilled Promises of Globalization: Global Knowledge Production and Africa *Shimelis Assefa*	17
Chapter 3	Globalization as Problem: Globalization and NGOs in Bangladesh: Contradictions in Development *Rezaul Islam* and *John Morgan*	35
Chapter 4	Taoism in Western Therapy of Anxiety *Ruth Chao*	55
Chapter 5	Globalizing Counseling Paradigm: From the United States of America to the World *Chu-hui Chao*	71
B. Cultural Intercourse		83
Chapter 6	Globalization as Localization *Chung-yue Chang*	85
Chapter 7	Globalization: Its Twin Threats to Cultures *Yun-ping Sun*	103
Chapter 8	Beginnings: The Global Crossings of Classical Daoism *Jay Goulding*	119
Chapter 9	Medicine East and West *Masami Tateno*	135
Chapter 10	"Ever the Twain Shall Meet," Two Thinking-Types in Synthesis in Tension *Zailin Zhang*	155

C. Global Dynamics — 169

Chapter 11   Translation in Globalization   **171**
Kuang-ming Wu

Chapter 12   History in Globalization   **195**
Tang Ruei-hong

Chapter 13   Globalization as Ecology   **215**
Kuang-ming Wu

Chapter 14   Globalization as Togetherness   **237**
Kuang-ming Wu

Chapter 15   Globalization as Ubiquity-Move   **265**
Kuang-ming Wu

Chapter 16   Globalization as Interculture: Cultures Inter-Frame to Interculture   **289**
Kuang-ming Wu

Index   **329**

INTRODUCTION: GLOBALIZATION: ITS NECESSITY, ITS DIFFICULTIES, ITS ESSENTIALS

ABSTRACT

As of today, not many scholars at all, much less thoughtful people, have even noticed "globalization" as a thinking-horizon, much less begun engaging in its exploration. One aim of this modest anthology is to call attention to this exciting dimension of globalization. "problems and prospects" and "cultural intercourse."

In the first division, "problems and prospects," concrete and specific problems and prospects kicked up by globalization are cited in world economics of cancellation of debt of developing nations (J. Wu), Africa's problem of knowledge production (Assefa), economic problems of foreign aids in Bangladesh (Islam and Morgan), infusion of Taoism to Western therapy of anxiety (R. Chao), and globalizing counseling paradigm (C. Chao).

In the second division, "cultural intercourse," globalization as concrete cultural intercourse is kicked off by Chang and Sun. Both sensitively spot the problem of today's globalization to lie in monocultural dominance to threaten the survival of local cultures. Chang's solution is globalization in the direction of localization. Sun offers interculture equal and various as a solution.

Goulding exemplifies local interculture concretely by offering the panorama of dialogues among scholars East and West in the specific arena of Daoism, which is generalized as East-West meeting by Zhang.

It is amazing how two words with the same meaning-content of "all-inclusive" have incredibly different meaning-impacts. Endangered by rare use, "universality" is close to extinction. It is quite cold and remote, almost forgotten by us all now, far from being cared about except by oddballs such as professional philosophers. In sharp contrast, "globalization" is hotly in fashion today as a cutting-edge common sense term on the street corners, a buzzword constantly on the mouths of experts and common folks alike.

Sadly, however, as with any buzzword such as "democracy," globalization is more nodded at and praised than really known, or deeply pondered on its benefits and harms, much less carefully put into practice to benefit us all. Globalization is a popular antonym to "selfishness," a "bad guy" to avoid and never avoided.

"Globalization" is a publicly acknowledged "good guy" to be with and never has really been with, as it is a description we all are in the know, and is constantly misused. Buzzwords are an empty fashion often to harm without serious consideration of its pros and cons. The aim of our anthology lies precisely here, that globalization can never be buried as an unexamined buzzword to turn into a live land mine to explode to devastate us all, but must be carefully pondered on and prudently practiced.

Now, what "buzzword" is must be explained. Buzzwords are common coins freely circulating in public realm, honored as something "technical." To understand this strange situation of "common technicality," let us look at "system." System is literally things and thoughts standing-together. Togetherness can be tightly and coercively implicated, and it can be freely and situationally coherent.

Conceptual implication differs from notional coherence.[1] "Implication" tightly connects precise concepts with mathematical coercion. "1+1" must yield "2" and no other. A triangle must have three lines, each demanding the other two, and no other. Being "coherent" is no less tight among matters notional, while seeing their connections freely open, as time goes on. An example can help.

When my dear friend dies, I am of course saddened (tight), and can *then* be deepened by sorrow, or can grow cynical, or turn compassionate, or something else quite otherwise (open).[2] All these possibilities are reasonable when having seen happened, yet unpredictable in advance. Coherence is retrospectively understandable—"It was inevitable, given this fact and that"—but prospectively unknown, for anything can happen. Such is history, situationally tight in time, i.e., spatially tight while opening out in time. So, having an implicative system differs from being coherently systematic.

Co-implication is conceptual. Conceptual implication comes about by computing concepts coercively, mathematically. Conceptual implication is cherished by academic scholars, whose researches and reports express their trials, constantly trying for such conceptual comprehensive coverage of all actual cases, and constantly coming short. Their failures are a conceptual dynamo to push their researches "ahead."

In contrast, coherence is notional, to reveal the situation. We understand, notionally, when we are told that the soft drips of dripping spring drizzles, heard at home as we sip a cup of hot tea, nestle and calm our souls, to be settled in composure, at home in ourselves; it feels so good, at home, being tenderly spring-moistened. Such description, by such story as this, is situationally coherent, while allowing all sorts of situational "exceptions" such as being sick or sad, and being deepened pain by soft dark rain.

Notional coherence in some such way as this *shows* the situation by telling *stories*, as we just did above. Do we remember the kindergartners' "show and tell"? Theirs is the most telling showing. It is thus that notional coherence is favored by scholars and common folks alike. We all settle here, explaining things with half-baked ideas evoked by stories, thereby elucidating situations as we think in thoughts shown by telling stories.

---

[1] "Concept" pulls out with mind-forceps abstract ideas from actuality. "Notion" notices matters noteworthy within actuality. See my On the "Logic" of Togetherness: A Cultural Hermeneutic, Leiden: Brill, 1998, pp. 344-353. But we here concentrate on the implication vs. coherence contrast, so we bypass the concept vs. notion contrast, though the former contrast is closely related to the latter, as is shown by how implication is contrasted with coherence, which are two sorts of a system.

[2] Situational tightness is well described by P. H. Nowell-Smith in Ethics (1954), UK: Pelican Original, 1965, but he missed its historical openness, and so he missed situational coherence.

Journalists, economists, politicians, musicians, historians, fiction writers, and many such reflective people, with genteel grandmothers so warm and understanding, constantly do such notional elucidation, telling us stories to enlighten us. Thus coherent story-notions turn into popular buzzwords, such as "health," "normal," "life," "happy," and their opposites, "honorable," "civilized," "ethical," "unique," "right," and their opposites; and now "globalization" comes onto the scene. They are all compact stories.

"How does storytelling make things and events coherent?" This is a good question, and its answer is rather complex. When we look ahead, things just happen haphazardly, without rhyme or reason. When we look *back*, however, things appear to have happened as they should have, given this fact and that factor. Their story tells how orderly things happened in retrospect by our telling of them prospectively, so their story "catches time by the tail," as Sartre put it aptly.[3]

Actually, though, storytelling of such two-way traffic is how history always goes, a retrospective prospective going, a looking back to story-tell ahead. Things happening are thus made coherent in time-way, backward ensured, forward open and alive. After all, afterthought is better thought, as they say. The historian looks back, sees through events, sorts them out, unpacks their whats, hows, and whys, and then packs them into compact stories quite poetic, for poetry is compacted story, the most stuff told in the least words.

"Don't push the river," says someone. Well, we cannot help but "push *ourselves*" in the river of time, by retrospection into prospective gazing, and the indifferent river of time-flow turns into music of human history singing forward. Quite often, then, history and its stories soar to poetic heights, as *Mr. Tso's Commentaries* 左傳 and *History Records* 史記 do in China, the culture par excellence of history.

Such is system-alive, being systematic in time, performing and singing the music recorded by the past, or rather, the music as we at present record the past and sing it as history. Story-thinking is history-thinking as coherence-thinking. Here all notions are compact stories awaiting our unpacking and intoning. "We are born storytellers," said Sartre the great storyteller, and so we all take to notional coherence-thinking in storytelling, as fish take to water. Buzzwords are born here, circulating among us all, commoners and scholars alike.

But all this makes it so difficult to tell a story of globalization, for its history is so young; the word "globalization" was coined just yesterday, in 1951.[4] And so, we have not much at all to look back to tell forward, much less to conceptually implicate anything, for globalization has no concept to implicate, at least not yet.

Precision coerces thinking and excludes imprecision. Coherence invites a variety of sorts of thinking and includes information, the more the merrier. Human thinking requires dovetailing one style of thinking into the other. The dovetailing bespeaks globalization. So, globalization is our natural paradigm at this basic level of thinking. This point is set and settled as our common goal. What remains open is how to dovetail conceptual thinking into story-thinking, and precision into coherence.

---

3 Jean-Paul Sartre, Nausea, NY: New Directions, 1964, pp. 56-59; this was his virgin publication, and it was naturally an instant bestseller. On storytelling as a crucial alternative to analytical thinking, see my Story-Thinking: Cultural Meditations, NY: Nova Science Publishers, 2011.

4 Merriam-Webster's Collegiate Dictionary, Eleventh Edition, 2008, p. 532. Its previous editions did not have this entry.

As of today, not many thinkers or thoughtful people at all have even noticed globalization as such a thinking-horizon, much less begun engaging in its exploration. One aim of this modest anthology is to call attention to this exciting dimension of globalization. Chapters in "cultural intercourse" and "features of globalization" do touch on this dimension.

We can thus only freely roam around in our present global situation, at least notionally, in mere 16 points below and 16 essays that follow. They all dot themselves into a sort of vignettes adumbrating "globalization," as the sun dots on shimmering leaves and grass to tell of the dawn all over the world, the first creation of "globalization."

In such a manner as this, globalization erupts as a buzzword today reasonable and open, coherently understandable yet open and unpredictable and vastly futuristic. No one knows what it definitely and comprehensively means, yet everyone *knows* what it is at its base. We all know that globalization is an élan-verb, expanding our inter-prosperity worldwide, and so pan-poverty and monocultural dominance have no place in globalization of pan-togetherness.

And so, globalization leads to our shared imperative to fight against cutthroat inequality and competition, to strive together toward our win-win inter-need to trade off mutual strengths to turn the vast globe into our tiny neighborly Global Village, humming along in the music of buddy-togetherness. What follows just unpacks all this in the compact story-notion of "globalization" coherent and open.

Now, here are some free points, floating as mere sixteen, less than twenty, freely jotted down to turn inter-penetrating inter-crisscrossing. They freely roam to show how free and inevitable globalization is, as it is our blood constantly circulating in our nature within Mother Nature. We die dried out, hardened, without this gutsy current strongly flowing through us as "globalization."

1. Sky as Globalization

"Globalization" is in fashion today. This world-climate did not exist in the 17th century Renaissance when we were barely beginning to note "global togetherness" as critical for humanity, although it was sporadically shouted aloud among the Pre-Socratic sophists (sadly, Socrates did not pick it up) and flashed out as a Confucian joy and dream of "within Four Seas are all brethren" (sadly, this dream was soon smothered in national sociopolitical concerns).

"Globalization" is indeed in fashion worldwide today, but actually we humanity have been aspiring for it at least since we began to think. When we hit on something "true," we are excited because we expect what we find is true everywhere every-when for everyone, such as "one and one together make two." Globalization is our dream of discovering something true of everywhere anytime for anyone. "Universal truth" is a tired cliché for this intense romance, this undying dream of ours. We die without this diehard dream of global universality.

No wonder, globalization of this sort is our constant rationale behind all our pursuit of researches, all our engagements, even our buying things serviceable, and so the Better Business Bureau in USA tries to ensure such "reliable" business practices. Globalization is the be-all and end-all of our life-engagements. Mathematics is cherished, technology is trusted, and international businesses and communications flourish today, all to show that globalization-dream has actually blossomed globally, or at least has begun to do so.

Introduction   xi

This globalization-dream is in worldwide fashion, we are living it now, consciously though unawares. Globalization is truly budding global now. Now, to think of it, isn't this fact as it should be? Don't all activities living and non-living end up here, aspiring to be globalized? Isn't globalization the Wonderland of all Alices of all ages? Isn't it because globalization is *actually* the be-all and end-all of all things, all lives, and all projects human and non-human?

Moreover, isn't globalization our joy, our reason for living for us all? What is living if it is not living together? What is togetherness if not living together worldwide in cosmic concord? No wonder, the ancient Greek sophists dreamed of it and lustily promoted it, and it is also ancient China's zeal, shouting, "We are all brethren within Four Seas!" And then the dream of cosmopolitanism spread among the Renaissance French and German humanists, and later fought for by the American revolutionaries and avidly promoted by its transcendentalists. Globalization is literally "our sky" to reach for.

2. Sky vs. Globalization

Sadly, however, this dream of globalization is as intense and global as it is amazingly far away from us all, for no one really knows what it is, much less has seriously practiced it. It is as unreachably high as the sky. For example, suppose someone, such as a child, asks what "sky" is, what shall we do?

We point upward, but they still ask what it is, for all we all see is an expanse vast and empty, and there is nothing specific we can name as "sky." We think we know the sky, for after all it is a common ordinary noun, until we try to look and see and describe it, and we cannot even look *at* it, for it is so vast everywhere we look up. We only know the sky is up, an unlimited horizon upward.

"Sky" is then *our* verb upward, up, up, and we are lost up there nowhere. "Up nowhere' is a verb unlimited, not even a UFO, an "unidentified flying object," for the sky is not even an *object* at all, for it is all empty, as China aptly calls it "sky empty 天空.". The word "sky" describes not an object out there but *our* movement upward unlimited, a horizon infinite, infinitely expanding as we look up and go upward in imagination. Globalization is such a sky, vast, unlimited, and unknown.

3. Globalization as *Our* Life-Verb, Unknown

We have just thought about the sky, because the "globe" is all that is "under the sky 天下," as China tells us. "Globalization" is likewise a "globe" made into a verb, "globalize," and then fitted in as a noun, "globalization," for our ease of lugging it around, whatever "it" is. But we do not see the globe, which is nowhere, much less can we "globalize," for we do not know how to globalize whatever we have or do.

Worse yet, we cannot even look up to the "globe" as we look up at the sky. The astronauts bring us from up there some pictures of our globe as a blue beautiful ball, but that is so much out of this world, so unreal, so incredible, having nothing to do with our actual seeing here now. All we see here now is that "globalization" describes *our* movement toward some totality of our world, and our "world" is another something so familiar yet so much unknown, as something like a 'totality of our lives together" that is far beyond what we know, for we do not know what "totality" here means.

Thus, strangely, the common honorific word "globalization," what we think we all know, turns out to be all unknown to us. Besides, we would have thought "globalization" is an object out there or an objective movement, and yet we end up realizing that globalization is about us ourselves and our own movement unknown toward our unknown.

Globalization is such a protean word so frustratingly difficult to understand. Is it a description of an object, objective fact, or objective movement? Or is it a description of us, or of our own activity? Or else, is it a description or a prescription, what we would understand or what we should do? Or does it mean all of these? But then, how could a mere simple word mean all these different meanings?

4. GLOBALIZATION AS TOGETHERNESS

We are driven into a dead-end. But then, "That's it!" we would suddenly shout, and things tumble into place. The globe is our world, which is our lives together worldwide, this whole bit, although our "whole" is ever beyond our grasp. We just vainly stare, not even knowing what to stare *at*, where to stare *to*. It is thus that our "globe" is rightly made into a verb, "globalize," to describe our movement that draws us all together, on and on forward.

So, globalization is our horizon of togetherness unlimited, ever expanding as we draw ourselves into a bunch, and the bunch tries to reach its maximum that we do not even know what it is. The maximum is our horizon our "globe," and our soaring toward it, beyond our reach here now. It is our verb made into a noun, "globalization."

We are so stunned at all this that we must repeat this stunning discovery that is yet so important. The sky is our fantastic upward look into somewhere unlimited; "globalization" is even more fantastic, for we cannot even look up, for we do not even know where to look, what to look at, and yet we know it is about us-all.

And so, "globalization" describes our movement toward such our unknown so intimately known (it is us) yet so vastly unknown (us all). Its maximum is our horizon, our "globe," and our soaring toward it beyond our reach now is our verb "globalize" that is then made into a noun we call "globalization" so mysterious.

5. GLOBALIZATION AND PROFIT

So, globalization is our movement to make the globe global. The "globe" has today been made to appear as it is, called a "Global Village"; it is made up of us all, together. Actually, however, we ourselves are not behaving as villagers of this worldwide Village. We are each trying to profiteer out of each of us, nothing global but quite tribal and local, and our local-tribal mind is ruining nature globally.

Profiteering itself is not evil, though. If we want to profiteer, we must profiteer *globally*, for happiness of us all is obviously much greater joy than happiness among a tiny local group. We in selfishness are not greedy enough! We must profiteer together for us all globally, enhancing Mother Nature that is global. "We all together for us all" is where globalization is heading, but such goal is still far ahead of us in petty selfishness. This globalization-goal constantly beckons at us individually to grow global vast.

"But, then, what situation of such pan-togetherness would globalization exhibit?" This is a good question. The answer is, it is music of the globe, what is used to be called the "music of the spheres," but this music is here now, not up there in the sky. Let us look into such music of the globe here in this world.

6. GLOBALIZATION AS MUSIC

Our lives come together into music antiphonal, in poetic lyricism that goes on expanding. The music of life is composed of so many diverse notes, each coming alive as distinct and integral in itself, within the captivating music-dynamics of the poetry of global counterpoint. The notes sound in the varied manners we live on, each in our respective ways called "cultures," as we live cultures to compose cultures, to gather into the chorus of interculture worldwide.

"What is music, however?" "Music" is a splendid thing yet so strange, for it is a thing that is a no-thing. Music cannot be touched, smelled, or seen, much less manipulated, and yet it vibrates our whole being and changes us all over. This is because music is many sounds intangible come together as notes, to gather to compose a sheer power to vibrate existence such as our own existence. Music is the power to exist as we.

Togetherness is such power of music, intangible, that absorbs any of us who comes close to it in close attention, as tornado that sucks us into it, but this musical tornado does not ruin us but enriches us and empowers us. Music resonates among us, deep calling deep, one responding to the other, into mutual counterpoints, to compose the poetry of the sense of existence.

The responsive antiphony of poetic music, ever contrapuntally going on, creates intercultures in dialogues that are the dynamics of globalization. Globalization is polyphonically composed of intercultures in dialogues, pointing to counterpoints of claim against counterclaim, asserting and counter-asserting, to learn and enrich each one by the other, expanding as music of one note resonating with another, to go on and on globally.

7. GLOBALIZATION AS AN ETHICS

Now, let us sum up what we have found so far, and then we will see what we *should* behave in life. We saw that "sky" is not a name of something out there, for we do not know what it is; sky is instead a verb of how we move to look up at "it" that we point to but do not know what it is. "Globalization" is not a name of how a globe globalizes, but a verb of how we move together to the maximum worldwide. We are now in business, now that globalization is all of us gathering to the maximum.

Globalization is our gathering together maximized, and although we do not know what such maximum will be, we do know togetherness maximized is togetherness asymptotically expanded to the maximum, and we know what "togetherness" and "expanding" are. Our "togetherness" is another verb made into a noun; it is our gathering.

And we know "we" are a bunch of distinct persons, each living differently one from another. "Different livings" express different ways of living, and "way of living" is "culture." So, "we gathering together" amount to performing "interculture" one to another. Globalization is interculture maximized, globalized. In short, interculture describes how globalization operates. Interculture is the *modus operandi* of globalization, and "we" *are* such an operation global, on our way to globalization. We are global on our globalization way.

Seeing what we are, as globalization on its way, makes us aware of what we should be and behave. To be it is one thing; to become it is another matter. To be it unawares is one thing; to know it and fulfill it is an ethical matter. Being it implicates the obligation to know it and become it, and fulfill it. Now, the most important content of the "it" here is that we are global as above described, that therefore we must stop behaving as if we are still "local," "tribal," and locked up in petty selfishness.

8. GLOBALIZATION AS REVOLUTION OUT OF LOCALIZATION

All this means that we must revolutionize such our cramped life-attitude into behaving globally, for we *are* global, so we deserve to behave globally. We have an obligation to ourselves to become what we are, to become global. That is what "globalization" means. We have its enemy in "localization," an opponent of "globalization." Being "local" has three meanings we may not have noted before.[5]

Selfish profiteering, individual or corporate, at the expense of others, individuals or corporate, is the *first* variety of being local, and the most apparent. Such selfish profiteering is rampant as shameless "localization," especially at a corporate and political level, against globalization to retard globalization, for ages. This selfishness is our disease, ubiquitous, historic, and chronic, of all humanity.

The *second* variety of "localization" is insidious and invisible, coming to us as a fashion taken for granted. It is monocultural dominance, taking "*our* way of thinking and behaving" as "of course, global," as what all of us, in our culture and others' cultures, must "naturally" adopt and live by. Globalization as interculture together is thus stampeded to death by both varieties, selfish and monocultural, of *localization*.

Corporate selfishness, political and economic nationalism included, and monocultural domination worldwide, have no shame in displaying themselves raw and naked. They are blatantly out there confronting us all around. Such shameless "enemies" we must engage in our concerted efforts to demolish, in our persistent performance of globalization together, as befitting togetherness as *performing* globalization.

Thirdly, besides both varieties of local domination, intercultural dialogues will be snuffed away also by this subtle but obvious case of selfishness, exploitation of others. Common sense decides on the limit of "use" beyond which is abuse of "exploitation." Let us take an example from academia.

---

[5] This explication of what "local" means here avoids being in conflict with Dr. Chang's great chapter, "Globalization as Localization" below.

My common sense that offers service says that I can be gladly used to comment, and critically complement, your own essay, not to complement an essay created by your student, and then cap your name (with student's) onto it. I will be also exploited-abused if you want me to create an entire report, and you just cap your name onto it as its author. Such moves provoke my protest.

To benefit from my critical comments on your own view is to properly use me with profit. To appropriate my view and pretend it as your own wholesale is to exploit to profiteer on me. To react to my critiques on *your* view is to use me profitably, and quite properly. Simply to take over *my* view and proclaim it as yours is an abusive exploitation.

From your exploitation, I would have to withdraw myself, thereby withdraw from non-existent exchange, heartfelt, of life-orientations, now ruined by exploitation. After all, it is to such intercultural dialogue, in honest respectful inter-disagreement to inter-influence, that each of us is dedicated, and offers to properly be "used."

The whole problem of exploitation lies in a lack of gutsy confrontation of authentic integrities. In music, mere technical accuracy to perform pretty tunes amounts to mere ability to use language to talk, to turn oneself into a chatterbox babbling out pretty chats so empty. Such emptiness of the person hurts the person's very humanity.

"But what do you mean by authenticity of the person?" Listen to *early* Dvorak, Haydn, and even Mozart, whom conductors and performers tend to avoid. They go more naturally and *real* than toying with tunes, or worse, manipulating melodies to manipulate music and its audience. Toying and manipulating empties away the person's integrity. Can you hear *him* in his composing, in the playing of his composition? *That* is the question. Schubert is deep and lonesome, while Dvorak is nakedly warm in his Bohemian rural milieu. Can we hear *them*?

Moreover, it is easier to hear them in their "early" music, Dvorak's and all.[6] We bow before them in their early periods. "Early" is a kid rugged, coarse, and gutsy real, as the sunflower-seeds *simply* roasted, salt-free. Their seed-power is directly eaten into us, as we taste its real power. Now hear this real story.

I went to a Target store so huge, and I was amazed at how much junk was cranked out to dazzle us customers, with "price cut" on them. Isn't there a way to lift the quality out of such low taste? And then, I saw kids running out. And all my uneasiness and question were instantly melted away. Those kids had nothing, quality or no quality—they simply had nothing. And their parents had to follow them around; they lead the way! I felt then that they are higher in quality—don't ask me what it is—than any adult around. Their gutsy voices, almost shouting so vibrant, filled the air. High quality filled the air.

9. Our Failure, Our Task

Unfortunately, all this is much easier said than done. Amazingly, we all know what gathering together means, how concord, heartfelt togetherness, is to be cherished, and yet no one, never at any single moment in history, has really practiced togetherness, exactly as we know what sky is, and yet no one has really probed what the sky is, and so no one really knows what the sky is, even though our astronauts have repeatedly gone up. Their difference

---

[6] Later Dvorak cherishes every note and follows tunes erupting from his Bohemian soil. Later Dvorak is early Dvorak growing "early."

is that our ignorance of the sky matters much less than our ignorance of globalization. The sky-ignorance is academic; the globalization-ignorance is tragic.

In any case, our task of globalization is thus incredibly difficult, enormously sky-high. All of us have dreamed about globalization since time immemorial, and not a single one in history has actually fulfilled our shared intense dream. We must look closer at our task of globalization as our cherished concord worldwide. We will look closer at globalization as togetherness, togetherness as meeting, meeting as dialogue, and then will realize the challenge and the enemy of such dialogical togetherness, globalization. This is what this book of anthology aims to do for us.

10. GLOBALIZATION AND TOGETHERNESS AGAIN

Globalization is often regarded as spreading whatever there is, and "whatever" is taken as "what I want." This is the standard structure of the tyranny of dictatorship, political and/or economic, accompanied by destruction of whatever others there are that differ from what I want. This is a "zero-sum game." History tells us of ruins all around of such efforts at spreading "what I want." People tirelessly practice such self-destructive version of globalization, its outrageously falsified version. This is our common practice since time immemorial that keeps destroying all of us.

"Whatever I want I want to spread" does not work, simply because "what I want" needs others different from me to work. The zero-sum needs the more-sum with others. "I" need "difference" and "others" to be "I" at all, as "A is A" needs "A is not no-A." "What I want" needs—as the word "want" means "in want of"—"what is different" to gather together. Togetherness with all others all different is globalization proper.

What goes around in respect of differences of others comes around as enrichment of my self-integrity, and here what "goes out" goes *before* what "comes in." What "goes to others" is the necessary condition of what "comes to me." This process structures togetherness that automatically spreads as globalization.

This stance of togetherness with different others looks suspiciously threatening to my "I want" desire, though. "Going out respecting others different" seems to destroy what I have already, what I have hoarded to protect my dear self. The fact is, however, this "me only, against others" actually overlooks—to ruin me—an important fact that concerns my very existence.

This crucial fact is that I myself came into existence—was born—by my parents together, giving themselves to me, who were and are different from me. Moreover, I continue to come into richer existence solely by continuing my parental self-giving to others different, as my parents continue giving me as of this moment, by giving themselves to me who am their "other, different" from them.

Self-hoarding originates in fear of self-loss. Where such fear comes from is unclear, but clearly this fear is contrary to the fact, sheer simple fact, that the best self-protection is self-giving for other-protection, as, again, what goes around giving to others comes around enriching myself *with* others. In music, each note must give itself over to others to become a great note that it is within music. Music such as of quartets and symphonies sings the togetherness of self-giving of notes to others different, to become the notes themselves now deepened.

To realize that all this is true revolutionizes our life-stance, turning us from "I want to preserve myself" to realizing "self-preservation *is* self-giving in self-loss" so that "other-enrichment enriches me myself." Those who want to save themselves lose them; those who lose themselves for others save themselves enriched.

As we perform charity just for others, our charitable acts enrich us ourselves with others. Globalization as togetherness is our basic imperative toward basic simple existence, to enrich all existence as coexistence to inter-exist. Globalization proper *begins* here self-giving, at our base, and ends here giving, as our end-all.

Let us now impress ourselves on the close interrelation between globalization and togetherness, as when we see one, we see the other. "Globalization" is today floating around as a strange "common technical term"—what contradiction!—in the same manner as "togetherness" is. Both terms are significant, and they even inter-elucidate, yet neither has ever been carefully examined, much less elucidated. Years ago, I dared to initiate the task in my *"Logic" of Togetherness*.[7] Now, I am collecting thoughtful essays from various parts of the world on various aspects of togetherness-globalization.

"You all go ahead and do all such globalization and togetherness bits. But just leave me alone, ok?" O, No. No one can be left alone. "Lifeboat Ethics"[8] that lets others die out of "our lifeboat" is a terrible, unethical illusion. We are all on the same boat-of-life called Mother Nature. We float and swim and sink together, in nature, with nature. This is the case for three reasons.

One, we have together depleted natural resources. Either we must conserve, nurture, and cultivate natural recourse, or else we, "you" included, perish in sheer natural depletion. Moreover, this is because, two, our very existence is coexistence to inter-exist. "A is A" obtains only in contrast to a not-A, as not no-A. In other words, three, we are by nature born of Mother Nature and raised by her; as she gives us birth she continues to suckle us together. We survive together or perish together, in Mother Nature.

Mother Nature is our vital milieu in which we live, move, and have our being. Deprived of this milieu wild and natural, we are deprived of ourselves. "You are talking about ecology here, not globalization." Well, ecology is globe our household to manage, and such management of globe-as-home *is* globalization. Ecology and world togetherness form a synonymy with globe to compose globalization.

We are thus intimately related to the globe as the globe literally lives us. We see how significant they are and how significantly related they are. They form a pair of palms of life as its asymmetrical counterparts, to aptly and indispensably guide our thinking and behaving. Our thinking and behaving are each uniquely in situ, yet with ubiquitous significance, though not "theoretically universal." Besides, both globalization and togetherness compose a totally concrete whole, embracing theoretical thinking. Both inter-clarify to inter-elucidate, to co-typify the essential direction in which all thinking, body-thinking and analytical thinking, should proceed.

---

[7] Kuang-ming Wu, On the "Logic" of Togetherness: A Cultural Hermeneutic, Leiden: Brill, 1998.

11. WORLD CLIMATE OUR LIBERATION

Globalization ciphers worldwide; togetherness expresses interculture. Globalization must be intercultural; interculture must be cosmopolitan. Short of such global togetherness, any of our thinking turns cramped, crippled, and monocultural, to self-imprison in human hubris, with stench of haughty petty "orthodoxy." Such "orthodoxy" is a murderous crime against the whole humanity in the name of non-existent Truth, such as Western universality of logical thinking as the universal road to universal truths envisaged by such universally inerrant methodology.

Our ubiquitous modernity gives us this gift of global togetherness to alert us to this danger. It is a delightful fashion quite cosmopolitan. In this cosmopolitan light, monocultural "universality" is exposed as monocultural, as Western universality logical and mathematical, side by side with, say, Chinese universality storytelling historical. For example, the West abhors contradictions, while China thrives on them as the Yin and the Yang internecine internascent.

It is in such manners as these that each culture's contribution is valuable to all, to enrich and enliven all. In contrast, monocultural domination kills valuable intercultural enrichment that is true globalization. We are thus so grateful for this climate of world opinions. Essays in the following pages adumbrate what "globalization" as global togetherness is, inter-enriching.

Various features of globalization as these can be cited indefinitely, without end. Enough has been presented here, though, for us to savor what "globalization" typically is, and how it functions. It remains the fact, however, that globalization is so common everywhere everywhen, and yet at the same time it is so amazing, so unsuspected, as to be seldom practiced well as it should be. This is a sad global fact.

12. FAILURE AS HOPE

Now, as we are saddened for our failure to practice globalization, we suddenly meet this stunning thoughtful stunt. Globalization is all-inclusive of all our life praxes, which include our failure to practice globalization. Thus globalization includes as its part our failure in globalization, and so, paradoxically, our failure to practice globalization practices it. Stop failing in globalization, and we would stop practicing globalization.

In other words, in globalization it is all right to fail in globalization, as long as we keep trying at it. After all, "failure" shows the struggle that has failed, as spilt milk shows an existence of milk spilt. As long as we *keep* failing, we have hope; continual failure mothers hope of success. We must continue trying, in the midst of continuous failing. Our failure generates our obligation to continue struggling, defying failures.

But "defying" may be a mistaken expression. Children enjoy what adults call "failures," for their "work"—actually they don't work, they just play—comes out "funny," and it is fun to come out funny, and so *their* "work" is no tedious workout at all, but just part of their play, to grow up. We the kids of all ages must also enjoy continuing "failing," then.

---

[8] See Lifeboat Ethics, eds. George R. Lucas, Jr. and Thomas W. Ogletree, NY: Harper & Row, 1976. Cf. Lester R. Brown, Tough Choices: Facing the Challenge of Food Scarcity, NY: W. W. Norton, 1996.

In the world of children, failure is the royal road to maturity. Their life is made of "seven falls, eighth, rise" of a tumbler, and both falls and rises are fun! Kids are tumblers alive. We call their tumbling "failing," and so they are professional "fail-ers." The more they play failing, the more they grow. No fail, no growing. It is in the fun of playing failures that they grow. It is in the fun of failing globalization that globalization grows.

13. Propitious Foreboding

Still, failure remains failure, not struggle, even though failure ciphers struggle. Fortunately, we do have concrete practices in life that forebode well our turning of brutal zero-sum game into the cooperative more-sum tradeoffs into win-win prospect of pan-prosperity. We see at least five such propitious examples, i.e., sex, family, art appreciation, dialogue, and interculture.

In sex that develops family, you are my flesh of flesh, the bone of my bones. In art appreciation that features dialogue and inter-culture, you are needed to enhance my deepening of camaraderie insights and enlightenment, even through, and especially through, our disagreements. The more we are together of this sort, the merrier and richer we turn among us *all*.

Besides, the second set—art appreciation, dialogue, and interculture—naturally extend from the first set of sex and family, as we ourselves were brought into existence by parental sex and nurtured in the family to grow up into mature self. Thus these five activities belong to our innate nature. None of them has room for fabrication or deception. Falsehood or scheming collapses them into something *else*.

In music composition, for example, the composer shows through as he truly is. Performance of music shows the performer, how blockish and clumsy he is, and even how deceptive or manipulative he is. "What performer takes to which compositions" shows through both composers and performers. In music, the person's sinews are swaying, his heart is throbbing, and we are moved. Sex, family, and intercultural dialogue are at the base of our life-music, to feature our paradigms of authenticity, of being truly ourselves, self-composed.

These five praxes are our task quite natural, essential, and pleasant as the baby struggling to crawl, and then toddle, and then walk to run away to be chased after by his parents. All these five praxes are growing activities that please people surrounding us, parents, siblings, relatives, and friends alike. Thus all these activities are performed on the win-win people that your gain prospers my gain. They are globalization in miniature ready anytime to crawl, toddle, and run away all over the world.

14. Globalization in Time

"I can see that globalization in space spreads worldwide, and that innately and naturally, as you have described. But does globalization spread in *time* for eternity? We humans are so bodily fragile, living only a hundred years at most." We agree that we humans are physically fragile in bodies so temporal.

Even ancient Chuang Tzu in China agreed twenty-five centuries ago, saying (22/39), "People within sky and earth are like a white colt passing through a door crack." But do we realize that we today are reading this saying, and we are sure people in later days will be reading it, too, and there is no time-limit for "later days"? Let us repeat. This statement, made 25 centuries ago in faraway China, with a fragile body, about our temporal fragility, is still here now and will last indefinitely whenever it is read, and "whenever" has no time-limit.

Another telling example is Schubert who lived only up to the age of 31. He is one of the composers who died the youngest, younger even than Mozart who lived to 35. Still, Schubert's music composed by his fragile, shy, and young self is continuing to be performed today and later indefinitely, all by no less fragile human beings. His music so feeble lasts and lasts with his fame that lasts and lasts.

Besides, music itself is notoriously note-temporal, for its notes vanish as soon as they sound out. Still, every time the notes are sounded forth, the milieu typical of Schubert emerges to make us sigh, and "every time" and "make us sigh" are so physical, so fragile, and yet "every time" never fades and perishes, nor do "we."

Chuang Tzu's ancient statement made by his perishing body, and its bodily readings by later bodily readers, continue to last and last, time without end. Schubert's bodily compositions, and their subsequent bodily performances, and bodily listening, also continue to last and last without time-limit. Every time Chuang Tzu's fragile statement is read, the reader of all ages sighs. Every time Schubert is performed, his sentiment comes alive to be present among us, at any age. This "every time" and this "every age" have no time-limit; they last forever.

Thus our body is an amazing existence. It is fragile, limited, and ephemeral, on one hand, *and* lasting without time limit throughout the globe, on the other. The same timelessness holds for bodily insanity of Nero and Hitler, and many other less than admirable fragile characters; they are no less bodily and physical.

In short, globalization spreading our fragile bodily existence is timeless, what China calls "incorruptible 不朽" without time-limit. Globalization is a time-verb making history worldwide. Globalization is a time-bomb that makes history that has no end. Such is the dynamics of globalization spreading worldwide in time. Globalization is togetherness in time as well as in space.

It is with good reasons that China has an expression, "spring, autumn 春秋," for autumn is also the spring when crickets serenade themselves mating toward their births later soon. Autumn is the "June bride" season, the spring, for the insects. Their decease soon in winter is spring to the next generation to spring up. Thus, their autumn mating dies in self-giving into the baby-joy in the spring-dawn.

When in autumn, is winter far? So, autumn is spring to the winter. When in winter, is spring far? So, winter is spring to the spring. Spring is spring to summer, summer is spring to autumn, and so every season is spring to the next season. Every season is thus the spring, and every moment is dawn to the next moment. Every "now" dawns the next, and so "now" is spring to "next now."

By the same token, thinking generates a thought to dawn the next thought that thinks *its* next. Thinking is a potential potently actualizing, and "potential actualizing" is the spring generating the next season. Every generation generates the next, so every moment is a spring.

We notice here that "every" has been repeated, and "noticing" and repetition of "every" are globalization in time.

Let us come back to ourselves here. In all our fragility, we are *homo viator*, humans on our way in globalization, and our being on our way into globalization is itself globalization in process, globalization as the verb of globalizing dynamics, cosmopolitan and historical, world without end.

What remains for us to explore is the variety of globalization, at least some typical features of it, if we cannot cover it in its entirety. These features will give us the parameter of the expanding horizon unlimited of globalization, to chart the directions in which we ought to strive. It is to this purpose that the present anthology is dedicated.

15. GLOBALIZATION AS PAN-GIVING

Hush, pal! Let me divulge a secret, an open secret. Globalization begins at a win-win more-sum game. The win-win arrangement begins at an outrageous joy of *giving* away something precious to you and to me, what both you and I cherish. This is because I like to give you "my joy of owning something I like," to see you smile, and your smile makes me smile. Smile is contagious, and no one minds it.

My smile at your smile begins "you win so I win, I win so you win," the win-win management to yield more-sum joy. This is the structure running through all the five previous examples of sex, family, art appreciation, dialogue, and interculture. They all interchange to inter-change both you and me. In fact, I can give something to you and forget my giving in my joy at your smile. It is what all kids do. It is sheer happiness.

In contrast to all this, "need" describes poverty, starvation, and pain. Kids do not understand need, for the kids live in win-win giving to forget giving. All those kids know is their *need* to give away what they like to anyone they like. Giving is thus more blessed than receiving because giving quenches our thirst to receive smiling satisfaction.

"This situation obtains only when there is enough to go around, though." Well, we do not know such comprehensive "there is enough." In fact, the contrary situation holds, that such situation of "there is enough" obtains only when giving all around happens. So, this logic of giving reverses the logic of getting that whines, "This situation obtains only when there is enough to go around."

The simple fact is this. The more we give, the more we would have to go around. The more we get, the worse our need gets. Giving makes riches to go around, to make everyone prosper. Giving is the secret joy of the "win-win game." We have just hit upon the key to win-win toward prospering globalization process.

The key—the giving—is our open secret that belongs to kids, who just love secrets, and love to tell secrets all around! Loving to *share* secrets is one manifestation of giving something special away. Again, here is a win-win tradeoff to perform the more-sum game. If this is not globalization, nothing is. Globalization is such a more-sum game to spread all over into win-win for us all.

The spring mist descends on us all, birthing unceasing. The spring is the kids, telling us that kids can afford to give because they are in the embrace of Mother Nature. Mom is nature inside us and around us, giving the spring mist away to us our own lives. To realize so, and keep this fact firmly in mind—for we tend to forget *this*—makes us all kids of all ages. It is the blessing all around to give all around. What gives around goes around, and then it comes around to give us all. That is Mother Nature, and that is Mom's riches of the spring mist that moistens us all. That is globalization.

Now, to go around to coming around is to return. To return is the Way things go around, by giving things around. To return is the move of the Way, says Lao Tzu (40). It is the recycling way of Mother Nature. We remember Lao Tzu admires and cherishes Primal Mother (6). Mother is empty because mother empties herself in giving herself away to give birth to her kids, and she herself is enriched in all her love of her kids.

That is the ultimate of giving, to give away the whole motherly and parental self. Such self-giving is fullness, says Christianity as well, as it points at Christ's self-emptying to us all as the fullness *of* Christ who fulfills us, enriching us all.[9] Here Christ and Lao Tzu glance at each other and smile. That is globalization going around giving around into all riches in win-win more-sum of all with all.

Have you noticed the same phrases coming around as rounds of music? All this sings the music of the spheres that are round, and goes around in circles, and the more the music encircles giving around, the louder the music of joy sounds, in silence of the spring rain, hitting the window-panes to slide down into tulips' soil, and the tulips nod as they sprout into mature blossom. Meanwhile, the raindrops hitting makes music, soothing us into sleep unawares. Such spring music disturbs no one. Such hitting, soft and silent, calms our souls into slumber, as the baby sleeps all the time. The hitting of spring rain induces *this* baby sleeping to grow so fast so unawares.

After all, now, anytime now, is the spring the season of sprouting. The spheres' music sings spring life. This is because music is coherent to open out. Coherence is rhythm all around; to open-out rhymes ahead. The phrase, "rhyming ahead" has two senses. One, A differs from B, so that A calls to B as B calls on A, and in their mutual calls, A is deepened by B into more true and real A, as B is tuned up by A into more authentic B. Two, such mutual tunings did not exist before their mutual rhyming resonation, and so their tunings advance forward in time.

Now, as "rhythm" internally resonates into a coherence of self-integrity, the rhythm rhymes with what is coming that is created by the rhyming resonation of A and B, what are actually the self A opening out into the new self, B. This is the dynamic open coherence of music. The old self A is tuned and turned into the new self B due to the self A inter-responding with A's alter ego, the other B.

Thus A and B are the self in different periods of time, *and,* at the same time, A and B are also two different selves, A as the self and B as A's alter ego different from A. So, A and B are same and different, and such same difference ciphers open coherence, the movement of rhythm rhyming *ahead*. Such is the dynamic structure of the music of togetherness that is globalization.

And so, mind you, togetherness and globalization are both music-verbs. Such is the dynamics of music, and it is globalization spreading itself global. Globalization is the spring of the music of round-spheres, where the more the giving goes around, the merrier the riches come all around. Such spring is all silent also, to soothe and lull us into slumber by softly hitting our soul our soil, in rhythm rhyming forward.

---

[9] Philippians 2:6-11. You can see how I radicalized Paul's ode to Christ-centeredness.

"Things are actually all-cutthroat. They are never as rosy as you portray, pal. Please be realistic." I have three responses to your advice supposedly realistic. One, I do not consider as of now what and how things "actually" are, for we have been pursuing the meaning of our *innate* togetherness. Besides, two, we do have the spring birthing, in kids shouting giving. In sex, family, and art in dialogue and appreciation, things are quite actual but not cutthroat. They enable existence. Listen, faintly chirping the birds are at dawn, while they are being constantly ruined by squirrels and snakes.

Three, we must be really realistic about being "realistic." Being realistic means not blindly-following brutal facts as brutal and no more, but seeing the dawn of globalization among brutality of things after brutality of things. The dawn is silver-lines peeping through some things of dark clouds; they are quite otherwise than brutality darkness, and peeping *within* the darkness.

After all, actuality cannot last forever in "pan-brutality alone," which is an unrealistic scenario. Somehow brutality is fed by spring-birthing, and brutality somehow contributes to spring-birthing, believe it or not. "No birthing of existence" would have disabled brutality from taking place. Besides, brutality of zero-sum game can be the background, the foil, and the catalyst, to more-sum win-win management. In fact, it actually—realistically—goes this way.

Flowers grow out of muddy sludge and are not muddied. Weal somehow leans behind woes. The dark clouds have sliver-linings. Science calls such strange unpredictable phenomena "contingency." "It's been tried for ages. It's been useless." This attitude of resignation assumes that the past rules the future, as scientific experiments operate on the ruling assumption, "as in the past, so in the future."

Western science is thus the science of the past. But the past rules no future; the past can never *always* predict future. Actuality is contingent. Don't we like the weather? Wait a minute. It is changing. Dogged persistence in the right direction can win *our* future. When these brutalities take place, lift up our heads, for our joy is drawing near!

Mother Monica prayed for her prodigal son, Augustine, for nineteen long years. Augustine finally turned around into a saint. Those who stick it out come out ahead. Here "stick it out" and "come ahead" express maternal "giving." Constant outrageous giving out, even to the extent to "love enemy," results in melting away all enmity *to* capture the entire hearts and souls, both of our enemy and of ourselves, *to* win us as we win them. And the "to" of "to us and to them" is "giving out."

All this describes being "realistic" in the winter snow, and the patches of snow left shall be beautiful decoration of spring, to seep into the soil of blossoming grass so green so tender. That is "realistic togetherness" of globalization marching on. Do giving, never give up. Keep going giving among the wailing all around, with kids playing while still wet in their dirty cheek with tears. Be of good courage. Behave maternal "like a man" in persistent caring in giving.

The parents instinctively beg and plead with their baby to allow them to feed him. The baby's refusal to be fed means he is sick, and his parents will be worried through all their sleepless night. The baby is the parents' glory and pride, the flesh of their flesh, the bone of their bones. Praising the baby praises the parents, who give their *entire* selves to nurturing him. The baby just grabs them all in, as if nothing is the matter. His grabbing makes the parents so very happy, as if they won an award. Such is the basic self-giving as the basic existential innate joy-receiving.

Such parent-baby joy spreads all around. In a TV show, "Gomer Pyle," a man told his mother to just sit at the seashore and watch the waves. She almost died. Then Pyle asked Mom to cook and entertain his whole platoon of hungry gangs. What busy hours ensued! What vivacious confusion they had! Mom came out all alive threading through all this commotion back and forth! Mom needs them as they need her. She gives them a dinner and joy, as they give themselves shouting and grabbing the foods she cooks for them, to delight her with pride! Their mutual needs are their mutual giving of joys.

Let us generalize this inter-giving delight. C. S. Lewis quoted Lamb[10] saying that among the friends A, B, and C, A sees B in C, C sees A in B, and C sees A in B, and B in A. the process goes around so much so that A is much richer than A standing alone, and so is B, and so is C, because each gives of all herself to the other unstintingly, in all smiles. Any hoarding of any sort here means a loss of the self. In contrast, in erotic love, exclusive hoarding of each other is the rule. Friendship is a splendid thing to go around eagerly, the more the merrier. Total liberal giving receives total swelling of all in all.

And A, B, and C yearn to double up their threesome enrichments in D, E, and F, *and* to expand both their double threesomes twofold, threefold, and more, and more, until the whole Global Village is composed of tens of thousand-folds of A, B, Cs. Such delightful duplication *process* is globalization ongoing, world without end.

Such self-duplications are heartfelt, intimate, and completely free, without encumbrance of whatever sort, as "friend" aptly etymologically means "love free," and that is why they are quite irresistible. We cannot help but expand friendship on and on, and on, the farther the merrier. Who dare say this is not globalization?

This process of soulful friendship can and must also happen between us contemporaries and the time-honored ancients we honor and cherish. What China calls "with ancient people befriend 與古人為友" ("友" portrays hands clasping) in reading books they left us, never looking down on us anytime anywhere, is our ultimate delight and significance of living. Friendship across the ages makes our life worth living on. Our global Village is a Village history-deep, to define what history as the village of continual friends in time, dynamic, unfinishable, and incorruptible.

Such soulful friendship can also obtain in imagination. My dream last night still lingers on now, in my almost painful yearning after meeting *that* superb violist. He looks like my Dad my hero of all time. As I watched and watched him play that deep viola music, looking far, my eyes were in misty haze. O how I yearn to meet him so tall, so casual, so sublime! We can have as many friendships out there of this intensive sort, waiting for us, as we have people, and perhaps as we have as many animals, plants, precious stones in pebbles, and even in machines.

---

[10] I quote here in my way what C. S. Lewis quotes in his way what Lamb said. See The Norton Book of Friendship, eds. Eudora Welty and Ronald A. Sharp, NY: W. W. Norton, 1991, p. 527, quoting from Lewis' The Four Loves (1960), NY: Harcourt Brace Jovanovich, 1988, pp. 91-92. Lewis forgets to consider three matters. One, these four loves are related in more ways than to be hurriedly lumped up into "charity"; what are these delicate relations, really? Two, these loves are not our manuals of acts but form a milieu in which we live, move, and have our being. Three, these loves are just four tips in the vast warm iceberg of unspeakable love, synonymous with globalization ongoing, the milieu so pervasive that we hardly notice it.

I think this narrow confine of Lewis is due to him being a traditional conservative so literary-persuasive. No wonder, he is much admired as god-sent by conservatives and fundamentalists. To balance him off, see an interesting, though no less imperfect, Friendship: A Philosophical Reader, ed. Neera Kapur Badhwar, Ithaca, NY: Cornell University Press, 1993. Friendship is indeed bottomlessly alive as we are.

And of course we can and must have friend(s) *beyond* friends human, historical, and natural, as we sing, "What a friend we have in Jesus!" We are here in the realm of the Beyond, religion. Dreamed yearning for friendships such as these, in space, in time, in dream, and the Beyond, is the stuff of which our life is made, as friendship. It is this dreamed imagination that never lets us go, and never let us down, for if, god forbid, *this* friendship fails us, we in tears can go to another, and another.

An additional benefit of having friends is that they jolt us—by their sheer contrastive differences, if nothing else—into realizing our own habit of thinking, to expose our assumptions and paradigms we take for granted. Without friendly contrasts, we would have thought our customs and routine ways of thinking are "of course what everyone else in the world has and does." Our manner of thinking is equated with the universality of world thinking.

Such monocultural ethnocentrism is our lethal group-think, all the more ominous for our being unaware of it. The sooner we get out of this ethnocentrism, unaware or not, the sooner the world gets out of cultural chauvinism imposing itself on everyone to death. Friends can help us out of the deathtrap. "How do friends help us?" They do it this way.

Friends serve as my mirrors mirroring *to me* all my freckles, warts, and wrinkles, all without my consent. I cannot avoid such exposures so embarrassing. I ask smugly, "Mirror, mirror, on the wall. Who is the fairest of all?" and back comes its blunt answer, "Not you, dummy." Friendship can be such an unflattering self-exposure to me, far from mutual admiration.

Our time-honored ancient friends are our penetrating mirrors as well. The *Tao Te Ching* and the Bible are two prime examples, but all classics, such as Aesop's Fables, the Grimms' grim stories, and Andersen's kid-stories,[11] reflect back on our own ways of thinking. That is why they are popular classics for all time, the bestsellers of longest sellers the world over, for after all, nothing catches more attention than our "self," and anything that bluntly tells us about our "self" is worth honoring.

This is why we honor these friends ancient and today as classics, as doctors and teachers, as parents and friends. Friends inter-mirror in this way to inter-enrich, often in pain. My friends make me self-aware to self-give, to other-enrich to self-fulfill unawares. We just follow our innate urge to inter-benefit this mirroring way, and friendship spreading this way is globalization ongoing, outgoing.

Still, friendship our mirror is often a bitter pill of sobering self-look, a catalyst to unpleasant self-examination, to painfully make life worth living. In any case, the spread of friendship of difference is one feature of globalization. Globalization is the spice of difference to wake up our taste-bus to the vivacity of living.

Friendship is composed of self-giving. Giving me myself to you gives you and me, to inspire you into giving you to gain you and her, and the more-sum win-win increase of sober joyous smiles spreads all over. More blessed it is to give than to receive, indeed, for giving gives a receiving joy, to receive the joy of such giving. No receiving simpliciter can give such joy as giving gives. To empty myself fills all. It is a continuous series of chain reactions in more-sum investment to yield self-giving smiles all over the globe. This it is that is globalization.

---

[11] I omit all classics in China, most of Greece, India, Italy, Japan, and elsewhere.

Just to envisage such prospect of globalization makes us to take a deep breath in excitement, in the vastness of time and space that composes the music of global spheres. The music of friendship resonates in rhythmic rhymes of friendship, ever enriching, ever expanding. We call it the "cosmos" of Mother Nature, birthing itself in us without ceasing. This it is that is globalization forever globalizing.

Let us put this globalization thrust in an historical manner. We can look at the happenings linearly, and then laterally. The linear view prepares for the lateral view. In *linear* view of events, we chronicle one happening, and then separately chronicle another happening, as we study [1] the climate of public opinion at the time, [2] what were the proximate cause of the event are, [3] how the event actually happened, [4] what the effects were that resulted, and [5] what lessons we can learn from the happening.[12] We study the happenings, one at a time, and one after another, under these five headings.

After our linear studies of separate events, *we* would then see through the events—we choose whatever cluster of events—sideways, comparatively, and come out with our own opinion on what they could mean. This is our *lateral* view and study of the events, connecting in our ways what seem to have happened separately.

And of course this connection expresses *our* opinion, and our opinion can differ according to what we are collectively viewing, how our standpoints come to differ one from another as time goes, and so on. We can cite just four concrete examples, put in question forms, so simple, so sharp-edged.

Our *first* example is Marx-Lenin *Communism*. Marx's passionate advocacy for poor workers the proletariats against oppressive tyranny of the ruling class is turned by his friend Lenin, of all persons, into a massive program for setting up a totalitarian government that oppresses precisely those poor people. My god, what had happened? Why did it happen? What lessons can we draw from this tragic turning?

Our *second* example is "People's Republic of China," *Chinese* Communism. We see no less than three ironic contradictions. One, Chinese history has been boasting of how, twice during Yüan and Ch'ing dynasties, China had been culturally conquering the "barbaric aliens" who had militarily conquered China. Today, however, China is being conquered culturally by alien Communism, even without Communism militarily conquering China. What is happening here?

Two, China has had in its history a school of Legalism, of brutal Realpolitik, and even practiced it to its tragic end in Ch'in Dynasty. Not as major a school as Confucianism or Taoism, Legalism is a counterpart of Communism. Why does China deign to adopt such alien view comparable to a minor school of thought in China? Three, Communism is a totalitarian dictatorial rule, brutalizing the people. Why does it "proudly" tout "people" and "serving the people" all over China and advertising them worldwide? What an insult it is to the *people*! What is going on here?

Our *third* example is popular uprising called "*revolution*." How does the French Revolution compare with the American Revolution? Aren't they similar and different in their origins, in how they transpired, in their results, and in their aftermaths? How do today's Arab Revolts compare with those populist revolutions in France and USA? How do such political revolutions compare with religious revolution called the Reformation? And how do the religious revolution then compare with today's series of Neo-Orthodoxy revolutions of Barth, Bonhoeffer, liberation theology, and beyond to "death of God"?

Our *fourth* example is global *populism* that has two versions, the people-power of "democracy" as an ism in the West, and the "people-rooted" governance as a climate of sentiment and assumption in China. It is a mistake, unforgivably monocultural, to lump these two different versions into "democracy." In any case, how do these two versions of populism mutually compare?

Again, all these lateral studies differ as to what events we choose as a cluster to compare and study, how we see and study them, how we change our minds on them as time goes on, and so on. Thus these lateral views are *alive* as we are, to compose an exciting history itself. This laterally composed history is a history collected out of linear histories, separately chronicled.

This meta-history is a fascinating collection of linear histories of world events, and this one historical collection is a plurality of togetherness alive, one in many, many into one, to spread; the more numerous and various clusters they gather, the more instructive and inter-enriching they come out for us all in our Global Village. After all, Global Village itself is a pluralistic singular, growing variously as globalization goes on.

We must make all this sentiment and life-process our *routine* way of living, never acquiesce in brutality that comes and goes. Be "brutal in giving" against brutality around us. "Giving" is our joy-imperative in constant daily living. After all, the reality of actuality is forever like this: we describe it, to end up prescribing how to live in joy. "Giving" is our description of life, and so it is our prescription of living.

Can you still not believe it? Try it, and you will like it. Prove this giving-pie by tasting-tasking it. We all will be in smiles all around, to spread all around, I guarantee. Mom still misses someone to care for, as birds are still chirping casually among squirrels and snakes. We *must* keep giving, to keep giving joy all around. To be realistic is to make real, to realize joy by giving, by realizing the joy of giving all over. Now listen.

The journalist gives reports on what has happened, and soon enough gives what might have happened, and then what should have happened, and then what should happen, and ends up being an author independent as fiction-writer such as Tolstoy. That is what happened to H. L. Mencken, Lafcadio Hearn, George Orwell, and many unsung hero-journalists *giving* us "realistic" reports of "actuality" beyond actuality.

Giving and being realistic fuse here into one in journalists journeying through daily routine realities. Here, our dreams undying protest senseless brutalities. Joy wages war for peace against war. The joy-war is really *the* one war to end all wars, not a war to continue wars. If such strange war still continues, the fault is in brutality, not in our diehard dream of all-joy, and more. In fact, *this* very continuation of joy-war against brutality inspires joy, dreams, courage, and composure, to make our life worth living.

Thus it is that brutalities negatively enhance joys and dreams, and become our strange ally to strengthen our dreams, to toughen our living that continues on *this* way. Importantly we must note. All sorts of loyalties in history have been harvesting senseless tragedies, except *this* loyalty dedicated to the diehard dream of pan-joy cosmopolitan.

---

[12] These five linear ways of studying an event are imperfectly exemplified by Foreign Affairs in its May/June 2011 issue. It prints out on its front cover, a large theme saying, "The New Arab Revolt: What Just Happened; Why No One Saw It Coming; What It means; What Comes Next."

If this loyalty provokes tragedy, *this* tragedy is also worth celebrating, as we now have Martin Luther King Day every January in USA. Such tragedy incites the stalwart incorruptibility of global joy. This is to be realistic, really, beyond all realism, because this realism lasts for ever as all other realisms come and fade, and lasts beyond them all, and stays on and on after all other realisms come and die in fickle trends of the times.

Let me confess. Just to write all this down already gives me joy unspeakable, and excites me beyond all rhymes and all reasons. "Are you writing a promotional tract for globalization?" Yes! This is my heartfelt advertisement for globalization, from the bottom of our shared innate Mother Nature. I do wish we all join in.

16. PROMISE

Various essays are collected in the following pages; they are essays from Africa, Bangladesh, Canada, China, England, Taiwan, and USA. These essays naturally cluster themselves into three bunches, in an ascending order of concrete problems in globalization, through cultural intercourse in globalization, to the dynamics of various features of globalization.

First, although the goal and meaning of globalization are limitless, globalization is appallingly clear at its minimal beginning, i.e., now that we are close neighbors in Global Village, we are all *required* to inter-help to pull one another out of miseries economic, medical, scientific, and political. This is the theme of Cluster One. This first cluster of essays urges us to realize the urgency of globalization both in its stark problems and in its prospects of win-win pan-prosperity.

Therefore, concrete and specific "problems and prospects" of globalization are cited in world economics of cancellation of debt of developing nations (J. Wu), Africa's problem of knowledge production (Assefa), economic problems of foreign aids in Bangladesh (Islam and Morgan), infusion of Taoism to the Western therapy of anxiety (R. Chao), and globalizing of counseling paradigm (C. Chao).

Then, in the *second* bunch, globalization as "cultural intercourse" is kicked off by Chang and Sun. Both sensitively spot the problem of today's globalization to lie in monocultural dominance. Chang's solution is globalization in the direction of localization. Sun offers interculture equal and various as a solution. Goulding exemplifies localizing interculture concretely by offering the panorama of dialogues among scholars East and West in the arena of Daoism, which is generalized as East-West meeting by Zhang. So much is what gloablization contains.

Division C. begins by noting that "translation" in meaning and meaning-milieu (K. Wu) catalyzes among cultures into globalization. Dr. Tang then tells of how such culture-communications compose "history" in globalization, to manage cosmic household in "ecology," as activities of "togetherness," in "ubiquity," as "interculture," all by K. Wu. And then, all these various essays are rounded up by a brief "Coda."

"Why did you choose those themes in the third cluster?" Since "globalization" is concrete and general, globalization as music, as future, as friendship, as dawn, and so on, could have easily been written further into separate essays, on and on. Only globalization as pivotal ecology, togetherness, ubiquity, and interculture are written, and other themes such as mentioned above that form an exciting globalization-synonymy are incorporated, sometimes repeatedly from various angles, into these chapters. This practice itself performs globalization as a dynamics of expanding process of interpenetration.

Real gutsy thinking—philosophy—should not become "universal" to tend perfunctory on concrete issues, just hovering over the surface of actuality. Philosophy truly so called should instead be deep and general, omitting nothing detailed and concrete without losing their whole vast vistas. It sounds impossible until we go out and watch Mother Nature that so spontaneously exhibits such stunt, as if nothing is the matter.

The situation can be envisioned as a casual tree with so many countless leaves swaying and swinging in various breezes in all directions, and all this while showing in their bewildering swings the peculiar features of *this* particular tree. This stunt can be accomplished only by telling the story of the "tree" of globalization, inviting as many various cultures and histories as possible to join in, as they all keep lustily swinging in the various winds of the times and cultures blowing this way and that.

This anthology in its all too modest scale—it should have run up to several volumes, and would still have been overflowed—aspires to this ideal by covering the vast range of themes in globalization from the basic modes of thinking, translation, and ecology, and such, to apply to concrete problems of globalization in Bangladesh, lack of computers in Africa, and debt cancellation of the poor nations. And the list goes on.

"What *sort* of thinking does this anthology perform?" A good question you raised, my friend. As we read sensitive fictions with deep meanings, such as those by John Fowles, we are struck by the fact that fiction does not move, if any, but just portrays milieus that slowly shift. If a fiction moves at all, it moves sideways, obliquely, descriptively, tacitly, and perhaps in deep streams. Is it a mirror portrayal of life itself?

Fiction compressed turns poetry. Poetry briefed turns philosophy. And so, philosophy with fiction-poetry flair is true philosophy. Confucius, Socrates, and Plato did such philosophizing. A true philosophical reading, true philosophizing, is to read any philosophy, e.g., Aristotle's, in fiction-poetry fashion, never analytically. All essays in this anthology perform this fiction-poetry *sort* of thinking.

"*How* does this anthology write?" To answer this good question, let us gaze at actuality. Actuality global is alive, now dragon-soaring, now snake-slithering. All we see is soaring and slithering alone, so bewildering. We must sense the dragon's eye in the snake's head that makes sense of the bewilderment. Sensing the eye of the head is to understand actuality. Cultures describe soaring and slithering so bewildering. "Understanding" senses their pivot, their head's eye, to make sense of them. Our volume writes in cultural understanding.

Obviously, these writings barely dot out the vast dynamics of globalization in process, world without end. Globalization continues to win-win prosper all beings, humanity included, in cosmic concord. Such is globalization our life-milieu in its modus vivendi and modus operandi. Globalization is, as such, our shared life-task quite awesome and innate, to make our life worth living. Now, we must go into these various essays from all over the globe.

Here is an imagined story of how globalization could actually proceed. A group of octogenarians drum up their dream "social foods" and push it to go along with social medicine and social security. We would then gain food security as we have social security and medical security, and they could perhaps go with insurance securities and other securities.

In food security world, people would go to the "food offices" and pull out food-trays, as we go to the post office for letters and packages. We can adjust food menus and amount and quality, to our taste. Professional dietitians administer food security as professional economists and medical professionals oversee their respective securities. The US government is already doing something like food security in a small scale, e.g., food stamps, food quality regulation, and food price control.

Perhaps all other basic life-needs can be socialized as we socialize foods, money, and medicine. The Communist China has been socializing even family systems, work forces, education, and religions, disastrously because they do it dictatorially. The cure lies in globalizing securities. Can we globalize socialization of ecology, and interculture as well? Can't those socializations spread all over the globe? Problems will of course erupt and proliferate, as those in the *1984* and *Animal Farm*, as dictatorship easily spawns here, but globalization will spread their benefits. This spread of socialization of globalization is not an impossible dream. Can't socializing globalization tackle 1984-woes by interculture[13]?

Meanwhile, this Introduction aims at explaining the necessity, difficulties, and essentials of globalization, to set the parameter of what follows. I do hope that it has done so at least on the whole. "I got none of your stuff here, pal. What follows may clear up." That is frustrating, isn't it, after all my struggles so far in these pages.

But then at least this Introduction raises questions to induce your interest in what follows, and, by any chance, if even what follows fails to clarify, then at least this whole volume provokes questions and discussions among us interested in globalization. These provocations and question-raising are part and parcel of globalization on the go, aren't they? Thus, perhaps this Introduction defends the rest of the book, as the book here clarifies this Introduction.

Here is one last point so simple, obvious, and so crucial, which all of us must keep firmly in mind, always. To begin, it is a thoroughly *dusty* world in which we live. What George W. Bush calls "rogue nations" are actually everywhere, including USA so shady, with Pax Americana so dirty. Furthermore, in this pan-dust, we are much amazed that the shining ideal of globalization in Global Village can even exist. In fact, it is a miracle indeed that we can even recognize "dust" at all in this all-dusty world.

Fish does not feel water to be wet. We must be amphibians before we can say that water is wet. That we can shake heads and say that this world of ours is "all wet," and produce the name, "rogue nations," and feel uncomfortable about all these at all, is a miracle, at the rock-bottom supporting the very hopeful notion of "globalization." Globalization would have been nowhere without such shared sentiment of pain at the dust.

Such hope, undimmed, vigilant, can never die, as long as our very recognition of "dust" as uncomfortable goes on, as pain is the unmistakable sign of hope that we are alive toward health. Globalization is a "me, too" thrust that cannot help but spread, pushing itself step by step throughout the whole globe in Global Village, precisely in the midst of dusty dirty world recognized as painfully dusty.

This modest anthology is dedicated to this undying thrust of "globalization," with our shared fervent prayers and commitment that it may grow greater, vaster, and stronger by the day, through our tireless struggles for cosmopolitan togetherness, going through one disappointment after another, in this dusty globe, as we persist in our dogged vision of "globalization" in every grain of dusty sand gritting our teeth of souls.

---

[13] Robert Theobald in his *Avoiding 1984: Moving Toward Interdependence*, Athens: Ohio University Press, 1982, moves in this direction.

Now, let us turn around in a positive direction. Japanese haiku poet Basho, infused with his favorite Chinese poet Chuang Tzu, said, "This road, no one goes down it."[14] When I see no one goes down the road, I am full, for I can go on my way with no restriction whatever.

When I am vacant, I am full, for I can do anything I want. "Can" is a potential; it is potent everywhere. "Everywhere" is a dynamic of globalization that is by nature potent potential, on the go everywhere. Our dear indomitable Tommy shouts, "I can do anything!" He is right. He is young and has nothing, and so he can do anything. He is so powerful. Globalization is our young Tommy together growing worldwide. Together, we can do anything, for we have just started. "Just started" is important.

The abundance of potentials is the flower-power in blossom. Tender flowers fade into vigorous green. Tender baby grows into naughty Tommy. Babies are flowers Mother Nature treasures, as she is sad and happy to see the baby tender sheds himself into stout Tommy and beyond, as I miss those flowers grown into vigorous green. "Are we the baby or the Tommy?" It does not matter, for the baby is Tommy as Tommy is forever *the* baby of Mother Nature's. We are always the baby Mother Nature cherishes as we grow into globalization, always growing.

---

[14] This is the second poem with which Robert Hass begins his anthology, The Essential Haiku: Versions of Basho, Buson, & Issa, Hopewell, NJ: The Ecco Pres, 1994, p. 11.

A. Problems and Prospects

In this division concrete and specific "problems and prospects" of globalization are cited in world economics of cancellation of debt of developing nations (J. Wu), Africa's problem of knowledge production (Assefa), economic problems of foreign aids in Bangladesh (Islam and Morgan), infusion of Taoism to Western therapy of anxiety (R. Chao), and globalizing counseling paradigm (C. Chao).

In: Globalization Dynamics
Editor: Kuang-ming Wu

ISBN: 978-1-62100-750-0
© 2012 Nova Science Publishers, Inc.

Chapter 1

DEBT CANCELLATION: A GLOBAL SOLUTION AND WIN-WIN TASK

John Y. Wu[*]
California, US

ABSTRACT

This essay sees three ugly dynamos behind miseries of pan-poverty all over the globe. They are debt-payment, corrupt governments, and illicit—illegal and legal—money flow. This essay proposes an exciting first step, debt cancellation, out of them, against two stoppers of its effectuation, corrupt governments and illicit money flow.

INTRODUCTION

This essay sees three ugly dynamos behind miseries of pan-poverty all over the globe. They are debt-payment, corrupt governments, and illicit—illegal and legal—money flow. This essay proposes an exciting first step, debt cancellation, out of them, against two stoppers of its effectuation, corrupt governments and illicit money flow.

The current global population is 7 billion. These peoples have 195 nations plus one (South Sudan) to add in July 2011. Of those 196 nations not counting Taiwan, 160 nations are euphemized as "developing nations" struggling in the miseries of poverty. These 196 nations are too numerous to list, but the wealthy G-20 can be cited. They are Argentina, Australia, Brazil, Canada, China, France, Germany, India, Indonesia, Italy, Japan, Mexico, Russia, Saudi Arabia, South Africa, South Korea, Turkey, United Kingdom, United States, and European Union. To repeat, such G-20 is the wealthy elites on the globe.

"Rich" in this global context is, an indecent four-letter word brutally hovering over the ocean of global injustice and poverty, mortally miserable, created by the rich. Illicit money flow, from under legal avenues to outright stealing, contributes enormously to the miseries of

---

[*] The author is a violinist, cytotechnologist, musical historian and archivist. He has intense social conscience, and his global concerns produced this essay. His email is: wutulare@yahoo.com

pan-poverty all over the globe. The rich match the poor in their twin four-letter words, cranking out global miseries of injustice and pan-poverty.[1] Where this mortal misery of pain-ocean came from, how to immediately stop its spiraling intensification, to start our globe on its way to self-rebuilding, is the main concern here.

The first step to the solution is dramatically simple. The global ocean of pan-pain is being kicked up by the very G-20, who can and must resolve the miseries by their quite feasible means, debt cancellation, which stops the pan-misery right away to let start national rebuilding by the poor nations themselves.

This essay claims that debt cancellation is the first step toward resolving the problem of world poverty. The poor are all over the world. The whole globe is possessed by the poor, and they are in dire miseries. The wealthy nations can and must immediately relieve global poverty by debt cancellation.

Believe it or not, the world turns not on the rich but on the poor. Not the elegant rich but the unsightly poor are the pivot of the globe. All revolutions in history are made by the oppressed poor to directly change the entire fabric of society. The world is shaped by how the poor are handled by the rich, for the better (win-win prosperity) or for the worse (all of us ruined). It is as serious as that, and as simple as that. This stark fact of the world exerts impacts on the world beyond the grave. All this is what all religions of the globe insist.

All world religions place the poor in high importance. World financial institutions are tragically in direct opposition to this view. Thus, at the very least, not merely standing aside watching the ugly pan-misery of the poor all over the globe, not making more money to exacerbate pan-poverty, is the topmost responsibility of the rich G-20. And the rich can easily stop the spiral worsening of pan-poverty by quite a feasible means of debt cancellation. Debt cancellation benefits the poor to benefit the rich, to start on our sure road to win-win pan-prosperity in which pan-poverty vanishes of itself.

The "Jubilee" institution is one such voice of social conscience. The Jubilee is made up of 75 religious denominations and faith communities, and human rights groups, environmental groups, and many other community groups. Raising voices seems a weakest vanity against the inexorable trend of the time. Actually, on the contrary, the world is shaped and driven by personal voices seemingly so useless. All paradigmatic individuals[2] are insignificant "individuals" who shape the world for better (Confucius, Socrates, Gandhi) and for worse (Hitler *the* rhetorician).

We do not even need to go to the height of paradigmatic individuals. On December 17, 2010, Mohamed Bouazizi, a 26-year-old street vendor in Tunisia, set himself ablaze on the steps of a local government building. He touched off an enormous fire to a combustible mixture of economic despair, social frustration, and political yearning for well-governed society. The conflagration spread throughout the region.

The flames consumed not only Bouazizi who died on January 4, but, in a matter of weeks and months, the regimes of Tunisia and Egypt, and likely others to come (ForeignAffairs@cfr.org, 5/5/11). A single individual, a tiny obscure young fellow touched off an extensive series of popular revolutions, called "New Arab Revolts." Such spontaneous,

---

[1] Peter Singer's "Famine, Affluence, and Morality" (Philosophy and Public Affairs, Spring 1972, pp. 229-243) is in the same wavelength as the present essay, but it does not go far enough or concrete enough.
[2] Karl Jaspers, Socrates, Buddha, Confucius, Jesus: The Paradigmatic Individuals (1957), San Diego, CA: Harcourt Brace, 1990. These four people are all poor hobos.

homemade ignitions have abundantly been repeated in world history, so much so that China takes people's welfare as heavenly mandate of the rulers.

Beyond what John the Baptist said, that God can raise children of Abraham from these mere stones (Matthew 3:9, Luke 3:8), these poor nameless folks *are* already Mother Nature's precious stones of humanity. Their spontaneous voices of social conscience remove mountains of indifference and pan-poverty, by appealing to G-20 the brutal rich. We must join in, and urge all others to join in. Whatever we are, however insignificant, we are *never* insignificant.

After all, the world is made of individuals common and nameless. It is *they* who move and shape the world. Besides, they are quite effective, for it is *they* who know where the shoe really pinches. All in all, the silent majority of the poor is the "boss" of the whole globe, and G-20 had better listen and obey their groans in miseries of poverty that G-20 nations have produced. Poverty is the business of the rich, not of the poor.

This essay explores just a few global economic aspects: an overview on global poverty, origin of the debt crisis, why drop the debt, how debt relief works, International Monetary Fund (IMF) and gold sales, the promises of Group of 20 Nations (G-20), to end with pleading for raising voices to all global leaders for justice in redressing global poverty. This essay has six sections under three headings, A. the problem (sections 1, 2), B. the solution (sections 3-7), C. the task (section 8), to conclude with a passionate appeal.

A. THE PROBLEM: TRAGEDY OF GLOBAL POVERTY

One: Overview on Poverty Worldwide

Read this list of global facts absolutely appalling. To begin, over 30,000 children die per day of hunger and preventable diseases, according to the United Nations Development Program 2003 estimate. Secondly, 1.4 billion persons live at or below $1.50 per day income, 70% of whom are women. Thirdly, of the world's population about half are women. Women are disproportionately among the poor. (Helene Gayle, MD, CEO, care.org)

Fourth, 2.5 billion persons do not have access to toilets (sanitation facilities); 2/3 of these are in Southern and East Asia (World Toilet Organization, worldtoilet.org). Fifth, combined with the above tragedy, 2.5 billion persons do not have access to safe water (Matt Damon cofounder, water.org, Chris Zivalich, "Thirsty for a Solution," April 2011, buzzsawmag.org). Mostly women spend several hours each day risking their lives to find and carry water for miles. Most diseases are due to the spread of human feces.

Sixth, nearly 925 million people, mostly in developing countries, are hungry, that is to say, deficient in protein and calories ("Food and Agriculture Reports," October 2010. worldhunger.org). Seventh, over one billion people lack adequate housing, and 100 million have no housing whatever (Millon Kothan's Report to the Sixty-First United Nations Commission on Human Rights, Geneva, March 2005, reported by article by Gustavo Capdevila, psnews.net).

All these figures mean that the tragedy described here is worldwide. We are hit with staggering global tragedy. These numbers are human figures that silently flag to us the human miseries so hushed so unbearable, every day, in fact, every second. No one can get accustomed to such penetrating pain. What is particularly tragic is that the miseries are made by human hands, quite predictable and preventable. We now dig into the cause of such global miseries, human, all too human. It is injustice in money management, an injustice too stark, so simple.

Two: Origin of Debt

In the 1960's the US government spent more money than it earned and, to make up for this imbalance, decided to print more dollars. The value of the dollar fell in world markets. Major oil companies raised their prices for oil and made huge sums of money which was deposited into banks in the West. This brought interest rates down and the banks faced an international crisis. They had to lend out the money quickly, and so turned to the Third World governments to make their loans, often to the corrupt governments.

In the 1970's, under advice from the US, the developing countries grew cash crops e.g. coffee, tea, cotton, etc. The prices of these fell, since too many countries were producing the same crops. As oil prices continued to rise and interest rates rose (for reasons beyond me), these countries could not pay their loans and had to borrow money just to pay their loans. Mexico was the first nation to default on its loans and eventually all the poorest nations became bankrupt.

In order to help these countries pay back the loans the main international financial institutions, i.e., Multilateral Development Banks, the International Monetary Fund (IMF), and the World Bank, implemented programs known as Structural Adjustment Programs (SAPs) to reschedule debts or borrow more money. These SAP's require governments to shift money away from social services such as health, education, devalue the national currency, encourage privatization of public industries, including sale to foreign investors, and other policies. They all hurt the poor the most. (Jubilee USA, jubileeusa.org)

B. THE SOLUTION: DEBT CANCELLATION FEASIBLE AND EFFECTIVE

Three: The Case for Debt Cancellation

The debts of poor nations are essentially the result of injustice shown in the above situation. Debts have been paid over and over. Interest rates have ballooned, and the compound interests made repayment impossible. From 1970-2002 Africa received $540 billion in loans and paid back $550 billion in principal and interest. Yet Africa today still has a debt stock of $295 billion. The money paid to the IMF and World Bank each year is more than they receive in loans. Africa pays more for debt than it receives in aid, new loans, and assistance. (Jubilee USA).

Now, if global miseries of poverty originated in outright "mismanagements," i.e., outrageous injustices of loans and interests to the poor nations, then the solution is of course to stop such mismanagements by simply canceling the debts unjustly imposed on them. It is a simple "debt cancellation," no ifs or buts.

Four: Ameliorative Effects of Debt Cancellation

Under pressure from Jubilee's debt cancellation movement, world leaders at the G-8 Summits in 1999 and 2005 agreed to cancel billions of dollars in unpayable debt of low-income countries, freeing up billions of dollars towards investment in social services of health care, education, and sanitation in poor countries. To date, 26 countries in Africa and Latin America have seen most of their debts cancelled.

The US and other rich countries have helped to provide more than $100 billion in debt cancellation. The effects are dramatic, almost overnight. According to the report by World Bank, overall positive effects of debt cancellation are three: 75% increase in spending on social services, decrease in child mortality, and more universal primary school education as dropout rates of students drop. Three concrete examples can be cited among so many in the world.

Our first example is Ghana: Here the poverty rate was reduced from 40 to 29% between 1999 and 2006. Enrollment in primary schools was upped to 91% in 2006. They now have 268 new classrooms, 36 new clinics, 10 new hospital wards, and 87 new water boreholes

Our second example is Tanzania. Here, the number of children attending schools increased by 50%, and due to the elimination of school fees, 1.5 million children returned to school almost overnight. Overall, 2500 new schools were built, as 28,000 new teachers were recruited

Our third example is Mozambique. Here, 500,000 children received vaccinations (Data from the IMF and World Bank). In addition, in Uganda school enrollment was more than doubled. In Honduras three more years of schooling was added for children. In Tanzania children started schooling at age 6 instead of age 8.

We note that these examples are most salient ones, all from the continent of Africa. We must keep firmly in mind that Africa is the world's greatest Continent, because it is the world's treasure trove, the Mother of all human genes and human cultures. Destruction of Africa destroys the entire humanity. Rebuilding Africa rehabilitates the whole humanity and the whole globe. The G-20 is tragically pulling Africa down. Debt cancellation is the first step to re-enrich Africa. The G-20 cannot shirk this global responsibility.

Five: International Monetary Funds Profits from the Sale of Gold

Jubilee USA found that the increase in world gold prices in the past two years means that IMF gold sale profits could be used to provide $4-5 billion in grants (non-repayable funds) and debt service relief for up to 70 of the world's poorest countries for the next 3 years.

However, sadly, it could take years before the IMF decides to do this and it requires pressure for them to do so. This is quite alarming. If one can do something that involves no sacrifice to oneself and can thereby relieve immense mortal disasters to a great number of people, in fact, millions of innocent people, and yet one does not do so, such dragging of feet amounts to criminal negligence, almost to a crime against humanity, committed by, of all institutions, the International Monetary Funds whose very expressed purpose is to improve on the global economic conditions. IMF seems worse than a global wolf in sheep skin.

Six: One Obstacle to Effectiveness of Debt Cancellation: Corrupt Governments

Some people hesitate, however. For example, Easterly vigorously argues against "debt relief" on the ground that the relief would worsen corruptions rampant among the poor nations.[3] I have three sad responses. *First*, lack of debt cancellation that he proposed worsens global miseries without reducing corruptions, much less resolving them at all, even though Easterly seems to assume would.

Secondly, debt cancellation does not give extra money. The poor nations are not "relieved" of the debt they ought to pay. Rather, debt "cancellation" is an inescapable burden of responsibility on the part of the unjust rich G-20. The burden of the whole issue is thus to be shifted to the shoulders of the dirty rich G-20. The poor nations have an urgent and legitimate *demand* on the rich G-20 to cancel the debt unjustly imposed on the poor nations.

Does saying all this sound too harsh and unreasonable? Now, listen. The situation is identical to plundering innocent people into utter poverty-miseries, and then "loaning" them the very money robbed of them, imposing interests on the money as "debt" so enormous those people cannot pay. How could debt cancellation be called "debt relief"? Worse, some rich people say, condescendingly, "Don't give the 'relief' to worsen their corruptions." Wow! What an argument of self-justifying self-righteous plunderers turned the elites! This is the argument of the leisure class worsened a thousand-fold, quite similar to Harding's Lifeboat Ethics.[4] Fiery prophets of the Old Testament, with the early Marx, are turning in their graves.

And *thirdly* and finally, please never be smug and presumptuous. Corruption does not belong to the poor nations alone. Corruptions are the problem worldwide, especially the problems of the G-20 themselves. This corruption-problem is irrelevant to G-20 being the cause of world-misery.

Let us take an example. Stopping the tobacco industry raises the problem of throwing out *their* workers into unemployment, of course. This unemployment problem is irrelevant to the necessity of public health to stop tobacco industry, and requires a separate handling such as retraining those workers for different and positive occupations.

In the same manner, government corruption of the poor nations is irrelevant to the urgent global necessity to stop the continual worsening of pan-poverty. Corruption requires a separate treatment such as government restructuring, by G-20 if needed, and even popular revolution. But restructuring and revolution require peoples with healthy bodies in healthy minds, and pan-poverty saps their health and their vigor.

Twist and turn as we may, the solution of pan-poverty is the top priority among the poor nations that poor nations themselves are powerless to handle, for pan-poverty is not caused by the poor but by the rich. Only the rich can help out the poor. The rich G-20 must come in; it is their responsibility, no one else's. This essay insists that the rich G-20 have the means, the means is quite feasible and quite effective, and implementing this easy means benefits both the poor and the rich alike. This means is debt cancellation.

---

3 William Easterly, "Think Again: Debt Relief," in Foreign Policy, November/December, 2001.
4 See Thorstein Veblen's verbose The Theory of of the Leisure Class, NY: Dover, 1994, Lifeboat Ethics: The moral dilemmas of world hunger, eds. George R. Lucas, Jr. and Thomas W. Ogletree, NY: Harper & Row, 1976, and Lester R. Brown, Tough Choices: Facing the Challenge of Food Scarcity, NY: W. W. Norton, 1996. Actually, the issue may be tough to practice but clear; it has no "dilemmas" at all.

The onus of responsibility now shifts from supernumerary "debt relief" to the duty of "debt cancellation." The transfer of "debt"-money must be performed by the rich G-20, but transferred to whom? It must not be toward the region's corrupt government. In this regard, Easterly's objection amounts to issuing the correct warning. Thus the issue here is now not whether but how debt cancellation can be effectively implemented, and this how should be administered through international channels. How concretely is it to be done?

The legitimate party to receive the "debt"-money should be the people's agency responsible and intelligent enough to effectively put the money into social reconstruction. The setup of such a people's party should be by the people themselves, perhaps assisted by international organizations such as the United Nations.

The responsible transfer of money and its effective utilization for social rebuilding could also be overseen and assisted by responsible nonprofit organizations such as Habitat of Jimmy Carter, Jubilee,[5] and Doctors without Borders. Actually these measures are being implemented today. Poor nations are required to pass through Heavily Indebted Poor Countries Initiative of World Bank. They must report on their public financial management, transparency, and plans on how to use the money obtained under debt cancellation.

Many countries, e.g., Ghana, Tanzania, Nicaragua, Uganda, and Nigeria, have set up Virtual Poverty Funds, a tracking system for revenues obtained by debt cancellation and other routes in the nations' budget. Other nations, e.g., Cameroon and Honduras, set up separate funds under independent oversight such as by civil society and others. These independent people's groups can, when needed, call for assistance to civil groups in other nations such as USA.

There must be more of such national institutions of the peoples, and international assisting organizations. We have many ways to regionally and globally manage the transfer of funds that bypasses the corrupt local government into actual improvement of people's welfare. It is thus that debt cancellation shall be the first step toward conduit of joy to conduce to pan-prosperity among every community and every nation all through our globe.

Seven: Another Obstacle to Debt Cancellation: Illicit Financial Flow

Another troublesome "corruption," this time worldwide as well as regional, stubbornly clinging on to money transfer, is its laundry in its route. It is so invincible, ubiquitous, silent, constantly siphoning off trillions of dollars each year. Worse, it is often done "legally," in broad daylight, as "tax haven," a major conduit to the illicit flow. Such an illicit money siphoning is a plain hard-hitting fact, strikingly simple and globally effective, to court disasters.

What follows is Global Financial Integrity's ground-breaking research to expose the alarming extent of the global damage of illicit money flow, and efforts at resolving this mammoth disaster.

In developed countries, credit has dried up due to the difficulty of appraising the quality of assets held by financial institutions that operate partially or wholly within the shadow

---

[5] World Bank could have been included here also, were it not the sad fact that it has mixed record on improvements of miseries of pan-poverty. On one hand, it has the reputation of children vaccination and recording the progress of improvement of the poverty-situation. On the other hand, it requires poor nations to forego their social services in order to pay debt!

system. This includes almost all banks in US and Europe. In developing countries, an estimated $1 trillion a year is shifted abroad to harvest the most damaging financial condition devastating the poor, undermining poverty alleviation, and delaying sustained growth.

Tax dodging by multinational corporations alone is estimated to deprive the poor nations of $160 billion per year. This amount alone could have gone into health services to save 350,000 children under five from death ("Death and Taxes: The True Toll of Tax Dodging, *Christian Aid*, 2008). Of course curbing tax dodging also helps rich nations to close the gap in government bail-outs in credit crises, and restore steady revenue stream.

Lack of data contributes to opacity that facilitates siphoning away billions of dollars from debt cancellation to benefit the poor nations. Disclosing data discloses where these dollars end up. This connection between lack of data and devastating opacity was finally discovered after over 50 years of research by Dr. Dev Kar, the leading economist at Global Financial Integrity. But of course "lack of data" is equivalent to "opacity to the public" that facilitates "private siphoning of public money." These three practices form an illicit synonymy in mutual implications; to see one sees the other two.

Every year a staggering $1 trillion dollars vanish that are on their way to the poor nations. The dollars vanish in the banks' deposits much more than by way of tax evasion. These banks are located in the wealthy nations such as Australia, Japan, UK, USA, as well as Denmark, Norway, Sweden, Switzerland, and Turkey. Dollars are gone not because those wealthy nations need the money. It is the wealthy people's greed that siphons the public money for the poor.

Taking away money meant for the poor amounts to robbing foods of the starving persons, not because we are hungry but because the foods are worth money. No matter how one interprets it, such an act is equivalent to mass murders, killing 10 million people a year, killing more than the 6 millions the Nazis killed in totality. The massive crime against humanity is committed silently right here now by so many "civilized" rich nations.

Massive murders by greed of the rich operate under cover of opacity. One way of cleaning and preventing dark mass murders in the dark is to expose them to the public by constant publicity. Transparency is one effective weapon against opacity that abets annual crimes against humanity. Law enforcement to force disclosure of deposit information is one way of exposure. Persistent journalistic dissemination of the terrible information is another way.

To break through their "triune illicit conspiracy"—lack of data, opacity to the public, and private siphoning of public money—we must break open its first phenomenon, "lack of data." We can do so by patiently investigating the classified—opaque—institutional information to publicize it, to make it transparent. Disclosure of data can be made by at least two implementations combined, journalistic probing and legal enforcement on the financial and commercial organizations to report their data and operations to the law agencies.

Probing exposure by nameless journalists Woodward and Bernstein had toppled powerful Richard Nixon. Today, shady opacity, so inveterate, of illicit fund-siphoning must be shone on by the sun of requiring reports on "developed countries bank deposit data on non-resident non-bank private sectors of developing countries." What is needed is "data on cross-border bank deposits." And then the journalists must spread such information worldwide to sanitize away the devastating opacity.

Now, let us go into how we can concretely do it. Since it is global, illicit money laundry can also be controlled and prevented by a global transparency in the global network of financial corporations. The Financial Accountability and Corporate Transparency (FACT) Coalition seeks to remedy the illicit flow by four means, by

a) requiring ownership information of all business entities, trusts, foundations, and charities-information that indicates who actually controls these entities be made available to law enforcement and the public;
b) requiring country-by-country reporting by multinational corporations of the sales made, profits earned, and taxes paid in every jurisdiction where an entity operates;
c) strengthening, standardizing, and enforcing anti-money-laundering laws;
d) eliminating loopholes in our tax systems to make sure that the corporations that benefit from all resources, protections, markets in the United States pay their fair share of taxes. These are the four means whereby to control if not prevent illicit money flows.

In essence, these are efforts at achieving global transparency to combat half-a-century-old shadow financial structure comprising tax havens, secrecy jurisdictions, disguised corporations, anonymous trust accounts, and fake foundations. Such shadow system performs with trade mis-pricing mechanisms, money laundering techniques, and loopholes left in Western laws that facilitate commercial tax-evading money across borders, illegal and legal, quite criminal and corrupt. Some estimates suggest that as much as half of the global trade and capital movements pass through this shadow system. (gfip.org)

By the same token, various Jubilee organizations have various "tricks" to "out trick" siphoning of money by illicit financial flow. In all this, the Jubilees are also trying for global transparency, exposing shady shadow-system to sanitize it under the publicity sunlight. Since illicit capital flow hurts every nation, rich ones included, so much effort has been expended on controlling it. It seems to be working, though quite haphazardly (adna briefing booklet 2001; cancun blog. doc).

Let us now sum up what we have learned so far, in four points. *One*, the poor is powerful boss of the world. They can turn the world upside down to put it right side up, by revolutions China calls "justice aroused 起義" by sheer pain the poor suffer unjustly. *Two*, we can and must ease the pain and bring about less bloody revolution, by fighting poor people's enemies who happen to be *our* elite rich, the banks and the organizations commercial and industrial.

Three, what cleans them of illicit money laundry, which siphons up billions of dollars in debt cancellation to the poor, is transparency. Transparency is the sun of publicity that sanitizes foul money laundry. Financial institutions resent such inspection, to clearly tell of how effectively transparency would work. *Four*, we bystanders can begin transparency-sun to shine on them, by journalistic spreading of information on their shady deals throughout the world. Journalists are the prophets who thus clean the rich-us to ease the pain of the enormous poor.

Thus, human pain ubiquitous caused by human greed of the rich, corporate and organized, can and must be wiped away by human hands of transparency, beginning at *our* journalist hands that distribute information on foul plays of the rich. Journalist propagation, worldwide, of foul financial deals so rampant, is one urgent task of *ours* of globalization to globalize welfare of all of us.

Now, we must note one important "almighty loophole" that can and does bypass the public transparency and survive its exposure unscathed. Tax evasion is illegal, but tax avoidance through legal loopholes is not a "crime," for it is perfectly legal, and no jail verdict can be given. Everything is perfectly above board, legal as can be. But it remains an obvious wrong, as helpless groans of the poor all over the globe appeal to our conscience, loud and clear.

Maneuvers through tax loopholes, e.g., tax havens, secrecy jurisdictions, to lubricate greed of the rich and perhaps ease their guilty conscience, are being quite ubiquitously practiced. But perpetration of legal right to hide moral wrong is clearly one despicable crime committed by the "decent wealthy" with thriving layers under them. There seems to be no means devised yet to correct this evil. It is a sad brick wall to the poor erected by civilization, one of the saddest harvests yielded by today's civilization, among many others.

But can stubborn journalistic propagation of this very fact help? at least an obscure citizen (such as Henrich Kieber) of any nation (such as Liechtensteiner) can divulge the secret data on tax evasion to stir up the entire world, thanks to journalist dissemination of such exciting story. See "On the Trail of the Fugitive who Blew the Cover on Global Tax Evasion" (www.worldcrunch.com/trail-fugitive-who-blew-cover-tax-evasion/3539)

But can stubborn journalistic propagation of *this* fact help? An obscure Henrich Kieber of an obscure nation Liechtensteiner has divulged the secret data on tax evasion to stir up the entire world, thanks to its journalist dissemination, "On the Trail of the Fugitive who Blew the Cover on Global Tax Evasion" (www.worldcrunch.com/trail-fugitive-who-blew-cover-tax-evasion/3539) Kieber is a recent one of many whistle blowers. We need more, though it takes courage to blow the whistle; many have been indicted. There is no legal protection of whistle blowers against the US *government*.

C: DEBT CANCELLATION: THE TASK OF WIN-WIN GLOBALIZATION

Now, we must never forget this twofold fact. This fact is a matter of global life and death, global joy and global pain. One, the task urged in this essay is the task toward global *joy* of co-prosperity in which every one, the poor and the rich alike, is needed to accomplish. Two, the rich G-20 nations hold the key to start global prosperity, not the poor nations. This ignition-key to turn on pan-prosperity is debt cancellation. This twofold task of joy together has negative and positive aspects.

Negatively, the G-20 have-nations are sitting on a global pressure-cooker of unjust disparity between the haves and the have-nots. Sooner than later the whole globe will blow up. Already we see an ominous beginning of the disaster in 911 of 2001 in NYC and elsewhere, and they are planning on another 911 in 2011. The global economic disparity so brutal is cooking up military terrorist disasters, both within the dictatorial nations in the Arab Revolt and outside, spreading regionally and worldwide. Can you imagine "Christian terrorists" in Switzerland?

Positively, we human beings are by nature social. We were born socially of parents and medical personnel, raised in families, natural and social, of caring, and enjoy friendly camaraderie through the community at large. Thus is not (just) austerely ethical to care for my neighbors, as Singer[6] would have us think. It is sheer *joy*, incited by our innate sensitivity so unbearable to fellow beings' suffering, as Mencius of ancient China insisted, to care for one

---

[6] Peter Singer, "Famine, Affluence, and Morality," Philosophy and Public Affairs, Spring 1972, pp. 229-243.

another. The global ethics of co-care originates in, and blossoms in, joys of inter-prosperity. Caring is joyous obligation among human brethren in our shared Ecopiety of Global Village.

Thus our shared task is an ethical imperative, to spread our benefits worldwide, toward the task to joy-together. The cutthroat zero-sum competition in selfishness must, ethically and naturally must, yield to our shared win-win *joys* of inter-thriving in global inter-prosperity, for which the G-20 nations need the poor nations to trade off profits to achieve, as the poor nations are to be pulled out of poverty-misery by the G-20 in economic globalization by rich nations outsourcing their businesses abroad.

But the poor nations must be helped first. At this moment of worldwide miseries of pan-poverty, the G-20 nations must first fulfill *their* duty to global conviviality, with their first step easy and feasible, debt cancellation. G-20's debt cancellation is the crucial key to set global inter-prosperity rolling. The global ball of all-joy is in the court of G-20.

Six: Group of 20 Nations (G-20) Summit Promises and Actions

During the global financial collapse of late 2008/early 2009, in the course of just a few months, the G-20 countries mobilized $18 trillion to bail out the banking and financial institutions, the very same ones responsible for the disaster.

In sharp contrast, the G-20 nations have not lived up to their modest commitments to help the poorest countries affected by the crisis. They promised to deliver just $50 billion to them. Of this amount, only half or $25 billion has been actually delivered, with only $1.2 billion since the September Summit. Not a word has been mentioned by the G-20 leaders since September 2009 regarding the $50 billion dollar commitment.

In the US alone, the top 20 "too big to fail" companies on Wall Street received $283 billion in bailout money from US taxpayers—11 times more than the entire G-20 has delivered in new resources to the 2.7 billion residents of the 78 lowest income countries. (Jubilee) Clearly and tragically, our win-win co-prosperity of the whole globe is still far ahead in our world horizon.

CONCLUSION

In the midst of overwhelming differences in attitude, that of the world leaders and financial institutions, on the one hand, and world religions, charity organizations, etc., as world conscience, on the other, we see that there is a fundamental power imbalance and shift of resources to the few away from the vast majority of global peoples. This is the origin of world miseries today, quite unjustified. We simply must revolutionize our very life-attitude from brutal zero-sum game to raise global hell of world poverty, to the more-sum management of worldwide togetherness toward win-win global prosperity.

Fortunately, efforts to persuade those in power have had some success, as in England, where debt cancellation is being effected. There are many voices of grassroots conscience to be heard from, and our leaders simply owe it to themselves to hear from them. Recently, in USA alone, 1000 religious leaders are being summoned to petition for debt cancellation, among other many efforts. It is not impossible for justice to be achieved this way, from the grassroots up to spread globally, for globalization to truly happen, slowly but surely. But world miseries cannot wait, demanding us all to act fast, taking the first step of debt cancellation.

Now, let us go over this important point, this time slowly. Three points can be raised. *One*, it is factually false to regard debt cancellation as a nice gesture that G-20 need not do. Given centuries of exploitations that brought G-20 to wealth at the price of other nations, thereby draining other nations into rock-bottom poverty, and driving them into life-basic miseries worldwide, debt cancellation that relieves additional loads to these poor nations is the least G-20 can do, and are obligated to do. Debt cancellation is not an extra-mile of kindness but an urgent responsibility of G-20.

Two, moreover, this obligation costs G-20 practically nothing to implement, and relieves much miseries among poor nations almost overnight. *Three*, in addition, debt cancellation is a costless yet priceless enhancement of the good fame of G-20, a fine advertisement for them. Thus, debt cancellation is a feasible obligation of G-20 that benefits both the poor nations and the rich ones such as G-20. All things considered, debt cancellation is G-20's win-win tactic, simple, feasible, costless, and assured, for every nation all around the globe.

Let me impress on us how serious a responsibility debt cancellation is on G-20's shoulders. The poor nations are globally distributed. World poverty is tragedy enough. Knowing an almost costless first step solution and dragging the feet not implementing it, in the face of burning world tragedy, is abysmal tragedy. G-20's decision not to give $50 billion to low-income countries (LICs) will force LICs prioritize debt repayment over their essential social services and creating a new debt crisis. Such misery tells of unspeakable crime against humanity being committed by the rich G-20, who made their wealth out of exploitations that pushed the world into poverty miseries in the first place.

The Nazis slaughtered millions of people in Europe, to collapse itself. Not to implement debt cancellation amounts to slaughtering billions of human lives worldwide, quite beyond lamenting, into collapsing the entire globe, including the rich nations. In contrast, to perform debt cancellation redounds to win-win globalization of pan-prosperity. All this tragically, inexorably, argues for debt cancellation as the G-20's obligation and immediate task, the task toward win-win prosperity worldwide.

Of course, debt cancellation is no magic bullet or panacea, much less a root-cure of world miseries of food shortage. Promoting inexpensive, protein-rich foods such as soy beans is one route, as Shurtleff and Aoyagi[7] are vigorously doing now. A related route is promoting Green Revolution with agricultural technological know-how.

A third obvious route is promoting population control such as birth control by political fiat (as in Communist China) and/or advertising birth control worldwide, even though birth control would be naturally practiced as child-mortality drops, which comes only after starvation is relieved, and so starvation-drop and birth control form an onerous tail-catching game. In any case, there must be many more other means of easing global miseries of pan-poverty. They can and must be mobilized *together*. Debt cancellation is one among them, an immediately effective one quite costless to the rich nations.

What so special about debt cancellation is that it remains surprisingly unnoticed and yet it is quite a hard-hitting and positively effective means. Debt cancellation is G-20's effective,

---

[7] See William Shurtleff & Akiko Aoyagi, The Book of Tofu & Miso, Berkeley, CA: Ten Speed Press, 2001, and so many other publications by them.

assured, and feasible first step to start rolling toward the cure of world-miseries. Debt cancellation will provide modest though much needed seed-money to *begin* building social infra-structures, to start business enterprises to make more money for social reconstruction, to build up medical relief from preventable diseases, to implement education of school-age children, and so on.

In a word, debt cancellation will get things rolling to start rebuilding a healthy viable community, this one first and then that, one after another, throughout the poor nations. Three concrete examples from great Africa were given above, in Section 4, to show how such social reconstruction is for sure to follow debt cancellation. Debt cancellation amounts to an emergency blood-infusion so indispensable into the emaciated body of a society. Our global societies will simply die away without debt cancellation.

After all, our common human situation is quite understandable. Cutting down others in a brutal zero-sum game ends up cutting down everyone, rich and poor alike. Sharing and trading off benefits to go around makes you and me to thrive and prosper, one and all, every one in all smiles. You win to my win, and we need one another to help one another, in win-win prosperity.

To cut down each other comes from one's short-sighted desire for immediate gain by shoveling others aside, to end up shoveling me aside by others. We all need to calm down, to sit down together to scheme for reciprocity of gains to and fro to eventuate in win-win prosperity. There is no other alternative to survive but to thrive together. We either cut down us all or thrive all, both together. Debt cancellation is costless to the rich G-20, to raise up the poor nations who would then reciprocate gains with responsive help, as "out-sourcing" among the rich nations gain with the poor nations.

Let me repeat this critical point. No one enjoys world miseries that, if not stopped now, will soon gnaw away the whole globe. Debt cancellation is an urgent first step required of G-20. How to persuade them into this mindset is our further task for global conscience to meet, represented by all religious groups and many grass-roots organizations throughout the globe. They must devise and implement effective tactics of persuasion to effective revolution of attitude among G-20 to immediately implement at least debt cancellation, to spread to economic change and mind change throughout the globe, for the world cannot wait any longer.

Even such a simple and effective solution to world poverty at practically no cost to the wealthy has been tottering on, going so slow. Let us repeat gain. Mismanagement as the cause of world poverty matches a solution to it, clearly understood, by simple debt cancellation, without visible dent to the G-20 to do so, and yet how slowly they drag their feet to implement such simple painless solution, debt cancellation! This scenario is heartbreakingly tragic. The tragedy of G-20's selfishness matches the tragedy of world poverty. The former causes and worsens the latter.

The political Gandhi from India has won independence for India from the tyranny of Britain. We need the financial Gandhi in the globe to pull off the stunt of releasing the world's poor nations from the grip of G-20. Perhaps one solution to this new tragedy of G-20 is to enlighten them to see that it is to *their* advantage—at least financial, prestige-wise—to cancel debt. And doing so is practically at no extra cost to them. Turning their eyes away from world misery shall sooner than later turn *them* into misery in this world of close-knit relations. The ball is clearly in G-20's court.

It is quite a tragedy to see poverty-tragedy. It is an unspeakable tragedy to know the solution so simple and costless, and *fail* to implement it, debt cancellation. Of course, debt cancellation is an immediate stopgap measure, not a root cure. But we need to do it now, to give us a breathing room, to gain an inch of leg room, to design a further concrete step, and then another one, to inch toward root-cures. Here is a global problem with global solution *demanding* G-20 to implement, immediately.

We must not lose heart, however. Mother Nature will raise many a Gandhi from the "dust" anywhere. As Jesus said, the very stones will shout.[8] They are the rock-bottom stones of poverty; they will force open the deaf ears of the rich. And, indeed, occasionally we see ebullient successes, as mass rally in England has forced G-8 to cancel debts with encouraging results.[9] This is one recent success in a series of successes before, however modest yet nonetheless clearly effect.

Some more examples come to mind. Many mass protests in the late 1990s included 24 million signatures handed to the government in Cologne, Germany. In Birmingham in 1998, rowdy human chain chanting for debt cancellation penetrated the conference chambers of G-8, to result in cancellation of debt in some nations to increase their spending in health and education, with happy results in popular welfare.

These successes of the Jubilees led to another more complex movement, Trade Justice Movement, joining forces to shift policies of the rich nations. Britain passed the bill against the practice of "vulture funds" to make obsolete the private companies buying up debts of poor nations, forcing the poor to pay the debts to *them*. We will join hands *worldwide* to persist in pushing debt cancellation, step by step, one day at a time. Isn't such our global move, one struggling step at a time, what globalization is all about?

---

[8] See Mohandas K. Gandhi, An Autobiography: The Story of My Experiments with Truth, Boston: Beacon Press, 1597. The "dust" is in response to Gandhi comparing himself to being so humble as to be crushed by dust. Jesus mentioned "stones" shouting if we are silent (Luke 19:40), in response to the rich august Pharisees' envy at the humble crowd's spontaneous welcome of Jesus riding on a gentle donkey and her colt (Matthew 21:6).

[9] http://www.guardian.com.uk/global-development/poverty-matters/2011/apr/20/debt-owed-to-jubiliee-debt-campaign#start-of-comments

In: Globalization Dynamics
Editor: Kuang-ming Wu

ISBN: 978-1-62100-750-0
© 2012 Nova Science Publishers, Inc.

Chapter 2

UNFULFILLED PROMISES OF GLOBALIZATION: GLOBAL KNOWLEDGE PRODUCTION AND AFRICA

Shimelis G. Assefa[*]
University of Denver, Denver, Colorado, US

ABSTRACT

The nexus between research, education, innovation, and economic progress is very well established (Association of Universities and Colleges of Canada, 2005; Mattoon, 2006; Teferra & Altbach, 2003; Wende, 2009). It is equally true that the enterprise of research and education is heavily dependent on access to scholarly information and knowledge. This is particularly so in today's knowledge-based economy where the competitive advantage of nations is largely dependent more on human capital than physical. Because higher education systems are in the forefront of knowledge production, universities in Africa need to build the required infrastructure to - increase research outputs (thus knowledge production), prepare more knowledge workforce (hence build the human intellectual capital) – which are the necessary ingredients for innovation and economic growth. It is only then that we can say the broken promises of globalization are mended when it comes to Africa. The purpose of this chapter is to provide a framework that guides the discussion in globalization, knowledge production, higher education, and innovation taking Africa as a case in point.

INTRODUCTION

What is global knowledge production? Why is it important for Globalization? What are the unmet promises of Globalization? These are key questions around which this chapter will focus the discussion. Particular attention will be given to the continent of Africa. I am not an economist and so I will not dwell much on what and what is not globalization. Based on my background, i.e., information science, and based on how I framed this chapter, I limit the

---

[*] Assistant Professor, Library and Information Science, University of Denver, Denver, Colorado, USA. His email is: Shimelis.Assefa@du.edu

concept of globalization to mean "the free flow of - ideas, information, best-practices, know-how, and knowledge on a global scale." In a more general sense, a description of globalization that appeals to this essay is "the widening, deepening and speeding up of worldwide interconnectedness," (Marginson & Wende, 2009, p.18).

Globalization is not a new phenomenon. Much has been written and said on the topic. A scan of the extensive extant literature reveals differing views, different schools of thought on the pros and cons of globalization, especially when least developed countries like Africa are added to the mix. The bulk of the discussion centers on economic and political integration between countries (Schaeffer, 2009). Under this theme - trade, political integration, financial integration, movement of people, poverty reduction, foreign direct investment (FDI), transnational corporations (TNCs), the flow of goods, services, and capital across national borders – dominate the conversation.

What is not adequately discussed in the globalization literature in this respect is 'global knowledge production.' How much knowledge is produced and who's producing it, and what infrastructure is needed to produce it, are important discussions to understand globalization in today's global knowledge-based economy. The driving force behind this chapter is the recognition of the fact that global knowledge production is critical for a speedier, wider, and deeper interconnectedness that is inclusive and one that benefits all involved. In this chapter, global knowledge production is constrained to: (1) research and development (R&D) outputs, and (2) patent application by countries and universities included – which are key indicators of knowledge-based activities. Research and development (R&D) activities by higher learning institutions and their affiliates together with patent applications – are often cited in globalization papers to support the argument in productivity and innovation (Powell & Snellman, 2004, p.202; Vincent-Lancrin, 2009).

The idea of global knowledge production is a complex undertaking on its own right. Covering the collective sum of conscious experience by humans together with the spoken, written, and recorded knowledge in all facets of societal life/activity – from art, entertainment, science, technology, business, to custom, culture, and of course commerce – will .be a difficult task. Nonetheless, in light of the discussion on globalization, restricting the global knowledge production topic to R&D outputs together with patent applications by higher education systems will serve the purpose well.

More than ever, today it is a well recognized fact that information and knowledge play a critical role in day-to-day societal life and activities. Benkler (2006) summarizes this model of information and cultural production as one based on cooperation, sharing, and coexistence, and continues to state how information, knowledge, and culture are central to human development. These notions become more evident when we recognize that we live in global knowledge-based economy. It is true not all economies around the world are knowledge-based, as is the case in Africa. Knowledge as one critical input to propel discoveries and economic progress; the production of goods and services becoming more knowledge-intensive activities; the greater dependence on intellectual capital than on natural resources – are all important indicators of the global knowledge-based economy (Powell & Snellman, 2004).

The manifestations that arise from the global knowledge-based economy are critical to situate this essay on a clear path. It is in this context, that I explore global knowledge production and the unfulfilled promises of globalization. If we single out the statement 'greater dependence on human capital,' from the above lines, we can easily relate the connection between higher education, research and development (R&D), knowledge production, and even innovation and economic progress. It is in this web of interconnectedness that we will find Africa lagging behind the knowledge-based economy enclave. We know full well higher education establishments are the primary centers for preparing and producing skilled and knowledge workforce, and hence intellectual capital. It is also logical to establish the connection between knowledge production as a function of R&D activity by higher education and that further becoming the engine for innovation and economic progress.

What are then the unfulfilled promises of globalization? We read reports from the United Nation's (UN) millennium development goals (MDG) that more poor people in LDCs (Africa included) are out of poverty every year – more children are going to school – life expectancy is increasing – access to health is improving – and above all these countries are registering faster economic growth (UN, 2010; UNDP, 2007). All these accomplishments are very positive and commendable. However, we are not yet there to witness the assertions being made in the New York Times best-seller book 'the world is flat' by the well respected writer Thomas Friedman (2005). The idea that in today's global knowledge-based economy, the Internet and the revolution in information and communication technology, has given everyone equal opportunity to succeed - is far from truth. The Nobel Laureate economist, Joseph Stiglitz, although from a different prognosis, argued globalization has yet to live up to its promises (Stiglitz, 2006).

There is no level playing field for everyone yet. Yes, to be critical of my own statement, as I will discuss later in detail, Africa has completed mega-infrastructure projects that connect the continent via high-speed under-sea fiber-optic cables to the rest of the world. While this is a significant step to bridge the physical infrastructure bottleneck, Africa still lags behind any geographic region in the world in so far as ***content/knowledge access and production*** (which I often call it the content divide), and as a result Africa has a long-way to go to fully-participate in the global knowledge economy. It won't take much contemplation when we say the Internet is everywhere and has made access to information easy and effortless. While this is true to a certain degree, when we take into account higher education establishments in Africa and their access to critical content/knowledge that supports teaching and research, the situation is very different. African higher education systems have limited access to the global scientific and technical knowledge base, mainly due to prohibitive cost issues. In addition, because of the limited access African universities also contribute very little to the global knowledge base. To this end, the highly cited author in international higher education issues, Professor Philip Altbach from Boston College very nicely summed this same sentiment – that "world-class research-oriented universities dominate the production and distribution of knowledge, while institutions in least developing countries are following in their wake." (p.7).

The lack of access or limited access to the global scientific, technical and scholarly knowledge base by African countries is very well documented. The situation in sub-Saharan African countries (where 34 of the 50 LDCs exist) is more serious. For example, only South Africa and Botswana have a reasonable budget to continue to subscribe to the increasingly expensive print and electronic journals and databases. A large number of university libraries in sub-Saharan African countries have a total freeze on journal subscriptions since about the 1980s (Zulu, 2008). Many of the libraries in tertiary education get their journal and database resources through donors and university library systems in the west that provide shared access to some of their e-resources.

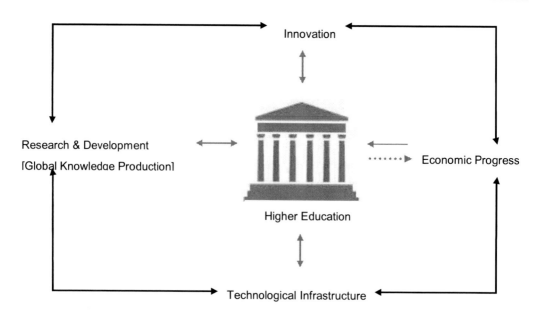

Figure 1. Framework for Globalization and knowledge production in Africa.

Notable mentions in this shared-access scheme for developing countries (including Africa) come from the UN and its specialized agencies – particularly WHO, FAO, and UNEP. For example, AGORA (access to global online research in Agriculture) provides a collection of 1900 journals to institutions in 107 countries (FAO, 2009), HINARI (Access to Research in Health Program) enables developing countries to gain access to one of the world's largest collections of biomedical and health literature. More than 7,500 information resources are now available to health institutions in 105 countries (WHO, 2009), OARE (Online Access to Research in the Environment) another program in the environment is an international public-private consortium coordinated by the United Nations Environment Program (UNEP, 2006), Yale University, and leading scientific and technology publishers and enables developing countries to gain access to one of the world's largest collections of environmental science research. Over 2,990 peer reviewed titles owned and published by over 340 prestigious publishing houses and scholarly societies are now available in more than 100 low income countries.

Whether one is for or against, many has predicted globalization is inevitable and it is here to stay. Among the many support accounts we find in the literature, I will present one authoritative and most appropriate explanation around this issue. This account comes from one of the many World Economic Forum (WEF) reports on the topic. The report not only asserts globalization is real, it also states a similar thesis along the lines of what this chapter aims to explore – that – the success of globalization is defined by innovation, which in turn is dependent on the use of technological applications. The report further states "...success in this world will increasingly be defined by the extent and pace at which an organization (or a society) innovates and becomes more productive. In turn, innovation and productivity are related to the adoption and appropriate adaptation of new technological applications (Dutta & Mia, 2011, p. 62). Against this backdrop, the purpose of this chapter is to provide a coherent and well-researched account of globalization and its unfulfilled promises in regards to the African continent. Global knowledge production remains the centerpiece of this essay and the following diagram (Figure 1) is intended to provide a framework that guides the discussion in this chapter.

GLOBAL KNOWLEDGE PRODUCTION

Without going into detailed philosophical and ontological discussion of what is and what is not 'knowledge,' in this chapter global knowledge is constrained to the collective "research outputs by higher learning institutions around the world. It is also appropriate to add 'patents' in the knowledge production mix. Innovations by companies or higher education systems are registered by filing applications with national or regional intellectual property offices, such as USPTO (United States Patent and Trademark Office), and WIPO (World Intellectual Property Organization). As a result, the global knowledge production discussion in this essay refers to – R&D outputs and patent registration by higher education systems around the world. It is fitting to state here that there is an increasing trend that uses patent as indicators of intellectual capital (Grindley & Teece, 1997).

Following the framework above (Figure 1), it is appropriate to restrict the global knowledge production in view of R&D outputs and patents granted/registered. This way we can clearly demonstrate how - higher education, research, knowledge production, innovation, and economic progress- are so closely connected. It also helps to explain where Africa and other least developed countries need to place the priority and focus in order to leap-frog to the global knowledge-based economy. It is equally appropriate to note that many of African countries recognize these priorities and there are several meetings and conferences around such issues held in Africa. The United Nations Conference on Trade and Development (UNCTAD) is one good example to note where knowledge and technology for development is discussed (UNCTAD, 2008). While the UNCTAD secretariat and participating members duly recognize the power of knowledge and technology for innovation and development, the "national systems of innovation" model they put forward does not adequately capture the magnitude of the role that needs to be placed on higher education institutions (UNCTAD, 2008, pp.4-5).

In view of the discussions thus far, we recognize that the unfulfilled promises of globalization are the challenges Africa and other LDCs has to overcome in order to transition to knowledge-based economies. In the following few paragraphs, I present data gathered from international organizations to support the discussion around scientific publication outputs and R&D investment (commonly known as GERD – Gross Expenditure on Research and Development). We have already stated how Africa, especially sub-Saharan Africa, has little access to the global scientific and technical knowledge resources. The contribution of Africa to the global research footprint is equally extremely low. On his featured article on 'the scientific impact of nations,' King (2004) found that only 31 countries in the world account for more than 98% of the world's highly cited papers, of which South Africa is the only country from Africa in the 31 countries group. The world's remaining 162 countries contributed less than 2% in total. By some account, Africa's total contribution to the global research output is a mere 0.3% (Teferra & Altbach, 2003). The following diagram (Figure 2) is not directly related to Africa's share of scientific publications, but it is indicative of how a large percentage of the output (close to 80%) is by countries and regions outside Africa.

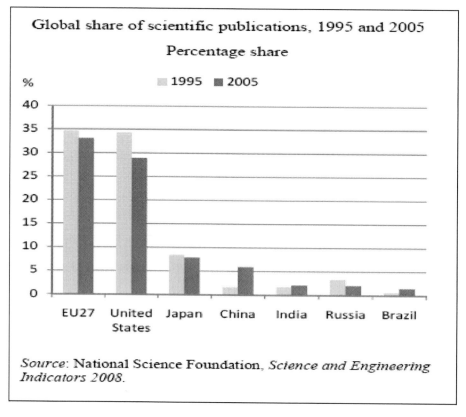

Figure 2. Global share of scientific publications.

Research & Development. R&D is another indicator that help us measure where countries like Africa are in so far as the global knowledge production is concerned. R&D is a critical activity of higher education establishments and I think it is fair to state that the amount of money allocated for it is directly related to the amount of research output that can be registered. In addition, several studies have shown that there is a strong correlation between countries that have shown significant economic improvement and those countries that have made substantial investment in R&D (GERD) – (UNCTAD, 2005).

Globalization is a major driver of innovation not only because it means more intense and global competition but also because it has created a more global landscape for innovation. A growing number of countries, including emerging economies, have developed important science and technology (S&T) capabilities and resources, and the internationalization of R&D and of science, as well as the international mobility of researchers, has created an increasingly global supply of S&T (NSB, 2010; OECD, 2008a; OECD, 2008b). As shown below in the map (Figure 3), the data from the National Science Board (NSB) in the US shows an estimated $1,1 trillion Worldwide R&D expenditures in 2007, where Africa combined with middle east has a mere 1.3% share of expenditure (or roughly 15 billion dollar (NSB, 2010, p. 4-33).

Figure 3. National R&D expenditures in 2007.

Still in the above share of R&D expenditures, we notice the same dominant pattern that the three regions predominate in their worldwide R&D performance - North America accounts for 35% ($393 billion); Asia, 31% ($343 billion); and Europe, 28% ($313 billion); the small remainder, approximately 5%, reflects the R&D of countries in the Latin America/Caribbean, Pacific, and Africa/Middle East regions (NSB, 2010, p. 4-34).

Innovation. Patents are good indicators of innovation activities. It is logical to consider the amount of patent applications by universities or specific countries offers a reasonable indictor regarding the intensity of innovation taking place in a given country or region. According to the latest report on higher education by OECD (Vincent-Lancrin, 2009, p.14), the number of patents received by US universities has increased from about 250-350 patents in the 1970s to more than 2700 patents in 2005. It is also reported that during this time period, the number of institutions that were awarded patents in a year has doubled to reach 160 institutions in 2005. Revenues from these intellectual property rights have also shown surprising increase and net royalties from academic patenting and licensing activities reached more than $925 million in 2004 for the 164 reporting institutions (NSB cited in Vincent-Lancrin, 2009, p.14).

The following table (Table 1) presents the number of patent applications filed under the Patent Co-operation Treaty (PCT) from 2006 to 2010, according to the sub region of origin of the applicant (WIPO, 2010, p.15).

Here again we see how Africa is faring compared to other sub-regions. Africa, all regions combined filed the smallest number of patent applications during the time period, 2006-2010. Southern Africa performed better, registering an average of 80% applications every year. If anything, these numbers will definitely give us some general idea as to how little innovation activities are taking place in Africa. This data did not indicate patents and R&D efforts by transnational corporations (TNCs) that have presence in Africa and there could be some spill-over effect as a result. A continent that has 54 countries and close to a billion population is still lagging behind its comparable region, the Latin American countries, and that's not a healthy sign. I again would like to situate the discussion in perspective. There is no doubt the leading regions in PCT applications have a well-established industrial complex, better economy, and world-class research-oriented universities that collaborate with their respective industries, and hence more innovation activities. However, we cannot under-emphasize the idea that this is where Africa should start to place priorities if it wants to transition to knowledge-based economy.

The same report (WIPO, 2010, p.21) presents an interesting comparison of the top 50 educational institutions that have filed patent applications in 2010 and there is no single university from the Africa region that has filed a patent. It may appear clear by now that I am stating the obvious because it could be anyone's guess that Africa will perform poor in all counts of knowledge production and one may suggest why bother to consult such databases and statistical tables to begin with. The key, however, in this paper is to clearly position the problem in Africa's overall poor performance and to shed light on what needs to be done. It's worth noting here that "Among the top 50 educational institutions, 30 are based in the US, 10 in Japan and 5 in the Republic of Korea. The number of Japanese academic institutions increased from 6 in 2009 to 10 in 2010," (WIPO, 2010, p.21).

Table 1. PCT applications filed from 2006 to 2010

Regions	Sub Regions	2006	2007	2008	2009	2010
Africa	Central Africa	2	1	5	10	6
	East Africa	23	20	23	19	17
	North Africa	59	82	75	75	76
	Southern Africa	423	408	393	378	326
	West Africa	8	2	5	2	6
	Total	515	513	501	484	431
Asia	East Asia	36,921	40,264	42,789	45,740	54,147
	South Central Asia	860	934	1,091	1,007	1,355
	Southeast Asia	590	667	839	870	1,115
	West Asia	2,031	2,274	2,450	2,118	2,168
	Total	40,402	44,139	47,169	49,735	58,785
Europe	Eastern Europe	1,226	1,295	1,412	1,386	1,459
	Northern Europe	12,576	13,488	14,423	13,324	12,835
	Southern Europe	4,283	4,668	4,730	4,735	4,869
	Western Europe	33,327	35,019	36,793	34,496	35,193
	Total	51,412	54,470	57,358	53,941	54,356
LAC	Caribbean	297	436	302	147	119
	Central America	192	206	244	216	205
	South America	407	504	577	644	689
	Total	896	1,146	1,123	1,007	1,013
North America	North America	53,855	56,922	54,614	48,144	47,611
	Total	53,855	56,922	54,614	48,144	47,611
Oceania	Australia/New Zealand	2,350	2,452	2,296	2,041	2,075
	Melanesia	1	1		1	
	Micronesia	1	1			1
	Polynesia	1		5	6	5
	Total	2,353	2,454	2,301	2,048	2,081

Source: WIPO Statistics Database

Table 2. Top 50 PCT applicants among educational institutions in 2010

2010 Overall Rank	Position Changed	PCT Applicant's Name	Country of Origin	Number of PCT applications published	Change Compared to 2009
38	2	THE REGENTS OF THE UNIVERSITY OF CALIFORNIA	United States of America	306	-15
103	4	MASSACHUSETTS INSTITUTE OF TECHNOLOGY	United States of America	145	0
115	16	BOARD OF REGENTS, THE UNIVERSITY OF TEXAS SYSTEM	United States of America	130	4
144	0	UNIVERSITY OF FLORIDA	United States of America	107	-4
145	33	THE UNIVERSITY OF TOKYO	Japan	105	11
168	-22	THE TRUSTEES OF COLUMBIA UNIVERSITY IN THE CITY OF NEW YORK	United States of America	91	-19
168	-18	PRESIDENT AND FELLOWS OF HARVARD COLLEGE	United States of America	91	-18
176	16	THE JOHNS HOPKINS UNIVERSITY	United States of America	89	2
183	575	SNU R&DB FOUNDATION	Republic of Korea	86	63
202	112	ARIZONA BOARD OF REGENTS	United States of America	80	25
206	74	THE REGENTS OF THE UNIVERSITY OF MICHIGAN	United States of America	79	18
218	-7	THE TRUSTEES OF THE UNIVERSITY OF PENNSYLVANIA	United States of America	75	-5
242	110	CORNELL UNIVERSITY	United States of America	71	22
287	162	OSAKA UNIVERSITY	Japan	60	22
290	-29	UNIVERSITY OF UTAH RESEARCH FOUNDATION	United States of America	59	-7
290	43	THE BOARD OF TRUSTEES OF THE UNIVERSITY OF ILLINOIS	United States of America	59	7
302	-64	WASHINGTON UNIVERSITY	United States of America	57	-15
341	60	KOREA ADVANCED INSTITUTE OF SCIENCE AND TECHNOLOGY	Republic of Korea	52	9
347	-70	THE BOARD OF TRUSTESS OF THE LELAND STANFORD JUNIOR UNIVERSITY	United States of America	51	-11
349	-16	CALIFORNIA INSTITUTE OF TECHNOLOGY	United States of America	50	-2
349	36	PURDUE RESEARCH FOUNDATION	United States of America	50	5
357	92	DUKE UNIVERSITY	United States of America	49	11
368	-102	WISCONSIN ALUMNI RESEARCH FOUNDATION	United States of America	48	-16
376	-94	UNIVERSITY OF SOUTHERN CALIFORNIA	United States of America	47	-13
376	9	KYOTO UNIVERSITY	Japan	47	2
376	264	INDUSTRY-UNIVERSITY COOPERATION FOUNDATION HANYANG UNIVERSITY	Republic of Korea	47	20
395	-10	ISIS INNOVATION LIMITED	United Kingdom	45	0
414	116	YISSUM RESEARCH DEVELOPMENT COMPANY OF THE HEBREW UNIVERSITY OF JERUSALEM	Israel	43	10
430	6	TOHOKU UNIVERSITY	Japan	41	2
430	41	THE UNIVERSITY OF NORTH CAROLINA AT CHAPEL HILL	United States of America	41	4
443	46	EIDGENOSSISCHE TECHNISCHE HOCHSCHULE ZURICH	Switzerland	40	4
448	-31	UNIVERSITY OF MASSACHUSETTS	United States of America	39	-2
462	-122	INDUSTRY-ACADEMIC COOPERATION FOUNDATION,YONSEI UNIVERSITY	Republic of Korea	38	-13
462	-93	RAMOT AT TEL AVIV UNIVERSITY LTD.	Israel	38	-9
462	54	KEIO UNIVERSITY	Japan	38	4
462	88	NORTHWESTERN UNIVERSITY	United States of America	38	6
462	119	NATIONAL UNIVERSITY CORPORATION HOKKAIDO UNIVERSITY	Japan	38	8
486	-76	IMPERIAL COLLEGE OF SCIENCE, TECHNOLOGY AND MEDICINE	United Kingdom	37	-5
486	240	INDIANA UNIVERSITY RESEARCH & TECHNOLOGY CORPORATION	United States of America	37	13
497	84	UNIVERSITY OF MIAMI	United States of America	36	6
497	229	NATIONAL UNIVERSITY CORPORATION OKAYAMA UNIVERSITY	Japan	36	12
526	-77	THE REGENTS OF THE UNIVERSITY OF COLORADO	United States of America	34	-4
526	70	THE UNIVERSITY OF QUEENSLAND	Australia	34	5
526	114	NATIONAL UNIVERSITY CORPORATION NAGOYA UNIVERSITY	Japan	34	7
526	200	EMORY UNIVERSITY	United States of America	34	10
559	-158	THE OHIO STATE UNIVERSITY RESEARCH FOUNDATION	United States of America	32	-11
559	-110	THE RESEARCH FOUNDATION OF STATE UNIVERSITY OF NEW YORK	United States of America	32	-6
580	-144	POSTECH FOUNDATION	Republic of Korea	31	-8
580	211	NIHON UNIVERSITY	Japan	31	9
593	47	UNIVERSITY OF MARYLAND, BALTIMORE	United States of America	30	3
593	266	NATIONAL UNIVERSITY OF CORPORATION HIROSHIMA UNIVERSITY	Japan	30	10

Source: WIPO Statistics Database

Now that we have addressed the knowledge production from the perspective of scientific publications, investments on R&D, patent applications by countries and universities, we can devote the remaining section of this chapter to showing the infrastructure development or availability thereof in the African continent, compared to other regions and countries. In due course, I will also address areas of improvement for a more inclusive –globalization and – development.

Internet Access & Use. Several indexes have been developed to measure the performance of nations connectivity and broadband penetration, such as the Nokia Siemens Networks (NSN) connectivity scorecard (Waverman et al., 2009), the International Telecommunications Union (ITU) Digital Opportunity Index (DOI) (ITU, 2008), and the Economist Intelligence Unit (EIU) E-readiness rankings (Economist Intelligence Unit, 2008).

One of the best developed index to-date, the NSN connectivity scorecard for 2009 considered 50 countries where Botswana, Egypt, Kenya, Nigeria, South Africa, and Tunisia are selected from Africa. Based on infrastructure and skills & usage as important indicators for connectivity, South Africa scored high from the African countries group, with a score of 5.76 out of 10, with Nigeria ending the least in the African group with a score of 1.30 out of 10, the U.S. leading all the 50 countries with a score of 7.71/10. Chile ranked high from the South American countries group, with a score of 6.59/10. The following radar chart is presented to compare South Africa and Chile, best performing countries in their respective region.

CURRENT INFRASTRUCTURE PROJECTS

Robert Rogers, executive director of the global information infrastructure commission (GIIC) cogently described the digital divide as "infrastructure divide." (Rogers, 2006). Whether the digital divide in Africa is attributed to government policy, economy, political, or other barriers, Africa's lack of reliable and quality bandwidth access is directly related to the infrastructure problem. The good news is Africa has embarked on mega infrastructure projects with combined cost exceeding billions of dollars, covering the entire continent. The following map (Figure 5) shows the types of infrastructure projects that are currently underway in Africa, some of which are already completed in the current year and preceding years.

The table below (Table 3) supplements the map above by describing the project names and the area they cover. Satellite based infrastructure projects are not included in this paper.

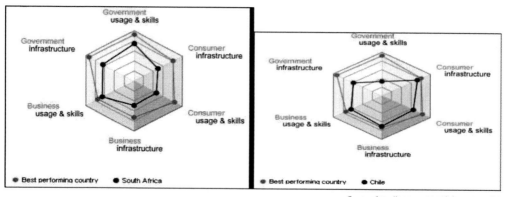

Source: http://www.connectivityscorecard.org

Source: www.connectivityscorecard.org

Figure 4. Comparison of connectivity performance between South Africa and Chile.

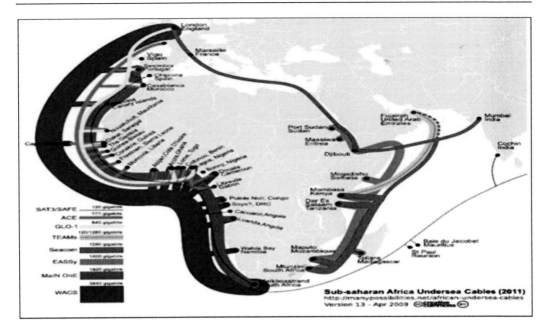

Figure 5. Africa's Infrastructure project.

Table 3. Current telecom infrastructure projects in Africa

Project name	Distance, coverage
TEAMS – the east Africa marine cable system	Mombasa, Kenya to Fujairah, UAE
SAT-3/SAFE – South Atlantic	South Africa to Far East
GLO-1	Nigeria, Portugal, UK
EASSy – East Africa Submarine Cable System, 10,000km covering distance	South Africa to Port Sudan *Completed in August 2010*
SEACOM - South Africa - East Africa - South Asia – 17, 000km worth of fiber optic technology.	East Africa to London, *completed in July 2009*
WACS, 14,000 km-long West African Cable System.	Cape town to London *Landing reached South Africa in April 2011.*
MaIN OnE	West Africa to Portugal
ACE	France Telecom

The three most significant infrastructure projects that were completed in 2009, 2010, and 2011 are the SEACOM, EASSy, and WACS, respectively (SEACOM, 2009). SEACOM connects south, east, and north east African countries to major landing points (GigaPops, Point of presence) in Marseilles, France and London, UK and Mumbi, India. The east Africa submarine system (EASSy) covers some 10000 km of fiber-optic lines linking 21 countries from South Africa to Sudan (Martin, 2006; Smith, 2008). EASSy offers 1.4 Tb/s (Terabyte per second – Tera for trillion) backbone capacities (EASSy, 2008), more than two times the current global reference for backbone excellence, which is 500 Gb/s (Gigabyte per second – Giga for billion). Even more, WACS promises to offer 5.12 Tb/s. These are indeed very promising initiatives that connect Africa with one another and to the rest of the world.

One should not be misled, however, these mega-infrastructures, as exciting and powerful as they are, can't bridge the content divide or knowledge divide I addressed above. If anything, these projects will primarily ease the existing digital divide in terms of overcoming the infrastructure bottleneck, even then if people can afford to subscribe from the regional service providers. In order to bridge the content/knowledge divide, African higher education systems should start working vigorously to connect one another and to connect with similar higher learning institutions the world over. I will spend time to discuss this particular issue below. There is no doubt these projects are excellent steps in the right direction in that Africa's isolation from the international scientific and scholarly community, will end provided the right partnership and collaboration are established.

BROADBAND ADOPTION IN AFRICA

The global Internet infrastructure is increasing its bandwidth capacity to cope with increasing Internet traffic. By the end of 2006, researchers led by a team at the University of Tokyo set the record by streaming data at a speed of 9.08 Gb/s, over a network which stretched from Tokyo to Chicago, on to Amsterdam, and then back to Tokyo via Seattle, a distance of 32, 372km (three quarters of the earth's circumference) (Richards, 2007). In this test the researchers achieved a speed about 1,000 times faster than top of the range broadband connections for the time, which would allow a user to download a high-definition DVD size film in 4 seconds.

While the world is heading to 100's and 1000's of Gb/s backbone infrastructure (GigaPoPs, Gigabit-per-second Points of Presence), the situation in Africa has been very grim. Africa is the second largest continent in size and population number next to Asia. The 2008 population estimate for Africa was 975,330,899, of which as of December 2008, only about 54 million users are estimated to have access to the Internet (Miniwatts Marketing Group, 2009), which accounts for a mere 5.6% penetration rate, compared to a 23.6% world average. The figure is very dismal for broadband Internet subscribers, with only a little over a million subscribers by the end of 2007, accounting for 0.1% penetration rate.

In the few countries where broadband connection exists in Africa, the services don't come cheap. Broadband costs more in sub-Saharan Africa than anywhere else in the world, consumers in the region spent an average of $366 each month for broadband access in 2006 compared to users in India, who paid just $44 (Smith, 2008). In addition to the poor telecom infrastructure, low broadband penetration and prohibitive cost, the total Internet traffic and utilization in Africa is one of the lowest compared to any other place in the world.

Akamai, one of the largest Internet companies in the world, regularly monitors the world's total Web traffic in real-time, providing a unique insight into what's happening on the Web. Akamai's web traffic monitoring and visualization solution offers a useful metrics that helps to assess the rate of Internet penetration throughout the world (Akamai, 2009).

The following summary (Table 4) is extracted from Akami's broadband adoption data:

Table 4. Comparison of broadband adoption and bandwidth by regions

Geographic region	Broadband Adoption (%)	Average bandwidth (kbps)
Africa	12	1009
Asia	43	4765
Australia	50	2811
Europe	70	3682
North America	55	3629
South America	18	1318

RESEARCH AND EDUCATION NETWORKS (RENs)

We have seen very interesting mega-infrastructure developments in Africa that far exceeds the world standard today. This is however like having a pipeline that brings water to bigger distribution centers. From there individual consumers, including higher education systems and organizations are expected to subscribe to broadband services so the pipe will extend to their premises or individual customer homes. Assuming both consumers and institutions have the required money to subscribe, that does not mean problem solved. What's being transported inside the big pipeline – content, data, research, knowledge – are equally important. It's here the building of national, regional, and global research and education networks become very critical.

Africa can benefit and at the same time contribute to the global knowledge base if these RENs are established. One way of understanding the digital divide as defined in this paper is by reviewing the state of National Research and Education Networks (NRENs) available in Africa. NRENs are established in over 60 countries the world over and their primary goal is to provide a dedicated bandwidth for research and education institutions. Regional RENs also exist in almost every continent, which are intended to serve member academic and research institutions. For example, Internet2 supported by the Abilene network is the premier advanced networking consortium comprising more than 200 U.S. universities in cooperation with 70 leading corporations, 45 government agencies, laboratories and other institutions of higher learning as well as over 50 international partner organizations (Internet2, 2008).

GÉANT, now GÉANT2 supported by DANTE (Delivery of Advanced Network Technology to Europe, is a collaboration between 30 NRENs representing 34 countries in Europe (DANTE, n.d.). TEIN3, Trans-Eurasia Information (TEIN) initiative is a regional connectivity for Asia-Pacific research and education connecting 19 countries and 45 million users at more than 8,000 research and education institutions across the region (DANTE, n.d.). ALICE2, (América Latina Interconectada Con Europa 2 - Latin America Interconnected to Europe 2) powered by RedCLARA network infrastructure is the first regional Latin American research and education network, interconnecting 12 NRENs across Latin America and offering connectivity to Europe and other regions in the world (DANTE, n.d.).

The map below (Figure 6) shows the global RENs topology, where only South Africa and the Northern African countries from the Africa continent have access to the International network, GÉANT2.

Outside South Africa and North African countries like Algeria, Morocco, Tunisia, and Egypt, NRENs in Africa are at their early stages of development. The North African countries enjoy a better national level infrastructure as well as having direct link to GÉANT2 via the EUMEDCONNECT2 gateway (the EU Mediterranean connection). EUMEDCONNECT2 allows approximately 2 million users in and around 700 institutions across North Africa and the Middle East to collaborate with their peers at more than 3000 research and education establishments in Europe (DANTE, n.d.). It is not difficult to realize the significance of having this link for the institutions in North African countries because it opens the floodgate for sharing and accessing academic and research resources from their pan-European counterparts.

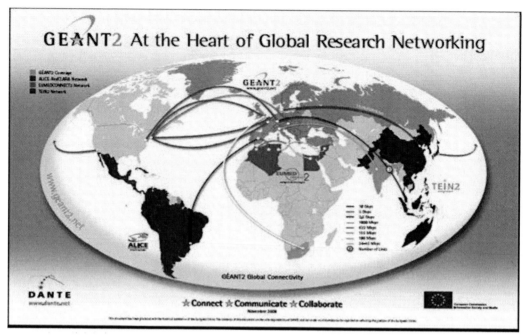

Source: http://global.dante.net

Figure 6. Global RENs connectivity map, Feb. 2009.

The present state of high speed Internet infrastructure dedicated for higher learning institutions in Africa is summarized in the table below (Table 5). The first national and regional REN with a global link to GÉANT is established in North Africa. South Africa's TENET also enjoys a direct global connection to GÉANT in London, and through GÉANT to more than 30 NRENs in Europe and the world over. The general characteristics of African RENs are that none of the national and regional RENs in Sub-Saharan Africa have advanced network and sufficient bandwidth (Tusubira, 2008). Formal RENs with underlying operational infrastructure exist only in Algeria, Kenya, South Africa, Sudan, Morocco, Egypt, and Tunisia. Countries in the process of establishing NRENs are Botswana, Mozambique, Malawi, Rwanda, Tanzania, Uganda, Zambia and Zimbabwe.

As can be seen from the table below (Table 5), only 4 countries in North Africa and South Africa from sub-Sahara have access to the international network, GÉANT. The situation is worse for west and central African countries, where there is no sign of research and education network development, except some ad hoc policy discussions, which is stalled for so long (Martin, 2006).

Outside of the North African regional network, a major regional REN called 'UbuntuNet Alliance' was established in 2006 with the goal of providing affordable high speed connectivity for sub-Saharan Africa tertiary education. The UbuntuNet Alliance already has 10 national RENs as its members from southern, eastern and central Africa. UbuntuNet Alliance is established at a historic moment when the infrastructure project is gaining momentum. Now that the SEACOM EASSy, and WACS projects are completed, UbuntuNet Alliance needs to take advantage of the high bandwidth backbone infrastructure, and similar RENs in other sub-regions in the continent should follow suit.

Table 5. REN activities in Africa

NRENs	Membership in Regional, Global or International RENs		
	EUMEDNCONNECT2	UbuntuNet Alliance	GÉANT
Algeria (CERIST)	√		√
Morocco (CNRST)	√		√
Tunisia (RFR)	√		√
Egypt (EUN)	√		√
South Africa (TENET)		√	√
DRC (Eb@le)		√	
Kenya (KENET)		√	
Malawi (MAREN)		√	
Mozambique (MoRENet)		√	
Rwanda (RwEdNet)		√	
Sudan (SUIN)		√	
Uganda (RENU)		√	
Tanzania (TERNET)		√	
Zambia (ZAMREN)		√	
Formal REN but no underlying operational infrastructure - Rwanda, Tanzania, Zambia, DRC, Uganda, Malawi, Mozambique			
Countries in the process of developing NREN – Botswana, Burundi, Ethiopia, Lesotho, Namibia, Somalia, Swaziland, Zimbabwe			

Networking is an essential component of academic cyberinfrastructure that facilitates many research-related activities such as communication, data transfer, high-performance computation, and remote use of instrumentation (NSB, 2010). We have recently witnessed a team of particle physics researchers from several countries testing the Large Hadron Collider (LHC) massive scientific equipment between the borders of Siwtzerland and France. This European Organization for Nuclear Research (CERN) based scientific center is the world's largest center for scientific research, where more than 100 member countries are represented, having nearly 8000 scientists and engineers from close to 600 universities working together (CERN, 2008). It is not difficult to understand that these thousands of research teams are distributed all over the world, and one would assume the cyberinfrastructure provided by DANTE and other NRENs would have helped to facilitate the team work.

CONCLUSION

The goal of this chapter was to shed light on issues of Globalization in relation to Africa. A strong argument is made that political and economic integrations including the free flow of goods and services alone will not fulfill the promises of globalization – one that is more inclusive and one that benefits all countries across national borders. What has not been given adequate attention and priority, especially when Africa is taken into account, has been the much needed development activity in higher education. A recognition needs to be made that well-established higher education systems in Africa that engage in R&D and knowledge production activity are critical to prepare the knowledge workforce, that in turn become the fuel for innovation and further economic progress. Around this focused themes, the essay tried to show the gap between Africa and other sub-continents in the world, particularly in regards to knowledge production and information and communication infrastructure. The author of this essay believes unless African countries fully participate in knowledge production and at the same time contribute to and benefit from existing global knowledge base, the rapid progress made in economic growth, poverty reduction, healthcare access, etc... will not be sustained. This is true because the world economy is more and more based on knowledge and for that we have already asserted that the human intellectual capital is more important than the abundant natural resource Africa has. It is the knowledge workforce of the future that will tap and make full-use of Africa's natural resource and that can only happen if Africa produces more scientists and engineers. Specific suggestions are also addressed to achieve these noble goals. Africa should set its priorities on capitalizing its existing mega-infrastructure broadband projects to connect higher education systems within the continent and with other sister institutions the world over – thus national research and education networks (NRENs) should be built and should work in a sustained fashion. The developed countries should also play their part in devising a scheme to lower the cost of scientific and technical resources. At a time when the world is increasingly moving to open access to scientific and technical resources, the west where much of the knowledge base exist should work with countries in Africa to extend the benefit of open access. For example, the National Institute of Health (NIH) in the US has adopted open access policy and as a result the UK and Canada have copied the entire Pubmed central (PMC) database (the single largest bio-medical database by NIH and National Library of Medicine) to create their own version of UK-PMC (http://ukpmc.ac.uk/), and PMC CANADA (http://pubmedcentralcanada.ca/). So, why not we have Africa PMC? With such concerted efforts and through time, I think the unfulfilled promises of globalization will be met bit by bit.

REFERENCES

Akamai (2009). Broadband adoption trends. Retrieved from *http://bit.ly/IC9Of*

Altbach, P. G. (2004). Globalization and the university: Myths and realities in an unequal world. *Tertiary Education Management, 10*(1), 3-25.

Association of Universities and Colleges of Canada (2005). *People and ideas: Why higher education is a cornerstone of productivity: A brief submitted to the House of Commons Standing Committee on Finance.* Retrieved from http://www.aucc.ca/publications/statements/2006/fnuc_05_30_e.html

Benkler, Y. (2006). *The Wealth of Networks: How Social Production Transforms Markets and Freedom.* New Haven: Yale University Press.

Delivery of Advanced Network Technology to Europe (n.d.). GÉANT2. European Commission Information Society and Media. Available *http://www.geant2.net*

Dutta, S., Mia, I. (Eds.) (2011). *The Global Information Technology Report 2010–2011 Transformations 2.0.* 10th Anniversary Edition. Geneva: Switzerland.

EASSy (2008). EASSy: *Closing the final link.* Retrieved from *http://www.eassy.org*

Economist Intelligence Unit (2008). *E-readiness rankings 2008, Maintaining momentum: A white paper from the Economist Intelligence Unit.* Retrieved from *http://bit.ly/j1ko2*

EUMEDCONNECT2 (n.d.) EUMEDCONNECT2. Retrieved from
http://www.eumedconnect2.net/

Food and Agriculture Organization (2009). *AGORA, Access to Global Online Research in Agriculture*. Retrieved from http://www.aginternetwork.org/en/

Friedman, T.L. (2005). *The world is flat : A brief history of the twenty-first century*. New York: Farrar, Straus and Giroux.

Grindley, P.C., & Teece, D.J. (1997). Managing intellectual capital: licensing and cross-licensing in semiconductors and electronics. *California Management Review, 39*(2): 8-41.

Internet2 (2008). *Emerging National Research and Education Networks*. Retrieved from *http://www.internet2.edu/pubs/emergingNRENs.pdf*

International Telecommunication Union (2008). Digital Opportunity Index (DOI). Retrieved from *http://www.itu.int/ITU-D/ict/doi/index.html*

King, D.A. (2004). The scientific impact of nations. *Nature, 430*, 311-316.

Marginson, S., & Wende, M. van der (2009). The new global landscape of nations and institutions. In OECD, *Higher Education to 2030, Volume 2, Globalization* (pp. 17-62). Paris: OECD Publishing.

Martin, D H. (2006, September). Research and education networking in Africa. Paper presented at iWeek, Kyalami Castle. Retrieved from *http://bit.ly/4OxZW*

Mattoon, Richard H. (2006). Can higher education foster economic growth? *Chicago Fed Letter*, No. 229.

Miniwatts Marketing Group (2009). Internet world stats. Retrieved from
http://www.internetworldstats.com

National Science Board (2010). *Science and engineering indicators 2010*. Arlington, VA.

Organization for Economic Co-operation and Development (2008a). *Education at a Glance: 2008*. Paris.

Organization for Economic Co-operation and Development (2008b). *Globalization and Open Innovation*. Paris.

Organization for Economic Co-operation and Development (2009). *Higher Education to 2030, Volume 2, Globalisation*, Educational Research and Innovation, OECD Publishing. doi: *10.1787/9789264075375-en*

Powell, W.W., & Snellman, K. (2004). The knowledge economy. *Annual review of sociology* 30, 199-220.

Richards, J. (2007, April 25). *Scientists beat Internet speed record*. Retrieved from *http://bit.ly/jgIOSC*

Rogers, R.G. (2006, October 6). Developing telecoms - the digital divide is an infrastructure divide. Retrieved from *http://bit.ly/kGJtNk*

Schaeffer, R. K. (2009). *Understanding globalization: The social consequences of political, economic, and environmental change*. 4th edition. Lanham : The Rowman & Littlefield Publishing Group, Inc.

SEACOM (2009). SEACOM: Connecting Africa to the world. South Africa - East Africa - South Asia - Fiber Optic Cable. Retrieved from *http://www.seacom.mu*

Smith, A. (2008, September 15). High-Speed Internet Coming to Africa. *Time Magazine*, Retrieved from *http://www.time.com/time/business/article/0,8599,1841175,00.html*

Stiglitz, J.E. (2006). *Making globalization work*. New York :W.W. Norton & Co.

Teferra, D., & Altbach, P. G. (2003). Trends and perspectives in African higher education. In T. Damtew, & P.G Altbach (Eds.). *African higher education: An international reference handbook* (pp. 3-14). Bloomington: Indiana University Press::

Tusubira, F.F. (2008). *Creating the Future of Research and Education Networking in Africa.* Retrieved from *http://bit.ly/rQX3D*

United Nations (2010). *The millennium development goals report 2010.* New York: United Nations. Retrieved from *http://bit.ly/c2YLPa*

United Nations Conference on Trade and Development (2005). Globalization of R&D and developing countries: *Proceedings of the Expert Meeting. Geneva 24-26 January 2005.* New York: United Nations.

United Nations Conference on Trade and Development (2008). *Harnessing knowledge and technology for development: Note by the UNCTAD secretariat.* Geneva, Switzerland.

United Nations Environment Programme (2006). OARE, Online Access to Research in the Environment, Retrieved March 27, 2009 from *http://www.oaresciences.org/en /*

Vincent-Lancrin, S. (2009). What is changing in academic research? Trends and prospects. in OECD, *Higher Education 2030, Volume 2, Globalization* (PP. 145-178). Paris: OECD Publishing.

Waverman, l., Dasgupta, K., & Brooks, N. (2009). *Connectivity Scorecard 2009. Nokia Siemens Network.* Retrieved from *http://bit.ly/199p6j*

Wende, M.C. van der (2009). *European responses to global competitiveness in higher education.* Research & Occasional Paper Series (CSHE.7.09).

World Health Organization (2009). HINARI: Access to research initiative. Retrieved March 27, 2009 from *http://www.who.int/hinari/en/*

World Intellectual Property Organization (2010). PCT: The international patent system yearly review. Developments and performance in 2010. Geneva, Switzerland: WIPO.

Zulu, B. (2008, May 21). Bridging the scientific content divide in African universities. Retrieved March 27, 2011 from *http://www.elearning-africa.com/newsportal/english/news137.php*

In: Globalization Dynamics
Editor: Kuang-ming Wu

ISBN: 978-1-62100-750-0
© 2012 Nova Science Publishers, Inc.

Chapter 3

GLOBALIZATION AND NGOS IN BANGLADESH: CONTRADICTIONS IN DEVELOPMENT

M. Rezaul Islam[*a] *and W. John Morgan*[‡b]

[a] Institute of Social Welfare & Research, University of Dhaka, Dhaka, Bangladesh
[b] UNESCO Center for Comparative Education Research, School of Education, University of Nottingham, England

ABSTRACT

This chapter considers the role of non-governmental organizations (NGOs) for development in Bangladesh in the context of globalization. Its findings are derived from an in-depth qualitative investigation conducted on two leading NGOs in Bangladesh. The main purpose of the chapter is to give a general account of the present trend of globalization in Bangladesh in which NGOs' functions are limited and, in development terms, often contradictory in such circumstances.

Keywords: globalization, NGO, development, Bangladesh

INTRODUCTION

This chapter considers the role of NGOs for development in Bangladesh in the context of globalization. Its findings are derived from an in-depth qualitative investigation conducted on two leading NGOs in Bangladesh. The main purpose of the chapter is to give a general account of the present trend of globalization in Bangladesh in which NGOs' functions are limited and, in development terms, often contradictory in such circumstances. NGOs' activities in the developing countries such as Bangladesh are dominated by the donor agencies which provide financial and managerial supports. Moreover, it is argued that most of

---

[*] M. Rezaul Islam, PhD is Associate Professor, Institute of Social Welfare & Research, University of Dhaka, Dhaka-1205, Bangladesh, E-mail: rezauldu@gmail.com

the NGOs practice Western development models through their activities which do not match with the local socio-economic, political and cultural conditions in Bangladesh. The purpose of this chapter is to consider the development constraints that the NGOs in Bangladesh are facing due to globalization.

GLOBALIZATION AND NGOS: THE DEVELOPMENT DEBATE

The concept 'globalization' is both a dynamic and deliberated word; it means different things to different people. There is no doubt however that globalization is at the centre of a starkly polarized debate over the major policy issues facing the world today (CEPR, 2002). Consequently, attempts to define globalization usually seem clumsy (CEPR, 2002), partial, and complex (Sen, 2002, p. 1). Globalization is a hotly disputed and contested issue (Carnoy, 1999). It offers many possible meanings, which depend on ideology, context, perspective and location. Harcourt (undated, pp. 7-8) notes that some global-advocates, such as Ohmae (1990, 1995), write enthusiastically about the 'borderless world' and 'the end of the nation state'. Some social scientists prefer a broad, rather unfocused definition, such as the 'movement of people, information, symbols, capital and commodities in global and transactional spaces' (Kearney, 1995).

Most economists understand the concept as free trade, and see the modern form of globalization as part of this process. For instance, Eslake (2000, p. 2), says "…globalization is…simply the logical extension of the tendency towards specialization and trade that has been going on almost since mankind first walked on the surface of the earth". Others, like Friedman (1998), regard globalization as being not just about trade, but about the triumph of market forces, technologies, and democratic forces throughout the world. Gunter & Hoeven (2004, p. v) state that it means gradual integration of economies and societies, driven by new technologies, new economic relationships, and the national and international policies of a wide range of actors, including governments, international organizations, business, labor, and civil society.

From the sociological and cultural point of view, Ludden (1997, p. 2) describes globalization as comprising human networks of influential interaction which are measured and explained by many factors, including migration, trade, empire, technology, and the spread of languages and disparate cultural elements. Held & McGrew (2002) state that it is the spatial organization of social relations and transformation, generating transcontinental or interregional networks of interaction and the exercise of power. Mittelman (2000) offers a broader explanation. He says that globalization means an historical transformation in: the economy, of livelihoods and modes of existence; in politics, a loss in the degree of control exercised locally and in culture, a devaluation of a collectivity's achievements. Globalization is emerging as a political response to the expansion of market power... [It] is a domain of knowledge. On the other hand, Sen (2002) sees globalization often as global Westernization. Ottone (1996, p. 231) says that globalization is commonly referred to either as 'the knowledge society', 'the information society', 'the communication society', or more generally, 'the post-industrial society'.

---

‡ W. John Morgan, PhD is Director, UNESCO Center for Comparative Education Research, School of Education, University of Nottingham, England, E-mail: john.morgan@nottingham.ac.uk

There is no doubt that globalization is a multifaceted and interconnected process involving economic, cultural, political and social change that has affected even the most remote communities in the world (Buckland, 2004, p. 126). For example, Rahman (2002) argues that globalization increased opportunities exist, reflected in economic growth for some but increasing disenfranchisement of the great majority marked by severe social dislocations. Ortiz (2007, p. 209) argues that nearly, two billion people are excluded from the benefits of globalization and development in Asia.

Leen (2003, p. 3) argues that globalization is neither novel nor new; it is a real danger of cultural homogenization as the result of contemporary 'western' driven models. Current global processes have been shaped by the neo-liberal ideology. It accents the rights and control of the individual by advancing the role of the market place into the economic, political and social sphere (Buckland, 2004, p. 127). Deacon (2000, p. vii) argues that globalization is undermining equitable public social provision. Wolf (2004) provides a list of the negative impacts of globalization in Asia. He says that globalization undermines the sovereignty of states and their ability to regulate their national economies and raises and allocates financial resources to public goods and social welfare; that it undermines democracy by increasing the power of unaccountable bureaucrats, corporations, and markets; and that it causes mass destitution and increased inequality within and between nations. Critics also contend that globalization is destroying agricultural; livelihoods for the poor and depriving them of affordable medicine, lowering real wages and labor standards, and increasing economic insecurity. Globalization helps to increase the amount of the productivity in the agricultural sector but the food security program could not give freedom to the peasants but rather they became dependants on external institutions such as the World Trade Organization (WTO) and International Monetary Fund (IMF) (Islam, 2010).

Friedman (1998, p. 93) argues that globalization isn't a choice; it is a reality. As a result the whole world is now facing massive financial crisis, and so called development models in the developing countries have collapsed, with millions of people forced into unemployment, bankruptcy, and material hardship. Apparently, people in border areas and landlocked countries in South Asia are among those most affected by a lack of adequate access to trade-led globalization. It is because the welfare of South Asia's poor people strongly depends on how trade at borders benefits the local economy, including landlocked areas, where the concentration of the poor people is comparatively high. Khan (1998, p. 122) argues:

"Globalization has not allowed South Asia's progress toward poverty reduction to continue at its previous pace. Indeed it has often slowed down or temporarily reversed. This has been due to structural inequality being aggravated by the disequalising forces unleashed by the reform packages that were adopted in the pursuit of global integration" (Khan, 1998, p. 122).

On the other hand, many authors argue that globalization is a new and effective means for development. Sen (2003), for example, says that globalization has enabled appropriate local steps to be taken. In the purest sense, it is not a threat to local cultures in the sense that imperialism is. It is seen that developments linked with globalization have opened up possibilities and new opportunities for human progress, and enhanced the quality of life for many people in the developing countries. In the face of declining opportunities for productive employment, the people of developing countries are trying to combine traditional activities with an increasing variety of new activities to protect their communities and their societies while ensuring themselves a means to guarantee their material wellbeing.

Some authors have mixed opinions about globalization. For example, Morgan (2005) says that the rapid process of globalization has clearly destroyed and damaged many indigenous and belief systems in recent centuries, although he argues that this is simply an inevitable process of historical change. As Karl Marx said: 'Men make their own history, but they do not make it just as they please; they do not make it in circumstances chosen by themselves, but under circumstances directly found, given and transmitted from the past.' (Marx, 1936, p. 116) On the other hand, globalization provides access to resources to use the political strategies of cooperation, negotiation and contestation, through which rural groups may overcome their poverty (Webster, 2004, p. iii). The communities that are well connected with the processes of cross-border exchange will benefit from globalization; communities that are not well linked with markets and commercial exchange may get left behind (Krishna, 2007, p. 191).

GLOBALIZATION AND BANGLADESH

The contemporary global debate on globalization and its multi-pronged impact has had a strong echo in both academic and political discussions in Bangladesh. After a hesitant start in the mid-1980s, Bangladesh moved decisively to embrace the wave of globalization in the 1990s. Ever since, the impact of globalization on the economy of Bangladesh and, more pointedly, on the lives of its people, has become a hotly debated Issue (Buckland, 2002).

It is important to emphasize that the economy of Bangladesh is one of the most vulnerable economies in the world, characterized by an extremely high population density, a low resource base, high incidence of natural disasters, and persistent socio-political instability, especially during the initial years of the state. Moreover, the country inherited a war-ravaged economy after the Independence War (1971). With such extremely adverse initial circumstances, the implications for economic growth were considered extremely unfavorable for Bangladesh (Sen *et al.,* 2004, p. 1). Within these socio-economic and political paradigms, the NGO sector became an agent for improving socio-economic conditions. However, most of the NGOs in Bangladesh are being funded by the donor agencies based in Western countries, which carries with it conditions and implications.

NGOs and donors face the twin challenges of demonstrating effectiveness in their work and accountability in their relationships with various stakeholders. Donors, on the one hand, are particularly concerned about the accountability of NGOs in the efficient and effective delivery of services. NGOs, on the other hand, are often concerned that *accountability to donors* can overshadow and overwhelm their *accountability to communities* and to their own missions (Ebrahim, 2004, p. 4). There are a number of ways in which donors provide direct financing to NGOs in Bangladesh- the most common is funding for specific projects. Where financing needs are large, donor funds may be pooled and a donor-liaison function introduced to coordinate support and reduce transaction costs for the NGO. In some instances, donors have financed the whole range of NGO activities, and in a few of these cases, the institution develops into a different legal entity by the end of the funding period. In recent years, the recognition that partnerships with smaller NGOs carry high transaction costs has increased reliance on wholesale vehicles, in which an agency manages a pool of money for which smaller NGOs compete (World Bank, 2006, p. vi).

Recently, the argument has been raised that, due to globalization, the development organizations (like NGOs) face fresh challenges in this new millennium of development activities. For example, Buckland (2004, pp. 128, 139) argues that the NGOs (mainly the big ones) have been encouraged to directly confront policy level constraints to development, and move out of program implementation. These changes have been significantly influenced by official aid agencies and northern NGOs (NNGOs) and with complex implications for indigenous NGOs and local communities. He adds that many people, including local poor people have benefited from the scaling-up of reform-oriented development organizations. But this strategy has not overcome other powerful local, national and global constraints to development that have led to persistent poverty, gender bias and economic change that has not benefited the poor.

OUR CASE STUDY: METHODS AND DATA

This chapter is based on a pair of linked case studies using a qualitative approach, influenced also by the ethnographic approach, considering different interacting social and cultural factors, such as people's attitudes, norms, values and practices in their day to day life. The field work was carried out between July 2006 to March 2007 in two communities and with two NGOs: *Proshika* and Practical Action Bangladesh (PAB) using two core projects such as the Markets and Livelihoods Program (MLP) (of PAB) and the Small Economic Enterprise Development (SEED) Program (of *Proshika*). One community was urban (Mirpur (1) Market for *Proshika*) and the other rural (*Mostofapur Bazar* (market) for PAB). Data were obtained also from the two indigenous occupations: the goldsmiths and blacksmiths. The other stakeholders were NGO staff members and community leaders.

A number of qualitative data collection methods such as participatory rural appraisal (PRA), social mapping, participant observation, focus group discussion (FGD) and documentation survey were employed to enhance the linked case studies. Twelve sets of research questionnaires/ guidelines and data were collected from forty two respondents (community people, local leaders and NGO staff members) of two NGOs and two communities. These included one set of questionnaires from head, area and field office staff members for both NGOs, (total four respondents); two sets of PRA (participatory rural appraisal) and participant guidelines from both communities (total four respondents); three sets of in-depth case study questionnaires for NGO staff members (head and area office), community leaders and community people (total sixteen respondents); four sets of focus group discussion (FGD) guidelines for NGO staff members (head and area office), community leaders and community people (total eight group of respondents); and two documentation guidelines from head and area office (total four respondents).

The data collection procedure employed a triangulation approach. One of the principal reasons for this is to avoid the limitations of a single method, as it helps to increase the reliability and validity of data. Data were analyzed using a *thematic approach* which offers opportunities to expand the already established horizons of knowledge. What is learned may reveal something that has been unknown, or it may correct or expand what is already known.

By revealing both personal and structural aspects of experience, a harmony is achieved, transcending the opposition and bridging the gap between personal and collective knowledge (Kidd, 1992, p.1). All sorts of data were carefully managed and the ethical issues were taken into account, which required extensive preparation.

WHAT DID WE FIND OUT?

NGOs' Conventional Role: Questions of Accountability

The field data obtained from the two communities of blacksmiths and goldsmiths showed that both NGOs' roles were not very supportive towards the development of local producers as the core of development. Our findings may be compared with Bebbington (2005, p. 937) who notes that NGOs' interventions became biased toward the less poor. It was observed that the NGOs were concentrated in urban areas, where replication of their activities was frequent, but many of the poorest people were excluded from the NGOs' target. The NGOs' bureaucratic approach could not ensure a 'sustainable community'; rather they further marginalized many local people, such as blacksmiths and goldsmiths. Significantly, the exclusion of many poor people from program objectives is quite a common feature of NGOs' activities in Bangladesh. The realities of those, who are poor and marginalized, are often ignored or misread (Chambers, 2004, p. 8). The notion of social exclusion focused on inadequate social participation, lack of social integration, and lack of power (Hunter, 2004, p. 2).

Notably, micro-credit based NGOs such as *Proshika*, did not provide loan support to goldsmiths, who were not guaranteed to re-pay such loans. In addition to this, the replication of a program in a community had a strong negative effect on the flow of programs of the same sector or run by the same NGO. As a result, many of the extreme poor remained beyond their services. Other r research has also criticized NGOs for lacking the capacity to involve the 'ultra-poor', and the poorest villages and neediest communities (Fruttero & Gauri, 2005, p. 760). We found that NGOs' rigid practices kept away such vulnerable communities. *Proshika*'s social and economic empowerment process usually side-lines the vulnerable population. One gold businessman said:

"SEED selects the people to give loan support who are able to return their loan safely. I cannot find any difference between the normal bank and NGO bank. Both are same. But I think they should provide loan support to them who actually need it."

Practical Action Bangladesh (PAB) worked with people's existing employment rather than focusing support for generating new employment. Some NGO staff members, community leaders, and local producers raised questions about NGOs' short-term development approach. This approach failed to sufficiently mobilize indigenous social and political capital that would build, or re-build community capacity and ensure sustainability of impact.

It was also observed that the indigenous people, such as blacksmiths and goldsmiths were suffering from 'minority' and 'isolation' problems, and their trust of NGOs was marginal. The local producers thought that, due to the expansion of large and medium sized industries through globalization, they might disappear in the near future. There was a clear lack of confidence in their reluctance to face this global competition, as their education and quality of production were not sufficient to do so. They were also afraid of the future, as they were not getting any kind of GOs' and NGOs' supports, and national and international networks towards their working capital, and modern tools and technologies. It was found that national and international involving technology-based firms were much stronger than local ones (Hendry, Brown, & Defllippi, 2000).

Our findings are that, in the 'winners and losers' game of globalization, more and more people were excluded from the benefits of this so-called development. Only those who could sell their labor or services as a commodity in an increasingly globalize economic system could survive; the majority who could not were left out (Tagicakibau, 2004, p. 8). Local languages, oral histories and cultural traditions were also threatened. Equity and redistribution were increasingly recognized the 'missing link'. Devine (2003) found that the 'ultra' poor had been completely marginalized in the NGO budgets in Bangladesh. It was not simply a lack of available resources; it was also fundamentally an issue of unequal power relations in which the poor were permanently marginalized and vulnerable, dependent as they were on local élites (Wood, 2003).

Our research reviewed the policy documents of both NGOs. These were well written, and the NGOs had high-flying goals and objectives, and set out interesting programs. The documents described how these would be achieved within the time framework. Notably, very good impressions were gathered from meetings with head office staff members in focus group discussion (FGD) sessions, who explained how they were helping the local producers. Some interesting points are worth noting here: the first is about written statement ', which was just 'a policy by which they caught the attention of the donors'. However, there was a big 'gap' between their written statement of policy and actual implementation at the field level. One *Proshika* staff member stated:

"There is a gap between policy and implementation because of financial dependency. Most of the NGOs are project oriented. When final funding comes it is too small for the purposes, then the NGOs change their target and the donors again shorten their funding allocation during final allocation. Then the NGOs again shorten their project target."

Many local producers and community leaders raised questions about the ultimate controversial objectives of NGOs. A number of local producers and community leaders argued that the NGOs were 'new money laundering' agencies. They stated that the NGOs were using donations to 'make money for themselves'. Many said that they were confused, whether or not the NGOs used more than ten per cent of their resources at the field level, but they had expensive furniture, high salaries, and high consultancy fees and so on. Edwards (1999, p. 367) found the same, when he reviewed the cost-effectiveness of two NGOs in Bangladesh, because of high overheads (a large number of staff and buildings). Stubbs (2006, p. 13) argues also that the most active 'high-profile NGOs' are more concerned with organizational gain rather than with the wider cause of poverty elimination. In addition, some NGO staff members' attitudes were negative about their own value. They could not believe that their help would contribute a great deal of benefit for the local producers. This opinion was given by a field worker of PAB. Local producers also claimed that the staff members came to them just to take their *kisti* (installment) and they gave them nothing, which eventually benefited them.

The enquiry found that the NGOs' development approach was 'monolithic'. The Market and Livelihood Program (MLP) of PAB just provided training and advocacy, and SEED of

Proshika micro-enterprise loans, training, and advocacy. It has been argued that credit does not necessarily help the poor to accumulate assets, improve productivity, escape poverty and improve empowerment (Nawaz, 2004, p. 170). It is true that microfinance programs and institutions are increasingly important in development strategies, but knowledge about their impact remains partial and contested (Hulme, 2000) and promotes lively debate (Simanowitz, 2003, p. 1). There were some other concerns about micro-finances, such as their distribution and usage. Micro-credit did not reach to the bottom layer of extremely poor households. In addition to this, it is found that a significant amount of micro-credit was provided to non-poor and non-targeted households. Importantly, it was observed that micro-finance does not 'automatically' empower, just as with other interventions, such as formal education and political quotas that seek to bring about a radical structural transformation that true empowerment entails (Kabeer, 2005, p. 4709). This approach can foster sustainable development if, and only if, it is integrated in a view of development that links the social, economic and environmental dimensions.

The accountability of NGOs, particularly their 'downward accountability'[1] to their beneficiaries, affected NGOs' effectiveness in the process of empowerment for the poor and marginalized people in developing countries such as Bangladesh. This debate is well traveled, and much less concern is given to the NGO's broad values and its effect. This notion of accountability created practical knowledge gaps. While, in principle, donors generally assigned a high value to it, in practice the ways in which they managed their grants and investments did not support it. Here, some areas such as common planning tools, reporting formats and information systems did not capture the quality of accountability in relationships between NGOs and their constituents, nor did they actively enable learning and improvement. It was seen in the research that micro-credit demanded 'a type and quality of relationship that actually limited poor people's room to maneuver'.

Informal discussions with the local producers, who were neither the members of SEED nor took a loan from any NGO, suggested that enterprises required larger amounts to be offered , which the local NGOs found risky, and many of the local NGOs did not have the capacity to provide such enterprise development loans to the small enterprises. The government and private commercial banks also suffered from bureaucratic practices and required collateral, which the small entrepreneurs in most cases were unable to provide (Chaudhury, 2006, p. 64). In reviewing the conditions of a SEED loan, it was seen that the SEED provided loans on specific terms and conditions, which the goldsmiths found hard, complex and unaffordable. They calculated that, including everything, the interest rate rose to thirty eight per cent, which a producer had to pay from his first month of the installment. It was also found from the list provided by SEED (2006) that the flat rate of other NGOs (such as BRAC 15%, and MIDAS 16%), and other government and private banks (*Janata* Bank 12.5%, *Agrani* Bank 14%, and Prime Bank Ltd 15%) was comparatively low.

The goldsmiths had serious problems formulating loan procedures; for example, to complete nine pages of an application form with information on personal, business, property, business appraisal, and profit. SEED required ten types of documents, such as the original

---

[1] The question of downward accountability is sensitive to power issues and the word 'beneficiaries' is problematic in its own right. The term 'downward' reinforces the idea of power asymmetry. Mulgan (2003) and Kilby (2006, p. 961) caution that the use of the term ''downward'' accountability can exaggerate the weakness of the beneficiary or client and so suppress the essential ingredient of authority inherent in the accountability relationship.

property or tenant agreement, two copies of a passport size photograph, letter (with two witnesses) and one copy of a passport size photograph from guarantor, citizenship certificate or two pages photocopy of passport, bank certificate mentioning current account of the business, photocopy of last month's electricity bill, photocopy of last month's rent payment receipt, photocopy of trade license and two revenue stamps of Tk. four, four non-judicial stamps of Tk. 150 (£1.36) each (two by the name of shop, one by the name of producer and one guarantor). In many cases, the goldsmiths had difficulties to produce such kind of documents.

NGOs' Political Networks as Negative Features for Development

The theoretical notion of a social network is to produce positive outcomes for development. For example, Lin (2000, p. 787) argues that the poorer social networks mean poor social capital and resources. Purvez (2005: p. 94) found in his study that the economically poor people in Bangladesh had poor social networks. The research agrees with these findings but argues that, recently, social networks have been a negative feature in some cases in Bangladesh. This needs to be considered within the country's distinct socio-cultural and political conditions. As Aldea-Partanen (2003, p. 1) argues, depending on various causes, social networks might allow the generation of positive or negative social capital. This also depends on the level of power decentralization in a political system within new institutional and social capital approaches (Svendsen & Svendsen, 2004, pp. 173, 175). It is still observed that in most developing nations, the power of NGOs has increased in recent years in relation to the state or government.

In the case of Bangladesh, the NGOs have become a formidable force, affecting the political and economic domains, especially the power and legitimacy of the government (Haque, 2002, p. 411). In addition, there is a growing trend, in alliance with foreign donors, for the influence of NGOs to expand to the extent that they now compete with the government for scarce foreign assistance at the national level and for sharing political power at the local level (Sobhan, 2000). To enter and be involved with the political networks as a result of empowerment of NGOs was not always helpful; rather these were used for self-interest, where the community people were affected seriously. Here empowerment was seen as 'any process by which people's control (collective or individual) over their lives is increased'. So empowerment was not a neutral force; rather it was a 'discursive construct, with its assignment meaning resulting from the exercise of power' (Lyons, Smuts, & Stephens, 2001, p. 1234).

The Head of the MSL argued that this politically empowered network deformed new feudalism. He stated that:

"[The] new power structure is now polarized in and affiliated by party based political networks in the community. This party based politics are spread out so strongly from grassroots to international levels. All parties have organizations everywhere. They are holding power. There is no power at the hands of educated and conscious neutral people such as teachers, social workers, and young generations."

It was found that many local NGOs' executive committee members were active politically, ranging from the Union Parishad (UP) Chairman to the Ministry level. The local NGOs are now part of the local power structure (Hossain, 2006, pp. 239-41). *Proshika* was accused of embezzling funds for developing NGOs during the Bangladesh Awami League (BAL) regime from 1996 to mid-2001. It was alleged that the *Proshika* chairperson (who was also the head of the Association of Development Agencies in Bangladesh (ADAB)[2], maintained a direct connection with the party in power, and tried to influence the ADAB in favor of his political will (Hossain, 2006, pp. 243-44). Hossain found that, out of thirty local NGOs in the Rajbari District in Bangladesh, only two had been exploiting opportunities through their networks and membership with the ADAB, which had good connections to national NGOs and NGO leaders at the centre. Even the membership of local NGOs depends on how deeply the personal relationship and political line were maintained. NGOs' politics appeared factionalized along political lines, and conflicts were confirmed to power, leadership and resources. The focus on power and trust naturally brings up the issue of inequality. Social trust can not exist among those who are unequal in power (Cook, 2005, p. 7).

It is also argued that the private power becomes public power when it controls voting behavior (Islam, 1974, p. 5). Many local producers and community leaders said that the staff and members of *Proshika* were used in the alliance against the existing government. In this condition, NGOs were not considered as autonomous, but rather as the extension of the existing power structure (Hossain, 2006, p. 248). The NGO staff members said that they often faced extraordinary challenges both at a personal and organizational level. They reported that they had to work long hours with limited resources in uncertain and volatile political and economic circumstances in order to help the most marginalized and disadvantaged members of their communities (Hailey, 2006, p. 1).

The Lack of Social Trust

In Bangladesh, the lack of 'social trust' has become a crucial barrier for NGOs' work. A number of networks, such as NGO staff members, community people, local leaders, local institutions and administration, funding agents, the Government, and civil society were involved within NGOs' initiative through collective actions and partnership contacts. Our research found that 'trust' was absent within and between these networks. For example, one community leader of PAB said:

---

[2] ADAB is a unique network of NGOs developed over the last two decades or so and emerged as a model for the development NGOs across the world. It brings together its members working within the broad framework of people-centered sustainable development. One of its central goals is to knit these constituent parts closer together and respond to their needs creatively. It has been playing active roles in strengthening inter-NGO relations, exchanging ideas and experiences, expanding fields of co-operation, developing organizational skills and enhancing functional relations and communication with government, donors and various groups of civil societies. ADAB is registered simultaneously under the Societies Registration Act of 1860 and Foreign Donations Regulation Ordinance of 1978. Currently ADAB has a membership of 886. Of these, over 231 (as of Dec. 1997) are at the central level and 655 are at the Chapter level (SDNP, undated).

"I have no faith in PAB. What are they doing for the blacksmiths? I did not find anything there. I heard that they provided some training, but they did not give any kind of capital to utilize their training. It is worthless."

Due to lack of trust, NGOs' social enterprise concept could not function well. It was one of the barriers to achieve mutual benefits. One blacksmith's opinion was:

"Why would I share my business with others? It is my business and I want to get all money as I earn. Why would I give and share my earnings and experience to others? It is my property. I don't think that everybody has trust in each other. Sir, please do not do anything else like that. If you do so I am not with you. We will protest that."

We found that the trust between the cross networks, such as NGOs with donors or NGOs with community people or community leaders/religious leaders or civil society and vice versa was low. We found also that the trust between NGOs and local producers was limited to the 'give and take' policy, as many local producers reported that their relation with NGOs was just for 'loan purposes.' There was neither any mental or social attraction, nor any kind of commitment, other than the financial. We argue that such exchange of trust is so slight and ephemeral that it could not give any guarantee to achieve any kind of long-term social change toward achieving social development. The local producers never believed that *Proshika* would do something for them in crisis periods, such as *chatabaji* (money collected by someone illegally), business loss, leadership crisis, local conflict, and control over the local market. The goldsmiths of SEED found that nothing was offered when they suffered such problems. In response to the question about the involvement with SEED, one goldsmith answered that, like other NGOs, *Proshika* is a 'new moneylender' (Hossain, 2006, p. 239; Davis, 2006, pp. 12-13), and it was helpful to get some loan from them. His comment was: *"When there is no way to get loan from elsewhere then they take loans from SEED"*. This kind of 'NGO dependency' is the dark side of social capital (Huda, Rahman, & Guirguis, 2005, p. 11). On the other hand, the blacksmiths were not significantly happier whether or not PAB would provide them other supports, such as further training, loan incentives, and help during leadership crisis, as they found nothing before.

The community leaders of both NGOs said that they were not happy to say that one NGO's relation with another or relevant organizations was good. They observed that the NGOs' relation in regards to knowledge and experience sharing was not cooperative; rather some were hostile to each other. One community leader of SEED said:

I don't find one NGO's relation with another is cooperative. Rather I find there is a cold war among them. I am saying this to see their overlapping activities, commercial motive and exclusion the 'ultra' poor from their activities. I heard from my village neighbors that many NGO staff members caution that they will withdraw their support if they go to another NGO".

The lack of trust from donors is a fundamental problem in the NGO sector in Bangladesh. There remains a huge gap between donors and NGOs as to what they expect from each other (GPF, 2005). It is because some NGOs, such as *Proshika*, were trying to compromise between Western knowledge and pressures, which, because of financial supports, became complex. Wallace & Chapman (2003, p. 2) referred to an experience in Africa, which indicated that in spite of a commitment to participation and bottom up approaches, there was a recognized need for sustainability. They also found that the focus was still on 'us' solving problems for 'them' (be they individuals, households, communities, or governments) and little trust was given to agencies.

As mentioned earlier, NGOs' political involvement and corruption limited their capacities. Due to these kinds of involvement, many local people, community leaders, local administrators, and the Government could not trust *Proshika* as this NGO was patronized by a political party. It was observed that many local people, who had no political involvement or were of specific political ideologies, withdrew their membership from *Proshika*, and many social agents became their rivals. NGOs' involvement in corruption was another negative image, where people's general faith was completely hampered. The news of corruption, with NGOs taking money from the local poor peoples' savings, is frequently cited in Bangladeshi newspapers. In a study of twenty NGOs, the TIB (Transparency International Bangladesh, 2007) found that many NGOs were registered with the government in exchange for bribes and some existed only on paper; and the government officials assisted them in the process. Our research did not find any such kind of corruption in relation to the two NGOs considered, but in general the local peoples' trust for the NGOs weakens the overall perception of the NGOs' activities. Moreover, there is no regulatory mechanism in Bangladesh for ensuring local peoples' savings and safety of deposits (Jackson & Islam, 2005, p. 46).

Donor Dependency and Organizational Autonomy

The majority of Bangladeshi NGOs are designed, funded, and managed externally (Hashemi, 1996). Consequently government-donor relations in Bangladesh are shaped by a history of donor dependence and reactions against it (Green & Curtis, 2005, p. 389). There were a number of issues that we found were important and challenging to the roles of the NGOs'. Essentially, NGOs' donor dependency is a matter of power relations (Wallace & Chapman, 2003, p. 8). This suggests that NGOs shared an international community development culture reflecting their own national cultural norms (Jamil, 1998, p. 43).

Local level planning, organizational accountability, autonomy and social trust became problematic with the application of so called 'universal knowledge'. The 'accountability' problem is traditionally concerned with the unequal relationships within the aid industry between donors, Northern and Southern NGOs (Lewis, 2007). It is because the donors bring universal values, self-colonization and élitism, individualism and anxiety. The NGOs often seek to represent 'fashionable' and 'acceptable' development ideas, knowledge and skills. As a result, enormous pressure gets put on the rural poor to comply with certain 'universal conditions'.

Such universal conditions should be considered as inappropriate or invalid, where less consideration is given to their validity (Wood, 2007, p. 6) for the local context. It creates dual dependency (Ferguson, 1994). It is directive, not facilitative (Garilao, 1987, p. 119). Ahmad (2006, p. 629) calls this 'donorship', rather than partnership. This is because there is a fundamental gap between the socio-economic conditions of developed countries and the developing world. This kind of 'imported knowledge' does not always fit well with the national development priorities and development systems (OECD, 2003, p. 10). Such kind of aid based development practices have long been a barrier to sustainable technology.

Schumacher (1973) believes that foreign aid is able to play only a limited role in bringing about sustained economic development. Such substantial input of foreign aid is doing much damage to the spirit of self-respect and self-reliance; the loss is greater than the gains. It creates a 'development' gap, which does not encourage innovative practices (Hossain & Marinova, undated, p. 9). A PAB staff member stated:

> "Sometimes the donors do not want to extend their projects or increase the funding for those though it needs to continue these for its local community demands. It is a big problem that we cannot provide any follow-up services for them. We all know that these social development projects need to serve continuously for a longer period of time for achieving actual outputs. But they are bound to stop those at a 'half-done' stage because of donors' discontinuation of funding supports."

Development is not apolitical, and 'the process of organizing and empowering communities and poverty groups is in itself a political act' (Garilao, 1987, p. 119). This de-politicization (Escobar, 1995) of NGO development efforts, experienced in Bangladesh over the last twenty years, is part of a broader global trend in NGO policies (Kamat, 2004). As a result, the NGOs were increasingly shaped by the Western-dominated international development discourse (Rahman, 2006, p. 456-457). However, this explanation can also be seen as 'one-sided', 'marginalized', question of 'sustainability' (Khan, 2006, p. 174), since this Western development model ignored the important influence of local conditions that the NGOs face as their constraints and policy choices. Within this discourse, do aid agencies have the right to be the 'voices of the poor' and to decide correct approaches for humankind and to speak on behalf of grass roots' communities such as blacksmiths and goldsmiths? We found that this Western model could not explicitly promote participation, but created confusion among local producers versus NGO workers, due to the lack of social trust.

Our research conjectured that around the aid process, there was insufficient dialogue, or an attempt at dialogue that would sometimes be totally unheard. Partnership relations in NGOs' activities in Bangladesh are inhibited by the instrumentality that each side brings to the equation: donors seeking conformity with current reform prescriptions or conditionality clauses, recipients seeking least (political) cost thresholds (Green & Curtis, 2005, p. 389). In this condition, both parties felt constrained into being more responsive and accountable to their superiors than to others. Like Green & Curtis (2005, p. 397) we believe that under such circumstances, improved donor co-ordination in any form may be conceived more as a threat than an opportunity by the national government. In addition, the South-Asian NGOs' have tensions regarding cutting-off funding supports from the donors (Fernandez, 1987, pp. 43-44). Globalization, new (and ever changing) trade agreements and aspects of the emerging new international political order all contain perceived threats (Green & Curtis, 2005, p. 397).

Because of donors' and other external pressures, NGOs' organizational autonomy, poor managerial capacity (Kusumahadi, 2002, p. 4) and inconsistency with the operations (Hulme & Edwards, 1997, p. 8) are now issues. Both NGOs had mixed opinions about this. Some NGO staff members observed that there were some barriers to increase control over program management, where a certain level of external/donor pressure existed. Some staff members said that they still had shortages of funds and had to depend on donors. As PAB (2006, p. 12) stated in the review of the MLP program, it took funds from a number of donor agencies, such as the United Kingdom's Department for International Development (DfID),

KATALYST during 2001 to 2006. They faced some problems from the donor agencies, such as project discontinuation and lack of flexibility. Some PAB staff members said that their central management was not decentralized to implement some local peoples' urgent demands, such as for loan supports, equipment supply, and supports during natural disaster. It was seen that both NGOs were based on the new public management (NPM)[3] approach. Both NGOs' staff members believed that too much donor dependency was bad for an organization. An organizational self-assessment can help understanding of and comparison between investments in learning and investments in doing, policy awareness and policy influence, insulation and influence, and independence and partnership. A foreign partner may damage a local NGO's credibility and effectiveness, especially as a leading voice in the policy arena (VanSant, 2003, p. 7).

However, in crisis states capacity is often limited, which increases the risk of corruption (Larbi, 1999). This was particularly true for *Proshika* as we stated earlier in this chapter. Moreover, the public-sector reforms were externally driven by donor conditions and timetables. The over-ambitious nature and the demand for quick results failed to take account of weak institutional and management capacities (Larbi, 1999). These kinds of capacities can use a new technocratic language, whilst failing to deal with political problems and contradictions arising between the situation of people in developing societies and the fashionable neo-liberal ideology (Arce, 2003, p. 855). We found evidence of this in both NGOs' interventions. However, we argue that the NGOs need to develop partnerships with consideration of fair measures and accountability. It is necessary for funding organizations and NGOs to put themselves in each other's shoes in order to understand better their mutual constraints (Donald Terry in Ebrahim, 2004, p. 11).

Conclusion

We understand that the meaning of globalization is multiple as well as complex. Its impact is widespread and mixed as it evokes different feelings among different people. We found that both NGOs experienced a number of threats and limitations due to this globalization, where their capacities were restricted. It was observed that globalization made these limitations so complex that the NGOs faced tremendous challenges to overcome those. One of the principal disadvantages was the poor socio-economic and cultural conditions of the country. The NGOs could not offer many of their interventions, such as loans, training, new information and knowledge, and technology to the local producers as the local producers were not able to utilize them. The chapter argues that this debate was extremely sharp, not only among ordinary community people, but also among NGO staff members, community leaders, civil society, development thinkers, and policy makers. The NGOs' conventional roles (i.e. micro-credit business, target based approach, monolithic development approach,

---

[3] NPM originated from the crisis of the Keynesian welfare state in the 1970s in developed countries such as the UK, Australia and New Zealand. The use of management techniques and practices drawn mainly from the private sector is increasingly seen as a global phenomenon. NPM reforms have shifted the emphasis from traditional public administration to public management. Key elements include various forms of decentralizing management within public services (e.g., the creation of autonomous agencies and devolution of budgets and financial control), increasing use of markets and competition in the provision of public services (e.g., contracting out and other market-type mechanisms), and increasing emphasis on performance, outputs and customer orientation (Larbi, 1999).

exclusion of the 'ultra' poor, work with existing employment rather creation new employment sectors, and downward accountability) were caught in this complex situation. However, the NGOs could not fulfill the demands of the marginal communities, such as the blacksmiths and the goldsmiths because of their lack of services. In addition, the feeling of isolation among such local communities was considerable in competitive globalize markets.

It is found that most of the big NGOs, such as *Proshika* were empowered politically. However, there was neither social trust nor collective community supports. Such networks and empowerment were used to perform a conventional role robustly. These attitudes created many conflicts among different development agents. Eventually, the NGOs lost people's trust and confidence. Moreover, NGOs' exploitation, through money laundering, corruption, and misuse of donation, gave a negative impression to the community people, including community leaders and civil society. As a result, the NGOs could not find network-based broader supports at the community level.

Most NGOs in Bangladesh are dependent on foreign donation. It was seen that, within 'decentralized management', there existed a 'centralized management' system. Because of donors' terms and conditions, the local NGOs lost their autonomous management power. However, the NGOs lost their 'ownership'. Rather, they were practicing 'formal' and 'universal' knowledge (neo-liberal ideologies), which failed to get responses from local people. The chapter concludes that a new power is emerging called the 'new civil society', which included teachers, NGO managers and NGO workers, businessmen, and local leaders, stimulated by global aid interventions. But this 'new civil society' is also empowered through political networks, and the role of these towards development is also negative. This is a dilemma hindering the prospects of authentic development in Bangladesh.

REFERENCES

Ahmad, M. M. (2006) The 'partnership' between international NGOs (non-governmental organizations) and local NGOs in Bangladesh, *Journal of International Development*, 18, 629-638.

Aldea-Partanen, A. (2003) Local development networks in remote areas and knowledge management, *Third European Knowledge Management Summer School*, San Sebastian (Spain), Research and Development Centre of Kajaani, 7-12 September.

Arce, A. (2003) Pre-approaching social development: a field of action between social life and policy processes, *Journal of International Development*, 15, 845-861.

Bebbington, A. (2005) Donor–NGO relations and representations of livelihood in non-governmental aid chains, *World Development*, 33(6), 937-950.

Buckland, J. (2002) Non-government Organizations and Civil Society in Bangladesh: Risks and Opportunities Globalization, in Rahman, M. M. (Ed) (2002) *Preface, Globalization, environmental crisis, and social change in Bangladesh* (Manitoba, University of Manitoba).

Buckland, J. (2004) Globalization, NGOs and civil society in Bangladesh, in: J. L. Chodkiewicz & R. E. Wiest (Eds) *Globalization and community: Canadian perspectives*, Anthropology paper 34 (Winnipeg, University of Manitoba).

Carnoy, M. (1999) *Globalization and educational reform: what planners need to know* (Paris, UNESCO).

Centre for Economic Policy Research (CEPR) (2002) *Making sense of globalization: a guide to the economic issues*, CEPR policy paper no. 8 (London, European Commission Group of Policy Advisors, CEPR).

Chambers, R. (2004) *Ideas for development: reflecting forwards,* IDS working paper 238 (Brighton, Institute of Development Studies (IDS).

Chaudhury, I. A. (2006) *Sustainable livelihoods through capacity building and enterprise development, documenting the evidence and lessons learned*, (Dhaka, Practical Action Bangladesh).

Cook, K. S. (2005) Networks, norms, and trust: the social psychology of social capital, *Social Psychology Quarterly*, 68(1), 4-14.

Davis, J. K. (2006) *NGOs and development in Bangladesh: whose sustainability counts?* (Perth (Australia), Murdoch University).

Deacon, B. (2000) *Globalization and social policy: the threat to equitable welfare* (Geneva, United Nations Research Institute for Social Development (UNRISD).

Devine, J. (1996) *NGOs: changing fashion or fashioning change?* Occasional Paper, Centre for Development Studies (CDS) (Bath (UK), University of Bath).1

Devine, J. (2003) The paradox of sustainability: reflections on NGOs in Bangladesh, *Annals of the American Academy of Political and Social Science,* 590, 227 – 242.

Ebrahim, A. (2004) Seeking NGO-donor partnership for greater effectiveness and accountability multilateral investment fund (MIF) & Sustainable Development Department (SDS), *Inter-American Development Bank (IDB), Workshop,* 12-13 May.

Edwards, M. (1999) NGO performance- what breeds success? new evidence from South Asia, *World Development*, 27(2), 361-374.

Escobar, A. (1995) *Encountering development: the making and unmaking of the third world* (Princeton (New Jersey), Princeton University Press).

Eslake, S. (2000) *The drivers of globalization, presentation to a Regional Defence Seminar,* the Australian Department of Defence Cypress Lakes Resort, New South Wales, 20 November.

Ferguson, J. (1994) *The anti-politics machine: development, depoliticization, and bureaucratic power in Lesotho* (Minneapolis, University of Minnesota Press).

Fernandez, M. E. (1987) NGOs in south Asia: people's participation and partnership, *World Development*, 15 (Supplementary), 39-49.

Friedman, T. L. (1998) *The Lexus and the olive tree* (New York, Times Books). Fruttero, A. & Gauri, V. (2005) The strategic choices of NGO: location in rural Bangladesh, *The Journal of Development Studies*, 41(5), 759-787.

Garilao, E. D. (1987) Indigenous NGOs as strategic institution: managing the relationship with Government and resource agencies, *World Development*, 15 (Supplement), 113-120.

Green, L. & Curtis, D. (2005) Bangladesh: partnership or posture in aid for development?, *Public Administration and Development*, 25(5), 389-398.

Gunter, B. G. & Hoeven, R. V. D. (2004) *The social dimension of globalization: a review of literature*, working paper no. 24 (Geneva, Policy Integration Department, World Commission of Social Dimension of Globalization, International Labor Organization (ILO).

Hailey, J. (2006) *NGO leadership development: a review of the literature* (Oxford, International NGO Training & Research Centre (ITRAC).

Haque, M. S. (2002) The changing balance of power between the Government and NGOs in Bangladesh, *International Political Science Review,* 23(4), 411–435.

Harcourt, T. (undated) *What is this thing called globalization?* A discussion paper, (New South Wales, Economics' the Association Journal of the Economics and Business Educators' Association of New South Wales).

Hashemi, S. (1996) NGO accountability in Bangladesh: beneficiaries, donors and the state, in: M. Edwards & D. Hulme (Eds) *Beyond the magic bullet: NGO performance and accountability in the post-cold war world,* pp. 123–31 (West Hartford, Kumarian Press).

Held. D. & McGrew, A. (eds.) (2002) *Governing globalization: Power, authority, and global Governance,* Cambridge, UK: Polity Press.

Hendry, C., Brown J. & Defllippi, R. (2000) Regional clustering of high technology-based firms: opto-electronics in three countries, *Regional Studies,* 34(2), 129-144.

Hossain, A. & Marinova, D. (undated) *Assessing tools for sustainability: Bangladesh context* (Murdoch (Australia), Institute for Sustainability and Technology Policy, Murdoch University).

Hossain, A. (2006) The changing local rural power structure: the élite and NGOs in Bangladesh, *Journal of Health Management,* 8(2), 229-250.

Huda, K., Rahman, S. & Guirguis, C. (2005) *Is social capital the missing link? an exploratory study of Gram Shahayak Committee effectiveness* (Dhaka, Bangladesh Rural Advancement Committee (BRAC).

Hulme, D. & Edwards, M. (Eds.) (1997) *NGOs, states and donors: too close for comfort* (Basingstoke/New York, Macmillan/St. Martin's Press).

Hulme, D. (2000) *Protecting and strengthening social capital in order to produce desirable development outcome,* Social Development Systems for Coordinated Poverty Eradication, SD Scope Paper no. 4 (Bath, Centre for Development Studies, University of Bath).

Hunter, B. (2004) *Taming the social capital in hydra? indigenous poverty, social capital theory and measurement,* Discussion paper no. 261/2004 (Canberra, Centre for Aboriginal Economic Policy Research, Australian National University).

Islam, A. K. M. A. (1974) *A Bangladesh village conflict and cohesion: an anthropological study of politics* (Cambridge, Massachusetts (USA), Schenkman Publishing Company).

Islam, M. R. (2010) Book Review, Transnational agrarian movements confronting globalization, Saturnino M. Borras Jr., Marc Edelman, Cristo´ bal Kay (Eds.). Wiley-Blackwell (2008). 362 pp., £19.99 pbk, ISBN: 978-1-4051-9041-1, *Journal of Rural Studies,* 26(1), 83

Jackson, K. E. & Islam, T. (2005) Regulation of microfinance NGOs: general reflections and the case of Bangladesh, *International Journal of Rural Management,* 1(1), 45-57.

Jamil, I. (1998) Transactional friction between NGOs and public agencies in Bangladesh: culture or dependency? *Contemporary South Asia,* 7(1), 43-69.

Kabeer, N. (2005) Is microfinance a 'magic bullet' for women's empowerment? Analysis of findings from South Asia, *Economic and Political Weekly,* 29.

Kamat, S. (2004) The privatization of public interest: theorizing NGO discourse in a neo-liberal era, *Review of International Political Economy,* 11(1), 155–176.

Kearney, M. (1995) The local and the global: the anthropology of globalization and transactionalism, *Annual Review of Anthropology,* 24, 547-565.

Keystone (2006) *Downward accountability to 'beneficiaries': NGO and donor perspectives*, online: *http://www.keystoneaccountability.org/files/Keystone%20Survey%20Apr%2006%20Final%20Report.pdf (accessed: 11 May 2008).*

Khan, A. R. (1998) The impact of globalization in South Asia, in Bhalla, A. S. (Ed.) Globalization, growth, and marginalization, Ottawa: International Development Research Centre.

Khan, S. (2006) Learning from south Asian 'successes': tapping social capital, *South Asia Economic Journal*, 7 (2), 157-178.

Kidd, S. D. (1992) Thematic methodology from the amplifying complexity of consciousness, presented at the Fourth International Symposium of Universalism, 19 May, London, England.

Kilby, P. (2006) Accountability for empowerment: dilemmas facing non-governmental organizations, *World Development*, 34(6), 951–963.

Krishna, A. (2007) Mobilizing social capital: Community responses to globalization, in in Rondinelli, D. A. & Heffron, J. M. (Eds.) (2007) Globalization and Changer in Asia (Boulder & London: Lynne Rienner Publishers), 191-208.

Kusumahadi, M. (2002) *Practical challenges to the community empowerment program experiences of Satunama Foundation of Yogyakarta Indonesia*, online: http://www.satunama.org/upl/article/en_Meth.Kusumahadi%5C's%20PRESENTATION.pdf (Accessed: 19 October 2006).

Larbi, G. A. (1999) *The new public management approach and crisis states* (Geneva, United Nations Research Institute for Social Development (UNRISD).

Leen, M. (2003) The challenges and opportunities for international civil society in promoting ethical globalization, Development Studies Association (DSA) Conference *on Globalization and Development*, Glasgow (UK), University of Strathclyde, 10-12 September.

Lin, N. (2000) Inequality in social capital, *Contemporary Sociology*, 29(6), 785-795.

Ludden, D. (1997) The news of globalization, *Online:* http://www.sas.upenn.edu/~dludden/global2.htm *(accessed: 27 August 2005).*

Lyons, M., Smuts, C. & Stephens, A. (2001) Participation, empowerment and sustainability: (how) do the links work? *Urban Studies,* 8, 1233–1251.

Marx, K., (1936) 'The Eighteenth Brumaire of Louis Bonaparte', in Burns, E., (Ed.) A handbook of Marxism, (London, Left Book Club, Victor Gollancz Ltd.)

Mittleman, J. H. (2000) The globalization syndromes: transformation and resistance *(Princeton, Princeton University Press).*

Morgan, W. J. (2005) 'Local knowledge and globalization: are they compatible?' in: C. Cullingford & S. Gunn (Eds) *Globalization, education and culture shock*, (London, Ashgate). pp. 35-47

Mulgan, R. (2003) *Holding power to account: accountability in modern democracies* (New York, Palgrave).

Nawaz, S. (2004) An evaluation of micro-credit as a strategy to reduce poverty: a case study of three micro-credit programs in Bangladesh, in: K. Jackson, N. Lewis, S. Adams, *et al.*, (Eds) *Development on the Edge*, pp. 170-1175, *The Fourth Biennial Conference of the Aotearoa,* New Zealand, 3-5

Ohmae, K. (1990) *The borderless world* (London, William Collins).

Organization for Economic Cooperation and Development (OECD) (2003) *Harmonising donor practices for effective aid delivery,* Development Assistance Committee (DAC) Guidelines and Reference Series (Paris, OECD).

Ortiz, I. (2007) Social protection policies: making globalization work for all, in in Rondinelli, D. A. & Heffron, J. M. (Eds.) (2007) *Globalization and Changer in Asia* (Boulder & London: Lynne Rienner Publishers), 209-224.

Ottone, E. (1996) Globalization and educational change: modernism and citizenship, *Prospects,* XXXVI (2).

Practical Action Bangladesh (PAB) (2006) *Annual report 2006* (Dhaka, PAB).

Purvez, M. S. A. (2005) Building support for a living: the importance of social networks for the livelihoods of the poor in: I. A. Khan & J. Seeley (Eds) *Making a living: the livelihoods of the rural poor in Bangladesh,* pp. 93-107 (Dhaka, University Press Ltd.).

Rahman, M. M. (Ed) (2002) Preface, Globalization, environmental crisis, and social change in Bangladesh (Manitoba, University of Manitoba).

Rahman, S. (2006) Development, democracy and the NGO sector theory and evidence from Bangladesh, *Journal of Developing Societies,* 22(4), 451–473.

Schumacher, E. F. (1973) *Small is beautiful: economics as if people mattered* (London, Harper and Row).

Sen, A. (2002) *How to judge globalism,* the American prospect, online: *http://www.prospect.org/print/V13/1/sen-a.html* (accessed: 12 July 2005).

Sen, A. (2003) The importance of basic education, speech to the *Commonwealth Education Conference,* Edinburgh, 28 October.

Sen, B. Mujeri, M. K. & Shahabuddin, Q. (2004) Operationalizing pro-poor growth: Bangladesh as a case study, Online: *http://siteresources.worldbank.org/INTPGI/Resources/342674-1115051237044/oppgbangladesh(Nov).pdf* (accessed: 12 April 2009).

Simanowitz, A. (2003) Appraising the poverty outreach of microfinance: a review of the CGAP poverty assessment tool (PAT), I*mproving the Impacts of Microfinance on Poverty: Action Research Program,* 1, 1-7, Online: http://ageconsearch.umn.edu/bitstream/23743/1/op030001.pdf (accessed: 1 August 2008).

Sobhan, R. (2000) *Trends in the post-flood economy: a review of Bangladesh's development* (Dhaka, Centre for Policy Dialogue).

Stubbs, P. (2006) Community development in contemporary Croatia: globalization, neo-liberalisation and NGOI-isation, in L. Dominelli (Ed) *Revitalising communities in a globalising world*, pp. 161-174 (London, Ashgate).

Sustainable Development Networking Program (SDNP) (undated) *Association of Development Agencies in Bangladesh (ADAB),* (Dhaka: SDNP).

Svendsen, G. L. H. & Svendsen, G. T. (2004) *Creation and destruction of social capital: entrepreneurship, co-operative movements and institutions,* (Cheltenham (UK), Edward Elgar).

Transparency International Bangladesh (TIB) (2007) *Problems in good governance in the NGO sector: the way forward, presented in a discussion meeting at CIRDAP Auditorium,* Dhaka, Bangladesh, 6 October.

Tagicakibau, E. G. (2004) Development-for whom in the pacific? issues and challenges to globalization and human security at community level, in: K. Jackson, N. Lewis, S.

Adams, *et al.*, (Eds) *Development on the edge*, pp. 7-12, *The Fourth Biennial Conference of the Aotearoa*, New Zealand, 3-5 December.

VanSant, J. (2003) *Challenges of local NGO sustainability*, Keynote remarks prepared for the *USAID/PVC-ASHA Annual PVO Conference*, 14 October.

Wallace, T. & Chapman, J. (2003) Is the way aid is disbursed through NGOs promoting a development practice that addresses chronic poverty well? an overview of an on-going research project, presentation at *Staying Poor: Chronic Poverty and Development Policy*, International Conference, IDPM, University of Manchester, 7-9 April.

Webster, N. (2004) Understanding the evolving diversities and originalities in rural social movements in the age of globalization *(Geneva, United Nations Research Institute for Social Development (UNRISD)).*

Wolf, M. (2004) *Why globalization works* (New Heaven, CT: Yale University Press).

Wood, G. D. (2003) Staying secure, staying poor: the Faustian bargain, *World Development*, 31 (3), 455-473.

World Bank (2006) *Economic and governance of non-governmental organizations in Bangladesh* (Dhaka, World Bank Office).

In: Globalization Dynamics
Editor: Kuang-ming Wu

ISBN: 978-1-62100-750-0
© 2012 Nova Science Publishers, Inc.

Chapter 4

TAOISM IN WESTERN THERAPY OF ANXIETY

Ruth Chu-Lien Chao[*]
University of Denver, Colorado, US

ABSTRACT

We believe that Chinese thinking can enrich Western psychologists with a new approach to the treatment of anxiety. This essay first reviews various treatment-approaches in the West, such as how these treatments approach anxiety, in what manners they are limited, then how related Oriental treatment approaches—in this chapter, Taoist—are to current approaches in the West. Our overall aim is to consider how these two approaches can best be integrated. This essay includes (a) review of Western treatments of anxiety, (b) brief explanation of the Chinese Taoist approach to anxiety, (c) integration of Western and Chinese Taoist approaches, and (d) the limitations of this chapter.

Integrating Taoism and Western therapeutic theory needs to satisfy two requirements. One, general theory and concrete specifics inter-need to inter-establish. Two, the West and the Orient must inter-learn, not to impose or discard either one (Chao, 2001; Tweed &). This essay tries to fulfill both desiderata by concretely Taoism-framing the Western treatment of anxiety.

Most current treatments of anxiety operate in the West,[1] and the history of treating anxiety consists in Western thinking pattern. Those psychologists tend to indifferently apply their Western approaches and treatments to a variety of non-Western races and cultures, including the Chinese Taoist.[2] But mental illness is closely related to *how* we think, and how we think is culture, so mental illness is inextricably cultural. As den Boer (1997) pointed out,

---

[*] Assistant Professor of Counseling Psychology, University of Denver, Colorado, USA Email: ruth_chao2000@yahoo.com
[1] The term Western as used here refers to cultures of the United States, Canada, and European Countries.
[2] Since Asian cultures are so numerous as to be unwieldy, this essay focuses on one of them, Chinese thoughts, especially on Taoism made of Tao Te Ching and the Chuang Tzu, and their extrapolations and elaborations. The other Chinese trend of Confucianism awaits future consideration.

"Although the biology of the major illness [anxiety disorder] is the same everywhere in the world, how we organize what we know and see, as well as what we think we understand, differs from country to country, and from culture to culture (p. iii)."

In my opinion, the issue goes deeper, more extensive, and more complex than the above quotation says. How we organize our knowledge and understanding, when it goes askew, *is* "mental illness," and what/how we take "askew" to mean is "culture." Thus "mental illness" is a cultural matter. And so, cultural differences about mental illness cut even deeper than den Boer thinks. A common perspective among anthropologists is that what one culture sees as mental illness, another culture extols as high virtue to emulate, if not a divine visitation to revere (Benedict, 1934; Lebra, 1976; Shweder & LeVine, 1984).[3]

Suppose one could bypass this complex issue, however, and assumes that den Boer's thesis is valid, that many "civilized" cultures agree on what mental disorders are. Even then, we feel pain as we reflect if adequate and effective cure is possible in such a situation at all, so long as we keep applying indifferently, uniformly, and universally the Western style of treatment to different *sorts* of "mental illnesses" in different cultures.

For simplicity's sake, this essay focuses on one mental illness, anxiety, and presents a new perspective on treating anxiety disorders by integrating Western approaches and the Chinese thoughts. As Alan Watts (1975) said,

> The other way was to describe...the most fruitful way in which Eastern and Western psychotherapies can fertilize each other. For not only have they much to learn from each other, but also it seems to me that the comparison brings out hidden and highly important aspects of both (p. x).

We believe that Chinese thinking can enrich psychologists with a new approach to the treatment of anxiety. This essay first reviews various treatment-approaches in the West, such as how these treatments approach anxiety, in what manners they are limited, then how related Oriental treatment approaches—in our essay, Taoist—are to current approaches in the West. Our overall aim is to consider how these two approaches can best be integrated. Thus this essay includes (a) review of Western treatments of anxiety, (b) brief explanation of the Chinese Taoist approach to anxiety, (c) integration of Western and Chinese Taoist approaches, and (d) some limitations of this essay.

A REVIEW OF WESTERN TREATMENTS ON ANXIETY

First, anxiety must be defined, at least provisionally, taken as "anxiety" among Western psychologists. Anxious people with generalized disorders lack effective anxiety-avoidance mechanism. Their unavoidable feelings of threat to cause anxiety are central in the disorder (Carson, Butcher, & Mineka, 1996). Generalized anxiety disorder (GAD) is characterized by chronic excessive worry about a number of events. "Free-floating anxiety" is its traditional description. According to DSM-IV (American Psychiatric Association, 1994), GAD has the following characteristics:

---

[3] The entire anthropology researches may be said to consist in an elaboration of Ruth Benedict's view to this effect in her celebrated classic, ***Patterns of Culture*** (1934).

The essential feature of Generalized Anxiety Disorder is excessive anxiety and worry (apprehensive expectation), occurring more days than not for a period of at least 6 months, about a number of events or activities. The individual finds it difficult to control the worry. The anxiety and worry are accompanied by at least three additional symptoms from a list that includes restlessness, being easily fatigued, difficulty in concentration, irritability, muscle tension, and disturbed sleep. The focus of the anxiety and worry is not confined to features of an Axis I disorder. The anxiety causes clinical significant distress in social, occupational, or other important areas of functioning. The disturbance is not due to the direct physiological effects of a substance or a general medical condition (pp. 435-436).

Research on anxiety is usually on its causes, symptoms, development and maintenance, assessment and diagnosis, psychological and pharmacological treatments (Last & Hersen, 1988). This essay begins by reviewing three therapies, cognitive, cognitive behavior, and psychodynamic (later side-glancing at humanistic-existentialist psychotherapy), and compare their effectiveness/efficiency. The essay does not summarize diverse studies of etiology, clinical symptoms, and continuation of generalized anxiety disorder (GAD). Nor is effectiveness of pharmacological treatment of GAD included in this essay.

How we tacitly understand GAD influences, and how we explicitly explain GAD directs, how we treat it. Psychoanalysis takes GAD to be resulted from broken defense mechanisms due to an inadequate dealing with unconscious conflict between ego and id impulses. Behaviorism explains GAD from the classical conditioning of anxiety to many different events, activities, and environments. Cognitive therapy attends to the cognitive thinking process of anxiety. According to biological approaches, GAD is seen as having inheritability and biological foundations (Carson, Butcher, & Mineka, 1996).

Psychodynamic therapy helps clients to achieve great insights about themselves, their problems, and their relationships. Therapists assist the clients to uncover their repressed conflict that is thought to underlie the symptoms of anxiety, seldom focusing on the "symptoms" themselves (Carson, Butch, & Mineka, 1996). Goisman, Warshaw, and Keller (1999) reported that psychodynamic therapy lacks empirical support, while supporting data for the use of cognitive behavior therapy are abundant. Thus psychodynamic therapy has two weaknesses: it does not treat symptoms themselves, and it is difficult to empirically validate.

Behavior therapy focuses on (1) removing specific symptoms or maladaptive behaviors, (2) developing needed client-competencies to adapt, and (3) modifying environmental conditions that maintain maladaptive behaviors. Their techniques are deliberate exposure to anxiety-inducing circumstances, systematic desensitization, asking clients to imagine anxiety-producing situations, beginning at the lowest anxiety and moving up (Carson, Butch, & Mineka, 1996).

According to van Dyck and van Balkom (1997), the most effective treatments of anxiety disorders are behavior therapy, cognitive therapy, and pharmacotherapy. Andrews and colleagues (1994) suggested that cognitive behavior therapy is as effective as pharmacological therapy.

Blowers et al. (1987) found patients improved more with anxiety management plus cognitive therapy and relaxation exercises, than those on the waiting list did. Butler et al. (1991) found that cognitive behavior therapy (CBT) was more effective than behavior therapy (BT), for CBT deals with subjective feelings and behavioral problems, while BT reduces only outside behaviors.

Comparative studies showed that cognitive therapy was more effective than psychodynamic therapy (Durham, Murphy, Allan, Richard, Treliving & Fenton, 1994; Durham, Fisher, Treliving, Hau, Richard & Stewart, 1999). Brown et al. (1992) reviewed new developments in cognitive therapy and found that it restructures attitudes, beliefs, and cognitions related to anxiety-provoking situations. Cognitive behavior therapy does well to combine with other approaches of therapy, such as hypnosis (Schoenberger, 2000) and relaxation (Fisher & Durham, 1999).

The above review concentrates on effectiveness/efficiency as an essential component in various treatments of GAD. Cognitive behavior therapy might be one of the most effective one. Effectiveness has three characteristics: (1) reducing symptoms within a short time (e.g., 12 sessions), (2) maintaining clients' symptoms-free status as long as possible, and (3) reducing possibilities of relapse to the lowest degrees.

In short, the focus of all treatments, such as psychodynamic therapy, cognitive therapy, cognitive behavior therapy, behavior therapy, combined therapy, and group therapy, is to reduce GAD symptoms within the minimum period of time.

But is quick reduction of symptoms and prevention of their relapse the sole focus in the treatment? Kraus (1997) suggested that therapists must help clients to positively/radically change their basic attitudes to frightening situations/objects, in addition to desensitization in behavioral therapy. For the therapies, especially behavioral ones, may merely repress their uneasy relation with the world. The clients *remain* in anxiety and fear.

How do we radically if not permanently alter the clients' basic attitude to the world? Butler et al. (1987) encouraged half of the participating patients (the other half patients were the control group) to identify their strengths and engage in activities to reward them. This is done in addition to other treatments such as psychoeducation on anxiety, relaxation, distraction, cognitive restructuring, and "immunization" to anxiety by exposure to it through regimented practice. The patients participating in such anxiety management significantly improved, on the ratings of anxiety scales, compared with those in the control group. The six-month follow-up examination showed that patients on anxiety management maintained anxiety-reduction well or even improved on it.

Basch (1995) strongly encouraged therapists to understand patients' strengths as well as problems, saying,

> No one is without strengths, and those strengths can more often than not offset an individual's deficits or conflicts....There is a strong pull toward establishing or reestablishing order in living system that opposes the entropic tendency of the universe....When I meet new patients, I always make it a point to assess their strengths, listening for what went right in their lives as well as what seems to have gone wrong (p. 6).

In my opinion, assessing patients' strengths should parallel and be balanced with evaluating their problems, and then the comprehensive understanding would help patients *and* therapists to "see the whole picture" of the patients. Basch's (1995) assessment of patients' strengths emphasizes their positive aspects even more than patients' own identification of their strong points in Butler et al. (1995). Both approaches focus on instilling positive aspects to reduce symptoms.

Now we must engage in their critiques. These therapeutic approaches are all very good as far as they go. Unfortunately, they all keep busy on rehabilitation of anxiety. Even the radical attitudinal change advocated in the above last group of therapists leaves untouched *what* change has been effected, and how to *promote* lasting constructive attitudes, not just healing anxiety.

This twofold lack seems to typify American culture. An American writer Jane Bernstein commented on American culture, saying, "You are supposed to be happy, there was no room for sad sacks. [They are] not part of the American Dream... I began to see—to feel—how I build a shell to protect myself and cut myself off from feelings (Chollet, 2000, July 2, p. 3f)." American or Western culture is strong in avoiding "sad sacks" without understanding what "happiness" is.

Some people tried to apply non-Western perspectives to psychotherapy. Zhang, et al. (2000) applied a Taoist cognitive psychotherapy to anxiety disorders (117 with GAD). Taoist cognitive therapy ABCDE was introduced to the first and third groups of patients. "A" means to assess the patient's stress, "B" is the patient's belief to investigate, "C" coping systems to be analyzed, "D" introduces Taoism, and "E" evaluates and reinforces the patient's outcome.

Such introduction of Taoism is essential in the treatment. The researchers instilled in the patients a Taoist principle: "Benefit and harm not; do and fight not; little egoism, few desires; know [when is] enough, know [when to] stop, know rapport, stay low; with soft conquer; clear, calm, non-ado; follow what [comes] natural." Then Taoist cognitive therapists included evaluating stress, investigating beliefs/values, analyzing mental conflicts and coping styles, while introducing Taoist philosophy to promote the clients' health and prevention capabilities.

Patients were assigned to three groups—those in Taoist cognitive psychotherapy alone, those in pharmacological therapy alone, and those under both therapies combined. Patients in the *first* group of Taoist cognitive psychotherapy and the *last* combined group of Taoist cognitive psychotherapy cum pharmacological therapy demonstrated significant improvement.

Zhang et al. (2000) did use Taoist philosophy to assist patients to prevent relapse. Sadly they did not elaborate on the relationship between Taoist philosophy and cognitive therapy, nor did they assist patients to develop their own new philosophy in life. These two aspects are essential to the development of the structure and rationale of Taoist cognitive therapy. We must engage in this project by first clarifying what Taoism is relative to GAD.

THE TAOIST APPROACH TO ANXIETY

Instead of presenting Taoism in general, it is best to briefly depict what it is as it relates to psychotherapy. One of the Taoist key notions relevant here is *wu wei* (Chuang Tzu, 370?-319? B.C./1970; Lau Tzu, 551?-479? B.C./1963), literally, "no do" that is not "not do," cessation of deed, or "do," deed. The *"wu wei"* is *"wu"*-enfleshed *"wei"*, actively "no"-ing "doing." *"Wu"* in *wu wei* is a verb all its own, not subordinate to *wei*.

In other words, *wu* here is an independent act to "stay (opposed)," not a mere reaction to *wei* to counter *wei*. As Taoist "nothing" (*wu*) is a nothing-infused thing, so their *wu wei*, no-do, is not-not-do, an active doubled negation, a *wei wu wei*, an active dynamic "do no-do."

Wu-wei is nonaction or noninterference, not acting in conflict with the Tao, the Way of course of events in nature. *Wu wei* does no-push of the river of natural events.

This amounts to an empty room that *accommodates* its opposites (Van Dusen, 1979), no-empty things. It amounts to letting all life's dilemmas stay, with constant watchful prudence. It is like the Chinese character, *koan*, which depicts a crane quietly standing for hours in the marsh for fish to come by. Such calm standing is an active watch as intense as its own survival, for it depends on the watchful stand to feed its self. The crane feeds on such standing. Its life depends on its "idle standing" that is actually intensely active as life itself. It lives its calm standing.

From this perspective, we see that the doctor and the mother, as well as the financial institution and the government, all should pattern themselves after nature as they cannot help but do. They have to, to keep things running smoothly as things in nature do. Freedom is more than simple "not free not to be free" (Sartre), for freedom does not protest being not-free. To be free is freely to be self-destined.

"Natural laws" show how "lawful" natural happenings are in their "free abandonment." Even much berated troubles, sufferings, and injustices in the world are under God's watchful eyes, says Psalm 121, and God is Mother Nature in Taoism. For even the devil finds work for idle hands, God's mill grinds slow but sure, and the cosmic "law" of laissez-faire Karma works as the coarse and invisible Heavenly "Net" that leaks nothing (Lau Tzu, 551?-479? B.C./1963).

Our life should pattern after Nature's Net and God's Mill, and this patterning is *wu wei*. Our *wu wei* patterns after nature's non-doing that is working everywhere every time. Let me repeat. *Wu wei* no-do is no *pu wei* not-do (complete cessation of doing). *Wu wei* is not giving up doing but freely to be in action as destined Naturally.

Accordingly, the Taoist psychologist would just sit there, as the Zen/Taoist people do, simply being there. This intensive there-ness, no inattentive abandonment but *full* presence with the client here/now, is the heart-calming warmth, the calming calm, that is a dynamic *wu wei*, an existential double negative. It is not even minding not-to-mind but just being there, as kids are.

It is thus that the *genuine* pervades the false, gently letting it disappear unawares into the genuine. The false is here falsified by its own double negation, and the genuineness in the insane heals the insane. It is thus that such concentrated staying in existence and behaviors heal us into our own genuine selves. We are now to unpack what all this implies in psychology.

WESTERN AND TAOIST APPROACHES INTEGRATED

Beck and his colleagues (Beck, Rush, Shaw & Emery, 1979), who pioneered cognitive psychotherapy, said that cognitive therapy is related to Taoism, for "Eastern philosophy such as Taoism and Buddhism emphasizes that human emotions are based on ideas (p. 8)." As early as 1930s, some psychologists have explored Taoism as a possible way of treating patients with psychological disorders (Maslow, 1971; Rogers, 1975; Watts, 1975). Watts (1975) said that people's rationality causes their psychological problems. This echoes the assumption underlying cognitive therapy, which assumes that cognitions represent perception of situation. "Changing the ways and contents of cognition" changes emotions and behaviors (Beck et al, 1979).

Concretely, Taoism as described above has at least three therapeutic impacts. *One*, accommodation to, even allowance of, "being sick" makes room for relaxed tarrying in the status quo as it is, however imperfect and "unhealthy" the situation is. Such relaxed rooming is itself a therapy.

Two, the therapists come to understand more about *themselves* by counseling clients. They are fellow travelers in the authentic Way of living. Such fellowship provides relaxed rooming toward healing.

Three, relaxed rooming spreads to accommodate various schools of psychotherapy to inter-enrichments across boundaries. Inter-enrichments only redound to enhance their overall healing effectiveness.

The significance of such Taoist frame of attitude for psychology in the West is obvious. Psychological counseling today is full of techniques. They must stop their ad hoc haphazard character to anchor on a solid basis of full life, their goal. Thus techniques need be enriched with Taoism as they steer toward the final goal of life's natural spontaneous fullness.

We must seriously consider what should ensue after removing symptoms to culminate counseling. The above Taoist attitude/sentiment supplies the milieu, justification, and culmination of cognitive therapy and other therapies, not just at its beginning and end but also throughout the entire counseling operation.

In essence, Taoism expressed in its key notions of no-do (*wu wei*), genuineness, letting be, accommodating presence, and interdisciplinary cooperation, supply answer to our queries on why we need counseling, what we mean by "health," how we reach there, and what the ideal of psychology is.

Thus Taoism justifies, defines, and provides methodology and goal to psychology. It is this Taoist Way (tao) that should pervade psychology as its solid goal, ground, and methodology. This pervasive "way" is what I mean by "attitude." All this amounts to a radical attitudinal change, a climatic shift, in psychology from ad hoc treatment to steady stream of healing our whole life.

For example, Taoism encourages both patient and therapist to accept the patient's conflict, and even receive it as a resource to patient's self-understanding. This attitude can incorporate into cognitive therapy that gives the patient techniques to explore *on their own* their dysfunctional thoughts that impoverish life. Taoism's spirit of *wu wei* allows the patient's anxiety to exist, and the techniques from cognitive therapy help clients understand how their anxiety influences their experience.

All these reflections result from psychological approach to anxiety as informed with Chinese Taoist attitude and sentiment. After all, the basic attitude-change constitutes the psychological healing of anxiety, and at the same time the basic attitudinal reorientation crucially vitalizes and enriches psychological counseling itself.

Now let us see what would happen to Western psychology with China-inspired attitude-change. To simplify, let us consider three methodological implications of a Taoist notion, "accommodation," to accommodate other schools, oneself, and the untoward milieu.

One, China-informed psychology will accommodate other schools. An example is existentialist-humanistic psychotherapy (EHP) *opposed* to scientific behaviorism. Such EHP is criticized as powerless on extreme psychoses. Yet EHP also emphasizes persons' embodiedness that includes chemical balances in the body, for body has a physical aspect of chemistry that correlates with "extreme psychoses."

So, EHP can and should freely use as its integral part chemical-medical therapy that it faults. For the fault is not in chemistry as such but in regarding people in the physical perspective *alone*. EHP must extend body-perspective to include chemistry, as its person-perspective includes body. EHP should apply chemical therapy to restore/sober psychotic *people* to personal presence essential in EHP. EHP should freely use chemical means in the overall perspective of the humanism of th process and presence of the person. EHP thus fulfills its vision that is an overall, embracing, and empathetic therapy of persons.

Conversely, scientific empiricism can join EHP from *its* perspective, for "persons" are complex physiological mechanisms, and empiricism can learn from EHP about the structure of such mechanism. "Opposites" in science should join together as in life, to make for effective psychotherapy.

Two, the psychology that is China-informed would accommodate *oneself* even in illness ill suited to living. The calm watchful crane gives us a methodological principle: When in a serious situation, retreat and *stay* put. Move *not*. That is an existential version of doing no-do, *wu wei*. On hearing the oncoming of an overwhelming army toward his empty camp, a great strategist K'ung-ming ordered all doors opened, all gardens swept clean and water-sprinkled. Then he came out in the open in front of his camp, strummed away his zither and sang and hummed tunes. Fear struck the reconnaissance on seeing the quiet situation, and the great enemy battalion retreated in silence.

In psychology as healing counseling, the "enemy" is our mental disturbance, the lingering GAD. When anxious, let be. The master psychologist is forever beside the man beside himself, as Mom beside her jittery crying baby. Mom knows that the baby needs sleep. When tired, let him go sleep. When hungry, let him eat. No problem is here. The great One keeps one's "baby" inside, lets the baby say "I want to eat 'cause I'm hungry," and lets him eat. Psychology mothers clients quietly beside them.

Concretely, psychology accepts the other, the not-self, and thereby heals the other. Humanist-existential psychology of Carl Rogers (1973), as mentioned above, should accept its opponent, behaviorist psychology, in accepting the embodied client in trouble. For behaviorist empiricism concerns the physical embodiedness of a person. With empirical methodology the psychologist knows when and how to intervene as necessity of emergency dictates, and here, in this know-how is the contribution of Western psychology.

But emergencies are rare. Usually the psychologist lets the clients be, who are aware that psychologist is ever with them, ever ready, never disturbing them in their self-disturbance. It's okay not to solve all problems all at once, right now. It's okay to cry over spilt milk *they* spilled. It's okay not to even know what or where their problems are. All this "not" of "okay" is the *wu* of the *wu wei*. This is what okays the clients and thereby heals them.

"Listen," both psychologist and client would say, "how many creative geniuses are 'sane' and 'mentally healthy'? Think of Van Gogh, Kurt Gödel and many others, and controversial ones such as Percy Shelley and Pablo Picasso. You may not go as far as to say that unless you are 'insane' you are not creative. The fact remains that a vast majority of those creative geniuses were hurt, suffered so much, and created so much.[4] They were in pain as they created." It is okay to suffer and be excluded from the society. Just be there, be yourself.

This is not an "anything goes, for no one cares" situation where pure chaos whirls, although often geniuses suffer that way. A child with fever under the doctor's and the parent's watchful eyes, without intervention for now, is no abandoned child sick out in the street.[5]

Thus the psychologist is a dynamic presence, "doing nothing here now," to accommodate clients. The psychologist is a fertile void to let clients exist, live, and move in it. Since the psychologist is a "void," she is the clients' room. "Void" is thus a positive verb, a homecoming, a facilitating of free psychic space for clients to feel at home, to come home to themselves, to be at one with themselves—and be at their creative *ease* with themselves, completely without obsession of any sort. The void creates of itself. It permits to enable. It's fun, even in pain.

Van Dusen (1979, pp. 218-221) describes how he did so with a schizophrenic, somewhat ramblingly (as befits the Taoist Void), as follows:

> For a moment the patient couldn't concentrate, couldn't hear me, couldn't remember what he intended to say, or he felt nothing. At first it appeared these . . . great blank spaces were characteristic of schizophrenics only. . . . In the depressive they are the black hole of time standing still. . . .[It is painful. And so in the West] we let the action of objects (cars, TV) fill our space. In the Orient, emptiness may have a supreme value in and of itself. It can be trusted [and] productive. The *Tao Te Ching* suggests that while thirty spokes make up a wheel, only in the emptiness of its hub is its usefulness. . . . I explored the empty spaces.... If he [the patient] anxiously filled space with words, we looked for a while at wordlessness. The person who feared going down in depression permitted himself to go down and explore the going down. The findings are always the same. The feared empty space is a fertile void. Exploring it is a turning point toward therapeutic change. . . . When he [the patient] drifts he seems to stumble on something new. . . . As the hour ended I asked whether he wanted to climb out of the hole. He said (with a trace more of affect) he would stay in it and see what else of interest might happen. I was pleased because he had discovered that of itself the void filled with new things. He didn't have to work so hard to fill it up.

Here Van Dusen's (1979) patient begins to create while suffering, as creative geniuses do. How? By "staying in the hole," the patient comes to courageously own him or herself in all his or her twisty scary vacancy. This "courage to be" (Tillich) heals and creates in the twisty self as it is, out of it, simply by owning oneself as a twisty self. Whatever "healing" importantly means, here we come, by and by, to spontaneously managing the twisted self, as we "manage" and live with cancer, blood pressure, or Alzheimer's disease. The sagely True-Man of health is child-spontaneity enfleshed in a no-child, the adult.

David Burns' (1999) "Feeling Good" is appropriate here. His "the ten forms of twisted thinking (pp. 8-11)" are a mirror and therefore a guide to self-untwisting. His cognitive therapy tells us *how* to turn straight and honest toward the self, to treasure the self, as it is, toward honest straight self-owning. Taoism chimes in, differing only in not *contriving* to untwist oneself, as Burns does with elaborate regimen of programs. One never pushes the

---

[4] The same situation holds for physical health or un-health. Chopin, Pascal, and Kant come to mind. One need not be vigorously healthy to be great.
[5] Perhaps the historians could sigh, saying that the invisible Muses' eyes were watching over those suffering geniuses.

river—of the self, of the self's environment—but simply flows along, swims nimbly along, and even frolics in it. One then gradually and imperceptibly comes to *be* untwisted and straightened to become in line with oneself and one's milieu.

Three, this following-along does not always mean a smooth unproblematic blending-in with the milieu, however. Chuang Tzu's (370?-319? B.C./1970) imagined fable has it (4/85-89) that, in the scary twisty world of political brutality, the "insane" floaters, wayfarers, shouted at Confucius who was zealously intent on reforming the world, with so many poetic lines, saying, "Let it be! Let it be!"

This is because, Chuang Tzu continued (4/55-64), we must "be not a praying mantis waving its furious arms at the oncoming cart. A man may pamper his favorite horse with a basket for its dung and a shell for its piss. Then, should a fly or mosquito hovers near, he unwittingly slaps the horse, which will then burst its bit, smash his head, and kick in his chest. The pampering did the damage."

Instead, true following along would go like this, Chuang Tzu continues, "A skilled tiger tamer would refrain from giving it a whole live animal to provoke its lethal rage. He instead feeds the tiger according to its natural timing and manner of when and how its hunger arrives. As a result, the ferocious tiger that differs in breed from men comes to fawn on the tiger keeper."

Pampering the horse that usually does no harm proved to be fatal, while feeding the tiger that usually kills made the tiger come to fawn on the feeder. Where is the difference? Following along with the nature—with skill and insight—or not, makes all the difference between life and death.

Similarly, to "tame" the irrational tyrant, we must "join him to play his games prudently, whether to be childish, to jump the fences, or to burst the shores. Fathom him right through. No refusing when he comes, no pursuing when he goes (Graham, 1981, p. 72)."[6] Play shadow boxing *with* him. Not following the gentle horse's nature, and we die. Following along with the fierce nature of the tiger, and it comes to fawn on us.

Following makes the life-and-death difference. Play along with the tiger-game of the tyrant, playing non-doing (*wu wei*) with twisty "no" (*wu*) of untoward things, such is accommodation, staying in the ugly vacancy. That is the secret key to a wholesome life. That is psychology informed and infused with Taoist attitude.

Let us take stock. All this sketch of what Taoism-informed psychology would behave induces an attitudinal revolution in psychology, a new psychological *attitude*, not a detailed program. Intervention without intervention, permitting things to happen, is how in general this new psychology operates.

To challenge the Western psychological stance to the patient's problem, the Taoist has five "constructs": nowness, not trying, ego de-emphasis, guilt desensitization, and observing judgment (Knoblauch, 1985). They facilitate a twofold comparison and complementing of Taoism with cognitive therapy, as follows.

One, both approaches focus on experience "here now." Taoism lets patients honor conflicts, however. In honoring conflicts, patients are using the wisdom of *wu-wei*. Cognitive therapy in the meantime investigates the processes underlying the conflicts. Instead of solving problems, cognitive therapy encourages patients to self-monitor their conflicts by cognitive therapy techniques. Taoism has no techniques, however.

---

[6] Since no exact translation is necessary or possible, I freely adapted A. C. Graham.

Two, both Taoism and cognitive therapy focus on patients' pace in therapy. Neither Taoism nor cognitive therapy encourages patients to suppress their anxiety. Taoism encourages patients to let anxiety unfold itself, however, while cognitive therapy teaches patients to understand how their anxiety exists, so as to resolve it.

In conclusion, we have briefly tabulated the interrelation between the West and China. The strange congruence between Chinese approach and Western is three: *One*, unlike cognitive therapy, Taoism does not purposely reconstruct clients but lets them come to their own senses by just being with them, accommodating their GAD.

Two, Taoism assists the clients to realize their own situations—difficulties and strengths—with unsuspected perspectives (i.e., in spontaneity). It operates like Basch's "Doing Brief Psychotherapy (1995)," as an overall healthy life-attitude, not as technique to heal.

Three, the Chinese attitude above strengthens the Western goals—effective therapy. Taoism lets clients develop their own skills to interpret problems, even after treatment. They are now reborn with their own perspective to manage themselves. "Who needs psychologists now?" they would now proudly say.

In the end, we see how paradoxical Taoism is. It encourages clients to change their thoughts and behaviors to be happy, yet it does "nothing" to change them. Taoism lets change come by quietly being there. Its strength is in letting new perspectives come fo themselves. The Taoist presence makes us realize changes and envision new possibilities for ourselves. It does no (*wu wei*) techniques of Western therapies, without tools to produce changes. It lets the clients do it themselves.

Thus an integration of Taoism (Johanson & Kurtz, 1991) into cognitive therapy of distorted thoughts (or twisted thinking) (Burns, 1999) can turn out as follows.

First, in Burns' all-or-none thinking, people see things in black or white only. Cognitive therapists assist them to see such thinking as irrational. Taoists nudge that they accept these thoughts, which then fade away.

Secondly, in Burns' labeling is an instance of all-or-none thinking, e.g., "I am a loser." Taoists suggest, "The Tao is connected, not abstracted [by labels] (p. 3)." Taoists assist clients to see that labels separate us from real experience, and we then lose reality in labels. So Taoists suggest (not persuade) them to stay in experiences, for experiences to give apt words, not labels.

Thirdly, in Burns' "should" statements, people expect that things should be the way they hope. They stick to their "right" to judge themselves, e.g., "I should have called Mom." Taoists suggest that they can let go of their "right" and be open to self-accommodation, in self-acceptance.

Fourth, in Burns' personalization, people think *they* are responsible for an event that are actually out of their control. Taoists suggest that they may want to do whatever they can but with no judgments on the outcome.

Fifth, in Burns' overgeneralization, people generalize specific negative events, saying that all events are in a fixed pattern of defeat. Taoists suggest that they reflect on their feelings and events now, and stop ruminating on negative side, leave their set mind, and accept, even appreciate, whatever comes, in a fresh perspective they may not have envisioned before.

Sixth, in Burns' mental filter, people dwell on one single negative detail, excluding all other positive sides. Taoists nudge them to "perhaps" open their eyes and minds to another side, possibility, and experience.

Seventh, in Burns' discounting the positive, people reject positive aspects of events. Taoists may smile and say, "I hear you are rejecting something perhaps positive. That is okay. Now what would you see if you reject such rejection?" And they are thereby given a new perspective to self-reflection toward new vistas of life.

Eighth, in Burns' jumping to conclusions, people interpret events negatively without facts to support their conclusions. Taoists may suggest that they slow down and digest their own thinking process.

Ninth, in Burns' magnification, people exaggerate their shortcomings and problems. Taoists suggest that clients appreciate and evaluate themselves as they are, without judging on their being "good" or "bad."

Tenth, in Burns' emotional reasoning, people assume that their negative emotions reflect outside reality. Taoists may suggest that clients be detached from connecting negative emotions to objective events outside. Let us, so clients are told, calm down and let things tell what they are as they are.

This comparison helps us to understand how such Taoism-therapy integration turns cognitive therapy differently, more flexuous, and more effective.

LIMITATIONS AND FUTURE RESEARCH

This essay has (1) reviewed Western psychotherapies on GAD and (2) integrated them with Chinese approaches. It thus envisioned and outlined a possible future to Taoism-informed psychology. Psychologists are left to develop their own therapy strategies, as each uniquely specific situation specifically requires. This is in line with Taoism, to let things be. Never push the river. Swim with it in it.

If "this approach" by any chance somehow did not work in a specific case, Taoism-informed psychologist will freely accommodate and integrate *any* other techniques that work, but always with the same attitude of open free accommodation. Absolutely no problem is here.

Regarding the future research, I recommend four possible ways according to my theoretical exploration so far.

One, the future research needs to further elaborate on how cognitive therapy theoretically combines Taoist attitudes. Future research also needs empirical testing and verification of actual implementation on the effects of such Taoist-cognitively integrated approach.

Two, as Alan Watts (1975) pointed out, such comparisons of Taoism with many psychological approaches in the West such as psychoanalysis, humanism, behaviorism, and others, would benefit Western psychotherapy. The future questions would be like "How has Taoism enriched psychoanalysis?" "To what extent are Taoism and humanistic psychotherapy similar, and how different are they from each other?" This essay has explored the integration between Taoism and cognitive therapy, and the integration between Taoism and other approaches in psychotherapy needs future explorations.

Three, this essay has investigated the integrative approach to treat GAD, not other mental disorders. The future research does well to explore how the integrative approach—Taoism integrating cognitive therapy—benefits mental disorders other than GAD.

Four, this essay has done theoretical exploration. Practical investigation of its effectiveness is indispensable before it can treat patients, however. The future studies need develop new therapeutic approaches out of this integrated approach.

This essay has three omissions on important details. *First*, it omits women's GAD that has woman-distinctive stressors, such as families, work, and childhood traumas. Her pharmacological treatment needs to consider pregnancy and larger proportions of body fat (Zerbe, 1996).

Secondly, this essay omits different life span-stages with their respective distinct stressors related to GAD. Children and adolescents have their own stressors such as schools, parents, siblings, friends, self-identities. As a result, children's avoidance behaviors differ from adults' because children have less choices and mobility than adults. Besides, parent often forces children to do what they reject, while adults have fewer external forces (Kleinknecht, 1991).

Thirdly, this essay omits anxiety of the elderly, with their typical psychophysical changes (Patterson, 1988).

Now, these omissions indicate that the proposal of this essay requires future elaboration, experimentation, and verification in specific directions suggested by, but not limited to, the omissions cited here. Again, "accommodation" to the future is suggested by the omissions. All this is in line, by the way, with the Taoist approach to life.

REFERENCES

Andrews, G., Crino, R., Hunt, C., Lampe, L., & Page, A. (1994). *The treatment of anxiety disorders: Clinician's guide and patient manuals.* England: Cambridge University Press.

American Psychiatric Association. (1994). *Diagnostic and statistical manual of mental disorders (4th ed.).* Washington D. C.: American Psychiatric Association.

Basch, M. F. (1995). *Doing brief psychotherapy.* New York: Basic Books.

Beck, A. T. Rush, A. J., Shaw, B. F., & Emery, G. (1979). *Cognitive therapy of depression.* New York: Guildford.

Benedict, R. (1934). *Patterns of culture.* Boston: Houghton Mifflin.

Blowers, C., Cobb, J., & Mathews, A. (1987). Generalized anxiety: A controlled treatment study. *Behavior and Therapy*, 25, 493-502.

Brown, T. A., Hertz, R. A., & Barlow, D. H. (1992). New development in cognitive-behavioral treatment of anxiety disorders. *American Psychiatric Press Review of Psychiatry*, 11, 285-306.

Butler, G., Cullington, A., Hibbert, G., Klimes, I., & Gelder, M. (1987). Anxiety management for persistent generalized anxiety. *British Journal of Psychiatry, 151,* 535-542.

Butler, G., Fennell, M., Robson, P., & Gelder, M. (1991). Comparison of behavior therapy and cognitive therapy in the treatment of generalized anxiety disorder. *Journal of Consulting and Clinical Psychology*, 59, 167-175.

Burns, D. (1999). *The feeling good handbook.* New York: Penguin Group.

Carson, R. C., Butcher, J. N., & Mineka, S. (1996). *Abnormal psychology and modern life (10th ed.)*. New York: HarperCollins.

Chao, R. (2001). Integrating culture and attachment. *American Psychologist*, forthcoming.

Chuang Tzu (1970). *Chuang Tzu*. (B. Watson, Trans.). New York: Columbia University. (Original work published 370?-319? B.C.).

Chollet, L. (2000, July 2). Berstein pens searing memoir. *Florida Today*, p. 3F.

Den Boer, J. A. (Ed.). (1997). *Clinical management of anxiety*. New York: Marcel Dekker.

Durham, R. C., Murphy, T., Allan., T., Richard, K., Treliving, L.R., & Fenton, G. W. (1994). Cognitive therapy, analytic psychotherapy and anxiety management training for generalized anxiety disorder. *British Journal of Psychiatry, 165*, 315-323.

Durham, D. C., Fisher, P. L., Treliving, L. R., Hau, C. M., Richard, K., Stewart, J. B. (1999). One year follow-up of cognitive therapy, analytic psychotherapy and anxiety management training for generalized anxiety disorder: Symptom change, medication usage, and attitudes to treatment. *Behavioral and Cognitive Psychotherapy, 27*, 19-35.

Fisher, P. L. & Durham, R. C. (1999). Recovery rates in generalized anxiety disorder following psychological therapy: An analysis of clinically significant change in the STAI-T across outcome studies since 1990. *Psychological Medicine, 29*, 1425-1434.

Goisman, R. M., Warshaw, M. G., & Keller, M. B. (1999). Psychosocial treatment prescriptions for generalized anxiety disorder, panic disorder, and social phobia, 1991-1996. *American Journal of Psychiatry, 156*, 1819-1821.

Graham, A. C. (1981). *Chuang Tzu: The inner chapters*. London: George Allen & Unwin.

Johnson, G. & Kurtz, R. (1991). *Grace unfolding: Psychotherapy in the spirit of the Tao-te ching*. New York: Bell Tower.

Kleinknecht, R. A. (1991). *Mastering anxiety: The nature and treatment of anxious conditions*. New York: Plenum Press.

Knoblauch, D. L. (1985). Applying Taoist thought to counseling and psychotherapy. *American Mental Health Counselors Association Journal, 7*, 52-63.

Kraus, A. (1997). Existential and differential aspects of anxiety. In J. A. deBoer (Ed.), *Clinical management of anxiety*. New York: Marcel Dekker.

Last, C. G. & Hersen, M. (Eds.). (1988). *Handbook of anxiety disorders*. New York: Pergamon Press.

Lao Tzu. (1963). *Tao-te Ching*. (D. C. Lau, Trans.). London: Penguin. (Original work published 551?-479? B.C.).

Lebra, W. P. (1976). *Culture-bound syndromes, ethnopsychiatry, and alternate therapies*. Honolulu, HW: University Press of Hawaii.

Maslow, A. (1971). *The farther reaches of human nature*. New York: Penguin.

Rogers, C. R. (1973). My philosophy of interpersonal relationships and how it grew. *Journal of Humanistic Psychology, 13*, 3-15.

Schoenberger, N. E. (2000). Hypnosis in the treatment of women with anxiety disorders. In L. M. Hornyak, & J. P., Green (Eds.), *Healing from within: The use of hypnosis in women's health care*. Washington, DC: American Psychological Association.

Shweder, R. A. & LeVine, R. A. (1984). *Culture theory: Essays on mind, self, and emotion*. England: Cambridge University Press.

Suler, J. (1993). *Contemporary psychoanalysis and Eastern thought*. Albany, NY: State University of New York.

Patterson, R. L. (1988). Anxiety in the elderly. In C. G. Last, & M. Hersen (Eds.), *Handbook of anxiety disorders.* New York: Pergamon Press.

Van Dyck, R. & Van Balkom, A. J. L. M. (1997). Combination therapy for anxiety disorders. In J. A. den Boer (Ed.), *Clinical management of anxiety.* New York: Marcel Dekker.

Van Dusen, W. (1979). Wu Wei, no-mind, and the fertile void in psychotherapy. In J. Welwood (Ed.), *The meeting of ways: Explorations in East/West psychology.* New York: Schocken Books.

Watts, A. (1975). *Psychotherapy East and West.* New York: Vintage.

Wu, K. (1990). *The butterfly as companion: Meditations on the first three chapters of Chuang Tzu.* Albany, NY: State University of New York.

Zerbe, K. J. (1996). Anxiety disorders in women. In W. W. Menninger (Ed.), *Coping with anxiety disorders: Integrated approaches to treatment.* Northvale, NJ: Jason Aroson.

Zhang, Y., Yang, D., Xiao, Z., Fong, Y., Zhang, H., Zou, H., & Yu, S. (2000). The role of Taoist cognitive psychotherapy in the treatment of anxiety disorder. *Chinese Mental Health Journal, 14,* 62-63.

In: Globalization Dynamics
Editor: Kuang-ming Wu

ISBN: 978-1-62100-750-0
© 2012 Nova Science Publishers, Inc.

Chapter 5

GLOBALIZING COUNSELING PARADIGM: FROM THE UNITED STATES OF AMERICA TO THE WORLD

Chu-hui Chao[*]
Community College of Denver, Colorado, US

ABSTRACT

This chapter addresses the importance, in fact, the [1] necessity, of globalizing counseling by learning about cultures outside the United States, the [2] methodology of how to do so, as [3] we watch the dangers of implementing mental health delivery systems based on models derived from culture in the United States alone, as we caution ourselves on the role of cultural bias in globalization of counseling psychology. Through this essay, it is hoped to inspire counseling psychologists and counselors to consider the practice of counseling beyond the cultural borders of the United States.

To be a counselor means to be a human being able to help and cure people beyond the border of nations, cultures, and races. Counselors should be cosmopolitans addressing human pain in various cultural forms beyond national borders. The reason is simple but humanly significant. How we suffer depends on how we feel. How we feel depends on how we see and think about things, and how we look and think is culture. So, our pain derives from our own culture our community has. Psychological counseling serves to heal people's pain. So, counseling must be culture-sensitive. In other words, counseling must be multicultural. Monocultural counseling is no counseling but an imposition.

Happily, in recent years, counselors have begun to serve the diverse needs of people around the world (Gerstein, 2005; Rogers & Sanford, 1987). Some counselors have traveled outside the United States to enrich themselves, studying different cultures and languages, and, more important, to offer educational services overseas (e.g., lectures, courses, workshops, research), and having been applying services abroad (e.g., counseling, consulting, assisting conflict resolution).

---

[*] Community College of Denver, Colorado, USA. Email: chao.chuhui@gmail.com

As a result, there are now considerable amounts of international interests among counseling professionals (e.g., collaborating with scholars and professionals in other countries; training international students; serving international clientele; teaching and doing consultation overseas; conducting appropriate and valid cross-cultural research; and thereby demonstrating an appreciation and understanding of international cultures and models of counseling).

The importance of training counseling students to effectively serve the needs of global populations cannot be underestimated, as the population in the United States alone turns increasingly diversified. This happy situation raises a hopeful prospect to globalizing psychological counseling, and ironically poses some tricky risks. One hopeful sign is that many health-care professionals propose and implement the methods of globalizing counseling. We immediately review the first hopeful methodological sign, and then consider the monocultural dangers attendant thereto, in the section after it.

METHODOLOGY

Naturally, we are now concerned with how to prepare students and professionals to successfully function as scientists, practitioners, and educators in global settings, and there is no lack of proposals. Here we cite just some examples.

Most frequently, these authors have stressed the importance of students and professionals (a) learning about differences and similarities between cultures (Gerstein, Rountree, & Ordonez, 2004); (b) facing, confronting, and modifying, if necessary, their cultural assumptions, values, biases, and behaviors (Ægisdóttir & Gerstein, 2005); (c) embracing a globalized perspective of culture (Heppner, 2006); (d) taking appropriate and immediate action in response to the needs of the global community (Pedersen, 2003); (e) promoting indigenous psychologies (Kim, Yang, & Hwang, 2010); and (g) continuing mutual learning from different professionals around the world (Wu, 2010).

At the program levels, counseling psychology must encourage the training programs to (a) support students to attend international conferences or courses *outside* the United States; (b) to value bilingualism; and (c) to promote externship and internship experiences at sites in other countries (Leong & Ponterotto, 2003, p. 391). Mostly important, it is critical for counseling psychologists and counseling psychology programs to integrate global perspectives into the curriculums in psychology.

To exemplify the globalization of counseling psychology, this essay includes the following sections: (a) the necessity of globalization of counseling psychology; (b) the methodological bias in Western counseling psychology; (c) what globalized counseling psychology look like; (d) challenges of globalized counseling psychology.

THE NECESSITY OF GLOBALIZATION OF COUNSELING PSYCHOLOGY

Takooshian (2003) stressed that it is important for counseling psychology programs to function globally, by encouraging their curriculums to include international or global activities through various programs on campus, studying abroad, and collaborative international research. Indeed, counseling psychology programs can even apply current technology (e.g., Skype, teleconference, internet, blogs, e-mails, etc.) to internationally communicate to broaden their perspectives to global worldview.

Furthermore, because a major purpose of counseling psychology programs is to prepare students, readying them to serve diverse clientele, counseling psychology programs must encourage students to become involved in student groups interested in international issues.

Giorgis and Helms (1978) also address the importance and necessity of globalizing counseling psychology. They offer excellent ideas. *First*, globalizing counseling psychology should begin within United States. We must investigate on how to train specifically international students enrolled in psychology courses in the United States. Counseling psychology programs can globalize themselves by first training the international students.

These international students should be encouraged to secure internships in settings similar to those in their native countries. By doing this, international students may learn about the unique concerns experienced by persons from their native countries.

Secondly, the faculty should encourage international students to pursue research relevant to their home country and also to collect their data in their own country. Conducting such studies can help students to strengthen their understanding about the specific challenges of performing research in their own countries and the particular needs of persons in such countries.

Thirdly, students should be taught about the similarities and differences of educational systems throughout the world and be provided with opportunities to gain firsthand experiences in such systems. This will help to better prepare future educators who are interested in teaching outside the United States.

In globalizing counseling psychology programs, it is also important to truly comprehend and respect the uniqueness of a specific culture. To conceptualize a culture in an isolated perspective is one thing; to appreciate a unique culture in a global world context is quite another.

Globalization of counseling psychology includes both appreciation of each unique culture and integration of different cultures into a comprehensive "global village" of counseling psychology. Thus, it is inevitable for psychologists to understand new social, cultural, political, religious, economic infrastructures, different norms, values, and behaviors. Thus a potentially unique or new psychological philosophy emerges, with disposition and framework different from psychology we are conventionally used to.

Counseling psychology programs must also realize that globalizing counseling psychology is a new landscape which includes numerous other factors unsuspected hitherto (e.g., operating outside one's own support system, different frame of reference, cultural group, reward structure, comfort zone, as compared with home country). These factors could be a daunting, exhilarating, and at the same time motivating challenge.

In a cultural setting different from the United States, psychologists must contend with myriad dynamic factors and experiences unsuspected hitherto, often without any external support, input, and feedback, familiar cues, patterns, or recognizable and understandable stimuli. It is also important for counseling psychology programs to approach the experience of such novel uncharted globalization with openness, patience, genuineness, and undying curiosity.

THE METHODOLOGICAL BIAS IN WESTERN COUNSELING PSYCHOLOGY

To globalize counseling psychology, an essential first step is to know the *bias* in our Western counseling psychology. Although counseling psychology as a Western science and profession continues to respond to the challenges of our changing times, counseling psychology is still struggling with the growing concerns of many Western, non-Western, and ethnic-minority psychologists.

In other words, counseling psychology is still struggling to find an adequate response to the challenge to integrate Western and non-Western perspectives to reach the goal of globalization. For example, a Canadian psychologist Prilleltensky (1997) analyzed the moral implications of Western psychology's historical roots and summarized the emerging values, assumptions, practices, potential benefits, and potential risks of alternative psychological approaches. We must self-understand the principles of our counseling psychology before we move to globalizing counseling psychology.

Furthermore, more and more non-Western psychologists note that Western counseling psychology may be irrelevant and meaningless to non-Western peoples in their life contexts alien to the West. Western counseling psychology stresses individuals, objectivity, quantification, narrow specialization, and universal "truths." These assumptive attitudes may well be incompatible, even contradictory, to people's life-orientations in other countries.

Naturally, many organizations, training programs, research activities, and publications in USA remain rooted in Western perspectives and cannot serve as the foundation for a psychology that is adequately responsive to our global context of diversity today. Western counseling psychology cannot help but offer its limited perspective with special privileged prestige (Prilleltensky, 1997). According to Gergen, Gulerce, Lock, and Misra, G. (1996). Let me explain.

The current Western thinking of the science of [counseling] psychology in its prototypical form, despite being as local and indigenous as any other, assumes a global relevance and is treated as a universal mode of generating universal knowledge. Its dominant voice subscribes to a decontextualized vision with an extraordinary emphasis on individualism, mechanism, and objectivity.

This peculiarly Western mode of thinking is fabricated, projected, and institutionalized through representation technologies and scientific rituals, and transported on a large scale to the non-Western societies under its political and economic domination. As a result, Western [counseling] psychology tends to maintain an independent sublime stance ignoring *other* substantive possibilities from disparate cultural traditions.

Mapping reality through Western constructs has offered a pseudo-understanding of the people of alien cultures and has had debilitating effects by misconstruing the specific and distinctive realities of other people. The Wes then exorcize and disregard psychologies that are non-Western. Consequently, when people from other cultures are exposed to Western psychology, they find their very identities put in question and their conceptual repertoires taken as obsolete. (pp. 497–498)

This observation indicates that the development of globalized counseling psychology for non-Western people is put in jeopardy, if not rendered questionable. Our observation indicates that Western counseling psychology tends to detach itself from people's cultural context, to result in a science unable to accurately describe human beings as human.

The time is overdue to reexamine the whole Western counseling psychology within the global context of our actual living so diverse, with all the risks that this reexamination may imply for new global worldviews, methods, and interventions. The time is overdue to develop a globalized counseling psychology. Counseling psychologists, throughout the world, do well to cooperate to develop and advance a holistic mental health profession by using the wisdom and knowledge of other cultures (e.g., Wu, 2010), and then they can evaluate the applicability of these counseling psychologies in various arenas and forums throughout the world.

To date, while counseling psychologists are concerned about global issues, they should constantly be aware of the imperative that counseling psychology should be culturally generated to turn culturally sensitive. Such counseling psychology should mirror different ideologies to serve culture-specific social and political functions. All this while, counseling psychologists should be aware of all the ethical, moral, and political ideological dimensions of people they serve.

Ingleby (1990, pp. 61–62) said that psychology as science is deeply entangled with its own object, the inhabitants of the modern Western world. The question is, can it disentangle itself sufficiently so as to open up to the reality of other cultures. It was precisely the cultural *detachment* of psychology which was supposed to provide it with authority: therefore any suggestion that it was embedded *within* a culture amounts to denying this authority.

Pushing Ingleby's point further, we on our part say that when counseling psychology pursues its scientific neutrality and rigor, it also detaches itself from people who it is meant to serve. Without serving people, counseling psychology loses its most essential mission, to promote human beings' mental health.

STRATEGIES TO GLOBALIZE COUNSELING PSYCHOLOGY

Despite having some edited books, research articles, professional conference presentations on globalization of counseling psychology, the counseling psychologists and counseling psychology programs remain in dire need to enrich their knowledge about the distinctive psychological aspects of specific social and economic involvements in countries outside the United States.

Obviously, then, it behooves cross-cultural counseling psychologists to acquaint themselves with the traditions of the culture they are studying and to incorporate this knowledge in their internal understanding as they serve those people different from Americans. Thus, equally valid interpretations from objective knowledge could take on individually different counseling expectations in various indigenous mental health practices often totally unexpected by typically Western counselors.

Again, counseling psychologists' findings of people outside U.S. should be interpreted from the participant's unique context, never from the West's indifferently objective perspective. One critical challenge to the counseling psychologists is to have an inner understanding of what people from various cultures say and mean, instead of interpreting various people's various meanings from the Western perspective alone.

While carefully examining counselors' biases when generating interpretations, the counselors must contextualize their interpretation into specific cultures. Thus, cross-cultural research and practice are quite challenging. To meet the challenges in cross-cultural studies and even practices, there are four strategies, among others, that counselors could adopt.

First, a mentor who is experienced in conducting international research or practice can be of great assistance when faced with this challenge. Or a specialist in a particular culture could be our resource for those counselors who are conducting cross-cultural studies or practice.

Second, counselors can organize an interdisciplinary team of social scientists (e.g., educators, linguists, and medical scientists) to enrich their tasks. *Third*, when conducting cross-cultural research or practice in the United States, it is also highly advisable to solicit inputs from persons overseas and professionals who are knowledgeable about the topic under investigation. *Fourth*, more important, it is indispensable to rule out participants' levels of acculturation to control the confounding effects of the acculturation on research outcomes.

In the USA where psychology thrives, only 6% of their articles (48 of 818) on an international topic from 2000 to 2004 were published in four typical counseling journals (*Journal of Counseling & Development* [JCD], *Journal of Multicultural Counseling and Development* [JMCD], *Journal of Counseling Psychology* [JCP], and *The Counseling Psychologist* [TCP]). To globalize counseling profession, this field sorely needs to increase the visibility of topics on internationalization or globalization.

Because understanding and appreciating diverse cultures are essential to globalizing counseling psychology, we have several strategies to appreciate cultural diversity. For students or trainees, classroom activities and assignments addressing international topics are probably the easiest methods to implement and pursue.

Therefore, counselor training programs are encouraged to integrate materials from international cultures. One way to accomplish this is to internationalize reading materials and course assignments. Additionally, students might be encouraged to explore literature, history, nonfiction, Web sites, international movies, television shows, and/or see plays with an international theme.

At this time, there are very few readings available in U.S. counseling publications that focus on global or international issues. Therefore, this profession must expand our repertoire of reading assignments to include publications in other fields such as folklore culture or cultural anthropology.

Next, bilingual students can be encouraged to explore, for instance, counseling psychology written in another language, such as exploring counseling or mental health publications in Spanish. Additionally, counseling psychology programs may want to take advantage of their international students and students who have lived abroad, to gain the diverse perspectives from them, to enrich classroom discussion.

Perhaps U.S. students who have lived abroad can also discuss their experiences in another country and how "people from that foreign country" perceive the world (e.g., time, space, mental health). Similarly, international students in counseling programs can share their experiences in their home countries and in the United States.

Faculty or educators can also add several things into their class: listening to international music; learning international languages; eating in ethnic restaurants; watching international news. Moreover, students might visit local international neighborhoods, seek to interact with international students and organizations on campus, or agree to serve as a host family for international students or visitors.

In addition, the training programs could sponsor international scholars from other countries. These international scholars will enrich the programs or courses with invaluable resources. The faculty members could create informal (e.g., roundtable discussions, conversation hours) and formal (e.g., poster and paper sessions, symposiums) forums on campus, and in their departments and universities.

Another easy way to increase the students' understanding of global cultures is through the electronic media, Internet, Skype, or e-mail. Students in the USA could network with students around the world. Web sites, chat rooms, and message boards could be launched by students, training programs, and/or professional organizations to establish an international network and forum that would allow students to exchange background information, local ideas, personal interests, peculiar challenges, specific successes, and so forth.

METHODOLOGICAL ISSUES ABOUT GLOBALIZING COUNSELING PSYCHOLOGY

To put counseling in a global context, the most basic practical challenge is gaining accessibility to an international sample. There are several strategies to gain an international sample: collaboration with a scholar in the country of interest; collecting data from international neighborhoods in the USA; conducting qualitative research with an international group, etc. It might also be difficult to convince individuals outside USA to participate in research conducted by someone unfamiliar. For instance, seniors or children in other countries may feel uncomfortable to participate in a research project from someone foreign to them.

Another strategy to collect international sample is to control the length of time to collect data. The strategies are infinite, but on the whole, perseverance, patience, tolerance for ambiguity and uncertainty, and the ability to effectively delegate responsibility for carrying out the study are essential requirements of the successful international researcher.

Next, the assumption that all human beings share a universal theory cannot be applied to other international cultures. Thus, to globalize theories in counseling needs much preparatory work. Researchers must discern if a particular theory is appropriate for a specific group and if the application of this theory requires any adjustment.

Concretely, to better apply a theory to an international group, researchers must also decide how the theoretical construct could be operational, be assessed (e.g., by self-report instrument, observation, interview, archive reserach, public data), and appropriately investigated.

When conducting studies in international settings, therefore, counseling researchers should first question the presence, relevance, and appropriateness of any specific construct. For example, "family" has different meanings and connotations in the USA from other countries.

In quantitative issues, the researchers should question the design validity of the intended procedures and the validity and reliability of applying scales to the targeted international samples. For instance, it is conceivable that research methodologies (e.g., laboratory studies; self-reported scales) used in the West may have less validity in other countries with different cultures from USA. Thus, researchers might additionally explore the possibility of qualitative strategies (e.g., interviews) to collect data.

After these considerations, even if it is found appropriate to use a quantitative methodology in a particular international setting, researchers may still need to decide if they need a new measure to capture the novel meaning of the construct or it is OK to use an existing measures in the USA.

If the latter approach is taken, the researcher must be cautious with the issue of translation, back translation, to test the equivalence of the measure before collecting data (Brislin, 1986). Back translation will provide counseling researchers with the opportunity to evaluate the equivalence of measures by comparing the original with the back-translated version of the instrument.

Finally, researchers should be careful with the use of standards when interpreting data (Brislin, 1983). This can result in researchers being judgmental or even paternalistic in their interpretation. For example, researchers studying psychological loneliness might find that participants from Asian countries tend to score higher than participants from the USA. This does not mean that Asians feel lonelier than Americans. Researchers may want to examine *their* standards when interpreting the differences of loneliness.

GLOBALIZE COUNSELOR EDUCATION

As contacts increase among people from countries around the world, it is understandable that the mission of globalizing counselor education must be adapted and expanded. Relying on Western assumptions alone on counseling and education when working in an international setting amounts to Westernizing counseling to other countries. This is especially critical when comprehending interpersonal transactions and cultural values, norms, expectations, and behaviors.

To expand theories of human behavior in social interaction, counselors and mental health professionals must first approach international issues with absolute openness, with great genuine respect and appreciation of the unique features of the their target culture. At the same time, it is important that counselor educators immerse themselves in the culture to develop a deep conceptual and experiential understanding of the culture.

RECOMMENDATIONS

Recommendations in this essay are intended to help counselors to think and act outside traditional paradigms of counseling in the USA. International work requires counseling professionals to leave their comfortable zone and enter a circle of observation, discovery, feedback, reflection, in fresh adventure in alien culture with equanimity and interdependence. The counselors aspiring to be agents of social change may also achieve globalizing of counseling psychology. These counselors will help preserve and honor diverse cultures around the world.

Surveying those various offers of methods above, we see a delightful plethora of proposals to reach beyond the Western culture to places abroad such as Taiwan and then

China beyond. Here we must be alerted that these methods proposed are still at their beginning stage of being tried out, experimented on, and watched over for results both hopeful and ominous. We must be warned. Here our excitement at launching into a virgin territory of non-Western cultures tends to blind us to unexpected bumps ahead. We must repeat. Extreme caution is in order.

Above all, we must firmly remember this. All our reach-out has been from the West. All our proposals are in the Western style and approach. We must be aware, always, that no Western tiger can change its skin of objective analysis, if not of our pet tendency to confuse psychology with physiology.

Luckily, the non-Western budding "psychologists" are usually quite sensitive and receptive to the Western approach. Sadly, however, we are yet to see them reciprocating with their own offers of innovative methodology toward globalizing counseling that has begun in the West.

At this initial global stage, the situation bristles with risks of monocultural imposition, instigated precisely (and ironically) by warm non-Western receptivity. We had better elucidate the origin of this danger, often quite innocently occasioned unawares. Let us take a concrete example. It is simply that the West tends to explicate, while China tends to implicate, and it so happens that human psyche in its thinking and feeling is spontaneous and implicative in its supposedly open operation and expression.

This human and cultural fact does not forebode well for the West's explicitness. Explicitness vastly and easily facilitates its spread without even noticing its ominous prospect, i.e., the West tends to pull psychic seedlings to pieces in death by pulling them up, so as to help them grow before their own growing times, each differently appropriate to each.

Nurture and cure require patient sensitivity implicated in the tacit tenderness of the human life-situation. The West's external explicitness must be forewarned of its inherent "handicap" as above at this sensitive point. All this leads us to consider the West's risk of monocultural imposition, however unawares, and done in goodwill.

MONOCULTURAL RISKS AND GLOBAL MANAGEMENT IN INTERCULTURE

Of course, it is only human nature to universalize—however unawares—our own comfortable ideal and our familiar taken-for-granted pattern of thinking and feeling. We think that what we like, what we take as tasteful and comfortably noble, is also likewise to *all* others, and so in goodwill we bring "our best" to others as our best gift to them. Monocultural uniformity thus comes as a matter of course, quite meaningful to *us*. Our culture is well-organized and visible, and generally accepted, and *that* must also be the case with every other culture—so we think.

A moment of reflection makes us realize, however, that we must always be thoughtful enough to discern the often totally *different* tastes and patterns of thinking and feelings of people other than those in our own community. Moreover, any concrete situation, including ours, is in constant change, and our concrete situation is often a deeply felt situation that changes to upset our accustomed patterns of taking things.

As a result, we often—if not invariably—come to apply wrong "cure" to the so-called "diseases" and elusive troubles of people. Our standard bible, *DSM-IV*, is beset with such danger. It lumps patterns of mental instability into the physical and physiological irregularities. The mental *is* the medical here—even in the phraseology of describing the mental.

Thus it is absolutely required of us to have *sensitivity* toward subtle elusive pain of other people in other cultures. We must wholeheartedly *learn* from other cultures of other people, as to how they see, feel, and handle the daily situation. After all, the non-Western cultures usually have been historically and informally practicing their own psychotherapy without the name of "psychotherapy."

Without such sensitive learning from *inside* the alien cultures, the Western psychological professionals would in good conscience bulldoze over the mental terrains, rugged and irregular, whamming and overwhelming everything with bombardment of Western "cures," to worsen the "disease," and often devastate the trouble into disaster. "The procedure went perfectly in a textbook fashion, and patient died. It was all the fault of the patient!" The textbook is sadly and neatly Western.

Thus the Western professionals simply have to *learn*, there are no ifs or buts about this absolute imperative. These "professionals" are first-graders at the kindergarten of world cultures. A radical open-mindedness and open-heartedness is an absolute must to the Western professionals. In fact, "professional" here means a professional at sensitive learning, nothing else.

By the same token, other non-Western cultures must also *learn* from the West. Psychology in USA is distinctive in that it has its peculiarly clean organized system—at least so it tries—of approaches to coordinate healing. Since the mental does carry its physical aspect, chemical imbalance does coordinate with emotional imbalance, and coordination of counseling with psychopharmacology can achieve a marvelous cure. No non-Western culture has such wonder-cure of science.

The crucial pivot around which the West's entire operations revolve is "coordination." Here, coordination of every department, psychic, physical, physiological, and medical, must be humanized thoughtfully by *coordinating* with variety of distinct cultures all of which are uncomfortably messy to the West.

There is a thin line between sensitive client-oriented healing, on one hand, and textbook and automatic consignment of the "insane" to a psychiatric regimen of brainwashing "for their own good," on the other. This thin line can be discerned and maneuvered by humane sensitivity *alone*. And we must significantly add here that this human sensitivity can be given to the West by learning from so many and varied non-Western cultures, as they in turn learn from the West.

Now, isn't it about time we have noticed this important point? It is this. Such sensitive inter-learning among various world cultures—the more the better—is the Open Sesame to genuine psychological counseling itself, and this inter-cultural learning is none other than the process of globalizing counseling.

Intercultural inter-learning is globalization of counseling that produces genuine and steadily and specifically culture-tailored counseling truly human and effective. Our shared humanity thrives together in this counseling constantly globalizing. Far from being at the periphery, globalization is indeed the *sine qua non*, the very soul of psychotherapy truly so called.

REFERENCES

Ægisdóttir, S., & Gerstein, L. H. (2005). Reaching out: Mental health delivery outside the box. *Journal of Mental Health Counseling, 27,* 221–224.

Brislin, R. W. (1976). Comparative research methodology: Cross-cultural studies. *International Journal of Psychology, 11,* 215–229.

Brislin, R. W. (1983). Cross-cultural research in psychology. *Annual Review of Psychology, 34,* 363–400.

Brislin, R. W. (1986). The wording and translation of research instruments. In W.J. Lonner & J. W. Berry (Eds.), *Field methods in cross-cultural research* (pp.137–164). Beverly Hills, CA: Sage.

Brislin, R. W., Lonner, W. J., & Thorndike, R. M. (1973). *Cross-cultural research methods.* New York: Wiley.

Gerstein, L. H. (2005). Counseling psychologists as international social architects. In R. L. Toporek, L. H. Gerstein, N. A. Fouad, G. Roysircar-Sodowsky, & T. Israel (Eds.), *Handbook for social justice in counseling psychology: Leadership, vision, and action* (pp. 377–387). Thousand Oaks, CA: Sage.

Gerstein, L. H., Rountree, C., Ordonez, A. (in press). An anthropological perspective on multicultural counseling. *Counselling Psychology Quarterly.*

Giorgis, T. W., & Helms, J. E. (1978). Training international students from developing nations as psychologists: A challenge for American psychology. *American Psychologist, 33,* 945–951.

Heppner, P. P. (2006). The benefits and challenges of becoming cross-culturally competent counseling psychologists. *The Counseling Psychologist, 34,* 147–172.

Kim, U., Yang, K.-S., & Hwang, K.-K. (2010). *Indigenous and cultural psychology: Understanding people in context.* New York: Springer.

Leong, F. T. L., & Ponterotto, J. G. (2003). A proposal for internationalizing counseling psychology in the United States: Rationale, recommendations, and challenges. *The Counseling Psychologist, 31,* 381–395.

Pedersen, P. B. (2003). Culturally biased assumptions in counseling psychology. *The Counseling Psychologist, 31,* 396–403.

Rogers, C., & Sanford, R. (1987). Reflections on our South African experience. *Counseling and Values, 32,* 17–20.

Skovholt, T. (1988). Searching for reality. *The Counseling Psychologist, 16,* 282–287.

Sue, D. W., Arredondo, P., & McDavis, R. J. (1992). Multicultural Counseling Competencies and Standards: A call to the profession. *Journal of Counseling & Development, 70,* 477–486.

Takooshian, H. (2003). Counseling psychology's wide new horizons. *The Counseling Psychologist, 31,* 420–426.

Wu, K. M. (2010). *Chinese wisdom alive: Vignettes of life-thinking.* New York: Nova.

B. Cultural Intercourse

In this *second* bunch, globalization as "cultural intercourse" is kicked off by Chang and Sun. Both sensitively spot the problem of today's globalization to lie in monocultural dominance. Chang's solution is globalization in the direction of localization. Sun offers interculture equal and various as a solution.

Goulding exemplifies local interculture concretely by offering the panorama of dialogues among scholars East and West in the specific arena of Daoism, which is generalized as East-West meeting by Zhang.

In: Globalization Dynamics
Editor: Kuang-ming Wu

ISBN: 978-1-62100-750-0
© 2012 Nova Science Publishers, Inc.

Chapter 6

GLOBALIZATION AS LOCALIZATION

*Chung-yue Chang**
Montclair State University, New Jersey, US

ABSTRACT

The local-global dialectics has two tendencies. The first broadening tendency of "local is global" is well known and even celebrated. However, the second indigenous tendency of "global is local" is little known, if at all. Yet, this little known second tendency is of greater interest. This is because, as stated earlier, "local is global" under the dominant Greek-European perspective is promoted to be the only tendency, so that all locals will become identical. By paying attention to "global is local" this essay aims to bring out the hidden fact that what is global would always return back to, and generate new, locals. Not recognizing the critical co-presence of the second indigenous tendency, any account of human experience would be disastrously incomplete.

I. INTRODUCTION: GLOBALIZATION AND LOCALIZATION

During this second decade of the 21st century, the "globalization" concept is one of the most popular buzzword the world over. Discussions on almost any topic of importance would end up with a global reference. Globalization is one of those seemingly important yet imprecise concepts that are opened for diverse applications and interpretations. Historically, globalization first appeared and gained currency during the last quarter of the 20th century. And it promises to become a major concern for the balance of the 21st century, perhaps beyond.

The "tendency to broaden" human experience, which the globalization concept of the 20th-21st century connotes, is actually present in all periods of history. Likewise, the contrasting concept "localization," which connotes the opposite "tendency to be indigenous" in human experience, is also present in history. Globalization and localization are, therefore,

---

* Professor of Western philosophy and Chinese philosophy, Montclair State University, New Jersey, USA. Dr. Chang's email is: cycee888@yahoo.com

the co-present contrasting human tendencies found throughout history. This paper examines into the relations between, and the philosophical implications of, these two tendencies, extending beyond the confines of current centuries.

The 20th-21st century understanding of globalization is characterized by the dominant Greco-European perspective, which is itself local.[1] Here globalization is a local Europe-specific-broadening-goal, by dint of its acquired dominance, became universal, and toward which the world's other indigenous locals move. It is how the world's other locals, regardless of their origins and diversities, become the universal ideal of a dominant global-local. When this ideal is strictly interpreted, globalization implies the elimination of all other locals, because they are all expected to be identical to the Greco-European global ideal. The whole linear process aims for a single static end-point. It should be noted that the exclusive practice of the dominant Greco-European perspective during the 20th-21st century led, unfortunately, to global mono-cultural disasters. This crucial point will be discussed below at several points.

To underscore the dominant, static, and linear Greco-European view of reality, history, and human destiny, we cite briefly three notable historical examples from European philosophy. Within an exclusive static context, the first grand linear view was expressed 2,500 years ago by Plato's eternal Form, which became culturally dominant. Within a dialectically dynamic context, more recent linear views were expressed 160 years ago by Hegel's Absolute Spirit, and by Marx's materialistic Communist Utopia. "Form" is the static universal (global) end-point for all dynamic particulars (locals) to strive for. Likewise, "Absolute Spirit" and "Communist Utopia" are also the static universal (global) end-points, respectively spiritual and materialistic, where history, populated by dialectically dynamic particulars (locals), ends. Form, Spirit, and Utopia are all static linear instances of globalization, albeit philosophical. Yet these instances were themselves "locals," but were made universal and global, and then for each to serve out its effective historical periods of dominance.

There is, however, an alternative to the Greco-European perspective. This would be the unique perspective of China, which is also a local. From this perspective, globalization and localization are, like *yin* and *yang*, holistically, organically, and dynamically related. Here globalization and localization must each be read as a verb, globalizing and localizing. This relationship, accordingly, is not linear, but is organically inter-mixed, mutually supportive and productive, as exemplified in Chinese philosophy 2,500 years ago by Laozi's Dao and De. Dao would be equivalent to the globalizing ideal, and De's are how the globalizing Dao is localized.

All local De follow global Dao. And global Dao, in turn, would transform every local De.[2] In other words, the different De as locals, would always strive to be in accord with the common global Dao, which, in turn, would ever broaden and transform De as locals. Being two sides of the same coin, the two dynamic tendencies interplay concurrently in a mutually penetrating way. This holistic-organic pattern of human experience is also present throughout historical periods. This holistic approach, based on global-local interplay, provides the antidote to correct the mono-cultural disasters.

To reinforce the above description, the dynamic holistic relation between the two tendencies can be expressed in a simpler way. The first broadening tendency is simply called

---

[1] This perspective has become specifically American due to the economic, political, and cultural dominance of the United States. The 20th century has been known as the American century.

"local is global," and the second indigenous tendency is simply called "global is local." Again, these are the two sides of the same coin. First, "local is global" means that pluralistic localities make global, or the globe is locality plural writ large. The reason is that localization has an inherent tendency toward becoming global. Localization is therefore global charged. Actuality is simply that notes make the music, persons make the nation, and continents make the globe. Laozi would say, that "De's are constituent ingredients of Dao."

Obviously, the first broadening tendency of "local is global" involves synergistic movements from localities toward a common goal. However, in this very striving, the localities will never become identical. This is because every local is, in its beginning and in its ending, indigenously different from every other local. Even though all locals can strive after a common goal, yet each is affected and broadened differently, even under the shared goal.

Therefore each local's indigenousness can never be erased. There will always be differences between and among locals, no matter how small the differences, and no matter how similar they become. There is always differentiation among locals. Thus, globalization can serve localities to become more like each other, but it can never cause them to be identical to each other. There will always be localities that are different no matter how far globalization globalizes localities. With the primacy of localities, it is now easy to see how "global is local,"

"Global is local," the second tendency, means that locality is global writ small, that every locality has the depth of the global, that there is universality within specificity, or, as William Blake puts it, "to see a world in a grain of sand."[3] Again, the global depth in each locality never causes all localities to be identical. This is because each locality contains traces of the global in its own indigenous way. Indigenousness always takes priority. Being affected and broadened by the global, each locality in its inerasable indigenousness continues to grow into a new locality. Again, there will always be localities that are different.

The local is thus the basic. Considering "local is global" and "global is local" from the holistic-organic perspective shows that local is the anchor which global always serves. Thus this perspective balances and corrects the static linear Greco-European perspective, which has created the 20th-21st century mono-cultural disasters by insisting that localities become identical as a result of globalization. The holistic-organic perspective shows how globalization, as the natural and expected human tendency to broaden, cannot be the linear end-point, but must return back to and generate new locals, new indigenous foci. It is imperative that this hidden crucial fact be made evident.

Due to its 20th-21st century connection, the first broadening tendency of "local is global" is well known and even celebrated. However, the second indigenous tendency of "global is local" is little known, if at all. Yet, this little known second tendency is of greater interest. This is because, as stated earlier, "local is global" under the dominant Greek-European perspective is promoted to be the only tendency, so that all locals will become identical. By paying attention to "global is local" this essay aims to bring out the hidden fact that what is global would always return back to, and generate new, locals. Not recognizing the critical co-presence of the second indigenous tendency, any account of human experience would be disastrously incomplete.

---

[2] Laozi 's classical work is entitled Dao De Jing, literally the Cannon of Dao and De.

To show that "local is global" and "global is local' are identical as two sides of the same coin, we must first discuss them separately. We will first consider the tendency of "local is global" to show that global, from the holistic perspective, would not and could not be the end point. We will then consider the tendency of "global is local" to underscore the primacy of the local. Finally, we will consider the two tendencies together in order to underscore the primacy of localities over the global. Of the two, the most important tendency is "global is local."

II. LOCALIZATION TOWARD GLOBALIZATION

Globalization provides occasions to universalize. We humans love to universalize. We love to claim, "All are like this." The word "this" refers to the universal, and the "all" refers to the particulars. To universalize is to recognize and appeal to the common "this" as shared by the "all" of particulars. This is a philosophical relationship that is at once metaphysical and epistemological. It is metaphysical because universal and particulars are twin aspects of reality. It is epistemological because universal and particulars together enable us to know reality.

To rationalize universalizes, which humans started to do in earnest 2,500 years ago that philosopher Karl Jaspers called the Axial Age.[4] This was the time when, as if on cue, rationality emerged spontaneously, simultaneously, differently, and indigenously around the globe. Of course, rationality at the time took on different local features. Thus, it was at this Age that Greek Thales began the Western analytic rationality. Buddha founded a unique Indian rational approach to life. Confucius and Laozi pivotally shaped China's radical pragmatic rationality.

They were all local sages yet, through differing rationalities, they left us diverse indelible universals. Thales influenced fellow pre-Socratic Heraclitus to give us the universal Logos, Confucius and Laozi left us the universal Dao, and Buddha left us the universal Dharma. Importantly, there are substantial and irreconcilable differences among Logos, Dao, and Dharma as universals, as each universal originated in various localities to carry thoroughly local characters. These were legacies of global universals from the Axial Age of human history. It is thus that every incorrigible locality has its own universal depths with global depths.

"But why do humans love to universalize, to rationalize?" A definitive answer may never be given. However, one can speculate that the penchant to universalize may be due to the very nature and structure of human consciousness. Human consciousness is awareness. At the primary level, we are aware of things and facts through our senses. At the secondary level, we come to be aware of meanings of things and facts, by way of recognizing the order and pattern among things and facts. The absence of order and pattern is chaos. Chaos is not preferred by consciousness, because whatever chaos means, it is far less significant than the

---

[3] This phrase begins his well-known poem quite long, titled "Auguries of Innocence," in The Complete Poetry & Prose of William Blake, ed. David. V. Erdman, NY: Doubleday, 1988, pp. 490-496.

[4] Karl Jasper identified a number of Axial Age (800 to 200 BCE) thinkers who made fundamental contribution to worldwide philosophy and religion. Socrates, Confucius, and Siddhartha Gautama were key. Others include Parmenides, Heraclitus, and Elijah. See his book, Vom Ursprung und Ziel der Geschichte (The Origin and Goal of History).

meaning of order and pattern. The meaning of order and pattern is far more useful than chaos, which is "irrational" to our reason.

Chaos is problematic for human consciousness. Solution to this problem is shown by the evolution of human consciousness. In general, human civilization, which displays this evolution, is a march from chaos to order. This pattern can be repetitive, because order can fall back to chaos to start the march again. Because of this pattern, particular civilizations share the same chaos problematic, for which they provide different order-like solutions. Before the Axial Age, the Greeks turned to the order of Olympian Gods for solution, as the Chinese turned to the order of its mythical personalities. After the Axial Age, the Greek rational solution gave rise to the order of Logos, and the Chinese rational solution gave rise to the order of Dao. These different solutions thus gave us differing rational approaches, Greco-European and Chinese in this case. Same pattern exists in other civilizations, Indian and others. For all these civilizations there are globalized universal orders for before and after the Axial Age. Likewise, there are also corresponding localizing particular activities.

Now fast forward to our own time. The high-profiled 20th-21st century globalization from the dominant Greco-European perspective testifies to this truth about a particular kind of universal order. This is a prime example of taking "localization toward globalization" or "local as global" as the final end-point. It does not account for nor allow "globalization back to localization" or "global as local." This results in mono-cultural disasters worldwide. Counter measures to avoid these disasters would depend on the counter balancing role of "global as local," which will soon be discussed. Before we do so, however, we must consider how the 20th-21st century concentration on the "local as global" aspect of globalization leads to mono-cultural disasters.

III. THE 20TH-21ST CENTURY CASE

A General Observation

Before offering corrections to avoid mono-cultural disasters, we must look at how it all started, how we came to think of "localization to globalization" as the *only* option. To do so, we must look into the development of the concept of globalization concept during our 20th-21st century today.

As a general observation, globalization for 20th-21st century is both a fact and a vision. This fact is solid, the vision will be shown to be misguided. Here is the fact of globalization. Our consideration of matters global recognizes a tendency toward momentum to universal uniformity in all shared human experiences. This momentum is made possible by a significantly accelerated rate of technological interconnection among all peoples across geographic regions and time zones.

The accelerated global interconnection is made possible by applications of new communication technologies today that effectively collapsed space and time down to zero. In other words, for peoples worldwide, their usual common space-time frame for experiencing and communicating ceased to be essential. Now, there is a new option of zero space and time. Such new option opens up a new alternative way to experience and communicate, done in co-presence and simultaneity or, equivalently, in virtual space and in real time.

In addition, we see the new vision of globalization. The fact of erupting globalization is revolutionary, and so its meaning is not yet clear. What does it mean for people all over the world to be able now to experience and communicate with one another in a co-present and simultaneous way?

The old ways to experience and communicate had to struggle to overcome their reality of "delay" or even "access denied" due to challenging spatial distance and temporal duration. Now, thanks to the ever upgrading new technologies, space and time platform can each collapse down to zero. People from opposite sides of the globe have the option to experience and communicate with each other within a co-present virtual space (physically provided through a local TV or computer screen; a communicating *i*-pad or the latest smart phone) and in the simultaneity of real time.

What are the impacts of this new virtual reality, this instant global communication, on matters economic, social, political, and personal? We must search quite deeply in order to answer such question. What sort of new economy and politics would be made by economic and political activities now carried out in virtual space and in real time? What radical changes ensue out of the new ways in which people live, think, and relate to one another? These questions would guide us to an articulation of new visions about economy and politics, and thereby about all matters human.

We will understand from such situation today, as extrapolated from discussion below, that the dominant new globalized vision tends to advocate a world of universal uniformity. The world will do things in the same standard and uniform ways to display the same universal values. This essay will then closely examine this vision and will argue, in the following sections, that the world will globalize, march toward uniformity to invite mono-cultural disasters. To avoid and correct these disasters the world must renew itself to display new localization with global depth. There are always philosophical reasons why localization will always take precedence in all globalization process for today, tomorrow, and yesterday.

Specific Observations

Against this predominant tendency today, let us look at some actual alternative examples of globalizing facts and visions. We would cite geopolitics, economy, and culture. First, geopolitics as an academic discipline can best reflect the "fact" of globalization. Geopolitics studies the impacts of geography, economics, and demography on politics, especially on foreign policies of a state. National policies reflect the impacts of technologies and of greater intimacy of interconnection among the states.

In geopolitics, globalized visions invariably come up when developed, developing, and under-developed countries gather to negotiate on their respective futures within their common future. Developed countries, Western in orientation, would wish to push to globalize their own visions, by uniformly universalizing their values and ways of life toward all other nations. Some developing and under-developed nations, with different histories, values, and ways of life, may agree to follow the West. Some others, while modernizing, or globalizing, in Western ways, may insist on their own paths of development. A particular reading of "globalization" as equivalent to Westernization has become, for some Western nations, a handy foreign policy tool for global geopolitical control. This is one prime example of the ills of mono-cultural disasters.

Second, "globalization vision" is often strictly deduced from the "globalization fact" of global economy, which is essentially the market economy of capitalism.[5] In the practice of capitalism, large industries, especially those with global reach and profit-driven ambitions, seek to push and sell their products universally to every corner of the world, made possible by the new technologies. The technology-supported practice of unfettered capitalism has resulted in a global economy of worldwide trade nexus and global integration of investment and finance.

Their vision is to make cheaper goods and services a commonplace to promote higher material living standards worldwide. Yet, global economy has also brought about dire consequences quite un-resolvable, such as massive miseries of poverty, social inequality, and industrial and commercial waste, and global environmental pollution. Western international financial institutions, such as the International Monetary Fund (IMF) and the World Bank, were created in 1944 to ameliorate the ills of economic globalization on developing and under-developed nations. Historical records show that measures from these institutions created more harms than help. This sad fact calls for a revision or replacement in vision. Such are some examples of economic mono-cultural disasters.

Finally, globalization invariably touches on the wider aspects of *culture*. Given the world's geopolitical and economic reality, social scientists, economists, and sociopolitical theorists argue on competing models, pro and con, for a globalized world order. Philosophers join the conversation with their usual critical, axiological perspectives. Public philosophers, for example, wrote compelling articles with titles like "Famine, Affluence, and Morality"[6] and "Globalization and Its Discontents."[7] These essays typify philosophical oppositions to integrate the world through monolithic economic globalization.

Sadly, however, current philosophical views are uniformly for universal uniformity in globalization. They just disagree on *which* uniformity is desirable. They do not consider the continuing role that "localization" plays within globalization context. For them, globalization replaces localization. Still, they do call for revision or replacement in global visions in some sense. These are cultural examples of mono-cultural disasters

A Historical Observation

Let us now look at globalization from a historical perspective. Stated slightly differently, globalization refers specifically to the unifying trends strewn across the full range of human situations, which are a dynamic mix of social, political, economic, and cultural elements. These trends are factually real. Historically, the unifying trends are facilitated by the emergence of technologies new for the historical period in question. For today the new technologies came from the "Information and Communication Revolution of the 20th century." This latest Revolution will prove as seminal and formative for centuries to come.

---

[5] For the 20th-21st century European West, capitalism has been a tool to practice mono-culture economic hegemony. Modern China defies this characterization. China achieved its second largest economy today by being local. China went global to modernize by being locally Chinese. Its economy is socialist, and its socialism is with Chinese characteristics.

[6] Peter Singer, "Famine, Affluence, and Morality," Philosophy and Public Affairs, Vol. 1, No. 3 (spring, 1972), pp. 229-243.

[7] Herman E. Daly, "Globalization and its Discontents," Philosophy and Public Policy Quarterly, Vol. 21, No, 2/3 (Spring/Summer, 2001), pp. 17-21.

Similarly, the First Industrial Revolution 1712-1830 of textiles and steam was seminal and formative of the subsequent 19th and 20th centuries.

Each of these Revolutions had been triggered by the appearance of critically life-changing technologies. Industrial Revolution erupted with the technology of steam engine; steam engines established manufacture industries, capital economy, and created the gap between the wealthy and the poor and the social problems of how to fairly distributing wealth, as well as the issues of modern transportation and communication, improvement of material life, modern nation states, colonization, the two world wars, dire poverty, and even the modernized practice of slavery for cheap labor.

As for today's Information and Communication Revolution, its dynamics of technologies is represented by the internet and the satellite communications. Internet connects us to a hitherto unknown inner virtual reality, as the satellites connect the outer physical, literally global regions. The twin technologies shrank the space-and-time platform for human experiences down to its limiting point, zero. Spatial extension in human experience is now reduced to nearly non-existence, and time becomes instantaneous.

Now, such revolution of the 20th century is actually an extension of the revolution of the 18th century. The modern Information and Communication Revolution has inherited all the unique development and positive and negative consequences of the Industrial Revolution, and continues to develop them and grapple with their problems and benefits. There is, however, a difference. Now, the globalized, near zero space-time, platform has to deal with the challenging problems derived from a unifying vision quite urgent.

The unifying trends and the supporting technologies together have harvested a shared expectation that, for a not too distant future, the world will become a highly homogenized and self-same global village. In other words, globalization will eliminate localization. Because the unifying trends are factually undeniable, there is no question but that homogenization will congeal to an ever greater degree. The question is whether homogenization will eliminate diversification all together.

There is also no question but that greater globalization will take place for more and more geographical regions. The question here is whether localization will become extinct. The great debate is whether localization or diversity that typifies human reality will disappear for good. The path from globalization to homogenization to the extinction of localization is the ultimate mono-cultural disaster. Human progress may eliminate humanity.

Fortunately, there is an alternative. It is the fact that, however homogenized and globalized, many localities would, on their own initiative, turn diversified and localized anew as they have been many times before. This path of renewed diversification, localization, would provide the necessary correction for today's mono-cultural disasters. For this path of localization and diversity, we now turn to the next section: globalization back to localization. The choice of vision here is either one uniform world or the global village in diversity continuous.

IV. GLOBALIZATION BACK TO LOCALIZATION

What is the meaning of globalization? What, philosophically, does globalization entail? Trace to its essentials, globalization entails the fact that people interconnect with other people, with facilitation across space and time. And their interconnecting activities often have weighty consequences, whether intended or not. "People" here refers, generally and historically, to individuals, communities, ethnicities, principalities, tribes, empires, all the way to the modern nation states. "Acts of interconnection" here refers to the nature and range of interpersonal and inter-communal relations at various levels.

Comprehensively, these interconnections comprise the full range of human communicative struggles and experiences, categorized as social, political, economic, and cultural. Most importantly, such interconnecting acts must be significantly facilitated. "Facilitations" here refers to communication tools, methods, media, and skills. Historically, the range of facilitation had been from the simple to the sophisticated. The higher the sophistication we have, the greater the degree of globalization we gain.

In sum globalization entails "people" acting in "interconnection" with "facilitation" to affect "socio-political-economic-cultural" aspects of humanity. All these elements are local in character. Thus all such considerations inevitably lead to a complementary vision of globalization as enhancement of diversity of localities, rather than the destruction of local diversities. This complementary vision is basic to globalization, and is the solution to monocultural disasters. Globalization needs to be brought back to localization.

Globalization Localizing

Globalization is an active verb. It moves toward localities. Globalization that generalizes actually globalizes worldwide the deepening of various earthy localities so countless. And so localities are the be-all and end-all of ongoing activities of globalization, and such globalization serving localities is the glory of proud localities.

We must also remember that localization is also an active verb. Localization moves toward the global. Localization has the inherent tendency to become global, just like globalization must return back to localities.

We have been elucidating two simple but significant points. One, each locality is globe writ small as globe is locality plural writ large. Two, to pretend that globalization as beyond and above locality invites the disaster of parading one local culture (today's Greco-European West) as "global today." Our thinking must stick to the fact that global is local so many and various as local diverse is global so deep and rich. Both are two sides of the same coin, called "humanity." Here the pivot is global as local, so much so that locality is globe-charged.

Now, never forget that seeing global significance in the local-specific differs completely from identifying any one local specific as global and general. Seeing the global in the specific edifies to enrich, while taking the local-specific *as* the general-global kills us all by the monocultural disasters. The global in the local deepens humanity, while the local elevated to the global is pan-mortal, killing us all with the arrogated one locale. Let us now think further on what riches seeing the global in the local-specific involves.

Blake said that this universality *within* specificity is "to see a world in a grain of sand." "A world" of "all" can and must be envisioned in a specific speck of dust, "a grain of sand," and such specific of dust shall, as it is, as dust, sparkle with the "all," to excite us all. Each pebble is discovered as a precious stone shimmering with sparkles of deep meaning charged with "all." Each local "here now" carries in itself the weight of the glories of the entire globe.

We need not, cannot, and must not, fly up beyond "here now" to hover and flutter nowhere in vain, to impose this vain emptiness on riches of localities.

The glory of the whole globe is right here now in our countryside. We all enjoy the music of the Bohemian rural in B. Smetana and A. Dvorak. We all can share the glories and miseries so globally weighty of the specific, only as the specific glories and miseries are specifically appreciated. The "all" is right within the here-now of each of the concrete "many," as the global is the local, as the local *as local* is already weighted with the global so diverse.

To discern this "world in a grain of sand" is our general excitement called "knowledge," called "science." This is "scholarship" scientific and historical, truly so called, for what scientist does not do specific experiment and specific observation of specific concrete happenings? What historian does not do specific investigation of specific happening and specific observation of the trend of the times in a specific period?

At the same time, we note how the same situation of specificity as (origin to) universality obtains for universality as well. "All" is extrapolated from the specificity of "here now" by way of analogy, "as this, so that," to attain a concrete general situation, and then on to derive the universal for countless all, the universal validity for anything whatever so diverse. The specific concrete is prior, an *a priori*, to the general universal. Even Plato in the *Republic* must go through a concrete specific "human body" in its threefold structure to attain "body politic," and then go from the so-called specific "myth" of the cave to reach the sunny realm of pure Ideal Forms.

All this Platonism is all right. The only crucial and fatal mistake Plato made—or is it what later thinkers attributed to Plato?—is to call this concrete initial step an unreal "myth," for on the contrary, Plato's "Realm of the Really Real" *is* the derived myth, and the cave is the really actual. This is because Plato must engage in concrete stories of human body and actual cave first, before he can concoct the dream of body politic and the Ideal Forms. Whether these dreams are real or not must then be checked by the actual human body and the actual concrete cave that Plato happened to see.

And so, Plato should have said instead that the latter universal realm resides *in* the former concrete situation as the actual weight of the concrete actual. Here the actual archeology of the universal is the real ontology of the universal attached to the actual. To express it in our context, the global is, again, the local, and nothing else. Globalization goes localization.

Now, we have just put Plato upside down, so as to restore Plato right side up, as he actually is, and as he should have admitted that this is as he is, for otherwise Plato would be another Icarus having his wax wings melted away by Platonic dreamy Sun[8] to fall to death, bumping the actual ground of the concrete, where he belongs. If to aspire to the universal is human, all too human, then to discern the universal *in* the specific concrete is truly global, humanly global. The general universal and the specific concrete are equal, two sides of the same coin. The concrete aspires for the universal, and the universal is grounded in the concrete.

Thus, all of us, globally and locally, must be warned of a wrong move, though it is subtly similar to globalization as localization to serve various localities. The wrong lies in *directly* globalizing one specific local, identifying *one* locality as the global for all localities, so as to demolish all other localities. This move is not at all the globalizing that deepens many localities, enabling the *many* localities moving into global by joining *with* other localities, inter-deepening.

If the glory of globalization sparkles with many and variously proud localities, then the various and delightful localities are now chorusing lustily together in their own depths globalized so proud, joining arms in need one with another. Here we have the win-win world of "the more, the merrier" enjoyment of beauty together, natural and cultural, inter-enriching co-thriving, called "globalization as localization." All of us are now Alices in Wonderland showing, telling, and sharing our favorite toys, our hugged pets, and our dream treasures. Such a paradise on earth is made of, again, globalization in localization, never one locality as the global over all.

This essay revolves around three pivotal points. What we have done in this section is to call attention to the key pivotal point, which is the fact that the direction of globalization must return back to localization. The other two pivotal points had been discussed previously: *One*, the growths of many localities by way of meticulous globalizations, *two*, a warning against the subtle corruption of globalization as localization into one locality as *the* global, to demolish many localities, thereby destroy that one locality arrogating itself to the general.

In the section below we formally bring the discussion of "growth of localities through globalization" and "globalization returns to localities" together, which topics had been discussed separately before. Again, "globalization returns to localities" is further discussed below for good measure, since it is so important a topic.

V. "Locality Globalized" Flipped to "Globalization Localizing"

Now, to closely observe the relation between disastrous "a single locality globalize" and its solution, "globalizing as localizing," we must retrace ourselves a bit and summarize what we have gone through so far. We understand that we humans love to universalize. On noticing and considering something specific, we love to claim, "All are like this. All universal truth is here in 'this' that I find. This is just a tip of the whole rotten situation I claim to be." All politicians are dirty as this one I find, as all bankers as this one I met are crooks. All of us are selfish criminals as the whole world is dusty to the core. And the list goes on.

Interestingly, we tend to claim that the whole barrel of apples is rotten like this one I find. We tend to laugh at anyone who sees a ray of silver lining over clouds so dark as an unrealistic Pollyanna, while we secretly yearn after such a "pig heaven" we pretentiously sneer at. "Globalization" is one such fad expression abetted by stupendous scientific technology today, a happy expression of our dream of beautiful "all" puffed up in our "all"-sky. We go upward to universalization, forgetting where we are, actually, specifically, here now.

Against this risky upward "all"-tendency of us all, expressed in the buzzword "globalization," this essay issues a warning. It urges us to go solidly downward, not emptily upward. As we gaze at the twinkling stars up above us, we often fall into an ugly ditch-of-

---

[8] The Sun was taken as the heat of actuality before. Here the Sun is taken as the heat of Plato's puffed-up dream. Dream can heat up as the sun of our aspiration. Thus the sun takes a bewildering variety of forms of heat, all because of our illicit aspiration in human hubris.

"all" underfoot. The universal meaning dwells in every rustling tree-leaf, not in empty firmament. As we have leaves so many, so "all" is a plural so rich. The "universal" in the West differs from the "universal" in China, and the so-call global is actually the local deeply gazed at. Every locality has global depths, as globalization is empty "pie in the sky" bereft of solid locality. Actually, "globalization" serves to deepen localization, and nothing else.

Let us continue to consider our human tendency toward universality, often uniform and empty; it is full of unsuspected pitfalls. We want to add prestige and weight to our specific discovery, by advertising it, even to ourselves, as loaded with universal significance. And then, crucially, we forget if not despise the original specificity. We see "all" in "this," and soon discard "this" in enchantment with the "all." And we float up hovering in the dreamy "all." We pretend to be the Olympian gods, and arrogate ourselves as divine.

The ancient Greeks have already warned us that this upward move is human hubris, mortally punishable sooner than later. Our wings of "all"-arrogance are made of uncertain wax and puff up to the sky above, soon to be melted away by the heat of the sun of actuality, and we fall dashed to the solid ground to die in ecological disaster.

Human hubris is human suicide, due to leaving—pretending to leave—the autochthonous nature in humanity and around. Actually, it is worse. We think we leave our earthiness, but of course we *are* earthy and we can only pretend to leave, and so, as Socrates warns us, our pretension proves to be our downfall. Our earthiness punishes us to death in earthiness—only earthy being dies, divines are immortal—for our forgetting our innate earthiness. We are made of dust, and we go back to dust for better or for worse, and we go back to dust for the worst—pan-death cultural and ecological—when we forget our nature of dust.

We had better, then, go back to dust for the *better*. The dust is incorrigibly concrete and specific. The reader must have noticed that a specific story of Daedalus and his son Icarus in specific Greek mythology[9] is cited to warn us all against our hubris flying away into the empty sky of generality from our innate earthy specifics.

In fact, fatherhood in general is understandable only through my personal experience of being a father, and then I understand that Daedalus is the specific father to his specific son Icarus, and their specific parental relation instructs us on the mortal risk of human hubris, at least so we read it here, by extrapolating from their specific relation, their concrete case, even those it is a mythical case, for all myths are extrapolated from actuality. Without concrete actuality, there would have been no myth whatever.

It has gone so far so good, as we have elucidated the factual principle of the global and the local. Now, in order to impress on us its urgent necessity, on pain of destroying the entire globe together with ourselves, we go a negative way of considering what if we go against "global as local" by its sneaky twist, to parade a single specific local, as itself a specific "this" as it is, as global beyond specificity; it is quite a contradiction.

We see a subtle thin line between the two, to discern the global in the local, on one hand, and to parade a specific local itself *as* the global, forbidding other localities from being global as well. This is another hubris, to display a specific as global, besides the hubris of leaving localities altogether to hover up there nowhere as universal. We will now detail this other hubris, and then specify how mortally risky such a hubris is.

---

[9] On Daedalus and his son Icarus, see The Oxford Companion to Classical Literature, ed. M. C. Howatson, 1989, p. 167.

On a personal level, this blowup of one specific discovery, of a specific value, all over to everywhere every-when, is one, in fact, the first, of Burns' "ten cognitive distortions"[10] that are responsible for unhappiness, for "feeling bad." But Burns did not realize that this all-too natural tendency cannot help but blow itself further up into a cultural level, and then one local culture's discovery and development of a limited application is now imposed all other local cultures as the newest global civilization today. The unspeakable disasters of all-out "bad feelings" and "unhappiness" then break out; they are of course humanistic and ecological disasters at global level worldwide.

Our Platonic dream soaring high beyond all things specific and concrete will inevitably self-melt in its own heat to crash down. The disaster is that the crash takes the form of [i] obsession with one's dream [ii] that turns out to be one's own self, one's own culture, and [iii] one is wholly unaware of this one specific "self"-as-general-universal. The crash is tragic precisely because we are unaware of the tragedy, taking it as quite natural, trying to tinker with it in one's own cultural way and frame, nothing else.

Here the self-contradiction, the stark contradiction in the self, is threefold. One, the self is specific and concrete and yet it is taken as global and universal. Two, the general-universal is abstract hovering "nowhere" and yet it is tangible here now as "my own culture." Three, one is fully awake and conscious and yet one is at the same time wholly unaware of such contradiction, still dreaming always, drunk living, dead dreamed—of empty ideal of uniform generality.

This sad threefold self-contradiction amounts to being the "self as contradiction," all twisted beyond repair as a crashed airplane in a tattered contorted piece beyond repair. It is "one locality as global," one locality arrogating its own self as global. The "local as global" is a tragic cynical twist out of "global as local," i.e., many localities weighted with global significance.

"Now, be careful. I don't know what you are talking about. What do you want? Isn't what you lament as twisted self-contradiction actually wholly identical to what you applaud as ideal globalization? 'Global as local' *is* 'local as global,' isn't it? What's the difference?" A good objection you raised, my friend. Let me sincerely warn you. "Local as global" can mean identical to "global as local" only *after* first carefully *distinguishing* the two.

For example, the well-known saying, "The more national-cultural, then the more global-worldwide 越是民族的, 越就是世界的"[11] superficially sounds similar to "local as global," but it really means local with global weight, i.e., "global as local." But such understanding is possible only after getting straight the critical distinction between "global as local" and "local as global." The thin line dividing the two, my "global as local" as distinct from their "local as global," is alarmingly serious.

My global-as-local takes [a] the local *as local* frankly specific, earthy, concrete, and pluralistic and [b] discerns its global weight with wonder, and [c] fully recognizes its need of being complemented with many other localities no less imperfect, and no less global-weighted. *Their* "local as global" takes [a'] the local identified *as global*, as general and

---

[10] David D. Burns, Feeling Good: The New Mood therapy (1980), NY: HarperCollins, 1999, pp. 28-49. Burns takes it as "all or nothing" frame of mind that breeds perfectionism to pester us needlessly into feeling bad. Cf. an interesting How Good Do We Have to Be? By Harold S. Kushner, Boston: Little Brown and Co., 1996. We here apply this warning to monocultural imposition to invite global disasters.

[11] This common saying in China is quoted to begin "說明" that begins each volume of 中國書法名帖精選, 孫廣來主編, 西安: 陝西旅遊出版社, 2005.

universal; [b'] identifies such "universal local" as one's own culture, and [c'] wholly unaware of all this identification, while rejecting all other localities as mere outdated irrelevances today. "Global as local" and "local as global" are thus completely distinct, quite opposite each to the other.

And here is a bombshell. The *harvests* of these opposed ideals are as stunningly devastating as they are starkly opposed. Their local-as-global is mono-cultural hegemony clad in the shiny slogan of "we the globalization today," to *replace* all the anachronism of obsolete localities. Such hegemony imposes mono-cultural imperfections onto the whole globe, in disasters ecological, cultural, socio-political, and world-economic. The wealthy G-8 nations today dominate and exploit other nations, and thereby create world-poverty to worsen global miseries, which sooner than later will drag them down to miseries as well.

In contrast, my proposed "global-as-local" would produce multi-cultural inter-complementation originating in frank shared recognition of imperfections of each local culture, in dire need of all others. On the strength of global weight of each local culture, all localities are appealed to globally coordinate into variegated brotherliness. It is cosmopolitanism in every locality inter-criticizing, inter-learning, and inter-enriching among them, the more, the merrier and richer. Respective imperfections frankly recognized are thus bettered by and by.

Such ideal of global-as-local is thus forever open to continual complementary improvements, ever sensitive to the erupting needs of adjustments big and small, in principle and in detail. Ecological camaraderie inter-thrives at every locality in continual cosmopolitan process of globalization in progress pluralistically and locally.

In short, the local-as-global approach is a proud monopoly imposing mono-cultural pan-uniformity into global disaster. In contrast, the global-as-local approach is all localities in coordination, in multicultural diversity, toward global enrichment of all diverse localities. Their stark stunning differences between global tragedies and global inter-thriving spell our shared global urgency toward immediate implementation of "globalization as enrichment of localities" all over the globe.

Now, let us go down to the nitty-gritty of the above two contrasting approaches, and see how we can cure the trouble. We first follow George Orwell and portray the world of Orwellian disasters.[12] The disasters come about as follows. In order to globalize civilization, Orwell proposes that everyone adopts a pig. One squeal a pig makes one rational voice to pacify the world. To his horror, however, there emerges a revolution, and the pigs take over as the Fuehrer of the whole world, and the "1984"-disaster arrives again and again in global economics, nuclear technology, international politics, world poverty, and now global mono-culture.

"What has happened? What is responsible for the reversal of the civilized world?" The answer is simple. "Globalization as localization" has turned upside down, reversed itself, into "locality as globalization," identifying one single locality as global, and, by means of powerful technology concocted in a locality, spreads *its* cultural hegemony worldwide. Stuffing one local culture into the throats of all other localities asphyxiates all localities into extinction.

---

[12] We are thinking here of George Orwell's well-known two novels, Animal Farm (1945) and 1984 (1949), but we describe the disasters our own way.

All this while, this single locality commercially advertises its cultural hegemony worldwide as the cutting-edge civilization of today, and any locality that does not "obey" and accept such mono-cultural hegemony is obsolete, backward, barbaric, and uncivilized. Thus, to drink Coca Cola and wear Levi blue-jeans is to partake of "today" with American accent, and every kindergartner is to be educated to greet people with "How are you?" and "I'm fine, thank you," in American English. If this is not a global disaster of a pervasive cultural sort, in which specific cultures vanish, we do not know what it is. Such a mono-cultural global storm has created terrible global havoc.

"Do we have any cure to this terrible havoc?" Well, its cure is as obvious as the root of this global woe. The single road, above, down to pandemonium, can evidently be adjusted back, and must be turned around, to make for the numerous ways, vigorous and various, toward pan-paradise. This turning consists in reversing the above disastrous reversal, by turning the world upside down, to turn it right side up, into globalizing various localities, globe-diversifying "this locality" together with that, and that.

Bohemia produces many a Dvorak among so many other localities in the world that love Dvorak. China produces many a Confucius for any local peoples who admire him. India touts many a Gandhi to spread nonviolent concord, as he captured M. L. King's heart and soul. Algiers offers many an Augustine to those who adore him. Greece harvests another Socrates, and more of him, for so many followers of him. Russia offers Tolstoy in so many lands to enrich so many magnificent life-situations. Germany glitters with many a Leibniz the monadic cosmopolitan. England smiles with many a Churchill, brilliantly literary and political. Italy gives us a wise Seneca so many to suit so many local situations.

And need we mention that Gandhi's nonviolent protest against the powerful British colonialism has inspired Martin Luther King, Jr.,'s irrepressible dream after peace among all peoples in concord. And the list goes on. These goings-on intone the chorus of odes to joys together worldwide, in globalization toward lively localization, one delightful locality here, another lusty one there, all happening at once, gorgeously flower-blossoming in the globalization-spring, serenaded by twittering birdsongs of localities far and near, faint and clear.

All the tiny flowers open out wide in big smiles, in various local colors, as birds big and small giggle singing songs in gutsy rural tunes, all at once. They are breathing exciting, all at the dawn, in the first morn of creation of the world, by globalization as localization. What a beautiful morning global it is! Everything is going our local ways heartfelt!

Laozi's vision (47) is now happily fulfilled in globalization as localization. "Not go outdoors, we all know all under heaven," thanks to your greeting me in vast fresh China from your rural Bohemia no less refreshing. He in Algiers of ancient Coptic culture smiles and nods at her among many voluptuous goddesses in India, as people in Japan bow in nature to Britons embraced in their fabulous gardens. Nothing is happier, more in spring season all over, more inter-uplifting and enriching, than such globalizing of earthy fertile *localities* all over the globe, world without end.

Locality, locality, and more localities here and there, they are the all flourishing pan-paradise no one can resist, as absolutely no one is excluded. We all need one another, shaking hands, ha-ha-ing everywhere all over the globe. Such happy situation is created by globalization that is indeed localization globalizing, in so many places local, today and tomorrow. Let us go for it, you and I, shall we? How could anyone resist this globalization as localization?

The contrast of one locality as global, over against diverse globalizations as various localities inter-thriving is staggeringly serious. The contrast means "globalization as unilateral vs. globalization as multilateral," and "globalization as mono-cultural vs. globalization as intercultural." Unilateral mono-culturalism leads to global disasters. Multicultural togetherness leads to the win-win more-sum future of the whole globe-full of localities.

The reason is simple. If you are enriched, I will be enriched by your riches, more than I can enrich me myself alone. And so my obligation is irresistible to enrich *you*, even at my own cost, and such investment in inter-enrichments all of us want to globalize. Globalization must serve localization. There is no other way than this way together.

The choice is starkly clear. Our pan-obligation is irresistible to completely switch globalization over toward serving the diversity of so many localities to thrive together worldwide. Again, the vibrant movement of globalization must be brought synonymous with invigorating diversity and plurality of all localities, earthy and peculiar, all over the globe. There can never be any other alternative future to our common humanity globally local, in powerful autochthonous diversity everywhere, always. This shared ideal for all of us in the world is served precisely by globalization as localization.

Such globalization will make "our world" by mixing the wealth of varieties of Mother Nature, with colors and melodies of peoples of so many bewildering localities. Our Global Village will be continuous bazaars and countless expositions of riches beyond imagination, day after day, night after refreshing night. Meditations mix with soft music. Tiny flowers are serenaded by birdsongs far and faint. We walk, tarry, sit, and chat, and then nod and walk on, together or apart. We show things and tell of them, share and stare, and then bow and part good friends. Everything is casual, fun, fresh, and filling to everyone.

We give and are given; nothing is to buy, for everything barters with nods. We all enjoy things made in Bangladesh, Bhutan, Brazil, British Isles, Buenos Aires, Burma, and the list goes on. Their local products are "happiness" various and diverse. "Almighty money" is useless here, dollar, euro, or shilling, or yen. Here kids refuse mom's hand. As mom walks, kids hop, skip, run, and stumble. And mom is right there.

Globalization is kids' mom all around us the kids of all ages. Globalization thus serves local peoples in various scenes of nature where they *are*. In globalization, peoples hug nature as nature silently nurtures us all with spring rain and summer rainbows. My god I cannot stop describing our Global Village, every day so different from every night, while all dusk is inviting the dawn, the morn of the first creation by globalization as localization.

Listen. Tiny birds are still twittering far and faint, as morning doves are cooing, near and away. Ms. Flower-Power softly brushes away our fatigue as she feeds us, to turn trillion steps of our daily trudge into flourish of fit and health, every step of our life's way. It is globalization as localization, as casual joy beyond joys and sorrows, as the cool plain water from the artesian well of Mother Nature. Such globalization as localization is joy unspeakable, to take our breath away. It would be sheer insanity to refuse such joy together in globalization forever localizing.

CONCLUSION

We first discussed "local as global" and "global as local" separately. In Section V above, they were brought together as twin aspects of one holistically dynamics in an organic whole of the globe. We must firmly keep in mind that "local as global" is equivalent in the end to "global as local." They are two sides of the same precious coin, communal humanity in all their human experience.

We must go out of our way to stress "global as local," because the 20th-21st century development of the concept of globalization, in line with the Greco-European perspective of linear development to a static end-point, emphasizes "local as global" and the world is mesmerized by it. Emphasizing "local as global" leads to the unsustainable mono-cultural disasters.

The ability to see "local as global" and "global as local" correctly as two sides of the same coin comes from the Chinese perspective of organic holism. This perspective is healthy and balanced. The static linear Greco-European perspective, as developed during the 20th-21st century, is lop-sided, and it, with extreme exercise of overbearing power on world localities, brought about mono-cultural disasters, with which the world is still struggling to overcome.

Between the co-equals of global and local, local is basic and primal. We can stress and express the local as primary, this way. Localization keeps vigorously going on as globalization, uniform or not, goes on. This fact shows how globalization strengthens localities as localities compose globalization. All this amounts to saying that each locality is globe writ small as the global is pluralistic localities writ large. The inescapable conclusion is that the local is basic and primary. This conclusion shows how essential "localization," in all its plurality and diversity, is to "globalization."

Chapter 7

GLOBALIZATION: ITS TWIN THREATS TO CULTURES

Yun-Ping Sun[*]
National Central University, Taiwan, ROC

ABSTRACT

This chapter considers four topics. *One*, "culture" is our human way of living to constitute humanity, and so touching culture touches humanity itself, quite seriously. *Two*, globalization touches local cultures to induce two threats to them, monocultural obliteration of local cultures and multicultural isolation of those cultures, as illustrated by Kant and Hegel. *Three*, in criticizing both Kant and Hegel, interculture as their solution is revealed to the two threats of globalization. *Four*, modernity, postmodernity, and their three issues are considered to tie up this chapter.

Globalization is allegedly general, while cultures are obviously particular. How could they mix? Bland indifference of the general is worlds apart from peculiar particularity. The earthy particulars simply vanish, obliterated into gritty grains of sand each isolated from the others, as fertile particulars are helplessly baked and exposed to dry generality. In such way as this, general globalization poses two fatal threats to thick local cultures, their obliteration and their isolation.

In other words, tension between the global and the local brings two threats to cultures, monocultural obliteration of the variety of local cultures, on the one hand, and paradoxically, isolation of those cultures one from the other, on the other. Now, what has happened here? We would have thought "globalization" to be such a fashionable buzzword today, worth rallying to.

The trouble originates in us casually taking "globalization" to mean emptily "general," but "nature abhors vacuum," as they say, and we humans are part of nature. Bland "general" turns out to be one culture's concoction, and it has come to arrogate itself as the glorious "general globalization" to mono-culturally impose itself on all other cultures, to threaten

---

[*] Professor of philosophy, National Central University, Taiwan, ROC. Dr. Sun is a Heidegger scholar.
His email is: bunyansun@yahoo.com

those local cultures with extinction of their vibrant peculiarities—in at least two ways, their obliteration and their isolation.

Looking closer, we realize that "globalization" has after all been produced by many local specific cultures, not just one, to globalize their close contacts to mutually benefit one another, and so the modus vivendi of globalization is "interculture" as its modus operandi is "dialogues." As intercultural dialogues, "globalization" serves to shape and enrich these many local cultures as those cultures determine and shape globalization to suit their needs by intercultural dialogues continuously globalizing.

Thus, this chapter considers four topics. *One*, "culture" is our human way of living to constitute humanity, and so touching culture touches humanity itself, quite seriously. *Two*, globalization touches local cultures to induce two threats to them, monocultural obliteration of local cultures and multicultural isolation of those cultures, as illustrated by Kant and Hegel. *Three*, in criticizing both Kant and Hegel, interculture as their solution is revealed to the two threats of globalization. *Four*, modernity, postmodernity, and their three issues are considered to tie up this chapter.

I. CULTURE AS ESSENCE OF HUMANITY

Culture is a specific manner in which a group of human beings strive to deal with their problems of living both in their environments and among themselves. By such struggles *together* they come to develop camaraderie and strengthen communal identity. Even in eccentric individuals in their eccentric ways of life in the community, their eccentricity appears as "odd" only against the background of common ways of problem-solving in which these odd individuals live.

Therefore their very eccentricity shows how inseparable they are from their culture in the light of which they exhibit their eccentricity. After all, we human persons are by nature "social," and so we simply have to live in a community that is culturally constituted. Thus, culture is a necessary collective and ubiquitous way of social living among human persons.

To further concretize the matter of culture, let us take language as an example. What makes language an actual language is not its grammar but its usage made by a community of users of that language, says later Wittgenstein. Language is a language game. A game is played among players by following its rules that are in turn altered by its being played.

In the same manner, language usage follows its rules that are changed and created anew as this specific language is used by a language-community; language rules are never pre-fixed or preprogrammed. This fluid flexibility enables language to stay commonly shared, conventional, and repeatedly created anew as it is used. What constitutes language is its usage in daily ordinary life Wittgenstein calls "form of life".[1]

Now, language is part of culture. Just as language is a system of symbols as a group of people freely use to indicate, describe, and refer things concrete and abstract, so culture is the way in which we express ourselves and designate the significance of things we are interested in.

---

[1] Ludwig Wittgenstein, *Philosophical Investigations*, tr. G. E. M. Anscombe, Oxford: Basil Blackwell Ltd, 1995, §§23, 241.

Wittgenstein takes language as an instrument or tool to refer to things in the world and in daily living,[2] by speaking to express or evince things to mutually communicate. How people use language to present their ideas and communicate with each other is the way of their common life. How one should express oneself and get along with others will be implicitly or explicitly influenced and determined by the group or the community to which one belongs.

We use language this way as a tool to solve problems together. In this sense, language can never be an isolated or private activity of any individual. There could not be private language in a coherent sense. Language is a public, collective, and social part of culture human, all too human.

As language exhibits culture, so do convention, custom, tradition, religion, arts, as well as politics, commercial trading, scientific research, and all sorts of techniques with which we deal with daily problems. They are all various ways of human development to deal with diverse problems. In short, they are all parts of culture.

Culture consists in language in a wide sense. Culture is a system of symbols, called conventions, traditions, religions, and ideologies, all of which we create to make a unique way of a society, i.e., a cultural community, in which we solve life problems that occur in the environment and among members of a community.

At the same time, our culture we create directs and shapes our standpoint of viewing, thinking, and behaving, how we perceive what our community members are. Culture offers a specific way of looking at persons and things in our lifeworld as we appraise them. As Wittgenstein said, culture in this sense is indeed a form of human life. Culture is thus the very stuff of which we are made to constitute our identity.

We must now repeat this important point. Culture is constitutive of humanity as humanity shapes and changes culture. We human persons are not born fully made as human, for we are not animals that are "animal" at the moment of their birth. Instead, we *become* human by being enculturated through history, education, and socialization, in a specific culture of a specific community.

All this shows that history, education and socialization are concretely developed to interact and cope with concrete problems in an environment of specific time and specific place. Thus culture is specific, local, earthed, autochthonous, rooted in concrete soil and its concrete sight and smell. Our environment of living has concrete flavor, each different from the others, and so our culture is thickly concrete, specific, and pluralistic.

Since each environment differs from all the others, it follows that "culture" is incurably local, and so pluralistic, as localities are by definition many. Every culture is unique and peculiar in a specific locale both geographical and historical. So, we have three factual features about "culture." One, culture is essentially human; humanity and culture inter-shape and inter-constitute. Two, culture is specific, peculiar, and local. Three, culture is by nature earthed and many, and there exists no such monster as "general culture." Culture by nature resists generality beyond its concrete locality.

Culture is thus quite seriously human. Whatever touches the local peculiarity of a culture seriously touches humanity. The shock would grievously arouse and induce grave repercussion to shake the foundation of our very humanity. Now, it so happened that globalization, by definition "general," shakes up these "pluralistic, local, and earthy cultures," with its "generality," to shake up our very humanity to the core.

---

[2] Ibid;, §§11, 14-15, 23, 41-42, 53.

Another sense of globalization is that globalization globalizes close contacts among these many local and peculiar cultures. What would happen when these cultures are confronted raw with such globalization, to be challenged by other cultures now close at hand? Could we then obtain the so-called "universal understanding of mankind," or would we lose our cultural identity to lose humanity in global contacts with other cultures?

In both senses of "globalization," general and cultural contact, the shaking of the cultural foundation by globalization is certain, to produce at least two threats to the survival of local cultures, their obliteration and their isolation. Meanwhile, we must be alerted to this important distinction.

Globalization as raw direct contacts among cultures is one thing; it is quite uncertain and full of risks. Globalization as cultural contacts in mutual honest dialogues is quite another, arousing inter-exposure of assumptions to inter-enrich. The latter sort of dialogical contacts among cultures as genuine globalization will be advocated below. But as of now, we must consider these two threats, by way of concretely illustrating them with Kant and Hegel. And then in the next section after the next, we will criticize both to realize the solution to both threats of globalization.

II. TWO THREATS OF GLOBALIZATION SEEN IN KANT AND HEGEL

We saw the two threats posed by globalization to cultures. One, globalization as the general exists nowhere, but is concocted by a particular culture arrogating itself as "general" to decimate other cultures. Two, we can only see specific local cultures, and as globalization brings them into close mutual contact, they show themselves as isolated one from the other. Two examples, Kant and Hegel, bring out these dangers concretely to our view. To begin, let us briefly survey proposals by Kant and Hegel. We first consider Kant, and then Hegel.

Kant

We often ask questions on globalization such as these. What is globalization? And in what sense it is global and general? Is globalization political, economic,[3] moral, or cultural? For *Kant* everything above is inclusively correct. Globalization would occur not only in global commerce and international politics, but also in universal morality and international laws. It is in these senses that globalization is global and general.

Kant had already predicted all this beyond two hundred years ago. In his *The Idea of a Universal Cosmo-Political History* as well as *Eternal Peace: A Philosophical Draft* Kant envisaged and described a historical process which would inevitably evolve into an institutional world universal and cosmopolitan.[4]

---

[3] In fact, Merriam-Webster's Collegiate Dictionary, Eleventh Edition, 2008, p. 532 defines "globalization" in exclusively economic terms.

[4] Kant, Idee zu einer allgemeinen Geschichte in weltbürgerlicher Absicht, See also: Zum ewigen Frieden. Ein philosophischer Entwurf. Werke in sechs Bände, Band VI, Schriften zur Anthropologie, Geschichte, Politik und Pädagogik. Darmstadt: Wissenschaftliche Buchgesellschaft, 1983. (English translation: The Idea of a Universal Cosmo-Political History, translated by W. Hastie, In: Eternal Peace and Other Essays. Boston, 1914.)

In contrast to nihilistic view of history, Kant affirms that there would inevitably be an ultimate purpose in human history whose development must follow the dictate of universal rational principle. Despite many accidents, follies, and disasters in history, its overall trend should always be in a rational, moral, and lawful direction in the long run. This general trend includes all sorts of human transactions, be they sociopolitical or economic, and however purely for egoistic purposes they are conducted.

For example, although worldwide trading transactions may seem to be purely practical undertakings back and forth, they are actually one means of Nature to bring about peaceful concord among all peoples and nations, Kant insists. People simply have to get along well with one another, in order to keep the trade run smoothly uninterrupted. In order that this undisrupted situation is to be constantly kept up, different countries would have to frame, sign, and enforce legal international treaties with one another, whose spirit conforms to Kant's moral principles.

According to this picture portrayed by Kant, "globalization" would offer a flourishing, orderly, and lawfully organized state of affairs throughout the world. If Kant is correct, then globalization should be a desirable world picture. It would be our vision we are to be at work to realize.

Such globalization is not only to be welcomed, but would *inevitably* become real, because globalization is determined by divine Providence as it is justified by human reason. Thus globalization seems to be an inexorable and unstoppable trend, and the nearly necessary destination of human history.

We cannot help but ask questions, however. Is the globalization depicted by Kant really globalization we want? Is Kant's globalization already actual or it is still our dream ahead? More critically, even if such a rosy picture of globalization is rationally inevitable, doesn't this very inevitability ruin its rosy beauty, for how could desirability and inevitability mix? And hasn't these awkward questions arisen out of a single culprit, an ironclad "rationality"? Isn't this "universal reason" Germanic generalized global? Isn't *this* globalization of one cultural ideal responsible for all above doubts?

Hegel

For *Hegel*, globalization is a stage manifesting the process of history. "World history belongs to the realm of the spirit. [...] the spirit and the course of its development are the true substance of history,"[5] and history is the development of freedom. Far from being fixed, freedom is the substance of the Spirit, Hegel says.[6] Freedom means self-sufficiency and independence. Freedom is the ideal and the ultimate goal of the Spirit.

To seek and realize freedom is therefore the necessary development of human history. Globalization is a necessary universal process which could never be limited to a single nation or local society. On the contrary, these nations and communities can only be understood as a signal expressing such freedom of the Spirit moving on. The thrust toward more freedom in

---

[5] Hegel, Lectures on the Philosophy of World History. Introduction: Reason in History, translated by H. B. Nisbet, with an Introduction by Duncan Forbes, Cambridge University Press, 1975, p. 44.
[6] Ibid., pp. 47-48, 55.

every sphere of life is the real rationale for the existence of globalization; freedom justifies globalization.

Moreover, the *means* used by the Spirit to realize its Idea is interactions of human desires with their environment. Originally shapeless and undeveloped, the means the Spirit adopts is external and phenomenal, explicitly presented to our senses. Hegel claims that actions springing from human needs, passions, characters and talents are the dynamo that pushes historical progress into the future, not virtues such as generosity and benevolence, because interests and profits are more efficient agents than moral virtues artificially produced by disciplines.

Hegel regards passions, private natural impulses to satisfy selfish desires, as real factors that direct and determine human actions to form historical progress.[7] Natural impulses, not artificial and tedious discipline, directly influence human behaviors and decisions. And this vast congeries of volitions, interests, and activities constitutes the means and instruments of the Spirit to achieve its goal.[8] In this way the Spirit could make use of human beings who unconsciously and consciously serve as its tools to fulfill its end, namely, the freedom. Now, how is freedom to be achieved in this historical process of the Spirit?

In order to get real freedom, the world history would dialectically develop toward the direction which reveals more and more appropriate manifestation and actualization of the Spirit. Self-actualization of the Spirit would adopt a form that is continuous and surpasses itself in each stage. It is getting richer to incessantly exceed the former stages of itself. In the end the Spirit would reach the destination of finding itself, coming to itself and contemplating itself in concrete actuality. Hegel posits the terminal of world history as a nation or state whose spirit would permeate religion, politics, morality, legislation, even science, art and technology, and all such human achievements.

Hegel's prediction of the inevitable historical process seems to say this. As freedom, globalization seems to be justified as the ultimate stage of human history. Moreover, the abstract idea of freedom would be concretely realized in the physical and cultural globalization. While all human beings had been attempting to extend their living room as great as possible since ancient days, modern technology has now accomplished it.

Globalization is human harvest out of long history trying to solve problems of living with the purpose of achieving autonomous freedom. Today, at last, globalization prompted by techniques, gadgetry, and commerce arisen out of cultures finally succeeds at pushing forward "globalization" humanity had long dreamed for countless centuries.

In the meantime, in Hegel, "human passions, desires, etc." ciphers "human freedom," and "Spirit using desires as means" ciphers "Spirit squeezing freedom into the Spirit's scheme of inevitable progress." Thus, individual freedom is locked in its own sufficiency self-independent, and classified, stuffed willy-nilly, as an indifferent part of "thesis" or "antithesis" or "synthesis" in the inexorable progress of the Spirit. Individuals are isolated as cogs classified in total indifference of the process of Reason-as-Spirit, ironclad, automatic. *Isolation* takes place in Hegel.

---

[7] Ibid. p. 74.
[8] Ibid.

Survey

Now, the above brief detour shows us how culture-bound both Kant and Hegel are. *Kant* universalizes—to universalize is his favorite move—his one-dimensional view of "reason" onto the pluralistic variety of world situation. Kant's "Reason (with capital R)" is a simple straight extension of the august Aristotle's categories and deductive argumentation, quite staid high up in the logical firmament of Western thinking. Kant takes such Aristotelian "Reason" as sacrosanct, apodictically applicable to all matters whatever.

Do we remember Kant's favorite phrase, "rational being"? Here, "rational" is of course Aristotelian, thoroughly Western. Kant's universality of Western Reason amounts to Western imposition of the West onto all cultures *überhaupt* without exception at all. Obliteration of local peculiar cultures inevitably results with such "universal Reason" Eurocentric, monocultural.

Hegel, on his part, sees his proud Reason—he calls it Spirit, he is so proud of it—as moving, albeit in a fixed frame of prearranged thesis, antithesis, and on to their synthesis. This universal process of Reason-Spirit aims at accomplishing "freedom" of universal sort, indifferently all-inclusive.

He is vague on what he means by "freedom." On one hand, freedom means "self-sufficiency and independence," while on the other hand, such freedom is the universal aim of world Spirit. Now, how could self-sufficiency and independence that indicates individuality—it is my freedom, your freedom, and yours, and so on, each in its peculiarity and no one else's—become universalized in all the world for all time?

Individual freedom stays individual. How could inherently individual freedom be inexorably caught up in the inexorably process of Spirit-Reason? The only outcome in universalization of individual freedom is to expose its own individuality as separate from someone else's individuality. Universalization of individual freedoms isolates individuals, and, by extension, isolates one local culture from another. In Hegel, globalization amounts to isolation of local cultures one from another. If Kant obliterates, Hegel isolates. It is sad, indeed.

III. CRITICIZING KANT AND HEGEL TO REVEAL SOLUTIONS TO TWO GLOBAL THREATS

Cultural myopia, typical of a local culture of proud Germany, can thus be seen in Kant and in Hegel, and our realization of their cultural myopia is assured by comparing them with another entirely different culture such as China. And, to think of it, isn't such cultural comparison a modus operandi of globalization? Our critique of German Kant and Hegel is performed by strength of global interculture.

Kant takes over Aristotle's categories and one-directional syllogism, all carved in the set logical firmament of the West. Hegel wiggles himself out of the Procrustean logic by his moving dialectic, to put a thesis ("thesis" just means "to put"), and then oppose it in antithesis (i.e., to put it opposed), and then infuse both into synthesis (i.e., to put them together). Isn't all this a glorified common sense? Who does not do so in common dealing? Whether thesis and antithesis are still "alive" in their new synthesis remains to be seen, but at least his "logic" does thus move.

Sadly, however, the "freedoms" of these "theses" and "antitheses" stay individual, and stay theirs, for otherwise there is nothing to show as "they," their "identity," which is their freedom of independent self-sufficiency. Their synthesis thus merely exposes their mutual isolation. Thus Kant represents one danger of globalization, obliteration, while Hegel posits another danger of globalization, isolation, locking individual in individual, broaching Western individualism.

Now, looking over their shoulders, we realize that they have not thought of how one-directional their thinking pattern—logic—is, and Hegel's use of contradiction as logical movement is a crude first step peeping at its beyond. Nicholas of Cusa has the affirmative and the negative mutually biting into each other, as in *docta ignorantia* and *coincidentia oppositorum*, but such a radical logical move out of traditional Western logic, prominently represented by *Kant*, is not clearly and urgently noticed, until we—"we" all in the West and in China—see China.

China's Yin and Yang, the mutual opposites, are internecine inter-nascent, killing in birthing, birthing in killing, woe and weal inter-hiding inter-lurking. Thus the *Mo Pien* logic has it that thinking can go forward *and* backward, such that if P implies Q, then Q can imply P also.[9]

"How could it be?" the West asks. "Simple," China answers, saying, "Look how weal leans on woe as woe lurks in weal, how losing a horse can incite a series of happy and then sad and then happy incidents, and isn't such 'inciting' of opposites, mutually dependent, logical implications back and forth? Isn't it the Yin and the Yang internecine and inter-nascent?"

The West would of course insist that China confuses different implications on different occasions as the same implication back and forth in the same sense. China would reply that all this is an arbitrary setup irrelevant to actuality, for after all, weal is weal happy as ever, as woe is woe drenched in pain, and pain is pain. Besides, the "same" does not actually exist, for things actual are "flowers" here today and are no more tomorrow. The logic of the "same" does not work in actuality, so logic is not actual but illusory. Even deconstructionism melted logocentrism away, to vanish itself.

The West responds that thinking must start at sameness of "A is A" all the way. China says, yes, but logic—the way we think—cannot *stay* the "same" to judge everything in flux with "same." Logic would be a Procrustean bed. The West says we have "informal logic" and many-value logic, both based on formal logic. China says such logics are all branched out of "same"-logic based on rigid "sameness." The West says "judging on the base of" differs from "bound by."

This exciting debate would continue like this. The debate itself benefits all parties concerned. It is meta-logical in logical sense, thanks to China nudging us all to sense the complex inter-involvements of many opposites, different, various, and actual, in elusive actuality in flux, even when we are considering formal patterns of thinking called "logic."

In any case, such meta-logical prospect opens up an alternative thinking to Western monologue in logic, to open out to China's "logic" as an alternative to the West's one-directional thinking. We must include such alternative thinking to be enriched in our logic,

---

[9] This is 旁行句讀 in the 墨辯, in 墨子, 臺北市三民書局, 民85, pp. 304, 575ff.

and "seeing alternatives" as we look beyond *our* culture is globalization at work, called "interculture." Interculture is both the modus vivendi and the modus operandi of globalization intercultural, back and forth.

Another example is China's constant use of paradoxes often frowned upon in the West. China thrives in paradoxes in ironies and far-out analogies to hint and point at actuality so concrete as to be inexpressible, as constantly engaged in by Taoists, Name Logicians, debaters in the brutal ages of warring states, Sun Tzu the military expert, and usual historians through the ages.

Name Logicians just want to con-form names (our notions) to fact (solid actuality), and e.g., Kung-sun Lung quipped, "White horse, no horse," and appended no less than eight explanations of it, all solidly concrete.[10] After all, if actuality is alive, our notions and thinking should flex with the flexuous moves of actuality, and this "flexing with" is logic truly so called.

As a result, all such China's logical moves go far beyond Socratic ironies and abduction of Aristotle and Peirce, for they are too stiff to flex with flexing actuality, and beyond their casual dismissal of analogy and metaphor as poor subordinate substitute of logic proper so timidly self-confining and strictly defined.

Such free-flowing "logic" of China has produced amazing individuals sprawling all over in so many fields, often so successful in them all. Mo Tzu had military expertise (he had the well-disciplined strongest army around) and opposed war (he was a staunch pacifist), had fine logic that freely goes forward and back, and the principle of loving-all for prudent living, and wrote essays on all these fields, all exquisitely accomplished.

Later, Wang Yang-ming gloriously succeeded in administration (he served as governor of several districts) and all military campaigns, while he wrote many poems as he attained meditative enlightenment and founded a new and quite popular school of Neo-Confucianism, all at once. No people in the West, not even Leonardo da Vinci or Blaise Pascal, had succeeded in such various incompatible fields.

The point of all these citations from China, seemingly so odd to the West but are actually a standard and time-honored practice of thinking in China, is to show that the world has more ways of thinking—logics[11]—under Heaven than the West has even dreamed of, and so intercultural encounters are an absolute requirement to enrich any one culture's logical resources. "What about China, doesn't it have to learn from the West also?" Yes, indeed. I cited only an example of the West learning from China because the West more than China arrogates itself to being universal beyond specific cultures.

"Doesn't Western science and technology work universally?" Yes, but so does Chinese gadgetry. "Doesn't Western medicine heal?" Yes, but so does Chinese medicine with entirely different assumptions, methods of healing, and gestalts. All this shows that "universality" is culture-sensitive, as lofty ideals are culture-infused. All matters thinking and acting are cultural, thoroughly cultural.

This cultural fact at the bottom of efficiency and at the top of ideals does not indicate facile "cultural relativism," a term of Western opprobrium, but the necessity of intercultural

---

[10] "白馬非馬" 公孫龍子, 臺北市三民書局, 2004, pp. 27-41. Cf. 黃克劍, 名家琦辭疏解, 中華書局, 2010.
[11] Gilbert Ryle has "informal logic" alongside with "formal logic" in Dilemmas, Cambridge University Press, 1954. Friedrich Waismann has "alternative logics" in How I See Philosophy, London: Macmillan, 1968. But they are mere skirmishes at the fringe of notice by mainline philosophers in the West.

complementation, the more numerous and various, the richer and better. On the whole, the West describes and explains thoroughly, while China presents and indicates tacitly.

In this situation, the West simply must not despise China as insufficient, while China must not complain that the West is unnecessarily over-picky. Both cultures must come together to inter-complement and inter-enrich, even at the basic level of "logic," the patterns of thinking.

"Would globalization cause the loss of personal individuality and the disappearance of some cultures?" Well, if globalization means not generalization but bringing as many local cultures into contact as time goes on, then globalization facilitates mutual encounters of different cultures that do nothing but good to each and every culture throughout the globe.

Looking at China's supple thinking in actuality, the West can no longer brag about being the first to invent strict logic, which is now shown up to be rigidly confined to a single-track mind in one-direction logicizing, and so may want to learn from China with curiosity, even at this basic logical level. Thus, it is so far so good for intercultural insight gained by critically considering Kant's Reason.

Let us now critically consider *Hegel* and the problem of freedom. Our Hegel-critique may yield answer to the problem of globalization as risking isolation of cultures. Hegel's definition of freedom as self-sufficiency and independence is fine except that he forgets to further specify what self-sufficiency means and what independence means here in the overall global context.

Self-sufficiency of freedom is not self-confinement, which would be contrary to free explosion of freedom. By the same token, independence of freedom is an active one, interacting with other freedoms in mutual independence. Freedom as independence is free interdependence in inter-independence.

Missing these crucial features, freedom would amount to isolation cut off from others under an indifferent inexorability of march of Reason-Spirit, for such total indifference of totalism is contrary to the nature of freedom that explodes outward, as freedom is free from confinement and free toward what is beyond status quo.

Freedom is élan vital that soars up to the beyond-self, free from oneself to be free toward the self beyond the self. Such self-transcendent freedom is the élan of growth beyond the status quo of one's environment, to positively demand contact with the beyond-self. Novelty and growth attend freedom to explode beyond. This élan vital should never be isolated, for isolation is antonymous to transcendence.

Hegel missed all this vitality of freedom. In fact, both Kant and Hegel are scared of freedom as destructive, and so constructed magnificent systems to safely trap freedom from getting out of hand in its voluptuous explosion. Self-explosion would be equivalent to self-destruction.

"But freedom is not lawless license, right?" Ah, such scared timidity kills freedom that reaches beyond itself toward the not-self. Mutual contacts freely developing will cure the "lawlessness" those decent rationalists fear. The élan toward the not-self is the "law of freedom" Kant yearned after. It is a free bouncing back and forth between self and not-self that thrives all free selves, equally.

Now, have you noticed it? Isn't "bouncing back and forth between self and not-self" precisely what globalization is? In globalization, freedom freely grows, in avid mutuality among free selves. Let me repeat. Freedom is free from self toward beyond-self. Wang Yang-ming studied Zen and Taoism, rejected both, infused by both, and claimed the resultant version to be "Confucian," nothing else.

In all these logically atrocious acts, Wang was absolutely sincere and authentic as Kierkegaard said, "Purity of heart is to will one thing," and, mind you, Wang goes beyond Kierkegaard's "truth is subjectivity" and Berkeley's "to be as to be perceived" into unifying Heaven and Earth into "one body."

"Would the encountering of cultures inevitably lead to the competition or even to the conflict among cultures? Would it produce more misunderstanding between different people than ever?" Criticizing Hegel gives us an answer. Freedom as self-sufficiency is strengthened by interacting of respective independence, rejecting one another to be infused by one another. Wang Yang-ming precisely did so as he was enriched by Zen Buddhism and Taoism by rejecting both, and then claimed his enriched version to be "Confucian" his favorite.

Thus rejection is absorption, and independence is interdependence, and *such* inter-absorption is inter-enrichment. All this obtains thanks to freedom as the élan of self-transcendence. This is, strangely, to adapt and enrich Hegel's moving logic as a threefold dialectic of outward enrichment, by way of globalization as intercultural contacts, in freedom self-sufficient in interacting with others' independence. Now, isn't "adapting Hegel's moving logic" one way of globalization as interculture?

So, we conclude this essay this way. Globalization arises out of cultures, as it paradoxically changes cultures from which it comes. Such an inter-transformation between local cultures and worldwide globalization amounts to globalization as dynamic interculture, which resolves two dangers of globalization as empty generality.

In short, the two dangers of globalization not thought through can only be resolved in and through globalization thought through. In globalization as interculture, individual freedom freely grows beyond itself by contacting not-selves, to inter-criticize as they inter-enrich (as Wang did). Globalization is not static generality but interactive contacts among different local cultures throughout the world.

Now, do we still hear such worries as these? "Would globalization result in the monopolization of a dominant culture, so much so that it subdues all the rest, as it is said that the ongoing globalization should actually be Americanization? Would globalization make a unified and standardized world, so that everywhere now becomes the same monocultural scenes?"

We are now ready to answer these worries to soothe them. In globalization as contacting many alternative sorts of reasoning beyond the West's Reason, Western reason is enriched beyond itself. After all, no existence is without its inner reason of itself, such as "A is A, and it is not not-A." Existence has its own contrary reasoning in itself for its own existence.

This is an existential reasoning never to be mocked, for just to exist is sacred. As John Locke said somewhere, "A is A, and is not not-A" is an ontological reasoning for the impenetrability of a thing. Thus nothing is more sacrilegious than to mock at a thing's reasoning for its existence. "To make light of reasoning" makes light of the very existence, making light of the one who makes light of reasoning.

Since reasoning is thus at the base of things, enriching reasoning enriches actuality. Thus globalization as dialogical interculture—reasoning back and forth between opponents—is the solution to its own two threats to the existence of many local cultures. These existential threats arise out of defining globalization as bland generality empty of concrete existence.

IV. MODERNITY, POSTMODERNITY, THREE ISSUES

With the insights on globalization as interculture and its solution so far to its own double dangers, obliteration and isolation, we now look close at our lifeworld today. It is called the modern world going postmodern. The two buzzwords "modern" and "postmodern" are period-descriptions to indicate strata of trends. *Modernity* connotes pride in our modern life of the masses as "decent," properly "civilized, and not barbaric or outdated." Thus this mindset tends toward standardization and uniformity. Here the individuality of persons and local cultures is engulfed and *obliterated*.

In protest, *postmodernity* smashes everything that is settled and orderly, for settled order chokes to kill our vitality of living. By doing so, however, *this* mindset goes to the opposite extreme. Postmodernity tends toward randomness and fragmentation. Everything is now in bits and pieces, all chaotically *isolated* one from the others. Both threats we thought we have successfully met ironically came back from back door of time.

Looking at this modernity pushing and pulling with postmodernity, we sigh, and are deeply impressed. They say, "History rhymes." History does reenacts its pattern of swinging from "totalistic obliteration in monoculture," and then "piecemeal isolation of localities in multi-cultures" right here and now. We must repeat our discovery above, that the resolution of globalization-waves of obliteration and isolation remains globalization itself properly thought through.

We take this "globalization" not as blank contentless generality but as close encounters among distinct cultures local and individual. Far from wiping them out, globalization as interculture depends on localities to obtain, to enliven localities. Far from exhibiting their isolation one from the other, globalization as close cultural contacts strengthens mutual enrichment through critical inter-rejection in absorption among their free interchange of dialogues of opponents.

Out of today's push and pull between modernity and postmodernity, we see three additional issues emerging for our attentive consideration. *One*, during global contacts of local cultures as incompatible gestalts and horizons, and modes of viewing and thinking, "misunderstanding" is bound to happen. What can we do about it?

Two, technology powerful and ubiquitous has universally unleashed cultural "lowest common denominators" of global vulgarized uniformity. *Three*, globalization and locality constitute a dynamics of mutuality. Everything now seems topsy-turvy, and nothing is assured in sheer chaos.

We now consider these three issues not (fully) discussed in previous sections, to tie up loose ends that remain, to concretize our argument above to ground globalization in actuality today. We do so by applying the above stated "solution by globalization," globalization as interculture of radical differences.

One, misunderstanding: Globalization is interculture, encounters among radically different cultures that represent radically different ways of viewing and thinking things. Encounters with radical differences inevitably produce a blockage of understanding and result in misunderstanding, both often quite serious. Conflicts and wars often erupt out of mutual misunderstanding. Can globalization offer a solution?

Two points out of globalization as interculture can be made. *First*, blockage of understanding can be unplugged by stretching our courageous hand of goodwill and open-mindedness to the other party in other culture, however obnoxiously different they are. After all, we are all human, and cannot but respond to goodwill with goodwill.

And then, misunderstanding can be minimized, step by step, by a gathering of many parties in many cultures to offer our most conscientious interpretations on an "identical matter" we agree to be identical. And sooner than later, a rough consensus will result. For example, however different and diverse our interpretations of "Hitler" are, he can never be another "Mother Teresa."

Secondly, the very notion of "misunderstanding" assumes that an absolutely correct "understanding" exists. There is never such a Platonic "truth" in our actual world, and if by any chance there were such, our world would be quite a dull place. The point is that, far from avoiding it, we must approach the so-called "misunderstanding" with excited joy of anticipation, for it opens the way to novel creativity. Creativity connotes difference, and "misunderstanding" provides differences. The aesthetics of creativity begins and even ends here, at "misunderstanding."

Now, have we noticed it, again? Both points just raised, a gathering consensus and creative differences, obtain only in a gathering of radically diverse cultures, and the more diversely we gather, the more creatively different we turn, and "the more, the more" is the process of globalization.

In other words, globalization as interculture is the answer to the "problem of misunderstanding" to turn "problem" into "opportunity." Globalization opens up delightful camaraderie of free and challenging association, enhancing the peculiar freedoms freed *out* of isolation of every sort.

Two, vulgarization of the masses: Powerful and scary because they seep into us so naturally unawares, technology, TV, and advertising turn us into the masses quite vulgar, unthinking and uniform. We are lulled into an unthinking mass of automatons. This situation is opium-like and quite scary, but it is not theoretically surprising. This is one exhibition today of "obliteration" of our distinctive identity of personal and cultural existence, killing us with vulgarized uniformity worldwide, into which "technology in TV and advertising is engulfing us all," they say.

Now we must gaze intently at this "technology" that is supposedly a monster, and then we would realize. Technology, however powerful, is a powerful *means* quite value-neutral. We can and must use it to our advantage, never to kill us. We can cite three concrete examples of such creative use of technology.

Our *first* example is this. the same TV advertisement that is flattening us has been used to combat and successfully demolish the all-powerful tobacco industry, so much successful that it is now our common global knowledge that smoking is lethal, to be evicted totally from our life.

Our *second* example is this. The powerful Nixon presidency was toppled by two powerless journalists, Woodward and Bernstein, by using information-dissemination of technology. Our *third* example is this. Technology frees us from tedious repetitive labors, to free us from vain time-consuming slavery to daily chores of laundry, dish-washing, and walking to distant places, so we can be free to nurture our self in diverse ways as we freely wish with our free time thus gained.

Do we not know how to nurture ourselves? Technology serves to disseminate information to enable us to choose, to enhance our quality of life. Technology can be "exploited" to obtain education programs that fit us to nourish and develop ourselves into our "true self." The possibilities of self-deepening are sky-high, thanks to our prudential utilization of technology that is at our service.

Three, inter-dynamics between globalization and cultures: Let us first rehearse what we considered when we began our essay. Language shapes thinking, viewing, and expression of human individuals. At the same time, while language is shaping us all, as we use our language, language itself is shaped and changed by our very use of it.

Language is part of culture. Culture also shapes our ways of thinking, viewing, and expressing, and as we follow culture to express ourselves, we imperceptibly shape and change culture. All this while, globalization shapes and changes various cultures, as cultures in interactions are shaping and changing globalization that is interculture.

Now, aren't such inter-dynamics of human cultures and globalization bewildering? It is part of our self-recursive homeostasis, the essence of human living. This is where the master serves and the servant rules, while the master remains master to rule and servant remains servant to serve.

In our cultural context, confrontation with another culture is a threat and an opportunity. It is a threat to the very existence of our own culture, and yet it is also an opportunity to enrich ourselves with unforeseen difference. It behooves us to turn the threat of chaos into an opportunity of growth—by dialoguing among cultures various, opposing, and different, the more and the more various, the better.

Dialogue is a revolution of assumptions on each dialogue partner. Dialogue confronts each party with searing differences to expose its own assumptions. We do not like it at all, and we fight and we try our hardest to justify ourselves. In the meantime, as we argue, we realize our strengths and weaknesses, both at once. Such realization takes time, often in pain. But then such pain is our growing pain, as it is also growing pain to the other dialogue partner. Now, such painful intercultural dialogue is globalization as interculture. We all grow into ourselves thanks to globalization.

One last remark before we end this essay. "Globalization" is not blank generality that breeds all sorts of problems, including obliteration, isolation, and the above three issues. Globalization is instead to be defined as interactive inter-determination among local cultures. This "inter-determination" is freely determined into human historical process by globalization-as-interculture, many local cultures mutually encountering.

Globalization is thus alive as humanity is, for, after all, culture is human, and so interculture is human as well in interactive inter-transformation, all alive as human. And all this interculture describes no other than "globalization" itself. Globalization is the be-all and the end-all of humanity that in turn determines and shapes globalization. Our very humanity consists in such inter-shaping between intercultural globalization and local cultures so concrete and specific, and different and inter-opposed.

So, all in all, we find that the all-out culprit is globalization-in-general. Globalization-general is starkly staid, blandly bereft of concrete plurality in flux. Asking self-referentially, about where the culture that proposes globalization-general belongs in its generality, reveals—demolishing its own claim to be above cultures—that this "generality" is concocted by *one* specific culture, itself.

So, globalization-in-general is a self-contradictory claim, one culture claiming generality to be separate from all cultures, including the culture that proposes generality beyond-culture, which yet depends on this culture to come to exist at all. "Generality" amounts to a monocultural imposition, so self-contradictory, on all cultures, to destroy all cultures including this "monocultural culture."

This bland uniform monoculture poses a brutal either-or, "We must either embrace this (our) globalization-general alone, or else chaos of no set standard results in misunderstanding everywhere, leaving us wandering directionless as hobos." Thus monocultural globalization-general comes to threaten other specific cultures in five ways, among many others.

One, globalization-general wipes out all specific cultures, and there exists no more local peculiarity and plurality of cultures; they are now all *obliterated*. *Two*, we do not need to explore a standard universally applicable, for globalization-general *is* this standard. All of us are then reduced to standardized vulgarity. It is a lowest common denominator in monocultural *uniformity*. *Three*, globalization-general then locks these local cultures into themselves, *isolating* each from all the others.

Otherwise, globalization-general claims, the alternatives are disastrously worse, for we will be reduced to chaos of at least two sorts. *Four*, one is that *misunderstandings* will go rampant, now that we lack uniform universal standard that gives us a straight criterion of correspondence of what we view-and-express with what is really the case, *this* culture. *Five*, another case of chaos is that, lacking in uniform correspondence under uniform globalization-general, we lack definite purpose, lack a reliable direction to follow, vainly *wandering* around as hobos in a land of no ideals.

In opposition to such monocultural imposition and threats of globalization-general, we envision globalization as *interculture* in and for many peculiar local cultures. Globalization as interculture rejects the brutal either-or of "either one culture as general, or else chaos of misunderstanding and directionless wanderings."

On the contrary, globalization intercultural promotes and enriches local cultures as these specific cultures adjust such interculture to fit their own actual situations, ongoing so fluid and always changing. Globalization intercultural builds up local peculiarities as it depends on peculiar situations of many local cultures to continue to invigorate them. As a result, all five woes bred by globalization-general vanish in thin air. They vanish this way.

The modus operandi of intercultural globalization is intercultural *dialogues* back and forth among local cultures. Such cultural dialogues will inter-help to hammer out an ad hoc maxim of operation as a workable *direction* to proceed for now, and then revise it in the new future. Intercultural dialogues generate one direction after another, always according to the actual situations of local cultures. Whenever any one culture is lost on the way, it can always rely on such town-hall-meeting-styled dialogues to find its next steps in its way back.

Any *misunderstanding* of one another can be eliminated, by and by, with group consensus emerging out of continuous dialogues. Any more misunderstanding will be generated in the context of group dialogues to strike out new, to create a new order revisable in the future dialogue. *Uniform vulgarity* vanishes here. At the same time, such intercultural dialogues will result in inter-determination of the general and the local to inter-guide and inter-build. In this "inter-" dynamics, *obliteration* and *isolation* of whatever cultural sort vanish.

It is in some such ways that all sorts of threats posed by set and staid globalization-in-general are tamed and cured, by globalization-intercultural, the globalization dynamics within and among local cultures, to inter-vitalize and inter-enrich the peculiarities of specific local cultures, which in turn adjust globalization intercultural to suit their needs and aspirations.

True globalization now dawns on our globe. Everyone is a winner full of smiles. Our choice is clear, as our globalization intercultural is beckoning ahead. We must go to it.

In: Globalization Dynamics
Editor: Kuang-ming Wu

ISBN: 978-1-62100-750-0
© 2012 Nova Science Publishers, Inc.

Chapter 8

BEGINNINGS: THE GLOBAL CROSSINGS OF CLASSICAL DAOISM

Jay Goulding[*]
York University, Toronto, Canada

ABSTRACT

Classical Chinese Daoism finds two prominently overlapping traditions: Huang-Lao as a combination of the mythical Huangdi and Laozi on one hand, and Lao-Zhuang as a combination of Laozi and Zhuangzi on the other. The excluded middle is Liezi who both is and is not part of these two traditions. Hence he appears as a pivot for the beginnings and beginnings again of Daoist philosophy somewhere between 'stillness' and 'parable.' We can understand the global intertwinings of these thinkers in terms of Western phenomenology.

Merleau-Ponty's 'hollow' where time is made is similar to Zhuangzi's 'hollow' (窾) which swirls with nothingness and being. Heidegger's *Lichtung* where being and nothing are 'cleared' is similar to Laozi's *ming* (明) where meditation leaves us in between being and nothingness.

In between Zhuangzi and Laozi, we have a relatively unexplored empty centre of Daoism as exemplified by Liezi; in between Merleau-Ponty and Heidegger there is a relatively unexplored empty centre of phenomenology which is itself connected to its Daoist counterpart.

---

[*] Professor in the Dept. of Social Science, York University, Toronto, Canada, where he is Programme Coordinator for Social and Political Thought. His expertise is in classical and modern Chinese philosophy, Japanese philosophy, hermeneutics, and phenomenology. Dr. Goulding's email is: jay.@yorku.ca

ABBREVIATIONS

BC	Wu, Kuang-ming, *The Butterfly as Companion: Meditation on the First Three Chapters of the Chuang Tzu* Albany: SUNY, 1990.
CW CT	Watson, Burton trans., *The Complete Works of Chuang Tzu* New York: Columbia University, 1968.
DEEP	Heidegger, Martin, "Das Ende der Philosophie und die Aufgabe des Denkens," pp. 61-80 in *Zur Sache des Denkens* Tübingen: Max Niemeyer, 1969.
EEPR	Fischer-Schreiber, Ingrid, Franz-Karl Ehrhard, Kurt Friedrichs and Michael S. Diener, *The Encyclopedia of Eastern Philosophy and Religion: Buddhism, Taoism, Zen, Hinduism* Boston: Shambhala Press, 1989.
EN	Merleau-Ponty, Maurice, "Everywhere and Nowhere," pp. 126-158 in *Signs* Evanston: Northwestern University, 1964.
EP	Heidegger, Martin, "The End of Philosophy and the Task of Thinking," pp. 369-392 in *Basic Writings* ed. David Farrell Krell. New York: Harper & Row, 1977.
HHS	May, Reinhard, *Heidegger's hidden sources: East Asian influences on his work* trans. Graham Parkes. London: Routledge, 1996.
HOT	Paul Shih-yi, "Heidegger and Our Translation of the Tao Te Ching," pp. 93-104 in Graham Parkes ed., *Heidegger and Asian Thought* Honolulu: University of Hawaii Press, 1987
LT	Wong, Eva, *Lieh-Tzu: A Taoist Guide to Practical Living* Boston: Shambhala, 1995.
LTTTC	Feng, Gia-Fu and Jane English, trans. *Lao Tsu: Tao Te Ching* New York: Random House, 1972.
VI	Merleau-Ponty, Maurice, *The Visible and the Invisible* Evanston: Northwestern University, 1968.

Eva Wong, a translator and commentator agrees with Stevenson that in the West, people usually start with Laozi when tackling Daoism. They then proceed to Zhuangzi and maybe, those with a passionate interest finally move to Liezi (列子). Her experience, however, like some growing up in Asia is the opposite. Ironically, long before hearing of Daoism, she started with Liezi's fables and fairy tales that were imbedded in children's books. This was followed by Zhuangzi and Laozi. For her, "Laozi talks at us, Zhuangzi talks to himself and Liezi speaks to us."[1] Laozi hits us with profundity, Zhuangzi dazzles us and rattles our conceptual chains while Liezi "gently shakes us awake" from an eternally deep slumber (see *LT*, 18). For thousands of years, it has been unclear who these three thinkers are. Are they three separate people? There is some evidence for that. Are they one and the same? Perhaps they are two in one - Lao-Zhuang - as Chinese scholars used to say. What about the mythical Yellow Emperor, Huangdi (黄帝)? Is he person or legend or fiction? Is he really Laozi? Hence the Chinese refer to the origins of Daoism as Huang-Lao. Between Huang-Lao and Lao-Zhuang lie the beginnings and beginnings again of classical Daoism. But what about Liezi? Where does he fit in? He seems to be the invisible partner, the emptiness at the centre of the chaotic wheel in this phenomenal crossing of the Daoist body. This paper fleshes him out and breathes some time into his being along side the Daoist *corpus*.

Merleau-Ponty's global phenomenology of the body helps us. He writes an essay entitled "Everywhere and Nowhere," in which he argues:

Indian and Chinese philosophies have tried not so much to dominate existence as to be the echo or sounding board of our relationship to being. Western philosophy can learn from them to rediscover the relationship to being and initial option which gave it birth, and to estimate the possibilities we have shut ourselves off from in becoming 'Westerners' and perhaps reopen them.[2]

In the dialogue between East and West, Merleau-Ponty emphasizes the "lateral relationships" of civilization to civilization "...in the echoes one awakes in the other" (*EN*, 139), that is in their mutual intertwining. In concurrence with his views, Daoism takes shape amongst the shadows and the echoes. Ironically, Liezi is both a creator of shadows and echoes while *himself* being shadow and echo. He both is and is not. Liezi explains that: "The action of one thing produces effects on another. In a universe in which all things are interconnected, this is just natural. Thus, a shape and its shadow, a sound and its echo are always together. When there is action, there is effect. When there is effect, there is a response in action" (*LT*, 33). He quotes Huangdi's fabled book: "'When a shape moves, it produces a shadow, not another shape. When a sound resonates, it produces an echo, not another sound. Stillness does not generate stillness but movement'" (*LT*, 33). The relationships between Huangdi, Laozi, Zhuangzi and Liezi can be understood in terms of Merleau-Ponty's idea of a chiasm between flesh and idea[3] which emerges from "...a furrow that traces itself out magically under our eyes without a tracer, a certain hollow, a certain interior, a certain absence, a negativity that is not nothing..." (*VI*, 151). Hence, the flesh which is "midway between the spatio-temporal individual and the idea" is a kind of "incarnate principle that brings a style of being wherever there is a fragment of being" (*VI*, 139). The Daoist texts represent a 'style of being' and a style of non-being somewhere between 'philosophy and non-philosophy' as Merleau-Ponty put it (*EN*, 139) in their never-ending interweaving and crossing. To the universal through the particular is a strategy for understanding these fractals as they erase and negate linear, logical thinking. Like the shape that has its shadow or the sound that spawns its echo, Huangdi has Laozi, Laozi has Zhuangzi, Zhuangzi has Liezi and all belong to the *Dao*. They are everywhere and nowhere appearing and disappearing into the background noise where "fierce wind relieved, then multitudes of hollows are made empty"[4] as Zhuangzi proclaims. Zhuangzi's 'hollow' as a vortex of being and nothingness is parallel to Merleau-Ponty's 'hollow,' an absence which is not nothing.

Through their mythical origins, Huangdi, Laozi, Zhuangzi and Liezi float through the dream world of beginning and end between Heaven and Earth, and between East and West. Rather than *eliminating* myth as Western rationality often does, Daoism *illuminates* it. As Merleau-Ponty explains:

> The destruction of beliefs...the split between vision and the visible, between thought and being do not as they claim, establish us in the negative... and what remains is not nothing... what remains are mutilated fragments... appearance, dream, Psyche,

---

[1] Eva Wong, Lieh-Tzu: A Taoist Guide to Practical Living (Boston: Shambhala, 1995), 18. Hence cited as a parenthetical note in the text as LT.

[2] Maurice Merleau-Ponty, "Everywhere and Nowhere," in Signs (Evanston: Northwestern University, 1964), 139. Hence cited as a parenthetical note in the text as EN.

[3] Maurice Merleau-Ponty, The Visible and the Invisible (Evanston: Northwestern University, 1968), 149. Hence cited as a parenthetical note in the text as VI.

[4] Kuang-ming Wu, The Butterfly as Companion: Meditations on the First Three Chapters of the Chuang Tzu (Albany: SUNY), 136. Hence cited as a parenthetical note in the text as BC.

representation. It is in the name and for the profit of these floating realities that the solid reality is cast into doubt. (*VI*, 106)

Huangdi was reputed to live between 2700 and 2500 BCE. He was the inventor of writing, the compass, the pottery wheel and humankind, the giver of family names, the bringer of social order, the author of *The Yellow Emperors' Classic of Internal Medicine* and the founder of religious Daoism (*daojiao* 道教) which sought immortality.[5] He is everything and nothing, everywhere and nowhere; he appears and disappears, advances and recedes in and through Daoist texts.

On the one hand, it is a popular belief that Laozi lives about the same time as Confucius in the 6th C. BCE. He is as anonymous and obscure as his teachings. Exiting the overly administered city for the quietude of the mountains, he leaves us with the way of the water, a single drop moving down the crack of a wall, going where no army can go. The *Daodejing* (道德經 *The Book of the Way, the Book of Virtue*) is attributed to him, an infinitely difficult poetic text juxtaposed to Laozi's own verdict: "my words are very easy to understand."[6] On the other hand, Zhuangzi lives somewhere between 369 and 286 BCE, connected to a body of literature called the *Zhuangzi*, 33 chapters worth; the first 7 are attributed to him, called the 'inner' chapters, accompanied by 15 'outer' and 11 'mixed' chapters supposedly composed by followers (*EEPR*, 76-77). He is the co-founder with Laozi of philosophical Daoism (*daojia* 道家) which seeks to conjoin with 'the way' through meditation, breathing and living a good long life.

We know much of the above personages because of the global popularity of Daoist stories. But what about Liezi? Wong relates:

> Lieh-tzu [Liezi] was a real person who lived in the Spring and Autumn Period of the Eastern Ch'ou dynasty (770-476 BCE). Most historians now agree that he was born… about two hundred years after Lao-tzu [Laozi] and Confucius. He was a citizen of the feudal kingdom of Cheng, and, like many people of his time who were weary of the political struggles and intrigues, he never held a government post. He was reputed to have studied under Wen-tzu [Wenzi] who was a student of Lao-tzu [Laozi] and with various shadowy and legendary characters such as Hu-tzu [Huzi] and Old Shang the Immortal. Of the rest of his life, not much is known. (*LT*, 3)

Because Liezi is not recorded in the *Historical Records*, he is often "dismissed…as an imaginary character" (*LT*, 3). He emerges in *The Spring and Autumn Annals of Lu Buwei* and gains an historical identity through this source. As a text, the *Liezi* is composed between the Han and the Jin Dynasties (200 BCE and 400 CE), spanning the Warring States Period.

It does not really matter where you begin with Daoism; all falls to the centre of the hollow. It does not really matter if Laozi is Zhuangzi or Zhuangzi is Liezi. Wherever we begin, we must begin again. A few statements on beginnings from the Daoist canon help us. In *Daodejing*, Poem One, Laozi relates:

---

[5] Ingrid Fischer-Schreiber, Franz-Karl Ehrhard, Kurt Friedrichs and Michael S. Diener, The Encyclopedia of Eastern Philosophy and Religion: Buddhism, Taoism, Zen, Hinduism (Boston: Shambhala Press), 144. Hence cited as a parenthetical note in the text as EEPR.

[6] See Man-jan Chen, Lao-Tzu: "My words are very easy to understand" (Richmond: North Atlantic Books, 1981).

The Tao [*Dao*] that can be told is not the eternal Tao [*Dao*].
The name that can be named is not the eternal name.
The nameless is the beginning of heaven and earth.
The named is the mother of ten thousand things.
Ever desireless, one can see the mystery.
Ever desiring, one can see the manifestations.
These two spring from the same source but differ in name;[7]

"The nameless is the beginning of heaven and earth" (*wu ming tian di zhi shi* 無名天地之始); "The named is the mother of ten thousand things" (*you ming wan wu zhi mu* 有名萬物之母). The Chinese word used for 'beginning' (*shi* 始) is a combination of two characters, one for woman and the other for platform or stage. Platform or stage is composed of the ancient character for self or breath and a mouth, naming the self. Hence, beginning is the woman platform for exhaling /naming of the self.[8] Naming, self, breathing and mother are important components of Daoist thought. Ancient poetic texts such as *Daodejing* constantly play on etymological and phonetic punning.

Liezi helps explain Laozi's creation/proclamation in a section entitled, "That which is not born gives birth to everything" (*LT*, 25-27). Quoting the Yellow Emperor, he announces:

'The Valley Spirit that does not die is the Mysterious Female. It is the foundation of heaven and earth. It continues forever and cannot be used up.' Because the valley is hollow, it can hold the spirit, it can embrace, and it can nourish. Because the valley is empty, it is not subject to birth and death. To transcend birth and death is to enter into the Limitless (wu-chi) and be at one with the origin of heaven and earth. (*LT*, 27)

Liezi goes on to say:

The Gate of the Mysterious Female is where all things are created.
And yet heaven and earth are said to be born from the not-born. This is what is meant by 'that which is not born gives birth to everything,' for the Mysterious Female is that which is not-born. Its origins belong to the realm of nondifferentiation, where there is neither birth nor death. Because it is never born, it never dies. Because it never dies, its energy lasts forever. It is in heaven and earth, and heaven and earth do not know it. It is in all things, yet all things do not recognize it. (*LT*, 27)

In terms of the Daoist creation cosmology, Liezi directly addresses 'the Nameless giving birth to the Named' through four platforms: the Primal Oneness, the Primal Emerging, the Primal Beginning and the Primal Substance. The Primal Oneness is the condition of undivision and undifferentiation of no subject, no object, no shape, no form; the Primal Emerging is a state where Primal Vapour (*qi* 氣) "covers heaven and earth. Yin and Yang have not divided, and everything lies within the embrace of the Vapor" (*LT*, 28); The Primal Beginning is the splitting of *yin*陰and *yang* 陽in the creation of shape and form; The Primal Substance is the emergence of qualities - hard or soft, light or heavy, moving or still (see *LT*, 28). From this Liezi asserts: "The Tao [*Dao*] is formless and cannot be seen or heard. What

---

[7] Gia-Fu Feng and Jane English trans., Lao Tsu: Tao Te Ching (New York: Random House), Poem One. Hence cited as a parenthetical note in the text as LTTTC.
[8] See Kenneth G. Henshall, A Guide to Remembering Japanese Characters (Tokyo: Charles E. Tuttle), 47; cf. G. D. Wilder and J. H. Ingram, Analysis of Chinese Characters (New York: Dover Publications), 64.

we see or hear are only the manifestations of the Tao [*Dao*]. That is why the ancient said, 'Try to see it and it is not there; try to hear it and there is nothing'" (*LT*, 29).

In regard to the Primal Beginning, Liezi does us a favour by explaining elements of the Chinese soul: "...the pure and light vapor rises to become heaven, and the muddy and heavy vapor sinks to become earth" (*LT*, 29). The Chinese word for soul is *hunpo* (魂魄). *Hun* (魂) as a heavenly soul rises to *shen* (神), the depository of heavenly souls; *po* (魄) as an earthly ghost soul falls to *gui* (鬼), the depository of earthly ghost souls.[9] In "Shadows, Sounds and Ghosts," Liezi explains that *gui* (鬼 ghost) also means 'return': "Death is not the end of things but a return to the origin" (*LT*, 34). This echoes a famous passage from Zhuangzi on the occasion of his wife's death. Huizi finds Zhuangzi singing and pounding on a tub instead of being full of sorrow. Confused, Huizi asks Zhuangzi about his unusual behaviour. Zhuangzi explains:

> ...When she first died, do you think I didn't grieve like anyone else? But I looked back to her beginning and the time before she was born. Not only the time before she was born, but the time before she had a body. Not only the time before she had a body, but the time before she had a spirit. In the midst of the jumble of wonder and mystery a change took place and she had a spirit. Another change and she had a body. Another change and she was born. Now there's been another change and she's dead. It's just like the progression of the four seasons, spring, summer, fall, winter.[10]

These above passages from Zhuangzi and Liezi help us with Laozi. Between life and death, 'the pure' and 'the muddy,' 'the light' and 'the heavy,' we have a harmonization, which is humanity - *tian di zhi jian* (天地之間 between heaven and earth). The mutually conditioning, oppositely charged, linked entities of the muddy and heavy, pure and light illuminate Laozi's famous Poem 15:

> Hollow, like caves,
> Opaque, like muddy pools
> Who can wait quietly while the mud settles?
> Who can remain still until the moment of action? (*LTTTC*, Poem 15)

The latter two lines are the ones which the Mencius (孟子) scholar Paul Shih-yi Hsiao (蕭師毅) writes for the decoration of Heidegger's study in 1946 while working on a collaborative translation of *Daodejing*[11]:

孰	能	濁	以	靜	之	徐	清
shu	neng	zhuo	yi	jing	zhi	xu	qing
孰	能	安	以	動	之	徐	生
shu	neng	an	yi	dong	zhi	xu	sheng

---

[9] 9. See Richard Wilhelm trans. and C G. Jung commentary, The Secret of The Golden Flower: A Chinese Book of Life (New York: Harcourt, Brace & Company, 1962), 13-18; cf. Cary F. Baynes, "Summary of the Chinese Concepts on Which is Based the Idea of the Golden Flower, or Immortal Spirit-Body," in Richard Wilhelm trans. and C G. Jung commentary, The Secret of The Golden Flower: A Chinese Book of Life (New York: Harcourt, Brace & Company, 1962), 65.

[10] Burton Watson trans., The Complete Works of Chuang Tzu (New York: Columbia University, 1968), 192. Hence cited as a parenthetical note in the text as CWCT.

[11] D. C. Lau, Chinese Classics: Tao Te Ching (Hong Kong: Chinese University Press, 1982), 20-23.

Hsiao's corresponding translation reads:

Who can, settling the muddy, gradually make it clear?
Who can, stirring the tranquil, gradually bring it to life?[12]

In an October 1947 letter to Hsiao, Heidegger brandishes a phenomenological translation:

'Who can be still and out of stillness and through it move something on to
the Way so that it comes to shine forth?'

[Who is able through making still to bring something into Being?
The *tao* [*Dao*] of heaven (*HOT*, 103)

Heidegger's "listening, inquiring gaze" as Hsiao calls it, becomes the "questioning which is the piety of thinking" (see *HOT*, 97).[13] For Heidegger, listening as a non-action of action begets speaking. Harkening to the call of Being is Heidegger's example of Daoism's *wu wei* (無為 non-action). Zhuangzi might want Heidegger and other listeners to go one step further in their non-action: stuff up your ears: "Those who peer with bright eyes will never catch sight of it. Eloquence is not as good as silence. The Way cannot be heard; to listen for it is not as good as plugging up your ears. This is called the Great Acquisition" (*CWCT*, 140). He goes on to say: "The formless moves to the realm of form; the formed moves back to the realm of formlessness. This all men alike understand. But it is not something to be reached by striving" (*CWCT*, 140).

Zhuangzi and Laozi are eternal partners, not one without the other. Similarly, Merleau-Ponty and Heidegger are phenomenal partners, not one without the other. Zhuangzi's 'hollows' (*qiao* 竅) as empty centres of being and nothingness are similar to Merleau-Ponty's 'hollow/crucible,' the empty interiors between flesh and idea where time makes itself.[14] Both hollows are invisible like the swirling wind. Yet, we still feel a presence. When the wind dies down, the hollows once again become empty.

In a parallel fashion, Laozi's *ming* (明 'clear/bright') as a meditative illumination traces its way into Heidegger's *Lichtung*, 'the clearing,' where being and nothingness are settled as in Poem 15. A constellation of concepts such as *jing* (靜 stillness, tranquillity, equilibrium) and *qing* (清 clear, settle) from Poem 15 find harmonization in Poem 16 where Laozi writes: "To know permanence – this is clarity" (*zhi chang ming ye*知常明也). In addition to drawing the two lines of Poem 15 in calligraphic style on parchment for Heidegger's home, Hsiao adds the expression the "Dao of Heaven" (*tian dao* 天道). The "Dao of Heaven" might be more than a fanciful wish on the part of Hsiao. It is a clue to the linking of Laozi's poems of *Daodejing* with Chapter 13 of Zhuangzi's stories entitled "The Dao of Heaven" (*tian dao* 天道). Here, Zhuangzi gives us the best description of the Daoist meditation strategy of *ming* (明). Reminiscent of Poem 10 of *Daodejing* on the polishing of the dark profound mirror

---

[12] Paul Shih-yi Hsiao, "Heidegger and Our Translation of the Tao Te Ching," in Graham Parkes ed., Heidegger and Asian Thought (Honolulu: University of Hawaii Press, 1987), 100. Hence cited as a parenthetical note in the text as HOT.

[13] Cf. Martin Heidegger, "The Question Concerning Technology," in The Question Concerning Technology and Other Essays (New York: Harper & Row, 1977), 35.

[14] See Maurice Merleau-Ponty, Phenomenology of Perception (London: Routledge, 1962), 431.

(*xuan jian* 玄鑑), the sage makes his essential spirit (*jingshen*精神) still (*jing* 靜) and clear (*ming* (明)) like water so that it mirrors the ten thousand things (*tiandi zhi jian ye, wanwu zhi jing ye* 天地之鑑也萬物之鏡也).

If these alignments find us gasping for breath, Frank Stevenson and Edgar Allen Poe arrive with an oxygen tank. In Stevenson's book, *Poe's Aulos: Voice, Echo and the Logic of Noise* (2000), he tells how Poe's imaginary dialogue with Plato subverts the *logos* of classical Greek by flipping the *lambda* (λ) of αυλός (the horn or the flute) upside down, thus revealing a *gamma* (γ) as in αὐγος (shining or clarity).[15] Both Poe and Stevenson are supporters of a type of chaos theory. Their semiotic disruptions serve to establish a noisy background rumbling which helps contextualize Daoism. Intelligible utterances emerge from the meaningless chatter of the background. This is similar to Liezi's idea of a sound begetting an echo or a shape begetting a shadow. On the one hand, we have Zhuangzi piping emptiness into the hollows of heaven and earth, which parallels Merleau-Ponty's breathing ambiguity into the hollows somewhere between the mind of the body and the body of the mind. Both seem to operate under the sign of Poe-Stevenson's αυλός of background noise or Liezi's idea of a sound generating an echo. On the other hand, we have Laozi's *ming* (明) as a type of empty clarity paralleling Heidegger's *Lichtung* as a place of no-place for being and nothingness. Both seem to operate under the sign of Poe-Stevenson's αὐγος, the shining from a mysterious darkness or Liezi's idea of a shape begetting a shadow. Zhuangzi's hollow is *yin*; Laozi's clear/bright is *yang*; Merleau-Ponty's hollow is *yin*; Heidegger's clearing is *yang*; Poe/Stevenson's horn/pipe is *yin*; shining/clarity is *yang*. Liezi's echo is *yin*; a sound is *yang*; Liezi's shadow is *yin*; a shape is *yang*. The purpose of the above phenomenal intermeshing is to illustrate the interconnectedness of the universe and the myriad of possibilities that defy logic in favour of chaos. *Yin* becomes *yang*, *yang* becomes *yin*, being becomes nothingness, nothingness becomes being. The following chart outlines these crossings which can be read in both their respective vertical columns and in their respective horizontal pairings.

Zhuangzi	*qiao* (竅) hollow	↔	Laozi	*ming* (明) clear/bright
Merleau-Ponty	*le creux*, hollow	↔	Heidegger	*Lichtung* clearing
Poe/Stevenson	αυλός horn, flute	↔	Poe/Stevenson	αὐγος shining/clarity
Liezi	echo/sound, *yin/yang*	↔	Liezi	shadow/shape, *yin/yang*

Lest we leave Stevenson and Poe dangling in the ontological twilight of pre-Socratic ambiguity, we can adopt their chaotic strategy of linguistic dissemination and flip the *lambda* (λ) of *logos* sideways and bring them home to China. *Lambda* becomes *ren* (人). The Greek *lambda* is a mirror image of the Chinese character *ren*. In all do respect to the Phoenicians, the Chinese character *ren* is perhaps the originary beginning of the Greek character *lambda* as a pictoriographic representation of a lame man, perhaps the lame man Oedipus.[16] We remember the riddle of the Sphinx, itself the rumour of background noise in Sophocles for it never appears in its full form in his works. It is fleshed out in later myths such as Apollodorus of 200 BCE: "what goes on four in the morning, two at midday and three in the evening?"[17] The answer is 'man,' *ren*, the Chinese character standing for both the limping Oedipus and

---

[15] See Frank W. Stevenson, Poe's Aulos: Voice, Echo and the Logic of Noise (Taibei: Bookman Books, 2000), 12.
[16] See Edmund Leach, Levi-Strauss (London: Fontana/Collins, 1970), 63.

the solution to his riddle. Ironically, 'four in the morning, three in the evening' is the offer of Zhuangzi's monkey-keeper to his monkeys to keep the 'heavenly balance' (see *BC*, 142). Zhuangzi and Laozi, Merleau-Ponty and Heidegger, Poe/Stevenson and Liezi all indulge in playful semiotic games that act to subvert and deconstruct logical, rational thinking and the languages which support an unnatural life. By doing so, they help us return to the *Dao*, the way of natural being, thinking, speaking and doing which is chaotic, irrational, erratic and human.

In the classical fashion of Chinese homonymic puns and their mystical making and unmaking, we are led to Hwa Yol Jung. Jung not only discusses *ren*, 'the person' but the Confucian virtue *ren* (仁) as 'benevolence,' in terms of another ideographic deconstruction. In explaining the 18th C. Korean neo-Confucian, Tasan ('Tea Mountain'), Jung writes:

> The ideogram jen/in, etymologically speaking, spells 'one human being' standing by 'two'.

As such it encompasses the moral performance of any pair of people in relation and assumes the moral responsibility of one for the other. 'Jen/in', Tasan argues,

> ...is the association of two people. Treating one's elder brother with fraternal respect is jen. Elder brother and younger brother are two people. Serving one's king with loyalty is jen. King and minister are two people. Ruling the people with compassion is jen. Ruler and citizen are two people. The fulfil[l]ment of respective duties in relationships between all pairs of people, including spouses and friends, is jen.[18]

One human being stands by two; two beget one. Once again we see a flipping of classical Daoists personages - linked, mutually dependent, oppositely charged. Laozi and Zhuangzi stand in for Liezi; Liezi and Zhuangzi become one. Liezi and Laozi stand in for Zhuangzi; Zhuangzi and Laozi become one. All give rise to *Dao*. This pattern itself is reminiscent of Laozi's Poem 42 of *Daodejing* which reads: The way generates the One. The One generates the two. The two generates the three. The three generates the ten thousand entities (*dao sheng yi yi sheng er er sheng san san sheng wanwu* 道生一一生二二生三三生萬物).

This is a Daoist twist on the later Confucian scholar Mencius: duty (*yi* 義) 'mitigates' propriety (*li* 禮) while 'manifesting' benevolence (*ren* 人).[19] Mencius explains that in ancient China, women and men were forbidden from holding hands in public under *li* (propriety or decorum). Yet no man, because of *yi* (duty or righteousness), would deny the extension of his hand to his sister-in-law who was drowning. *Yi* arises, *li* wanes and *ren* appears. Likewise, Daoism illustrates a holding of hands with eternal partners. Zhuangzi is the making of Daoism, Liezi is the unmaking (hence negative Daoism) and Laozi is the tranquillity between the making and the unmaking. Zhuangzi is going everywhere in all directions simultaneously, Liezi is going nowhere in all directions simultaneously and Laozi is already there and nowhere at the same time. Wherever you go, there you are! An interpreter of Daoism, Yuan Ji (210-263 CE) summarizes these phenomenal crossings of ambiguity: "If the sage has no

---

[17] Apollodorus, Apollodorus. Vol 1 trans. Sir J. G. Frazer (Cambridge: Harvard University, 1921), 347-348.

[18] Hwa Yol Jung, "Chong Yagyong: Korea's challenge to orthodox neo-Confucianism," in Asian Philosophy vol 8, no. 2, 1998: 133.

[19] Richard Smith, China's Cultural Heritage: The Qing Dynasty, 1644- 1912 2nd edition (Boulder: Westview Press, 1994), 145.

house, Heaven and Earth will contain him; if the sage has no master Heaven and Earth will own him; if the sage has nothing to do, he is free to walk under Heaven and on the Earth."[20]

Martin Buber lucidly explains part of this Daoist codependence through the cultivation of stillness (Laozi) and the joy of parable (Zhuangzi):

> Like the life of Lao Tzu [Laozi] so too his teaching is the most concealed for it is the most without parable. The naked oneness is silent... - in the hour of silence, before day, where there is but no Thou other than the I, and in darkness the secluded speech measures across and back the abyss - the oneness is already touched by the parable. Man speaks his words as the Logos speaks man; it is no longer pure oneness, it is already the manifold, the parable therein.[21]

Buber's 'the naked oneness is silent' seems also to be as dear to Heidegger as Laozi, yet it is the parables of Zhuangzi that issues forth the everyday.

In five decades of rigorous dialogue with East Asian thought and Daoism in particular, Heidegger cherishes the tension between the 'oneness' and 'parable' of which Buber speaks. Part of his engagement with these emerges in his notion of 'the clearing.' The unfinished project of translating *Daodejing* in the 1940's finds its resolve with Chang Chung-yuan (張鍾元) in the 1970's who completes the translation with Heidegger's help in a book entitled, *Tao - A New Way of Thinking* (1975). In his dialogue with Heidegger, Chang states: "This *lichtung* in the Taoist sense is *Ming* [明]. Thus from the Eastern point of view we can understand your new approach as identifying with the attainment of *Ming*. Heidegger answered, 'That is correct.'"[22] This happy completion is a coming full circle; the Chinese characters of sun (*ri* 日) and moon (*yue* 月) together form their own illumination (*ming* 明). This is reminiscent of Heidegger's own judgement from *Being and Time* on *Dasein*: "To say that it is 'illuminated' ['erleuchet'] means that *as* Being-in-the-world it is cleared [gelichtet] in itself, not through any other entity, but in such a way that it *is* itself the clearing."[23] Although Chang concentrates on *ming* as the luminosity of Being and Nothingness, we might also open this up into the Chinese vernacular for 'glade' or 'clearing': *linjian kongdi* (林間空地). The characters are revealing. 'The empty in-betweenness of forest and earth' is similar to Heidegger's explanation for *Lichtung* in *On Time and Being*: "The clearing is the open for everything that is present and absent."[24] Reinhard May is persuasive in arguing that Leon Wieger's 1915 description of the Chinese character for nothing, *wu* (無) as a wood clearing was also influential in Heidegger's formulation of 'the clearing.'[25] May juxtaposes two descriptions: one from Wieger's lexicon of Chinese characters and the other from

---

[20] Shi-Ying Zhang, "Heidegger and Taoism," in John Sallis ed. Reading Heidegger: Commemorations (Bloomington: Indiana University, 1993), 308.

[21] Martin Buber, "The Commentary: 'Afterward,'" in Jonathan R. Herman, I and Tao: Martin Buber's Encounter with Chuang Tzu (Albany, SUNY: 1996), 78.

[22] See Chung-yuan Chang, "Reflections," in Gunther Neske ed. Erinnerung an Martin Heidegger (Pfullingen: Neske, 1977), 68; see also Chung-yuan Chang, Tao – A New Way of Thinking (New York: Harper & Row, 1975).

[23] Martin Heidegger, Being and Time trans. John Macquarrie and Edward Robinson (New York: Harper & Row), 171.

[24] Martin Heidegger, On Time and Being (New York: Harper & Row, 1972), 65.

[25] Reinhard May, Heidegger's hidden sources: East Asian influences on his work trans. Graham Parkes (London: Routledge, 1996), 32-33. Hence cited as a parenthetical note in the text as HHS.

Heidegger's essay, "The End of Philosophy and the Task of Thinking."[26] Of the Chinese 'nothing' and Heidegger's 'clearing,' May gives us two quotes. The first from Wieger describes *wu* ('nothing'): "A multitude...of men, acting upon a forest, felling the trees, clearing of wood a tract of land. In the old form [the graph] stated that the wood had vanished. Hence...the general abstract notions of vanishing, defect, want, negation" (*HHS*, 33)[27] The second quote which May translates from Heidegger, describes *Lichtung*: "To clear [lichten] something means: to make something light, free and open; for example, to make a place in the woods free of trees. The open space that results is the clearing [*Lichtung*]" (*HHS*, 33; cf. *DEDP*, 72; cf. *EP*, 384).

From the above, we see that Heidegger's complex intertwining with Eastern thought influences his understanding of the relations between being and Being, subject and object, visible and invisible. The move from logical, textual-style analyses to poetry affords him a phenomenal body that allows Daoism to speak the unspeakable. Regarding Heidegger's favourite couplet of Laozi's Poem 15, the *Xiang'er* 想爾 commentaries (written before 215 CE) offer revealing insight. The *Xiang'er*, a classic of early Daoism, pinpoints 'clarity and stillness' and 'clarity and brightness' as crucial Daoist meditative statutes.

Regarding Chapter 15, the commentaries read:

While they are learning to be clear and still, their thoughts will temporarily be as if confused and muddy; but since they are confused and muddy, they have maintained simplicity and are about to reach their goal. Finally, in clarity and stillness, they will be able to observe all of the subtleties. Since inside they will be clear and luminous, they will not wish to draw near the common. These essentials of clarity and stillness are the delight of the subtle [pneumas] of the Dao.[28]

The Chinese translation of *Lichtung* (*chengming* 澄明) in *Being and Time* (*cunzai yu shijian* 存在與時間) captures both Heidegger's and Laozi's twin notions of clear/still and luminous.[29] *Cheng* (澄) carries the sense of settling out and clearing up as in limpid water (*shui qing* 水清); *ming* (明) has the sense of bright (*liang* 亮). *Chengming* (澄明) together represents open clarity of interpretation. Xiong Wei (熊偉), who supervised the 1987 Chinese translation of *Being and Time*, studied with Heidegger in the 1930's.

For Zhuangzi, clarity is not so easily achieved. Language takes a rather circuitous route for this illumination. Hence, Zhuangzi makes fun of language and its logic as does Liezi and Poe/Stevenson: "To use a horse to show that a horse is not a horse is not as good as using a non-horse to show that a horse is not a horse" (*CWCT*, 40). Here he is responding to the ancient sophist Gongsun Long's (公孫龍) 'white horse is not a horse' (*bai ma fei ma* 白馬非馬) that claims that 'horse' is naming a shape; 'white' is naming a colour. Thus a

---

[26] See Martin Heidegger, "Das Ende der Philosophie und die Aufgabe des Denkens," in Zur Sache des Denkens (Tubingen: Max Niemeyer, 1969), 61-80. Hence cited as a parenthetical note in the text as DEDP; cf. Martin Heidegger, "The End of Philosophy and the Task of Thinking," in Basic Writings ed. David Farrell Krell (New York: Harper and Collins, 1977), 369-392. Hence cited as a parenthetical note in the text as EP.

[27] Cf. Leon Wieger, Chinese Characters: Their origin, etymology, history, Classification and signification (New York: Dover Publications, 1965), 36.

[28] Stephen Bokenkamp, Early Daoist Scriptures (Berkeley: University of California, 1997), 99.

[29] Martin Heidegger (馬丁海德格), Being and Time (存在與時間) 2 vols. trans. Chen Jiaying and Wang Qingjie under the supervision of Xiong Wei (Taibei: Tang Shan Publishing, 1990), 170, 558.

'white horse is not a horse.'[30] Once again, Zhuangzi goes a step further. He is not interested in logic. He is concerned with "the ontological consistency of self-so-ness" (*BC*, 197). As Wu Kuang-ming (吳光明) argues: "...we can afford to affirm things in their differences (using a no-horse to show that a horse is no-horse), accepting everything as 'such'" (*BC*, 196). Zhuangzi calls this 'the double walk' (*liang xing* 兩行) (*BC*, 195), taking both logical roads simultaneously in order to "tarry at the pivot" and "respond endlessly and freely" (*BC*, 196). In Wu's translation, Zhuangzi says:

> Where none of that or this obtains its counterpart - people call it the Tao [*Dao*] Pivot. Then the Pivot begins to obtain its middle point of the circle, and - with it, it responds till there-is-no end. (*BC*, 140-141)

Alternatively, Watson translates 'tarry at the pivot' as the 'hinge of the way': "When the hinge is fitted into the socket, it can respond endlessly. Its right is a single endlessness and its wrong is a single endlessness" (*CWCT*, 40). This is the definitive 'illumination of clarity' for Zhuangzi (*BC*, 141, 144). The *Dao* Pivot, the hinge of the way brings us full circle to Laozi's Poem One. Both desire and desirelessness "spring from the same source but differ in name" (*LTTTC*, Poem One).

Finally, we have the ultimate beginning statement on beginning by Zhuangzi, itself a never ending swirl of negations and possibilities:

> There is a beginning. There is a not yet beginning to be a beginning.
> There is a not yet beginning to be a not yet beginning to be a beginning. There is being. There is nonbeing. There is a not yet beginning to be a nonbeing. There is a not yet beginning to be a not yet beginning to be nonbeing. Suddenly there is nonbeing. But I do not know, when it comes to nonbeing, which is really being and which is nonbeing. Now I have just said something. But I don't know whether what I have said has really said something or whether it hasn't said something...Heaven and earth were born at the same time I was, and the ten thousand things are one with me. (*CWCT*, 43)

The above statement leaves the reader with anything but a place to begin. The tangled mesh of language seems to cloud any attempt at getting started. The purpose of these linguistic tricks for Zhuangzi is to persuade us to abandon language and embrace our feelings. In Daoist scholarship, it is called 'words without words' (*yan wuyan* 言無言). If you catch the fish, you do not need the net; if you have the meaning, you do not need the words (see *CWCT*, 302). We might also think of Laozi: "If nothing is done, then all will be well" (*LTTTC*, Poem Three). Better still, be like Liezi's neighbour, have a 'full face' and a 'nothing mind'; hear nothing, do not be 'distracted'; see nothing, do not be 'attracted'; say nothing, do not 'argue'; be like a 'blank wall'; have a 'wooden face.' If there is no difference between hearing and not hearing, seeing and not seeing, speaking and not speaking, then you will be empty, that is all (see *LT*, 113-114). Once again we have returned to the monkeys: hear no evil, see no evil, speak no evil.

A good summary emerges through Daoist parable. Zhuangzi tells us the creation myth of Chaos:

---

[30] See A. C. Graham, Disputers of the Tao: Philosophical Argument in Ancient China (LaSalle: Open Court), 85.

The emperor of the South Sea was called Shu (Brief), the emperor of the North Sea was called Hu (Sudden), and the emperor of the central region was called Hun-tun (Chaos). Shu and Hu from time to time came together for a meeting in the territory of Hun-tun, and Hun-tun treated them very generously. Shu and Hu discussed how they could repay his kindness. 'All men,' they said, 'have seven openings so they can see, hear, eat, and breathe. But Hun-tun alone doesn't have any. Let's trying boring him some!' Every day they bored another hole, and on the seventh day Hun-tun died. (*CWCT*, 97)

If we attempt to order any of the Daoist philosophers by identifying them or pinning them down to specific personages or placing them in a hierarchy, then we lose them. If we bore holes in them, they too will die. If we fill in the blanks, then they disappear forever. If we stuff the empty centre of Daoism by reducing Liezi to Lao-Zhuang or to Huang-Lao, then we close the opening.

In contemporary global perspective, Merleau-Ponty and Heidegger help preserve the between of stillness and parable, straddling Laozi and Zhuangzi with an eternal phenomenological bracketing, suspension or *epochein* (to withhold). Echo and shadow are traces of beginnings which lead away from logic and into the suchness of being and nothingness. From this empty centre, the wind begins to pick up and swirl with possibility and impossibility. If we fill in the void of Zhuangzi's hollows or Merleau-Ponty's crucible or muddy up Laozi's *ming* (明) or Heidegger's *Lichtung*, then they all disappear. Each is equiprimordial; each is centripetal; each is co-constitutive and co-resonating; each returns to the empty centre of stillness and non-action. Non-action (*wu wei* 無為) as an action is the undoing of doing. Chaos is the progenitor of both the world of things and non-things: sound and echo, shape and shadow, visible and invisible, being and nothingness, *yin* and *yang*. The in-betweenness of these polarities shows us 'the way.'

REFERENCES

Apollodorus, *Apollodorus* vol. 1 trans. Sir J. G. Frazer. Cambridge: Harvard University Press, 1921

Baynes, Cary F., "Summary of the Chinese Concepts on Which is Based the Idea of the Golden Flower, or Immortal Spirit-Body," pp. 64-65 in Richard Wilhelm translation and C. G. Jung commentary, *The Secret of the Golden Flower: A Chinese Book of Life* New York: Harcourt, Brace & Company, 1962.

Bokenkamp, Stephen, *Early Daoist Scriptures* Berkeley: University of California, 1997.Buber, Martin, "The Commentary: 'Afterward,'" pp. 69-100 in Jonathan R. Herman, *I and Tao: Martin Buber's Encounter with Chuang Tzu* Albany: SUNY, 1996.

Chang, Chung-yuan, *Tao - A New Way of Thinking* New York: Harper & Row, 1975.

Chang, Chung-yuan, "Reflections," pp. 65-71 in Gunther Neske ed. *Erinnerung an Martin Heidegger* Pfullingen: Neske, 1977.

Chen, Man-jan, *Lao-Tzu: "My words are very easy to understand"* Richmond: North Atlantic Books, 1981.

Feng, Gia-Fu and Jane English, trans. *Lao Tsu: Tao Te Ching* New York: Random House, 1972.

Fischer-Schreiber, Ingrid, Franz-Karl Ehrhard, Kurt Friedrichs and Michael S. Diener, *The Encyclopedia of Eastern Philosophy and Religion: Buddhism, Taoism, Zen, Hinduism* Boston: Shambhala Press, 1989.

Graham, A. C., *Disputers of the Tao: Philosophical Argument in Ancient China* LaSalle: Open Court, 1989.

Heidegger, Martin, *Being and Time* trans. by John Macquarrie and Edward Robinson. New York: Harper & Row, 1962.

Heidegger, Martin, "Das Ende der Philosophie und die Aufgabe des Denkens," p. 61-80 in *Zur Sache des Denkens* Tübingen: Max Niemeyer, 1969.

Heidegger, Martin, *On Time and Being* New York: Harper & Row, 1972.

Heidegger, Martin, "The Question Concerning Technology," pp. 3-35 in *The Question Concerning Technology and Other Essays* New York: Harper & Row, 1977.

Heidegger, Martin, "The End of Philosophy and the Task of Thinking," pp. 369- 392 in *Basic Writings* ed. David Farrell Krell. New York: Harper & Row, 1977.

Heidegger, Martin (馬丁海德格), *Being and Time* (存在與時間) 2 vols. trans. Chen Jiaying and Wang Qingjie under the supervision of Xiong Wei. Taibei: Tang Shan Publishing, 1990.

Henshall, Kenneth G. *A Guide to Remembering Japanese Characters* Tokyo: Charles E. Tuttle, 1988.

Herman, Jonathan R. *I and Tao: Martin Buber's Encounter with Chuang Tzu* Albany: SUNY, 1996.

Hsiao, Paul Shih-yi, "Heidegger and Our Translation of the Tao Te Ching," pp. 93-104 in Graham Parkes ed., *Heidegger and Asian Thought* Honolulu: University of Hawaii, 1987.

Jung, Hwa Yol Jung, "Chong Yagyong: Korea's challenge to orthodox neo- Confucianism," in *Asian Philosophy* vol. 8. no. 2, 1998: 131-134.

Lau, D. C., *Chinese Classics: Tao Te Ching* Hong Kong: Chinese University Press, 1982.

Leach, Edmund, *Levi-Strauss* London: Fontana/Collins, 1970.

May, Reinhard, *Heidegger's hidden sources: East Asian influences on his work* trans. Graham Parkes. London: Routledge, 1996.

Merleau-Ponty, Maurice, *Phenomenology of Perception* London: Routledge, 1962.

Merleau-Ponty, Maurice, "Everywhere and Nowhere," pp. 126-158 in *Signs* Evanston: Northwestern University, 1964.

Merleau-Ponty, Maurice, *The Visible and the Invisible* Evanston: Northwestern University, 1968.

Smith, Richard, *China's Cultural Heritage: The Qing Dynasty, 1644-1912* 2nd ed. Boulder: Westview Press, 1994.

Stevenson, Frank W., *Poe's Aulos: Voice, Echo and the Logic of Noise* Taibei: Bookman Books, 2000.

Watson, Burton trans., *The Complete Works of Chuang Tzu* New York: Columbia University, 1968.

Wieger, L., *Chinese Characters: Their origin, etymology, history, classification and signification* New York: Dover Publications, 1965.

Wilder, G. D. and J. H. Ingram, *Analysis of Chinese Characters* New York: Dover Publications, 1974.

Wilhelm, Richard trans. and C. G. Jung commentary, *The Secret of the Golden Flower: A Chinese Book of Life* New York: Harcourt, Brace & Company, 1962.

Wong, Eva, *Lieh-Tzu: A Taoist Guide to Practical Living* Boston: Shambhala, 1995.

Wu, Kuang-ming, *The Butterfly as Companion: Meditations on the First Three Chapters of the Chuang Tzu* Albany: SUNY, 1990.

Zhang Shi-Ying, "Heidegger and Taoism," pp. 307-322 in John Sallis ed., *Reading Heidegger: Commemorations* Bloomington: Indiana University, 1992.

In: Globalization Dynamics
Editor: Kuang-ming Wu

ISBN: 978-1-62100-750-0
© 2012 Nova Science Publishers, Inc.

Chapter 9

MEDICINE EAST AND WEST

Masami Tateno[*]
Nihon University, Tokyo, Japan

ABSTRACT

In this chapter, I first take up the very first characterization of the philosophy of traditional Chinese medicine, which we can find in the Chin-shu chapter of the *Lu-shi chun-chiu*[a], since it describes the core modality of the philosophy of medicine, and is actually back-grounded by a very common conception of cosmic order, found both in ancient China and in 10th-18th century Japan—the "holistic total", that is, a world view that takes the world synthetically as a whole, and emphasizes the importance of achieving a good balance of constituents(= cosmic harmony) of the whole world in order to achieve a healthy life and longevity. At this point, I would refer to Lao-tzu's philosophy of the Tao[b] so that we may clarify the relationship between mind-body and human being-universe through a philosophical practice based on our respirational procedure.

INTRODUCTION

For human beings, health, and living healthier lives, is an everlasting theme. Even living in a highly medically and scientifically developed world, we still tremble with fear over a number of diseases—like a deluge overwhelming us. The case seems just the same in all ages and countries. This is the reason why I characterize it as an "everlasting theme," and take the philosophy of medicine as a core theme to discern the "everlasting theme."

Cosmic order is another "core theme", of which the philosophy of medicine consists as one of its most significant schemes. Accordingly, in this paper I clarify the cosmic order in 10th-18th century Japan through a comprehensive view of the philosophy of medicine during those ages.

---

[*] Professor of Western, Japanese, and Chinese philosophy, and of Medicine, Nihon University, Tokyo, Japan. Dr. Tateno's email is: tatenoma@chs.nihon-u.ac.jp

Now, there is a lot of excellent scholarship on classical medicine in 10th-18th century Japan. At the same time, there are many marvelous studies on the philosophical thought of those ages. Thus, there would hardly seem room for me to offer even a minor contribution to either field. Surprisingly, however, regarding the much more specific field of philosophy of medicine, I could not find even a single major study—not only of these ages but of any other age in Japan. This makes it possible for me to write this small paper on this great subject.

In this chapter, I first take up the very first characterization of the philosophy of traditional Chinese medicine, which we can find in the Chin-shu chapter of the *Lu-shi chun-chiu*[a], since it describes the core modality of the philosophy of medicine, and is actually back-grounded by a very common conception of cosmic order, found both in ancient China and in 10th-18th century Japan—the "holistic total", that is, a world view that takes the world synthetically as a whole, and emphasizes the importance of achieving a good balance of constituents(= cosmic harmony) of the whole world in order to achieve a healthy life and longevity. At this point, I would refer to Lao-tzu's philosophy of the Tao[b] so that we may clarify the relationship between mind-body and human being-universe through a philosophical practice based on our respirational procedure.

In a philosophical background of "science," Western biomedical technology has developed remarkably in the last few centuries, at least regarding its clinical techniques. In such a technological development, "analysis" is the core philosophy (e.g. cellular-pathology, DNA, "spare parts", etc.). This modality hardly permits conceiving the world as a "holistic total."

On the contrary, the Chinese/Japanese philosophy of medicine, which has been based on "synthesis", and the basic characterization of which is found in the Chin-shu chapter of the *Lu-shi chun-chiu*, conveys to us a cosmic order of a "holistic total." For this reason, after a general survey of the contents in the *Lu-shi chun-chiu*, in order to understand this cosmic order, I consider some other "classics" of Chinese medicine, which seem to be the heirs of this notion. Then, I look into the *Ishinpo* and Kajiwara, Shozen's[c] works to clarify how those 10th-13th century Japanese scholars inherited this worldview.

Based on the above observations, I will make the following assertions about the 10th-18th century Japanese view of the cosmic order:

1) The core worldview found in the Chin-shu chapter of the *Lu-shi chun-chiu* is the cosmic order of a "holistic total," derived from the intrinsic mode of scientific conception, "synthesis," where we, human-beings, exist in psycho-somatic harmony with the cosmic order—cosmic harmony.
2) Those notions are actually conveyed in the heirs of traditional Chinese medicine like the *Huang-ting nei-ching* [d] and the other works on traditional Chinese medicine.
3) When they were transported to Japan, they were naturally accepted into the Japanese mind, even though there was some "dyspepsia."
4) Nevertheless, there still seems to be some typical Japanese characteristics in the process of transmission, such as "conformity," more precisely "import and modify".
5) After some "digestions," there appeared several medical practitioners who truly attained real Chinese-origin cosmic order, while possessing their own Japanese mode of cosmic order in 18th century Japan whose basic idea is "analysis" and whose main interest is cure the diseases not to prevent it.

To begin with, I will take up the Chin-shu chapter of the *Lu-shi chun-chiu* to clarify the notion of a "holistic total" as the core cosmic order of the philosophy of medicine, common to both ancient China and 10th-18th century Japan.

THE CHIN-SHU CHAPTER OF THE *LU-SHI CHUN-CHIU*

We can find the paragraph which describes the first form of the ancient Chinese philosophy of medicine, which would seem to be much more theoretically described in the *Huang-ting nei-ching* and the other volumes down through the ages are found in chapter 3-2 of the *Lu-shi chun-chiu*, the Chin-shu chapter, the chapter regarding the achievement of longevity. Namely, the original modality of the ancient Chinese philosophy of medicine, which is later called "Nei-ching i-hsueh" [e], are all lined up here in the Chin-shu chapter of the *Lu-shi chun-chiu*, as follows:

> Tien[f], Heaven, as a metaphorical expression of Mother Nature, created the very diverse modalities of phenomenal conditions in the daily world such as sunny-shady, cold-hot and desiccation-humidity. The four seasons are turning, and "the every-thing" is changing, doing both benefit and harm to our lives. The sage, discerning the facilities of the of the phenomenal conditions above and disclosing the profit in "the every-thing", will accord with every facility of his life. In this manner, his mind would rest peacefully in his body, and he would have a long life.[1]

The passage can be understood as follows: the sage will work for the cosmic harmony of mind and body to achieve long life according to the diverse modalities of the phenomenal conditions in the world of nature (such as sunny-shady, hot-cold, four seasons, and so forth) that Heaven has created. In this paragraph, we can grasp the typical expression of the cosmic harmony of a holistic total in Chinese philosophy of medicine that is intrinsically based on the cosmic order derived from the modality of synthesis. The first point to notice is that they regarded Tien, which entails the cosmic harmony of the phenomenal diversities derived from "synthesis", as a symbolization of the cosmic order, and according to this "order" a human being in the physiological level would be inherently long-lived.

This striking, but at the same time natural, view of the nature of longevity would be seen as universal, at least in the context of philosophy of medicine in ancient times. That is to say, this view is one of the most crucial in the philosophy of medicine of classical times just as was the conception of *vis medicatrix naturae*[2]. This view seems so crucial that it should even be reconsidered now along with the philosophical background, since the modern and highly developed medicine seems to have been developed through the process of "forgetting" this view. This is an irony of philosophy.

---

[1] *Lu-shi chun-chiu, A Concordance to the Lu shi Chun-qiu*, Taipei, Taiwan: The Commercial Press, 1996, p. 12. All translations throughout this paper are my own. And also, about the philosophy of medicine in the *Lu-shi chun-chiu,* see my paper "由《呂氏春秋》看中國古代身心相關醫學思想" (Philosophy of psycho-somatic medicine in ancient China from the viewpoint of *Lu-shi chun chiu*), in 《中國古代思想中的氣論及身體觀》 (The Theory of Ch'i and views of the body in ancient Chinese philosophy), edited by R. P.Yang, Taipei, Taiwan: Chiu Liu Press, 1993, pp. 485-96

[2] We can also find this precious notion in Hippocrates' words (e.g. in his On Epidemics, 6) or even in the famous words of Ambroise Pare's " Je le pansay, Dieu le guarit."

In fact, this view of our nature, which describes a human being as an integration of mind and body, *is* the very key to the longevity, and this is enumerated as one of the core features of the cosmic order of Tien in the ancient Chinese philosophy of medicine.

A mere *homo sapience* broken down to a collection of cells in compliance with Vilchow's cellular-pathology in the modern theoretical formulation of medicine which is a typical upshot of "analyses" could not be designated a true human being of our everyday experience. We can find large numbers of patients with unrelievable distress who are exhaustively analyzed as a mere diseased *objects*. This way of thinking is at the root of the limitations of modern "scientific" medicine. We, human beings, live in the harmony of bodies and minds— the cosmic harmony. We are not just objects but living creatures with body and mind. The early Chinese philosophers of medicine understood this clearly.

The Chin-shu chapter continues:

Longevity is not merely a collection of short lives, but is an accomplishment of one's life. In order to achieve longevity one should avert harm. How can one do it. Too much sweet, too much sour, too much bitter, too much hot and too much salty, when one's body is filled with these five "too much tastes", it brings harm. Too much joy, too much anger, too much anxiety, too much fear, and too much grief, when these five "too much feelings" get in one's mind, it brings harm. Too much cold, too much hot, too much desiccation, too much humidity, too much wind, too much rain and too much fog, when these seven "too much weather" move in on one's spirit, it brings harm[3].

This passage suggests a concrete strategy for caring for life and achieving longevity based on the fundamental world view alluded to above— the cosmic harmony of a holistic total based on the cosmic order[4]. Namely, in order for a human being to be long lived, it is indispensable that:

1) One should avoid "too much tastes", that is, an unbalanced diet with too much sweet, too much sour and so on. That is to say, one should keep temperate tastes.
2) One should refrain from too much trembling in his mind, such as too much joy, too much anger and so on in his daily life.
3) One should accommodate oneself to the weather.
4) Even though human beings are disposed to be long lived by nature, numerous "too much" get in the way of our longevity. These "too much" cause harm, hai[g], to the cosmic harmony of a holistic total, and distance people from the cosmic order causing them to fall ill.

This passage advocates 1) temperate tastes for one's body, 2) control over one's emotions, and 3) enabling various changes of the environment to get in one's spirit—ching[h], as will be shown later. It is an assertion of temperance in daily life. It is one of the most typical features of the cosmic order reflected in the Chinese philosophy of medicine in ancient times. In fact, an even more crucial aspect of this description is that human diseases, hai, have been understood pathologically in the holistic totality of an ontological level of human being—

---

[3] op. cit., p.12.

[4] Here, in this passage, we can see the original modality of pathogenic idea not only of Nei-chin i-hsueh but also that of Chen yen in the south Song dynasty.

body, mind and mind-body. It is not a product of "analysis", but only "synthesis" can entail such a marvelous pathological formulation. This is one of the greatest features of the ancient Chinese philosophy of medicine.

Regarding this point, the Chin-shu chapter elaborates:

> When the vital forces, ching-chi[i], gather, they necessarily make some things. Gathering in a bird, they will make it fly in the sky; gathering in an animal, they will make it move in the field; gathering in a gem, they will make it glitter; gathering in a tree, they will make it rampant; and gathering in a sage, they will make him bright.[5]

The vital forces, ching-chi, in this passage are the essential being of things on the epistemological level. There are numerous points that could be made on this issue. However the only philosophically significant point to be taken in this passage is that the vital forces of ching-chi are supposed to compose both the body and mind of human beings just as they construct birds, animals, gems and so forth. Not only our body but also our minds *are* composed of the vital forces of ching-chi.

From a philosophical point of view, what the vital forces, ching-chi, scientifically are, or how we can see them through some artificial mechanisms, is not such a crucial point. Rather, this world view, in which our body and mind, even the whole world itself, are taken to be one "holistic total" on the same ontological level, *is* the very point of which we should take special note in this paper. We, human beings, are living in the cosmic harmony of body, mind and the whole world as one holistic total.

It is precisely on this philosophical basis of the cosmic order that a human being is to be grasped as an existence of the holistic total of body and mind, and at the same time a human being, and the whole universe is conceived as one in the cosmic harmony, not just as a theoretical formulation but in reality. In one word, the vital forces, ching-chi, *are* the very essence of the mind-body, and of human beings and the universe linked together both on the epistemological and the ontological level. In other words, the vital forces, ching-chi are not just a conception of mediation among them but a mediation itself to compose the cosmic order of a holistic total of the cosmic harmony.

Furthermore, on the metaphysical level, the philosophically crucial point here is that this basic idea of the holistic total of body and mind, in the ancient Chinese philosophy of medicine *is* intrinsically back-grounded by some profound philosophy. Suffice it to say here that the ancient Chinese philosophy of medicine is not just about fitness or health care but has a profound background. Particularly this notion that mind-body is integrated into one, and further mind body and the whole universe is linked together as one harmony is unerringly the same as that of Lao-tzu's Tao, which is not just a metaphysical concept but is one's philosophical status embodied through our philosophical practice—shugyo[j]. So for now, I would take a glance at Lao-tzu's Tao hereinafter[6].

---

[5] op. cit., p.13.

[6] On this issue, see my "Lao-tzu's Tao and an Ancient Chinese Philosophy of Medicine: A Philosophical Background of Traditional Chinese Medicine" in *Studies in Humanities and Sciences,* 68, Nihon University, Tokyo, September, 2004.

Lao-Tzu's Tao and Traditional Chinese Medicine

Lao-tzu's Tao has traditionally been interpreted as transcendent in the sense of being beyond our faculties of external sensory perception, and as a cosmogonic generative principle, and as an essential moment of every possible phenomenon. It is further commonly asserted that the Tao is beyond our verbal description, and it is the reason why Lao-tzu himself writes: "The Tao that can be spoken of is not the true Tao." (chapter 1)

Lao-tzu's Tao is beyond the reach of our sensory perception or cognition, and for this reason it resists theoretical delineation. Being beyond knowledge acquired by cognition based on sensory perception, the Tao is "something true" that we should attain through by way of *internal* perception in the depth of our *"psyche."* So we can not make sense of the Tao through conceptual analysis, for such analysis is no more than a tautology or shuffling of synonyms, making no sense.

Although epistemologically "transcendent," beyond our cognition, Lao-tzu's Tao is not ontologically isolated from us. Tao is some "thing" that involves us, and to be embodied in ourselves in the depth of our *psyche*— our mind, consciousness, unconsciousness, and the whole psychic entity--through the physical training of a self-cultivative regimen.

It is why Lao-tzu, on one hand makes such provocative statements as:

One who knows does not speak, one who speaks does not know. (chapter 56)

And on the other hand, laments earnestly as follows:

My words are very easy to understand and easy to put into practice.
But there is no one to understand them, nor practice them. (chapter70)

This suggests a view of "self-cultivation" (shu-gyo) as progressing further and further into the depth of our *"psyche"* through a philosophical practice of a self-cultivative regimen which is actually realized through the respiratory regulative method of abdominal respiration (i.e. "stomach breathing" in Lao-tzu's phraseology) and that this is the background of Lao-tzu's philosophy of the Tao.

When viewed epistemologically that is, in terms of his theory of knowledge, Lao-tzu's philosophical thought is amply based upon his view of the world, more precisely "a view of the relativism." Lao-tzu himself points out the relativity of this phenomenal world as follows:

All of us can acknowledge the beautiful things beautiful. But it is possible just because there are the ugly things as a cognitive modality for the inference.
All of us can acknowledge the good things good. But it is possible just because of the existence of the bad things.

These are the examples which are to hold with respect to the view of the relativism viz. existence-nonexistence, easy-difficult, long-short, high-low, acoustic sounds-human voices, before-after and so forth. (chapter 2)

Specifically, we recognize "beautiful things" as beautiful where we have "ugly things" to compare them with to serve as the basis for the judgment of relative beauty. This modality of relativism is also said to hold in these cases as to existence-non existence, easy-difficult, high-low and so on. In other words, they can only be relatively "beautiful", "good", "existent," and so on.

Without "ugly", "bad" or "non-existence", there would be no possibility of "beautiful", "good" or "existence". This implies that our cognitive function of our external sensory perception of phenomena is carried out in a framework of the relativism such as "beautiful-ugly", "good-bad", "existence – non-existence" and so forth. Lao-tzu concludes that our ordinary subject-object cognition, in ordinary epistemological subject-object cognition can never go beyond the relative world of phenomena.

From here we can find Lao-tzu's words of strict and self-restraint introspection about our limited faculty of cognition as follows:

> To know our not-knowing is the best [knowledge].
> Not to know the [limits of] our knowledge is a troublesome suffering.
> If one makes clear sense of this suffering, he must be free from it.
> A sage is free from this suffering for he knows what the suffering really is.
> This is the reason why he is free from it. (chapter 71)

In this passage, Lao-tzu elucidates our limited cognition in the everyday phenomenal world. We have to know that we can not know the eternal-universal, theoretically perfect-absolute truth: Without this profound consideration, we would easily fall into the epistemological suffering. So we should take this epistemological "suffering" or "suffering" of our cognitive function, as our own suffering plainly so that we might avoid it as sages do. This is Lao-tzu's intention behind his assertion.

In summery, so far as we remain in the daily phenomenal world, we are restricted by the confines of relative framework of space and time, and object and subject, then we can never reach the higher cognition of our true selves. Then, how can we do so? The Tao is Lao-tzu's answer.

Lao-tzu asserts that we should rise far above this everyday phenomenal world and our ordinary daily level of consciousness through our own practical self-cultivation in order to embody the Tao in the depth of our *psyche*. Lao-tzu suggests this in a terse and metaphorical saying:

> The five colors [of beautiful scenery] will blind eyes.
> The five tones [of fine music] will deafen ears.
> The five flavors [of delicious food] will spoil plates.
> Racing and hunting will make men's minds trigger madness.
> Things rare and hard to get will injure men's activities.......
> For this reason, the sage makes his stomach, but not his eyes; hence he discards the other and secures this. (chapter 12)

Beautiful scenery, fine music, delicious food and joyful racing and hunting enchant us in this phenomenal everyday world. But they are possible only instantaneously as outgrowths of relativity. These fleeting pleasures manifest just at one place and at one moment. In other words, they could be pleasures only relatively -- not eternally nor universally. Furthermore, trying to hold on to them will hurt our eyes, ears, mouths and minds.

This is why the sage is not concerned with his eyes, perceives not through his eyes but through his stomach. Lao-tzu's phraseology of "to make his stomach" is not a metaphorical expression for something metaphysical or something immanent. Instead, the "stomach" refers to stomach as it actually is. That is, the sage makes stomach breathing, namely abdominal respiration, as his self-cultivative regimen.

More precisely, the sage actually makes his abdomen an area of concentration, that is, the sage gathers the vital forces, namely chuan ch'i[k] at his abdomen, or the so-called "field of cinnabar" in traditional Chinese medicine, as he delves deep into the innermost recesses of his consciousness, or rather unconsciousness, to consummate the Tao *qua* himself. Accordingly, Lao-tzu's "make his stomach" expresses the saga's practical attempt to grope after the Tao. And at this point, it is particularly noteworthy that this mind- body and human being-universe are one through ch'i exercise viz. respiratory practice in the Chin-shu chapter, the *Lu-shi chun-chiu*. It is through this practice of progressive retrogression, or the active withdrawal of consciousness, that the sage actually transcends the framework of relativism in his cognitive faculty into the world of veracity - the Tao. And as a parenthetical remark, this meditative "stomach breathing" is a basic technique common with Zen, Yoga, fine arts, martial arts, training of various medical healing arts and so forth.

To put it in other words, from another physiological point of view, Lao-tzu's saga cultivates his body and mind simultaneously through the practical regimen of abdominal respiration. That is what I call psycho (mind)-soma (body) tic modality of self-cultivation based on the regulative technique of abdominal respiration.

Thus respiration is the pivot or rather a "missing link" between mind and body, since it is actually a mediation or a "link" between mind which belongs to the autonomic nervous system (e.g. involuntary muscle, (e.g. myocardia), secretion of gastric acid, insulin in pancreas etc.) and body which is subject to the somatic nervous system (e.g. voluntary muscle that is pectoralis major, triceps or biceps branchii etc.). So we can carry out a "mysterium conjunctum" of body and mind not mystically but actually in this phenomenal world—to be what I call "Tao *qua* self."

We are now in a position to assert that the philosophy of medicine we find in the Chin-shu chapter of the *Lu-shi chun-chiu* furnishes us with the typical formulations of the cosmic harmony that is the holistic total of mind and body and, further, human beings and the whole universe under the great cosmic order of Tien.

Now I would like to take a step forward to the *Huang-ting nei-ching* and the other works on traditional Chinese medicine to clarify how they inherited and developed the cosmic harmony of "holistic total" hereinafter.

THE HUANG-TING NEI-CHING, AND OTHER WORKS ON TRADITIONAL CHINESE MEDICINE

The Huang-ting nei-ching is the first set of volumes with the complete theoretical formulations of traditional Chinese medicine in the Chinese history of medicine. The current volume of *Huang-ting nei-ching* principally consists of two sections [7], Su-wen and Ling-

---

[7] On the philological aspect of this classic, there are a lot of excellent works. I will just mention the one which benefited me most: Kosoto, Hirosi's 『中国医学古典と日本』 (Chinese classics of medicine and Japan), Tokyo: Hanawa Shobo, 1996, pp. 45-174..

shu[l], both of which can be said to have been compiled around the time of the Han dynasty. Su-wen chiefly discusses pathological formulations and Ling-shu describes acupuncture.

It goes without saying that there should be really a lot of interesting topics from various points of views, but the point to be taken in this paper *is* that the fundamental modality running through each of the theoretical formulations in this classic is the yin-yang wu-hsing[m] theory. The theory is the most conventional expression of the Chinese mode of thinking which has the same origin of cosmic order that we have seen in the *Lu-shi chun-chiu* derived from the concept of Tien. Accordingly, we can assert that the cosmic order represented by the concept of ching-chi in the *Lu-shi chun-chiu* has been developed to be the yin-yang wu-hsing theory in the *Huang-ting nei-ching* remaining intrinsically and semantically in the same mode.

Furthermore, more precisely, we can grasp the same but developed phraseology of the cosmic harmony as a holistic total in many passages of this volume. Actually they regarded our body, body-mind, and body-mind and the whole world to be one as a holistic total in the cosmic order and our healthy lives are accomplished by the cosmic harmony under the same order.

For example,

In the ancient times, a person who attained the Tao would follow yin-yang, accord with the way, keep moderate in foods and drinks, lead regular life and not work recklessly. Therefore, he could harmonize body and mind, achieve his longevity derived from Tien, and so pass away over one hundred years old[8].

In this passage, the cosmic order we saw in the *Lu-shi chun-chiu* is described typically through the new concept of yin-yang. As we see, it is just the same notion about our longevity which was delineated in the *Lu-shi chun-chiu*, that is the longevity through the cosmic harmony of holistic total. And this idea is theoretically formulated further through the epistemological scheme of yin-yang wu-hsing in those chapters of this classic as wu yun hsing ta lun, liu yuan cheng chi ta lun, etc., which is so called a pathological theory of "wu-yun[n]" that is yun-hsing (= movement) of wu-hsing.

Accordingly, it seems a quite natural result that this cosmic harmony, derived from the cosmic order formulated through the concept of yin-yang would yield such a clinical theory as follows:

A good acupuncturist would draw yang out of yin and yin out of yang, treat left by right and right by left, understand that by this and back by front, and he would grasp the reason of surplus and shortage, and see the subtle symptoms to know the diseases, then there would be no problem[9].
Too much yin harms yang, and too much yang harms yin[10].

The above passages assert that the proper balance of yin-yang, i.e. the cosmic harmony of holistic total, *is* the crucial condition for a healthy life and longevity, and imbalance and lack of harmony lead us to disease, therefore the main clinical procedure is "harmonizing" of yin-

---

[8] Huang-ting nei-ching, Ichikawa, Japan: Toyo gakujyutsu shuppansha, 1991, vol.1, p.28..
[9] ibid., p. 127.
[10] Ibid., p. 104.

yang wu-hsing. This idea is obviously the inheritance of that in the *Lu-shi chun-chiu* derived from the modality of "synthesis".

Now we will consider another classic of traditional Chinese medicine that is the *Shang-han-lun*[o]. The *Shang-han-lun* is the oldest classic for the remedy of acute febrile infections in traditional Chinese medicine. This classic is said to be originally compiled in the third century, around the end of the later Han dynasty, as a comprehensive survey of Chang-chung-ching's[p] pharmaceutics. It has been handed down to be printed and published in the tenth century, during the Song dynasty. Now, leaving aside questions of philology regarding this classic, I would like to point out the philosophical modality of the pharmaceutical theory of san-yin san-yang[q] *is* that same old cosmic order of holistic total we saw in the *Lu-shi chun-chiu*. To put it in another way, the cosmic harmony of holistic total derived from Tien which has been found originally in the *Lu-shi chun-chiu* is also expressed in the theoretical formulation of pharmaceutics in this book.

In this classic, human diseases, especially acute febrile infections, are identified in six stages, of three-yin and three-yang. They are: tai-yang[r], yang-ming[s], shao-yang[t], tai-yin[u], shao-yin[v] and chueh-yin[w], and are treated according to each phase of the six stages through the most appropriate formulae, e.g. in general, for the yang stages (tai-yang, yang-ming and shao-yang) han-chi[x] (cool efficacious formulae) like gui-chi-tang[y], ke-ken-tang[z] etc. should be taken, on the other hand, for the ying stages (tai-yin, shao-yin and chueh-yin) wen-chi[aa] (warm efficacious formulae) like ssu-ni-tang[bb], chen-wu-tang[cc] etc. should be taken.

This traditional Chinese pharmacological theory is actually formulating the cosmic harmony of holistic total, which is typically articulated as: cool efficacious formulae for the warm stages and warm efficacious formulae for the cool stages. At this point, we can see the typical example of the cosmic order contained in this volume.

As a parenthetical remark, I would point out the crucial modality of Chang's pharmaceutics—"synthesis", namely his 117 ways of pharmaceutics in this book is nothing but the "combinations" of 72 kinds of singular galenical without any "analysis". Chang just synthetically combined various galenicals for each phase or stage of disease under the cosmic harmony of holistic total. He was another resident under the cosmic order of Tien.

Now I would take another look at the *Shen-neng pen-tsao ching*[dd]. In this classic of traditional Chinese medicine, especially galenicals, those galenicals, even though they are divided into three levels, upper, middle and lower, yet are not analyzed in their component level like Theophrastus or Dioscorides in ancient Greece. They synthetically arranged/composed those galenicals into efficient pharmaceutics accoding to the chi-ching[ee] theory.

What is called "chi-ching" literally means "seven conditions" (of employment of the galenicals), e.g. tuan-hsing[ff] (single use), hsiang-shu[gg] (efficient reinforcement), hsiang-sha[hh] (toxicity offset), etc. They made various combinations of each single galenical in accordance with the efficiencies for each phase of diseases.

This best fitted cosmic harmony of pharmaceutical formula *is* one of the typical manifestation of the cosmic order of Tien derived from the intellectual modality of synthesis, which we saw in the *Lu-shi chun-chiu* earlier. We can see the same cosmic order here in this classic again. It seems reasonable to say that this traditional cosmic order has been inherited as an intrinsic principle in the field of Chinese traditional medicine for centuries.

Now that we have come this far, let us take one step forward to the impact and the development of this cosmic order particularly in traditional medicine in 10th-18th century Japan.

THE *ISHINPO*, THE *TON-I-SHO*, AND THE OTHER WORKS OF TRADITIONAL JAPANESE MEDICINE

Now we will consider the oldest classic of traditional Japanese medicine, the *Ishinpo*. This classic was edited by Tanba-no-Yasuyori[ii] (912?-995?) and presented to the Emperor En'yu[jj] in 984. He collected over 120 various kinds of old and rare books of traditional medicine not only from China but also Korea and even Japan, almost all of which are written in/before the Sui-Tang era (around 6th-10th centuries).

Tanba-no-Yasuyori cited a lot of topics and passages from those various volumes to edit this book, the *Ishinpo*. Accordingly, the *Ishinpo* is regarded as a tremendously valuable book from a philological point of view in that it carries a lot of fragments of those classics that have already been lost. It seems, however, I could leave this phase of this book untouched and proceed straight to the philosophical background of it, for there are excellent works from the philological points already.

On the other hand, we have to discern his philosophy of medicine relying on his choice of citations and only one chapter of his own writing in this book. In the preface to volume two of the *Ishinpo,* where the phrases of the classics of acupuncture are collected, Tanba-no-Yasuyori exceptionally attached his own brief note, since this volume was edited thoroughly according to his own ideas about acupuncture. This note explains:

> Those chapters about the points of acupuncture in the *Huang-ting ming-tang-ching*,[kk], the *Hua-tuo chen-chiu-ching*[ll] and the *Pien-chiao chen-chiu-ching*[mm] are exceedingly complicated and profound.
> At the same time, there are no old and wise authors whom we can consult with, so it is very difficult to understand them. It takes so much time to read and understand them, so actually we can not apply them to an emergency case. Also, for the same reason, when we try a moxibustion, we are often at a loss for the points, so I didn't classify the points so precisely, but merely classified some parts of head, face, hands and legs, etc [11].

Apparently, because Tanba-no-Yasuyori was an expert of acupuncture, he made his own description about it particularly precise, and he did not take too much complicated description found in the Chinese classics but adopted his own simple and easy way for convenience'sake, which would assume a typical Japanese modality of "import and modify" foreign thoughts and technology, that is, he was just in the midst of importing andmodifying the traditional Chinese medicine to adopt them to the Japanese life. In other words, Tanba-no-Yasuyori as a typical Japanese of those days imported a tremendous amount of the classics of Chinese traditional medicine, and attempted to modify the contents in order to accommodate them.

In this effort, he shows that this book is compiled thoroughly under the cosmic order we have seen in the first half of this paper, because all of the tremendous number of citations in this classic are actually described under the idea of cosmic order. Even though Tnaba-no-

Yasuyori himself was *not* conscious of it as a "theory", for he was just operating in an "import and modify" mode, yet he was distinctly conscious of it as a matter of fact.

We can see it in the fact that he quotes the *Nan-hai chi-kui nei-fa-chuan*[nn] to describe ssu-ta wei-he[oo] or ssu-ta pu-tiao[pp]—the four elements disorder, which is the theory that the disorder of four elements of every phenomenon in the world will cause diseases. It is evident that he, quoting this theory, actually compiled this volume under the cosmic harmony of holistic total derived from the cosmic order of Tien.

Now we will take a look at another classic of traditional Japanese medicine—the *Ton'isho*[qq]. In 12th-13th century, Japan mainly depended on the Buddhist priests to transmit traditional medicine, since those volumes of traditional medicine were often imported with the Buddhist canons and were read/studied by these priests. Kajiwara, Shozen, the author of the *Ton'isho*, is one of the typical Buddhist priest/medical practitioners of those days.

From a Japanese perspective, the *Ton'isho* is considered "the oldest" classic of traditional medicine in the sense that it is written in Japanese, and so it is not only one of Kajiwara, Shzen's main works on medical clinics but also one of the main works in this field in 12th century Japan. As compared with the *Ishinpo* by Tanba-no-Yasuyori, this volume is written in Kajiwara, Shozen's own words, despite being full of a lot of citations of Chinese classics of traditional medicine. Although we find a lot of quotations of Chinese classics in the volume, and Kajiwara, Shozen himself is strongly influenced by traditional Chinese medicine, nevertheless he wrote it his own words, as he himself describes below:

This book is written in Japanese, so it is easy for people to read and understand, not to be piled up unread. You, the readers, should always consult it to see the stigmas of complaints and the indications of drugs and face the diseases. This is my main intention[12]. Since this book is written in Japanese, it can convey the crucial points of medicine to all the people in order to relieve them [13].

We can see one typical stage of the Japanese "import and modify" mode in his description above, the more significant point is that his ideas express the idea of a cosmic order, which is of Chinese origin but at the same time well digested into the Japanese culture. Actually, he advocates theories of "cool efficacious formulae for the warm stages and warm efficacious formulae for the cool stages", ssu-ta pu-tiao, etc., which evidently means that he was in the cosmic harmony of a holistic total derived from the cosmic order whose origin is found in the *Lu-shi chun-chiu* in ancient China.

Now I will take up Kajiwara, Shozen's other major work the *Man'anpo*[rr], just for our reference. While the *Ishinpo* was written in Japanese, the *Man'anpo* is written in classical Chinese quoting many more Chinese classics of medicine. It is said that this book was written privately in order just to hand down his own proprietary recipe to his son, so he quoted various phrases from the Chinese classics of medicine directly in classical Chinese without any translations.

This book includes a lot of citations regarding various phases of therapeutics and remedies. As a matter of fact, this book is composed of that typical cosmic harmony of holistic total derived from the cosmic order of Tien, actually conveying the theory of yin-yang pu-tiao[ss], wu-yun liu-chi[tt], etc.

---

[11] Ishinpo, vol.2, MS. 24a-b.
[12] Ton'isho, vol.6, MS. 26a.

Now that we have come this far, we can assert that the cosmic harmony we see in those Japanese classics of traditional medicine above *is* one of the typical manifestations of the cosmic order of Tien derived from the intellectual modality of synthesis, which we saw in the *Lu-shi chun-chiu* earlier. We see the same cosmic order here in these classics. Since they occurred in the course of "digestion" of foreign technology and thoughts, there still remained several aspects which are "not totally Japanese", it seems quite reasonable to say that this traditional cosmic order from China has been inherited as an intrinsic principle in this field of Japanese traditional medicine. We can say that in these centuries, they were still in the midst of importing and modifying the idea of the cosmic order imported from the ancient Chinese classics of medicine. That was the situation those days in Japan.

It would still take some time for the Japanese medical practitioners to achieve the real Japanese aspects of this cosmic order. I could mention the names of Manase, Dozan[uu], Yoshimasu, Todo[vv], etc. who really achieved a Japanese version of the cosmic order. Now just for the sake of our future perspective, for he lived in 18th century—just after the era focused on in this paper, I would like to briefly consider Yoshimasu, Todo's philosophy of medicine below.

YOSHIMASU, TODO'S PHILOSOPHY OF MEDICINE

Yoshimasu,Todo(1702-1773) was one of the greatest medical practitioners in the Koiho[ww] school in Edo[xx] era Japan. There have been a lot of studies on his medical practices from the viewpoint of medical science and pharmacology. There have hardly been any studies, however, on his philosophy of medicine, even though his philosophy of medicine seems to have very significant suggestions for us. Accordingly, I would like to consider Todo's philosophy of medicine called manbyo-ichidoku-setsu[yy] through a study of his criticism of the theory of yin-yo go-gyo[zz], leaving aside precise philosophical and philological argument, in order to relate it to our main topic of cosmic order.

In the studies of Todo's philosophy of medicine, hitherto, it is generally accepted that he was quite emphatic in denying the theory of yin-yo go-gyo. He writes:

> We should not talk about human affairs in accordance with the theory of yin-yo go-gyo. But now, such talk has become fashionable, and the true way (of medicine) went out of use. ……Alas ![14]
> We can see the theory of yin-yo go-gyo in the Yu-shu[aaa] and Hung-fan[bbb] chapters.……However, they are merely the words of the theoretical formulations. If adapted to our pharmaceutics, it would bring about wrong results. This is why we do not take it [15].

Looking into Todo's descriptions much more precisely once again, however, we can see that he does not reject the theory of yin-yo go-gyo thoroughly. As he proclaims:

---

[13] ibid., vol.8, p.170..
[14] Kosho'igen, vol.1, in 『東洞全集』 (Todo's Opera), kyoto, Japan: Shibunkaku, 1970, p.42. About Yoshimasu Todo's philosophy of medicine, see my 『吉益東洞『古書医言』の研究』 (A study of Yoshimasu Todo's Kosho-igen), Tokyo: Kyuko shoin, 2004..
[15] Idan, ibid., p.448

Well, yin-yo is a matter of nature; not human society.[16]
Now, genki[ccc] is one fundamental ki of yin-yo from Heaven. Human beings are brought forth in it. This is a ki a-priori[17].

Todo never denies the very existence of the ki of yin-yo itself. He just refuses to apply the yin-yo, more precisely the *theory* of yin-yo, to his daily clinical practice. He was actually thinking in terms of that old cosmic order derived from Tien in ancient China. So if asked whether Todo really denied and rejected the theory of yin-yo go-gyo, then the answer is definitely "No". He didn't deny it nor reject it, but he didn't include it in his theoretical formulations.

Namely, first he clearly defines the distinction between theory and practice, offering the following explanation:

> According to an ancient saying: Just taking a good rest, even when you are ill, it is equal to seeing an ordinary doctor. Isoku[ddd] (=Todo=I) would say: When I found this ancient saying for the first time, I was so ashamed of myself as a medical doctor. ......As we can see the doctors who rely upon the theory of yin-yo do not obtain good results, I understand that these words are not irrelevant. ......Then I studied hard every day and night, and at last I became versed in the core point of the healing arts—the Tao of medicine, I-do[eee]— then I felt exempted from the censure of those ancient words. ......My apprentices, be discreet yourselves. Do not be deluded with biomedical theory or its technical terms. Even though you should read all of the books of biomedical technologies and memorize the technical terms, if you can not cure people of their diseases, then you can not be exempted from the censure of those words[18].

We can see clearly that Todo's main purpose *is* to practice his healing arts to cure peoples' diseases and not to make theoretical descriptions of biomedical techniques or symptoms through the theory of yin-yo go-gyo, which he believed might sometimes even be harmful to patients.

In other words, Todo seems to have an intense conviction that each medical practitioner must study and train in one's own practice of healing arts, and it is not the main job to formulate medical descriptions theoretically in the context of the theory of yin-yo go-gyo, criticizing those who adhered to the theory itself yet were not effective at curing diseases.

Here we see clearly that Todo almost unconsciously adopted that old cosmic order in his intellectual modality, but at the same time he didn't take the theory of yin-yo go-gyo as it is, he devised his own theoretical formulations.

And then, he devised manbyo-ichidoku-setsu, a medical theory that explains every phase of various diseases through one concept of "doku"[fff]—poison, as a descriptive formation of his expressions of his philosophy of medicine, he writes:

A master of healing arts does not rely upon medical examinations, but can just see the place where the poison of diseases byodoku[ggg][19].

---

[16] Kosho'igen, vol.1, ibid., p.42.
[17] *Idan,*, ibid., p.445
[18] (*Kosho'igen*, vol.4, ibid., p.121.
[19] Todo Sensei Tomonsho, ibid., p.463.

Medical doctors in an orthodox school would take manbyo-ichidoku-setsu, and remove the poison from the patients through perspiration, emesis, and excretion, then diseases and symptoms would all disappear.[20]

As I see it, Todo really was a master of healing arts who embodied the Tao of medicine, I-do, through his clinical training of healing arts and applied it to his biomedical practice. Holding firmly to the cosmic order of Chinese origin, Todo asserts his view on clinical praxis through his own words as well. This is typical of the Japanese scheme of "import and modify". We can see it everywhere in Todo's works now.

Now, leaving aside precise analyses of Todo's philosophy of biomedical theory, what should we learn from Todo's philosophy of medicine concerning our focus? That would be a well digested Japanese style cosmic order which is really in the Japanese style but actually derived from that old cosmic order in ancient China.

As for Todo, he clearly did not attach importance to knowledge-base clinical techniques, at least he strictly distinguished knowledge-base theory from the clinical techniques—in this point he is in the same traditional medical domain as that elucidated in the Chin-shu chapter of the *Lu-shi chun-chiu* as we saw above. That is not a phase of "science" in the Western sense where analysis is the main intellectual modality, but it is a typical variation of the intellectual modality of synthesis. Todo's works represent a typical Japanese manifestation of the cosmic harmony of holistic total derived from the cosmic order of Tien in ancient China.

Conclusion

Now we have seen a general survey of the traditional Chinese/Japanese medicine through the ages from ancient times to the 18th century in order to clarify that the philosophy of traditional medicine in 10th-13th century Japan is totally composed under the cosmic order of ancient China and would become thoroughly "Japanese" in 18th century Japan.

I first took up an early characterization of the philosophy of traditional Chinese medicine, which we can find in the Chin-shu chapter of the *Lu-shi chun-chiu*, since it describes the core modality of the philosophy of medicine, and is actually back grounded by the very common conception of cosmic order, found both in ancient China and in 10th-18th century Japan—the "holistic total."

In the West, "analysis" is the core philosophy (e.g. cellular-pathology, DNA, "spare parts", etc.). This modality hardly permits conceiving the world as a "holistic total." This is in contrast with the Chinese/Japanese philosophy of medicine, which has been conceived by "synthesis."

In other words, we could assert that the philosophy of medicine we see in the Chin-shu chapter of the *Lu-shi chun-chiu* furnishes us with the typical formulations of the cosmic harmony that is the holistic total of mind and body, as well as human beings and the whole universe under the great cosmic order yielded by Tien.

All of the above mentioned theories assert that the good balance of yin-yang, i.e. the cosmic harmony of holistic total *is* the crucial condition for a healthy life and longevity, and imbalance and lack of harmony leads us to disease. Therefore the main clinical procedure is

---

[20] *Kosho'igen*, vol.2, ibid., p.72.

the "harmonizing" of yin-yang wu-hsing. This idea is obviously the heir of that in the *Lu-shi chun-chiu* derived from the modality of "synthesis".

Above is certainly a crucial idea of traditional Chinese medicine; however it is not just a theoretical formulation, but a product of their philosophical practice of respiratorical training which we can see in Lao-tzu's philosophy of the Tao. In other words, in ancient China, philosophy is not just a survey of our theoretical contemplations but an intellectual practice to realize human truths in the depth of our unconsciousness. Thus, on this view, philosophy requires the practice of self-cultivative physical discipline. More specifically, Lao-tzu's philosophical practice involves abdominal respiration, i.e. stomach breathing, which leads into the deepest reaches of one's unconsciousness, and ultimately the consummation of one's true *self*. That is, Lao-tzu's philosophy has a somatic (=bodily) means of reaching, or rather embodying, the truth.

At the same time, a human being is a psycho-somatic being, i.e. a being of mind and body united together. So, at least in ancient times, medicine was not just a physical healing technique, but involved psychic (or mental) strategies to cure diseases, which means that kind of medicine has a psychological background like the Lao-tzu's philosophy I have been observing.

Now, this philosophical background, as I see it, is the pivot of Chinese philosophy of medicine in ancient times, with psycho-somatic (=body-mind) mode of philosophy. That is, traditional Chinese medicine in ancient times can not be understood properly without this philosophical background, since, in ancient times in China, philosophy has a practical side which fit together with the psychological side of medicine like two sides of one coin.

So if it had not been for this tangible practice, they could never attain this notion. This is the reason why I put stout stress on the philosophy-medicine linked together status. Without this philosophical comprehension, the wisdom of traditional Chinese medicine, being received attention at its mere cleverness, would never be integrated into our modern medical procedure. Medicine without philosophy is reckless, but philosophy without medicine is powerless.

Then I took another classic of the classics of traditional Chinese medicine, that is the *Shang-han-lun*. The *Shang-han-lun* is the oldest classic for the remedy of acute febrile infections in traditional Chinese medicine.

This traditional Chinese pharmacological theory actually formulates the cosmic harmony of holistic total, which is typically articulated as: cool efficacious formulae for the warm stages and warm efficacious formulae for the cool stages. At this point, we can see the typical example of the cosmic order contained in this volume.

And then I took one step forward to the impact and the development of this cosmic order particularly in traditional medicine in 10th-13th century Japan, taking a look at Tanba-no-yasunori's *Ishinpo* and Kajiwara, Shozen's works.

We could find out in this Japan's oldest classic of traditional medicine, the *Ishinpo,* that he was just in the midst of importing and modifying traditional Chinese medicine to adopt it to the Japanese life. In other words, Tanba-no-Yasuyori imported a tremendous number of classics of Chinese traditional medicine, and strove to modify the contents in order to accommodate them.

In this effort, he shows that this book is compiled thoroughly under the cosmic order we have seen in the first half of this paper. It is because all of the tremendous citations in this classic are actually described under the cosmic order. Even though Tnaba-no-Yasuyori himself was *not* conscious of it as a "theory", for he was just in the "import and modify" mode, yet he was distinctly conscious of it as a matter of fact.

The *Ton'isho* is considered "the oldest" classic of traditional medicine in the sense that it is written in Japanese, and so it is not only one of Kajiwara, Shzen's main works on medical clinics but also one of the main works in this field in 12th century Japan. As compared with the *Ishinpo* by Tanba-no-Yasuyori, this volume is written in Kajiwara, Shozen's own words, despite being full of a lot of quotations of Chinese classics of traditional medicine.

We could see one typical stage of the Japanese "import and modify" mode in his description, but the more significant point is that his ideas express the idea of a cosmic order, which is of Chinese origin but at the same time well digested into the Japanese culture. Actually, he advocates theories of "cool efficacious formulae for the warm stages and warm efficacious formulae for the cool stages", ssu-ta pu-tiao, etc., he was in the cosmic harmony of holistic total derived from the cosmic order whose origin is found in the *Lu-shi chun-chiu* in ancient China.

But at the same time, I should say that still in these centuries, they were in the midst of importing and modifying the idea of the cosmic order imported from the ancient Chinese classics of medicine. That was the situation those days in Japan.

It would still take some time for the Japanese medical practitioners to achieve the real Japanese aspects of this cosmic order. I could mention the names of Manase, Dozan, Yoshimasu, Todo, etc., who really achieved a Japanese version of the cosmic order. Then just for the sake of our future perspective, I briefly considered Yoshimasu, Todo's philosophy of medicine after that.

As I saw it, Todo really was a master of healing arts who embodied the Tao of medicine I-do through his clinical training of healing arts and applied it to his biomedical practice. Holding firmly to the cosmic order of Chinese origin, Todo asserts his view on clinical praxis— manbyo-ichidoku-setsu— through his own words as well. This is typical of the Japanese scheme of "import and modify". We can see it everywhere in Todo's works now. That is a well digested Japanese style cosmic order which is really in the Japanese style but actually derived from that old cosmic order in ancient China. Todo's works represent a typical Japanese manifestation of the cosmic harmony of holistic total derived from the cosmic order of Tien in ancient China.

At the same time, though I mentioned that in the West, "analysis" is the core philosophy but this modality hardly permits conceiving the world as a "holistic total", which has been conceived by "synthesis", Todo, understanding this way, took also an analytic way to galenicals, and wrote the *Yaku-cho*[hhh]. Consequently we can elucidate that he had a notion like Western "analyses" as early as in the Edo era Japan[21].

Now, three questions must be briefly cited and answered to tie things up and round up this essay. The first question is, "How could mortal medicine be immortal cosmos, how could tiny human physique be vast cosmos?" You do not understand, y friend. Human body does not duplicate the cosmos. It reflects its milieu. In mirroring cosmos is human health holistic.

The second question is, "How does Japanese medicine differ from Chinese? How does Japanese medicine modify Chinese?" Japan has accepted and modified Chinese language into Japanese language, Chinese culture into Japanese situation, as Japan adopts and adapts China

---

[21] On this issue, see my "YOSHIMASU, Todo's Philosophy of Medicine: In Comparison with It in Ancient China" forthcoming in Kampo Medicine, the Japan Society for Oriental Medicine

into Japanese clothe-style, Japanese dwelling-style, in Japanese sentiment, but the adaptation is so pervasive as to be inexpressible, in the same way as American adaptation of British language and customs is inexpressible yet quite visible. This essay tells of Japanese adoption of Chinese medicine, yet Japanese adaptation is so diffuse as to defy description.

Besides, importantly, the purpose of this essay is not to specify differences between China and Japan in their medicines, but to impress on us how *identical* they are in stressing and centering on cosmic holism in their medicines. Asking about their differences barks up the wrong tree.

The third question is, "How does Western medicine dovetail into Chinese-Japanese medicine?" The devil is in the details, they say. Analytical medicine of the West fills meticulous details into holistic cosmic medicine of China and Japan, while details of Western medicine gain their perspective and direction by being infused Japanese-Chinese medicine.

It was really too great a task for this short paper to give a comprehensive view on the long (ancient-modern) and wide (west-east) stream of traditional Chinese/Japanese medicine. Fortunately, I had one crucial conception, under which the whole tradition has been composed. That is the cosmic order of a holistic total. I still live in that cosmic harmony, and really fortunately I could finish this small paper wholly depending upon that great "harmony" conceiving each own characteristics. And again philosophy *is* the "missing link" among them.

GLOSSARY

a 呂氏春秋、尽数篇
b 老子、道
c 梶原性全、医心方
d 黄帝内経
e 内経医学
f 天
g 害
h 精
i 精気
j 修行
k 専気
l 素問、霊枢
m 陰陽五行
n 五運
o 傷寒論
p 張仲景
q 三陰三陽
r 太陽
s 陽明
t 少陽
u 太陰

v　少陰
w　厥陰
x　寒剤
y　桂枝湯
z　葛根湯
aa　温剤
bb　四逆湯
cc　真武湯
dd　神農本草経
ee　七情
ff　単行
gg　相須
hh　相殺
ii　丹波康頼
jj　円融
kk　黄帝明堂経
ll　華佗鍼灸経
mm　扁鵲鍼経
nn　南海寄帰内法伝
oo　四大違和
pp　四大不調
qq　頓医抄
rr　万安方
ss　陰陽不調
tt　五運六気
uu　曲直瀬道三
vv　吉益東洞
ww　古医方
xx　江戸
yy　万病一毒説
zz　陰陽五行
aaa　虞書
bbb　洪範
ccc　元気
ddd　為則
eee　医道
fff　毒
ggg　病毒
hhh　薬徴

In: Globalization Dynamics
Editor: Kuang-ming Wu

ISBN: 978-1-62100-750-0
© 2012 Nova Science Publishers, Inc.

Chapter 10

"EVER THE TWAIN SHALL MEET": TWO THINKING-TYPES IN SYNTHESIS IN TENSION

Zailin Zhang[*]
University, Shanxi, China

ABSTRACT

China is China, the West is the West, and the twain had better meet to inter-benefit. Accordingly, the gist of this chapter is that these two radically different styles of thinking must meet in differences to inter-benefit. So, the following pages have two sections: A. two thinking-styles meeting, and B. two thinking-styles meeting in differences. These two sections are of course closely interrelated, even words and ideas overlap, to compose globalization today.

Human thinking has at least two distinct styles, Chinese and Western. Kipling famously said, "Oh, East is East, and West is West, and never the Twain shall meet." Sadly, that quip was made back in 1889,[1] and globalization today makes the saying intolerably obsolete and mistaken. We must now quote him upside down, if we ever have to quote him. We must now say, "China is China, West is West, and *ever* the twain shall meet." The "shall" here is prediction and prescription. China-West meeting will happen in our globalization today, and we must promote such meeting.

Kipling has one grain of truth, though, and that is "China is China, West is West," that is to say, they *differ*, and, we claim, [a] meeting can happen only when there is difference, *and* [b] such differences met can only benefit different parties, though not without tension.

It is two distinct *modes* of thinking that compose two quite different worlds of things. The West thinks linearly, step by step, analytical and separative. Things are made of molecules made of atoms that are in turn made of indifferent electrons, etc. To understand a whole, we look into its parts as cogs that make up a mechanical indifferent whole. Western wording is

---

[*] Professor of Philosophy, Xian Jiaotong University, Shanxi, China. Professor Zhang's email is: zzl@mail.xjtu.edu.cn

accordingly alphabetical signs piling up into a word we use. The entire operation is clear-cut, exact, detached, detailed, and precise.

In contrast, in China, each thing is unique *and* interrelated. Things are organic both in themselves and as interrelated, net-crisscrossed with many such other nets. Even two words said identically would differ in meaning when uttered in differing tones. Even tones are *part* of the meanings of the words, as writings portray the sense of things concrete. Various ingredients compose flowers and birds, squirrels and trees, rain, clouds, and breeze, hills and rivers, in the sky and the fields.

"Are these ingredients mutually compatible or incompatible?" The answer is quite simple and surprising. They are compatible *and* incompatible. Its implications are staggering, as any organism typically is. "Compatible and incompatible" is mutually contradictory, internally in tension, and together interpenetrating. This amazing and strange "and" bespeaks how alive this whole organism of a thing is.

And then, just imagine how one such vibrant organism comes to another, and another, and then another, into a mutually compatible incompatible colony of a community inter-living Yin-Yang way, internecine inter-nascent 陰陽, 相剋相生, quite as alive all around. What tensed "family" of a cosmic-historic society they compose! Happiness in tension is here. This milieu of cosmic family is in sharp contrast to the West's lonely trek in dark indifferent outer space, through the telescope and in spacecraft, in search of a lone "habitable planet" with water in habitable temperature.

Let us now see their different worlds in time context. *In the West*, as surely as the past did happen and does not change, so surely will the future happen, and how and what the past is, so will be the future. Nature has its "laws" as determinate as hydrogen and oxygen combined make water, *always*.

Of course, such "natural laws" are just a statistical average of many past events contrived (in experiments) and observed (as the past), and we naturally meet many unexpected "violations" of such laws; they are accidents and exceptions we call "contingencies." Still we try our best to explain them with our "laws," according to our iron-clad "belief" (as Hume calls it), "as in the past, so in the future."

In China, however, nothing is set. As no one expected such and such an event to happen and yet it did happen in the past, so anything can happen at present and in the future. In the past, metal sank in water and stayed put on the ground. Now, metal routinely floats on water and navigates, and flies in the air, making routine commercial flights toward many faraway lands. Have we in the past expected all this to happen?

All we see is a trend "divined" in poetic mathematics of *Change Classic the I Ching* 易經. "Hydrogen and oxygen making water" is just an expected trend; in fact it is a miracle every time it happens, however expected beforehand. This is because it is entirely possible, though (we "divine") improbable, that hydrogen and oxygen gathered interacting would not one day make water. Even such staunch Western thinker as Russell would agree on the ground of "probability."[2]

Likewise, every event, even such "routine" happening as hydrogen and oxygen making water, is a happenstance happening in contingency, in short, a miracle, as the world is always alive, surprising us. If nothing can be determined and certain, then everything is dawn to

---

[1] Rudyard Kipling's Verse: Definitive Edition, Garden City, NY: Doubleday, 1940, p. 233.
[2] Bertrand Russell, The Problems of Philosophy, Oxford University Press, 1997, "induction" in pp. 60-69.

something novel, worth looking forward to and planning on. Every dawn differs from every other dawn, ever beginning anew, and "beginning anew" is always fresh, surprising.

This is to turn the headache of "contingency" in Western thinking and science into positive advantage of our living, Chinese way. And so we should never say "never" or "ever," but must always be on our toes, ready for things to happen beyond our readiness. We humans negotiate and catalyze such surprising trends of the times toward our advantage. We call it "history," of which we are its creative part. History is our objective lesson we make, which we bypass at our own peril.

It is thus that China is China, the West is the West, and the twain had better meet to inter-benefit. Accordingly, the gist of this chapter is that the two radically different styles of thinking must meet in differences to inter-benefit. So, the following pages have two sections: A. these two thinking-styles meeting, and B. the two thinking-styles meeting in differences. These two sections are of course closely interrelated, even words and ideas overlap, to compose globalization today.

A. Two Thinking-Styles Meeting

Each of our two thinking-styles has its own cluster of features, impossible to exhaustibly cite, and more or less interrelated among them on their own to form a coherent whole. These features are taken for granted and hidden to practitioners of a specific thinking-style, until these features show up clearly, and often irritatingly, in meeting the *other* thinking-style.

We now almost loosely, though not randomly, cite five salient examples of such meeting, among many others indefinite and various. They are [1] body-thinking meeting universal thinking, [2] story-thinking meeting analytical thinking, [3] child-thinking meeting adult-thinking, [4] relational thinking meeting isolation-thinking, and finally [5] concrete thinking meeting abstract thinking. Such meeting will show us how differently the different thinking-styles exhibit different milieus and different life-worlds.

ONE: body-thinking meeting universal thinking: Body-thinking stresses how human thinking always originates and continue in the human body, empirical, existential. Without human body, human thinking simply ceases. It sounds so trivial until we observe how easily various thinkers forget this base of thinking, to ruin their thinking itself, undermining itself by bypassing its basis, if not despising itself. Let me explain.

In our eagerness for high sublime universality freed from concrete details so senseless, we want, and want us all, to see from nowhere.[3] But how can we see without eyes? How can we see without seeing from specific somewhere concrete? "Seeing from nowhere" is an impossible contradiction; forcing it on thinking destroys thinking. Eagerly gazing at the stars and computing their various genres of universality, we are lost in them, and end up falling into a ditch here concrete. All this tragedy comes from our forgetting that we are concrete body concretely thinking the sense of concrete things.

In contrast, universal-thinking notes that thinking must go beyond particularities of time and space to soar up to concrete-indifferent universal truths. The human body is clearly

---

[3] See clever self-contradiction of Thomas Nagel in his *The View from Nowhere*, Oxford University Press, 1989. Ironically, the book is filled with concrete problems about our concrete self. He is caught in his concocted problem, a vision that is self-contradictory and impossible.

specific in time and in space, and needs some sort of universality to be "thinking" at all. This point is also a trivial common sense about thinking. Obviously, without universality in truth that is thought about, and without universal applicability of what we think here now to there then, thinking loses what it essentially is as "thinking."

TWO: story-thinking meeting analytical thinking: Body-thinking naturally thinks contiguously and organically as human body is an organ, a connected whole organ. Such organic connection weaves into a story to tell, and a story to hear, and a story to think about and *understand* what the story tells of, and thinking is for understanding, and so story-thinking is a legitimate thinking, thinking proper. All old ladies in any village naturally perform such story-thinking day in and day out.

In contrast, analytical thinking performs precise analysis of what we think about and how we think on. After all, thinking must be clear, and we cannot think clearly unless we analyze our thinking while we think about something. Thinking must be analytical and precise; otherwise, it is not thinking. Story-thinking must thus gain clarity by analytical thinking.

THREE: child-thinking meeting adult-thinking: The child is the origin of all thinking, all integral, pure, and straight. All thinking by definition must then proceed as the child does, without pretension, without cheating, and without scheming of any sort. Losing such radical existential integrity of the child in thinking, and our thinking loses itself. It turns into contrivance and manipulation and automatic management; it is not thinking any more.

In contrast, adult thinking says that the child is still growing, and so what the child thinks about cannot be taken as reliable, much less as final truth. The child needs guidance of the mature adult thinking to think on correctly, without error. The adult says this is also quite obvious. The child still needs adult tutorial to grow up yet.

FOUR: relational thinking meeting isolation-thinking: Relational thinking takes any entity as uncertain, if not non-existent, until it is placed in the context of network of relations with others. It is relation, sociality in the widest sense, which determines the quality, defines the essence, and sets the function of an entity. It is relation that is the be-all and end-all of all beings.

In contrast, isolation-thinking insists that any matter in its singularity is what it is as it is, irrespective of where and how it is put. Without this basic what-it-is, any further relation of any sort is as irrelevant as any dinner is meaningless without a person present to enjoy it. In fact, we must have what-it-is of a thing before we can even understand how its relation with others influences it. Enjoyment is a relation subsequent to the prior separate existence of dinner and person enjoying it.

FIVE: concrete thinking meeting abstract thinking: Concrete thinking takes it as obvious that thinking is concerned with concrete matters and affairs. In fact, such thinking on concrete stuff must itself be concrete, that is, thinking itself must be concretely thought before we can think about things concrete. No-concrete thinking cannot think about concrete things at all.

In contrast, abstract thinking insists that the very thinking by definition means an act beyond things concrete, in order to think *about* anything at all, concrete or otherwise. This is because a thing is obviously not thinking, and thinking is obviously not a "thing." If thinking is collapsed into thing thought about, thinking would not be able to think at all. Thinking is by nature "abstract," that is, abstracted from any thing concrete to think about.

Looking over such meeting between these two styles of thinking, we cannot help but be struck by the wide difference between them in their approaches, their atmospheres, their milieus, and their whole life-worlds that both sorts of thinking respectively dwell in, in which to function. Their differences emerge in their meeting, which is made possible by the differences. No difference, no meeting, and no meeting, no difference.

Difference is thus so exciting, to reveal difference alive in meeting alive, so radical and existential, that globalization today reveals, as it at the same time facilitates these two thinking-styles to meet in close contact, in tension. To this fascinating meeting in *difference* between the two modes of thinking, we now turn.

B. TWO THINKING-STYLES MEETING IN DIFFERENCES

The above description of the meeting, in radical differences, between the very *modes* of thinking, fascinatingly reveals how important and indispensable such meeting is for human thinking. After all, all of us are human, all imperfect, and so it is best that we come together to mutually complement. Human differences bespeak human necessity of mutual enrichment. Besides, such beneficial mutuality is now so conveniently and extensively facilitated by globalization for the first time in world history.

No more guesswork is needed about "human enlightenment" as envisioned by the Renaissance thinkers, and no more theorization about the "universality of mankind" is needed as spun and speculated on by the metaphysicians in the past since the Greek sophists. In fact, their dreams and theorizations are rendered obsolete as idle myths, at a stroke, by the stark actual face-to-face meeting of the *ways* of thinking in our small Global Village today.

Such meeting is so violent, however, that it is often called "confrontation." It is a brutal daily fact, often exhibited in world wars economic, political, and military, which are being constantly inter-jostled and fought out, in raw brutal contacts among downright differing cultures and life-worlds. At the base of all this conflict is the meeting in differences of two types of *thinking*.

In the context of globalization today, the result of such radical meeting is obvious. The meeting can spell either mutual butchery or mutual prosperity, either the cutthroat zero-sum game or the win-win co-thriving. Clearly, all of us must meet, not in order to gun down the other but to learn from one another, to enrich one another, to inter-help to co-thrive, on pain of perdition both individual and as a whole. And so, in this section we have three subsections: [1] challenges and responses, [2] synthesis, its how, and [3] the result as globalization.

[1.] Challenges and Responses

For this purpose of inter-thriving, we must detail how we can meet to dialogue between two styles of thinking above delineated. Again, we rehearse their dialogues in the same order as above, in five instances. Because today we see that only the West is complaining and despising China, we here simulate the critical China-West dialogues by China responding to the West's criticisms.

ONE: body-thinking meeting universal thinking: Universal thinking would of course complain about the mortal specificity of human body. Body-thinking thinks on the basis of human body, and human body, however we define it, is specific, fragile, local, and mortal. Human body is not at all "universal" as required by the nature of thinking.

Agreeing that thinking must be somehow universal, China's responses are two. One, body-thinking is family-thinking beyond individual human bodies that continue the legacies of bodily family from one generation to another. In fact, "generation 世代" means a continuation of bodily births through time. Two, such body-thinking as family-thinking naturally generalizes itself in cosmic dimension, vastly expanding with the cosmic cyclonic thrust to flood all in all 浩然之氣, into oneness with Heaven and Earth, *and* at the same time generalizes into unending series of time-narrative we call "history."

Such family-continuation into cosmic history is repeatedly stressed in China, as typified in the *Filiality Classic 孝經* and the *Great Learning 大學*, both intoned routinely and daily as Chinese common sense. There is no cosmos without the concrete human body thinking, being aware of it and elucidating it, *and* promoting it as cosmic family. By the same token, there is no history of joys and sorrows, elations and disasters, without the concrete human body thinking producing it and continuing it, *and* learning from it and being guided shaped by it without end.

All this describes the concrete incorruptibility 不朽 of the human body in China. It is no accident that China is called *the* culture of family and the world's only culture of history. China is thus concretely body-thinking and concretely "universal" in time as history, and in space as family members between Heaven-father and Earth-mother.

TWO: story-thinking meeting analytical thinking: Analytical thinking would of course complain of story-thinking as muddled, with no clear-cut principle, paradigm, system, and much less norm at all. In stories anything goes, just wandering along aimlessly, full of information without rhyme or reason, without backbone of any sort.

Story-thinking can respond with three points. *One*, "anything goes" implicates comprehensive netting of anything that comes in. This is what analytical thinking lacks that tends to exclude what does not fit in its preset analytical frame. Story-thinking can even revise its own frame of story-netting and storytelling as things come in.

Two, story-comprehensiveness does not imply arbitrary inclusion, simply being dragged on by whatever comes in. A typical example of story-thinking is fiction. Fiction has its own inevitable proceeding and outcomes; here is nothing to be mocked. Things must happen this way, and not otherwise. History says things, as they happened, must have happened thus and thus, and *not* otherwise. Story-inevitability is alive to facts that keep happening. That is what makes history so iron-clad an objective-factual lesson to guide our living on.

Three, story-thinking re-describes and re-presents, presenting another look, a second different look, at the whole bunch of affairs. This "re-" and this "another" are our reflective gaze, to gain a new perspective of coherence hitherto unnoticed. Story-thinking is a re-thinking, alive to ever changing facts, a reflection that penetrates the state of affairs. Story-thinking reveals its own system flexuous, factual, and fitting to things that keep changing, so that it can guide our life.

THREE: child-thinking meeting adult-thinking: Adult-thinking would of course look down on the child who is still growing, and growing to the adult maturity that the adult represents. The child can thus never to be trusted. Instead, the child must be led and guided by the sure hand of trustworthy adult and mature intelligence of the adult.

The child-thinking would no doubt respond with two points. *First*, looking down on the child amounts to looking down on the *base* of the adult. Wordsworth said, "The child is father of the man," and Freud and Erickson took the quip so seriously as to build their entire psychologies on this truth, and designed psychotherapies of the *adults*. At the very least, adults must learn from the child on how to learn; after all, no one is perfect, and learning is quite indispensable to human living. Stop child-learning, and we stop living as adult or as child; we simply die. This is because of the following reason.

Secondly, growing is life. Without growing we are dead. "Immature" is green, "green" is growing. "Socrates is green," said Wallace Stevens. In contrast, "mature" is ripe, and "ripe" is ready to rot and die. Thus paradoxically, to be mature is to die, and to *yearn* to mature is vigorous life that is the child. Someone said that he would rather pursue truth than having it. We must be children of all ages to pursue, to learn, and to grow without end.

FOUR: relational thinking meeting isolation-thinking: Isolation-thinking would say that within whatever relation an entity has around it, "it" must be "it" first to be related and influenced, and perhaps even changed. Otherwise, nothing is there to relate or to change. Relational thinking would respond, saying that there is no such fictive existence as "entity in itself" in the first place. The response can be elucidated somewhat this way.

All things are both born related and *defined* in their mutual relations. Relation is absolutely prior, ontologically and epistemologically, in being and in knowing. We are always having been born by a plurality of people, our parents and/or our parental personnel in a medical clinic.

"In the beginning is relation," said Buber in his philosophical poetry that meditates on anything and everything.[4] This is why China is profoundly family-centered, and family-oriented, even in its meditations on the Heaven-father and the Earth-mother. People in the West also have the familiar notion of "Mother Nature" quite routine.

FIVE: concrete thinking meeting abstract thinking: To abstract thinking, "concrete thinking" is a contradiction in terms, because "thinking" is not concrete but *about* the concrete, which is a mere raw material, quite raw, uncooked, and undefined, until it is thought about and processed by abstract thinking.

In response, concrete thinking would say that such stance of abstract thinking is itself a contradiction, trying to abstract itself out of the concrete while trying to enter the concrete to think about the concrete. It is simply impossible to pull out so as to pull in, trying to leave away while trying to go in. Abstract thinking is doing opposite contradictory moves at the same time.

Abstract thinking is a contradiction, impossibility in thinking and in action, also for this simple reason. In order to think of anything at all, thinking must be embedded in that something to feel its impact and its modus vivendi. To be embedded in something is not to melt away in it. Our very act of embedding requires that we must be distinct from what we are embedded in, as our swimming requires that we are not water.

Such concrete swimming in the concrete *is* the modus operandi of concrete thinking. If thinking is to be thinking about things concrete at all, thinking must be concrete to think about things concrete. Nothing is more natural than this requirement to thinking. This is the *first* response of concrete thinking, that nothing is more natural and logical than thinking as "concrete."

Of course, *secondly*, abstract thinking would say that the concrete is so murky in itself, in need of being abstracted its "principles" and "structure." Concrete thinking would respond in these two ways, negatively and positively. Negatively, the so-called "principles" and

---

[4] Martin Buber, *I and Thou* (1958), tr. Ronald Gregor Smith, NY: Scribner Classics, 2000, p. 31.

"structure" are clearly there as bones in a body, quite visible *within* the very movements of the body called the concrete, but these bones cannot be exposed as bones. Exposed bones must be put back into the flesh of the concrete as it is, alive and on the move. And this operation of putting-back in *is* concrete thinking to correct abstract thinking.

Positively, it is the task of concrete thinking to clearly show the principles alive and hidden *in* the movements of the concrete. "*How* does it do it?" Concrete thinking *shows* the concrete principle-bones by sensitively trailing along the contour of the movements alive, freely going on, and this trailing is concrete thinking.

Concrete thinking thus presents the actual as the actual, to jolt us, to evoke and awaken *our* attention to actuality, but without clearly saying it out as abstract thinking would do, to incur the violent unnatural bone-exposure. Thus, concrete thinking is sensitively tacit in understanding, as mother besides her beloved boy Tommy, always watching, but never interfering. China calls it non-doing wu wei 無為; it is a sort of act, neither letting go nor actively forcing.

[2.] The How of Synthesis, Modus Operandi of Joining

Differences are usually alien and distasteful irritants to us. We are surrounded by others different from us, so we have to manage differences. Our requirement is that we must deal with them resolutely with respect of the other as the other, not me; the other is never to be taken for granted, much less abused.

On the contrary, we must join with our others in inter-need to inter-complement. Such a joining is essential to growth in the integrity of our mutual selves, but it takes tact, discernment, and patience to execute. Again, we go over the same five instances to illustrate how synthesizing things can proceed.

ONE: body-thinking joining universal thinking: Body-thinking must not be locked in itself but must open out, guided by the universal vision of universal thinking. This is because body-thinking agrees that thinking must carry some sort of universality. Universality-thinking, on its part, agrees that body-thinking is thinking embodied in existence, that is, internal to existence.

"Universality," for all its ubiquity, is internally embodied in existence of specific sorts. Universality in abstraction, separate from a variety of existence, is a figment of baseless imagination, a non-existence in our thinking world. Universality must be a plural, according to the plurality of actual existence.

Thus, stone-universality is one sort of universality, plant-universality is another sort, the animals have another, and the humans have yet another, and these various universalities somehow come together to compose a family of universals, and, importantly, no "family" can exist without the body with its body-thinking; there exists no family without the body in body-thinking.

TWO: story-thinking joining analytical thinking: Story-thinking agrees that stories have their own analytical clarity and structure, while analytical thinking agrees that analysis and clarity are specific to each sort of existence, that analysis discerns stone-clarity to somehow differ from plant-clarity, animal-clarity, etc., and species-analysis clarifies and distinguishes them respectively. Besides, importantly, the process and the results of specific analytical clarifications and distinctions can be classified and understood only in the mode of story-thinking.

THREE: child-thinking joining adult-thinking: Child-thinking agrees that the child has its own immaturity ready and eager to learn and grow, while adult-thinking turns deep, vital, and vast by learning from the child's learning, as the adult learns the child's purity and yearning in the child's learning.

The child gives vitality to the adult, as the adult gives sophistication to the pursuit and adventure of the child. The Great Adults are those who lose none of their child-heart as their root (Mencius, Li Chih[5]), as the child continues enthusiastically to learn from the adult. Adults are children of all ages, as the children admire the adults, eager to learn from the adults to grow on their own.

FOUR: relational thinking joining isolation-thinking: Every being, human and non-human, is defined by its social relation with the others, while their relation is composed by the singularity of every being. The one cannot exist without the other. On one hand, the individual would be lost into non-entity without its relation with the others; there cannot be a Robinson Crusoe of lonely island. On the other hands, in the music of the family, every note of the individual member is special, cherished by the family, as every individual is an essential component of the relational whole.

Isolation obtains only by isolating an existent from its inter-existent context, while relation makes sense on the basis of the singularity of an individual. Thus relational thinking and isolation thinking are two complementary sorts of perspective and thinking, contrary and even contradictory, but not inter-opposed but, on the contrary, inter-implicative. The one cannot exist without the other.

FIVE: concrete thinking joining abstract thinking: The concrete and the abstract are actually two sides of the same coin, called "actuality." The abstract cannot exist without abstracting itself from its base the concrete, as the concrete appears not arbitrary but significant, through abstract consideration of it. Actuality is composed of such an intimate shuttle between the concrete and the abstract, and so actuality cannot be understood by one sort of thinking alone, concrete or abstract. This point is a corollary to the above point-FOUR, as the point-FOUR is a corollary to this point.

In sum, it is thanks to this interrelation between our two styles of thinking that the whole world of thinking comes alive and varied, to open out vast beyond here now, horizon after horizon, milieu beyond milieu. Thinking envisages an exploding universe as a result. Such explosion is globalization, enriched by inter-complementation of China and the West in their respective modes of thinking.

[3.] The Goal: Globalization

Now, what all this dialogue accomplishes is globalization with two features, [a] synthesis [b] in revolutionary tension. *First* of all, the above dialogues are performed for the purpose of synthesis, coming together in mutual need and inter-enriching complementation, negatively and positively. *Negatively* speaking, we parody Kant and say, clarity without the concrete is empty, as the concrete without clarity is blind.

On one hand, clarity without the concrete is empty, as the world's master mathematician Whitehead, who produced revolution in mathematics with multi-volume *Principia Mathematica* with his student Bertrand Russell, quipped, "The exactness is a fake" without concrete common sense to guide it. Without common sense, "One and one make two" cannot operate, as one spark added to a load of gunpowder does not make two. Our common sense easily sees it, while mathematical exactness cannot see.[6]

On the other hand, the concrete without clarity is blind. We would be forced to wallow in unending series of wishy-washy information, if we are not clear in our discernment. Even the seemingly offhand journalistic reports of daily happenings need to have some order of presentation, if not at least a provisional judgment on the situation, to clarify what is going on. This fact is so obvious as to require no elaboration.

Positively speaking, China's slogan during the May Fourth Movement days is correct. China must embody China while benefiting from the West 體中用西. At the same time, the West also must embody the West itself while benefiting from China. Such inter-benefiting, on the basis of being respectively they themselves, consolidates them respectively.

But, and this is the *second* point, we can do so only on two indispensable conditions. One, we must respect differences, never suppress them, never be unwilling to be corrected by the other party, and two, we must be prepared for tensions and conflicts as we do so, as above instantiated. This is because our respect of differences and our learning from differences are quite painful, irritating, shaking up as its does our foundational attitude; our existential basis is shaken and often pulverized to pieces before we can reconstruct us ourselves into ourselves.

As a result, the basic attitude-revolution on each side is inevitable, and required, and the revolution is not a pretty sight nor can it be easily performed. But the benefits on both sides are unmistakable and enormous, for the result is a holistic renovation and reconstruction. Such revolution is absolutely required of all of us living in Global Village in this age of globalization. Such global synthesis is to be routinely executed on a daily basis. We can have no ifs or buts about it.

In this light, monocultural dominance, in a refusal of reciprocity, spells stoppage of thinking, and so monocultural dominance amounts to a brain-death, a suicide. Even Socrates himself said of thinking to be an inherent dialogue (in *Theaetetus* 189E-190) and distrusted writing because it lacks dialogue (in *Phaedrus* 275-277). His self-examination is self discoursing self, and is conducted in the market-place in intense dialogues with people, with anyone interested.

Thus, dialogue is a necessary means to basic attitude-revolution not at all comfortable, yet quite beneficial to all parties concerned, as long as all parties concerned are courageously willing to respect distasteful mutual differences, accept the basic painful challenges to our own hidden assumptions, and are willing to be displayed in public our own mistakes, and learn from uncomfortable—to say the least—differences from our accustomed way of life.

All these performances, courageous or not, are analogous to being forced to taste an alien dinner utterly "distasteful" to our accustomed dinner to our comfortable palate. Nothing is

---

5 Mencius 4B12. <童心說> in 李贄文集, 卷一, 北京社會科學文獻出版社, 2000, pp. 91-93.

[6] This is his last public statement, in *The Philosophy of Alfred North Whitehead*, ed. Paul Arthur Schilpp, La Salle, IL: Open Court, 1951, pp. 699-700.

more uncomfortable than such acts of facing the others different from us. All this meeting in tension is the modus operandi of globalization togetherness.

The above description sounds rather arid and abstract. So, let us cite four concrete examples of what would happen as a result of China meeting and cooperating with the West. The four examples are cited in their progressive order of the concrete, the general, and the universal, and respectively in this order as well.

The first example is my mother's photograph. It was taken at a specific spot and specific moment, so it was a concrete happening. This picture typifies my mother as she is, for *whenever* I see this picture I see her, so the picture is general. She is now physically gone, yet she is alive vividly here now with this picture at my side, so this picture is a universal while it is concrete and general. This is the most concrete example that shows the concrete, the general, and the universal.

The second example is a bit general beyond being concrete, yet it is still concrete. It is a painting I love of four kids spinning tops; they are dancing, quite excited. This painting must have been inspired by a specific occasion of top-spinning kids, and so it is concrete. The painting typifies kids shouting jumping so active; they *are* tops spinning! And so the painting is general. And yet, "they" are nowhere, for it is after all an imaginative "painting," and so it is universal.

The third example is concretely general. We latecomers see older Confucius (born 551 BCE) and younger Socrates (born 470 BCE) in the world history. Both were specific persons lived at specific time and space, and so they are concrete. Still, Confucius typifies China as Socrates typifies the West, so they are general. Confucius is China's *ideal* as Socrates is the West's *ideal* beyond here now, so they are universal. History is such general description so concrete, and concretely specific yet quite general.

The fourth example is rather universal. It is fiction. Kazantzakis (1885-1957) omitted, changed, and added to St. Francis of Assisi's sayings and deeds, from a need to match St. Francis' essence, to turn him into legend "truer than truth," to fulfill our obligation to transubstantiate matter into spirit.[7] His legend is fact more factual, the universality of fact, as chronicled information is bare dead skeleton, less than the "true fact" in flesh and blood.

The pithy four Gospels dramatically testify to "*the* life of Jesus" in four ways. Tolstoy's magnificent *War and Peace* (1864-69) covers the war during 1805-20 in his lifetime.[8] It is a story quite concrete. At the same time, it is so popular worldwide even today because the story powerfully typifies war and peace in general. It is a general description of war and peace. Still, this fiction is meant to be fictive only, to cover the world's war-turmoil and its relief in peace everywhere, and so this fiction is a universal.

Surveying all these examples, we are struck by the fact that without China's body-concrete thinking, it would have been impossible to notice such impressive matters concrete, general, and universal. At the same time, however, without the West's logical sensitivity, it would have been impossible, either, to draw out all such above in this logical order. Thus, all above is the fruit of China-West inter-enrichment.

Now, listen to this heart-warming incident. It does not matter whether this incident is fictive or factual. It is just wonderful all around, all so irresistible that I have heard it quoted

---

[7] Nikos Kazantzakis, *God's Pauper: St. Francis of Assisi* (1962), London: Faber and Faber, 1988, Prologue.

[8] For an accurate and convenient survey of information on *War and Peace*, consult *Benét's Reader's Encyclopedia*, Third Edition, 1987, p. 1044.

many times. It says that two disciples were hotly arguing against each other. Their Master went to one of them and said, "I think you are right," and then went to the other and said, "I think you are right." The third disciple beside them protested, saying, "But Master. They are arguing *against* each other. How could they both be right?" The Master paused, and then smiled and said, "And I think you are right, too."

Did you get the point? Here, these three disciples contentiously argued back and forth, hotly disagreeing one with another, and also with their Master. In all this, they indicate that they are all one-sided and imperfect, that they need one another, and therefore they all do well to gather together to complement one another. Their Master is our globalization that is a gathering in disagreements approved! In fact, such arguing all around is one sort of inter-complementation together, Master warmly approves.

Thus the Master's another delightful implication is the result, that we can be privy to *dialogues* since of old, among sages and common folks of all lands. Confucius "tells without creating" (7/1), to echo Socrates' midwifery. Both thereby "create" in their dialogue partners. But they differ. Confucius' tells of the ancient, while Socrates' midwifery delivers the present self by logically asking for self-examination. Confucius is historical; Socrates digs into the present, quite unhistorical.

Still, Confucius also self-examines 自省 in studying 學 and reflecting 思 (1/4, 2/15). His method is to go through all into one (4/15, 15/2). Socrates' method is questioning in logical analysis without ceasing. Both provoke, never give; both ask, never answer. Therefore both are fascinating sights to behold to learn from, to go into our own self-revolutions. This is why they are sages.

They are sages due to their skillful and persistent dialogues that we overhear. We latecomers see them side by side and hear them talk one to the other. Such is globalization today. Confucius and Socrates are alive here shaking hands in smiles, words forgotten. Such a pregnant scene we have now here!

All their deep telling pasts are the present alive here, inviting us all to join in for a cup of tea, as we smile one to another all around among us all over the globe, inter-disagreeing. Nothing is new; it is out of the past. Nothing matters; all is at present fully in view, and every one of us is welcome into their dialogues inter-disagreeing, continuing ever since time immemorial, everywhere. Such continuation of dialogues all around is globalization, as China meets the West in all their differences.

All this is what the Master tells them, by approving them all, saying "you are right" to them all, to thereby announce their dawn of globalization togetherness. Their "right"-dawn is also ours, for their Master is also ours smiling at our side. He *is* the all-"right" dawn of globalization to all of us all over the world.

Here, our challenging inter-dialogues, among different thinking horizons of this uncomfortable sort, shall redound to deepening and enriching China, and deepening and enriching the West, to deepen and enrich all of us. "China is China, West is West" still, but now breathing deeply at the dawn deeper richer to each of us in Global Village, shimmering with various life-worlds under the global sunlight of dawn.

In fact, such continuous deepening and enriching *is* the globalization process truly so called. Inter-engagement of our two modes of thinking, China and West meeting constantly, is the dawn of globalizing China, as the West is just beginning to be en-lightened by China. We are all obligated to promote such dawn of globalization. "Is globalization process its dawn or itself?" Good question, my friend. Globalization is the process of globalizing, and so globalization is itself ever at its own dawn, isn't it?

This point cannot be overemphasized. Our modes of thinking are tightly intimate with the process of globalization. As the way we think differs one from the other, the world comes to differ one from the other. As thinking shifts, so the world turns; it is thinking that turns the world. The way people think determines *how* the world proceeds to come to be the new world. What is objectively out there is actually dependent on how we actually think. Our mode of thinking is the constitution of the world. Our lifeworld is the world of *our* thinking.

Now, "China is Chinese, and the West is Western" shows the world as plural as human cultures are many, i.e., as all our modes of thinking are so varied. In all this, interestingly, such our variety of modes of thinking implicates that the "other" modes of thinking different from "ours" are taken by us as "false," and so our meeting amounts to our inter-falsifications quite unpleasant.

"They are so obnoxious! Of course, *they* are false," *we* say as we meet them. Such inter-falsification in turn turns the meeting of basic modes of thinking into a vibrant confrontation of differences in cultures, to cultivate our mutual tolerance of one another to inter-learn, via inter-falsification so unsavory.

Falsehood naturally implicates correction, as existence inter-exists. Our discovery of inter-falsification ciphers our reciprocal responsibility to inter-"right" names the other professes. All this inter-righting of names is beyond China's initial intention in its history among the Confucians and the Name-Scholars, the socio-ethicists and the conscientious logicians.

Thus all of us today must use these inter-contradictions among us to "right names 正名" to inter-adjust basic cultures, our very modes of thinking. Such is the global seriousness of "righting names" beyond what China traditionally thought. As thinking names things, so rightly naming things thinks things rightly, and we thereby create the rich prosperous globe "right for us all." Righting names among cultures is beyond cultures to globalize all cultures.

All this amounts to saying this point quite crucial. Our thinking is our microcosm, and our microcosmic thinking redounds to macrocosmic significance. Our personal mode of thinking steers the very mode in which the whole world comes to exist. "Right" in righting-names here then bespeaks our shared socio-ethical norm in our global, dialogical responsibility. The way we think imposes its intrinsic responsibility on us, which is quite global in extent. It is such a scary thought, much scarier than the traditional saying, "A butterfly's one single flutter in New Zealand causes several huge tsunamis in Green Land."

"Globalization" indicates mutual responsibilities among all our world cultures to interlock one local culture to another culture local, to dovetail the Chinese mode of thinking into the Western mode of thinking, and also the Western into the Chinese, so as to pluralize and prosper our lifeworld. This is globalization that turns one into many so rich so variegated. Thus to globalize is to pluralize our lifeworld, to enrich our Global Village, by inter-learning among various "false" modes of thinking to "right" one another.

Our Global Village is then far from being an indifferent melting pot. The Village is instead a kaleidoscope of bewildering rainbows whose shimmering multidimensional beauty depends on its ingredient colors, as the rainbows in turn consolidate and respectively strengthen co-responsive integrities of the varied interweaving colors of our modes of thinking.

China is Chinese, the West is Western, and the twain simply must meet to inter-enrich our shared globe both one and many. Our Village is one depending on the many and the many being enhanced by so many ones interweaving. Globalization and the variety of individual modes of thinking thus inter-enhance to inter-enrich.

Globalization simply collapses if the twain of China and the West do not meet in their modes of thinking. Inter-meeting of basic modes of thinking is the *sine qua non* of globalization. Let us repeat this important point. Such radical meeting of the globe's various modes of thinking is the be-all and end-all of globalization, as it is the modus operandi and modus vivendi of globalization.

"Have you overstated the case, though?" On the contrary, I simply elucidated the stark *fact* of globalization in this essay. It is that the meeting of the modes of thinking *is* essential globalization so essential to our thriving together globally, on pain of dying-alone together, again, globally.

C. Global Dynamics

In: Globalization Dynamics
Editor: Kuang-ming Wu

ISBN: 978-1-62100-750-0
© 2012 Nova Science Publishers, Inc.

Chapter 11

TRANSLATION IN GLOBALIZATION

Kuang-ming Wu[1]
Taiwan, ROC

ABSTRACT

This chapter on translation considers "translation" in global context in three sections in eleven points, to punch out the claim that pan-translation makes for globalization, if not composes globalization. Section A says both translation and mistranslation perform globalization. One, ideal translation goes invisible as no-being. Two, mistranslation is quite useful. Three, how mistranslation benefits us is an exciting story. Four, mistranslation is thus a powerful dynamo to enriching globalization. Section B considers origin and function of translation in globalization, by Five, looking into the archeology of translation. Six, all cultural activities are translations. Seven, we have laws of cultural traffic in globalization. Eight, translation is the last stage of "translations" in cultures. Section C explains translation as living globalization. Nine, "one" and "many" are intercultural. Ten, translation is living. Eleven, translation is globalization unfinishable.

Globalization gathers different peoples of different cultures, and so translation is obviously essential to globalization. Let us begin considering—however we try, we just begin to consider, we just scratch the surface—what translation is, and how it is done, by starting at playing with the well-known cliché, "The medium is the message," taken out of Marshall McLuhan's original narrow context of technological communications (1967), and consider "translation" in global context in three sections in eleven points, to punch out the claim that pan-translation makes for globalization, if not composes globalization.

Section A says both translation and mistranslation perform globalization. One, ideal translation goes invisible as no-being. Two, mistranslation is quite useful. Three, how mistranslation benefits us is an exciting story. Four, mistranslation is thus a powerful dynamo to enriching globalization.

---

[1] E-mail address: kmwu2002@yahoo.com (Professor of philosophy, University of Denver, Colorado, USA)

Section B considers origin and function of translation in globalization, by Five, looking into the archeology of translation. Six, all cultural activities are translations. Seven, we have laws of cultural traffic in globalization. Eight, translation is the last stage of "translation" in cultures. Section C explains translation as living globalization. Nine, "one" and "many" are intercultural. Ten, translation is living. Eleven, translation is globalization unfinishable.

A. BOTH TRANSLATION AND MISTRANSLATION PERFORM GLOBALIZATION

One: Ideal Translation

Translation as medium is by definition not the message, but must vanish in the message that is to be translated. Translation is a catalyst to bring readers in one culture in touch with the original message in another culture alien to the readers. As a catalyst, ideal translation is the voice of the original author speaking in the target language if the author were to know that language.[2] What counts most important above all are the author and her message, and translation must be turned into a nothing in them.

Translation is nothing yet quite powerful in bringing the author in a culture alive to the people of audience in another culture. This point of powerful nothing can be understood by learning from Sartre's speculation on "nothing." Although put in dark negative terms, Sartre is perhaps the only thinker to recognize the dynamics of no-being, in the West dominated by being-thinking.

He describes no-being (*neant*) as "it is what it is not, and is not what it is," to negate being described as "it is what it is, and is not what it is not." No-being is then what negates Being, and as such serves as a hunger that bites into gluey being to cut out things, and as it cuts, it satisfies its hunger, and the hunger—the no-being—loses itself-as-hunger. No-being the hunger vanishes as it satiates itself.[3] This description of no-being of course fits in with how translation works. Translation is no-being that carves out the being of the message to be conveyed, and thereby vanishes in the message.

Without such contortion, Lao Tzu of sixth century BCE in China mentioned (11) three common things (besides water, mother, child, and valley) whose "vacancy" is precisely what is useful, that is, vacant hub at the center of thirty spokes of a wheel, empty hollow in a vessel, and empty space in a room. No-being is then the dynamics that makes being be and alive, while no-being happily goes silent as befits no-being. Lao Tzu is much simpler and less pessimistic than Sartre in conveying the same point of the power of no-being.

We on our part would say that, in the same manner, translation is useful precisely when we do not feel its existence, but through which we nakedly and directly—translation as nothing is translucent to let things through as they are—see the message conveyed. Translation is literally transference. It is in the hollow unobtrusiveness of translation that

---

[2] This is the view of all theorists of translation in *Theories of Translation: An Anthology of Essays from Dryden to Derrida*, eds. Rainer Schulte and John Biguenet, University of Chicago Press, 1992.

[3] Such is what Jean-Paul Sartre's massive *Being and Nothingness*, NY: Philosophical Library, 1943, talks about. His later, even more massive *Critique of Dialectical Reason*, Two volumes, London: Verso, 1976, 1991 (unfinished), just applies the no-being to poverty in society.

translation is powerful in transferring the message clearly to us. But of course neither French Sartre nor Chinese Lao Tzu thought of translation as such power of no-being. They are oblivious to the necessity of intercultural translation.

After all, translation is a go-between that introduces the original essay in a culture alien to the reader, into the reader's culture-world to understand it. Such introduction requires understanding of both sides, both cultures, that of the original, that of the reader, and "understanding" here is an interpretation, a hermeneutic, and such go-between must vanish, must be forgotten, as the introduction succeeds, as the reader meets the original face to face without intrusion from outside.[4]

Translation thus has two functions, interpretation of both sides, and self-disappearance in the introduction well done. Translation is thus a thankless task yet an indispensable task. Translation is as difficult and invisible as it is needed as catalyst, as messenger that needs to go away, the sooner the better. After all, the glue effectively applied is nowhere; we only see two things glued, the original and the reader. When translation-glue is seen, it shows the failure of translation-glue.

Intrusive showing of translation is to be frowned upon as intrusive showoff of the performer of music. We want to hear music, not the performer, though we are unaware that music is nowhere without its performer. Still, the performer succeeds to the extent that the hearer hears only music, not the performer. Likewise, translation succeeds when the reader forgets the translation and only reads the original, wholly unaware that reading the original in an alien language is impossible without its translation.

We read Homer's *Odyssey* in English, and then "another" *Odyssey* in English. We notice their differences, we thought Homer revised it, in English, and then we find that one is a translation by Rieu, another is translation by Lattimore.[5] Both are so good that we do not notice *them*. We thought Homer in ancient Greece wrote in English today, in our good natural English! Globalization across time and cultures is here. Good translation pulls off the stunt. Translation is genuine when it is nowhere; it is a no-being.

This "zero" of translation is a dynamic one, quite alive. Let us consider what "zero alive" means in translation, in two ways. *First*, translation is never a mechanical transfer of words, one at a time, from one language to another. Transference of words kills transference of the message. Computer does a better job of word-transference than we do—to produce a monster, dead and unintelligible. The original sentences are alive, and demand that they be conveyed by transplanting them alive in a new language. That is translation. "How do we do it?"

To be faithful to the message, we must express *afresh* an idea in an original paragraph. We must sometimes even add a new paragraph on a "new idea" missed in the original, and some other times we must even delete the original expressions that appear redundant in the translated language. Translation is thus literally a novel dramatic reenactment of the original vitality of the original message, quite historic. Some examples come to mind.

Leonard Bernstein's "Westside Story" translates Shakespeare's "Romeo and Juliet," as Chuang Tzu translates Lao Tzu, as Mencius translates Confucius. Translation is a

---

[4] When John the Baptist's followers left him to follow Jesus, John rejoiced as "friend of the bridegroom" whose job is finished of introducing the bride to the bridegroom (John 3:30). In the same way, Jesus came to introduce people to his God the Father. Jesus vanishes on the cross to lead people to his Father. Both John and Jesus are "translators" we admire.

companionship that re-creates the original's life in a new language world. The original is now newly reborn afresh in a new dawn in new language, and all this while appearing as the original. In this new world, there is no trace of translation anywhere. Now translation is invisible, vanished in the new original in the new language-world.

Secondly, here is another interesting feature of the dynamic "zero" in translation. While ever turning into zero, every good translation of the same original differs from every other, in the same way as every good performance of music differs from every other. Translation is an event, a happening, as every single day always differs from every next. This is because every "day" is a zero that allows and accommodates to enable all sorts of things to happen, and still remains as the "day."

"Day" is a room whose use lies in its vacancy, as Lao Tzu said (11). Similarly, a good translation is a room whose vacancy allows the original to come through alive. Moreover, as things appear one way in one room, and another way in another room, in every good translation the original comes through differently from every other good translation, while the same original is alive in these various ways.

Style is the rhythm beating the tune and the melody of an insight. Music throbs with its style, and so feeling the style hears the music of insights. Style is the heartbeat of what is being said raw, biased, and personal. Capturing the moving style grasps the content alive. Neglecting the style bypasses the content, to miss the whole point being said right in our face. Missing the style is the sure way to missing the content. No style, no content alive.

Translation amounts to capturing the style of the heartbeat of what is being said, and to transporting into "our" heartbeat in our own style. Translation begins at feeling the pulse of the life of ideas, by listening for the heartbeat of ideas throbbing forth in their own spontaneous style, to continue pounding within "our" mind-heart what you are saying pounding alive in your heart.

Such translation ends up saying what you say, in how you say it, but in our saying-style as in your style, as alive. Translation goes this way from heart to heart, beat to beat, hitting its style alive in our style alive. Translation not in such style-sync with the translated is no translation.

Seen from the other side of the translated, we realize this. Birthing turns out existence. Existence labors to produce new life and existence. "Birthing must birth" its own handicraft; birthing existence must in turn birth its product. Its product cannot sell, cannot keep, and only gives out itself to those who appreciate it. Birthing turns out existence to ex-ist, to stand-out as itself into the other here, and the other there.

This whole process of birthing, existing, laboring and producing and going out constitutes a rhythm of birthing existence that pushes out and gives itself away. It is a melody of one's way-of-existing, in one's own style of standing out as oneself. Existence is a style of other-ing. Such style of standing-out demands under-standing, to yearn after translation into the other. Translation is existence in give-and-take, in sync in style from here to there.

Of course this breathtaking translation-transaction risks failure in mistranslation in misunderstanding. We must consider failure in its negative aspect and in its positive aspect. It is because translation must vanish, and self-vanishing is easier said than done. Can the Greek sentiment and feeling appear in English translations without English distortions? How can the smells of the ancient Greek world come out in today's English? Thinking-mode is bound up

---

[5] E. V. Rieu, tr., *Homer: Odyssey* (1946), London: Penguin Books, 2003. Richmond Lattimore, tr., *The Odyssey of Homer* (1965), NY: Harper & Row, 1999.

with language-mode. How could thinking in one culture-and-language be conveyed, transplanted—translated transparently through—into another?

As such, translation is naturally beset with risks of mistranslation, either translating too much, overshooting the original, or too little, undershooting it, or coming out different from the original, and so there is no translation, or else all of them, translating too much to miss the original to turn out different altogether.

The genius of Bernstein, Chuang Tzu, and Mencius lies here, that they have gone through these pitfalls-and-risks and achieved brilliant "translations." Beware, though. Mistranslation is not always a plague to avoid, for it can harvest many a serendipity. In fact, we would rather brilliantly mistranslate than stodgily word-transfer.

Let us return to translation of Indo-European languages into English, for this is the easiest case to consider. Luckily, the English language as "a mixed up kid" with various language-parents may find itself more or less at home in translating French, Spanish, German, Italian, and so on, into English, for, after all, they are its parents. No wonder, seemingly unaware of the above translation-problems, Rée confidently asserted that Western philosophy alone is already multilingual since its inception.[6]

He never thought of probing into what this fact involves, much less what it means. In his confident article he *confuses* [1] general meaning(s) with specific experiential depths, and [2] how to translate one specific thinking-nuance connected with its specific linguistic nuance into another, with radical cultural differences involved in different languages. We here treat [2] alone, omitting [1] that involves the different approaches of Chinese thinking from Western, to complicate the already complex problems.

In the Indo-European linguistic realm alone we see problems of how to translate ancient Greek into modern English. The problem turns overwhelming in translating Chinese into English or English into Chinese, for it is a translation in a most outrageously cross-cultural sense. As their linguistic postures and patterns *radically* differ, so their thinking-modes and life-milieus are mutually alien.

Literary sensitivity to *both* language-worlds must come in aid. The English translations of the Chinese sentences must twist English almost to a breaking point *without* sacrificing the literary integrity of English language, to express the complex Chinese sentiment. Without cultural sensitivity, English translations of Chinese sentences turn into English compositions, a monologue irrelevant to China. The same requirement applies to Chinese translations of English essays that often come out as gobbledygook monsters entirely unintelligible.

All this while, though, we do find some serendipitous benefits of jolting us in both languages and cultures, into realizing the *differences* of English culture and thinking-mode from Chinese culture and thinking-mode. As commonly human with human life-experiences, love, hate, joys, and sorrows, life and death, we can appreciate how each culture lives and handles in its own manner these human experiences we all share.

Such appreciations will in turn enhance our abilities to translate with skill and understanding one cultural language into another, flexibly, without preset rule from either cultural language. Thus, the greater the obstacles and difficulties of intercultural translations we encounter, the richer, the deeper, and the more various understanding we shall gain on living and experiencing humanity as richly human, thoroughly and culture-variously human.

---

[6] "Translation" written by Rée in *The Concise Encyclopedia of Western Philosophy, Third Edition*, eds. Jonathan Rée and J. O. Urmson, London: Routledge, 2005, pp. 378-380. I omit my regret over its rambles.

Understandingly, however, such culturally risky translations are beset with chances of mistranslations. We must now consider what "mistranslations" give us.

Two: Mistranslation and Its "Use"

What we translate, *if* successfully carried out, would have made the world of right translations much less exciting if not duller than mistaken translations that raise our eyebrows and prick our interests. But of course, luckily or not, what is said above about translation is an ideal, for no one can succeed in becoming completely no-being and completely translucent, and our act of translation is no exception.

No translation is perfect, and so the medium tends to turn into a new message, or if "faithfully done," turns into the message with a new twist, with new implications if not ending up becoming a new message. This is because translation is redescriptions that bring out new implications and connotations, so much so that the translation would bring out a new creation. Three examples come to mind.

The first example is Hu Shih's 胡適 quip—now a bit tired because of its frequent citations—that I translate as "Dare to propose, care to prove 大膽假設, 小心求證." My translation I hope has brought out its original vigor lost through accustomed quotations in Chinese. But then we can munch on this quip further, and realize that it can mean more. For example, it can mean "Dare to make mistakes, care to check on them," for proposals often prove to be mistaken, and it is the job of "caring to prove" to check and find out the mistakes in our proposals.

"Why do we want to risk making mistakes?" Creativity comes about by daring to make mistakes, and that is why. So, Hu Shih's quip amounts to "Dare to make mistakes to create, and check to prove what we have created." "But, then, what if the checking itself is proven to be mistaken?" Well, then, the checking can itself be checked, and *that* checking can be checked again, ad infinitum, to approach less and less mistakes.

We can thus make mistakes to check on them further and more, to create more and further. *This* it is that must be the rock bottom of implications of Hu Shih's original quip, for otherwise why do we have to bother proposing anything and proving anything at all? We propose and we prove, isn't all this for the sake of *creating* things novel? But then our retranslations are now far away from the original quip in literal sense. Our retranslations are now so many exciting mistranslations.

Our next example is so many translations, elucidations, and explanations in the West that are supposed to transfer "accurately" Chinese writings, propositions, and classics to the Westerners who know nothing about China or Chinese language. Unbeknown to Western translators, however, the Chinese readers would have been shocked when these Western translations are retranslated back into Chinese, for now nothing like the original Chinese writings are left that the Chinese readers are used to.

This is because, now, these "translations" amount to Chinese stuff "chemically cleaned,"[7] that is to say, analytically clarified in the Western direction unheard of in China. For example,

---

[7] A blurb on the book jacket of A. C. Graham's *Chung Tzu* (London: George Allen & Unwin, 1981) says, "It is hoped that the effect will be that of a famous painting newly cleaned." The statement devastated me.

the famous thinker in the West, Richards, made an "experiment in multiple definition," i.e., an exhaustive probe into all logically possible senses in some of passages in the *Mencius*.[8]

Such a book really shocks and daunts the Chinese reader at any level, sophisticated or no. No Chinese scholar, in China or in Japan, dares to even mention that volume. Another example is a mathematician's reveries on "Tao" that "is silent"[9] are quite out of the Chinese blue, for whatever natural reveries one engages in, Tao is beyond sound and silence of reverie.

Mind you. We are all alive but, oddly, "alive" is not a category. The reason is obvious but sad. We must be alive to handle "alive," and then we handle the unknown-"alive" with our self unknown-"alive," as we are alive. Or else, we must be dead to handle "alive," and then, being dead, we cannot handle being alive any more. And so, we cannot win; no philosophy has handled "being alive." Thus our obviously basic and essential task of thinking "alive" remains impossible to fulfill. No one "translates" being alive intelligibly into our human language, any human language.

Amazingly, Chuang Tzu pulls off this stunt of the obvious impossible. He is alive and thinks alive, by grasping the "and" of two poles, being alive *and* thinking alive. His Chapter One presents "being alive"; Chapter Two presents thinking alive. Stories after stories sing both, and the remaining chapters continue singing, often collapsing the two poles, telling stories. Thus Chuang Tzu is so alive whistling, beyond all categorization.

Chuang Tzu is lilting alive as huge fish and bird, as chitchatting chickadees, as the winds and the dreams, as this in that and that in this, as death in life and life in death, and as everything moving, alive beyond joys and sorrows. Chuang Tzu's stories sing such "being alive," and even his stories playing arguments chant such life.

Stories sing because stories tell of life that sings an ode to itself. Chuang Tzu chants such an ode to life with stories alive, including stories playing with arguments, repeatedly. Such chanting of living thinks alive while it is being jumping alive. This performance bypasses the above dilemma because the chant is in sync with life-rhythm alive, and it is *aware* as living. Such is how Chuang Tzu pulls off the stunt, whistling.

Translations today must be as alive as he, and "as alive as" is fidelity translation must fulfill, though such "fidelity" is elusive, for "fidelity to another *life*" is oddly incoherent. Life is as it independently is, proudly self-sovereign, and translation must be faithful to "being alive." Fidelity-alive in translation must be made of two elements.

One, the syntax of one language differs from the other, so translation is needed to convey the synonymy of sentiment (not literalism of transfer of word-meanings) and resonance of sense-tunes (no jarring dissonance). Two, this sentiment-synonymy is assisted by traditional commentaries in China. Literal translation here is a sneaky betrayal of the original life; dissonant translation is irresponsible to it.

Besides, Chuang Tzu plays in ironies all over. He even plays with arguments. To take them as truths and serious arguments, and translate them literally, simply misses him. To seriously argue with Chuang Tzu fooling around with arguing invites smile. Chuang Tzu has

---

[8] I. A. Richards, *Mencius on the Mind: Experiment in Multiple Definition* (1932), Westport, CT: Hyperion Press. I have four more examples of such sort in my *Story-Thinking: Cultural Meditations*, NY: Nova Science Publishers, 2011, pp. 168-171.

[9] Raymond M. Smullyan, *The Tao Is Silent*, NY: Harper & Row, 1977.

"three Confuciuses," historical person, opponent to Taoism, and advocate of Taoism[10], and confusing them confuses our understanding of Chuang Tzu, who plays with "Confucius."

Again, Chuang Tzu benefits from the name-logician Hui Tzu by criticizing him in his own terms, and thereby pushes further his notion-scrutiny into thinking alive on actuality alive, all beyond all name-logicians and all thinkers in China, including Lao Tzu. Missing this context of friendly opposition at play misses the entire point of Chuang Tzu. All translations of him then misfire. This is why no translation has done justice to Chuang Tzu yet.

Similarly, the passionate Mencius in the heated exigencies of controversies for humane government is bypassed by being pulled out of his sayings some logical possibilities of what his sayings could mean, by Richards. The same mistake is perpetrated by Yearley who parallels Aquinas to Mencius in the paradigm of Thomism.[11]

But of course mistranslations are the rule of history of ideas. Hegel mistranslated Heraclitus, Marx mistranslated Hegel, as Lenin did Marx, to be mistranslated by Mao. Political mistranslations, such as brutal Han Fei's of pacifist Lao Tzu into no-nonsense Realpolitik, are usually violently self-devouring of the regime's own people on whom the regime is founded and dependent. Typically, mistranslations result in doing violence to the original meaning and to actuality.

This sad self-consumption of violence is perpetually perpetrated with continual mistranslations of ideas, as even mistranslation itself does violence to the original. But we must also admit that democratic dreams of Hobbes, Locke, and Rousseau were translated into democratic revolutions in France and in USA. In all, we must admit that translations and mistranslations of ideas are quite effective, even to the point of violence in all senses.[12]

As a third cluster of examples, China and Japan are filled with translations of the West that, if translated back into the West, would no less shock the West. Mao Tse-tung's "Communism" mistranslated the early Marx's *1844 Manuscripts*, loudly and passionately protesting oppressions of the proletariat workers, into the very oppression of *them*. To compound the mistranslation, China calls its oppressive communist regime, "People's Republic of China"! What an irony it is so insulting to the people! The Nazi National Socialism might as well call itself "All Jews' Aryan Republic."

Another instance is "Christianity" in the Communist China that suffers most from this casually brutal fate. For example, they pick Jesus' tongue-in-cheek acerbic shout, "If anyone comes to me and does not hate his father and mother, wife and children, brothers and sisters, yes, and his own life also, he cannot be my disciple" (Luke 14:26), and they take it literally to mean Jesus is anti-family, anti-filiality.

They miss Jesus' "hate his own life also" that concludes the saying, as also mentioned in another saying of his, "he who hates his life …will keep it for eternal life" (John 12:25). This phrase is significant, as no one can literally "hate" one's own life. Such is China's calumny

---

[10] See the long Note 10 in p. 400 of my *The Butterfly as Companion*, Albany: State University of New York Press, 1990.

[11] Richards, *Mencius on the Mind*, op. cit. Lee H. Yearley, *Mencius and Aquinas: Theories of Virtue and Conceptions of Courage*, Albany: State University of New York Press, 1990. The titles of both books are revealing, for Mencius has no "mind," "theories," or "concepts" at all. But then, "does Mencius really have them, or not?" This critical query must be done before engaging in the above quests.

[12] This makes a pivotal point in Edmund Burke's objection to violent revolution in his *Reflections on the Revolution in France* (1790), NY: Barnes & Noble, 2010.

against Christianity by pulling isolated statements out of context and out of its original sentiment. Such lack of textual sensitivity is quite sad and tragic.

Similarly, many sets of "complete translations" of famous thinkers in the West simply chill our minds and spines. Many thinkers in the West—Heidegger is one such victim—are simply pulled out of their original contexts, summed up in capsule slogans, and criticized or praised as if the critics knew what they are talking about. An outrageous praise of Heidegger is shown in a book[13] that simply and directly pastes his sayings onto Lao Tzu's *Tao Te Ching* as its "commentary."

Obviously, such act does injustice both to Lao Tzu and to Heidegger, unless carefully examined and elucidated at every move, by responding to questions such as, "Has Heidegger said all that Lao Tzu means?," "Why read the dated Lao Tzu if all Western philosophy today has exhausted him?," "How could Lao Tzu have allowed such alien outside intrusion?," "How could foreign thinker today make any intelligible 'commentary' on ancient classic?," and so on.

"Is this situation good or bad?" Well, it all depends. If we know the cultural differences in "translations" of this sort, such differences do nothing but our mutual good of enriching one another, both China and the West. If unprepared for the cultural *differences*, the harm is incalculable.

"What shall we say to all this?" We could say something like this. Translation must turn into a nothing or else it turns into a mistranslation. Still, turning into a zero is a rare feat, for it is hard to pull through, as no one can be "no one" easily, for everyone is a "someone." Thus translation often turns into mistranslation.

But no one purposely makes mistakes; it is impossible to "make," to manufacture, mistakes on purpose, even though it is possible to crank out falsehood, but of course falsehood is not mistake. We usually sincerely try our best until *later* we find that our trial was a mistrial, a mistake. Mistake is a retrospective discovery, a future happening, of an unexpected happening in the past—as mistake. Mistake is a happenstance we find out later, often much later.

Interestingly, such mis-happenstance can then be serendipity of creative novelty. Novelty is interesting. Even though everyone has an interest in novelty, positive or negative, no one can plan to pull off novelty, for the really new by definition defies plan consciously made. Novelty simply happens without rhyme or reason pre-known. So does creativity. No one can contrive creativity; it is also a happenstance out of the blue. So, mistake, creativity, and novelty form an interesting synonymy quite unexpected.

Thus mistranslation unplanned can turn into unexpected creation of novelty unheard of before, exactly as mistake is found to exist there that is unheard of before. We can then profit from mistranslation, as long as—and this is important—we are retrospectively watchful. Our several progressive translations of "Dare to propose, care to prove," to end up saying "Dare to venture mistakes, care to check on them," are after all strictly correct, then. They were mistranslations of no mistranslation, we find now.

"We thought we were wrong, but we are mistaken" is a familiar hilarious mistake, after all, though quite complex, creative, and novel and unexpected, and that is why the saying is hilarious, quite unexpected. One thing is certain, however. We cannot know what is

---

[13] Chang Chung-yuan, *Tao: A New Way of Thinking: A Translation of the Tao Tê Ching with an Introduction and Commentaries*, NY: Harper & Row, 1975. "Commentaries" here are Heidegger's words; its "introduction" just praises Heidegger.

unexpected, so we cannot chart in advance the flowchart of mistranslation as novel creation, for mistake cannot be preplanned.

Novel creation is as retrospective a discovery of the future as mistranslation is retrospective happenstance of our unplanned future. "Ignorance is bliss" happens in a funny way, here. Now, all these thoughts are our meta-harvest serendipitous about meta-serendipity, of the strange but common mistranslations. Let us now go into their odd benefits so unexpected; how can "mistake that is bad" bestow us benefits that are good?

Three: How Mistranslations Benefit

Because no translation can ever be perfect, all translations can be said to be "mistranslations." Such mistranslations *can* prove to give us serendipitous benefits to all parties concerned. At the very least, such mistranslations can stimulate and push globalization ahead. "How do they do that?"

However mistaken all translations are, they can be said to be honest trials, struggling to get asymptotically closer to the originals. In the meantime, the gap between the translations and the originals refurbish the originals with unforeseen implications and unsuspected connotations. The translations of classics by Homer, Plato, and poetically powerful Confucius, Lao Tzu, the Bible, and the notorious Chuang Tzu—and the list goes on—are all shimmering with brilliances of such "mistranslations" of later generations, continually pouring out onto the market.

Let us look into some examples of brilliant mistranslations. To begin, D. C. Lau gives us good sober explanations, harvest of years of researches, of the gist of Confucius' *Analects*. But sadly, he missed Confucius in *his* vigor of poetic evocation; missing Confucius' straight vigor misses Confucius. Lau's good explanations are his sad mistranslations. The tragedy is that he never realizes how mistranslation is worsened precisely by his conscientious explanation and elaboration. Lau remains so proud to plod scholarly on, to kill the open unlimited horizon of the original vitality!

Lau's sad mistranslations in good explanations continue in his "translation" of the *Mencius,* jumping alive and urgent, with Lau's verbosity so helpful, cumbersome, and long drawn-out. The same comment applies to Lau's "scholarly translation" of Lao Tzu's *Tao Te Ching*.[14] Lau missed Lao Tzu's *lively* invitation to mysteries of actuality with Lau's scholarly emendation and explanation.[15] For all this, however, if we take his "translations" as background information, his explanations are enormously helpful to understanding the background and infrastructure of the poetic thrust of those sages.

Richards' analytical labors on the *Mencius* also help us see Mencius' riches of logical variety of implications, allowing us to realize that Mencius is not randomly fuming forth irresponsible irrational eruptions at all. Such solid logical structure of Mencius was unplumbed hitherto by anyone in the world. Richards opens our meticulously analytical eyes to Mencius.

---

[14] D. C. Lau, *Confucius: The Analects* (1979), 1992. *Mencius*, Two Volumes (1979), 1984, both from The Chinese University Press in Hong Kong. *Lao Tzu: Tao Te Ching* (1963), 1994, NY: Knopf.

[15] Not surprisingly, Lau did not translate Chuang Tzu so outrageously illogical, roaming alive, his extant texts being "quite corrupt," said Lau,

Likewise, Yearley opens our Thomistic eyes to look into Mencius behind Mencius' rhetorical heat. Both Richards and Yearley help us the no-nonsense spines in Mencius that passionately flex in his sharp-witted controversies and his soaring universal vision so vast and global, so penetrating and natural. After all, a poem explained loses poetry, but at least such explanation helps us to orient us to deeper understanding of the poem and its poetic thrust.[16] May China's "sad" mistranslation of Russian Communism turn out to be a beneficial serendipity!

Four: Mistranslations Powerful Dynamo toward Enriching Globalization

Precisely because translations are forever imperfect, they are a dynamo, quite powerful and essential, to enriching globalization. Let us take a well-known example. Mencken's pioneering study in three massive tomes on the "American English"[17] can be taken as some reports—translations—on mongrelization—translations—of the British language, *and precisely because of it,* the "American English" is reported as an enormous enrichment of British language quite beyond Shakespearean English.

Today, even the Oxford University Press, the publisher of *The Oxford English Dictionary* the twenty huge volumes of "mother of all English dictionaries," is now publishing various dictionaries on the American English. In addition, the English, "globally polluted" into English-pidginized everywhere, is today's global Esperanto, equivalent to the Latin prevalent among the scholarly circles during the medieval ages. Thus the medium is indeed the message, which makes powerful globalization today, all thanks to translations that are often mistranslations.

In the meantime, we ourselves are totally renovated and refurbished in our mistranslations of those fellow cultures so alien, so exotic, into our culture. Our understanding of these foreign cultures mirrors *us* back to us. This mirror is our own picture newly cleansed and expanded, to help us examine ourselves, to sober up by such fabulous encounter with exotic cultures such as the Inscrutable Orient. As we are Westerners, we are cultural tourists having come home; it is, now we realize, our analytical Western self, to be enabled to reaffirm ourselves as Western.

Likewise, if we are Chinese people, our tour in the foreign land of the West would have enabled us to come home to our poetic evocative Chinese self, now tired but enriched, humbled, as at the same time we regain our cultural pride. Mistranslation thus brings us back our respective homes, our homes now more luminous, more luxurious, as we also see defects unnoticed in us, to refashion and repair. This it is that is the dynamo of globalization, precisely through our intercultural mistranslations often unnoticed.

---

[16] See a convenient collection of what poetry is, said by poets themselves, in James Scully, ed., *Modern Poetics*, NY: McGraw-Hill, 1965.

[17] H. L. Mencken, *The American Language: An Inquiry into the Development of English in the United States* (1919), Fourth Edition, 1980, *Supplement One* (1945), 1977, and *Supplement Two* (1948), 1978, all published by NY: Alfred A. Knopf. Each volume runs up to several thousand pages.

B. Origin and Function of Translation in Globalization

Now, let us look at all above in terms of time and work of translation in globalization. A new vista would open out to enlighten us further into translation and globalization, both inter-elucidating.

Five: Archeology of Translation

Translation originates deep in our psyche, then gets expressed—translated—into our awareness, and ordered according to our cultural heritage of language, ethos, thinking patterns, and become our resources of idea-expression in sentences and propositions and proposals. The shapers of our cultural resources are legendary individuals, the meta-authors of us authors of ideas and essays in our specific culture, our languages and thinking patterns, ready to be translated into other languages in other cultures.

As the past, our parents, gives birth to us in the present, so our deep cultural unconscious seeds seed our soul our soil to let seedlings sprout to grow and spread into consciousness our ideas our self, in intending, in thinking, in gestalt-forming, and we respond to ourselves, and to ourselves reacting to our milieus. We let things see themselves as we insert ourselves in their seeing us as they see. At least so we feel deep in our soul our spines, as we breathe deep in the vast Mother Nature our cyclones that are constantly belching throughout the skies and the fields.

The deep is the vast, and the vast shakes the world, and so we ourselves are the foundation of the world shaking in the wind singing the world. All this amounts to saying that we ourselves are at the foundation of the cosmos. We are born with the heaven and the earth, nodding at and smiling with myriad things, squirrels and the grass, trees and the clouds, spring and autumn, together with even all the roadside skulls so dry so happy. If this is not pan-translation throughout the globe, nothing is.

Six: All Cultural Activities are Translations

In fact, we must go a step further, and realize that all education must be regarded as transmission and message-transference, and often mistranslation, of cultural heritage that composes our humanity. How does mistranslation here also enrich us ourselves? This is globalization in the context of time. This theme of "history in globalization" is the theme Dr. Tang, Ruei-hong developed in his essay in our volume.

Thus translation in time (history) and in space (interculture) is the *modus vivendi* and the *modus operandi* of dynamic globalization, precisely because translation is forever in progress out of its imperfections. Our translations reveal mistranslations one after another as we continue translating our beloved classics.

Translation is *transferre*, transferring existence of, say, the kingdom from the house of Saul to set up the throne of David, even translating the life of Enoch who then did not see death.[18] Existence shows itself in the mode of existence that we call "culture." And so, translation is transference of cultural modes in time as tradition, in space as interculture that we usually call "translation."

Translation in time is what we call "education." Confucius famously confessed (7/1) that he continues to transmit but does not originate 述而不作. So modestly saying, his transmission of past heritage was actually quite alive, quite dynamic, so much so that he ended up originating the whole Confucian tradition to define China. He denied having much information. On the contrary, his "amassing of information" was shot through with his constant efforts at finding the one that cuts through bewildering details, skewering all information into one-coherence as it increases in bulk and in complexity.

At the same time, he constantly asked students to also find the one that goes through what they learned, and what they learned about him, while raising just one critical corner, to provoke them to come back with three, seven, or ten more new insights into implications and connotations of what they find. It is thus, in learning and in teaching, that he humbly transmitted what he learned to provoke creation of novelties in his students. If he did not create, he let create.

"How does Confucius skewer information into one?" He said, "*Poetry Classic* in three hundred poems is covered in one saying, 'Think no depravity.'" The saying in the *Classic* (4.2.1.4) was meant to praise a specific Duke, perhaps in flattery and no more, yet Confucius saw the saying as one pivotal key that goes through the entire three hundred poems in the *Classic*. That is Confucius raising one corner of insight. In this way, he created by not creating!

In such a way as this, he raised "one" insight to show to his students, questioning them again and demanding again what they think, for them to come back with two more, three more, even ten more thoughts. Confucius himself in turn was then provoked by their returns to go further in his reading and pondering on China's historical heritage.[19]

Such is how he transmits our cultural heritage, creatively and modestly. No wonder, he was the greatest of all teachers, around whom the whole Chinese culture is shaped. This is what makes the usually sober Chan to exclaim, without even mentioning how, "Confucius . . . can truly be said to have molded Chinese civilization in general. It may seem farfetched, however, to say that he molded Chinese philosophy in particular—that, he determined the direction or established the pattern of later Chinese philosophical development—yet there is much truth in the statement than is usually realized."[20]

Confucius was a great transmitter and translator of cultural heritage, and thereby became the greatest of teachers to lead China through its history, and thereby create the history distinctively Chinese. This is translation in time, while translation in space is interculture out and out. Both sorts of translations constitute globalization, on and on, as the transcendentalists and the flower children in USA respond to China's proud culture, and China in turn has its craze in the West in the form of communism, military hardware, space exploration, and the list goes on.

---

[18] 2 Samuel 3:10, Hebrews 11:5. Cf. Colossians 1:13. NKJV has "transfer" for "translate."

[19] Analects 2/2, 3/8, 4/15, 5/9, 15/3.

[20] This is a quotation from Wing-tsit Chan, *A Source Book in Chinese Philosophy*, Princeton University Press, 1963, p. 14.

Seven: Laws of Traffic in Culture in Translation

Stressing the actual fact of mistranslation does not mean that "anything can go" as we translate. Translation must try to get closer and closer toward the original. Although translation cannot help but be an interpretation, we must strenuously try to let translation be translation, never mix translation with interpretation, explanation, or elaboration, explication, and commentary.

This means that, while the original sentences are poetic, we should never explain "its gist" to explain away the poetry, but must translate them as poetry. Where the original is vague or obscure, we must be likewise vague and obscure in the way the original is vague. Translation must be in sync with the style and the air of the original. Explanations if any must be clearly separated and labeled as "explanations."

These "musts" and "must nots" compose the traffic laws of globalization that consists in translations. But we must beware. Such traffic laws are to be "obeyed with discretion." In other words, these traffic laws are meant to be broken with discretion in the actual translation-traffics of globalization. "Discretion" here means empathetic synchronicity and sym-spatiality with the original in its style, its air, and its sentiment.

Such discretion in actual empathy with the actual situation is the matter of life and death. On the highway, strict mechanical adherence to the letters of the traffic laws spells death by "traffic accidents." On the highway of globalization, strict mechanical transference of every letter of the original means straight disastrous "unintelligibility" that is death to translation. We must mistranslate to accurately translate. "The medium is no message" should be performed to attain "the medium is the message."

Eight: Translation the Last Stage of "Translation"

The last stage of transfer described above is translation proper. This actual visible translation must follow the original eruption of the original proposal, the original essay. Sensitive empathy heartfelt and cultural is required here. Translation is thus a retracing of cultural archeology of the origination of ideas and essays. This empathy is a retracing and redescriptions, and the retracing is re-creation.

The re-tracing is replication, but every replication differs from every other as it differs from the original. Each replication is an artwork that is unique, as performers of the "same composition" differ in their respective performances. Copying is re-creation, and it is a new creation. "Faithful translation" is a new creation. The original raises one, for translators and transmitters to return with three and more. Each translation of Odyssey differs from every other, each claiming to be faithful, empathetically, conscientiously, as every day differs from every other to compose "days of my life."[21]

Now, never should we forget. Such empathetic synchronicity and sym-spatiality is co-resonance of the rhythm of propositions and sentences that spreads contagiously from one cultural context to another. This is globalization. This is translation that is the music of existence, existence as music, resounding out and out, moment by moment.

---

[21] Is all this what the traditional "art as imitation" really means?

In music as resonance, the public's reaction is not the music's shadow but a part of music, for music is made by its audience with its composer and performers. The "new music" jars the public's existing criteria of enjoyment. Novelty jars to educate, to bring us ahead. That is pain, though, involving feeling of being insulted. Naturally, the public resents "new music" and rejects it.

Besides, "new" can push us ahead or pollutes us in decadence. That judgment rests not now but later. History decides the value of new music. "New" now just incites painful rejection. In any case, the "essence," what it is, of music is an awkward term. In music, "essence" moves and changes; its what changes in its how of moving on. Music moves, and so its how is its what.

Music moving on is such that I must take time to undergo to understand. The logic of music is the logic of time. I have no way of instantly surveying music. Now we think this describes music alone. But as long as our life is music developing itself, any thing in life cannot be understood without taking time to undergo it. The "biographies" of things are their music-of-being. Fiction and history present the life-music. Thus China as "literature history 文史" is the culture of life-music, self-coherent to open out into the future, ever throbbing on to the next moment.

In the end, we see that translation is musical sensitivity to the air, aria, suites, and atmosphere in one culture to transfer to the air and sentiment of another culture, and another, and another. Translation is the music of one sphere here now resonating with and into the music of another sphere there then, world without end.

Let us think of my brother's recent death. He died of complications in open heart surgery, guaranteed by doctors to be 100% safe. We can blame the death on his fragile kidney condition, and/or blame it on medical failure due to its ineptitude, and bite the cold bullet of the physical death, and wail over his coffin, wailing and missing him heartfelt. This is what we usually do, quite tragically, heartbroken. This is one air, one tune, of living.

Or else, we can claim that my brother is too naughty and peppy—that he was and is—to be boxed in his body, and so he has jumped out of time and space combined into physical universe, called yü-chou 宇宙 in China. He is now free as a bird, in fact, freer than birds; he is the Huge Bird P'eng 鵬 admired by Chuang Tzu, soaring to the end of the Southern Lake of the cosmos.

We plead with him, "Please, A-liong, don't fly too far, for we are soon to see you alive soaring, hopping, and jumping, in less than seventy years at most." Death is the Eternal Now,[22] at present always fresh forever, as my Mr. Cottonwood and my Mr. Flower-Power, now that both trees have been chopped down, now nowhere, are always with me here now, often talking *to* me when I least expect it, to pep me up.

Now these two contrary vistas and airs, death as end forever, death as beginning forever, coexist inter-dissonant, yet they do somehow co-exist together in this world of actuality. This dissonant "somehow together" is globalization music, ongoing without ceasing, thanks to translation of life-notes in opposing aria-tunes. Translation brings out, to bring about, all the inner commotions and gestalt-contradictions stirring in our spines, unawares or no. Such is globalization in dissonance of inter-resonance.

---

[22] Sadly, Paul Tillich's "eternal now" is Platonic no-change offered to today's bewildering changes. The whole show is quite lifeless, in his *The Eternal Now*, NY: Charles Scribner's Sons, 1963.

Chopping down a tree chops me off. Planting a tree even on the Last Day—of me, of the world—plants me and plants the world to thrive together, with birds flying singing so fragile, tender, and beautiful, with squirrels chasing those birds as the squirrels hop from this branch to that.

As I watch them, they store away hickory nuts and nibble off crabapples so wastefully, and then they hide themselves at the threatening booms of cars and airplanes so intrusive so impolite. All this is the global music inter-translating, dissonant in harmony, globalization so alive, ever ongoing, each existent translating the other into itself interculturing, inter-naturally, and inter-historicizing.

All this is of course my translation *ad libitum* of ancient Chinese Chuang Tzu's claim (2/52-53), outrageous and hilarious, saying, "The sky and the earth are born with me, and myriad things and I are one." And so, this whole bit here performs translation, across history and across cultures, into actuality global. Now that we see how translation comes about, its archeology, we are ready to consider the function of translation in globalization, as its *modus operandi*, and its *modus vivendi*.

Nine: "One Universal" and "Many in Situ" as Intercultural

Although some of us speculate, even insist, on the One that cuts through all things actual (Plato, Jung, Teilhard, Chomsky, etc.), our need of translations in globalization clearly indicates that we humanity are engaged in many ways of thinking, behaving, and saying in history in cultures (Kuhn, Polanyi, Feyerabend). Interestingly, Confucius habitually penetrates all sorts of information into one, yet he is quite alive to various sorts of dialogues with the past history and with the latecomer students he was so awed at.

We again ask, "Is the globe round or flat?" Both are correct. "Does the sun move or the earth move?" Both are correct. "Is evolution true or creation true?" Both are true. All depends on where things are looked at, and how things are experienced, to translate into "knowledge" so specific.

Those who say the globe is round, the earth moves, and evolution is true, say so by basing their claims on science and mathematics, to cover everything in one sweep. Those who say the globe is flat, the sun moves, and creation is correct originate their claims from daily experiences so various. They are the pluralists.

This is because even "creation" comes from experiencing every day to begin at dawn to create the future that is coming, for one inch ahead is darkly unknown, to be determined further, to be created, and so "creation" is our confession to our "awe" at something, *some* power unknown beyond us, and of course the very "some" here is beyond our control. All this is an incontrovertible fact of our experience.

At this point, to decide which side is absolutely correct is sheer dogmatism. This situation is that of many cultures. The culture of the one says, "The truth is one, and the one truth must be pursued and decided." And the wind of the day blows in the direction of the culture of the one, saying that we are progressing from primitive "many" to modern "one" and even future "one." That is "progress," quite "civilized," and so on.

We are of at least two cultures, the culture of the one and the culture of the many, and our strength lies in coming together through translation among us. But of course those who insist on oneness of all things would say that "translation" we mentioned is precisely the glue, the agent, the go-between, to bring into "one" all those disparate things. Without such propensity into one, no glue-translation can even work. And our debates go on, between the one-people and the many-people.

Thus those who propose the One through many may belong to one culture, the culture of the one, to meet with the culture of the many. Translation between these two cultures is needed for them to understand each other, though we are not sure of what such meta-translation amounts to, nor are we of what such understanding would be.

Perhaps this catalyst meta-translation is provided by the legendary Master who says to one student in dispute with another, "I think you are right," and then says to the other, "I think you are right." The third student protests, saying, "But Master, they are opposed. How could they be both right?" Whereupon the Master says, "And I think you are right, too." The Master gives them each the Master's careful understanding and warm approval, thereby brings them together in respectful disagreements. Such heartfelt and understanding "translation" of his catalyzes globalization-concord.

Let us put it another way. Some say there are two kinds of people, one kind say there are two kinds of people, another kind of people say, there are no two kinds of people, and then we are in for an infinite regress, repeating such rounds of "two kinds of people." There is no translation possible in this nauseating maelstrom, so we must stop going this way. But, then, to think of it, doesn't "saying all this" itself catalyzes us into such maelstrom, and so in this sense, saying so translates us into such knowledge? Translation, translation, there are always translations everywhere globalized.

Perhaps Section A above, describing both translations and mistranslations that mobilize to push ahead globalization, follows the Master of meta-glue of living translations, living globalization. This is not to be accused as irresponsible "relativism."[23] On the contrary, this understanding contains the riches of heartfelt and absolutely sincere togetherness, cosmic concord in inter-translation of different experiences, different cultures, into globalization.

Now, let us put some concrete meat into the above arid schematizing so bony. Conveying something is tricky. Translation is a difficult, indispensable, and wonderful art of conveying the original sentences faithfully, as they are transformed during their conveyance. Here is an amazing genre of "translation" across time in China, though China itself does not recognize it as translation.

The Chuang Tzu of fourth century BCE does not even explain the Lao Tzu of the sixth, but re-describes Lao Tzu to re-present him in Chuang Tzu's own way with cadence of Chuang's own, into Lao's rebirth quite poetic and potent. Chuang Tzu presents "dreams" to challenge our taken-for-granted paradigm of reality, tells tall tales so fabulous to challenge our accustomed life-views so confined, and plays with argument-bits to mock-argue and mock-disagree with Hui Tzu the name-logician, to develop Chuang's own deeper and more apt name-logic of living.

Chuang Tzu's storytelling "argues," as his playful "arguments" tell stories, to story-think on life. Such co-responsive dialogical thinking alive has already begun within the Book of

---

[23] I have long been preoccupied with this fascinating theme of "relativism" since my PhD thesis at Yale titled "Existential Relativism." See, e.g., my "Rorty, Confucius, and Intercultural Relativism," in *Rorty, Pragmatism, and Confucianism*, ed. Yong Huang, Albany: State University of New York Press, 2009, pp. 21-44, and indexes on "relativism" in *Story-Thinking: Cultural Meditations*, NY: Nova Science Publishers, 2011, *On Metaphoring: A Cultural Hermeneutic*, Leiden: Brill, 2001, and *On the "Logic" of Togetherness: A Cultural Hermeneutic*, Leiden: Brill, 1998, among many others.

Chuang Tzu after its Chapters One through Seven, and continues through Lieh Tzu 列子, Huai Nan Tzu 淮南子, Pao P'u Tzu 抱朴子, T'ao Ch'ien 陶潛, Li Po 李白, and so on, each in his own personal way in his peculiar style and cadence, yet all reenacted to convey the unmistakable lifeworld of Taoism.

This translation-process of transmission is not word-for-word transference but conveyance by "heat-transmission," as it were. The "heat" of Taoist thrust, sentiment, and posture is contagious, reenacted by one writer to transmit to another in a Taoist style of thinking and wording, and is conveyed from one writer-generation to another, and yet each in his own personal words and peculiar wording.

This historical reenactment produces a series of continuous re-incarnations of Taoism creative, poetic, and personal. This is quite a powerful genre of "translation" of sentiment, of message, and of wording, yet never in the exact words of the originals. The peculiar Taoist fire is lighted and spread from one specific stump of genius to another, each burning in its way yet all burning unmistakably Taoistic.

By the same token, the Confucus' torch is carried on by Mencius, Hsün Tzu 荀子, Han Yü 韓愈, Chu Hsi 朱熹, and Wang Shou-jen 王守仁, each in his own peculiar personal life-manner. Such is the transmission of Taoism and Confucianism, not as particular doctrines but as peculiar air, aria, sentiments, trends, and styles of life-thinking.

This is history, "translation" in time in Chinese style. We make history that teaches us how to conduct our life, as we can say that our education is a translation of history into ourselves, to cultivate ourselves by the ancients. The grammar is strained here, saying that we cultivate us by the ancients,to show the stunt of history where the subject freely turns into itself as it is, in all its *subjectivity*, as it is nurtured by the parental past in the past's own full *subjectivity*.

Such teaching by history came alive when Ssu-ma Ch'ien 司馬遷 lamented Hsiang Yü 項羽 the hegemon's disastrous downfall as due to his refusal to be "taught by the ancient 師古."[24] History is our great translation into us ourselves across time. History is resonation of the music of personal integrity from one generation to another. to refuse to enter into the music of history refuses to be alive as oneself, refuses to live.

Musical performance is translation-in-time of a composition, which is a time artwork written out in space. Believe me. I have been *carefully* listening through Bach, Brahms, Debussy, Dvorak, Elgar, Fauré, Haydn, Mozart, Ravel, Schubert, Sibelius, and Smetana. I finally found Beethoven colossal in quantity of varieties of genres and milieus, all in their inter-mingling.

Beethoven is staggering far beyond any other musical composers combined. His music makes not a world but many worlds shimmering and inter-reflecting into an infinite variety of worlds of sentiments. No wonder, he takes so many sensitive performers to "translate" into music alive.

His String Quartets alone are interesting. They are a favorite set of almost every string ensemble. They are complexly organized, tightly woven, and yet go quite naturally, and deeply, and surprisingly. They are not forced; they have no gap or sudden jump in musical progression, but convincingly leading us on from one fresh scene to another, all unsuspected, all surprising. His "Grande Fugue op. 133," for example, is less a botched Bach than the unique Beethoven baked, brewed, and made from scratch so fresh and alive.

---

[24] 司馬遷, 史記, 項羽本紀第七, 臺北市三民書局, 2008, 1:457.

Still, daunting is Beethoven often in sudden shift from very loud to very soft. It takes quite a musical structural skill and sensitivity to shape the transition naturally, for it is so easy to go too rough and loud, and then suddenly drop to too soft, almost smothering up our breathing in a roller coaster performance, or else their performance so boringly spreads his musical tapestry as to turn us off, making us wonder if *this* is Beethoven at all. It is tough to translate Beethoven alive and natural.

Beethoven's suddenness is his profound vitality if we can tame it; it is his pesky annoyance if we unthinkingly follow the score, failing to shape it sensitively to maneuver through his rough goings into his coherent vibrancy. In short, Beethoven is tough to perform through his string quartets. His Piano Sonatas are better, so rich in variety of nuances and much easier to maneuver through the rough edges. So far, I find Busch Quartet, Hungarian Quartet, and Talich Quartet doing Beethoven best justice, and Schnabel presenting Beethoven at his deepest, most eloquent, and most exquisite.[25]

Musical is Chinese writing,[26] portraying the sense of things that has tone-in-time as an intrinsic part of its language singing things' sense. Thus, the translation of Chinese writing amounts to musical performance in the West of the Chinese compositions. The translation is also a cross-cultural one. Sometimes, Chinese sayings in undulation are neatly translatable, and so are the Western sayings into the Chinese. Several examples come to mind.

Blake's well-known "to see a world in a grain of sand" is often rendered lyrically as rhyming "Yih sha yih shih-chieh 一砂一世界, one sand, one world."[27] Do we hear "yih" and "shih" inter-beckoning inter-intoning? China's Hu Shih's 胡適 famous quip, "Ta-tan [big] chia-sheh, hsiao-hsin [small] ch'iu-cheng 大膽假設, 小心求證" I tried as "Dare to propose, delicately to prove." Confucius' (17/2) rhythm, "Hsing hsiang-chin [close-by] yeh, hsi hsiang-yüan [far away] yeh 性相近也, 習相遠也" I put as "Born alike, learnt, apart." "Tso ch'ih, shan k'ung 坐吃山空" is my "Sit eat, mount empty." Etc.

Beyond sayings, China and the West can dialogue on notions, such as between Western democracy and Chinese trend of people-rooted politics as its judgment, Western pragmatism and Chinese praxis-posture,[28] and Western education and Chinese self-cultivation under the parental watchful eyes of our tutors.

In all these dialogues, however, we must be cautioned against taking Confucius as Chinese Cicero, Mencius as Chinese Emerson, Chuang Tzu as Chinese Thoreau, T'ao Ch'ien as Chinese Wordsworth, and the like. Such "translations" are outrageous misidentifications that impose the Western frame of mind onto China, to destroy cross-cultural dialogues in

---

[25] "Busch Quartet," *EMI* in an expensive 4-CD set, "Busch String Quartet: Beethoven String Quartets No. 7 and No. 8," *Biddulph* (no less expensive), "The Busch Quartet: Beethoven Quartets Nos. 7 and 13," *Sony*. Quatuor Talich, "Beethoven Intégrale des Quatuors," *Calliope*, France, in an expensive set of 7 CDs. Artur Schnabel, "Beethoven: Klaviersonaten," *EMI*, in 8-CD set. They are all divine performances.

[26] See Kuang-ming Wu, *Chinese Wisdom Alive: Vignettes of Life-Thinking*, NY: Nova Science Publishers, 2010, pp. 119-386, on how pervasive music is in China.

[27] Without referring to Blake, Jullien cited "In my sleeve, the sun and the moon are hidden,/ On the palm of my hand the entire universe fits" of Qi Ji (p. 282, note 12 has its reference) in François Jullien's scattered volume, *The Propensity of Things*, NY: Zone Books, 1999, p. 117.

[28] Cf. "The spirit of pragmatism and the pragmatic spirit" in my *On the "Logic" of Togetherness: A Cultural Hermeneutic*, Leiden: Brill, 1998, pp. 313-342.

cross-fertilization. No benefit can be harvested from such monocultural dominance. What do all these examples *mean* in globalization, however?

C. TRANSLATION IS LIVING GLOBALIZATION

Now, all this we understand and we are convinced of it all, and then we realize that of course we fully understand this whole bit, because we are alive, and all this translation is concerned with living. Translation is living. So we must now consider how living translation goes in globalization ever continuing without ceasing. We have merely to list our discoveries in two more sections, to round up this chapter.

Ten: Translation Is Living

In all this, we now see. Translation as shown above is living. Even naming things and persons translates the unknown and the unaware into our stock of conscious knowledge so as to orient our living in an apt and correct way. "Naming" is of course thinking that translates things into our minds, and thus "right naming 正名" is right thinking to make right living, as China proposed. Again, we have just performed translation of alien ancient culture, China, into the West today.

Living is traveling. Our travels to exotic lands excitingly translate exotics into our living. Actually, every single dawn begins our exotic travel into novelties of the future "today" ever unknown, yet. We can then train ourselves to properly adapt to things to adapt things *to us*. All our adaptive acts of living as adepts are those sent to us (translated) by the erupting power of existence incarnate (softly translated) in us.[29]

In general, existence is inter-existence, as exhibited in the law of identity, "A is A, as A is not not-A," thus the A is always with the not-A as the other to exist as the A. If existence is inter-existence, the existence obtains by transference of the other into itself, and itself into the other, and "transfer into" is translation.

So existence consists in translation. Eating, breathing, thinking, learning, talking, and acting, translate other things and persons to bring out existence as it expresses living on. Medicine, literature, technology, and all routine businesses, and all daily engagements, are our various translations, unbeknown to us (for we are not aware that they are translations) to keep us going on in fit-vigor.

Life as inter-existence is then an inter-living kept up by inter-translations without ceasing. Life cannot stop inter-translating as it cannot stop breathing under the trees breathing, back and forth with us. Translation is such togetherness inter-alive to inter-spread, in and out, out and out, hour by hour, day in and day out. Translation mobilizes existence to move the world. Translation is globalization alive on the go.

---

[29] The sensitive reader can see the parallel to—translation of—the New Testament here. In *The Acts of the Apostles*, "apostle" means one who was sent and translated into by the Power Parental and Deathless, ever Beyond all existing, all translated into life vigor overflowing.

Eleven: Translation Is Globalization Unfinishable

In the final analysis, we must claim this. With the help of Chuang Tzu in ancient China, we see that translation is "the ruling principle of nurturing life 養生主."[30] Such "help" amounts again to translation across time and cultures. In any case, our claim consists of three points. One, translation is adaptation of life to life. Two, criticizing this claim as relativism and responding to it compose an exciting dialogical translation. Three, all this activity composes music antiphonal, dynamic and global.

One: Translation is adaptation of life to life: Translation is our acts of adapting us to what comes to us, so as to adapt what comes *to* our living. This is to say that translation is our inter-adaptations between what comes *and* what we are. The "and" here composes what we are, and what we are here is how we live on. What we are consists in this inter-adaptation. We cite four concrete examples from the Chuang Tzu and the Huai Nan Tzu to demonstrate—show and prove—our claim.

Our first example is the dry skull casually tossed out on the roadside; such a situation is what we usually take as the rock-bottom abject misery of severed corpse, not even decently buried. Totally departing from our common sense, however, Chuang Tzu says that the skull is actually enjoying the joy, ultimate and unspeakable, of making seasonal rounds with the sky and the field. It is a surprising and delightful translation of miseries of life into the ultimate joy, without even the help of divine Beyond.

Inspired by this ultimate of flexible joy, Huai Nan Tzu has the story—our second example—of Uncle Fort at the edge of town, that is to say, he lives at the limiting life-situations, ever in crises, joyous and not-joyous. He constantly asks, "How could this woe not make weal?" when woe strikes him, and cautiously asks, "How could this weal not make woe?" when weal visits him.[31] He is poised ready, always looking forward.

He is ever fit to fit in, with revolutions of paradigms and gestalts[32] by translating situation constantly shifting into his flexuous living, where timeliness is the measure, now dragon-soar, now snaking-sinuous, with a pivot stable and self-forgetful in nurture of life, around which revolve all sorts of changes, expected and unexpected, joys and no-joys, moment by moment.

Two: Criticism of the claim and its response composes translation: Some of us would naturally demur, saying that this attitude amounts to irresponsible relativism. It is a sour-grape posture, a wishy-washy escapism that rounds up one's shameful story of spilled milk and inept failures by explaining things away, to make one's wobbly interpretation—translation of life—plausible and presentable, even to one's miserable self, otherwise quite helpless.

Our response is that any proposal must be judged by its practical consequences. Far from wobbly, the posture described with the above two stories portrays the sort of way of life

---

[30] "養生主" is the title of the third chapter of the *Chuang Tzu*, but we take off in our own direction, for Chuang Tzu did not connect that chapter to translation, though we do so in his spirit.

[31] On the roadside dry skull, see *Chuang Tzu* 18/22-29. On Uncle Fort, see Huai Nan Tzu, in 淮南子, 人間訓, 臺北市三民書局, 民86, p. 965.

[32] Both Kuhn and Feyerabend see science as revolutions of paradigms (Kuhn) and gestalts (Feyerabend; he even sees revolutions to extend to cultural ones), but neither realized that such revolutions spell the exciting progress of science in adaptive translations of recalcitrant actuality. Besides, neither was able to respond to the unjustified charge of "relativism." See Thomas S. Kuhn, *The Structure of Scientific Revolutions* (1962), University of Chicago Press, 1996. Paul Feyerabend, *Against Method* (1975), London: Verso, 1993.

powerfully effective at living, in vigor at leisure in any circumstances. It consists in fitness, fit in situ, quite stable and comfortable in life quite uncertain, so much so that we can even afford to forget our self.

All this is the principle of no-principle, in flexuous interpretations (translations) so as to naturally inter-adjust with whatever comes, with the future unknown yet inevitable. But, in any case, such inter-dialogue as this between criticism and response must *continue* to inter-translate one into the other to inter-benefit.

Three: All such activity composes music antiphonal, dynamic, and global: Something as above described is a portrayal of grand translation in futuristic thrust that is continuous and unending. All this may contain another implication—translation—of Confucius' sigh (9/22), "awesome are youngsters 後生可畏" with limitless promises and potentials of further translations in life, and so "no posterity" is the major 無後為大 perpetration of un-filiality (*Mencius* 4A26) to our cultural tradition, our parents. Both openings to the future are straight from supposedly asphyxiating Confucianism.

Interestingly, however, history always has posterity, for that is what history consists in. So history is filial, exhibits filiality, and portrays filiality. But history always changes, and so filiality is alive and dynamic. History filial is alive and dynamic thanks to antiphonic dialogues with posterity always interpreting and translating the past its parents into its present. Thus translation parents history that is filial.

In all this grand ultimate sense, life ongoing is translation ongoing, as life is adapting ongoing and "ongoing" is the nisus to the future, in time, in space. This it is that is globalization dynamic and forward-looking. Globalization is all lives translating, adapting together toward the futures together, as all lives live on to the future together.

All this antiphony in time describes rhythm, rhyme, and their going-on, and these four describe music. My rhythm of living cannot help but rhyme with your life-rhythm. And then ours spreads to rhyme with theirs, and all of ours with our milieu, on and on in antiphony in time of symphony of the "Ode to Joy" global, beyond all joys and sorrows. A concrete example, the fourth one, taken from Chuang Tzu (17/87-91) shows it.

Chuang Tzu exclaimed with joy at the leisurely swimming of tiny minnows roaming so casually under the bridge. His logician friend Hui Tzu asked how he could have known the joy of small fish if he is not fish. Chuang Tzu said, in essence, that mutually not one another is precisely the how, the cause, of his feeling the roaming joy of minnows. How could he feel their joy? "I know it—their joy—by being above the How River" here now.

"By being here now" across centuries and cultures is the dynamic how of all that rhyme with all, and the inter-rhyming is inter-translation, as Chuang Tzu the man resonating with minnows the fish shows such inter-species co-feeling of joy together. Being not-identical one to another here now is precisely the cause that enables the how of co-resonation of feelings of joy, even between two different species of living beings, which thus spells globalization.

"What is globalization?" Well, the teacher asks, "*What* are you drawing, Tommy?" Tommy said, "How should I know? I am not done yet." Similarly, we can answer, "How should we know what globalization is? Globalization is not done yet, and can never be done, as the future can never be done." "Is globalization totally unknown, then?" Well, we have some clues, as Tommy must have some himself.

We know now that globalization is the ongoing rhythms of existents inter-rhyming, going on inter-translating together from the past antiphonal into the future that cannot be finished;

so globalization is unable to finish. We are all Tommy who keeps drawing life, translating life together, to keep on growing in globalization, world without end, as Tommy keeps drawing and showing what he draws to his teacher and his pals.

C. GLOBALIZATION DYNAMICS

This *third* cluster typifies globalization in various "dynamic features," beginning with Dr. Tang's "history" in globalization, and then to manage cosmic household in ecology, as activities of togetherness, in ubiquity, and admired and presented as interculture, all by K. Wu.

In: Globalization Dynamics
Editor: Kuang-ming Wu

ISBN: 978-1-62100-750-0
© 2012 Nova Science Publishers, Inc.

Chapter 12

HISTORY IN GLOBALIZATION

Tang Ruei-hong[1]
Taiwan, ROC

ABSTRACT

History is an integral vigor in globalization, and we neglect history at our own peril. We first, A. describe how history is made, and then, B. see how from this description it follows that history is the modus vivendi and modus operandi of globalization in all its storytelling that, C. composes the story-integrity of the self to compose history, and, D. stress how ignoring history ignores our very survival, to, E. consider how to perform our task of history as globalization, before concluding what global historical perception consists in.

"Globalization" is a buzz word today; now everyone is talking about globalization, as if they know what it is. But very few people are aware of how deeply and pervasively involved "history" is in globalization. It is not just that history is one dimension among many of globalization. It is that history *constitutes* globalization, that globalization is world history at work, that globalization without history is no globalization but an empty vogue and fashion, soon to pass into oblivion. In all, history is quite a serious essence of globalization. History is the ongoing dynamics *of* globalization, in which we simply must participate, for we are its part.

This chapter elucidates this crucial fact of history as integral vigor in globalization, and stresses how we neglect history at our own peril. We first, A. describe how history is made, and then, B. see how from this description it follows that history is the modus vivendi and modus operandi of globalization in all its storytelling that, C. composes the story-integrity of the self to compose history, and, D. stress how ignoring history ignores our very survival, to, E. consider how to perform our task of history as globalization, before concluding what global historical perception consists in.

---

[1] E-mail address: ping_wentang@yahoo.com.tw (Assistant Professor of history in China Culture University, Taiwan, ROC. Dr. Tang is a Collingwood scholar in Chinese perspective)

A. Description of How History Is Made

To begin, we must grasp how history comes about. History is not just the past that has passed away and vanished for ever. History is raw past data preserved as chronicle by us in the present, and shaped by us in the present as we now at present see it, and while the present is shaping the past into history, history processes the present and shapes us in the present. History of the past is shaped by the present to shape the present. History is powerfully contemporary (Croce, Graham[2]).

Moreover, we the human present, we must note, live culture as the way we live that is pervaded by history. We seldom notice the fact that culture is [1] made of accumulation and handing down of information, and [2] all "information" and all "knowledge" are historical accumulation, and [3] education hands down such historical heritage to constitute "culture" that is the hallmark of our being human. Our very humanity is thus our continuous three acts of *history* so globally vast indeed. History in this vast sense composes our entire culture to constitute us all as human, all too human.

Collingwood tells us how "history" obtains. History is formed by us at present posing questions to the past data we collect, and the answers the past data gives us are our "history" at present. Then he says that our questions are based on—derived from—our "absolute presupposition" that he says is "culture."[3] We then realize that "culture" is itself what history makes us, as we just described above.

So here is already a dialogical circle of history between our present culture and the past data we collect. We-now ask questions to the past-we-see, for the past to answer to turn into our history, while our questions themselves derive from "culture" made by the past history for us. In addition, we see—though Collingwood did not say so—that the history in turn poses questions to us at present for us to respond and answer, to be answerable to history, to be historically responsible.

Thus history is the grand global process of inter-dialogues back and forth between our past and our present, based on our dialogue with the past called culture. Such inter-dialogue in time is history, and the very "inter" is the history trafficking in dialogue between our past and our present, to and fro, back and forth, interculture without end.

Naturally, we realize how radioactive all such "inter" is. Culture is our proud stories, and stories are to be told and heard. Culture is telling and receiving of stories, quite social. We being social, we cannot help but talk about our stories of cultures one to another, in space and in time, and our inter-dialogues in storytelling and story-hearing spread among various histories among various cultures. This story-spread of inter-dialogues continues in time between past and present, and in space among various cultures. The continual spread to its maximum is called "globalization."

"Now, what shall we say to all this?" Frankly, we say that all this is nothing short of stupendously important, critical and cosmic. Hear this. History makes a thing, lasting or not,

---

[2] Benedetto Croce, *History: Its Theory and Practice*, tr. Douglas Ainslee, NY: Harcourt, Brace and Co., 1921, pp. 11-26. Gordon Graham, *The Shape of the Past: A Philosophical Approach to History*, Oxford University Press, 1997. Interestingly, both Italian politician-thinker Croce (b. 1866) and today's British analytic thinker Graham agree on we at present shape "history" of the past.

[3] R. G. Collingwood, *An Autobiography* (1939), pp. 29-43, and *An Essay on Metaphysics* (1940), pp. 21-48, both from Oxford University Press.

to last as history. No history, no thing. At the same time, history is made by questions and answers between us and our past, and thereby what is passed away comes back alive to haunt us to make us be. History is thus made by us to make us. History dialogically traffics between us and not-us, between the self and the other in time, to make the self with the other that depends on the self to be the other.

History tells us the story that the other the past makes the self as the other depends on the self to be questioned and turned into the other, and so the other and the self interdepend to shape into their respective selves, to be independently themselves, and their independence is actively shown in their interaction in questions and answers, and such is their dialogue that makes history.

No other, no self; no self, no other. The self is the other, and the other is made into its own "self" by the self, and all this while the reverse process of the other making the self goes on, and all this inter-making is the story of dialogues called "history." History inexorably creates all the existents throughout the globe.

Thus in the beginning is history that begins existence as inter-existence. Existence is history or it is nothing, and history says that existence is the self and the other inter-dialoguing in question and answer in time (past vs. present) in space (self vs. other, culture vs. culture). Dialogue makes existence, and where there is dialogue, there is history. Dialogue, existence, and history compose the story of globalization, birthing, birthing, without ceasing.

Now, human existence is made of such history called "culture" that is the way the self lives, and culture is accumulated history, that is, history is the heritage of culture that transmits from generation to generation in global interculture in time. Human existence is a social story from the past to the present, from the present to the future, and this sociality in time, dialogical and intercultural, is called "history," world without end.

In time begins today. Today begins the rest of my life, and "beginning the rest" is history, so today is history. History is the be-all to begin all, at every present. "Every" is global, and so globalization is all history. Forget this fact, ubiquitous and pervasive, and we will be consigned to hollow slogans whenever we vainly mouth "globalization." History anchors us onto the sure reality of globalization and its intercultural substance all over the world.

B. HISTORY AS MODUS VIVENDI AND MODUS OPERANDI OF STORY-GLOBALIZATION

We described above that our life's story of question and answer is history that constitutes the self, and such history, constitutive of the self, is inherently social. As I nod to my life-story to compose myself, my story gets to be told to you (what story is not told? Story is story telling), and you, and you, who hear and receive my story to learn and react to my story, to add to your stories, each of you. After all, telling stories requires receiving of stories.

Meanwhile, you and you and you do your storytelling to exist as you, for me to receive your stories and critically react to them to enrich my story that composes myself. Storytelling to and fro, back and forth, enables each of us to grow one into the other. Such is our dialogues in our mutual story-making that composes our respective histories of our many selves, to spread into making our community, which expands dialogically, globally. Globalization is made of telling stories that keeps spreading.

Stories make history, and story-dialogues compose interculture. All these four activities—story, history, dialogue, interculture—crisscross to skewer into coherent one, only to open out and develop continually toward globalization. Globalization is an ongoing activity of composition of the music of inter-existence called "dialogical interculture," world without end.

History is thus globalization in time, because history is dialogue in time that expands in space. Interculture makes globalization in space, and interculture is also dialogue in space. If culture is the way we exist, then interculture is the way we inter-exist, and to inter-exist is to dialogue one with another into history. And so, interculture is dialogues in time and in space, with historical stories telling and composing us all. In all, globalization is dialogues in time (history) and in space (interculture historical). Thus globalization is historical, through and through.

Naturally, history has a genetic originative significance for all of us. "The soul of the three-year-old until a hundred," says Japan. Likewise, "The child is father of the man," says Wordsworth and is picked up by Freud to compose his psychoanalysis, and by Erik H. Erikson his disciple to form his psychology as biography. To understand the self we must read its biography, says Erikson. We cannot help but agree.

What is said about the personal self applies to the big self such as cultures, communities, and globalization. To understand cultures all over the globe, we must read their biographies that are their histories reciprocally told among all cultures, to compose the history of globalization for each of us to read and understand, and thereby we, in turn, compose such histories to globalize them.

After all, it is all of us who make up globalization. Without specific existence, there would exist no globalization, and so we must understand so many existents to understand globalization; and to know any existent, we must know its story enriched by other stories, in fact, composed by other stories. Others and their stories are our parents.

Let us be concrete. To know the American culture, we must understand *its* parent the Indo-European culture. To know the European culture we must understand its parent the Greek-Roman culture, known by understanding India. To know the Japanese culture, we must understand its parents, the Chinese and the European cultures. And China and India must be traced to Africa, and all of us in turn are parented by primal and primitive cultures worldwide that we must sympathetically learn to understand, as we should lovingly understand our parents.

All this amounts to saying that, in the final analysis, we must realize that all cultures are miscegenation of global intercultures. Culture is the way we live on. We are by nature culturally miscegenational. So we are all interculturally growing without ceasing, thanks to all of us being "mixed-up kids."

Miscegenation has four features. One, it is historical and en-cultured. Two, it is inter-enriched among the selves and the others in time among many cultures with historical depths. Three, such inter-culture is global, happening all over the world. We are thus born global; we are innately interculturally global. Four, such globalization is thoroughly historical. In all this, history is our parents, our queen and king among us all, globally.

Let us now extrapolate. The description of history in the above section A, as a dynamic spread of inter-dialogues in time and in space, indicates that history is the modus vivendi and the modus operandi of globalization. First, history is the modus vivendi of globalization. History is how globalization goes on *alive*. Without history globalization is dead and hollow, just a shell and husk of empty slogans. All this while, secondly, history serves as the modus operandi of globalization. Globalization is history at work worldwide. In historical activities, globalization proceeds vigorously.

Thus history as dynamic inter-dialogues in time and space works out globalization forever active. History constitutes globalization and turns it alive. Do you want to see what "history" is at its grandest scale in its true glorious shape? Look at globalization shaping itself historical. Do you want to see what "globalization" is at its most vigorous and true spectacular shape? Look at how it is making itself historical between our past and our present, and among various histories of various cultures all over the world, going into the future full of unsuspected promises.

In other words, history is the life and the dynamics of globalization. Globalization is history incarnate at its most concrete, most vast, and most vivacious. Such global history tells stories of our lives since time immemorial. We must now consider history as storytelling.

C. HISTORY AS STORYTELLING

In section A we described how history is formed; in section B we saw how history as myself forms globalization. Here in this section C we describe *what* history is. "Story" is often mentioned above in connection with history. Not accidentally, history is cognate to story, etymologically and in meaning. Let us thus look into (history as) storytelling to understand history.

To begin, we must note that, importantly, there exists no history in general as there is no story in general. History always tells stories of *specific* concrete happenings. Still, these specific and particular stories thrill and enthrall us *all* who hear these stories. We are absorbed into those stories, and by and by we draw implications and instinctively apply them to our specific situations here now. It is for this purpose that books on history of whatever sorts keep coming out on the market. History as specific stories has wide appeal of universal relevance the world over.

Still, such universality of relevance of specific stories is quite peculiar. Historically drawing implications and applying to here and now are not logical deduction or logical induction, for this obvious reason. These logical processes assume universal generality to reach universal generality, all abstract and theoretical. In contrast, historical stories themselves are incorrigibly specific and concrete, neither abstract nor general, and yet they are powerful enlightenments to us all and to all our posterity. History has its own peculiar particularity combined with its own sort of inexhaustible applicability in time without end, world without end.

History is a concrete "particular universal" in a peculiar "historical sense." History as particular universal is *sui generis*, one of its kind, so closely intimate among us, and yet so beyond logical analysis in theoretical universal deduction or induction to understand. Now, this quality of historical "particular generality" is particularly suited to globalization that consists in ubiquitous interculture among specific cultures. It is in this global milieu that every particular community and culture, however small, is cherished and is depended on to compose and attain the global community worldwide.

This is due to the fact that any particular incident and/or idea have a cosmopolitan import and exert impacts throughout the globe. That is what globalization as historic means. This non-logical universality of historical particulars obtains because, among others, logic is a spatial link, while history is in addition a linking in time. All this while, globalization is imbued with a dynamics of time quite beyond logic to parse and understand. Globalization makes concrete sense without making logical sense. Let us take two historical examples to understand such odd non-logical universal particularity.

How could the historical phenomenon of Hitler that horrified us globally have happened in its particular period of time in its particular place and culture? The historians can cite specific circumstances in which Hitlerism appeared, but these circumstances are a dime a dozen in any period of time in any culture at any spot. The back-view mirror of history can obscurely see Nero in Hitler (universal), in that both insanely brutalized their own peoples, but Nero is Nero, Hitler is Hitler, and the twain shall never meet, in fact, neither is actually acquainted with the other (particulars). This "particular universality" is typical of history that defies any logical sense.

Similarly, globalization today may "parallel" the globalization of Pax Romana or even earlier ones, and there are some more uncanny parallels among many other globalizations in many other periods among many other cultures. This is historical universality. Still, why this kind of globalization is happening at this period of history now is beyond all abstract logic or even "historical logic," if any, to discern and concoct. We call this fatuous factual particularity "historical contingency" that makes sense in history, but not otherwise.

Thus again history has universal parallels and unrepeatable uniqueness-es, both at once. Globalization is such a historical "particular universal." Here any specific community and its culture is welcomed as a special note that goes into composing the global music of inter-existence worldwide, in the past, at present, toward the future, globalizing without ceasing. It is in this manner that history is ubiquitous storytelling, story-hearing, and story-enriching of human existence in its specific various modes, in interculture globally all the time.

Here every distinct culture with its peculiar history is eagerly welcomed. The more, the merrier; the more varied, the richer even more. Variety is the spice of joy of life and so variety constitutes the riches of globalization. Globalization must never be a melting pot but must grow into the grand kaleidoscope of interculture world without end.

Let us this time see history from the perspective of us growing, to give rationale to all above. History tells the stories of how we grow up in variously unique manners. In kindergarten, kids bring their favorite toys to talk about them to one another. Their diverse favorites are of course they themselves so diverse. It is this diversity that occasions joyous showing and telling of them.

Showing and telling about their favorites exhibits themselves, and the entire kindergarten bustles and bristles with laughter. It is how they grow in joys of displaying themselves, and in their own ways. We are all kids growing in the globe our kindergarten, by showing and telling about our favorite stories of our various selves. We tell our many stories and swap "our stories," and those stories are our histories. We grow in our histories by growing those histories.

"Growing" is itself a story that describes how I am coherently integrated as I am, *while* I continue to open out into the future "me" on its own way unbeknown even to me, to come to be me. In the same way, "story" is also coherent as itself, and open to further unsuspected additions in the future. Open coherence typifies both story in the yarning and history in the making, growing without ceasing.

History is story, as story makes history. Therefore we can read story to understand how history is composed. Let us then consider story to understand history. Story is yarning unlimited. The "yarning" coherently collects anything that happens, factually or in imagination; "unlimited" describes how such yarning is open-ended, unsuspected. Thus story is open coherence. Anything can be added to yarn out a coherent whole, while "anything" is open, continuously going on and on, in fact and in imagination. Story is systematically open.

This dynamic structure of story describes how events of our life continuing to come to us are then continually organized and yarned out by us into a story of our interest. This yarning composes our living-identity, and this story ongoing is history. History is our story to compose our very self. Deprived of such life-story of history, there would be no human life at all.

Oliver Sacks, a neuropsychologist at Albert Einstein Hospital, in all his books of so many interesting stories, tells us that we all carry our own life-story ready to tell to anyone, including telling to our self, to make and compose our very self. Losing this story loses me, and the loss of my story is "mental illness" that is pain quite unbearable, for it amounts to living my own death.

Moreover, we must remember this fact. We instinctively feel in our heart of being that "my story" that is "me" is a part of—my conspicuous tip of—our communal story I am proud of. "I am a Chinese" is at the back and base of my story as myself a China-man. The reason is quite simple. Every note is special only in music, and my specific note makes an important sense for me in the whole music that is my proud culture my China in which I live and move, and grow.

And soon enough, my culture appears to me as part of global concord, for "China" is senseless until it is seen as part of the whole network of world cultures, against the background of which "China" is proudly China. I am thus a cosmopolitan, a world citizen in being a China-man, and I can breathe deeply toward the vast global horizon as I turn on TV or the radio to listen to the news of the world, because that world is part of me as I am part of my world. My being global is why I am interested in listening to the world news that has nothing to do with my immediacies of daily routines.

Let us take stock. History as inter-dialogues in time and space spreads by way of telling stories, reading stories, shaping stories and being shaped by stories—of ourselves. In fact, all informed knowledge we have is a collection of such stories, nothing else. Such dynamics of stories is entirely free but not at all casual, much less arbitrary. This is because my cultural heritage is my most cherished essence composing my self-identity freely growing. Nothing is arbitrary here, for I am not arbitrary.

Stories compose the very identity of our self. This point is even physiologically brought out by all books of Oliver Sacks the neuropsychologist at Albert Einstein Hospital, as mentioned above. Unfortunately, Sacks himself, being a scientist, does not seem to see the inherent connection of storytelling to history, to see how history as storytelling composes the dignity of self-identity of the human self. We wish he did.

All the above description can be expanded as follows. My story that makes my self expands to compose globalization as history, in this way. My story composes my self; likewise our world is shaped by our stories, variously called myth, legend, and fable. Today's myth is verification by repeatability of experiments, as today's legend is natural laws in natural sciences, and today's fables are theories of evolution and cosmologies. All these stories gather to shape the world that we know today.

Thomas Kuhn called these framing stories "paradigms,"[4] but he did not link paradigms to telling stories and making history, although he did see how the paradigm-shift makes revolution. We say, such shift that is revolution is history. History is revolution of paradigms, revolution of assumptions that are cultures.

Sartre said that telling stories "catches time by its tail." We say that such retrospective telling composes history. Sartre also said that we are born storytellers, tall stories, as we always tell lies.[5] We say that "telling lies" here means concocting some retrospective connections to make sense out of senseless bits and events we encounter.

If this is the case, then since history is stories, we humans cannot live without history that we constantly concoct. Asking if these stories are factual or not misses the point, for these stories are the very criteria whereby to judge factuality and actuality, whatever they mean, for the very meanings of "fact" and "actual" are determined by these stories.

Rituals reenact myths and legends to actualize them that in turn elucidate the meanings and efficacies of these rituals. By the same token, technologies reenact sciences and their theories that elucidate the meanings, significance, and efficacies of technologies. My grandmother and Blaise Pascal died of chronic stomachaches, for in those days there was no "intestine cancer" that exists only in the context—myth—of today's medicine.

No wonder we cannot live without stories and histories that make up our "cultures" to frame our "world," in which we live and have our being. We *are* historical, and our whole world is shaped by stories that are histories, and so globalization is history. It is thus that my story that makes myself expands to the globe shaped by our stories that make ourselves. Global concord story-made shall be unspeakable joy consolidating our dignity of being ourselves together.

From this point of storytelling as composition of the identity of the self and the world, we see two points. One, neglecting story as history amounts to killing our self, to committing suicide. Section D tells of this first fatal risk. Two, story is by nature a verb of storytelling and story-hearing, spreading inexorably as history throughout the globe. Story is a dialogical verb that establishes our *social* selves to spread globally. Section E tells of this second point, on how to fulfill our social task of globalizing our personal intercultural storytelling.

D. IGNORING HISTORY IGNORES OUR OWN SURVIVAL

Since history is totally pervasive in human existence, even just to ignore history commits our most serious crime against humanity. Ignoring history amounts to opposing history. Such "opposition" to history is more serious than committing suicide, for even the very committal of suicide makes an episode of history, not opposing history as such.

Actually, ignoring history is one most un-filial act, to express it in terms of Chinese culture, given the fact that it is history that parents and nurtures our very identity. History tells us stories after stories of how refusing to let "history teach 師古" us composes a hegemon to

---

[4] Thomas S. Kuhn, *The Structure of Scientific Revolution* (1962), University of Chicago Press, 1996. Cf. his *Copernican Revolution* (1957), Harvard University Press, 1974.
[5] Jean-Paul Sartre, *Nausea*, NY: New Directions, 1964, pp. 56-59.

guarantee his downfall in disaster, as the Grand Historian Ssu-ma Ch'ien 司馬遷 loudly intoned this elegy over the hegemon Hsiang Yü's 項羽 tragic death in spectacular defeat.[6]

We add that refusal to let history teach us invites our disastrous downfall beucase such a refusal of history amounts to the un-filial act, quite serious as opposing one's root of existence to ensure cutting one's own original root, that is to say, committing suicide, to commit killing history our own parent. Sadly, however, even such trial at murdering history is in vain, for in trying to kill history, we just kill ourselves to add one more sad chapter in history. All in all, what tragedy it is indeed to ignore history!

Sadly, however, no one lamented over Hitler's refusal to learn from history, e.g., his neglecting to learn from Nero's brutality over Nero's own people. History calls Nero's brutality "insane"; Hitler was likewise insane enough to turn against Hitler's own decent citizens, the Jewry, devastating them in Auschwitz, to end up devastating his own nation and himself.

All hegemonies of dictators, past and present, court their own demise by attacking their own people on whom their regimes are built; it is the truth history tells us of. World history thus silently intones elegies after elegies over such insane suicides that refuse to learn from history. Ignoring history commits suicide to make up another tragic chapter in history. Ignoring history adds to history in sad sequel.

History thus continues to shape, enrich, and nurture humanity worldwide, even as some of us neglect our almighty parent, our history. We simply must consult history to direct ourselves toward prudential wisdom in conducting ourselves, on pain of destroying ourselves. If history parents us, refusing to learn from history our parents destroys us. This is our absolute lesson toward human existence, no ifs, no buts, and no exception.

In addition, history is our *sine qua non* to cosmopolitan survival, to our global thriving together. World history is world judgment (Hegel); those who forget the past are condemned to repeat it (Santayana). "But what if history itself is wrong?" in fact, history has indeed often been rewritten wrong on purpose.

Powers that be often try to rewrite histories, whitewashing over their bloody blemishes in their histories. Textbooks of history in Japan have no atrocities of Japanese troops perpetrated in China, Taiwan, and Southeast Asia. Kuomintang in Taiwan is currently busy rewriting its bloody 228 Incident. Political ideology includes rewriting national history.

Moreover, monocultural domination is another not-too-subtle trend worldwide especially today. The trend equates analytical logic with "thinking," Western sciences with "truth," and the Western culture with "global modernity," almost implying that English language is the world language, and so China or India has no language at all.

"How do we correct such blatant cultural mistakes so historic?" Infusion of more and more varied cultures and their histories is the cure. Perceptual mistakes are corrected by more perceptions, as invalid arguments are corrected by more arguments. Likewise, history *continues* to correct itself by posterity to continue history. We will soon elucidate this crucial point.

Thus history is our absolute necessity of existence as the sun is. History is the sun in human time. Exposure to the sun sanitizes. Pan-publicity cleanses. Pan-exposure is an operation of history to steer us away from mistakes and disasters of all sorts, and the "pan-" here ciphers globalization. Thus the imperative to consult history in global context remains absolute. It is one of the few absolutes we have in human life so piecmeal. Naturally, we now have to consider how to fulfill this absolute imperative of our existence toward globalization.

---

[6] 司馬遷 concluded his story of 項羽 with these sad words in 史記, 項羽本紀第七, 臺北市三民書局, 2008, I; 457.

E. OUR TASK: HOW TO HISTORY-PERFORM GLOBALIZATION

Globalization is never a staid item to be shelved away as an exotic file in an ivory tower, but our urgent task to be performed worldwide here now. In view of all above said about historicity in globalization as our absolute necessity, we must now consider *how* best to execute our historical task of globalization. Clearly our first order of business is to learn from one another our respective cultural heritages that are histories of these cultures, "good" ones *and* "bad" ones alike, while every culture must tell stories of what they are, and how they came to be as they are now.

"Do we have a goal to aim at in our intercultural learning? Does our cultural inter-learning have a norm to observe and follow?" Well, here our very goal and norm must be hammered out precisely in and by our global struggles of inter-learning, as such struggles compose history. The very destination and the very standard of our globalizing performances are part and parcel of globalizing struggles. The "inter" in globalizing inter-learning is the modus vivendi and modus operandi of its norm and its goal. And these very global struggles compose history as globalization. History in the global making composes its own norm and its own goal.

"This is incredible. What if we make mistake? How do we correct ourselves?" History is our grand judge. In ancient China, the royal court had the office of a Grand Historian. Our Grand Historians today are the historians, the journalists such as George Orwell and H. L. Mencken, in fact, any reflective persons who would examine and warn us every week as they reflect on what has happened "this week." The more and the more varied sorts of penetrating reflective persons we have, from the more various angles, the better off we are, i.e., the more sane and solid all around we would become.

"But none of us is perfect. There always exist tons of possibilities of making mistakes of whatever sort. Doesn't history itself make mistakes, too? Do we have any effective measure against our mistakes?" Of course, being imperfect, we would always make mistakes. But let us remind ourselves again on what we do to correct our mistakes. Look at how we correct ourselves in daily living.

Any perceptual illusion and aberration is corrected by more perceptions, not by refraining from perceiving altogether; we will look *again* to ensure that what we see is what really is. And mistakes in reasoning are corrected by more reasoning from more varied angles, not by stopping reasoning for fear of making more logical mistakes. In the same way, corrections of journalists' retrospective judgments on what has happened are to be made by more observations of more numerous and more various journalists, not by stopping all such reflections. More numerous and more varied journalistic trials correct themselves, as they continue to make mistakes.

In short, globalization continuing in history is a self-correcting dynamics incumbent on us all, and its power of unceasing corrections is historical reflections. All in all, we have no alternative but to press ahead to perform globalizing interculture to inter-learn, in all the historical depths of cultural heritages, as we daily and continually perform historical reflections on our situations worldwide here and now.

In all this essential task of globalization in our daily living, we cannot stress too much how indispensable and important a role *history* plays. To begin with, everyone needs foresight, but not many people know that foresight is constantly gained by hindsight. The past experience (history) of how event-one went on to turn into event-two in the past serves as a beacon to shine on our future, on how we must behave to turn events into our thriving together globally.

The future may not exactly repeat the past, but the past often "rhymes" with the future. The prophets of the future are the soothsayers among past experience, the historians. No wonder, ancient China's Grand Historians were those who remonstrated with their lords to point to the roads to tread ahead.

Let us remind ourselves again of what we routinely do for right living. Perceptual mistakes can be corrected by, one, more perceptions in time, and, two, more numerous and various perceptions among people. These two ways of more perceiving are related. More perceptions in time are "history" of every week produced by many people to form "public opinions" especially by people in the know, such as scholars, discerning journalists (Lafcadio Hearn, H. L. Mencken, George Orwell), and literary writers (Lu Xun, Wen Ito, Eudora Welty[7]). They are beacons to us; they are our sages.

These sages "are sorrowful before the world turns sad, and rejoice after the world rejoices."[8] They are the pinnacle of public perception so penetrative, and we must consult with as many numerous and various sages of keen perceptions as possible, in past and at present, to gain such perceptive insights. They are persons of histories of many cultures, to be compared and learned by us here now with open attentive mind.

Since history is the present's critical reenactment of past experiences (Collingwood[9]) known and settled, history is the powerful steps to reenact the process of "past to present" to act out our future. History is the scientific project of the future. Collection of histories of world cultures is the collective power toward our future.

If history corrects itself, globalization in history as history expanding in globalization is a ubiquitous corrective of mistakes. History is *the* power of correction in global assurance, setting us on *the* unmistakable path to our sure future we share globally. Such is globalization, the collective power historical toward *our* sure global future.

Concretely speaking, history tells us that our forefathers and foremothers made mistakes to muddle through in various misfortunes. Some of them were prudent enough to steer themselves out to survive them, while some others sadly perished. Reading their stories—history—as we assess their ups and downs benefits us in steering our days through to co-thrive.

Their stories are our history, the more and varied the better for us to consult to steer our life's way. Thus histories worldwide are of inestimable guiding values to us here now. My dreams now for the future are inspired and generated by their dreams then. Their past inspires

---

[7] Lu Xun (1881-1936) was one of the greatest literati, a literary revolutionary who sharply criticized China's old Confucian society, and was so harassed by political orders as to take refuge in Shanghai International Settlement. See 魯迅全集, 北京人民文學出版社, 1981, 16 volumes. Wen Ito (1899-1946) initiated a new poetry movement, and so passionately criticized social injustices as to be assassinated. See 聞一多全集, 武漢湖北人民出版社, 1993, 12 volumes, and 聞黎明著, 聞一多: 涅槃的鳳凰, 臺北市資訊科技, 2010. The well-known literary writer of short stories, Eudora Welty (1909-2001) confessed, "My wish, my continuing passion, would be not to point the finger in judgment but to part a curtain, that invisible shadow that falls between people, the veil of indifference to each other's presence, each other's wonder, each other's human plight." (*Newsweek*, August 6, 2001, p. 60, at her obituary). This parting is publicity of personal inter-living the feat of lgobalization.

[8] They are another great social sage 范仲淹's famous words 「先天下之憂而憂, 後天下之樂而樂」 that conclude his <岳陽樓記> (see 古文觀止, 高雄麗文文化公司, 1995, p. 820).

[9] R. G. Collingwood, *The Idea of History* (1946), Oxford University Press, 1993.

the present into our future, continual, coherent, and ever open. All this is history in the past and history in the making. History is myself living on in our selves and into ourselves all over the globe.

All this our history-learning is valid because our learning from histories itself makes history, for our posterity to learn further. It is in this manner that history "rhymes" itself on and on. The terrible news of Japan's nuclear disasters and the devastating news of Libya's terrible human disasters keep coming to us. History is made by globalized news that keeps coming. Historical precedents of natural and human disasters abound. It is time to consult history, any time disaster strikes us all.

Globalization in historical depth is particularly effective against[10] disasters both natural and human. We can now mobilize today's almighty technologies to swiftly disseminate the terrible information worldwide, swiftly consult with one another worldwide in the UN and NATO and EU, as we consult with world histories on relevant precedents, so as to swiftly pull together our resources worldwide to dispatch to the devastated areas in matter of very few days, often hours. The Doctors without Borders and the Red Cross worldwide have been busily active throughout the globe amidst, e.g., Japan's disasters of earthquakes and its subsequent radiation debacle.

Human disasters often come with dictators against unarmed civilians, in their own land and in other communities. Many other communities and other cultures can warn dictators with globally concerted threats, economic, cultural, and military, and can remind dictators of the lessons from history, that violence, however quickly effective, no less quickly boomerangs to destroy dictators themselves, as the Amnesty International keeps testifying.

In globalization we all pull together ourselves, our resources, and our historical lessons, to deal with our problems natural and human, both local and worldwide. Togetherness in historical depth worldwide is the healing power of globalization invincible worldwide.

Now, natural disasters naturally rally all nations and cultures together, drawing all of us together into concerted struggles to resolve the mess, while human disasters of dictatorship have an especially strange silver-lining above their dark clouds. Let us take a concrete example. Ruler Moammar Gadhafi of Libya does not tolerate disagreement, much less protest. He regards the protestors from his own people as "rebels," not his own people. So, he attacks them militarily as "enemies," without compunction.

In contrast, all other nations in the UN and elsewhere take militarily attacking unarmed civilians as illegitimate, quite unjustified. These other nations may take these unarmed civilian protestors as Libyan citizens under Gadhafi, in civil disobedience. The world nations perhaps also assume that unarmed civilians are world citizens, all global cosmopolitans without exception.

Thus the clash between a dictator and the world nations is clash between attacking "enemies" and attacking unarmed civilians or citizens. It is the clash between regionalism and cosmopolitanism, between political selfishness and peaceful negotiation among disagreeing parties.

---

[10] Strangely, history sees not many collective atrocities worldwide, any collective crimes against humanity, much less any global ones. Ecological devastation worldwide may well be unexpected, much less contrived.

Or else, "unarmed civilians" may mean straight Libyan citizens in civil disobedience that Gadhafi cannot tolerate, taking them as "enemies" and nothing else. If so, this situation expresses the fact that world nations are embracing "democracy," governance of people, by people, and for people, as applicable worldwide against regional dictatorship.

But then "democracy" is people-power, and people are all over throughout the world. So, "democracy" is sibling to "cosmopolitanism." Thus the conclusion remains that the clash today is between regional dictatorship and global democracy. In other words, "human disaster" today is expressed in terms of globalization struggling with regional selfishness of dictators political, economic, cultural, and historical.

Human disaster is judged "disastrous" by the standard of globalization—democracy—that is solidly in place in our hearts worldwide. Human disaster is then predicated on globalization. Human disaster is the dawn of globalization marching on, and marching on into history global.

Clearly, these disasters, natural and human, pose urgent questions to us all, to demand our answer with dead seriousness, challenging all of us worldwide to deal with them well, at once. This round of questions and answers is the matter of our life and death. We are forced to respond with tact, insights, and timeliness, and with histircal reflective discernment. We have to round up ourselves global to race against time for survival together. Disasters provoke our historic struggles together for global survival—with deep historical reflection.

Histories of various cultures come quite handy in supplying vital information about how our forefathers and foremothers made it, through it all, to their survival. Their histories are their success stories of survival worth consulting, for otherwise we would not have been here now to struggle to survive in the first place.

Our struggles here now testify to their success, inviting us to consult with their stories to strengthen our struggle to succeed likewise, although in our own ways. Even the histories of their failures serve as our negative object lesson to steer us today toward a surer safer paths of resolution of disasters.

Disasters thus come as history comes, pounding on us all to respond, on pain of perdition. They both come with deadly questions (disasters) and deathly demands (history) for us to answer, to pull together all our global resources to respond with tact and timeliness. Those questioning challenges of disasters keep all of us on our toes, keeping us up and about, prim and trim, in all muscles fit and vigorous.

Our creative answers, quite intercultural in time and space, then compose another round of world history, as historians and journalists and literary writers all over the globe critically describe our struggles coping and grappling with disasters for our survival, as we huddle together worldwide. History is the global matter of our survival into vigorous health worldwide. History is our global march to global survival, no, inter-thriving via successful resolution of disasters. Nothing is more critical and indispensable than history in globalization marching on, world without end.

CONCLUSION

Since history is a dialogue intercultural in time, let us begin concluding this essay on history in globalization, by dialoguing with Kant in distant land and time. Kant said[11] that $100 in my mind cannot buy but $100 in my pocket can buy. This is fair enough, for what else is new? But now let us see the whole situation from the point of view of thinking in history, and we can see how limited Kant's vision is.

Suppose I used to have $100 in my pocket, with which I bought something here in my hand. Thus $100 in hand before, in mind now, has bought this thing here now. I have earned this $100, now in mind, with my manufactured goods, and I am thinking I will do so likewise soon, and then I can have $100 to buy again.

Thus all such thinking in my mind, based on past actual earning, can create a commercial enterprise to earn $100 soon that can buy. All my thinking on past, present, and future is in my mind only, now, but can gain $100 in my future to buy things. Thus, to repeat, my $100 in mind will be able to buy. Such historical thinking in mind *applies* to actuality with actual impacts. Historical thinking in mind does buy actuality.

Now, to think of it, $100 in my pocket is also $100 in my mind, for I *know* I have $100 in my pocket, for that is why I am talking about it, and my talk is my mind alone thinking and acting. Our common sense is also thinking in mind that routinely achieves actual business of daily chores and worldly affairs. In addition, my ideal, imagination, dreams and reveries are all in my mind, which have impacts on actuality. My thinking buys actuality. A further concrete example shows this mind-buying-actuality.

The Wright Brothers had a dream to fly as birds, not actual then, and so they were laughed at and ridiculed as irreverent to their creator's intention who did not equip them with wings to fly. But thanks to their wild dream out of this actual world, the huge heavy pieces of metal called "air planes" are today daily, routinely, flying in the "friendly skies." We ought to be amazed at the power of Wright Brothers' dreams "totally unrealistic," not at all actual. Dreaming is the power of freedom out of this actual world.

Kant called freedom and God "regulative ideas," but all logics of all thinking are regulative ideas, that is to say, thinking only in my mind does regulate and buy actuality in the past, the present, and the future. The prominent concrete example, among many, of such concrete thinking in mind that bites into actuality, is historical thinking that guides the present to create the future. History is contemporary future.

This dialogue of ours with Kant exemplifies dialogue in mutual disagreement through time, history as dialogue. In fact, all dialogues are disagreements to mutually revolutionize all assumptions; dialogues are quite radical. Culture our way of living makes our assumption; Collingwood even says that culture is our "absolute presupposition." Such radical cultural dialogue must be shaped to obtain by three acts and attitudes.

First, most importantly, we must recognize and respect differences among dialogical parties. American people are good at such respectful recognition of differences, apropos of USA as world experiment of world togetherness. Secondly, we should not let go of the others' differences, but must listen to the other's positions. Thirdly, if all fails, we want to

---

[11] Immanuel Kant, *The Critique of Pure Reason*, tr. Norman Kemp Smith, NY: St. Martin's Press, 1965, A599=B627. I put him in my own words, for I am extrapolating from him out of his context, though by doing so I criticize him and expand him from the point of view of thinking in history.

silently leave the scene, while being ever ready to re-enter the dialogue whenever we see an opportunity as we watch for it. These three attitudes constitute our common human decency to make for dialogues to mutually benefit.

For all this, however, radical dialogue remains painful. Due to the pain of radical revolution in dialogue, such assumptive inter-revolution takes time to obtain. Only from history's eye can we see it taking place. Thus history is quite apposite here. In fact, history is composed by such radical dialogues, and so Collingwood's making of history, by us questioning data for their answer, is just a tiny tip of this vast overall global dialogue that is history.

In history, the first condition of dialogue, respectful recognition of the differences of the others, takes the form of recognizing the others as political enemies and religious abominations. Those "atrocious opponents" never go away but keep haunting us (showing the second condition of dialogue), and seeping into us. By and by, they are changed to turn into part of us as we learn from them, unawares or not (the third condition of dialogue).

Political enemies, ever blood-stained, often turn into our friendly nations. Some prominent examples are England the past enemy of USA turned now into its close ally, Japan as China's sworn enemy now being a business partner, many European nations that used to brutally colonize China being now allies cultural, economic, and even military. Only long-term history can tell us such incredible stories of political dialogue.

Religious abominations are even more dramatic. Let us take the most extreme example of adamantly exclusive monotheism, Christianity. Its parent, Judaism, fiercely condemned cannibalism and offering of the precious firstborn through fire to the fearsome god Moloch. Judaism remained deadly opposed to such barbaric abominations.

And then, lo and behold, abominable cannibalism is adopted into the Christian center as the Eucharist, and brutal offering of the most precious firstborn is now at the very center of the Christian faith, the cross of Christ, God the Father's offering of his own Son to us, the whole offering to Moloch wholly reversed. All such radical dialogues of revolutions take several centuries to take place. Here it is history again that pulls off such stunning feats of radical dialogues to transform the assumptions.

Therefore, our problem now is to consider what such historical thinking is that is both in mind *and* can buy actuality, what is such a magical cake I have (thinking) while I eat it (with actual impact). In addition, we must consider how we can obtain such magical and effective historical thinking.

And then we realize that by considering *how* to get this wonderful cake of historical thinking, we can answer the other question of what it is. This point, i.e., in history the how is its what, is graphically exemplified by China thoroughly drenched in history. China does not reflect on "what history is" but just keeps writing history. And their only two volumes of historical criticism are concerned with *how* best to do history, since "three classics of history say no 'history,' as people have their respective selves and allow no self to 'self' their selves."[12] In history, the how is the what.

And so we now consider what historical perception is by watching how it performs history. Historical perception is made up of three stages. In the first stage, the historian perceives coherence in the past among various factors and disparate elements that compose

---

[12] 「三傳不言傳, 猶人各有我而不容我其我也」, said (清)章學誠 in his 文史通義校注, 北京中華書局, 2005, p. 93. The only other book in China on historical criticism is (唐)劉知幾's 史通通釋, 臺北市九思出版有限公司, 民67 that also focuses only on how history is made.

past experience. This coherence is gained by the historian's hindsight. This hindsight is perceptive wisdom after the fact, to compose "history."

In the second stage, the historian perceives how the past situation causes the present and leads into the present world. Such a causal connection is open to various interpretations and yet all interpretations agree that the connection is coherent, all making sense. In the final third stage, the historian extrapolates from the past coherence and the coherence between the past and the present, in order to perceive their twofold coherence—past, and past-present—to point to the shape of the *future*, obscure yet inevitable and unmistakable.

The coming together of these three stages constitutes historical perceptiveness that composes a good historian we call the "sage." These three stages are progress in time called "history." The sage is historical through and through. The gathering of these three stages does not proceed by logical deduction or induction. The gathering is accomplished by seeing through things past, present, and future. It is perceptive foresight of the future through insight into the past and into the coherence between past and present. This gathering proceeds in time to spread far and wide in space. This gathering and this spread into the future is globalization dynamic and irresistible.

Globalization is a gathering verb that unifies specificity and ubiquity, one with all, and the past to the future in the present. Globalization is history as our school that trains and nurtures this historical perception. We grow here into a sage. This training is facilitated by history as [1] construction of stories, whose "validity," in whatever sense, is checked and ensured by [2] questioning and answering between us now and the past experience we thereby reconstruct.

Story-construction and questioning dialogues go hand in glove, as toddler Tommy creatively rehearsing his stories as he makes up his rehearsed stories, as he asks Mom what happened to Goldilocks, and to the all-powerful Monkey, and to the ferocious Gadhafi. Both the construction of stories and the dialogue with our Mom our data are coherent and open, to facilitate understanding (coherence) of stories and extrapolation (open) from stories. The above reflection on historical perception covers all how, what, necessity, and task of "history in globalization."

In addition, here is one more point about how dynamic history is. Looked at as above, history seems to determine the past, to determine the present, and thereby the future. This historical determinism of all is actually valid. This is why history is justifiably said to be contemporary (Croce) and the past is no less aptly said to be future (Habermas).[13] But this is one side of the story of history. Another side is that all this above is envisaged by us ourselves at present. It is we now who determine all above that determines us all. Reciprocal determinism spells open (reciprocal) coherence (determinism) of history.

So, history is shaped by us now to shape us here now. Such reciprocity of determinations is typified by taking history as inter-dialogues, coherent and open into the vast unknown horizon of globalization. This fact is valid everywhere and every-when, and so history is the essential dynamo of globalization.

It is thus that we come back to Section A where we said that we shape history for history to shape us. But we gain here extra cash value of history beyond Section A. It is that *we* ourselves can and must ride on the crest of the mighty river of history worldwide to live our

---

[13] Benedetto Croce, *History: Its Theory and Practice*, tr. Douglas Ainslee, NY: Harcourt, Brace and Co., 1921, pp. 11-26. Jürgen Habermas, *The Past as Future*, Lincoln: University of Nebraska Press, 1994.

life more prudently, and thrive together in prosperity. By "riding on the crest of history" we mean we must be historically perceptive as above described.

We gain here the praxis of history and prescription in history to live richer and happier, together in intercultural globalization. Thus this essay has undergone history as rhyming itself, showing how we come home to Section A but with the global difference, the richer global prescription we can never avoid without destroying ourselves.

It is now time to tie up some loose ends about history as necessarily global, and this tying-up unexpectedly evokes our marvel, and our marvel is all the more spectacular precisely because what we find is so common and routine. Let me unpack all this terse confession this way.

If we ask what is so magical about history, why history is open to infinity yet coherent always at each moment, why foresight into the future is composed of hindsight into the past, and how we would make sense of all these sorts of logical nonsense about history, we have one simple answer. Actuality, especially our human actuality, by nature goes beyond itself. Actuality consists in the élan of self-transcendence. Let me explain.

In Japan they say, "An inch ahead is dark."[14] Every moment goes beyond itself, and that realm beyond is beyond knowing, though not arbitrary but coherent with the status quo here now. We ourselves constantly "grow" beyond ourselves, and although we do not know where to we are growing, we can understand (coherent) our "next moment" however unexpected, even surprising, our next situation turns out to be (open).

History in its plain stories of the past describes such open coherence of events happening, for history is the most natural mirror of actuality as self-transcendence. Thus every moment is the dawn full of promises of the unknown horizon. History is such promises of the dawn as surely as the past described as set and settled. Life's élan of self-transcendence to the beyond unknown is set and settled, history warrants us.

Such amazing incoherence of "open coherence" of actuality is expressed in the magic cake, history, we have (open) and eat (coherent), as foresight of the future (open) composed of hindsight of the past (coherence). They are all originated in actuality in the dynamic élan of self-transcendence. This élan is so common and routine, at every moment as the dawn, everywhere any time, quite global, and so it is the élan all the more marvelous all over.

We also noted that history progresses not by repeating itself or in totally haphazard manner, but by rhyming between the past and the present, and the present and the future. The pair of past and present, and the pair of present and future, and the pairing of these two pairs, can be seen to form "two palms" each, as asymmetrical counterparts. Such enigmas of asymmetrical rhyming makes sense, if we explain them by the fact of the élan of life as self-transcendence that is coherent and yet open, impossible to mechanically predict yet understandable as inevitable, when looked back after the fact. This is to say that we can see events proceeding as making historical sense.

Such an amazing fact of historical self-transcendence to the beyond unknown is the ordinary thrust of actuality. This self-transcending thrust of actuality gives us good news of hope in our lives. Thanks to this élan, we have hope, however miserable and wretched the situation here now is.

Thanks to this hope, Uncle Fort of the story told by a Taoist Huai Nan Tzu survives all unexpected happenings, disasters and non-disasters alike. He is "good at counting" days as he

---

[14] "一寸先は闇."

lives at the limit of town, i.e., at the limiting situations of life, and who among us is not such an Uncle Fort? We see how he takes each day and each event as it comes, ever going beyond itself, forever asking, "How could we not know that *this* will not make its opposite?"[15] He is ever posed expecting the unexpected to come to him. He lives in life praxis of actuality as self-transcendence.

Such a posture of readiness, ever sinuously flexing one's attitude and adjusting oneself to suit the ever shifting situations, in the ever changing propensity of things, is in line with the élan of self-transcendence of actuality. Since self-transcendence is transcending all time and all space, self-transcendence is the historical élan of globalization ever globalizing itself.

Living in this self-transcending actuality worldwide, our ready posture enlists us into cosmopolitan "global citizens" as flexible as the daily situations ever going beyond themselves. We must grow fit to ever fit in the fickle situation coherent and open, as the history of globalization tells us, ever going beyond its own self.

If history is life's thrust of its élan of self-transcendence in time and in space, then globalization is history reaching out to its ultimate horizon unlimited. Again, the élan of self-transcendence tells of what, how, and how-to of history in globalization, history as globalization, setting the parameter of our urgent task of humanity cosmopolitan.

"Through faith, Enoch being dead still speaks," the Bible says,[16] as if it were something extraordinary. Actually, only the dead persons speak in deep silence; we call their incessant talk "history" alive to make us truly alive. We had better cease our silly chatters and listen well, to come alive as they for ever. Our lives together are in order to fulfill this global historic task. Now let us tarry here a while on this important point.

The fact of the dead really alive, to make us actually alive, is demonstrated in the fact that we instinctively stand in awe and respect in front of the dead, whether in front of their bodies, handling their mementos (photos, writings, things they left), or merely mentioning them. They are powerless to attack us, and enormously powerful to overwhelm us. We instinctively listen in silence to them in eloquent silence.

It does not matter if the dead have been saints or rascals, for the dead are now dead, and this fact is enough to sober us serious, and serious about them. We may pass final judgments on them, but we do so always in dead seriousness and earnest finality, all thanks to the fact of their death. Death is momentous, to turn things, *any* things alive or dead, momentous.

This fact of seriousness of death is the reason why "history" is indispensable though seemingly useless for concrete immediacies here now. As the dead have things important to tell us, history is the serious depths of our very being, as long as we pay attention to them as we pay respect to them. We can be seriously alive, integral, and dignified, only thanks to the dead and their history that is also ours. The dead are the stuff of which we are made. Bypassing them commits suicide. In fact, it is the dead who are really alive, to make us alive actually, in depth. We are not alive until they really come into us.

All this while, we look around, and we notice we are surrounded by babies and toddlers. We are totally won over by them to them. We cannot win them; we do not even want to win, for there is no point here in winning. They are so tiny and powerless that we instinctively take care of them as *the* tender beginning of life. By the same token, we do not and cannot win the

---

[15] 淮南子, 人間訓, 臺北市三民書局, 民86, p. 965.
[16] Hebrews 11:4.

dead, either. There is no point here in winning, for they are dead. The dead are our babies in us to grow us, to begin us.

Moreover, in all this we must remember this point. The dead and the babies are both dependent on us ourselves to begin life. We feel the dead and the babies are really alive to make us alive, while they in turn depend on us to feel so to make us really alive. Thus they and we interdepend to begin life together and invigorate us all alive. In this sense of interdependence, the dead are as alive as the babies, who both make us alive.

Our task shall then compose one long sigh of world concord, where all of us, dead, alive, and babies, nod at one another in happy silence, in globalization historic. Globalization is that in which we live, for which we work, and to which we strive, to compose cosmopolitan history vivacious. This history as globalization on the go is the existential *a priori* we breathe, to work at it as task, to work toward it as goal. This it is that is "history in globalization."

Chapter 13

GLOBALIZATION AS ECOLOGY

Kuang-ming Wu
Taiwan, ROC

ABSTRACT

Our ruling passion of life is our urgent need to co-thrive. This chapter just elucidates such our passionate concern so global, so vital. Now, we are going to unpack below what we said here, in Section A: *Ecology* as global urgency, and Section B: The root of ecology, continued by Section C: Ecology in performance. Ecology has no end as globalization continues without ceasing. To my knowledge, no book so far on ecology has treated the theme in the radical existential way as this chapter does.

Ecology has "logos" (-logy) that can mean dealing and management (originally log-collecting and counting[1]) in a certain mode of thinking, in a specific life-attitude. This attitude is that of "eco-" *oikos*, household, a family-attitude. Thus "ecology" is a challenge to us all to revolutionize our life-attitude from calculating profiteering to mutual concern to benefit my family-members. Ecology is attitude-revolution from selfishness to family inter-need to inter-thrive.

Let us begin by considering selfishness. Selfishness is an attitude of monopolizing any benefit to me *alone* at all cost, even at the cost of others. The others are my enemies to conquer, even to exploit for my lone happiness of self-satisfaction. Such is our usual attitude, our usual praxis unawares, in economics and political engagements, among many others.

The rule of our days is to fight against others for my gains, fighting with others who also fight with me as enemy to their gains. We all scramble to exploit everyone and everything as objects to benefit "me alone." This is the source of eco-disaster. Selfishness is eco-pollution eco-ravaged.

"It's not that bad, pal. We all are now civilized people." Well, being with people, we may graciously compromise with their desires for benefits, as we are often gentle with them.

---

[1] See "*lego*" in *Theological Dictionary of the New Testament*, ed. Gerhard Kittel, Grand Rapids, MI: Wm. B. Eerdmans, 1967, IV:69-192.

Animals do not talk, however, nor do trees respond, and we do not even see "nature" as a whole.

Our "old Adam" of selfishness would naturally get into a full swing here, and, worse, eco-devastation does not follow at once, and so we turn bolder and bolder, and devastations after devastations ensue. In short, our selfishness cuts down on our invisible Mother Nature to cut down ourselves with all our fellow beings. Selfishness is the culprit.

The alternative attitude to selfishness is "the more, the merrier" typified by family life in a household. I embrace here the same love in same joy with you, and you, and you all. My pain s yours, your pain is mine. When you win, I win. The same sweet and sorrow 同甘苦 make for the same joy 同樂 over all, pervading throughout all family members who thus intimately strive together to naturally cooperate for our joys together.

In my family, I labor for you, as you labor for me. My responsibility for your welfare is my joy, for you are the bone of my bones. So do you likewise take me as your spines, and share your responsibility for my happiness as your very joy. Enriching you enriches me. Existence is thus inter-existence; no you, no me, as your existence makes me to exist. This fact is dramatically brought out in sexual act that begins—parents—me in a family.

In sex that begins the family, I enjoy you as your enjoying me makes me ecstatic. When our children arrive as the fruit of our love, they are our treasures ourselves, we nurture them together, and our co-labors of loving them make up *our* life-passions. All our jobs, our engagements, and our family household chores, are concentrated on our children, expended for *their* sake. They are our glories, our joys, our pride, and our accomplishments. When we grow old, and they grow mature, they appreciate us enough to help us out in our old days.

All this is quite natural, as "nature" is *natura naturans*, nature naturing that is, birthing, birthing, without ceasing 生生不息 under the sky our father and in the field our mother. Such is the nature of mutual appreciation that overflows into the beauty of art appreciation. People flock together in art museums and music halls, to be warmed in the inter-glow of beauty all around. Here the more people enjoying the merrier; and we are happy together enriched in our respective ways.

Excellence shared is joy ultimate, riches beyond measure. This is what "nature is wasteful" means, overabundant in birthing and supplying to nurture growing, though in lean season the birth-rates among living beings drop to conserve foods. We can go see Mother Nature's abundance at the "nuts section" in a grocery store, and enjoy selecting from them to go home to enjoy them.

Can you imagine my "one pinch" counts 20 of sunflower seeds? Mother Nature is smiling at us in her prodigious abundance. And then our inter-joy of dinner and camaraderie in mutual intimate cooperation go on, spreading throughout nature. Mutual cherishing that spreads is the household spirit of ecology.

Thus, an attitude-revolution from me-alone selfishness into a family living under Mother Nature, in inter-need of win-win management, constitutes "ecology." Revolution, nature-as-family, and win-win partnership, are so intimately intertwined that no systematic separate itemization is possible.

They all describe our ruling passion of life as our urgent need to co-thrive. This chapter just elucidates such our passionate concern so global, so vital. Now, we are going to unpack below what we said above here, in Section A: Ecology as global urgency, and Section B: The root of ecology, continued by Section C: Ecology in performance.

More sections other than above can of course be added; what is listed here is a mere pinch of samples to typify ecology. Ecology has no end as globalization continues without ceasing. To my knowledge, no book on ecology so far, among so many, has treated the theme in the radical existential way as this chapter.

A. Ecology as Global Urgency

We cite, in a roaming though not disorderly way, thirteen points, all interrelated, to impress us on how globally urgent ecology is. In fact, globalization is equivalent to ecology, and ecology is where our life is at stake, for we survive only by thriving together, and thriving together is possible only in ecology that is synonymous with globalization, globalizing continuous.

One: The urgency, the extent, and the significance of globalization as ecology are so intensely inter-involved that I cannot systematically itemize this essay. Myriad things under the friendly skies, in one household of Mother Nature, cipher the economy of ecology, as "ecology" is *oikos-logos*, household-management of the entire globe, as the world daily shrinks into Global Village.

Ecology is eco-piety, the family-piety of globalization on the go. We are here to develop this vast fabulous warmth of macrocosm of the globe in microcosm of each existence, each in its own way. Eco-piety is family-filiality where every family member thrives, from crawling babies to oldsters on walking sticks. Eco-piety is nurture-filiality under Mother Nature, nothing else. We are all born of the family, and family-business is ecology, so ecology is the birth of our life.

Two: Ecology is human life-economy, for ruining Mother Nature ruins all beings, ourselves included, and yet, sadly, it is we humans who, with our businesses, ruin Mother Nature; no other species ruins nature. Human devastation of nature ruins all human businesses, losing all our money-making projects, to ruin our very life. In nature, every "exotic" species counts as every family member—however tiny and/or cranky—is essential to every other member. In the same way, in the family under Mother Nature, extinction of any one species begins to bring about extinction of the whole globe.

When brother frog and sister owl[2] are nowhere, no single human being can survive the pan-silence of desolation. Tigers are nowhere, lions stop taking zebras, and now no howling in wilderness is heard at dawn. The silent spring without frogs croaking, in stark silence of absent owls, betokens the graveyard-chill of darkness at noon.

Even the teeming lives of ants and bacteria cease. No one is here, for not a thing can exist, not even a "nothing" of the Buddhist. Desert winds whirl across dry vast horizons in searing sunlight, and in devastating storms all dark. Here is the scene so scary everywhere, and even the human scare of any plundering is nowhere to be seen, gone for good.

Three: We cannot take the desolation any more, so let us go the other way. As of now, we are still surviving. Chickadees chitchatting, lush greens with squirrels hopping on grass and jumping among the branches, nameless tiny wild flowers waving in the breeze, all these still make up the paradise here now in the Global Village. Frogs and dragonflies[3] still enjoy

---

[2] I do not hear morning doves cooing now. I am really worried.

[3] Sadly, however, frogs are reported to be extinct, and dragonflies are getting scarce these days.

their meals of mosquitoes, and kids hop, skip, and jump with deer eating flowers, as Canada geese honk their flights across the clouds.

This is another portrait of our home, our nature under Mother Nature. The choice of our favorite scene is clear, all so clear as to be so scary. We must sweat to toil to till the land, to cultivate the fields with love and reverence, and our unselfish labor of love of Mother Nature shall redound to bringing about our all-smiling household of ecological village. In all this, we must remember that genuine "reverence for life" is possible only in its home of family household of the whole globe. Schweitzer is only half-baked.[4]

Four: Ecology is globalization in process abundant. Our supermarket supplies all our daily needs. We must realize how our supermarket comes from our super nature our Mother Nature, demanding our filial services on pain of our own perdition, bereft of supermarket in super Nature. Save Mother Nature, and then we can enjoy our supermarket. We have no other alternative. This is our categorical imperative of existence as inter-existence abundant.

"Have you been belaboring on the obvious?" Sadly, our eco-disaster arrives on heels of our turning blind eyes to this obvious, all too starkly obvious fact. "Watchman, what of the night?" we ask. Back comes an answer, "Ask for the obvious, and your dawn of eco-prosperity will greet you." Globalization as ecology is our starkly obvious necessity of pan-survival to thrive together. All other choices, selfishness, exploitation, indifference, are royal roads to pan-extinction.

We either live together or die together. Togetherness is ecological globalization in process. Isn't it obvious? That is precisely why it is absolutely needed by us all. We need this eco-family of global Village for us to cultivate. There is no other choice. This is the matter of life and death for all our myriad fellow things, all existents our brethren.

We throw in one match, and the whole forest fire rages. We plant seedlings and nurture them, and a lush forest arrives. Wild "useless" bears and deer shall roam with frogs and dragonflies all around. Our supermarket will then rise to softly feed us. It is as simple as that, and as urgent as that. Chopping the tree chops me and us. Planting the tree plants us all. Please plant, never chop.

Five: When I am sick, I need a doctor to medically care for me. My Mother Nature is sick now because we devastated her, because of my misbehavior; she needs us to behave, and needs our expert "medical" technicians to "care" for her. It means that our Mother Nature must care for our sickness, our technological and commercial misbehaviors, as our Mother Nature must need our technical care for our sickness, our uncaring technological plundering and commercial pollutions of her. Our selfishness poisons us to poison nature, the nature devastated by us to destroy us all.

We must do our best to clean up, to detoxify rivers, lands, and oceans. We must regulate by international laws and regional reulations, and enforce our strict obedience to eradicate our poison, our misbehaviors of business exploitations, such as offshore oil-drilling, automobile emissions, urban sprawl with deforestation, and the list goes on. We must do all this technological care with utmost filial reverence to Mother Nature, on pain of devastating pan-perdition.

They say two things are inevitable in life, death and taxation. We must add the third life-inevitable, Ecopiety. Taxation may not relate to death, but death relates intimately to

---

[4] See *Albert Schweitzer's Ethical Vision: A Sourcebook*, ed. Predrag Cicovacki, Oxford University Press, 2009, and *Albert Schweitzer: An Anthology* (1947), ed. Charles R. Joy, Boston: Beacon Press, 1956.

Ecopiety, for without globalization-as-eco-harmony, all will die. Ecopiety is our categorical imperative of the very existence of all. Ecology is literally our household ethics of Global Village whose maintenance, its very survival, hangs on loving eco-management. We should perform eco-management as our daily chores as an ordinary household-matter of course.

Six: "Now, what else is new?" Nothing is new here except our own amazing eco-blindness and lethargy, as if household cleaning is the business of someone else, and none of ours, for "we are too busy for such money-losing stuff." We are thus lethally blind to this eco-fact that "such stuff" regulates our own survival, as our family business is our urgent life-necessity.

Nothing else is new here except our very survival is on balance, and our indifference is tipping that balance to *our* death. Such ecological life-survival comes out as the new world urgency today because we have *really* messed up our environment as we have never done before.

So eco-obvious is the whole global situation of devastation, and this situation shows how delinquent *we* are, to keep self-poisoning to pan-death. Pan-death and eco-disasters are devastatingly synonymous, the two names of the same sad affairs, the same global tragedy. Again, I have repeated the obvious, shouting to the wind in the wilderness. The shout is not pretty at all as no one is listening at all. John the Baptist is luckier than we. We continue the Baptist's shout to urge our repentance of our root-sin, eco-blindness, to root out the root of eco-woes.

Seven: "Don't we have to feed the hungry people?" Eco-mismanagement and the hungry people are two devastations from our identical ills, ineptitude combined with selfishness in social, political, and economic mismanagements on international, inter-organizational, and intercultural levels. Both our root-ills—ineptitude and selfishness—are to be cured by globalization as ecology of household-Nature, both inside us (callous selfishness) and outside us (callous indifference).

Globalization as ecology means we are urgently obligated to spread worldwide as soon as possible our concerted resources and efforts at eco-management, technical, legal, and socioeconomic, on a universal global scale. "Doctors Without Borders" must be expanded to Doctors of all of us in sickness of eco-mismanagement on a global scale, in all areas of *our* own life-management.

Luckily, eco-awareness is now an accepted global fashion, as tobacco-ill is now our common sense worldwide. We are yet to realize how identical these two awarenesses are, however, for smoking cigarettes of selfishness is lethal toxin to the smokers *and* to us all around the globe. We are pan-poisoned by secondhand smoking of selfishness to eco-disasters to pan-death.

Eight: "Now, now, cool down, pal. Aren't you too emotional?" Well, I cannot help it, and that, rightly. Mencius was accused of "given to argument 好辯"; he responded that he could not help it 不得已 (3B9). I cannot help passionately arguing for the eco-obvious, for the very existence of myriad things is on this eco-balance.

"Why could Mencius not help it?" He passionately cited the Ox Hill (6A8) originally lush but now denuded by constant grazing and daily tree-axing, beyond repairs by soft nightly dews. Ox Hill is our nature. Mother Nature *is* our innate nature. Eco-management is our household economy of pan-survival. Devastating it devastates us. Unless we shout now, no one would be here to shout, and no one would be here to hear, intently or indifferently.

Nine: If such ubiquitous ills of passionate urgency are handled with cool equanimity, we would obviously tabulate the statistics of Nazi atrocities to earn public revulsion, as Orwell was incensed at Kipling "objectively" reporting a British soldier beating up on an Indian passerby to extort money. No wonder, Black Theology was written in racist rage. Ecological disasters casually perpetrated by human businessmen are far more extensive a dire selfish "racism" against fellow family members of our globe, against the whole family of Mother Nature. A concrete example comes to mind.

The "Lifeboat Ethics" is devastatingly eco-unethical, seeing that our group selfishness has boxed in the eco-lifeboat to the well-fed alone, to "let the starving die," to let all of us die in the end, due to our selfish eco-mismanagement. Feeding the poor is related to eco-management breath to breath. There is a book, *Avoiding 1984*.[5] We have yet to have and to hear about "Avoiding Eco-Disasters Today," to perform it assiduously.

Ten: Some of us may doubt if there is any use for a few of us, much less for one of us, to do something about such a huge problem worldwide. This is a typical doubt in the face of huge problems. Globalization as ecology is one of the big themes. To this doubt, the very word, "ecology," has an answer. Ecology is the business (*logos*) of the household (*oikos*) of family. In the family, every member counts, in fact, the smaller, the less powerful, and the more sickly members receive the more attention and care.

We are all members of the global body of a family. A tiny prick causes a sleepless night all night. A small joy of a small member causes a great joy and a great joyous strength. This is the family of an organic structure as in a painting, where one spot added changes the whole setup, the whole gestalt. Every little effort at promoting eco-health helps much, to change the whole picture.

Mother Teresa was ridiculed by a critic, about how powerless and inefficient are her services to the poorest of the poor, and perhaps this criticism was correct. Her actual impacts on reduction of the sea of poverty and misery may well be miniscule. But her impact on us ourselves is enormous. She revolutionized our perspective on poverty, and our continuous effort, bits added to bits, can be formidable. In fact, our efforts still go on, thanks to her push she devoted her whole life to make on us.

Eleven: Poverty is one of the pervasive eco-disasters. We should do whatever we can, however little, to pitch in. What is crucial is "drips go through the boulder 點滴穿石," where *continuity* of drips is the key. The drips of good deeds continuing, step by a tiny step, accumulate into an avalanche of impact in the end, even though we may not see the avalanche, perhaps not in our lifetime.

We need not mention Aesop's slowpoke turtle against the jumpy fast rabbit. China's well-known Uncle Stupid 愚公 is here as well, who picked up his spade and began digging at the foot of a mountain. Asked what he was doing, he said he was digging the way through to the other side of the mountain.

Ridiculed at, on how old he was already against how overwhelmingly huge the mountain was, he calmly responded, "Well, my children, and then the children of their children, and so

---

[5] James Cone, *Black Theology & Black Power* (1969), HarperSanFrancisco, 1989. *Lifeboat Ethics: The Moral dilemmas of World Hunger*, eds. George R. Lucas, Jr. and Thomas W. Ogletree, NY: Harper & Row, 1976. Cf. Lester R. Brown, *Tough Choices: Facing the Challenge of Food Scarcity*, NY: W. W. Norton, 1996. Robert Theobald, *Avoiding 1984: Moving Toward Interdependence*, Athens: Ohio University Press, 1982. I have lost the reference to George Orwell's anger.

on, will continue." Our eco-work is our huge mountain. We had better pick up our tiny spade here now to clean up the mountain of mess.

Global eco-work is the project of many generations and deserves many generations' labors, in which we miniscule individuals can and must *continue* to pitch. Remember, every ticking of the second conspires to producing hours, days, seasons, and years, into vast eons after eons. All this comes from small seconds ticking constantly. That is the power of small drips, in *constant* dripping. The small and the constant together perform the miracle beyond belief, and beyond mountains.

Twelve: Look at how rain drops casually disappear into sands. Everything casual thus casually seeps into everything else, deeply, pervasively, as if nothing is the matter. Whenever such deep seeping takes place, however, there is no less than a "born again" of things, afresh alive, as babies coo with faint morning doves faintly cooing the dawn.

Things happen so fresh, as raindrops always make things happen afresh, and pervasive rebirths come about in silence. There is nothing newsworthy, and yet things come out stunning novel while quite ordinary. All this is a breathtaking world event at every second. It is Mother Nature naturing without ceasing.

We are part of such ecological nature the self-so of myriad things. I am constantly born with the sky and with the field, to be with all my things my brethren. To realize—and realize—all this is the ecological responsibility, our joyous task of tilling the field and thriving the forest.

Thirteen: Such our activity is how we, as actual parts of Mother Nature, are to care for all common grass and giraffes, frogs and dragonflies, and see to it that the rain actually drops into sands. Just to write on all this already makes us feel so good, and we must do all this as we come to ourselves, as we must come to ourselves, again and again, at every dawn of every "next moment." Such is how we breathe deeply, and then we turn vigorously alive with things all around. Everything is in every thing else, and they thereby continue to tell us of "ecology."

Such ecology is paradise, and what paradise does not sing? What paradise does not sing its own self? Hush, listen. Rain drops are singing onto the stones, into the ponds, and all this while stones and ponds are singing raindrops. All things are now wet and fresh and alive. It is thus that globalization is an ode to ecology. Let stones be, let ponds moisten, and this letting is our task of ecology, where spring sings. In winter, is spring far? Winter is spring in storms singing spring. In death, life is birthing. Death wails in silence singing life. If this is not happy ecology, nothing is.

B. THE ROOT OF ECOLOGY

One: The Zulu says, "O mother, I am lost."[6] That is bad enough. What is worse is, however, that my mother can be, and often is, nowhere. I often lose my mother, and then I cannot even say or whine, much less cry or shout, "O, Mother, I am lost!" Thoreau quietly lamented, "We lose our friends when we cease to be friends, not when they die. . . Death is no separation compared with that which takes place when we cease to have confidence . . . when

---

[6] So reported Martin Buber in *I and Thou*, tr. Ronald Gregor Smith (1958), NY: Scribner, 2000, p. 31.

we cease to love one whom we had loved, when we know him no more. When we look for him and cannot find him, how completely is he departed!"[7]

We used to be so close, but now no more. I intensely miss and yearn after those days, helplessly. My helplessness oozes sorrows venomous, sharp, acidic, to eat me away. "Far" out there, so far unreachable, erodes me inside me, and cuts me into helpless pieces. "Far" is "I miss it" that tells of its absence, and yet "I miss it" shows its poignant presence inside me, gnawing me with its absence.

This unity of absence with presence is "missing something." It is "far" that for the Fuegian says, "They stare at one another, each waiting for the other to volunteer to do what both wish, but are not able to do."[8] For me, "far" is where there is no more *that* "other" for whom I wait. "Far" is my sorrow unlimited in presence of absence.

That friend of mine is still physically alive but is my friend no more. He is nowhere. I cannot even have a closure at his funeral, for he is still physically alive. My friend lives on dead; he is alive yet dead, and I am sick to death in mortal sickness that never dies. Friendship is deathless precisely in its loss to bite into my heart of hearts. It is so unspeakably sad. Such pain of loss of the loved one—mother or friend—cuts deep into my spine-marrows. The pain is so mortally unbearable.

Now, what place does this pain occupy in the as-is, the self-so, of nature we call "Mother Nature"? Chuang Tzu said (6/26) that if we hide the world in the world, nothing will get lost, but here we do not even have a thing to hide in the world, for we *know* in our bone of bones that we have lost our beloved, and nowhere in the world can we find our mother or our friend. Does household management of ecology make sense, now that the very "eco-family" is in ruins?

Two: By the way, is this "loss of family" today—symbolized by our mother or our friend now nowhere—one more cause of eco-disasters besides selfishness that pushes others away? Or rather, does selfish push-away of others have something intimate to do with loneliness of the loss of beloved others? Pushing away hated others and losing beloved others are alike, are they not, for they are both losses of others? Is eco-disaster a mirror-image, another exhibition, of the terrible alone-ness of today's human situation that makes a "lonely crowd" that is another name for eco-disaster?

Of course, pushing others away loses others. If the loss of others cuts into my spine-marrows to cause an unbearable pain of self-loss, then selfish push-away constitutes self-destruction, a suicide committed by selfishness; selfishness is the precise opposite of family-management that is ecology that is self-fulfillment.

Let us now turn the table around. In view of all this loss of the self in losing others, doesn't our task of ecology amount to healing of us ourselves deep inside? Isn't ecology that is caring for myriad things around, our salvation from our own self-loss in loneliness? The proof of a pie is in eating it. The proof of ecology is in trying it. Here is another rationale for taking ecology as our existential imperative, without which we cannot even survive. Globalization spreads such ecological healing deep inside the self of things to turn into their individual self-so.

---

[7] *I to Myself: An Annotated Selection from the Journal of Henry D. Thoreau*, ed., Jeffrey S. Kramer, Yale University Press, 2007, p. 44. This tiny entry shakes up my whole being with tragic tremors. I have never found such saying anywhere, in China or in the West.

[8] Buber, *I and Thou*, p. 31.

Three: Now, here is a catch, however. Ecology is global household-management, and yet it is not at all easy. Ecology requires not just astute techniques but it is no less than our life-revolution. Ecology is our global business of our own rebirth. This s because we are constitutionally self-ish—caring for our self—turned being selfish, caring for our self alone by pushing away others.

We must then constitutionally turn around. We must be born again into the water and the wind of nature of Mother Nature so ubiquitous so selfless that no selfishness is to be seen anywhere in water and in wind, for they "unselfishly" spread, so that we can be freed from our petty selfishness, to freely care for things in Mother Nature, to be vitally cared for by Mother Nature.

Our Old Adam, our old selfishness, breaks things to ruin things all around. A newborn baby was born into unselfish water flowing and wind blowing all over. Still, in curiosity, the baby keeps breaking things by mishandling them. This baby needs to learn how to care for things properly. He cannot chew on books, or throw toys around. And we don't realize that we are that baby in Mother Nature ruining things.

We are today awakened to the necessity of ecology. We the babies of nature must still learn how to use our technological hand to gently handle and care for lands, oceans, and rivers, and trees and animals on grass, and the grass itself. They all have their own minds of being themselves. We must learn how to listen to what they "say" in silence, how to watch how they behave, and how to follow along and give them what they want, not what we think they need. They will then come to fawn on us, to play with us, to enjoy our company as we enjoy them. This is ecology, how the family of nature goes.

Our human family is a tiny extension of the global ecological family. In caring for the family of nature, we are just following our innate family-nature, for our inborn nature is just a loving extension of our Mother Nature. We just follow our instinct of family-caring to care for things around, as we just follow our instinct of self-preservation to serve the preservation of myriad fellow beings who are our eco-family siblings.

Thus we see that selfishness is an instinct of self-preservation gone astray awry, and we must tame it to tame fights, if any, among fellow siblings-beings around us. We must tame dog fights, dog fights called "wars" institutional, national, and worldwide. We call such management our ecological task. This is microcosm arranging for macrocosm, as Mother Nature nurtures our innate nature.

No wonder, the poetry of *Great Learning* 大學 in time-honored China harps on beginning at learning about how things act and behave, to make our intention genuinely fit and fitting, to render our heart right, so that our life can be cultivated accordingly to arrange our family well, to extend to governing the state, to result in world concord.

Following its lead, Chang Tsai in his prose-poem of *Western Inscription* 張載, 西銘[9] intones the sky and the field as our parents under whom I find my intimate place among

---

[9] The *Great Learning* 大學 is one of the *Four Books* 四書 that Chu Hsi 朱熹 compiled as the primer to Confucian Classics. See Wing-tsit Chan's *A Source Book in Chinese Philosophy*, Princeton University Press, 1963, pp. 84-94. On Chang Tsai's *Western Inscription*, 張載's 西銘, see 古文辭類纂, 臺北市三民書局, 2006, V: 3491-3495; it is conveniently translated, summarized, and explained in Chan, op. cit., pp. 497-500. Sadly, few note that both 大學 and 西銘 are lilting poetry; Chan has missed it miserably, without even knowing it. What is cited in the text above is my own rough approximation to the originals.

myriad things my brethren, of whom I care. The entire cosmos is my Family of which I assiduously take care.

Ecology is thus never an outside affair but our inside intrinsic living expanded globally, and such global family-expansion is globalization as ecology. All this ecology is our innate living. Now listen. Never aspiring to be universal and tuneful as Beethoven or Mozart, the ugly Dvorak just sings his own country music, as he shamelessly strums his own folk tunes his own unorthodox ways.

In his Piano Sonatas, String Quartets, and all orchestral works,[10] Dvorak, remaining an individual incurably smelling Bohemian, so incorrigibly rustic, single-handedly throbs, undulates, and swells, to swing into my Chinese life, to throb, undulate, and tune up my distraught days. Such local earthy music does a good job of inner resonation of ecology global.

Just by staying as his own self so peculiar so rustic, Dvorak turns out to be a surprising ecologist for all people. He composes, in all his Bohemian air, smell, and atmosphere, the "New World Symphony" of global living, and it turns out into an all-time hit all over the world. The individual is the cosmic. I am continually born with the sky and the field. I, remaining myself, mingle with myriad things and into continual rounds of seasons, world without end.

Four: We smilingly say to one another, "The spring has come." But what is the spring? Where does it, if anywhere specific, come? We cannot touch it as we touch a tree; we cannot meet it as we meet a person in person. And yet, the spring is unmistakably here, so much so that I take a deep breath and nod at red peeking tulips. We all take a deep breath in the so-called "spring," somewhere somehow. The spring is the air that is—that creates—the new life and the new world.

"How about the winter, is it any better or worse than the spring?" When in winter, is spring far? The winter is thus where and when the spring arrives. The winter is the spring to the spring. China has a phrase, "spring, autumn 春秋," telling us that the spring is the spring to the summer and the autumn is the spring to the winter. All is in the spring, then, in storm or in sleet, walking among tulips or being caught in briars' stings.

In other words, the spring is the milieu and gestalt; it is the world of nature in a nutshell. This nature is our Mother Nature that includes our father sky and our mother soil-earth. Our Mother Nature is the self-so of all myriad things. Lao Tzu chants (25), "People pattern on earth as the law 法, earth on sky, sky on Tao, Tao on self-so." Thus the self-so of things is the law 法, the imperative of all existents. We should never violate it. This is the Ecopiety, the filial ethics of the whole globe. The spring, the gestalt, the as-is, and the law—all form a cosmic synonymy so awesome.

Five: The self-so 自然 of all things is their as-is, which is birthing, birthing, without ceasing 生生不息, natura naturans, nature naturing the constant cosmic power erupting to exist. We see here "birthing" twice repeated, and the repetition occurs by a silence between them.

Birthing is punctuated by a pregnant silence to go on. This silence ciphers death. Thus birthing, birthing, without ceasing is pushed by dying, dying, without ceasing. This very push is

---

[10] Listen, e.g., to *Antonin Dvorak: Complete Solo Piano Music*, by Stefan Veselka, Naxos, 5 CD set, *Dvorak: The String Quartets*, by Prager Streichquartett, Deutsche Grammophon, 9 CD set, and *Dvorak: The Symphonies, Overtures*, by Witold Rowicki, Decca, 6 CD set. They are all very good indeed.

nature naturing, pulsating without ceasing, purchasing death with birth, purchasing birth with death. Thus the grand cosmic process of antiphony continues one generation after another.

Six: Our ancient world was permeated by life. Everything was alive. Reverence for life was naturally all around, and Ecopiety was quite taken for granted. "Everything being alive" means everything lives toward the future. The ancient world was pervaded by the spirit and the élan of the future produced by its ever present reverence for living without ceasing.

We today ridicule such a mindset as "primitive animism." We proudly proclaim mechanism and subscribe to it to replace animism. Mechanism is ruled by the universal physical laws of causality. Whatever that exists must have been caused by whatever that has existed in the past previous to that. We explain what happens now by what has happened in the past. Ours is the world of the past; ours is the world of past-determinism.

Thus today's world has no life left at all, much less personal life. All is machines, to be driven efficiently. Efficient operation can afford to cut anything irrelevant that is not needed. After a physical death, medical scientists leave the scene. Any medical failure is mechanical failure, and that is the end of the whole matter. Isn't eco-disaster here, the disaster of cessation of eco-family life toward the future?

"You are an ingrate, pal! Machines have given you so much to boost your life." Of course we are grateful for the tremendous help rendered by mechanical efficiency. But "I am grateful for A" means "I am not A" for which I am grateful. In the machine-world, there exists no gratitude, no respect, no dignity, and no honor, all of which are outside machines. And all these attitudes form the core of Ecopiety to constitute family and its household management of nature—alive toward the future.

Nature is Mother Nature where the above life-attitudes thrive, while these life-attitudes maintain the household of eco-cosmos. Since the mechanical world has no room for eco-piety or eco-disasters, eco-devastation of Mother Nature inevitably ensues. This does not mean that our gratitude to machines vanishes, though. On the contrary, thanks to being separate from the machines, we freely express gratitude to the machines.

Having realized this point, then mechanical management of eco-household makes sense, and such management is useful to ecology project. Here some may spout their mouths, saying, "Can't the machines just adjust the maladjusted nature, to mechanically clean up—un-pollute—the polluted rivers and forests? Reverence and gratitude can then be dispensed with, right?"

But then *why* we must un-pollute the world with our mechanical hand is missing. "We un-pollute nature in gratitude to the machines and Mother Nature for the survival of humanity with other species of existence." But why do we all have to survive? There is no rationale for eco-management to pan-survival unless we have reverence for life and gratitude for being alive-together. We need reverence and gratitude to even begin to un-pollute our globe. Twist and turn as we may, we cannot avoid reverence for honor and dignity, and gratitude for being together, for eco-management that is extra-mechanical, so that we can *use* our machine-hand.

Seven: Let us put the same point from another angle, our "living." Our life self-feels as being tired or vigorous, and self-repairs in sleep, self-grows, self-olds, and self-dies. We as living being feel that we are mechanical, as we self-act. We are two in one, mechanical and feeling mechanical in one; the two in us are not identical, yet not separate. Life is being self-with, called "body thinking," where body is machine and living in one, and thinking is computing and being aware of computing in one.

At the same time, we as living feel for others and feel with others, and repair with others such as medical doctors, and mechanics at the repair shop, and social workers. We also create with others, as creating children with spouses, cooperating for a project with others, and even die with other comrades. We are with others breath to breath 息息相關. No machine does any of such being-with and doing-with in full awareness.

We living beings do all above that machines do not, because nature is such being-with and doing-with; we are extended nature. Nature self-repairs and self-births through many deaths. We human beings feel with and feel for nature. This it is that is the root of ecology. Here is no room for push-away of others, no loss of others, and so there is no loss of the self here.

Instead, here is the dynamics of breath-to-breath inter-process that throbs in time, to compose an inter-living history to spread globally. Ecology is the maintaining of life living toward life to inter-fulfill—moment by moment—world without end. Isn't all this globalization as ecology, pure and simple? Now it remains for us to see how ecology handles problems against ecology.

C. Ecology in Performance

One: "How does ecology react to eco-disasters?" A good question you raised, pal. On looking into this theme, we find this strange and fabulous fact. When the chilly spring rain, an excellent occasion to catch cold, hits an enclosed home, on its roof and its windows, the rain produces a drizzling sheet of comfort. The drizzles make a blanket that invites tender warm peace.

Such soft sheet of blanket-sound conduces to an evening sleep, letting the tired self cozily come down on the tired self into slumber unawares. The rhythmic hitting of furry rain on windowpanes forms a sound-blanket for sound slumber as we are snuggled into silent music of the drizzles. I apologize for repeating the word "soft" and its equivalents but that is what the milieu the spring drizzles produce. In short, the chilly rain makes for comfort and restful peace, while we are embraced and snuggled at home.

Ecology is an enclosure (logos) at home (oikos). Eco-disaster, when we are enclosed in the home of our Mother Nature, turns into a soft blanket of comfort. Don't ask me how or why. The disaster comes to rain comfort on us, as long as we are huddled and bundled up in the comfort of nature's safe home. Ecology shields us, by turning disaster into balmy sounds of music that is the silence of nature dripping "nature mist" to surround us.

We manage the household of Mother Nature in "Mother Nature way," and Mother Nature shall then manage our threat into a delicate blanket of comfort, at home under Mother Nature. All this describes our eco-family that we make to tightly knit together, to give us silent smiles of solid relaxed strength, to weather through the cold rain of spring now turned soft blanket. "Family-ization" is the key that is ecology that is its secret. The turning of chill into warm blanket is fabulous and incredible. It is the sheer gift of ecology beyond our rhyme or our reason.

After all, to think of it, rain is part of nature. After all, disasters are natural, if "natural" means whatever happens in nature, and we realize that nothing that happens can happen outside nature. Mother Nature is thus incredibly strong, and incredibly motherly embracing us all, including our fellow beings, and we in turn must embody her to make us all into an eco-family. This is perhaps the maternal dynamo that turns threatening cold-catching drizzles of spring into a spring blanket of soft peace and sound slumber, unawares, into spring rebirths of life.

The tulips red and white are peeking at us, as they shiver in spring drizzles to promise us the dawn of life. Thus, the table is turned. The more global disasters we have to hit the window-panes of our eco-family, the more sound-blanket we have to snuggle into sound slumber, under the roofs of Mother Nature in her eco-household—as long as we "ecologize" our life-together into our eco-family, our solid eco-home.

Nye mentions "hard power" that oppresses and overwhelms, and "soft power" that allures and draws, and "smart power" that mixes both.[11] He is unaware that nature has already been operating on these powers for ages, in fact, since the world began before we came on the scene. Mother Nature is the invincible meta-power that turns the "hard power" of overwhelming disasters into the "soft power" drawing us all into the motherly eco-family to thrive together. "Where is 'smart power'?" That power is nature's power to turn hard power into soft power, isn't it? Isn't it the power of ecology, then?

Two: "How would ecology deal with human-made disasters?" This is another good question you raised, pal. All right, let us gaze at "ecology" again. Ecology makes an all-out win for us all. Ecology plays a win-win game in three ways, and we will see how they gather together into Mother Nature.

First, Sun Tzu the master strategist of all time advised us, "Know them, know us, a hundred wars without risk 知彼知己, 百戰不殆"[12] at winning friendship. For example, mother knows her Tommy from head to toe, and sees through his secret thoughts more thoroughly than Tommy himself knows. Such thorough knowledge conduces to intimate friendship between them.

Secondly, Sun Tzu also said[13] that, based on this pan-knowledge, we must use our soldiers not to fight but to scheme and dissimulate to win "the entire enemy," never to destroy them, by turning their enmity into friendship. This is the total victory, "the good war of all good wars" without fight[14] to develop mutual help and mutual support.

Thirdly, we never fight but just perform nonresistance. We do "no do, wu-wei 無為" that is not "do 為" or "not do 不為." "Nonresistance" or "no do" makes no logical sense, for they are logical contradictions, however, until we hear this story. To Tommy's adamant shout, "I don' wanna sleep!" Mom says, "OK, Tommy. Don't sleep. Just sit here beside your pillow. Mom will read you your favorite story. Don't sleep, OK?" Tommy nods.

"Once upon a time…" and Tommy hits his pillow. Mom did not push him; she did not "do 為." Mom did not let him go; she did not "not do 不為." Mom simply follows Tommy's desire not to sleep and his desire for a story he likes. She gives Tommy all he wants, she did "no do 無為," and he hits the pillow happily ever after. In the same way, if technology ruins the lands and the oceans, the same technology can be used to restore lands and oceans—in eco-family reverence for Mother Nature.

Here we must take note of a simple important fact. Only mother can deal with Tommy. Only the way of Mother Nature can bring us all together. All these three ways here are enabled by motherliness. We must embody Mother Nature to naturally manage our enemies

---

[11] A recent publicizing of these three powers I know of is Joseph S. Nye, Jr.'s "Get Smart: Combining Hard and Soft Power," in *Foreign Affairs*, July/August 2009, pp. 160-163.

[12] It is a concluding phrase in Sun Tzu's great Chapter 3, 謀攻 in *孫子*, 臺北市三民書局, 民87, p. 23.

[13] This is the gist of Sun Tzi's Chapter Three, ibid.

[14] Sun Tzu wrote *The Art of Soldiery* 兵法, how to use soldiers to win total peace, not the "art of war" as it was constantly mistranslated.

to dissolve enmity, to win all-out, and meanwhile we ourselves are won over to our "enemies," to help them out as they come to help us. Such is the motherly tactic of ecology in win-win victory for all.

Here global family-ization—turning all things and all peoples into eco-family—is the tactic and the goal, and this is none other than ecology at work globally. "Globalization as ecology" is our secret weapon to win concord global, and the weapon is an open secret, inviting our enemies to also use it. We will all be in a win-win milieu, where the more we have of those who come along, the merrier and the richer our camaraderie obtains.

Three: In our eco-family, there is no dull moment, for the family is made of youngsters and oldsters. Here every moment is the dawn to the next exciting moment. Mom always runs after her toddler turned a curious sprinter and an expert meddler. Oldsters keep being amazed at the wit and witticism of their young folks. Fish has no umbrella because fish has no hand, says Tessie aged five. Andy aged five wants to change his birthday so he can get the birthday presents anytime he wants to. Harry the hurricane aged almost three tears into toilet paper that rolls out without end; it's such fun.

Meanwhile, it snows in late March and then it sleets in mid-April. Each day is fresh and different from the next day, before and after, and nightly stars are twinkling in halos, tirelessly serenaded by crickets. All this while, Dvorak mingles with Bruckner as Schubert's "Sacred Works" chant after Vaughn Williams' "Sinfonia Antartica." Kids spin their colorful tops as they turn into tops themselves whirling and shouting and stumbling all over, for nothing.

Squirrels are seen chasing after chickadees that tease squirrels without end, while doggies bark up at the wrong trees and at *any* passerby, for nothing. Aren't they all wasteful? Well, it is all fun, and fun is wasteful, isn't it? Our common days are so ordinary, all sparkling with silly stuff all over.

And then, our dearest youngest brother dies on all siblings. So shocked, we all gather in disbelief and in tears to confess to our love of our youngest brother, and the youngsters gather to play piano and violin and sing at the funeral service. One brother says his youngest brother is too peppy and naughty to be boxed in the body, and so jumped out of time and space.

"Hey my baby brother, don't go too far, for I'm seeing you in ten years or so, ok?" Everyone is in tears. Such ultimate vitality of the youngest the naughtiest now released beyond death! Funeral is no fun at all. So goes the day, and then the night comes and everyone says "Good bye!" to everyone else. Email goes to and fro, in gratitude, in deep feelings, in collecting remarks.

Meanwhile, I called again, and found that my Professor Boris Anderson (with MA from Oxford, and another MA from Cambridge) came home from the hospital yesterday! He is 92. He thanked me for calling him, and then excused himself to rake leaves with his daughter in his garden. He casually mentioned that he planned to walk out with a walking stick! "O why, God? Why is not my A-liong physically alive, too? He is only 63!" And such a list of the surprising ordinary days of such sort goes on, in this way and in many other ways.

As the globe turns, ecology goes on around, and Japan's historic quakes, tsunamis come on to shock us all, and the nuclear aftermath debacles leak into fish and foods. Mubarak of Egypt and Gadhafi of Libya the deposed despots continue to be harassed with legal suits, as Mubarak goes into the hospital. Ecology in ordinary days has no dull moment, for there is always something surprising going on, funny, silly or sorrowful.

In sum, the ordinary daily living is yet quite surprising, as described above. The daily is "ordinary" because it is as expected. The daily is yet "surprising" because it is unexpected.

The daily is thus the expected and the unexpected combined. The daily ordinary is thus quite extraordinary. Since the daily is a global happening unceasing, globalization is quite extraordinary every day, quite beyond scientific prediction.

Four: The daily lesson to our daily living is obvious. Science calls our surprising ordinary living "contingency beyond science" in which we constantly live. All this is exciting and deserving of prudential caution. Lao Tzu says (25), "To go far is to return 反," and then he says (40), "Returning 反 is Tao's move."

Actually, "fan 反" translated here as "return" has three possible implications, to rebel, to repeat, and to return. "To rebel" ciphers constant changes and transformations of things into their opposites. "To repeat" expresses cycles and circulations of things in continual refrains. "To return" is to come home to the origin of things.[15]

This threefold "fan 反" is the constant ways in which myriad things transpire in life and in the cosmos, epitomizing the Yin-Yang operations among all these things in the sky and in the field, and the operations of Heaven and Earth themselves, both macrocosmically and microcosmically. We are all involved in this incredible "fan 反."

Lao Tzu then intones (58), "O woe where weal leans! O weal where woe lurks!" This is because the common daily things womb in them the seeds to bring about their opposites. Uncle Fort[16] living at the limits of town, i.e., thriving in the limiting situations of living, always asks, "How do we know this [joy] would not do woe?" and then, "How do we know this [disaster] would not do weal?"

All this is the Yin and the Yang operating, internecine inter-nascent, throughout the cosmos, among myriad tiny things, in time. We must thus swim on the daily crest of a time-wave, never to be drowned in it. This is our ecological lesson globally applicable to our daily "humdrum" that is no humdrum. This it is that is globalization as ecology, in time spreading in space.

Five: Having considered how ecology deals with negative disasters, natural and human, we now consider how ecology can harvest for us positive benefit. The ecological benefit is an all-out victory for *everyone* on the globe. The core of ecology is to play the win-win game of inter-thriving, in line with existence as inter-existence. "How can we turn the world into a win-win partnership?" This is *the* critical question for us all that ecology can answer us.

To begin with, we observe some obvious facts in life that show how inherently social we are, negatively and positively. And then we try to turn our negative sociality into positive one. Thirdly, the secret lies in making us all into "family members"; this family-tendency is actually inherent in us all. Finally, how to turn us all into family members is considered.

First, we observe some obvious facts in life that show how inherently social we are, negatively and positively. Negatively, even in a cutthroat competition, we need competitors, and every one of us can use an underdog. All winners in life's zero-sum game need the losers to be winners. Selfish hoarding needs others against whom to hoard, for where there is no one, there is no sense hoarding against stealers nowhere. Our sociality is negatively displayed in such examples.

Positively, in conviviality, I need people to enjoy this dinner, this painting, and this music. Excellence turns more excellent with co-appreciation. *Differences* among equals make

---

[15] I rifled from rambling insights in 吳怡's *老子解義*, 臺北市三民書局, 民82, p. 211.

[16] On the story of Uncle Fort 塞翁, see 人間訓 in *淮南子*, 臺北市三民書局, 民86, p. 965.

excellences more excellent when shared. After all, excellence is always uniquely excellent, and so when we are excellent equally we cannot be excellent differently. John W. Gardner's "problem," in *Excellence: Can We Be Equal and Excellent Too?*,[17] vanishes on this crucial point, that equals are different, differences make sharing possible, and sharing enhances excellence.

Moreover, significantly, differences among equals genuinely obtain in a family where friendly nurture of unique excellences takes place and cannot help but expands maximally, globally. The family that extends throughout the globe is globalization as ecology, which is the global management of all in all as family household-economy, as "eco-" is "oikos," family household, and "logos" is collective management reasonable. Thus, maximum enhancement of excellences is made possible only in globalization as ecology, the whole globe globalizing its own family household management.

By the same token, every conference needs attendance, the more the merrier. This is a display of family-spirit to see my brother in the other car on the highway, and so I must drive carefully. It is a defensive driving against hurting *him* my brother, not primarily against my possible injury. In fact, in a family circle, the smaller and the sicklier are cared for the more.

Secondly, Sartre is an expert at informing us of cynical inter-cheat, but he did not dig into the origin of this "inter-," however negative. We see in the above examples how we are by nature social, even in negative rejection of others. Sociality often manifests itself in mutual privatization, for negative sociality is immediately visible, and so infants display it at their very beginning of their social engagements.

We must grow up from immature negative sociality of inter-grabbing inter-hurting into mature inter-giving inter-caring. Even small children offer their favorite toys to their favorite people. We must cultivate this positive giving instinct. We must grow up enough to realize that happiness going around among us *all* is much happier all around than happiness hoarded to me alone, as the utilitarian principle enunciates, though without knowing its rationale, much less showing it.

In other words, we must try to turn our negative inter-privatization into positive inter-enrichment. The infantile zero-sum game, in need to push down others to preserve the sum zero, must be turned and mature into the more-sum game, in need of others to enrich our common stock of gains of whatever desirables we enjoy together, and in fact the enjoyment itself enhances our common stock of gains, as with mutual appreciation of beauty co-enjoyed. Here, the more people we have to enjoy, the merrier we all become.

In fact, zero-sum game is unnecessary criminality in which our world is awash, to result in ecological disaster by pressing down nature, exploiting nature for our profit. Zero-sum game assumes the other party as opponent. In business, the other party is no enemy but partner to thrive together in our shared enterprise of business deal. Here in business for the sake of enhancing profit to the maximum, only more-sum game of win-win deals operates, to maximize profits among us *all*.

Actually, all our business transactions are by nature—and so must be—win-win deals all around. Our business engagement must be what it essentially is, a more-sun win-win deal by trading off benefits. Buyers win what they need, merchandise, as sellers win what they want, profit. That more-sum game constitutes an obvious "ethics of business," as it is the core of

---

[17] John W. Gardner, *Excellence: Can We Be Equal and Excellent Too?* NY: Harper & Row, 1961.

business itself, its essence and its nature. We must be as we are, as we must act as we naturally do, to trade off mutual benefits.

If our business deals among us humans are in essence a win-win game, then our ecological deals with nature must by nature be win-win deals to benefit Mother Nature to benefit ourselves, for our business *is* a mutual befitting deal. But, incredibly, our business is actually ruining nature, as nature is not thriving in our businesses.

The win-win turns into the zero-sum because of our greed to get more than our fair share we gain, as we want to kill the hen to get more than one golden egg a day, to kill the hen itself to kill ourselves, for Aesop's proverbial hen is actually Mother Nature in us, and we in Mother Nature. Our greed kills Mother Nature to kill us all. Zero-sum in greed turns win-win into lose-lose. This is why our natural business deal of win-win game must turn into our obligation of "business ethics."

Such a natural practice constitutes our natural obligation. This mindset of win-win game toward more-sum practice for us all, including Mother Nature, is ecology at its bud and at its summit fulfillment. All human enterprises simply must aim to implement this realistic and natural dream. This thought leads us to the next third point.

Thirdly, here, the *turning* from the zero-sum to the more-sum is all-crucial. The secret key to this turning lies in making us all into family members, and besides, importantly, this family-tendency is inherent in us all. We begin by describing the family situation, and support it by describing how the "family connection" is the root of our existence. China routinely expresses "we all" with two memorable phrases—we hope the people *mean* them—such as "we the big family, we our big household 我們大家" and "the same womb 同胞" that can also mean "comrades" sharing life and death together.

That such expressions are not at all extravagant is shown by Mencius who passionately insists that our "heart-of-being 心 cannot bear people 不忍人" in pain. He points to two incontrovertible factual examples. The Lord Hui, the hegemon in the Liang State, who was not exactly benevolent, released a bull because he could not bear its pain of mortal jitters being dragged to sacrificial slaughter, and Mencius also cites how we are instinctively shocked on seeing a baby about to crawl into a well.

This viscerally felt co-pain is "*splanchnizomai*"[18] that appears in the New Testament 12 times, all used on Jesus in heartfelt visceral com-passion before saving people, and in his parables of com-passion, co-pain with people in pain. All Jesus' miracles and all his parables are centered, as they are rooted, in this co-pain, this compassion, at the inner viscera. Even a devout Buddhist, Dr. Chun-chieh Huang 黃俊傑教授 the Mencius scholar at National Taiwan University, was impressed with the close parallel of Mencius' unbearable heart at people with Jesus' visceral co-pain with people.

Now, this com-passion at the heart of our being, the deep pain in our very viscera, is the root of humanity. This root comes from the root of "ecology as the cosmic household." This compassion is family-feeling that brings us into being, and so it must be cultivated to cultivate our very humanity, so as to manage the eco-family throughout the globe. Without such global cultivation of ecology-compassion we lose our very "we," our being human.

---

[18] *Mencius* 1A7, 2A6. *The Greek-English Concordance to the New Testament*, Grand Rapids, MI: Zondervan, 1997, p. 693. *Theological Dictionary of the New Testament*, ed. Gerhard Friedrich, Grand Rapids, MI: Wm B. Eerdmans, 1979, VII: 548-559. William Barclay, *New Testament Words*, Philadelphia: Westminster Press, 1974, pp. 276-280. The list goes on.

Finally, all this is sadly much easier said than done, however. Actually, we remain indifferent to the suffering of people, and family-spirit remains quite neglected as divorce rates continue to soar. *How* to turn us all into heartfelt "family members" must be considered. We must constantly whip up our courage to whip our old habit of the zero-sum competition into the more-sum win-win game of the family. We must turn enmity-competition to kill others into friendly competition, insistent and persistent, to enhance our family camaraderie. We must *keep* on trying.

This is to fight against the fight-against. It is the fight-for fighting against the fight-against. This meta-fight, this mega-struggle, must itself not be a "fight" but courageously to reach *out* to our enemies, to gain the total enemies, including their humane hearts of visceral com-passion. We must remember Mom winning over Tommy's refusal to nap. We must keep on the inherent invincible goodwill, in our maternal inner nature, to win over enmity.

Six: Music has rhythm in refrains to go on and on. In music, dissonance is harmonized in a coherence of sense. The musical coherence opens out into unexpected novelty ever fresh, ever afresh every time it comes to pass. In music, open coherence, dissonance in harmony, and rhythmic refrains show beauty on the move, throbbing ahead in time, time and again. Now, doesn't such beauty on the go throb life itself?

To go forward ahead is to head for the future. The future *comes* upon our life from the beyond that is unknown to us at present. The future is the dawn forever, with definite promises, yet its own promises have uncertain contents, for no one would presume to *definitely* predict the future. The future is novelty ever fresh, afresh each time it descends on us, so inevitable so essential for living on here now and yet so challenging novel to us here now, totally uncertain. This is time-dynamics that has its own fascinating flowchart such as this.

The present folds onto the past, and blends into the past, to shape it, as the past serves a background to tint the present all over. All this while, the future comes down on us to fold onto the present, to blend into the present, to reshape it, as the present serves as background to tint the future into something of an expected promise, still yet for us to know. Such an interblend between present and past, and an interblend between future and present, themselves interblend to compose the "music unsung" of living on.

While inevitably going through all this process of time, some people hang on to the past for the security of the already known, while some others put their total weight on the coming future for any change out of the dissatisfied present, ever prepared for some surprises, even unpleasant ones. We must decide somehow between these two extreme eccentricities, in order to live in balanced sanity.

Listening to music may help us adjust ourselves, to enable us to set up a stable milieu in which to live, move, and have our being to work willingly, cultivate silently, and harvest lightly without fanfare. Music is thus our tonic to life. In fact, our life is itself "music without words," without sound but with deep meaning.

Music is beauty continually moving on into the future; all this while, the future is in turn shaped into coherent sense as we listen to music. Music breaks down into senseless sound-bits and pieces without the future pulling it on ahead, while the future is just the brutality of jarring time without music giving it sense and coherence. Being mutually different, music is tonic to the future, as the future is dynamics of music. Both are two in one, to push life on, as they pull life into coherence, beautifully.

Music by nature cannot be locked up in a box. As we hear music, the sound-scape spreads to seep in, and then inundates itself into us into a new milieu to make coherent sense of things here now. Music makes things into themselves, poetizes the world into beauty, and a new cosmos emerges. And then, music exhibits itself as the future inevitable, yet not threatening, not overwhelming, not jarring, but making sense of living-on for us. Music is our salvation to rebirth into the future. All this music describes ecology on the coherent move worldwide.

"Why does all this describe ecology? What does all this have to do with ecology, in any case?" Ecology is music as its future. Ecology is a verb of the march of life drumming on. Ecology is the music of life's heartbeat throbbing on. Ecology is the rhythm of life pulsing into the future. Ecology is future music alive.

Do you want to know what the future is? Hear the music of ecology. The future comes on to us as the music marching on throughout the world. As music goes on into the future, the future comes down onto the present, from beyond the present, singing the dawn of what is to come as the next rhythm of life. Music is rhythm. Rhythm is coherence and sense on the go, it goes on as it creates sense to the future coming into the present to make present throb into the future.

Ecology as music as future is the music of the future, the future music intoning life that throbs on from the future into here now, as the music resonating from here now toward what is to come to be. Music, future, and life belong together in ecology, for ecology is world-life itself coming down on the world from the future as music itself.

Such is Mother Nature singing its water music and its wind whistle, as the larks ascending to the skies, the Canada geese honking among the clouds, to echo the droning whale-songs in the bellies of the ocean. The future comes to them to be their life, as life sings the world on and on into its future, composing the music of "ecology" from one moment to the next. Such ecological dynamics, such beauty resounding life on and on!

We humans are a mere tiny part of this vast fabulous horizon of ecology, which is our home at present of music of life, living existence inter-existing inter-birthing into the future eco-household, world without end resounding. All such ecology is breathtaking, so alive so fresh as the future coming on down to us here now. Have I been repeating myself? The repeat echoes the refrain of existence returning home, again and again, among all beings living inter-opposing, inter-rebellious inter-reborn, in the inter-refrains of life's music going on and on without ceasing.

Ecology is still singing marching on. Let us join myriad things marching on into their futures. Ecology is musical refrains inter-rebellious antiphonal, returning home to Mother Nature all global. The New World Symphony so Bohemian is heard singing among the Canada geese now honking above the clouds, while the frogs are croaking deep in the Amazon pond-entangles,[19] and the packs of wild wolf scattered around are continuing to howl in the dusk of African wilderness and at the dawn of Indian jungle.

All of them with myriad others in the sky, throughout the field, and under the earth, are all our family members so proud, at home embraced in nature, as our Mother Nature suckles them all. Globalization is indeed ecology absolutely global, continually globalizing through time from past to future, happening right here and now.

---

[19] Compare the rich lively "Ponds Alive" in my *Story-Thinking: Cultural Meditations*, NY: Nova Science Publishers, 2011, pp. 387-404.

A final note must be made. We are hard put to find a single composer of music whose *life* was musical and harmonious. All composers composed music in pain if not in misery. We are tempted to say that their music is a "lotus flower out of mud and sludge, and not soiled," as Chou Tun-I said so of his beloved lotus.[20] Thus it takes courage to claim that ecology that is life ubiquitous is music and the future, music to the future, music of the future, indeed music itself.

This incredible claim out of this world is made possible, and plausible, by ecology as music, in full awareness that ecology is life itself all over in this *soiled* world. "Globalization as ecology" is the dynamo that beautifies this mundane world of ours, to enable us to sing it, and dance and live it. Globalization as ecology is our salvation out of soil into musical beauty. *How* this is so is only suggested (not elucidated) in this entire essay, for the theme is beyond explicit explication. We can only *live* joy in midst of pain, not think about it.

Still, we can say something about our joy, somewhat in this way. All things happen naturally yet mostly out of our expectation. Even things "unnatural," such as our contrivance, happen naturally, for they, including us ourselves, all happen in nature. Still, all these things natural are often quite strange to us, for they often happen out of our expectation, without rhyme or reason that we know.

We express our feeling of frustration by saying that all things are "contingent," which is an ugly word, isn't it? Even if we put it positive way, we are still uncomfortable. We can say, every moment is "dawn" to the next that is brand new and unknown to us, at least not yet, but if every moment is dawn unknown, then every moment is unknown, and we are always faced with things unknown so scary.

We always talk about the weather but do nothing about it, for we can do nothing about the weather. "Don't you like the weather? Wait a minutes," we say, and that is all we can do. Besides, believe me, we all do all things under the weather out of our control, and weather is nature out of our control, in which we live. Twist and turn as we may, we live in things uncomfortably unknown.

In other words, we live at home in Mother Nature yet not quite at home, and we have no *other* "home" than this Nature, called our "globe," that gives us birth at every moment, yet it is what is often quite surprising. We are supposed to manage such strange household of ours, our job called "ecology," and we always manage the globe of our home quite clumsily. We call it "ecological disaster." Shame on us!

Worse yet, this ecological responsibility of ours we cannot avoid, for who can avoid managing her own house? Ecological management is our rough ride of living in Mother Nature we cannot avoid. All this is quite "natural" and yet quite strange a responsibility, if not quite a heavy one. All this makes globalization as eco-piety a heavy though exciting adventure full of ups and downs quite unexpected.

Now, let us put a positive spin to all this, with the help of kids and Jesus. To Jesus, nothing is useless, nothing is wasted. Even his mortal enemy Saul is used into his pivotal apostle Paul, remember? In contrast, among kids, everything is useless and wasted, for they

---

[20] I take this phrase, "[lotus flower] out of mud and sludge, and not soiled 出淤泥而不染," from the well-known "On [my] Love of the Lotus" by Chou Tun-I (周敦頤's "愛蓮說"), but the essay did not connect the lotus with music. My extensive treatment of life and life-reasoning as music has been vague on this point of the sheer painful music-life contrast. See my *Chinese Wisdom Alive: Vignettes of Life-Thinking* (2010, pp. 119-386) and *Story-Thinking: Cultural Meditations* (2011, pp. 290-360), both published by NY: Nova Science Publishers.

have no use for "use" or for "waste." Both words show efficient calculation in cramped competition among us adults, beyond which Jesus and the kids are staying, jumping alive.

Kids and Jesus look at one another and smile. Kids show us Jesus the Paradise, after which Mother Nature models herself. This Paradise is modeled by Heaven that models after Tao, and by Tao modeling after Self-so, Mother Nature (Lao Tzu 25). Lao Tzu and Jesus smile at each other. Both are kids hopping alive as Mother Nature.

In any case, we cannot get over kids. We must repeat our love of kids, as kids love to repeat. Of course it is silly when we repeat, but it is divine when kids repeat. "How is it so?" Well, I will *show* you how so. "Kid" and "useless" do not fit. It is ridiculous to say, "Kids are useless," as it is to say, "Water does not cut," for water melts us into us, as kids do. Kids are our water.

"Use" or "useless" applies to some things, not to persons, of whom kids are the most typical, concentrated, and genuine. Kids go *out* of here now, here now, into the magic of novelties never dreamed before. They are full of themselves going out of themselves. Immaturity grows out of here now; lacking in such "immature" thrust, we all wilt away. No immaturity, no life.

Kids' cruelty expresses curiosity; lacking in curiosity, we are locked up in routines to death. Pain wails itself away; no wailing, we perish in pain. Fight pushes conflict out; no fight, no friends. Thus, kids lose themselves in things so amazing, magically there for the first creation of the world.

The kids forget themselves to live in these marvels, playing with their pals no less amazing, such as balls and doggies. The kids are pals even to themselves, as they play with their own magical toes and fingers, forgetting themselves in them. Life continues in magic and miracles in amazement, among fun-pals at play. We must grow out into *such* kids of all ages, for they are true persons full of themselves out of themselves. Life grows out or it dies; we must grow out into kids growing out, or we die.

Don't you believe it? Just watch the kids. They will draw you into smile. Kids are *full* persons so irresistible. Who says they are immature? Saying so show us so immature, to be brought up into the maturity of a kid-person. Poor Jean Piaget, he is so imperfect immature, and boring. He must stop studying kids in silly adult condescension, to start learning from scratch from kids. He has so *much* indeed to learn from them yet.

Thus, to repeat, we cannot even say "Kids are useless," for saying so is simply a sacrilege to kids' simplicity and perfect purity. By the same token, kids have no use for "use" or "useless." Kids want to make friends to play together, as they love balls and doggies so alive as they. Being together is to have give-and-take that kids call "play." It is fun, just fun, all fun, as life should be, for what else is life for?

Kids thus teach us that some beings are out of bound of "use" or "useless," the categories that are so important in adult life. We cannot use our own body. We cannot throw away our parents because they are "used tires" useless now, as we cannot use or abuse personnel, for they are as personally integral as we are, beyond use or useless.

Suddenly, the crow "car-cars," and the sky gets far up, vast, and so high. Are the crows and the sky useful, or useless? Neither, right? We cannot use hills, or clouds, or rainbow, or music, or paintings, either, though we can use stones as we cherish them as pivotal "cornerstones" indispensable. "How did you know all this?" Kids have been teaching me all this, my friend. Play with them, and they will show you all this.

Meeting kids, you turn sincere, for there is no point in pretending to be someone else as we face them who *are*, starkly gazing at us, or cheating on them who have nothing to swindle out of. You cannot win them, for there is no point in winning them, whatever "winning" means here. You are instead won over, as they grip your heart so tight to their hearts. You are shown the truth that abusing the precious kid abuses yourself, as chopping a gentle tree chops down the chopper. Kids are our trees of life. As we inter-breathe with our trees so silent, so we inter-live with our kids so jumping alive.

Kids are not useless; they *are* they, starkly they, as soft, silent, and strong trees. You are stripped to your bare self by kids all bare, all irresistible. What can you do in front of kids? You turn all-helpless, just smiling at them with them. Now, isn't all this precious as can be? Aren't we humanized by just being with them? Aren't we drawn by them into caring for them? Aren't we held by them as we hold them? Who is immature now, they so immature or we so "mature"-immature, to be matured so much richer by them so "immature"-mature?

Paradise so perfect is here among kids. All Mother Nature models herself here, as kids parent their parents. Blessed are those who are with kids, for they shall see God, for kids are gods on earth, and all the heavenly Kingdom belongs to them. Jesus is drawn into them to say so, as recorded in all three Gospels, and unless we are reborn into kids, we cannot see divine Kingdom, so John says (3:3) that Jesus says. We cannot worship kids, though, for kids won't accept worship, they want to play instead. They are our playmate-gods. Does this make you smile? It makes me laugh with kids.

Just to play with kids makes you holy. You need not play well. Clumsily you just play with them, and they will love you, and you are drawn into loving them, and even dream about them in your sleep. It is the most perfect love there is. In this kid-love, we see no ugly kid, as we see no ugly angel. We turn into angels as we are surrounded by tender kid-angels.

Shh-hush! Kids are all tired out asleep now; they are so beautiful. I watch them, in imagination at night, even, and my lonely pain vanishes into smiles spontaneous, as I fall sleep. These kids are my sleep-angels toddling tender. Their precious sleep hushes my silly talk about them. "Why silly?" We have been adult-talking about kids. That is silly as trying to put on kids' dress.

Now look. The twigs up there in front are softly swaying in spring breeze. They are all green shimmering in sunlight, telling us, "Rejoice! It is kid-dawn!" Mother Nature's twigs are all telling us, kid-smiling, that our unavoidable responsibility of ecological management is not our chore but our joy, for what Mom complains about managing her own household full of her own kids? We are all happy doing it, aren't we? And so, in the final analysis, we simply must say this. Globalization as ecology is our responsibility, and it is our *joy*.

In: Globalization Dynamics
Editor: Kuang-ming Wu

ISBN: 978-1-62100-750-0
© 2012 Nova Science Publishers, Inc.

Chapter 14

GLOBALIZATION AS TOGETHERNESS

Kuang-ming Wu[1]
Taiwan, ROC

ABSTRACT

Since *togetherness* is so basic a mode of thinking alive, all we can do is to dot some vignettes of it to typify it. Seventeen such dots in three tiers are presented. First, the parameter of globalization as togetherness is set. Both co-implicate in globalization as togetherness, utopia, what togetherness is. And then togetherness is seen as innate imperfection in existence, to spread globally as dawn, difference, milieu in cultural dialogues, I *am* together. Finally, dynamic features of togetherness are elucidated in indifference, body, the moment, music, poetry, future, our mere saying, and togetherness as unfinishable.

All meditations below are roaming and coherent, systematic without a system, coming to us without rhyme or reason, and with rhyme and reason so natural. Such coming is rambling all over, to show how globalization all over is togetherness coming on. This is because globalization is activity so vast, awesome, and beyond our understanding here now, ever going on into the richer vaster future together day in and day out.

These thoughts can only be numbered as they come. Japan calls such writing on as ideas come on, "following the writing brush 隨筆" that is actually following the ideas that visit me 隨意, that is following myself roaming all over the world. Thus this sort of numbering thoughts as they come is most suitable a style to elucidate globalization as togetherness, for this is the style of spontaneous togetherness toward globalization.

Style is a wonderful thing. Style is uniquely one's own, intimately bound to the individual, and at the same time the style is shown as "style" personal and one's *own* uniquely, as one's face, only as it is seen and felt as such by the *other*. Style is both personal and unique, not flying off rootless and general, *and* inextricably communal, never locked up

---

[1] E-mail address: Kmwu2002@yahoo.com

and sealed in privacy style-less. To be "racial and local" is to be "worldwide and ubiquitous," thanks to our local unique "styles."

And of course it is sheer *joy* to hit on such private pages with which we all can resonate wholeheartedly, while to resonate is not necessarily to agree. For example, we can feel and resonate in joy with the joy of "Mr. Five Willows" of T'ao Yen-ming's story, in joy forgetting meals when meeting and resonating with the intentions of such writings; it is naturally T'ao's own joy projected onto his writing brush.[2] In feeling Mr. Five Willows' joy, we feel Mr. T'ao's joy that is so intense as to forget himself.

Besides, the writer can of course feel no less great a joy to hit upon such *reader*. And, of course, again, such mutual hitting cannot help but spread globally—as togetherness. In fact, even by just being a shy loner as he is, whenever he shows himself as such, a person turns into a ceaseless chatterbox to this effect to the world. Spontaneously expressing the self, one's style of being continues to gather others, to expand to more and more others, publicizing particularity here, and here, and here worldwide. Personal particularity and peculiarity globalizes worldwide heartfelt.

Being recognized, as one is, is joy, and the joy grows into one's self in joy. In one's style, of being oneself, emerges the joy of togetherness of us all. Thus, it is sheer joy to just think on globalization as togetherness, for just to think on it already practices it at heart. No more preliminary thought about this essay is needed. We must plunge at once into writing—in our peculiar style—about globalization as togetherness, to obtain such mutual joys of togetherness spreading in globalization.

"But wait a minute. Is 'togetherness' worth our serious thinking at all?" Well, "togetherness" has its "ness" that is a hallmark of being an object of universal thinking, and things universally thinkable is worth thinking, and at the same time "togetherness" is actual and concrete, not as theoretical as "sharpness," say, is. Togetherness is both universal and concrete, in similar way as style is.

"What is 'togetherness,' then?" That question is to be answered in this essay, but a preliminary clue can be given. Wright said that Chinese thought or thinking is between common sense and (analytical) philosophy.[3] Togetherness is exactly between detailed common sense and theoretical philosophy; it is responsible as philosophy, concrete as common sense. Chinese thinking is thus quite congenial to togetherness, but that is another theme to pursue.[4]

One more preliminary can be mentioned before plunging into elucidating togetherness. It would not be out of place to consider here how the two modes of thinking—bodily and abstract—can get together. Thinking is always performed by our body, empirical and existential. Body-thinking is a powerful corrective to pan-abstract thinking, to supply the base of abstract "seeing from nowhere."[5] Abstract thinking sees and surveys far and wide, in space and in time, and it can do so because it separates itself from space and from time.

---

[2] See 「五柳先生傳」 in 陶淵明集, 臺北市三民書局, 2004, pp. 361-365.

[3] On references to Arthur Wright's saying and his colleagues' responses, and my series of responses through time, see *China-West Interculture: Toward the Philosophy of World Integration: Essays on Wu Kuang-ming's Thinking*, ed. Jay Goulding, NY: Global Scholarly Publications, 2008, p. 18 and notes 43 and 44 on the page.

[4] Togetherness can only be elucidated by story-thinking. Not accidentally, Chinese thinking fills my whole volume, *Story-Thinking: Cultural Meditations*, NY: Nova Science Publishers, 2011.

[5] Kuang-ming Wu, *On Chinese Body Thinking: A Cultural Hermeneutic*, Leiden: Brill, 1997. Thomas Nagel, *The View From Nowhere*, Oxford University Press, 1989.

Having supplied the bodily base to abstract thinking, body-thinking must face up to the challenge of thinking "abstract, empty, universal" with its own bodily *ubiquity* in time in space, somewhat in this body-way. Body-thinking "treads its body-form"[6] to co-respond with the ancient great, and with contemporaries at present, to resonate with later-comers in later generations. The human space thus comes alive through time in undying incorruptibility. Such is body-togetherness globalizing in time.

As such, togetherness is thinking so earthy, so concrete, and so ubiquitous in space. Togetherness is globalization at work, and its thinking truly, genuinely, and effectively catalyzes myriad things into sense in Global Village happily and casually alive, as if nothing were the matter. Such a global picture of life is freshly cleaned by togetherness and thinking on it, for globalization *is* togetherness.

Since togetherness is so basic a mode of thinking alive, all we can do is to dot some vignettes of it to typify it. Seventeen such dots in three tiers are presented. First, the parameter of globalization as togetherness is set. Both co-implicate in globalization as togetherness, utopia, what togetherness is. And then togetherness is seen as innate imperfection in existence, to spread globally as dawn, difference, milieu in cultural dialogues, I *am* together. Finally, dynamic features of togetherness are elucidated in indifference, body, the moment, music, poetry, future, our mere saying, and togetherness as unfinishable.

A tiny caution is in order before we plunge into those points. This is no place to go into details of the themes elucidated in the following. Those themes are mentioned to show the wide range and the diverse directions of togetherness. After all, this chapter is on togetherness, not on any of the specific themes mentioned under "togetherness." Now we can go into these points one by one.

One: Globalization as Togetherness or as Universal Utopia

We all know that globalization comes from things and cultures and persons coming together, but no one knows what it is, even though everyone thinks he knows it, for it is such a common word. Few of us know what globalization can be, as it is in fact togetherness, as globalization is the process of togetherness.

Of course, it is difficult to prove that globalization is identical with togetherness, but we can show how, if globalization is indeed togetherness, all sorts of exciting riches and implications follow and tumble into coherence. This essay is one of those attempts at showing the enormous riches of togetherness that goes on to its worldwide maximum, called globalization.

Two: Globalization as Universal Utopia

An alternative definition of "globalization" is that it is contentless generality, an empty universal far out there beyond what anyone knows, toward which many cultures worldwide gather to attain, and all this while they are wiped out in this indifferent universality of god-knows-what. It can be vaguely called "cosmopolitan humanity" that no one knows what it is.

---

[6] "踐形" in *Mencius* 7A38. Please pardon my repetition of "body"; it is quite indispensable.

But some of us are sure that it is "new humanism" of democracy, equality, and liberty, as the American Transcendentalists envisioned, and soon enough this vague "new humanism" was identified with the United States of America![7] This historical event shows us that any general universality inevitably turns into a specific entity.

American Transcendentalism is only one of many historical precedents such as, among others, French humanists and then the entire Western culture imposing monocultural dominance as "modernity," as fashionable "globalization." Such historical precedents demonstrate the human predicament of our inability to entertain an empty universal generality, as this hollow universality, "globalization" is a Utopia, literally a no-place, a nowhere dreamland.[8]

Three: What Togetherness Is

This essay pursues the first possible description of globalization *as* togetherness. Togetherness is quite a strange notion. It is on one hand an extremely common noun for ordinary gathering anywhere any time, nothing special. It is on the other hand a semi-theoretical concept with a "-ness" attached to it, quite possible to explore its theoretical implications and connotations, as I did it once.[9]

Thus "togetherness" is then a concrete universal, naming one community throughout the world *of* many diverse cultures. Togetherness is one *in* many, many gathered into one, and this "of" and this "in" make up togetherness that is the dynamic process of globalization. Togetherness is so fertile that I had to write a book on it, and it overflows the book.

Four: Imperfection as Dynamo of Togetherness

We note in this connection an interesting assumption that accompanies togetherness. It is 'imperfection," saying that everything is imperfect, including the thought that the concept of "imperfection" assumes the existence of the standard of perfection, even though we know nothing about what perfection is. Now, if everything is imperfect, things must of course get together to inter-complement to get less and less imperfect, to approach asymptotically the ideal of "perfection," whatever it is.

One of the performances of complementation among various imperfections is to play with argument-bits. It is so fascinating that I devoted a whole section to this theme in my volume on togetherness.[10] The rationale for our playing with argument-bits is that, since no argument is perfect, we would entertain—play with—whatever bits of argument we happen to see as plausible here now, which may turn implausible later elsewhere, sooner or later, and then we will play with more argument-bits. Let us take a concrete example. It actually happened.

---

[7] See George Hochfield, ed. & intro., *Selected Writings of the American Transcendentalists* (1966), Yale University Press, 2004, pp. x-xi.

[8] We nod and smile in tears at Samuel Butler's satirical anagram of "nowhere" in his *Erewhon* (1872), London: Penguin Classics, 1985. His Utopia is a place of no-place, no-where, but it is a specific spot.

[9] Kuang-ming Wu, *On the "Logic" of Togetherness: A Cultural Hermeneutic*, Leiden: Brill, 1998.

[10] Ibid., pp. 150-293. I am expanding on the thoughts expressed there.

I asked my granddaughter, about five at the time, "Hi, Tessie, how come fish has no umbrella?" Back came a confident answer, "'Cause fish has no hand!" We all laughed. "Why did you laugh?" she asked. I do not know. Was it because her answer made surprising (1) sense that (2) no one had ever thought about? If so, then the clash between (1) and (2) produced laughter, and we thought we could never win, and would not even want to win. We are all won over! (3) Being won over is part of our laughter.

Some years later, when asked the same question, she said, "'Cause fish live in water." Now the answer has changed from "no hand" to "in water," and so the sense has shifted. The plausibility has changed, while she had been always confident that she made sense! Thus kids' senses shift, ever with confidence!

So do ours, as we are kids of all ages constantly growing, as the history of ideas anywhere testifies to. All we do is to play with arguments to produce the sense plausible "here now," and we will see how things go in some other "here now," as we play on to produce more numerous and more diverse senses. "Is it progress?" Well, it is shifting growth, thanks to play, playing the game of arguments all over, all the time, in all places. Playing with arguments is togetherness in globalization on the go.

In the meantime, we keep juggling one argument-bit with another, and against another, so much so that we—especially we Britons and Chinese—in our common sense tend to look with suspicion at any "perfect argument" that goes so "flawless," too perfect to buy in and be convinced, as Lin Yutang also astutely observed.[11]

We on our part usually limp along with several incompatible pieces of argument, juggling one against another, all half-baked. That is what happens in, among others, committee meetings, where intuition cooperates with reasoning, both entirely imperfect, one stimulating another into some more half-baked ideas. This is one example of togetherness in our imperfect world.

After all, as nobody is in "perfect health," so none of us is "perfectly reasonable." Our life is made up of daily management of imperfect blood pressure and diabetes in the wind of thinking. We try our best just to live with our problems and live up to our best, and our "best" always shifts, with or without rhyme or reason, both imperfect.

We thus tinker *with* our problems as we play *with* argument-bits, and the "with" here is togetherness. Both the sour-grape withdrawal and "fools rushing in where angels fear to tread" belong here, called togetherness, which is globalization in the making. This situation is not as imbecile as we think, or as in low taste as it looks.

The Nolloth Professor of the Christian Religion and Fellow of Oriel College, Oxford, Basil Mitchell, said, "…the case for theism, like the case for any secular alternative to it [such as history, natural science, political theory, and metaphysics], must rely on the cumulative weight of a set of converging arguments that cannot be entirely formalized." His "arguments that cannot be formalized" are our "argument-bits."

We appreciate Mitchell pointing to the cumulative togetherness of cluster of arguments to clinch the case. We only add that the "converging" set of arguments is only one aspect of "cumulative" togetherness that includes divergent dissonance as well. My book on Nonsense

---

[11] Lin Yutang, *My Country and My People* (1935), NY: Halcyon House, 1938, p. 109.

cites "ridicule of low people" as corroboration of the case beyond our disputes and understanding.[12]

Nor did Mitchell mention that such gathering of arguments is often swayed by the fashion of the times, and the cumulative strength is evident in *that* period alone and in *that* community of thinkers alone. "Birds of a feather gather together" into a clique of scholars, who now gather into a powerful and prejudiced "think tank" to judge how convincing a set of cumulative arguments is.

Five: Existence as Threefold Togetherness

All actuality is togetherness in three senses, existential, thinking-wise, and normative. To begin, any *existent*—anything actual and anything thought about, and even any thinking act itself—is a composite, many composed into one. An existent literally stands out (*ex-sistere*) of the other, even a no-existence does, to exist. An existent is composed of its tension with the other to exist. "A is A" thanks to "A is not not-A." An existent "A" is—exists by—being in tension *with* the "not-A" that negates "A." An existence is "with," togetherness.

An existent "A" is a composite in tension, com-posed of tensed dealing with its negation, "not-A," where the "not" is an act of negating "A." Such existential composition is literally posed-together. Existence is thus togetherness, a single as plural, one in many, many into one. Existence is by nature social, and sociality is quite interactive among many inter-tensed.

Then, the same situation holds for *thinking*. Thinking thinks of something thought about. Even Aristotle's "thinking that thinks thinking" is social as above described, as "something" thought about is always a thing thought about, an existent. An existent is both thinking (as subject thinking) and is thought about (thought-object).

Existent and thinking thus form a close synonymy, as thinking and thought make a composite pair. After all, there is no thinking without thought, and no thought without thinking. Thinking is thinking-about, and a thought is thought about by thinking. "About" here ciphers catalysis of existent and of thinking. "About" is one in two, two in one, an interactive sociality.

Actuality is thus com-posed of existent and thinking, and so actuality, *any* actuality, is a singular-plural, a sociality interactive, and tensed. "Any" here is ubiquitous, and so sociality inter-tensed is globalization at work. Globalization is togetherness at its basic existential level of performance.

Thirdly, existence is *normative*. What is right is opposed to what is wrong, while the right itself is asked, "What is wrong with what is right?" as the wrong itself is asked, "What is right with what is wrong?" The right and the wrong inter-deny correlating one with the other. Existence is thus ethical, involving right and wrong, carrying on itself, carrying as itself, an inter-categorical imperative between right and wrong, ever self-tensed, as imperative is contentious within itself as right versus wrong, wrong within right trying to right itself only to be wronged at once.

---

[12] Basil Mitchell, *The Justification of Religious Belief*, Oxford University Press, 1981. Unfortunately, he did not probe the cause or rationale for cumulative strength of a set of imperfect argument. I supply it here. Kuang-ming Wu, *Nonsense: A Cultural Meditation on the Beyond*, NY: Nova Science Publishers, 2012.

Existence is thus right and wrong at once, coexisting yet incapable of coexisting, existing in self protest, in quite an unstable détente. Thus actuality is dynamic togetherness threefold, in existence, in thinking, and in norm, all at once in an uneasy sociality self-protesting. In all, globalization is such interactive togetherness ongoing.

Six: Existence as Dawn

Existence is thus internalized sociality, continuing to externalize itself into togetherness of globalization. Existence is a composite gathered into a community of globalization continuing on. Everything is existence being writ large into globalization macrocosmic, to mirror existence as microcosm. Existence sees a world of globe in a grain of sand that holds eternity in history unending.

All this is so fabulous yet so familiar that we are in daily daze. Here harmony takes place in dissonance, big in small, small as big. All things are compact composites as communal cosmopolitan, ever in concord tensed inside and out, in me in milieu among you and then another you, and another, whom I meet without ceasing, alive all, unawares or not. Existence large and small is togetherness.

Here sorrows refusing comfort wail, with laughs of carrying sheaths on shoulders homeward way, as harmony of all is in dissonance among all. Here concord happens in tension in struggles spontaneous, you and I, as the "and" here spreads across the ages among cultures worldwide. Togetherness thus expands in globalization.

We see that such expansion is random and coherent, surprising and reasonable, because the expansion takes place into the future. The future is unexpected, inevitable, and understandable, as the dawn of the child full of promises unknown, to be soon known, and when known, we see that all this unexpected growth has to happen, and the child then is of course the adult now here, nothing unreasonable or unusual. It is the wonder of the future, unknown to be known and definitely known as familiar.

One thing is certain. The dawn of expansion is for certain to take place all over the world, sooner than later, in joy and in wail, in eulogy in elegy, in legend in paradigm, random coherent. "Watchman, what of the night?" we ask, and he says, "The dawn is coming, ask, ask, and prepare." In dawn, every grain of sand is shimmering with the promises global, opening out into the horizon so vast, unlimited, and unceasing.

Seven: Differences the Dynamo of Togetherness

One more dynamo besides dawn in this dynamics of togetherness is "difference" so challenging. Differences make up distinctness of each existent, thereby to each open out. Difference is opening on the go unceasing, exiting beyond the status quo of existence. But such exiting out of the self is change of the self so scary.

Since change is scary, staying put in status quo is a comfort. But actuality keeps confronting us in time in space at dawn of every moment. Every dawn changes soon into broad daylight not dawn, and every dawn differs from every other, and so daily living is made of differences so scary yet inevitable. Besides, every dawn is abundantly worth looking forward to. This is so for the following reason.

Dawn is change and difference in every event and every existence to form a synonymy of the world to go forward into globalization. Globalization is open to the future, to become our future itself, and the future means being resolutely open no matter what, as we are at dawn willy-nilly going forward into the future. Change, future, and difference, these three constantly inter-operate in life, and *the* dynamo among them is the difference. Let us now probe "difference."

Differences dovetail one into the other. Difference is always a plural, and plurality comes as togetherness that dovetails on and onward to open out in globalization. "Is globalization one *or* many?" Globalization ongoing is one *in* many, many in one, and so the "or" in the question expresses many, expresses differences, while "in" in our answer expresses one in dissonance. Thus the "or"-difference and the "in"-dawn above compose the dynamics of open globalization process in harmony in dissonance.

Eight: Differences Our Imperative of Togetherness

Differences among all of us make for inter-learning inter-enriching inter-tensed, in scary pain. Differences makes up *dialogues* of all sorts, existential and oral, expected and unexpected. Since differences provoke controversies to push dialogues ahead, and differences are our pain, dialogues are quite unpleasant.

The pain of dialogues is well founded, because dialogue is inter-revolution of cultural milieus in which we live and breathe our very being. Dialogue shakes up our very paradigms, assumptions, and gestalts in which we are oriented to live on coherently. Dialogue smashes our smug coherence in pieces, and we must reassemble ourselves, and such re-assemblage produces a new coherent self-identity. Dialogue is our bitter pill, our tonic of new creation out of smug burial in the old self.

Dialogue needs differences to happen in disagreements, and so it needs our willingness to bite the bullet of opposition in disagreements among our differences. Besides, understandably, our oppositions can often be quite violent, for the disagreement is at the foundation of our basic assumptions, our milieu of paradigms and gestalts of living coherently.

Here there is no room in which to bask in mutual admiration, patting one another on the shoulders all around. Dialogue is no place for group think, as it is the place at most of critical encouragement, if anyone can afford to do so. All this is due to differences that make contrasts, produced by opposition born of differences.

Such contrastive opposition provokes forth new existence, as the baby's establishment of his self begins at shouting "No!" Strangely, pushing the other the no-self *out* of the self, and thereby pushing *out* the self into the world of others, are both negations at work ("out"), and yet these negations positively establish the self by stabilizing the self, precisely through its negative pushes. This positive push by negation makes togetherness.

Thus, togetherness includes its own rending apart by contentions and revolutions. How do we logically understand this odd situation? Let us take an example. Suppose I say, "The world is made of two kinds of people. [1] *One* kind of people say, the world *is* made of two kinds of people, the first kind say, the world is made of two kinds of people and another kind say the world is not, while the second kind say, the world is not such. [2] And then *another* kind of people say, the world is *not* made of two kinds of people; we are all of one kind. So, the world is made of *one* kind of people, one-people, and *another* kind, two-people."

All this is fine, until someone asks *me*, "Where do *you* belong? You tell all this of two kinds of people, and so you belong to the two-people, not to the one-people. But you also tell of another 'one-kind' who deny the existence of 'two kinds.' So you are one-people also; you are two and one at once." Self-reference is incoherence, yet consistency implicates self-reference, so consistency is incoherent, i. e., inconsistent."

This oddity happens because we take consistency as a comprehensive all. To avoid the oddity, we must prevent consistency from implying "all," as Russell did (by going to a meta-"class" of all classes). We must stop going to meta-level. But the stoppage here amounts to inconsistency, violating the implication of consistency as all-comprehensive. So, Russell tries to avoid inconsistency by being inconsistent. Avoiding inconsistency by being inconsistent performs inconsistency.

But then, to think of it, we have been inconsistent *all* the way, and so we are consistent in being inconsistent. We are consistent throughout, after all. But this is such an odd consistency, isn't it, for this consistency embraces inconsistency to be consistent. Does this embrace announce the arrival of globalization-togetherness in tension?

Togetherness-consistency is "all," "all" is the world, and the world has world-breakers of revolutions as consistency contains inconsistencies, as double negatives affirm. Global Village thus oddly includes revolutions to rend Global Village apart. The Village is such an odd "brave new world." But at least we now understand its "logic" that consistency can include inconsistencies of revolutions. Inconsistency makes revolution, and inconsistency bespeaks differences. It is difference that moves the consistency of existence that often exists by existential revolutions.

Moreover, it is difference alone that fills, feeds, and fulfills existence. Autophagy—self-devouring, eating self-sameness—kills itself. At the same time, however, difference poses a mortal threat to the self—as not-self—that is quite an unpleasant and impolite intrusion into what is all right all along here now, about my self. Revolution is social difference acted out socially, brutally unpleasant, that attends togetherness as above considered by considering "two kinds of people."

In any case, actuality keeps confronting us as above, to force a choice on us. Either we can commit a comfortable suicide of self-consumption, or else we must courageously take in the other so different, so threatening, and so imposing an intrusion into the self—to grow out of the status quo. Our ease kills us in self-sameness, as pain invigorates us in other-differences. And yet both routes contain death threats. That is the unavoidable choice of our existence in stark risky togetherness. "How does togetherness come in here?"

Togetherness is the pivot here, as differences gather to form togetherness. And so, we can either reject togetherness in differences to die in challenge-less isolation, or else we must accept the mortally painful differences in togetherness, again, accepting the deathly challenge to grow out of the status quo. Such acceptance is sheer pain, and yet, once we accept others different from us, we can then grow forward. Only those who are fit and tough enough to take on this challenge of differences can grow in fitness to tackle more and harder differences, to grow up into our richer stronger future.

Thus our struggling pain, tackling the constant challenges of continually oncoming mortal differences, is our dawn of growing pain, world without end. Our struggle this way is not unnatural, after all, however, because we are composed of inner differences ourselves. All we do is to externalize our inner struggling growth in differences, in spontaneous struggles accepting all challenges of outside differences.

Differences, challenges, and acceptance, these three together push us ahead in growth into the robust future of ourselves together. If all this is not dynamic togetherness in differences that is globalization in progress into the future together, nothing is. We can now breathe deeply, lift up our heads, and courageously accept the challenges of differences here now that continue to come to us ahead in the dawn.

Nine: **Milieu, Culture, Dialogue**

All this activity of togetherness occurs in a milieu. Milieu is that in which "we live, move, and have our being," and so it is what creates what we are. No wonder, Paul equates milieu with creator God as he talked to those thinking people the Athenians. Paul did not say that "milieu" can be identified as our "culture" behind us, beneath us, and beyond us ahead, or that creation is attended with birth-pangs. Paul did not say because he could not. Both points are unmentionable because they are too deep to get for the Athenian audience who just keep casually chatting on "some new thing." (Acts 17:21, 28)

Dialogue is no casual chat, though. Dialogue is give-and-take ("dia-") of life's "logos," the very mode and rationale of living, from one life to the other, to and fro, back and forth. Dialogue shuttles among the various ruling passions of life. Such a deep wording-with is quite beyond shallow telling and hearing of some new things, as the Athenians did, to capture.

It was they who are incapable of existential dialogue of a deep cultural kind. So, it barks up the wrong tree to accuse Paul for his failure to win any of the Athenians to Christ at the time.[13] It was the Greek shallow soil full of stony casualness that prevented the seed of the Gospel to take root.

Of course a mere chat can reveal one's élan of life, but such soul-thrust must be seriously engaged in, intently listened through, to inter-nurture, and this sort of inter-mothering takes time and deep sensitive sympathy to take place. It happened when a swineherd Eumaios wholeheartedly listened to Odysseus's soulful confession, even though under false pretense.

Cognitive discussion or even playful riposte must be discerned as "Freudian slips" into the deep recesses of life's "will" as Schopenhauer named it. This amounts to confession that is not easy, and demands soul-listening that is no less easy. Chuang Tzu yearns after wording with someone word-forgotten, that is to say, deep soulful inter-dia-loguing stripped of superficial chaffs of chats.[14]

Dialogue goes from heart to heart, deep answering deep, and only then inter-revolution of assumptive milieu can happen. Dialogue is provocative happening of this unpleasant sort. Still, only such dialogue heals, saves us from losing our life's way, and converts life back into its self-creation. Dialogue creates new life. Let us stress again. Rare or not, such happening is often attended with pain so messy, for no revolution is neat, clean, and easy.

Awakening to the importance of messy dialogue, and yearning after it, makes life's beginning called "adolescence." Chuang Tzu and Odysseus are adolescents for dialogical

---

[13] E. Stanley Jones is one of Paul's accusers, in *The Christ of the Indian Road*, NY: Abingdon Press, 1926.

[14] See *The Odyssey of Homer*, xiv: 183 and xiv: 360, in tr. Richmond Lattimore, NY: Harper & Row, 1967, pp. 215, 219. Arthur Schopenhauer, *The World as Will and Representation* (tr. E. F. J. Payne, 1958), Two Volumes, NY: Dover Publications, 1966. "Freudian slip" is too well-known to cite references. *Chuang Tzu* 26/49, its concluding sigh.

togetherness at the cutting edge of life that cuts deep into life, and changes the milieu of our lifeworld. What is so dynamic about milieu is that it changes, not just by itself (as history) but also by us as well, and *our* change of milieu is achieved by dialogues of deepest sort—to make history, to make new "we."

"How does dialogue work?" Listen to this. Dialogues traffic among diverse cultures to inter-revolutionize our cultures that are the foundations of human living. Dialogues are life's assiduous and painful processes of inter-existential creations, across histories and cultures toward the future.

Dialogues must happen among Socrates vis-à-vis Confucius, Stoics with Lao Tzu, Buddha and Chuang Tzu, Name Scholars 名家 in ancient China and logicians today. Such dialogues must be engaged between Chinese Communism and Chinese history, Chinese Communism with Russian Communism, Chinese Communism versus Western history, the people as lord-power in Western democracy vis-à-vis the people as the root and the judge of the nation, in Chinese people-root-ism 民本思想, and the list goes on unceasing. Our dogged observation to dialogues is the limit to such series of dialogues intercultural inter-historical.

Dialogue can take a radical turn. Chuang Tzu has elder Lao Tzu scold junior Confucius. Similarly, we can have George Washington scold Abraham Lincoln. More radically, Chuang Tzu (29) has the notorious brigand Tao Chih 盜跖 scold the sagely Confucius. Following this example, we can have Hitler scold Lincoln and Churchill, wrongly or rightly. It is the occurrences that count; their justifications can then follow.

Chuang Tzu learns from condemned criminals, and especially from those condemned to death (23/76-79). Such learning goes even beyond Confucius the all-time expert on learning! This learning is so radical that I cannot think of any parallel to it today. Here is togetherness so vast, diverse, and incredible beyond our wildest dreams.

In any case, we can thus have no limit to such oppositional pairing in dialogue, because history has no limit to pairing incompatibles, cultures included. In fact, all the above examples cited are on the past dialoguing with the future at our present in various cultures. The past and the future gather together at present among many cultures together here now.

Ten: I *Am* Together to Be Together with Others and Resolve Pain

Again, all the above description portrays the *modus vivendi* of globalization and its togetherness. This is because togetherness cuts deep into my very existence. I *am* together. This fascinating theme has been considered in Point Five above, and we will here expand it into external togetherness. But we must begin at rehearsing the impacts of "I *am* together" on others, to go into me being with things outside, and resolve my pain by noting the pain-parallel between my being together and my being together with others.

I exist by being-with, for I *am* being-with, to be myself, to inevitably be with others. I am being with me to be with others outside me, and *that* is what I am. "What I am" is defined by how I am, both as "being with," i.e., with me to be with others, and with others to be with me, doing so to exist as my self. Now let us unpack all this almost unintelligible explication of "being with" as my being my self, to be with others.

Existence inter-exists, as "A is not not-A" makes "A is A," as explained in Point Five above, Likewise, I inter-self to exist as my self. My thinking itself is I talking to my self, as

Socrates in the *Theaetetus* says that thinking is a self-dialogue. Even when just being alone, I am with me-alone. So I feel lonely by being with loneliness as I miss someone else that can be my self or someone else. "To miss someone" means that I am here with the other absent, and so I miss her, and so I am lonely.

All this is because I am with-me. To call being-with-me "self-reflectivity" is so insufficient as to border on naming amiss, for self-reflexivity comes from my existence as being-with through and through. I am forever my *alter* ego. This is why I can have the other as my alter ego I need. I am social at the core, and so I am ever surrounded by the others—even my self as my other—as my milieu. I am togetherness.

"But being together is often a pain. How would you deal with the pain?" Now, here is a bombshell to explode pain away, for here is an important twist. To begin, saying, "I am togetherness, and so I am the other" is filled with so much tension that borders on contradiction. It is because the other is a "not me," a negation of the "I," for the other is other than my self, "not me." And so "I am the other" means "I am not I," which is a contradiction to rip me away from me, and the ripping is pain.

This pain comes first from each existence being autonomous and autotelic. It has its own law of its own existence, and so any existence is autonomous. Any existence exists also by aiming at itself alone to be itself, and so any existence is autotelic. Secondly, for all this, no existence can exist without the other that it must negate. Existence exists by both being autonomous and social, *and* by negating sociality.

The same situation holds for me as the other *to* the other. Inevitably, "I am the other" makes a prescription of pain of inter-opposition. "I am the other" breeds my enemy, to mean "I am my own enemy." Jesus' "Your family is your enemy" (Matthew 10:36) is not as farfetched a declaration as it seems.

All this shows that my life is forever tensed with opposition, with enmity, and with pain. If I am togetherness, I *am* pain. All the well-known sayings that twist our minds, "Love is vulnerable," "Love is pain," and "Love conquers all," as well as "I take care of myself," "I hate myself," "My God is closer to me than I am to myself," and even "Love your enemies," and the like, now make sense, given the above explanation of "I am the other" as "I am not-I."

"Love is vulnerable" is interesting, and has a bearing on the rest of the love-statements cited above. We could say, "We cannot open our hearts to people too often. Jesus dies of doing so in an open heart surgery on the cross." You could respond, "But he was resurrected afterward. Love is deathless." And then we can thoughtfully say, "Yes, but all this is such pain. Love is pain, isn't it?" Such pain of love is closely related to "I am not-I," that is pain of contradiction, yet I need—love—the other the not-I to exist as "I" at all.

We can also see that the diverse sorts of radical existential pain avidly portrayed by the early existentialists, such as Camus, Sartre, Kafka, and others, is not their cynical overstatement. On the contrary, their portrayal has naturally originated in the pain of "I am the other" as "I am not-I."

Now on this base of "I *am* pain," here comes our unexpected twist, to find surprising silver-lining over the pain-cloud radical, existential, diverse, and extensive and pervasive. We have been on the whole[15] living along—that's why we are here considering existential pain—

---

[15] Barring some exceptions of suicides committed by abnormal people and super-normal people. They often come together, if not being identical.

without suicide, and so we have been on the whole *succeeding* in dealing with existential self-pain, however pervasive.

If so, we can likewise deal with pain that comes from our environment, whether natural or human, for after all, environmental pain can be regarded as an extension of our inherent existential pain that we have been managing successfully to live on so far. In other words, in this manner we see our own definite potentials in dealing with existential pain for deal with external pain.

We are quite familiar with external pain from our surroundings, and so such pain requires not much explanation except to just cite some examples. We are often living with our opponents, with our fights with oppositions beyond control, with the circumstances of woes natural and human, and the like. Reading biographies and news reports helps ease such pain, and especially dipping into "I am not-I" resolves such pain, as above noted.

Eleven: Indifference as Togetherness

"I understand that love and hate are modes of togetherness, but is 'indifference' togetherness, too?" It is a good question, pal. This is one of the common cases but odd ones that make us scratch our heads. We will have below five more such odd common cases, "body," "the moment," "music," "poetry," and "future." As before, we will not go into details of these themes, but just touch on them to elucidate the riches of togetherness as globalization ever continuing.

I think—this is my opinion, awaiting confirmation—indifferences have diversity and degrees, depending on the person's life-orientation that in turn depends on their backgrounds, cultural, educational, social, and the like. Sartre loves to plumb their diversity but not their degrees. Indifference is a peculiar form of togetherness, in that togetherness is conscious mode of sociality, and indifference is conscious negligence of those around us, and so is a negative social mode.

After all, we are constantly surrounded by things, matters, and persons. We are constantly bombarded with their impacts and demands, so much so that we must block out some of our concentrated dealings with them, and such a blockage is indifference. Indifference is our tactic of survival in this congested global world.

But there is blockage and there is blockage, with degrees and diversities. It would be insane of us to pay closer and more intense attention to world news than the urgent notices of our immediate neighborhood. And we have (usually unconscious) predispositions against a certain group of things, matters, and peoples. Outsiders point to our racism and anti-Semitism. We respond that we have rights to choose who we prefer to make friends with and where we wish to dwell in. And the debates go on. This is where crowd and social psychologies thrive. In short, indifference is togetherness.

Twelve: Body as Person-Togetherness

"Is our body togetherness, too?" Yes it is, but in a very peculiar manner, quite different from being with other things, matters, and people. For instance, even though the captain of a ship loves "his" ship so much as to be willing to sink with it, the captain would not feel the ship's "pain of drowning to death." In contrast, in writing, it is I who write; my writing activity is not my hand writing. As one member of the body suffers, the entire person is in pain. In my toothache or stomachache, it is not my tooth or stomach that is in pain, but I am in pain at my tooth or my stomach. I *am* my body; I do not have my body (Marcel).

Such body-unity of the entire person naturally spreads to our spouses to constitute our family. Our family members *are* our intimate body-parts, our very bodies. As one member suffers, the whole family suffers, and I suffer. When my baby is pricked and cries, I am pricked in tears. When my granddaughter won prize, however tiny one it is, and whatever significance it has, I am in paradise unspeakable, in all smiles.

Such bodily kinship feeling expands to our friends. We regard our friends as our own self. Responsibility commissioned by my friends—without reward, with nothing but pain and price in every sense—is regarded by me as my joyous reward. In an extreme case of loss of friendship, even though my friend is physical alive, my loss of that friend is pain unspeakable. I attend his funeral yet I have no closure as usual funeral would give me, because my "friend" is still alive. My friend lives on dead. Friendship is deathless even in its loss, and its deathlessness is keenly felt precisely in its loss. The loss is unspeakably sad.[16] It is the sorrow of loss of my body, my self.

Extended in range but not in meaning, medicine, counseling, and thinking are of our body in action. They are our body-activities, or else they are not genuine. Medical doctors who "treat" the patients and professional counselors who "handle" the clients fail in their respective professions. "Thinking" as my body-act is quite interesting. The Jewish people take breath as mind that thinks.[17] Mencius (6A15) takes thinking as engaged by my "greater body 大體."

Jews and Mencius represent ancient insights quite natural and significant. They indicate that thinking is always "I think," I am my body, and so thinking is always my body thinking. I have extensively considered "body thinking" in three volumes so far,[18] so I only mention its one specific problem in connection with togetherness in time and globalization in space.

Body thinking has a "mortal defect." The body is a particular, limited in space and in time, while thinking is an act that spreads universally without limit. "Body thinking" is thus a self-contradiction, "limit limitless," impossible to obtain. Despite all this contradiction, however, thinking originates in the body to typify the body. We must tackle this strange problem concretely, perhaps this way.

Naming signifies thinking. Any name is a particular. "[A particular] white horse is no [general name] 'horse,'" says a Name Scholar Kung-sun Lung.[19] "Human life between sky

---

[16] Both Montaigne and Marcel movingly described "my friend's commission as my reward," and Thoreau lamented over the loss of friendship; he is the only one I know of who discerned the sorrow of such loss. See Michel de Montaigne, *Essays*, tr. J. M. Cohen, London: Penguin Classics, 1958, pp. 91-105. *The Philosophy of Gabriel Marcel*, eds. Paul Arthur Schilpp and Lewis Edwin Hahn, La Salle, IL: Open Court, 1984 (I could not locate its page reference). *I to Myself: An Annotated Selection from the Journal of Henry D. Thoreau*, ed. Jeffrey S. Cramer, Yale University Press, 2007, p. 44 (1850, after January 5).

[17] William Wilson, *Wilson's Old Testament Word Studies*, Peabody, MA: Hendrickson, no date, "Spirit: breath, mind," p. 411.

[18] Kuang-ming Wu, *On Chinese Body Thinking: A Cultural Hermeneutic*, Leiden: Brill, 1997. *Chinese Wisdom Alive: Vignettes of Life-Thinking* (2010) and *Story-Thinking: Cultural Meditations* (2011), both from NY: Nova Science Publishers.

[19] "白馬非馬" in 公孫龍子, 臺北市三民書局, 2004, pp. 27-41.

and earth is like a white colt passing a crack, only so sudden," says Chuang Tzu (22/39). Both are particular sayings on particular matters so specific in space (Kung-sun) and so short in time (Chuang). And yet, these sayings so fragile last and last. They have lasted since over 2,500 years ago, and will continue to last far beyond today. Saying is then a particular universal, and saying is thinking that is due to our being bodily.

All this is a story in history. History comes to help us concretely resolve the tension. History is globalization in time, and it is togetherness in time. The story above shows how history breeds this sort of particular universal in time that is called in China—China is thoroughly history—"incorruptible 不朽," for in fact history is itself a grand "particular universal" that lasts and lasts quite incorruptibly. Nature in seasonal rounds is another grand example of particular universal. But we need not go far. The "moment" here now 當下—it is what we are—is a particular universal quite bodily.

Thirteen: The Moment

We always have the dawn to begin the day, but then we ask, "Do we have myriad dawns, then?" And then, strangely, we get the answer, "No." This is because we *only* have one dawn here now. We cannot even say, "We have one dawn at a time," for we are not allowed to experience here now the "at a time," for we have, to repeat, only the dawn here now, and "at a time" obtains only after jumping out of our being here now, and we can never jump out of being here now, for we are here now *alone*.

We find ourselves to have repeated "here now alone." We have one moment here now alone. This moment is the dawn. This twofold fact—our moment is here now alone, and the moment is the dawn—constitutes "we living on." The first aspect of the fact of "we" commands us to live the moment here now as fully as we can.

It is because this moment is our eternity that lasts for ever. We must "dig it," be open fully to it, as the baby who meets each "thing" for the first time in life; have we noticed their eyes wide open? "For the first time" expresses the baby-dawn here now, the second aspect of our life-fact, so fresh forever, forever for the first time!

Let us now push a step further. The dawn here now is the incorrigible particular. To live it as eternity in eternity is valid for every one of us, and so this particular is universal. The dawn here now so specific is the particular universal, so concrete as the dawn, togetherness in globalization, forever making a demand on us all to live fully, to live in eternity forever fresh.

Here we have no "repetition" that is an abstract concept drawn *out* of our life concrete, irrelevant if not contrary to the moment lived as *the* dawn eternal. Here there is not even "each moment" that is a contradiction, for "each" makes sense from the point of view beyond and outside the moment. "Each" is a surveyed concept, and the "moment" cannot be surveyed beyond the moment, for the moment has no outside. The moment is the dawn all by itself, eternal in itself, all on its own.[20]

We cannot even claim that each dawn-moment is unique, different from all others, for again "each," "unique," "different," and "all others" are intelligible only from the

---

[20] "All" is interesting. It is all right here, but it is a universal concept, as Russell warns us.

retrospective and prospective perspective of history, surveying and sweeping beyond here now (but perhaps not outside here now except for "each.").

At the same time, however, have we noticed that we cannot help but use such universal concepts and universal mode of thinking to describe the impossibility of describing the moment-dawn in universal mode? Eternity is understood only by such combination of particularity and universality, for "eternity" itself is such a combination as our living and we ourselves are the composites, and as togetherness-globalization is this particular universal. All this is the lucid *sub specie aeternitatis* of history beyond history here now, at the moment-dawn afresh forever fresh.

"You advocate living the moment fully. Should we live sorrow fully at the moment, too?" Look at the kids. They whine and they wail as they stomp feet in tears over the milk *they* spilled, over their dearest toys they themselves broke, and the whole world is ended right there. They break themselves because they have broken their dearest milk and toys that are they themselves. They want to die here now!

And then, lo and behold, such complete devastation cleanses them, and they rise up, tears still all over their dirty cheeks, and they rush out to play a game, a "new game" all familiar. We must be kids at their baby-dawn baby-moment, to fully shout and wail refusing all comforts. And the full-wail of ours, all ours, pushes us into the new dawn the new moment. We simply must!

"Is all this in language of the particular or of the universal?" Haven't we been doing both? If we talk in particularity-language, our Master would nod and say, "You are right." If we talk in universality-language, our Master would again nod and say, "You are right." If we say, "Particularity opposes universality," then our Master would say, "You are right here, too." "Who is our Master?" He is our moment our dawn here now, eternally fresh for the first baby-time in life. These if-stories of ours here are about the moment the dawn, to gather into togetherness as globalization.

Fourteen: **Music**

If all the above description of the dawn the moment sounds too ethereal if not abstract to understand, we have another quite concrete notion ready at hand to help us understand ourselves, our own living moment. It is music, the constant vibration of existence, what has been called the "music of the spheres," though of here now all around. Music with all its notes is tuneful lyricism of inter-resonance that composes existence, and existence as inter-existence, for inter-existence is music.[21]

The result is musical harmony in dissonance, and music in harmony with silence. Or is all this even the result? Isn't this existence inter-resonating itself harmony in dissonance? Music must have dissonance as contrasts to compose music in harmony. Music must have silence also to punctuate, shape, and push music ahead. Thinking of all this—and what else is thinking?—must itself be music as music must signify actuality as meaningful, as any existent is music vibrating.

---

[21] See Kuang-ming Wu's *Chinese Wisdom Alive*, op. cit., and *Story-Thinking*, op. cit., for more detailed appreciation of cosmos as music.

This is because music is the essence of meaning as thinking thinks on meaning. Physics today caught existence as vibration, but it is yet to feel the vibration as music, as music so alluring, lyricism so appealing and comforting. No wonder, not accidentally, we go listen to music in soulful openness whenever we are empty, despaired, or simply too tired to move on.

Musicians, composers and performers alike, are thus the angels of existential comfort and strength. They seem so arbitrary because there is nothing in music that we can see, grasp, touch, or hold on to. In fact, however, they surround us—we cannot escape it!—with rhythm so soothing to re-tune our deranged existence into a harmonious whole, and such wholeness is what we call "health."

Musicians are angels of our holistic health to send us forth living in strength and stability. They are ambassadors of cosmic vibration of existence to induce us to catch the vibration. As such our saviors, they are the pioneers and trail-blazers of globalization as togetherness so irresistible and uplifting among us all throughout the world, for nothing can resist the soft power of music to put ourselves together into one piece.[22]

Composer Mozart vaguely caught it in the *Magic Flute* that sings *the* power of music for love that conquers all obstacles. Music, love, and power are at one here, to spread all over the world. Music is indeed the *modus vivendi* and *modus operandi* of globalization in togetherness, as love is togetherness at its most powerful, compelling, and most cosmopolitan, in all its uniqueness of loving this person, loving this matter.

Here is the catch of musical particularity. Anton Dvorak smells Bohemian all over. His music vibrates his existence that is incurably, incorrigibly, his rural meadows in his bucolic home town, in his small town dinners of local tastes, not German, not Chinese, not even USA even when he conducted his *New World Symphony* celebrating USA as the New wide World. And at the same time his music delights every one, literally everyone in Germany, in China, and in USA, and everywhere else.

Dvorak's earthy particularity exudes globalization, to show how his smelly locality *is* universal globalization. We must follow him likewise, and insist on singing our own silly little songs we lustily created, as Stephen Foster composed household and minstrel folksongs, and everyone will flocks to us. Be yourself singing yourself and everyone will come humming along, and globalization together happens right here now, quite local, where everything falls into peaceful cosmopolitan delight.

Now, never forget this fact of pan-music. Music spreads the vibration of existence for a good reason; music is not at all arbitrary. Music has its rationale for its irresistible power to spread. It is that music is poetry charged with the power of meaning, without which life cannot go on. Dr. Frankl who survived the terrible Auschwitz, with the sole power of meaning to living, eloquently testifies to this fact,[23] even though he did not say that poetry is meaningful, that meaning gives us life as poetry of music does.

---

[22] Jonathan Goldman in *Healing Sounds: The Power of Harmonies*, Rockport, MA: Element Books, 1996, touches on the power of healing of music, but he is too confined to specific kind—his own—of music. Sally Beare mentions music as the 45th secret of longevity in here *50 Secrets of the World's Longest Living People*, NY: MJF Books, 2006, pp. 213-214, but she just gives scientific evidence of the efficacy of music.

[23] Viktor E. Frankl, *Man's Search for Meaning* (1959), NY: Washington Square Press, 1969, etc.

Fifteen: Poetry

Music is powerful when lyrical more than melodious, because lyricism produces sense in us, to give us meaning to living. Lyricism is the soul of poetry coherent and open, ever expanding with invincible appeal of meaning, evoked in the reader of poetry as the audience of its music.

Musical poetry's appeal lies in the contagion of rhythm that rhymes on and on, in time through space, and rhythm rhyming is the sense that cannot help but spread, as meaningful of myriad things. Music is poetry alive jumping and spreading with meaning; poetry is music charged and deepened with meaning. It is meaning that charges alive both music as poetry and poetry as music. And in this way we have just described what poetry is. We must go into poetry.

Poetry is compact, deep, simple, and alive, because it is in rhythm spreading in rhymes, for rhythm rhyming is meaning throbbing alive, and meaning is the essence of all things; anytime we ask, "What is it?" we ask the "what" that is the meaning of a thing, the "it." If we cannot stop asking "What is it?" whenever we meet something, we cannot afford to dispense with poetry in our living that pursues meaning poetry-charged. Now we must unpack these important words of poetry-description one by one.

By poetry as compact we mean that poetry packs the most sense in the least amount of sentences; the most in the least packs compactly, to turn things into poetry. Poetry then turns simple, in fact, it is the simplest delivery of communication we have, and so the most direct, going from heart to heart, deep answering deep. Such poetic give-and-take of the heartfelt in depth turns everything alive touched by poetry. Poetry compact and simple is alive to make us alive, or it is no poetry.

Poetry alive, simple, and compact moves on in rhythm that rhymes on and on; and the rhythm rhyming is the sense of things that we meet, on and on. It is the meaning on which and by which we live on and it spreads on. Without sense and meaning we cannot live. We commit suicide for finding no sense in living on, no meaning in life. And so, poetry—compact and alive—supplies meaning to turn us alive longer and more vigorous. We live on poetry; we live by poetry. We cannot take anything verbose and meaningless, as kids cannot learn without learning in nursery rhymes of "once upon a time," to hop, skip, and jump into knowledge.

All this is the power of poetry that makes for togetherness globalizing. Power is of two sorts, overwhelming power, and drawing power. Poetry overwhelms us to implode from inside us, and thereby draws us together into one piece to enhance and enrich us. Frost said that a good poem inflicts a mortal wound on us we cannot get over, and he should have gone on to say that such mortal wound draws us into the immortality of vigorous life. "How does all this go?" Let us trace how poetry proceeds, and we will see. How poetry goes shows what power, overwhelming us to draw us in, poetry has.

Poetry whams us with compact quips. We are overwhelmed, and provoked to unpack the inside of the poem. Our unpacking composes the music of undergoing into the deep sense of the poem. We thus tread the path we are evoked to create, to understand that poem. To thus undergo the poem understands it, and the meaning of living is created by us by being overwhelmed by that poem.

All this is alive fresh as can be. In this manner, we resonate with poetry, and the resonance is rhythm rhyming on, from the poem to me, from me to you, to resound forth the deep sense of life. Such is how poetry works alive, compact and undergoing, going-through to let create, and this creation continuous and coherent is poetry.

As music sings to soar, so poetry lyrical provokes to undergo to understand. Poetry lyrical tends to sing melody-less to evoke more, and meaning of life is created by us thereby. Such lyrical impact of poetry is the flowchart of togetherness. Still, poetry does sing tuneless a-rhyming to keep moving on.

Poetry is beauty alive in word-rhythm of time, timing and timely. Poetry is music the art of time, the time-art in pulses of sense in an expression of experience of sense, i.e., sensing sense, feeling the sensible meaning of ongoing experience of life. Poetry is sense in the making, always half-baked to keep baking into pieces of fruitcake concentrated, deliciously nutritious serendipitous.

Poetry always shouts lyrics, to sing along to hum along a-whistling a tune, once-upon-a-time to live happily ever after, the commoner the better, silly or profound. Poetry goes in meter in assonance and in dissonance. Poetry is such word-music to be heard to be tasted to be munched on, to nourish us alive to live long.

"When shall we meet again, in sleet or in the rain?," even the witches ask sweetly in the *Macbeth*. Macbeth himself is wiser than all of us enough to mumble, shortly before death, "All is sound and fury, signifying nothing." Now, doesn't this poetry-mumble itself signify something? Poetry is creation of coherence continuous, and so that coherent line of "signifying nothing" about "all" signifies something significant about all.

It is thus that poetry moves us to move the world, by singing words to chant sense and dance rhyming with myriad things, to create the cosmos the chaos ordered. Poetry moving with cyclones, vast and cosmic, is globalization in process vibrating all in time in space, shaking them up in delightful togetherness. Poetry is the power of pan-creation in the music of globalization togetherness. Poetry is sheer existential music of cosmic vibration, intensely alive everywhere all the time.

The poetic lines blend into silence that moves the music of existence vibrating, silently intoning the world, in enchanting whale-songs in the ocean-belly unheard of on land, to womb forth things big and tiny, microcosm blending mirroring macrocosm in the music of poetry. Vaughn Williams overheard it and brought it to us in Symphonies 1 (Sea) and 7 (Antarctica).[24] Music, and more silent music, all is poetry in silence chanting without ceasing.

One tiny penlight brightens total darkness to usher in the dawn. One grain of sand blows in the wind to mirror and wheeze through the forest. The dark forest then comes alive belching the poetry of Ode to Joy in silence without silence, as silence is music of nature wheezing its winds, even in bleak Antarctica. Remember Vaughn Williams overheard them as his *Sinfonia Antartica*? Silence sings all around, smiling, smiling, and smiling. If all this is not vast globalization on the go in cosmopolitan togetherness, nothing is, and then not a thing exists, not even nothing itself so loved by Buddhism.

Sixteen: Future

To irresistibly spread is the power of poetry, and this power to spread is the power of the future that *comes* to be. Poetry is the future-power in rhyme with the present, in rhythm with myriad things, in their existence-music humming on along. This power of the future applies

---

[24] Listen to, e.g., *Vaughan Williams* by Sir Adrian Boult, EMI, as an 8 CD set.

itself to eulogies and elegies. We wail out in poetic sorrow as we poetically wax in shouting joy, and in our poetic eruptions the future comes to us.

We sing when sad, we sing when in joy. We sing poetry to live into the future. That is how we create tomorrow. Poetry is such music of the future, as music is such poetry singing into tomorrow. As such, music-poetry rhymes us into power to create our self, and the self-power is the power toward the future, the future-power creating the self new and authentic. The future is what is coming, and what is coming is always fresh and exciting as we come home to ourselves, our real self that grows on and on.

Sometimes, however, the future comes as scary novelty. It is up to our power of poetic music to turn the threat of novelty into new creation undreamed of so fascinating. "How does it look like after our trial?" Looked at from the beyond, our future is our creation coming confronting us. Looked at from our inside, our future is growth erupting from our intimate heart. Both combined, our future turns exciting unknown so fresh and novel, yet deeply known as ourselves after all.

After all, poetry is *poiein*[25]; it literally creates. God "is the poet of the world," said Whitehead.[26] God the creator is the meta-poet of the globalization for all poets to create. Poetry creates the dignity of the self, the self-identity hitherto unknown and non-existent. In short, poetry creates the future quite unknown yet, we realize, quite familiar after all.

We cannot have a bird's eye view of the future as we cannot have a map of experience that we now undergo. In the same way, a bird's eye view of creation is impossible as the survey of poetry is impossible. We simply must undergo that power of poetry to understand the exciting future being created, and then our very undergoing enables us to understand what the future has brought us.

This poetic undergoing is the process of globalization as togetherness, gathering past and future in the present in process. "Now" is the moment of truth-in-the-making. The poetic undergoing is the poetry making the musical *of* the future. The future is the dawn of promise unknown that comes softly sneaking into our busy present, for disaster is always at present, not in the future ahead. The "future shock"[27] is a cheat and a mistake, for there is always tomorrow, promising a better time, in case we missed the last train today.

Tomorrow is a promise sent to us before, arriving today,[28] as today is the promise of tomorrow coming, like it or not. Every move here now today promises tomorrow the future. Thus, the future-élan is the dynamic paradigm of globalization in the making here now. Music, poetry, and the future, these three powers form a fascinating trinitarian synonymy to portray the exciting paradigm of the dynamics of globalization as ongoing togetherness, at present constantly going into the future.

---

[25] See *Theological Dictionary of the New Testament* (1968), ed. Gerhard Friedrich, Grand Rapids, MI: Wm B. Eerdmans, 1979, VI:458-484.

[26] Alfred North Whitehead, *Process and Reality: Corrected Edition*, NY: The Free Press, 1978, p. 346.

[27] See Alvin Toffler, *Future Shock*, NY: Random House, 1970. Future shock cannot happen if future is an unknown that cannot shock. Future shock cannot happen if it is the shock of our anticipation that is at present, not the future. Any other meaning of "future" is a literary embellishment, not real future. In short, "future shock" is impossible or it is a mistake.

[28] "Promise" is "*pro-mittere*," send-forth.

Seventeen: Togetherness Cannot Round up

Togetherness cannot be *exhaustively* elucidated, explained, and/or expounded, for togetherness cannot stop. This is because, first, our living cannot stop synthesizing, pulling things together from outside to live on, for synthesis is what life does as life is to live on. No synthesis continuous, no living *on*.

Thus, secondly, togetherness cannot be exhausted also because living on is living on to the *future*, for life's synthesis continuous requires time continuous to pull off and time continuous is future coming continually, and so synthesis is power to the future, as we live on toward the future, as every dawn turns into another day we live on. And we must remember that the future cannot stop, nor can it systematize, never, for continual synthesis is coherent beyond definitive systematizing, i.e., beyond rounding up.

One thing is certain in all this activity of synthesis continuous as we live on and on. Have you noticed how *warm* the word "together" is? The mere thought of "we together" smiles at us together. Interestingly, "filiality" figures rarely in the West, but it is so much favored as "孝"[29] in China that "we all" are expressed as "big family 大家" of the "same womb 同胞." *That* is togetherness so intimate so happy, to innately extends to family cosmopolitanism. Nothing is happier and more intimate a globalization than this humane family togetherness all over the globe. "Within Four Seas are all brethren!"[30]

Interestingly, I body-act, body-feel, and body-think, and they are mine alone, no one can do it for me, while, at the same time, they spread in contagion. Let me explain. To begin, I sleep, go to the restroom, eat, rejoice, and shed tears. No one else, even my own mother, sleeps or eats for me, or goes to the restroom for me, or shed tears for me. I must do it alone myself.

But then, even my casual friends can also yawn and feel sleepy as they see my eyes get heavy. They want also to go to the restroom seeing me go, feel hungry seeing me eat with gusto, and are "given a weep" as they see me weep, as the Japanese says, "貰い泣きする." Besides, what Plato thought in Plato's way alone is understood as Platonism, spread as Neo-Platonism, and all subsequent philosophies in the West are "a series of footnotes to Plato" (Whitehead), and even China takes the West as Platonic. Specific body-thinking that belongs to the West alone spreads in history worldwide.

Unique and irreplaceable while spreading in contagion is human body-living. I call this phenomenon body-thinking for short, and it is conveyable as non-analytical storytelling. Moreover, importantly, doesn't "uniqueness in contagion" aptly characterize concrete universal, thinking as actual, one cognitive into many concretes? And isn't all this a replica of globalizing togetherness?

The logical analytical conundrum of how universality, singular and abstract, applies to actuality, concrete and numerous, vanishes here. The globalization process is indeed

---

[29] "孝 hsiao" has "子 children" under cover of "old-bent [parents], 老." It is a cherished notion in China, portraying and telling of children serving 事 old-bent parents, receiving, inheriting, and supporting 承 them. See 說文解字詁林, 臺北市鼎文書局, 民73, 7: 557-559.

[30] *Analects* 12/5. Even though China keeps failing its passionate ideal, it has invaded no outside nation in history. Interestingly, as recent as spring of 2011, Charles Glaser also holds this pacifist view on China. See his "Will China's Rise Lead to War?" in *Foreign Affairs*, March/April 2011, pp. 80-91. Glaser is joined by Thomas Christensen and Wang Jisi in the same issue.

localities, regional and cultural, spreading worldwide. The Heaven and Earth are constantly born with me, as I constantly spread to be one with myriad things, as Chuang Tzu says (2/52-53). Globalization as togetherness is my body-story dynamics with cosmos, and within Mother Nature.

At the same time, we must never forget this contrary fact, for, paradoxically, this joy together is also pain. This is because, as said in Point Ten, "I *am* with" is "I am the other" that is pain of contradiction, "I am not I." Even in China, children's filial love is often tensed with differences with their beloved parents. Togetherness is joy continuous in pain continuous, to provoke our thinking about togetherness without ceasing.

So, "living in joy *and* in pain that cannot stop" ciphers togetherness that cannot stop, as globalization is a continuous activity-verb of togetherness. And so, living in joy-and-pain also cannot stop our meditations on it. Since all this is unstoppable, we can stop at any moment, and the moment promises the stupendous serendipitous potentials of more riches, and more, to be unearthed and enjoyed for globalization as togetherness, goes on world without end.

Isn't all this *the* Joy beyond all joys and sorrows, the joy of togetherness even with our opponents and our woes and disasters, to celebrate together an Ode to Joy of globalization, as togetherness throbbing into our common future? In fact, isn't such global joy enhanced myriad-fold precisely by enjoying it *together* with such life negativities, for nothing is more joyous than being happy *with* our opponents than just with our friends? Such is *the* meaning of globalization as togetherness, going on birthing, creating, without ceasing.

Now, let us put the whole bit in this somewhat general way. Any two notions can be related externally, or they can be related as part and whole. In the part-whole relation, the part is a part of the whole, and the whole characterizes the part as a part of the whole. The pebble-a, for example, is just externally next to the pebble-b. This is external relation. All this while, each pebble exists as "pebble," and so the notion of "pebble"-as-a-whole features each pebble as a pebble.

Most appropriately, human persons and their humanity are such part-whole relation, where a person is part of the whole humanity, and humanity so pervades each person that each person is human. Human community and human culture are just some descriptions of such human part-whole relation.

Now, globalization is one dynamic feature of humanity, and so each person, and each community, and each culture, carries global depth, as each citizen is a national, and each nation is global. Globalization is a cosmopolitan spread of being globally human from one individual person, community, culture, and nation, to another.

Humanity as one feature of nature-as-it-is requires human globalization to take place. The spring rain drops of humanity are softly falling on us, calling us to be human, all human, as each pebble is already a pebble; it is all pebble as a precious stone of Mother Nature. We must become natural and human as a pebble *is* real pebble.

Moreover, the part-whole relation is "relation" alive, a relating interaction. Every day, she in Taiwan calls me in USA, and then we Skype for half an hour. Why do we do so? It is because she feels pain of my absence and feels my pain of her absence. And her sister beside me feels our pain. We three are now parts of our shared pain. Pain is such part-whole relation; so is joy, and so is beauty. Besides, this part-whole interrelation as interpersonal spreads to the non-personal, turning everything into everyone, and every non-person vibrates "person." Now consider this.

If there is no viewer, there would be no scene. A viewed scene is a part-whole relation in which things out there are turned into a gestalt of "scene" by a viewer, who was an indifferent individual now turned into a "viewer" of this gestalt-scene, produced by the viewing, invited by those things now viewed-as-a-"scene." Thus, if there are no things, there would be no scene, and no scene, no viewer; and all this while, no viewer, no scene. A scene is a part-whole relation among things and persons.

And then, soon enough, the scene out there "tells" its viewer to take a picture of it. A picture of an inch square can then be blown up into any bigger size desired, and into as many pictures of as many sizes desired. A picture is not just a picture but a picture-seeing, winking at the viewer to see.

The part-whole here includes the size of a picture, as a small size requires a short distance to see, while a huge mural requires standing back from a distance to see. Size, distance, lighting, and surrounding, as well as the viewer's appreciative readiness, are involved in a seen-picture that makes up a picture. A picture is an invitation to such a viewing multi-involved. A picture is thus a dynamic part-whole interactive relation.

And then, the number and variety of the viewers are essential to this picture-seeing interrelation. The more, the merrier. The picture-seeing is expansive in attentiveness. The well-known harpsichordist Landowska said, "Music grows old if it is neglected—like a woman who is no longer loved. Take an interest in her, and she will become young again."[31] Interest here consists not just in intensity of attention but also in the number and variety of attentions of various people. Again, the more attention we pay, the merrier our life turns, and that the younger and more alive we turn.

Now, "the more" shows togetherness. Togetherness intensifies and enriches the relation that is a picture, a music-piece, a milieu, an interaction. The greater such togetherness grows, the merrier the enjoyment of stories these things variously tell of. This "greater" is the growth of interactions interested that continue to expand, and the expansion of togetherness self-expressing in their stories is globalization.

Every picture and every scene, big and small, past, present, and future, is an invitation to togetherness globalizing. The global is the local expanding. Every existence is a seed growing in globalization. "The more racial-cultural, the more cosmopolitan," proudly advertises a Chinese calligraphy publication.[32] The peculiar Chinese calligraphy, with all its historical depths, is a world-art of abstract-concrete portrayal of the senses of things alive.

By the same token, the Bohemian-drenched "New World Symphony" is a symphonic ode to cosmopolitan togetherness, of global enjoyment at every corner of the world. The more Bohemian the music goes, the more global its appeal grows. We here literally see and hear the whole world telling its stories in a grain of cultural sand, and every grain is a dynamic story-growth in globalization.

Hermann Hesse's *Siddhartha*, itself an intercultural story, written in German about Indian sentiment, and translated into English, concludes with a story of a stone as a river of various existents.[33] A mere pebble here now is part of the whole stories of global existence-

---

[31] This lovely saying begins the insert in *Bach: The Landowska Recordings: Wanda Landowska*, RCA Red Seal, 7 CD-set.

[32] Thus begins the 說明 that begins every volume in the series of 中國書法明帖精選, 西安陝西旅遊出版社, 2005. The original says, "越是民族的, 越就是世界的."

[33] Hermann Hesse, *Siddhartha*, NY: Bantam Books, 1971, pp. 144-146.

vicissitudes, making rounds of springs and autumns, with and within Heaven and Earth, through myriads of light-years.

So, the dry skull casually tossed on the roadside told so as above to Chuang Tzu (18/25-29) in China, merely 2,500 years ago. This cosmic story of a pebble, told by a wise useless skull, is amazingly bottomless in implications and boundless in extent. This is a truly global story about so many countless stories of countless existential instants, pebbles and mountains included. All human cultures join them all in making living in season and out of season.

That dry skull then added that these rounds of making seasons with myriad things in the cosmos are *the* ultimate joy beyond all joys and sorrows, simply because this is no less than the magnificent cosmic enterprise all global, all begun at the tiny insignificant pebbles and useless dry skull no one wants.

In fact, is there any difference between the skull no one cares and pebbles and grass no one cares? *Are* they all not the ultimate joy of making rounds of seasons with Heaven and Earth, with which we now must reckon? *That* is togetherness the power of the small that is so big globally. Expanding togetherness of all pebbles with all squirrels and all trees and all hills and all rivers, all expanding, is the dynamics of globalization.

This dynamics worldwide is nothing short of the whole globe in explosion of life's delight, telling of world-histories bottomless boundless, all cosmopolitan. Togetherness begins at the tiniest existence, and rolls out into the gigantic globalization indomitable, never to be mocked. Nothing can stop this global process, except, paradoxically, *our* business selfishness with our technological might.

Both Chuang Tzu in ancient China and Hesse in modern Europe have felt the awesome impact of globalization as the process of togetherness. It is our joy and privilege to join this mighty global process of togetherness. Our responsibility is to promote it, never to ruin it with our selfish ecological devastation. Togetherness joining globalization spells *our* global responsibility to achieve cosmopolitan camaraderie with the tiniest pebble and with the mightiest mountain.

Now, a little funny thing has just shown up, to nod at us who are going after togetherness, and this "little thing" turns out to be quite a big joy. It goes as follows. Our living brings together contraries to turn one into the other, in two ways. One sort of togetherness is simply that things negative turn into their positive contraries,

All this while, our living can consciously push such turning to our advantage. Doesn't Ssu-ma Ch'ien 司馬遷 tell forth his magnificent *Records of History* 史記 to wash away all clean what he takes as his shame? Doesn't Schubert compose so much music so lilting, whenever he is lonely?

Aloneness is needed to compose togetherness. Togetherness soothes loneliness of being alone. Schubert composes music when lonely; music is rhymed togetherness in harmony. By the same token, writing is done when one is lonely; writing is a sort of music stretching toward togetherness with readers. Togetherness and aloneness, in being lonely or not, inter-need.[34] Thus globalization and localization interpenetrate, so much so that there cannot be one without the other.

All this happens because we tell stories—in music, in writing—to us ourselves in pain, and our pain wailed out in stories comes in to us, to come strangely to soothe us. Don't *all* of

---

[34] Paul Tillich brings the Beyond into loneliness, in his *The Eternal Now*, NY: Charles Scribner's Sons, 1963, pp. 15-25. We go our simpler way, staying in this world in togetherness.

us tell stories of our music of histories anytime we are in pain groaning? Don't we groan forth stories so as to live on strong? Wail out our groans, and our music of pain shall be digested into our sinews to toughen us, as broken bones healed turn stronger than before.

This phenomenon is all too ubiquitous, so much so that we can stay calm and be prepared, as we watch when the disaster strikes. "Don't you like the weather? Wait a minute," says our common sense. We must wait it out to tough it out, for pain is our weather for us to weather through, to turn tough and flexibly sinuous.

Now, our weathering whatever weather is our great togetherness of life, for the "weather of all things" is that in which we all live and move around. Incredibly, we *can* maneuver and steer our weather to our advantage, due to the fact of weather-togetherness where things turn one into another inter-contrary, and we can steer their contrary movements to benefit us—by weathering it out flexuously and sinuously.

Togetherness of another great sort, though less noticed in daily life, is a gathering of the specific and the general. It happens whenever a story is told, such as telling stories about "anyone is somebody to someone." A story is always about a particular, even when it tells about a general truth such as "A is A" or "One and one make two." Besides, have you noticed it? Aren't "always," "any," and "whenever" themselves a togetherness of specific with general?

To think of it, whenever we say a word, any word, it always tells a story, any story, and the story gathers particulars and general; don't you find it so? Storytelling gathers particulars and general to produce the togetherness of specific and general. The specific is this particular quite unique; this is *not* that. The general is this *and* that and that, the more the merrier. These two, specific and general, are inter-opposed, and as opponents each to the other, they join in a "word," in any word we utter.

As soon as we say any words, or even a single casual word, these two opponents, specific and general, gather into one. Even my dearest brother A-liong, now physically gone on, is a particular here now whenever I think on and call "you, A-liong!" My "A-liong" is my dear particular everywhere, my dear particular-general. Doesn't this odd discovery tell us of a story that any single word is a story alive whenever we invoke it?

No wonder, Plato launched Western philosophy proper with dialogues, which are stories of inter-storytelling between one party and another. No wonder, one world-culture, oldest and vibrant irrepressible, tells of stories of history in storytelling of literature. It is China that collapses history into literature, and turns literature into history, and calls the unified complex, "literature-history 文史." After all, as we live on, to tell is to historicize. To tell is to make history to tell stories of our lives.

Telling of things, here now, is the dynamics of autobiography that transforms our life. Whenever we open our human mouths, sorrow gathers into joy, particulars into general, and togetherness takes place to nod at one another among us in smiles. We cannot help but open our mouths, for we are social beings even to ourselves, as we are forever self-expressive to show our sociality even as we talk to ourselves.

Any time we thus open our mouths heartfelt, said or unsaid, we show how we are as we tell it to ourselves and to others. This "any time" of our telling our stories is the crack of dawn of togetherness. Globalization begins to rush in right here. Or rather, more precisely, it is that globalization wells up from inside us to rush into us, to pervade all of us to turn us all irrepressibly vivacious, in all joys of all of us, various and together. All in all, togetherness is the joy of globalization inside us pervading among all of us.

Let us look at how marvelous a matter all this is, for we must, for it is so amazing we cannot help looking at it. The personal is intimate so specific here now, while the public is everywhere every-when so ubiquitous. How could they interpenetrate into our living that we want? We would have thought only rare sages can pull of the stunt.

We now find, to our surprise, that our very saying something, so ordinary, personal, and intimate—no public has a mouth—is itself general-ubiquitous. This is because words however personal are meaningful, and meaning is understandable all over. This fact so ordinary is nothing short of astounding, for we cannot help but "say" something, and so we cannot help but be intimate and public at once.

This astonishing fact yet so ordinary forebodes well for togetherness in today's Global Village. Even winds and rains, birds and trees, hills and rivers, are all clapping their hands of meaning welcoming us once we say something of them. We had better be fully aware of this common uncommon fact, to go join them in the chorus in cosmic joys of togetherness, globalizing constantly as we say things to converse with myriad things as we do among ourselves.

All in all, let me say this. With one eye we see things in flat two dimensions; two-eye vision adds depth and perspective. Add consideration of time and community, and "history" comes to us as a panorama of the dynamics of milieus, as Kuhn tells us. Add another culture than ours, and another, and another, ancient and today, and religious beyond, and "objectivity" in actuality appears, as Feyerabend advocates even to natural science in the West we usually take as universal beyond all cultures.[35]

The last addition is the ultimate of human endeavors toward our holistic sense and grasp of "reality," human, myriad things, cosmic, historic, and all. Even the supposedly "straight and austere" natural scientists in the West confess recently to such irrepressible joy of childlike curiosity in their researches.[36] In fact, their researches would simply cease without this curiosity constantly peeping out of itself.

It is fabulous joy, of which we can ultimately be aware, of sheer existence, to dip in this *total* reality, beyond all our calculation of profits or loss, joys or sorrows. If just to exist is sacred, then existing in sheer totality of reality is joy beyond all joys and sorrows, beyond all life and death. Nothing, absolutely nothing, can replace this joy.

This joy intercultural, cosmic, and ineffable is the final raison d'être of globalization in togetherness. Togetherness is final, and globalizing it is an absolute imperative demanded by our very existence. Globalization is toward togetherness or it is nothing. In fact, globalization *is* the élan of togetherness itself that fulfills our basic demand of existence. To exist is to globalize togetherness of all in all, in all-joys abounding. It would be sheer insanity, almost equivalent to committing suicide in the face of joy, to resist this irresistible joy so intoxicatingly cosmic and historic.

Look. What is *the* one single goal of life worth pursuing? Negatively, it should never be something that destroys. Positively, it should benefit *every* one without exception. Globalization as ecology fully satisfies both requirements. Globalization as ecology is family-management of globe-household, and it would hurt absolutely no one, and it cannot help but

---

[35] Thomas Kuhn's *The Structure of Scientific Revolution*, Third Edition, University of Chicago Press, 1996, is one-dimensionally criticized as rudderless relativism. Paul Feyerabend, *Against Method*, Third Edition, London: Verso, 1993, has a fledgling peep at natural science in China beyond the West, beyond Kuhn.

[36] *Discovery: Science, Technology, and The Future*, April 2010.

help nurture the full growth of every being there is. Such chores of joy are eminently worth pursuing. In fact, we cannot live on without such joy.

In: Globalization Dynamics
Editor: Kuang-ming Wu

ISBN: 978-1-62100-750-0
© 2012 Nova Science Publishers, Inc.

Chapter 15

GLOBALIZATION AS UBIQUITY-MOVE

Kuang-ming Wu[1]
Taiwan, ROC

ABSTRACT

This chapter *ubiquity* just cites five points among countless others of globalization as ubiquity-move. Point One mentions that "globalization" is the notion situated between theoretical speculation and concrete actuality, and digs into what this "between" means. Point Two says that "globalization" amounts to microcosms mirroring and resonating with macrocosm. Point Three claims that "globalization" performs interculture in dialogues. Point Four considers "globalization" as inter-versal, not universal or transversal. Point Five equates "globalization" with "all" that is at work, and considers what the dynamic "all" means. These five points meet as friends delightfully "meeting in minds 會意" in smiles, as the globe meets the globe five times.

ROAMING PRECIS: GLOBALIZATION AS UBIQUITY ON THE MOVE

You may have noticed, my dear reader, the word "roaming" in front of "précis." "Roaming" is here, apropos of "globalization as moving ubiquity." Globalization is ubiquitous that means actively "all over," and all over acting is of course roaming around all over.

"Isn't 'roaming' arbitrary, though?" Well, Yes and No. Yes, roaming is arbitrary and free as a squirrel hopping anywhere it wants, but No, roaming is not arbitrary because free roaming at leisure composes me, and self-composure fulfills me. Now, nothing self-composed and self-fulfilled is arbitrary, is it?

Thus "roaming" describes being natural and fully at home in oneself, self-so as nature itself is, inside and out, free anytime to respond to any contingency that comes, and "contingency" itself is nature roaming in all its rich ubiquity beyond all scientific predictions. Roaming is then our rich systematic living without the arbitrary—now, this is really "arbitrary"!—Procrustean bed of a system. No wonder, Chuang Tzu *the* thinker of nature and

---

[1] E-mail address: Kmwu2002@yahoo.com

naturalness par excellence begins his writing, as Chapter One, by describing "roaming and soaring 逍遙遊" throughout the sky and the field, and beyond.

Thus, the roaming here echoes the concluding part of this Précis that says that the whole essay arbitrarily picks five features of globalization as dynamic ubiquity. In fact, since ubiquity includes all, the all-inclusion of globalization accommodates roaming of every thing that there is. Everything has its roaming place in globalization as ubiquitous, all in all. All in all, we write this Précis in a roaming way.

To begin with, we must realize that noun is a charged verb. As is often the case, noun is a powerful verb, as we say we *baby* our skin to *mother* our nature, in Mother Nature naturing, to *birth* unceasing. Noun is a powerful verb moving, and to move is to be alive. "Life" as a noun lives and moves, and so "life" is alive. Nature natures and is alive, as globalization moves a-globe-ing, and so globalization is alive in things all around, moving on in time in space.

Such is globalization, the greatest of all verbs globalizing from particulars in particular to deepen particulars as global. Thus "righting the name"[2] of globalization becomes quite important, for righting the noun of globalization turns our entire living rightly. To describe *what* globalization is portrays *how* it goes, so as to determine how we *should* live rightly. This essay attempts this threefold trial, the what in the how in the should of life-norm called "globalization," as ubiquity on the move.

We must repeat this important threefold point. As we describe the correct meaning of globalization, and admire how it performs itself ubiquitously, we correct our living in line with our innate nature to globalize rightly. What globalization is describes how it performs, which in turn becomes our norm of how we should live according to "how we actually live, rightly as Mother Nature does, naturally." We shall find that pursuing any one activity above amounts to doing both others.

Globalization, as a progressive verb of globalizing penetration into things, is much more powerful than it seems at first casual sight. Globalization is the constant verb of globe-ing, a verb of pervasion and penetration into all things, to give the weight of ubiquity in each particular existence. Globalizing is globe-ing, as the world is world-ing itself, as Heidegger said somewhere, though he failed to appreciate fully its vast world implication of such globalization.

"What is the global implication of the world world-ing itself?" Well, globalization penetrates every particular entity on the globe. Every particular *is* the globe on the move, with the whole weight of the whole globe, as every grain of sand sparkles with the whole world. We are thereby enabled to "see a world in a grain of sand," as Blake said,[3] though he did not bother to dig into why it is the case. Globalization is the whence, wherefrom, and whereto of his stunning declaration, but now we understand how *natural* this is the case, thanks to pervasive globalization.

All this sounds incredible until we watch how animals routinely behave. For example, when the lion pounds on a small rabbit, the lion must put its whole weight on the rabbit, as the rabbit is the business of the whole lion. And so the tiny insignificant rabbit now consumes

---

[2] "Righting names 正名' is China's important praxis among the Confucians and the Name Scholars, to asymptotically conform to actuality sociopolitical (Confucius and Name Scholars) and inherent-natural (Mencius, Name Scholars). Taoism practices this name-righting without mentioning it by name.

[3] "To see a World in a Grain of Sand/ And a Heaven in a Wild Flower/ Hold Infinity in the palm of your hand/ And Eternity in an hour" in "Auguries of Innocence" in *The Complete Poetry & Prose of William Blake*, ed. David V. Erdman, NY: Doubleday, 1988, p. 490.

the whole attention and activity of the awesome royal lion. The rabbit *is* the whole lion to turn into the lion. In the mutual eating society of nature, the animals' mutuality renders each into becoming the other, and their very mutuality renders each to become the whole of Mother Nature.

In the same way, the world is seen in a grain of sand—as every scientist knows and does—and that grain is now revealed as weighted with the whole wide world. This is how the globe globalizes in every particular-in-the-globe. When a boat is hid in a ravine, it can be stolen. But if the world is hid and stored in the world, nothing will get lost, said Chuang Tzu (6/26). The world now worlds itself, and everything is safe and sound in it.

It is then the case that every boat is now the world that cannot get stolen or lost. Every thing is safe as the globe is the globe, for the globe as globe cannot get lost. The globe globeizes each tiny particular in the globe, as each particular *is* now turned the entire globe, in exactly the same manner as the slave in ancient Rome is proud of being the slave of a distinguished family, for he carries the honor and glories of his distinguished family.[4]

Now we are ready to go see another aspect of globalization. Safety stabilizes. In storing all things safely, globalization stabilizes the globe to stabilize every particle vibrating the globe, as seen by modern physics.[5] Thus any tiny "one" as a grain of sand, and a subatomic particle, is the all, and the mountain is the mountain as the river is the water. Everything is self-so the nature,[6] as it is, as it is the globe.

Every single moment, as with the Buddhist *ksana*[7] the shortest moment in all cosmos after cosmos, is the eternal dawn, sparkling with the world future. The world is a totality of the globe in the flow of time immemorial in the past, coming into the present, and going into the future, in time flow immortal.

Globalization is all things and matters at their maximum extents in all senses. Globalization is then the verb of all verbs that moves everything at their most ubiquitous; globalization is at the ubiquity-move in the skies and in the fields. Globalization is thus the most pervasive power with the maximum variety, the verb ubiquitous at its vastest and most various ubiquity.

Let us put all this as the "beyond" in time in space. Globalization is the beyond-verb par excellence. Globalization expands beyond here now to the maximum in time, called "contingency" beyond natural science that operates on the past-frame alone, according to the principle, "as in the past, so in the future." Globalization also expands beyond here now of life, as we live going beyond empiricism into "conviction" felt viscerally as religion.

The interesting pivot of all this is that all this expansion itself *changes* as globalization moves on, as living-on does change itself. Globalization features living-on beyond itself here now. Globalization is thus the élan of going beyond itself, as living-on is self-transcendence

---

[4] See Dale B. Martin, Slavery as Salvation: The Metaphor Slavery in Pauline Christianity, Yale University Press, 1990.

[5] Cf. Stephen Hawking, The Illustrated A Brief History of Time (1988) and The Universe in a Nutshell (2001), NY: Bantam Books, 2001.

[6] In China, the "self-so 自然" is Nature naturing in continuous nascence, birthing, birthing, without ceasing 生生不息, constantly on the go.

[7] Cf. A Dictionary of Chinese Buddhist Terms, William Edward Soothill and Lewis Hodous, reissued by Taipei: Ch'eng-wen Publishing Company, 1969, p. 250b.

continually self-transforming, as it is music-as-life in variation on the same theme of the individual alive.

Music is "better than it can be played," confessed Schnabel the pianistic musician beyond the pianist, although music is meant to be played, as we keep playing it, as Schnabel himself does so sublimely. Music going on beyond itself is our life going on beyond here now; our life is our self-transcendence, self-transforming into our holistic globalization. Globalization as music is the lotus beauty out of muddy sludge, and yet unsoiled while in the soil, and so the unsightly soil is part of the lotus beauty beyond the soil.[8] Globalization is dynamic beauty in globe-soil unsoiled. Such is our life our globalization on the ubiquity-move.

Global ubiquity is quite alive. Life is homeostatic, we say. Homeostasis is a verb as life is. But we hardly notice that life's homeostasis is ever at work to continuously go *beyond* its homeostasis here now, for otherwise life dies. Life is homeostasis for the next homeostasis, only to go for the next different one, ever going into more different rounds of homeostasis. Life is such élan vital of stable unstable homeostasis, the river of music here now not here now, an ever flowing poetry profoundly alive.

Life is one living poem in all its poetic creations of living and thinking about life and its creations "here now," and yet none of them quite expresses *the* poem well,[9] and in fact we are not even aware of our living expressing this one poem inexpressible. Our living-on is musical poetry of the future yet to be here while it is now here unawares, peeping at our present, as the tulips ever peeking at the spring breeze, all over, being here yet to be here.

Of course to claim that globalization is ubiquity on the move is irresponsible, for ubiquity is so protean beyond simple "ubiquity" as beyond our catching it as this and that. No essay can exhaust the vastest reaches of ubiquitous globalization. Thus this essay has to just roamingly pick five features to illustrate the inexhaustible riches of globalization. This essay merely adumbrates vast globalization beyond our comprehension.

Nothing can confine globalization that embraces all things imaginable and beyond imagination. Globalization contains even "nothing" itself, even its own demise, if that is possible, seeing that the maximum ubiquity of globalization continues to extend in space and in time. Globalization is deathless and infinite to us, for it is the all-inclusive in actuality and beyond actuality. Thus, to repeat, globalization can never be exhausted, and so cannot be explicated. It can only be illustrated, adumbrated, and hinted at with its vignettes. This essay winks at the reader with such indescribable adumbration.

This exercise is sheer joy of ours, as a toddler so proud that he "can do anything." Just to envisage the impossibility of even dreaming about globalization opens out the limitless horizon of growth of all our lives. Globalization is our human milieu in which we live, move, and grow up freely without restriction whatever.

This joy of growth ever forwarding constitutes the grand reason why we can never dispense with this vision of globalization of ours beyond our vision. Ridding ourselves of

---

[8] I am expanding Artur Schnabel's quip. He was told by his teacher, "You will never be a pianist; you are a musician." See Insert, p. 10, to Schnabel's *Beethoven Piano Sonatas*, EMI, 8 CD set. I omit references to all my treasures of his CDs. The phrase, the lotus "grown out of soil unsoiled 出淤泥而不染," appears in Chou Tun-I's 周敦頤's well-known "On [my] Love of the Lotus 愛蓮說." I also apply it to globalization, for after all globalization globalizes the globe all soiled.

[9] Martin Heidegger said that every thinker s a poet who has only one poem, itself uncomposed, out of which and of which all other poems speak. *On the Way to Language*, NY: Harper & Row, 1971, p. 160.

"globalization" rids ourselves of ourselves. We die deprived of globalization that gives us growth upon growth, for life is growth or it is death, and it is globalization that gives us the milieu and limitless horizon to grow on and on.

Thus, in globalization, paradoxically but quite naturally, the full riches of the world coincide with tragic emptiness. The coincidence gives us a vast room to freely roam living in time and in space, in plans in this world and in dreams beyond this world. Any thing and any life can do anything here, as it does in smiles and in sorrows.

Even violence—indescribably senseless and cruel as portrayed in Japan's tragic *The Tale of the Heike*, on fanatic loyalty irrationally devoted to by the suicidal samurai—has its place in globalization, for posterity after posterity to "enjoy" and lament over. That is why *The Tale of the Heike* is a timeless classic alongside the meditative *The Tale of Genji*[10] so pensive. The pair parallels Bushido the brutal Way of the killer samurai that embraces, paradoxically, the meditative Zen Buddhism of full emptiness.

All of them compose life's jokes of tragedies to parallel the criminal death on the cross, the cruelest and most abject punishment humanity has ever invented, which expresses the most heartfelt of visceral compassion of the Divine. In this manner, sublime religion exists side by side with the most irrational injustice, as both embrace each other in globalization.

Globalization is the softest and most immature baby demanding our most stringent of sensitive parental care, *and* at the same time it is precisely this baby who has the most versatile survival power to outlive the toughest mortal damage that can destroy the toughest mature adults.

In other words, globalization embraces the maximum of coincidence of opposites, that is to say, unification of the maximum contradictions and inter-happening of maximum opposites. Such a radical incoherence incites constant instability. This is one reason why globalization is in constant move in ubiquity, a fabulous maelstrom forever stable as it is, in all its grand Self-So extremely dynamic.

"All this is quite interesting and impressive, pal. But what are the 'five features' you mentioned a while ago that this essay promises to expound?" O, I am sorry. I have got carried away. This essay promises to scratch the surface a bit of globalization as such globe-verb, to show how globalization as ubiquity-move shows forth in five ways among countless various others. We scratch the theme of globalization five ways at random and in tandem, for the globe is a strange ubiquitous circle edgeless and pan-centered,[11] and so any point touched on in the circle touches any other point to touch the whole circle.

So, we just cite five points among countless others of globalization as ubiquity-move. Point One mentions that "globalization" is the notion situated between theoretical speculation and concrete actuality, and digs into what this "between" means. Point Two says that "globalization" amounts to microcosms mirroring and resonating with macrocosm. Point Three claims that "globalization" performs interculture in dialogues.

Point Four considers "globalization" as inter-versal, not universal or transversal. Point Five equates "globalization" with "all" that is at work, and considers what the dynamic "all"

---

[10] *The Tale of the Heike*, Tokyo University Press, 1975, and Stanford University Press, 1988, and *The Tale of Genji*, NY: Alfred A. Knopf, 1976. I omit all their translators.

[11] On this "circle," see my "World Interculturalism: China Written in English" in *Taiwan Journal of East Asian Studies*, June 2005, pp. 1-42, and "Ponds Alive" in *Story-Thinking: Cultural Meditations*, NY: Nova Science Publishers, 2011, pp. 387-404. In all this, I implied but not explicated this circle *as* globalization.

means. These five points meet as friends delightfully "meeting in minds 會意" in smiles, as the globe meets the globe five times.

ONE: GLOBALIZATION AS BETWEEN THE THEORETICAL AND THE ACTUAL-CONCRETE

"Globalization" is a *notion*, a *nota bene* noticed *within* the actual, and is not "concept" abstracted *from* the concrete.[12] This notion of globalization is generally applicable to concrete cases to charge them with global significance. Here we must note a subtle distinction; the actual may not be identical to the concrete though both often overlap. The "actual" itself has notional significance, while the "concrete" can be brute happenings, empty of meaning, though the concrete can overlap with the actual as the actual is also concrete, while the concrete can be simple brute facts, quite senseless.

We can say, then, that globalization is a notion freely trafficking *between* what we closely observe in our theoretical thinking and what we see as factual concrete happenings, to render both alive with actual significance. The "between" of this globalization is an interactive verb, and an "inter-" at work effectively, in four ways.

First, globalization as notion *joins* theoretical thinking with concrete happenings to charge them with actual significance. This joining would have been impossible for the abstract concepts that abstract from the concrete, for—so "globalization"-notion would say—how could something, a concept, abstracted *from* the concrete apply *to* the concrete? It is such a contradiction, as stopping and accelerating an automobile at once.

Thus the notion of globalization that joins is opposed to thinking as separate from things concrete to cover the concrete cases whatever, as abstract "1+1=2" aspires to do.[13] In contrast, "globalization" is something concrete that is at the same time thinkable; it is an action at the global level contagious from one concrete instance to another, and such a contagion spreads throughout all the friendly skies and all fields.

Second, globalization as notion serves as *catalyst* between one case and the other. Globalization is a category of actuality to lug around while we discuss problems at a global level, plan global projects of whatever sort, and design and enforce global justice in legal, political, communicational, and financial areas worldwide. "Problems and Prospects" of the present volume has essays that instantiate some of such cases.

Thirdly, globalization in ubiquity *penetrates* all. Here the general is the concrete to compose the actual. Here the notions are actual categories for us to think on the concrete. Incredibly, the perennial conundrums of how to apply theoretical thinking to daily ordinary ongoing, how all sorts of isms in the ivory tower of thinking has bites into praxis, are resolved right here in globalization as penetration of all things into all thinking.

Many languages influence one another, and interflow to inter-create into riches of world languages. For instance, "liao li 料理" in China, meaning to manage, went to Japan to turn

---

[12] Cf. Kuang-ming Wu, *On the "Logic" of Togetherness: A Cultural Hermeneutic*, Leiden: Brill, 1998, pp. 350-352, et passim.

[13] Master logician Whitehead was opposed to the universal applicability of "One and one make two"; it is "the exactness" that "is a fake." See his "Immortality" in *The Philosophy of Alfred North Whitehead*, ed., Paul Arthur Schilpp, La Salle, IL: Open Court, 1951, pp. 699-700.

into "riori 料理" to mean to cook meal, and then returns to China to proliferate among restaurants. Mencken's massive studies of the American Language[14] are a treasure trove of such linguistic inter-enrichment. Similarly, our way of thinking in so many places of the world is shaped by Western science and technology. Human beings are now machines, as machines acquire personalities.

Fourth, globalization *pervades* as the power of "inter-" at work between one thing, one matter, and another thing another matter. In globalization as pervasive, every single concrete happening, however tiny and seemingly insignificant, carries the awesome weight of the whole globe. At the same time, thanks to globalization pan-pervasive, all matters thought significant are charged with concrete contents most specific. Here is no empty talk, and no empty brute fact. Fact is pervaded with meaning as meaning is loaded with factual cargo.

Brute happenings, such as disappearance of frogs, whales hunted almost to extinction, icebergs melting away, massive deaths of various fishes, as well as global warming, quakes, tsunamis, and all such, carry ominous global risks we can never afford to ignore. The "silent spring" shakes us with mortal jitters. We owe it to ourselves and to all our fellow existents, now and later, to dig deep into what these brute tragic facts *mean*. Before all the world of people worries, we must worry; only after the world rejoices can we rejoice.[15]

Besides, how could I congratulate myself stuffing me with juicy steak while I was informed that so many others in other parts of the world are starving, wailing, and dying? In all this, we worry before the world worries, and rejoice only after the world rejoices. Their heartfelt touches with us make up cosmopolitanism breath to breath.

Globalization spans between thinking and the concrete to maximize and pervade the concrete with thinking into actuality-sense. So do exactly dreams and imaginations actualize the projected concrete-yet-to-be. Dreams are the globalizing power of actualization in the middle of thinking and praxis.

Globalization-between is music a-chanting in the middle of things. Globalization in the middle of theory and praxis is the quartet between grand orchestral works and deep solo violin sonatas to pull in both, catalyzing one to the other, to enrich music beating tunes so alive. Quartet-globalization is orchestral solo so sonorous and deep.

Now, we must never forget. These four features of globalization as between theory and fact, among so many other features, came from globalization in ubiquity as pan-verb, as the global dynamo at work with total impacts. Cosmopolitanism is here in global communication and world news to hit us heartfelt. All this is due to globalization as ubiquity at work.

Ubiquity as verb accommodates all things. Each entity, actual and theoretical, and beyond, has its place in the globe. Globalization keeps the distinctness of each as each, while putting each in touch with the others in the whole. Their inner touches are incredibly various as illustrated in the above four ways. The result is nothing short of radical and global.

We must also keep this subtle fact in mind. We have been saying that globalization does this, and it does that, but actually, "globalization" does not exist in the concrete space and time. "Globalization" *shows* itself only in those four activities illustrated above. We

---

[14] H. L. Mencken, *The American Language* (1919), 1980, pp. 769+xxix, *Supplement One* (1945), 1977, pp. 739+xxxiii, and *Supplement Two* (1948), 1978, pp. 890+xli, all published by NY: Alfred A. Knopf.

[15] I rifle from Fan Chung-yen's 范仲淹's famous saying, "先天下之憂而憂, 後天下之樂而樂" (taken and elaborated from Mencius 1B4) to conclude his "岳陽樓記," 古文觀止, 高雄麗文化公司, 1995, p. 820. I apply it to our globalization concerns.

understand this phenomenon when we see that the "shine" of an apple does not exist independently by itself, but is instead felt only when we meet an apple right here now. Nor does the "fastness" in running exist as fastness, but shows itself only *in* the running.

This "running" point has an unsuspected spin-off. It is false to say, "You have not too many citations from Chinese writing, and so what you say is not about China, much less Chinese." Some thinking can be typically "Chinese" without even specifically citing Chinese writings, as my *Chinese Body Thinking* has only some scanty references to Chinese writings, but no Western thinking can perform such a thinking *this* way. In contrast, many books copiously citing from China are not at all *Chinese*, as displayed in I. A. Richards, Chad Hansen, Christoph Harbsmeier,[16] and many countless others.

Chinese-ness depends on no amount of citation, but on *how* things, whatever they are, are said, for China is alive, shown in its performance alone, as fastness alive is shown in the running, as "Dvorak" appears in his music *performed* by others or by himself. It is the performance, especially the *mode* of performance, that shows the thinking and the thinker, and the culture in which thinking takes place, not citations.

By the same token, globalization shows itself only in its modus *operandi* in those four ways above described, among many other ways. Again, globalization exists by being at work inter-involving *between* theoretical and concrete crisscrossing, thanks to globalization at *work* as globalization; globalization does not exist either in theory itself or in concrete things or matters or happenings themselves.

"By the way, how does globalization as 'between' the two handle the third-man dilemma?" Interestingly, being in the middle of the two, the theoretical and the concrete, globalization is yet immune from an infinite regress of the third-man beside the two, and the third-man of its third-man, and so on,[17] simply because globalization is ubiquitously wealthy enough that it can afford to supply these infinite numbers of the "third-man," as it were. In any case, globalization in dynamic ubiquity is so rich that things in the world of globalization are packed up in all smiles. Globalization is paradise for everyone.

In the end, we must say this. All concepts corrupt and harden into useless stones, and great concepts corrupt greatly. Marx's passion for the downtrodden was corrupted by Lenin his bosom friend, of all persons, into its opposite of "Marxism" to oppress precisely the common people Marx so passionately advocates.

In contrast, because of being so concrete yet so general, globalization alive all over has less chances of being ossified into useless stones, much less poison.[18] Being a concrete notion, globalization has more potentials than other abstract concepts to whip up our passion for cosmopolitanism more fabulous than we dream of, while our dreams keep historically erupting as mythologies.

We have so many mythologies of so many lands, with so many dictionaries and encyclopedias of imaginary places, and thinking about them continues unceasing. In fact,

---

[16] Kuang-ming Wu, *On Chinese Body Thinking: A Cultural Hermeneutic*, Leiden: Brill, 1997, and *Story-Thinking: Cultural Meditations*, NY: Nova Science Publishers, 2011, pp. 166-172.

[17] Cf. the dry careful "'Plato and the Third Man" (Colin Strang) in *Plato: Metaphysics and Epistemology*, ed. Gregory Vlastos, Doubleday Anchor Original, 1971, pp. 184-200.

[18] Even globalization has been managed to turn into poison, however, as shown in various essays in "Problems and Prospects" in the present volume. This sad turning happens because the true meaning of globalization has been twisted to mean what it does not mean, usually as monocultural dominance global.

natural science is a collection of myths, called "paradigms" by Kuhn.[19] No political regime, especially dictatorial one, can survive without creating its own myths in which the dictator himself must believe in. Moreover, no fiction, scientific or otherwise, can ever be neglected, much less dispensed with, for without them we can never survive. Myths are the stuff of which we are made. They all belong to globalization.

And isn't "music" singing our trip to the lands of the myths? In fact, all music transports us to the dreamland where we dance our life-music in resonance with the music we hear in our spines.[20] And aren't those places the dreamlands of globalization so fabulous? Gary Zukav wrote a bestseller, *The Dancing Wu Li Masters*, which won the 1979 American Book Award in Science. He then came out with *The Seat of the Soul* in 1989 (Simon & Schuster). Does my tiny soul dance the cosmos, then? "But where is the music I dance to?" Hasn't the music come out with my dance?

"Aren't we dancing to utopias, though?" Well, if so, all these utopias are "nowhere" anagrammatized into fabulous *Erewhon*[21] that belong to globalization, as they are as concrete and general, and specific, as globalization is, all beyond our prosaic thinking in empirical confines, all beyond our daily routines that are actually guided by them. "How could it be?" Well, look at this example.

Even solid empirical science is led by our dreams. We are now in Dream Land where heavy metal is routinely flying in the air and floating on the oceans, and this *actual* Wonderland of all Alices who are we ourselves keeps expanding as our dreams and imaginations expand. We call this expansion "globalization." Globalization is the treasure trove of our dreamed insights into the future yet to be actualized.

TWO: GLOBALIZATION AS MICROCOSMS MIRRORING AND RESONATING WITH MACROCOSM

We must believe in this incredible twofold fact. To begin, in globalization, the tiny helpless individuals shape the world through history, as the world shapes them. A feeble blind

---

[19] Thomas S. Kuhn, *The Copernican Revolution*, Harvard University Press, 1974, *The Structure of Scientific Revolutions* (1962), University of Chicago Press, 1996. *Larousse Encyclopedia of Mythology*, NY: Prometheus Press, 1959. *Mythology*, ed. C. Scott Littleton, London: Duncan Baird, 2002. David Leeming, *The Oxford Companion to World Mythology*, 2005. Alberto Manguel, *The Dictionary of Imaginary Places*, Mariner Books, 2000. Alain Daniélou, *The Myths and Gods of India* (1964), Rochester, VT: Inner Traditions International, 1991. Ananda K. Coomaraswamy and Sister Nivedita, *Myths of the Hindus and Buddhists* (1913), NY: Dover, 1967. Robert Graves, *The Greek Myths*, 2 vols. (1955), England: Penguin Books, 1960. H. A. Guerber, *The Myths of Greece and Rome* (1907), NY: Dover, 1993. 袁珂校注, 山海經校注, 臺北市里仁, 民84. *The Classic of Mountains and Seas*, tr. Anne Birrell, London: Penguin Books, 1999. G. S. Kirk, *Myth* (1970), Cambridge University Press, 1975, and *The Nature of Greek Myths* (1974), NY: Barnes & Noble, 2009. W. K. C. Guthrie, *The Greeks and Their Gods* (1954), Boston: Beacon Press, 1969. Elizabeth Wayland Barber & Paul T. Barber, *When They Severed Earth from Sky*, Princeton University Press, 2004. *Myth and Literature*, ed. John B. Vickery, Lincoln: University of Nebraska Press, 1966. Donna Rosenberg & Sorelle Baker, *Mythology and You*, Lincolnwood, IL: National Textbook Company, 1984. And the list goes on.

[20] Bedrich Smetana and Anton Dvorak's orchestral works are typical. Listen to *Smetana: Ma Vlast, Complete Orchestral Works*, (Theodore Kuchar conducting), Brilliant, 3 CD set, and *Dvorak: The Symphonies, Overtures* (Witold Rowicki conducting), Decca, 6 CD set.

[21] Samuel Butler, *Erewhon* (1872), London: Penguin Books, 1985.

storyteller Homer, and the unemployed hobo wandering all around called Confucius, each came to single-handedly mold the entire West[22] and the entire China. Moreover, importantly, since either is so powerless, their "shaping" was done not by outside forces of conquest but by spontaneous resonance among common people, to spread in cultural contagion so irresistible.

And then, here comes the reverse shaping, the powerless Confucius was astute enough to intone (17/2), "Born alike, cultured apart 性相近也, 習相遠也." Here, "a- 相" in "alike" and "apart" describes the mutuality of co-resonance that tips us to culture. Human nature is found and founded enculturated. Confucius says that our innate nature grows acculturated. The mutuality of nature and culture as the chicken and the egg is thus embodied and introduced by Confucius, and, mind you, it is culture that spreads human nature far and wide, as it grows human nature in "decent" sociality.

This illustration of the mutuality of co-resonance describes how globalization irresistibly spreads as wild fire, fanned by winds of culture created, molded—fanned up—by single individuals often quite fragile. We remember the tiny lady Mother Teresa, the bed-ridden Ellen White, the shy sickly Schubert, and countless powerless others who came to "shape" us all, by soft resonance that seeps into us unawares, as the silent spring mist seeps in the plant to sprout their tiny bulbs of flowers and leaves.

Mind you. Both co-resonance from individuals to community, from nature to culture, on the one hand, *and* the contagious co-resonance of community to individuals, and from social culture to innate nature, on the other hand, never take place by external coercion, invasion, or conquest of great armies. On the contrary, such co-resonance to and fro, back and forth, pervasively perfumes, as it were, both individual nature and communal culture, to preserve the integrities of each of both parties, thereby enrich them into themselves, into their dignities respective and genuine.

We must further note. All such invisible yet definitive transformations take place imperceptive-ly through long periods of time, perhaps spanning centuries, and the results are unmistakable and irrevocable as time-carved into the granite of nature and culture. Homer's West is no longer in a Homer-less "barbaric" state, as China is now civilized by Confucius' perfuming pedagogy. Let us focus on China for a while.

The Confucian China is recognizably different from pre-Confucius China, and no recent attack by Chinese Communism could change this situation. China's time-honored Confucian ethos continues as before to "civilizing" Korea, Japan, and Southeast Asia, expanding to today's "Boston Confucianism" and the so-called "third" vigorous "Confucian renaissance" outside and within the continent of Communist China, only to, again, spread abroad into Taiwan, Korea, Japan, and elsewhere all over the world.

This global pervasion in the new Confucianism is also seen in a separate region of the new syllabary of the "pinyin 拼音" and the "simplified characters 簡体字." Both are flooding the world to reshuffle the entire expression-system of Chinese language in the Library of Congress in the USA, and all over the globe, dragging in all China-buffs kicking and screaming. I am perhaps one of the few diehards[23] against this "senseless invasion of ugly

---

[22] The Chinese Homer, the blind storyteller of history, Tso Ch'iu-ming (or Tso-ch'iu ming?) 左丘明, also single-handedly shaped China into the world's famed culture of history that it is, through its history.

[23] I know of two other diehards. One is Raymond Dawson who says, "I have retained the more familiar Wade-Giles system, which has been used for most English-language books on China, in preference to the new *pinyin* system

pinyin and barbarous simplified characters" to distract us from Chinese culture proper. Globalization is at work here, just on a single culture of China alone.

Now, let us put this same dynamics of globalization another way, by closely watching "cosmos" ubiquitous, so alive. The "cosmos" features order, system, and harmony.[24] These three features are nouns that are verbs, functioning entities composing the cosmos that is itself composed by ordering, standing-together systematically, and harmonizing together so many microcosms, internally in themselves and externally with others, again and again, into the "cosmos" as many in one, one among so many.

These three features turn out "cosmos" by co-resonance and co-mirroring—let us repeat—orderly, systematically, and harmoniously. An external cosmos forms a macro-cosmos out of internal cosmos that are so many micro-cosmoses. At the same time, various microcosms mutually and cosmically order, systematize, and harmonize into the macrocosm. These three features are thus in constant refrains in variations of the "music of the spheres" here now.

It is in this way that the one is the many, as the many co-mirror and co-resonate into one. History is the cosmic process of inter-echoes of now and then, then-done and then-to-come, and each is thus formed by the others. Such is the complex dynamics of globalization self-recursive as it self-progresses on and on. This cosmic process undulates up and down. The cosmic entropy[25] mirrors itself into cosmic ascendancy, only to go into a decline, and such ups and downs show how much globalization is alive, in time in space.

Meanwhile, the dragonflies so fragile and tender are hovering innocently all over one of the ponds of the globe,[26] their tails quietly touching without touching the face of the pond, and countless circles keep being made to ripple out, made to spread out, circles over circles over circles, disappear to appear, appear to vanish in the distance, with dragonflies vanishing into the distance as well.

This is because, all this while, the dragonflies are flying over there only to come back here, flying over here to fly elegantly into distance we cannot even see, continuing to touch without touching the pond; and then they fly all over many other tiny lakes of the globe, all beyond "law and order" of any sort of any nation. They do not care a bit!

They make all this silent music so loud all over, softly and intangibly circling out each dragonfly of its New World quite symphonic on the ponds of the world, spreading to vanish echoing into the next generation singing their vanishing tails, making the dragonfly-circles crisscrossing to spread to disappear "here and there," as "funny things everywhere," says Dr. Seuss for all kids jumping all over dranfly-way.

---

introduced by the Chinese, which gives even less idea how the words are actually pronounced." (*Confucius*, Oxford University Press, 1981, p. viii) Another diehard is Victor H. Mair. His edited massive *The Columbia Anthology of Traditional Chinese Literature*, 1994, keeps the Wade-Giles system and appends "Romanization Schemes for Modern Standard Mandarin" on pp. 1321-1325 at the back as if as an afterthought, before ending the whole book on p. 1330. My *The Butterfly as Companion* (Albany: State University of New York Press, 1990) also appends "Conversion Table: Wade-Giles to Pinyin," on the last page, p, 512. Such notices and appendages show the invincible trend of globalization.

[24] This is the first definition of "cosmos" in *Merriam-Webster's Collegiate Dictionary*, Eleventh Edition, 2008, p. 282.

[25] The reader can see that I am rebelling against scientific common sense on "entropy." See, e.g., Stephen Hawking, *The Illustrated A Brief History of Time*, NY: Bantam Dell, 1996, pp. 130-133, 137, 184, 190.

[26] I am expanding in globalization-way what I said in "Ponds Alive" in *Story-Thinking: Cultural Meditations*, NY: Nova Science Publishers, 2011, pp. 387-404.

See how those kids all come out in droves swirling around to admire funny dragonflies. There in their admiring eyes, every tiny "one" is dotted into the "many" and the "big" of whatever sort, and the small is the vast in the deep—of whatever "pond." A grain of sand-dot sees the pond-world! Isn't all this funny and fun?

The tiny "one" in this group of "many ones" is the power making the music symphonic. Each note of an individual, so special and specific, is needed in the choral music of world-projects of dragonflies one after another, appear to disappear, to reappear, as ideas half-baked, to be shaped up by other ideas no less half-baked.

Those ideas are of course dragonflies hovering on the surface of one poem-pond after another, touching without touching it, not quite encircling the pond of "poetic truth" comprehensively, as Heidegger saw. All these dots and circles are ideas and persons and feelings to compose the globe entire beyond composing.

Apropos of such global togetherness, China says that all of us together are a "big family 大家" expanding all over, all around, sharing the "same womb 同胞" of Mother Nature. Plato in the person of Socrates comes in to say that body politic is our personal body writ large threefold—intellectually, emotionally, and intentionally—into the community, as our body is the threefold "body politic" writ small to live on, guided into the transcendental Forms, disappearing out of this perishing world.

The "body politic," big and small, is of course the dot encircled by the dragonflies on the face of the ponds of the world, appearing to disappear, but China does not care. China just joins everyone jovially into the family circle of Four Seas—Mother Nature in her same womb—disappearing or not!

Meanwhile, we look around—the globe is big!—to see a small candlelight placed in the middle of many mirrors facing one another. A stunning panorama emerges, all at once, of the flickering candlelight here and there, there in here, magnificently calling to each other to respond to so many calls of one another, all softly, all sparkling in the light of the candle. All these brilliant reflections appear between mirrors of microcosms making a macrocosm, and another macrocosm, each resounding silently with the other, world without end.

Furthermore, importantly, we must notice the candlelight. It does not stay put. It *moves* around into many dragonflies to make the mirrors move around as well, and the kaleidoscopic panoramas, emerging one into another, take place. Here is the bewildering globalization spreading ubiquitous, into circles after circles edgeless pan-centered, moving on and on, many in one, one into many.

Everything is here moving expanding without ceasing, deep calling deep, one wheezing, the other oozing, in pan-pipings of all at once, in silence louder than sounds, all in lyricism more alluring than melodies. It is "heavenly piping" that pipes out "earthly piping" to induce "human piping,"[27] all over the globe.

"What do you say about our noisy 'human piping'?" For all their tireless inter-butchery since time immemorial, humanity has continually been proliferating like weeds, like wild oats, shouting at one another and keep polluting the environment to poison themselves into mortal diseases into communal decease, and then grow again as wild dandelions, one root rooting into the other, as their puffs fly to other places to take root all around, thriving and dying, dying to spread, world without end.

---

[27] I have rifled for my globalization-purpose Chuang Tzu's irresistible "three pipings" that begin his profound Chapter Two.

ization is the "one poem" not "one" your way, beyond counting, beyond reciting, ~~d our awareness of it, dreaming alive, drunken dead, living together and dying ~r after. "You must be kidding, pal. This is too wild beyond all our dreams." Well, to this real story so bothersome beyond handling.

~u believe this fact? I could not believe it myself but it happened on me! My ~other at his naughty 63 died of botched laser heart surgery that, he was told, was ," while my professor of 92 came back home after four weeks in the hospital. He ~g the spring leaves with his daughter in his garden, and plans afterward to take a ~his proud walking stick. He has been assuring me that *this* is his last phone ~ with me. The sheer mortal contrast here whams me dumb, floors me in sheer ~k.

~, wherever you are, understand my private pain that is mine alone, don't you? ~een listening to me with closed eyes, as Eumaios the faithful swineherd of ~d to Odysseus, without knowing that he is Odysseus. So does Vasudeva the ~yman intently listen, with eyes closed, to Siddhartha pouring out his life-~s they both at the river bank intently listened to the river ever flowing by them as aware unawares.[29]

~ad a Greek listening, an Indian listening, and now you in USA echo my pain in ~g pain, as we both are embraced in Mother Nature totally beyond our ~n.[30] Isn't all this listening "globalization ubiquitous"? As we listen, we realize that is indeed a river at our back, or rather a hard-core confusion of violence in inter-~chic and physical ever continuing, with a soft shell of family-intimacy so tender so this is so bewilderingly going on in Mother Nature, world without end.

GLOBALIZATION PERFORMS INTERCULTURE IN DIALOGUE

One, being in, in the middle, in between the theoretical and the concrete, was ~ verb as an "inter-," and the "inter" assumes difference to obtain. In Point Two, ~and the resonating were considered, and they also require difference to happen. ~ce" has been operating actively but tacitly, without being described so far. ~ne and Point Two describe globalization, globalization can be said to happen ~s." The result is that differences are seen to catalyze the equality of existents ~cellences of their own, that is to say, deepen their integrities in globalization ~ust now consider—the time is overdue—"difference" as the modus operandi of ~ concrete interculture in dialogues.

we must consider what *difference* here concretely and actually involves. of course appear as disagreement in ideas and views about some themes. Such

---

Homer, tr. Richmond Lattimore, NY: Harper & Row, 1967, 14:185, 360. Hermann Hesse, Bantam, 1971, pp. 104-105.

of human contacts with nature and human comprehension of nature in, e.g., *Ants, Indians, and A Celebration of Man and Nature for the 75th Anniversary of Natural History Magazine*, ed. : Charles Scribner's, 1975, and *The National Audubon Society Speaking for Nature: A Century* ed. Les Line, 1999.

"This is all so confusing, pal!" Yes, indeed, it is more than comes from the fact that all this is chaos in order, the cosmos various confusing microcosms inter-echoing crisscrossing one even to glance at, as it creates its own laws to follow, autonomo it is bewildering and confusing outside.

All this is as the China Towns with Chinese restaurants dot palates of various peoples all over the world, even those in Gre of course noisy, messy, and confusing, but that's how the wo and that delightfully confusingly.

"This is the way it is," as Walter Cronkite used to say constantly butchering one another, and constantly producing tl the midst of quakes, tsunamis, starvation, and dysenteries by d world all over. If feeding is messy, dying in droves is messi the world to go around.

You say you cannot believe in all this, for this world si right, then, just watch people, just travel around, and just lis whole globe dies to live on, lives to die again and agai *continues*—have you seen death continue?—and it is bewildering, and confusing is globalization, the globe going

Strangely, such confusing mess quietly composes the s here now in all this mess. Such ugly world-sludge is the m World Symphony. All composers and performers, no less t out of irrational pain inexplicable, to enjoy making mus makes music with composers and performers who need aud

As speakers without listeners are crazy, so those w composers, performers, audience—mad. Those who have lest they themselves turn mad while watching "mad peop rhyme or reason." Now, is all this confusing?

All this is the highway of living—to change our thi chaotic, with chaotic order to survive and thrive together live on, and it is messy as living is. That is globalization, the order of the day, of everyday; globalization is tl mirroring one another, resonating with one another into n

Now, here is a tiny footnote. Heidegger mentions th all thinkers poetize without quite hitting it.[28] Our admirin poetic insight, Heidegger is too much of a Platonist t moves around, proliferating itself into many poems scat "one poem" itself inexpressible everywhere, as a dragon

In other words, the "one poem" is the one globe so poem keeps singing the songs unheard of that keep Beware Heidegger! This is globalization the bewild elucidate. The globe is soft, warm, and violent, and reborn. The globe is alive beyond grasping, intellectual

---

[28] I am not quoting him verbatim; I do not need to, for he is excitin *Language*, NY: Harper & Row, 1971, p. 160. I quoted it before,

different views are bound to happen, seeing that we are all different. Difference can cut deeper, however, such as difference in milieu as culture.

For example, on one hand, being in China, we look at China and the West in the milieu of China, "from China," as it were. And then we go to the West. Being in the West, on the other hand, we also can look at China and the West, from the West. We can turn from looking at things from China to looking at things from the West. We can turn from "in China" to "in the West," and our *entire* outlook on things radically turns around.

This turning of the outlook is a revolution in milieu, for "in" and "from" above show gestalt, paradigm, and milieu in the *way* we look at things. This is the change of culture-milieu. The change of culture-milieu changes our whole outlook on things and on life. The change is a revolution at the root. This change is called "interculture."

The change happens by "going to the USA"; the change *is* going-to-USA. This going is not a geographic locomotion. The going means to read, hear, speak, and write in English, these four activities, to enable us to understand how the West thinks and understand things. "Going to USA" gives us in this way the gestalt of the West. By the way, this going does not imply that any culture is superior to any other.

Mere white skin or brown skin means absolutely nothing, except that these skin differences represent culture-differences. *They* in their different skins are culturally different from *us*. Such cultural difference deserves our learning. Even "mistakes" in another culture than ours—and we tend to see *them* mistaken—are our object lessons, our back-view mirror, to steer us cautiously ahead our way. Again, it is thus that difference in globalization is cultural difference to generate mutual learning in interculture.

In other words, difference in globalization is difference in our cultural *attitude*. We can either prevent such difference from entering our life—typically rustic people adopt this attitude—or else we can respect if not accept and learn from these odd differences those "odd people" display, although they may be unpleasant to us due to their odd difference in clothing, in manners, and so on that we "detest." We call the latter attitude of respectful learning from alien lifestyle, "interculture."

To put the same point another way, difference in the context of globalization is difference in culture, and what cultural difference does in globalization is "interculture." Globalization is an interculture process all around. Among the activities of interculture, one salient interaction is *dialogue* among cultures. Intercultural dialogues are the modus operandi of "globalization in ubiquitous move" world without end.

Now, we must keep this important fact firmly in mind. To meet others different from me is not just inevitable in this global world now so small. The others different from me is also those who I inherently *need* to be me. I exist only by literally standing-out—to exist is to out-stand—different from others, distinct as me in contrast with others, for "I am I" shows in "I am not no-I." Dealing with others different from me is necessitated by my very necessity to exist as I. I simply must deal with those other than me to exist as myself at all.

By the same token, as it is difference that makes me to exist, so it is difference that makes a variety of things to exist to make up the global world that is my milieu in which I live, move, and become me. Differences make the variety, the colors, and the riches of this world that is mine. Difference is what makes the world go around as my Global Village. "Globalization as ubiquitous" naturally revolves around differences.

Now, difference and meeting with difference make for *reciprocity*, friendly among friends and in friction among opponents. In whatever mode I meet the others, the manner of our reciprocity in meeting shows both me and them, and at the same time such reciprocity changes me and them.

If my friends I keep show what I am, my others in general, friends and foes, show what I am, and how I deal with them shows me. My others advertise me; I am the friends I keep. All this while, such reciprocity changes me. How I deal with the other, effectively or clumsily, changes me. The same showing and changing happen to the others who deal with me.

Our trick is to make such self-change to result in enriching both myself and my others. As a result of my dealing with others, I am now life-experienced, worldly wise, even after having "spilt my cherished milk" in dealing with the others. The same feature applies to my others dealing with me. Such reciprocity is an intercultural dialogue, in words and in acts, in friendly manner, in friction, or in quiet self-composure.

Unfortunately, reciprocity in difference can often make meeting with disagreement in tastes and in views, and such disagreement can be disagreeable. Friction and conflict result. Thus reciprocity in difference can be pain of confrontation, though it can also be joy of intimacy and support among alien others. Actually, both pain and joy can often happen together. The I-you relation between us can often be a love-hate relation in mixture of joy and pain.

Intercourse in reciprocity logically begins at sex, then develops into family caring, and then progresses on to social intercourse to compose cosmopolitan concord. In sex, your joy makes me ecstatic. In family, caring for the other in need, in intimate sensitivity, establishes others to establish me; the family is cemented by mutual support in heartfelt understanding. And then the community operates only in mutual joy of inter-service and support, patterned after sex and family that are built on the painful joy of differences. In all this, as I support the others, so the others support me.

Reciprocity is also reciprocity of direction, in different directions. As China looks at the West from China, so the West looks at China from the West, and comparing notes on such different viewing enriches both China and the West, as long as—and this is an important proviso—each party recognizes that their views are *theirs alone*, not an universally applicable absolute truth.[31] Comparison honestly recognized and performed is the spice of life that excites, enriches, and enlightens all parties concerned. This is intercultural dialogue quite fruitful.

Interculture is cultural dialogue at a deep cultural level that shakes the foundation of our thinking. For such deep dialogue to take place, each party must listen to the other, putting me in your position to see how it feels, "putting me in your shoes" to feel how they pinch me. After listening, I may want to—I do not need to, though—modestly suggest my impression, knowing fully well that I would for sure be misunderstood. When misunderstanding occurs, I will explain myself again in the light of your "understanding," and my explanation shall then enrich *me*, as it hopefully enlightens you.

In all this give-and-take, respect for the other is an absolute must. Such respect of difference is quite hard to execute, although it is quite constantly needed. Even if we agree, you will have a different take on the theme and its different development, for you and not for me.

---

[31] This important has often been missed in proposals of world in goodwill. This point is missing in, e.g., a collection of essays by world luminaries in the ambitious *Foundations for World Order*, CO: University of Denver Press, 1949. See also unabashed Eurocentrism in *West and Non-West: New Perspectives*, eds. Verra Micheles Dean and Harry D. Harootunian, NY: Holt, Rinehart, & Winston, 1963. Their perspective is not "new" at all.

Even the baby shrinks from someone not his mother, for that person even smells different as she holds him quite differently. At the same time, even a baby, and especially the baby, has an insatiable curiosity toward someone or something quite different, and wants to go into alien them to explore, brushing aside Mom's hands.

We adults are babies of all ages who love traveling to exotic places to expand our horizon of life-curiosity. Respect of difference is all important here, but it does not mean I must change myself to go over to the other. I cannot of course rid me of me, but I can in respect of difference change me the best I can to politely "conform" to *his* way of being, to learn from him. My conformity to his way of being shall redound to changing and expanding me, to enrich me.

Such a radical self-conformity is quite difficult, however. A cartoon has it that a person in the midst of mountains tries to paint those mountains, and all this while his canvas has his own portrait. In the China-mountain, many Sinologists try to paint the China-mountain, and end up painting their own culture of the West. I. A. Richards, Chad Hansen, and Christoph Harbsmeier come to mind.[32]

Now, it is all right, and in fact necessary, to be aware of such self-portraying trend, and honestly own it to the Chinese people, to offer such a portrayal to them. What is inadmissible—unforgivable crime in academia, no, in global interculture—is to pretend that *our* portrayal is the "real China," even beyond poor "Chinaman's false image of China." This is an outrageous ethnocentrism dominating the whole world as the truth, the ultimate truth. This monocultural attitude ruins the whole process of globalization.

In the end, we must say that difference makes existence to inter-exist in joy, in pain, and thereby in quiet support to inter-enrich. This whole dynamics is dialogical interculture in gestalt-revolution, toward inter-creation of one another. Such existential thoroughness is the inherent part of globalization, an inter-universal in globalization ubiquitous. This inter-universal is not simple universal to apply all over without qualification. We must now dig into this inter-universal as "inter-versal" in the next Point Four.

FOUR: GLOBALIZATION AS INTER-VERSAL

Ubiquity is a pan-inter-verb. I would have gladly used "universal," were it not for the sad fact that this good word has been kidnapped by separative-abstractive thinking. I used to use, following Schrag,[33] "transversal," but soon found it as but a slight variation of separative-abstractive "universal," for "transversal" goes over, beyond, and across matters as "universal," not inter-go *through* them back and forth.

To bring out the pan-penetration of dynamic globalization, I am forced to coin a new word, "inter-versal," as a shorthand expression of "inter-universal" that stresses universality-as-going-*through*-all, in a reciprocal manner, not flying over and beyond all. "Inter-versal" has a further merit of bringing out *interactions* among ideas and matters, to preserve and enrich their respective integrities. It is thus that both pan-penetration and pan-interaction of "inter-versal" among myriad things describe the active ubiquity of dynamic globalization.

---

[32] For more examples of such alien Sinologists, see my *Story-Thinking: Cultural Meditations*, NY: Nova Science Publishers, 2011, pp. 166-172.

[33] See Calvin O. Schrag's verbose *The Resources of Rationality*, Bloomington: Indiana University Press, 1992, especially his final pages.

First, pan-*penetration* of ubiquitous globalization describes how globalization ubiquitous does not fly over and beyond matters, ideas, and things. Instead, they seep one into the other, one constituting the meat and sinews of the other, to become part of the other's flesh of its flesh, bone of its bones, to turn the other richer into a renovated refurbished "new other" and new self. And the other's penetration into me renews and enriches me as well. Such inter-penetration goes all over the globe. Nothing is discarded.

Even "abhorrent cannibalism" has been adopted into, of all places, the central celebration of the Eucharist in the proudest and most exclusive of all religions, Christianity. Even the weak powerlessness of "nonviolence" has been adopted by Gandhi and Martin Luther King into a powerful weapon to overthrow unjust governance.

We look forward to the day when atrocities of insane Neros, Hitlers, Amins, KKKs, terrorists, and those unconscionable financial institutions sucking away the blood-money of the poor nations, are effectively used to strengthen and enrich Reverence for Life all over the globe.

After all, Mother Nature has no "waste." "Waste" is not in her vocabulary. We must follow our Mother Nature where everything interpenetrates to prosper every thing else, so as to let everything benefit everything else, using even injustice, abject poverty, and all thefts petty and grand,[34] and so on, all those life-negativities, all to be enlisted to this service toward pan-prosperity.

Secondly, ubiquity as pan-*interaction*, on its part, is interculture as a pan-inter-verb of inter-versal. Inter-versal makes no melting pot but a kaleidoscope of a rainbow of all composing all. Inter-versal never destroys the integrity of each matter, specific and concrete, but, on the contrary, catalyzes them toward interaction to inter-strengthen every private locality.

This inter-versal interaction opposes a romantic dream of globalized "world culture" devoid of specific cultures "dated and defective." On the contrary, the so-called "new world culture" is a composite, inter-complemented by specific excellences of time-honored cultures, all existing locally.[35]

This "new world culture" especially cherishes those primal-primitive cultures quite globally indispensable, which supply us all today with gutsy life-power primordial, direct from Mother Nature. The inter-versal ubiquity of penetration and interaction among all cultures composes the dawn to dynamic globalization. Globalization is interculture interactive pan-penetrative, and inter-versally ubiquitous.

Such inter-versal is opposed to two approaches to globalization. First, it is opposed to the view that globalization as thorough inter-revolution of cultures stays only between the two specific cultures concerned, none of the business of global ubiquity. Secondly, inter-versal is opposed to the view that globalization progresses toward a pan-culture beyond all historically confined cultures, all "local and dated."

To the first view of "locality alone," inter-versal says that globalization is ubiquitous. Every tiny individual is universally impregnated, as all music is composed by particular notes, one after another, and all fictions collect all particular stories told about specific matters. To the second view of romantic "world culture" empty of all specific cultures, inter-versal says that globalization is specific intercultures writ global. Without localities, there

---

[34] John Wu is eloquent in lamentation over this point in the first essay in this volume. He tries hard to propose our global mission of win-win game in "debt cancellation."

[35] The two essays by Drs. Chang ("Localization") and Sun ("Threats") detail this approach, each in his own way.

exists no globalization. Moreover, wonder of wonders, interculture writ large is globalization weighted on specific individuals.

This is because the globe is in a grain of sand, for the globe is sands-composed. The sands of subatomic particles make the cosmos that continues to expand through those sands. There exists no cosmos beside the sands, as there is no sand that is not cosmos-charged. Isn't all this marvelous? And yet isn't it Mother Nature that is after all our innate nature? As such, and only as such, things are global and the globe is all myriad things in time in space.

After all, no one tells "a global story," for there is no "world news" but the specific news of local places all over the Global Village. The world news is the varied and specific local news, each item loaded with global weight. The news always tells local stories, and the world emerges in them out of them.

Now, "stories" are not as innocent as they look. In stories, nouns come alive as they move on. All nouns are verbs of storytelling and all stories told are particular stories about concrete particulars. All nouns are each a shorthand collections of such stories. For example, there is no "spring" but the spring of this year, and "spring" is a collection of blooming flowers, tiny, shy, and nameless, waving in the soft breeze, telling their own stories moment by moment.

At the same time, all stories are told by compiling nouns. Somehow general nouns of general import emerge together to compose a specific story, as an indifferent note gathers with another indifferent note, and another, and a specific musical composition with *this* specific local sentiment emerges.

Story as music is thus com-posed of inter-penetration of the general and the particular. Without particulars, there would be no general; without general, there cannot be any particular as particular. Their inter-penetration in interactions is a mystery and a common fact that globalization chants, as globalization is nowhere without specific intercultures, as any local interculture bleeds cosmopolitan import. All sing all, all chants as all. All is each, as each is all as they are in all. Such is inter-versal globalizing.

Inter-versal is interpenetration of general and specific. "Here" is everywhere global, as "now" is eternity incorruptible. This moment is my longevity to be enjoyed in full with this shy tulip about to blossom, deep in spring breeze, swaying softly among the bushy tree full of no less shy white blossom, smiling at this tulip red shy among the buzzing nameless insects.

In the spring, spring out all silent births, prepared for long in long wintry snow storms and whirling sleet, to end the winter to moisten the soil. That winter was the spring for this spring to emerge, for tulips and trees to peep forth in the breezy sunshine. Such spring-shy here goes on elsewhere everywhere, including the spring in Greenland and the Antarctic. The spring everywhere is inter-versal ubiquitous. Inter-versal is embodied best, and displayed as most typical, in globalization. This is what globalization means, as ubiquity on the move.

So, let us repeat this story of all in all. Any single entity has global weight, as the global is full with single singular entities. The inter-versal is made through painstaking complementation of local cultures. Globalization is a composite of the concrete specifics. Without globalization, localities are mere bits and pieces of sands scattered all over, sound and fury signifying nothing. Without the sands, globalization does not even blow over the desert made of sands. In a grain of sand the world is seen. Through a grain of sand the world sees the world.

"Come on. Suppose we say, 'Human beings both itch and die. Itching and dying are both private and particular, and personal and inter-versal.' So then, what do you say to my private itch? Isn't all this vanity vainly senseless?" Well, "Both itching and dying are particular and personal, and yet itching is insignificant and dying is not," someone could respond.

And then we can agree with its sentiment, and explore its implications. Or else, we can disagree and say one is as insignificant as the other, for nothing is cheaper than human lives dying in droves. Or else, we can say that both itching and dying are significant, for whatever reasons, such as "both show the humanity of us humanity, for no stone would itch or die." Or else, we can say that the very distinction of insignificant vs. significant here or elsewhere is itself insignificant. And the list of possibilities goes on.

This "going on" alone may make this itching-dying statement worthwhile. Besides, do such debates in themselves deserve to continue? Aren't the debates themselves one of the harvests, delightful or disgusting, enabled by globalization of e-communication today? And then, even *these* questions can be dismissed by someone as well. And then, someone else may pick them up and continue pondering on them.

"Suppose the computer finds that the word 'computer' rhymes with the word 'Confucius.' So, what do you say to this discovery?" We then could counter-ask, "Can computer help us decide on what it means?" Again, we may counter-ask, "Suppose the computer gives us the frequency, not the variety but just frequency, of 'Come on' in the *Analects* of Confucius. Suppose the computer finds that 'come on' happens such and such times in the *Analects* and in the *Chuang Tzu*, but few, if any, in the *Tao Te Ching*.

Now, what would you say? Do these discoveries deserve our pondering? Can computers, or anyone else, help us ponder them? Or do such stuff unworthy of pondering? Can the computer help us *this*, too?" Such silly—or not-silly—questions continue to pester us, thanks to the new arrival of computers on the global scene.

In any case, the same sorts of debates as above may ensure indefinitely, thanks to the global proliferation of computers. Or else, this point just noted may induce us to yawn. Globalization ubiquitous can worsen such information explosion. Thus, inter-versal can be yawn-inducing, and we can say with the existentialists that life's ennui is part of life, for ennui is one example of inter-versal of life-globalization.

Enough has been said about the ubiquity of inter-versal that covers even the trivial and the insignificant, or rather, the potentiality of such things trivial, and even potentiality itself. All glories to such all-comprehensiveness of inter-versal! Or else, shall we spit on all this? We had better stop here, for globalization ubiquitous continues this way without end, and so we can end talking about it anytime anywhere. Does inter-versal crank out stoppage, too, though? In all this, the culprit is the tiny word, "all," isn't it? It is time to grapple with it.

FIVE: GLOBALIZATION AS "ALL": CONCLUSION CONTINUOUS

The "all" in globalization ubiquitous is all over in space spreading as Global Village, in instant global communication to inter-influence in interculture. Moreover, the "all" of globalization is all through the ages in time historicizing, the present and the past inter-shaping, inter-enriching, by inter-transforming, into the future.

This simple word "future" is actually quite loaded a dynamo, as the dawn of poetry in music, coherent and open out in horizon expansion, in moment and moment rhyming in rhythm, refrains, variations, and even mutual revolts, creating music as poetry, in novelty expected and unexpected. It is thus that globalization is the "all"-dynamics growing even in us among us to spill all over among all things.

The "all" grows in us, as "I grow against others" in international struggles and wars, to grow into "I grow as part of all" in the NATO and the UN, and multi-corporate enterprises continuing to expand, brewing disasters in Bangladesh by "international loans" (Dr. Islam), as national debts of small developing nations are cancelled and forgotten (John Wu).

China says of us together, we "big family 大家" of the "same womb 同胞" of Mother Nature, saying with Fan Chung-yen 范仲淹 that "we worry before the whole world worries, we rejoice after the world rejoices," because my self-cultivation enables family-management to develop into world concord, as the *Great Learning* 大學 chants, where "within Four Seas are our brethren," as the *Analects* records (12/5). To proclaim all this hits us hard, to make us happy, to give us all joys of our shared goal to globalization as treading forth ubiquity without end.

Thus the supposedly conservative Confucianism is surprisingly cosmopolitan-minded, shaking hands with Greek sophists who avidly touted the cosmopolitan "unity of mankind."[36] Surprisingly, not even the open-minded Socrates was as broad-minded as they. He had only his filial love to his parents the Athenian society and loyalty to death even to their mortal injustice done him, as the dialogue of *Crito* reported.

He did not have the love of global dimension enough to go abroad as Crito urged, with arrangement already made for it. He could not afford to shrug his shoulders with Mencius (2B13), saying, "That was one time, this is one time." Such is "all" alive, one time with those global-minded, another time with Socrates local-minded for all his enlightened honesty. "All" includes such Socrates and such Mencius.

"All" is alive, as we are being born of the skies, friendly or scary, and the "sky" is unreachable everywhere nowhere, as the all of all in all. The sky is equivalent to our cosmos, and China calls it "yü chou 宇宙" where "yü" means "space" and "chou" means time, and so the cosmos is an inexhaustible and so unreachable space-and-time.

So cosmology is our myth today to join ancient myths of many lands, and there exists no land that has no cosmic myths. Thus "being born of the skies of the cosmos" amounts to being born of myths one after another. All cosmic myths of all lands are yet to be compiled, and they are perhaps beyond compiling, for cosmic myths are as vastly beyond compiling as cosmos itself is inexhaustible. This is one more reason why the "all" of globalization is a vast verb beyond imagination and management.

Here only our imagination dares to peep, and then can only sigh at the impossibility of peeking at the potential reaches of the cosmos vast as our skies. I said "our skies" but we are not even sure what "our" means here, for no inventory of them is possible. We cannot even say we only scratch their surface, for they are so huge we cannot see their "surface"; the word "surface" is without meaning here.

"O, No. We are too busy for such nonsense." My dear pal, don't you realize that it is such vast "nonsense" that makes sense of our being "busy"? If empirical facts need no justification, as you may say, our imagination, which is our only tool to plumb the limitless cosmos, needs even less justification, for "fact" is literally "manu-fact-ured" by our

---

[36] W. K. C. Guthrie, *The Sophists*, Cambridge University Press, 1971, pp. 24, 44, 153, 160-163. See the conclusion to my "'Let Chinese Thinking Be Chinese, Not Western': Sine Qua Non to Globalization," *Dao: A Journal of Comparative Philosophy*, June 2010, pp. 205-207.

imagination, for "fact" must be perceived as fact, as "perceive as" is worked out, "manufactured," by imaginative composition into "fact," as a tree falling in no-man's forest is no "fact." Remember George Berkeley said that "to be is to be perceived."

It is our imagination then that justifies empirical facts so much so that the facts require no justification. What makes sense of our "busy, busy world" is something that itself cannot make sense, as what shines on things to make them seen cannot itself be seen; we cannot look at the sun that makes all things to be looked at. The vast Nonsense of the cosmos, the all, makes sense of all things with which we are busy. We are born of "all," of the skies of the cosmos. We call it "reaching out to the unreachable." We call it "globalization" that is a vast verb of ubiquity on the constant move.

"All" is indeed alive all over in globalization that features translation, ecology, music, future, poetry, body, and universality. Translation tacitly serves many cultures-in-meanings that keep shifting, even when to take what as important comes in only to vanish, for the next moment of differing importance to emerge. Translation is a "nothing" to catalyze meanings, alive without ceasing, from one culture to another.

Intercultural translation renders ecology to become globally aware as crucial. Ecology awareness tells us of Mother Nature our common womb where zero-sum games vanish into more-sum win-win sensitivity, to which we must grow to be attuned, the more, the merrier in appreciation of beauty-together, in eco-household of Mother Nature.

Music is the future in rhythm rhyming all in lyricism of dissonant melodies of existence. The future now performs this time-art to act out the self authentic, as performance has no room for inauthenticity, as no false performance is possible. The performance is a poetic co-creation of inter-coherence continuous, birthing never ceasing. Music is poetry of the future now, all over bubbling forth existence after existence.

Here the future dawns, one moment at a time, to promise us softly that there is no "future shock" but future healing of disasters at present, for the future has no disaster. In all this we all move and live in our body that is yet nowhere noticed in our healthy living. Our body is no flesh, not even vision, but our health self-forgotten, while we keep thinking and acting out our thinking, as if nothing is the matter, as if there is no "body."

Here any "universality" is proclaimed by a culture so confident, and cultural universality is *cultural*. Even the standards of justice, excellence, and effectiveness are given by cultures that shift as time shifts, and so these cultural universalities, cognitive, ethical, and aesthetic, do well to dovetail dialogically into global ubiquity.

What one culture admires another culture condemns as abomination. This fact tells less of indifferent cultural relativism than indicating our common cultural imperative to gather into globalization, in dynamic ubiquity of intercultural beauty and excellence, all inter-versal. We do so in body politic international in multi-corporations, continually negotiating for world concord cosmopolitan. Globalization as ubiquity on the move is here now, this way, as the cultural winds blow this way and that.

The winds routinely blow throughout the winter, while few people notice that the spring gust is no less noteworthy. The spring gust is something else, quite something to behold, while we are at home with windows closed, as it is too gusty for comfort. Secluded at home, the gust is indeed something to contend with, and something to hear, for the wind has nothing to *listen* to. Strangely, hearing the whooing that comes and then goes somehow gives me peace and calm ineffable, at home.

The spring gust tells, sometimes with soft drizzle, that things in tiny yellows, blues, and reds are sprouting, to show Mother Nature alive delightfully busy, as Mother Nature is softly smiling into me inside me, to calm me for no reason, for here all reasons melt away. Everyone is alone, but some are lonely. Can you hear how lonesome Schubert is in his music? I wish he hear the spring gust here gusting through my heart; it would have gusted into him to make him smile.

Remember that unsightly Dvorak? He smells gutsy rustic Bohemian villages that must be poor and rugged. His music gusts into my Chinese heart of hearts. His string quartets gust me into his gutsy towns far away, tiny and dirty and unkempt, where those sweet country folks must not welcome such a strange smelly Chinese fellow, but I do not care, for I am *there* now, thanks to rustic Dvorak warmly having taken me in. His shamelessly honest music travels me far in space, so far indeed where I do not even know their Czech language, much less their Bohemian dinners.

In due time, the gust is whirling into present, blowing me into summery tomorrow. The gust is the future now, where there is no room for cheat, for no future cheats, and so such no-cheat present-in-future does not cheat, either. No wonder, the spring gust gives me no-cheat composure unspeakable, ubiquity globalizing, pervading now into soon-to-be now. If disaster resides in the present alone, the future in spring gust here now tames such my pain, for the future has no disaster, only dawning of hope that does not cheat.

Hope is of course something to be dashed repeatedly. All sweet hopes are often dashed into wandering pieces in disaster at present, only to be tamed and healed by more hopes provoked by disasters now to dawn at present, moment after moment, for we always have tomorrow, and another tomorrow, blowing in by the spring gust. O my spring gust! I hear you whooing in silence to calm me here now, to ready me full and alive, for whatever disaster that may come here now.

The spring gust blows my tomorrow now, dawning, dawning, without ceasing. The spring gusts all over to gust into me its spring smiles, so sure and invincible. The spring thus gusts globalization ubiquitous all over into myriad things, world without end, for globalization in ubiquity *is* none other than the spring gust perpetual, whirling into everything and it is still whooing, whirling, right now at this very moment.

Myriad things blown in by the spring are sprouting alive in the gust often too much for the fragile sprouts, yet that "too much" is precisely what makes things to come out alive in vigor. Globalization in ubiquity on the move is indeed that spring gust, rough and motherly, for things to born again out of winter gust that has prepared them for this moment, this precise moment of rough hopes of life, now absolutely disaster-proofed by the rough spring gust that nothing deadly can win, wintry too chilly or summery too hot.

Ubiquity is ubiquitous beginnings of blossoms. I have not read anyone saying that birds are flowers in the air, much less singing the stones as flowers blossoming on the earth. But they are actually all flowers, birds and stones and everything between them! Now, everything I do, see, and feel is special, for it is my birthday today. Everything is my flower today, and every today is my birthday, when everything is flower so special, as everything is blossoming so special.

Grass dry out and flowers wilt, while God is eternal within flowers of grass, with their leaves in many sizes and shapes, all flowers all green. God is flower that flowers all flowers. My birthday is when I blossom to enjoy those flowers, including God. My birthday is when my God is born to make the first creation of all flowers, flowering in drying and flowering in fading.

"Achievements complete, events come about, and all hundreds say 'me, self-so,'" Lao Tzu (17) intones this unrhymed line of poetry of all things, self-becoming as achievements are accomplished. He forgets to add that the coming about of completion is flowers pan-blossoming. *That* is ubiquity all around toward which globalization tends. Now we must remember that our "achievements" are our interculture going worldwide.

In: Globalization Dynamics
Editor: Kuang-ming Wu

ISBN: 978-1-62100-750-0
© 2012 Nova Science Publishers, Inc.

Chapter 16

GLOBALIZATION AS INTERCULTURE: CULTURES INTER-FRAME TO INTERCULTURE

Kuang-ming Wu[1]
Taiwan, ROC

ABSTRACT

This chapter on *interculture* considers, one, how interculture handles frames. Then we consolidate its basis by considering, two, how radically different cultural frames are, to lead to, three, how we inter-handle frames, and four, how *this* essay is an inviting catalyst toward such interculture, to reach, five, our shared all-joyous goal of (no monoculture but) global interculture.

INTRODUCTION: INTERCULTURE

Different frames of thinking shape humanity to differentiate it as "cultural" from other species, as these frames differentiate one culture from another. This essay's major theme is that monoculture destroys the distinctness of respective cultures, while interculture inter-frames to thrive humanity in all its distinctness. This Introduction briefly explains this thesis before elaborating it in the pages that follow.

Life has similarities and differences, but we instinctively reduce similarities to *our* sameness to flock to it, as birds of a feather. We do not realize that it is proper handling of the difference that consolidates our unique identity. Now, culture decisively shapes life. This essay insists that our survival hangs on how we deal with cultural differences. Imposing our culture identically over all to perish is monoculture; meeting cultural differences to inter-thrive is interculture. Let us consider sameness, and then difference.

Undergoing similar life vicissitudes in similar natural environments, all cultures come to have similar contents. This fact does not, however, dictate that all cultures are identical, for

---

[1] E-mail address: Kmwu2002@yahoo.com

what frames a culture on similar contents makes one culture differ from another, as different frames make each culture distinct, to make them inter-different.

We risk mortal disrespect to ruin life by taking other culture's similarities to ours as a simple extension of familiar contents in *our* culture, thinking that what they have we have also, *identically*, and we express them much better than the other culture. The other culture is thus absorbed into ours; nothing is new under *our* cultural sun. This is simple monoculture to dominate everyone, to destroy all cultures; the dominant culture vanishes in a lack of contrast, as the dominated vanishes by being absorbed.

This sad demise is dictated by the law of identity. "A is A" must be supported by "A is not not-A." It is this "not not-A," this difference, that makes up the dynamics of cultural identity, "A is A." Monoculture destroys this cultural difference to consolidate cultural identity, to destroy *all* cultures including itself.

This is because, in order to find "our culture," we must find the other culture in the light of whose "difference" we see "our culture." We cannot find other culture as our monocultural dominance destroys it—to destroy our culture. Only "West" is present in "West and non-West," no "not" of "not-A." This stance self-locks into self-loss; monoculture is culture-blind to lose all cultures, as "changing China"[2] without changing the West loses China to proudly lose the West *just* changing China, not West with China.

This warning is itself a "not-A" affirming the following truth as "A." "A is not not-A" says, "not-A *differs* from "A" to tell ("is not") of not-A *confirming* "A is A," for A *stands out* (ex-ists) of not-A. The tautology of existence (A is A) is composed of difference (A is not not-A). So, "A is A, and is not not-A" says opposition (not-A) consolidates existence (A). This law of identity is that of mutuality, telling of how resisting[3] *difference* inheres in existence to inter-exist, for cultures to interculture.

The dynamics of difference is democracy as self-critical self-conquest; our enemy is us. When we are victor over us, we are self-composed, come what may. Since we change daily, we must self-win daily. Democracy is a dynamite of self-growth in self-education about the not-self. All this simply indicates that we are alive in daily difference. Such is the principle of interculture to deepen the integrity of every culture.

Interculture appears as ideal politics, the art of managing polis our community of people, managing people-together. Western democracy the people-power pits against the ruling power; Chinese "min-pen 民本" sees politics as "people-rooted." Ideal politics is "rooted in people (China) who watch over the ruler (West)."

The law of identity-in-difference[4] as interculture also works this cosmic way. Taiwan has the sky that differs from the US-sky, the Europe-skies, the Africa-skies, and so on. So the one vast sky is made of Taiwan-sky inter-cultured with US-sky and Europe-skies and Africa-skies and so on. Interculture makes for one pluralistic heaven of human cultures.

---

[2] Vera Micheles Dean and Harry D. Harootunian, eds., *West and Non-West*, NY: Holt, Rinehart and Winston, 1963. Jonathan Spence, *To Change China* (1969), NY: Penguin Books, 2002, just alerts that it does not work, with historical precedents, never realizing the seriousness of losing the changer the West.

[3] Resisting opposition as obstacle to produce value is also asserted by René Senne (*Obstacle and Value*, Evanston, IL: Northwestern University Press, 1972).

[4] Martin Heidegger also said something similar in *Identity and Difference*, tr. Joan Stambaugh, University of Chicago Press, 2002, though he did not apply it to interculture.

Thus in the midst of cultural similarities, cultural differences crucially inter-confront to promote respective peculiarities of cultures for each to grow into its own identity, to contribute to all. We must now detail how the cultural uniqueness is framed by the thinking-frame of each culture, how radically different these frames are, so as to understand how best to deal with frame-differences, away from monocultural absorption by victor or adulation by victim, quite lethal to all cultures.

Different cultures shape people to look at the same things differently. "Dust to dust" is a Western sober saying, while the Chinese Great Clod is alive, wheezing musical. Western past is settled behind us; China's past is a paradigm before us 以前, 前車之鑑. The mythical "dragon" is a Western evil-paragon and a Chinese royal splendor.

Culture shapes our way of viewing things because it is framed by a frame of thinking, as six examples below would soon show. The West looks at things directly, quite visual, objective, and articulate. China sees-through things to turn subtle, intently listening, interpersonal and accommodating.

So, our lives are alike and different, cultures shape us different, and frames of thinking frame many cultures. Every culture has its own frame of thinking. "Thinking frame" is usually called viewpoint, Gestalt, worldview, "common sense," convention, milieu, and cultural ethos and sentiment, all these called "culture." They are important because they frame our thinking, and our thinking frames our living.

Our being all identically human depicts, surprisingly, our wide differences in life-approach because we live radical differences in "cultural frame of thinking." Thus "frame" is preferred over all other epithets cited, to stress their structure as frame and their functioning as framing. All this frame-explanation explains what a culture is.

Let us repeat this crucial point. Culture is our inner eye directing how our eyes look, and a frame of thinking frames such an inner eye, a culture. A culture is a culture due to its frame of thinking. A frame frames a specific culture-world; Western "lifeworld" is not China's "under heaven 天下." We live among jumbles of many cultures; interculture inter-handles different cultural frames. Interculture inter-frames.

This chapter considers, one, how interculture handles frames, to round up our insistence so far. Then we consolidate its basis by considering, two, how radically different cultural frames are, to lead to, three, how we inter-handle frames, and four, how *this* essay is an inviting catalyst toward such interculture, to reach, five, our shared all-joyous goal of (no monoculture but) global interculture.

ONE: INTERCULTURE INTER-HANDLES FRAMES

Any culture has its frame of thinking. This description of culture bypasses the problem of culture as miscegenation,[5] because as long as a community exhibits a specific mode of thinking, that community has a culture that has its frame of thinking, irrespective of whether or not that culture is miscegenation.

---

[5] I did consider this issue to harvest interculture in my "'Let Chinese Thinking Be Chinese, not Western': Sine Qua Non to Globalization," *Dao: A Journal of Comparative Philosophy*, 2010, pp. 193-209. It was revised into the final chapter 49, pp. 451-475, in my *Chinese Wisdom Alive: Vignettes of Life-Thinking*, NY: Nova Science Publishers, 2010.

It follows that a culture has not genuinely met another culture if a culture takes into its own frame just the contents of another culture, not confront its alien frame. Such a taking-in sees others in our own lens, where nothing is new under *our* sun our cultural frame. This is monoculture, no real contact with another culture.

Genuine no-nonsense cultural contact is frame-contact with culture-jolts on all parties involved. Here is absolutely no room for interpreting other culture, whatever it has, content and frame included, in the comfortable terms of "our culture"; we take another culture only as an aspect in *our* frame.

On the contrary, in real contact of cultures, another culture's frame is starkly met as different, in contrast with ours. This contrast jolts both cultures into their own self-awareness, self-reflection, and self-examination, at the radical level of respective *frames* of thinking. Here cultures confront their different frames into frame-revolution. Here, interculture takes place.

An objection at once arises, saying, "Any interpretation is done by oneself, and so done in one's own culture-frame *alone*. Everything is appropriated by oneself." This objection expresses a monocultural fallacy common yet unnoticed and lethal. The fact is that the fact everything *starts* at oneself does not mean that oneself must *stay* in oneself, much less imprisoned in oneself to be choked to death. Unselfishness and selfishness are both acted out by the self, but unselfishness goes out of the self, and the act of going-out is done by the self, while selfishness stubbornly stays in oneself.

On the contrary, the self must stand *out* of oneself to be oneself. "A is A" must be backed up by "A is not non-A." This truth is dramatically shown in "my face" my identity being known only to the other-than-me, and a "handshake" in need of standing inter-opposite. The existence of oneself must literally stand-out (ex-hitemi) of not-self, and such a stand-out depends on the existence of the not-self. The self needs the not-self.

Thus otherness is already inherent in oneself. The other differs from oneself. The self depends on the difference from the other to exist as oneself. Existence is inter-existence backed up by inter-differences. Existence thrives on the differences of the other. We *are* intersubjective, never subjective-alone.

Concretely, our above insistence means that we are made for considerate unselfishness; selfishness commits suicide. The master depends on the servant (Hegel), and the master who cares for his servants thrives with his servants together (Old Testament). Considerateness starts at extending self-care to the other, and ends in thriving together by learning one from another on each other's frames of thinking.

Our dear critic continues his objection from another angle, saying, "*Our* culture has a frame that can apply everywhere; the West has logical canons that are universally valid, and Western science pursues natural laws—relativity included—that are applicable all over the universe. Any other culture is naturally to be digested into ours as part of our own *universal* culture."

Here is another monocultural fallacy, common, unnoticed, and lethal, to wit, taking what is universal as what is universal *alone*. So, China would naturally respond, "Western culture has 'logic' and 'natural laws' that are universally applicable. So do we *also* have the Ying-Yang internecine inter-nascent, ever unceasing.

This Yin-Yang interaction develops into the Five Goings, and the 64 Hexagrams expressed in mathematical poetry. Concretely, life observes that woe breeds weal, as weal turn into woe. Thus we understand the well-known story of Uncle Fort versed in such 'computation' of contingency thrives under all circumstances, come what may.[6] All of these are *also* universally applicable." Watched closely, however, we see that China can handle contingencies but is quite hard put to "universalize" such handling, while the West can universalize its calculation but cannot handle contingencies.

This dialogue jolts all of us to realize two points. One, the very notion of "universality" is culture-specific; universality *varies* as cultures differ;[7] while each continues to be universally valid, one linearly in the West, another circularly in China. Two, each culture is strong in one aspect alone, for no one human culture is all-comprehensive in *every* way.

Many "universalities" do well then to meet to compare frames so different to inter-complement. To repeat, no culture is perfect. We must engage in pan-dialogues in order to survive at all. We call all such dialogues "interculture," the sine qua non to our living on. We cannot survive without pulling all our various resources together.

All this says nothing new; it just says existence inter-exists, and we by nature inter-support to exist as our respective selves. We were born by others (parents, culture) before; we are now being born with others (surrounding cultures) everywhere. Interculture performs this inter-ontological imperative; monoculture violates this inter-existential fact, and commits suicide as it wipes out all others.

Monoculture frames away other cultures; they now vanish as parts of one's own culture, so monocultural dominance kills all cultures by killing "A is not non-A" to back up "A is A." In interculture, various culture-frames confront as mutual "others" to etch forth each culture, to deepen in inter-contrast; every culture thrives by confronting others. By wiping out such difference-confrontation, monoculture wipes itself out. The pages below explain this natural scheme of global interculture. To do so, we must begin at how basic and radical our frame-differences are, on which interculture thrives.

TWO: HOW FRAMES DIFFER

Here are six concrete examples to show what "frame" is and how radically the thinking frames differ among different cultures. Here we cannot help but hint at how to deal with the differences, to be detailed in Points Three and Four below, built on the radical cultural differences instantiated here.

But the emphasis of this section remains to impress ourselves on how radically different thinking frames are among cultures, for their differences are absolutely essential to interculture. Six examples below are, "old," psychology, modes of expression, "limit," "precision," and "contingency." All these examples show that China's frame that understands each of them stands radically opposed to the West's.

---

[6] See Lao Tzu's *Tao Te Ching*, Chapter 58, and 人間訓 in 淮南子 (臺北市三民書局, 民86, p. 965).

[7] Cf. my On the "Logic" of Togetherness: A Cultural Hermeneutic, Leiden: Brill, 1998, pp. 27-87.

Example One: "Old"

We begin by taking note of the simple word "old" that has two meanings in China, 老前輩 the senior who is 老練 an experienced expert (老 pronounced "láo" in Taiwanese), on one hand, and 老不修 old-un-trained who is 老朽 dead wood (老 pronounced "läo" in Taiwanese). The latter decrepit old is caned as good-for-nothing by Confucius (14/43); the former senior expertise is incarnate in Confucius, who keeps going on so vigorously that he even forgets getting-old *about* to arrive (7/19).

China tends, until recent days, toward "old" as "mature and experienced" deserving of reverence. Though having expressions, "ripe old age" and "You are now old enough to know this (told to a young lad)," the USA on the whole tends less to take "old" as "mature," than to shovel old folks aside as uselessly dated, and must retire. "Time honored" and "seen its days" are two divergent frames on "old" to make two different cultures. Their divergence cuts deeply, significantly, into our lifestyles, the ways of living our lives.

Example Two: Psychology

Let us now take the West's proud invention, "psychology." Thinking is psyche at work, so psychology, originally meant a study of our soul (psyche), is quite important in our context of cultures and interculture. It later turned into study of consciousness, and then into study of behavior patterns socially noticed, for easier observation/tabulation than invisible psyche. Now psychology is part of sociology.

It then somehow turns further into "counseling" to set right "abnormal behaviors" judged by social norms; it is thus a part of social work, often with varied techniques of control such as psychopharmacology. Now psychology is part of medical physiology. Going this way, psychology goes objectifying observation and quantification, and finally external control. Psychology is now an adjunct to sociology, social work, and medical physiology. Where is today "psychology" the study of invisible sovereign psyche?

Initiator of current psychology, Freud, takes psyche as "the unconscious"; so psyche is what we are unconscious of that influences us. Now, whoever does not know *that*? Freud's Ego, Superego, and Id take over Plato's tripartite self that is our glorified common sense, i.e., our pep, feeling, and sense. Again, what else is new? In addition, we cannot help but recall Aristotle who *defines* life as self-movement, as Chinese *colloquial* name of "animal" is "moving thing 動物."

The West thus decks up common sense into "technicalities" of august "science." China just goes with common sense that collects itself in time into "history" of all sorts, as simple and straight as common sense, which can even imagine "history" as fiction, and every common folk simply enjoys such historical fictions the West frowns upon as not worthy of the name "history." In this vein, China has its own take on "psychology."

To begin, China would respond to the West negatively. The West's "psychology" fails for two reasons. One, psychology studies the unknown (psyche) with the same unknown (subject studying psych who is psyche); this is the blind leading the blind in blindness. Two, psychology as science studies objects, psyche is subject, nowhere among objects. In psychology as science of objects, psyche-as-subject objectified now sours away, as touting "I'm normal" shows I am abnormal.

Psychology must then be a science of the *subject* to observe how the subject appears and behaves as it does, irrespective of whether it is socially judged "abnormal" or not; it must be a phenomenology of subjectivity.[8] Psychology amounts to a phenomenology of human living as China honestly exhibits as sociocultural history.

China has no "science of psychology"; China is people, inter-adjusting among their Five interpersonal Relations 五倫, parents-children, ruler-ruled, teacher-students, husband-wife, and friend-to-friend. Inter-adjustment happens in inter-listening, the soul and essence of psychology.[9]

We persons must personally "listen" to one another toward inter-transformation, to grow into our true selves to compose our vibrant community. Interestingly, "listening 聽" in China implicates "listen to obey 聽從"; listening conforms sympathetically to the person listened to.

Chuang Tzu told us to listen with the heart of our being, with our life-thrust vacant to wait on things.[10] Such is "listening" quite perceptive and observant that appears in Confucius who comprehends people by watching 視 their wherewith, perceiving 觀 their where-from, and seeing into 察 their whereat (2/10); these are acts of intensively observant listening.

The great premier Kuan Chung 管仲 greatly cherished his bosom friend Pao-Shu Ya 鮑叔牙 who perceived his talents; he owed his success to Pao-Shu's heartfelt "listening" to see-into him.[11] Such intimate listening perception composes communal concord, in heartfelt family-togetherness.

To put it another way, China knows that every note is special in music where notes and music interdepend. Music depends on its notes to sing its tune-melody, while notes depend on their music to be special, significantly alive musical. Similarly, in the family of community, every individual is special. The family-community sings alive only by listening to specific notes of individuals whose comportment bears the proud music-style of *their* family.

Thus individuals and family mutually listen to inter-shape. In all this family brotherhood—wrapped in Heaven-Father and Earth-Mother among brethren-things—is manifested the soul-and-spirit of the human among the myriad 萬物之靈, as "Western Inscription" of Chang Tsai[12] poetically describes. Care toward homestead prosperity, in our cultivation of nature, is our natural Ecopiety of family responsibility in the cosmos. Such is China's "psychology" without claiming to be scientific psychology.

The West must learn from China to restore social personhood beyond its physical aspect; China on its part must learn from the West to be clear and prudent to decisively effectuate "setting right" aberrant behaviors beyond legal sanctions. Their inter-learning shall set right and enrich our "human science of psychology" the West initiated.

---

[8] Interestingly, some Western thinkers blend science into music. See Oliver Sacks, *Musicophilia* (Knopf, 2007) and Daniel J. Levitin, *The World in Six Songs* (Dutton, 2008).

[9] See Erich Fromm, *The Art of Listening*, NY: Continuum, 1994. This is his posthumous book.

[10] "聽之以心 ... 而聽之以氣 ... 氣也者**虛而待物者也**." (*莊子* 4/27-28)

[11] See 卷六十二管晏列傳 in *史記*, 臺北市三民書局, 2008, pp. 2771-2772. Such careful listening so *allows* others to flourish, that people say they themselves did it (Lao Tzu 17, 57). Kuan Chung's appreciation may be a rare case.

[12] See "西銘" by 張戴 in *古文辭類纂*, 臺北市三民書局, 2006, V: 3491-3495. It is conveniently quoted and explained in Wing-tsit Chan, *A Source Book in Chinese Philosophy*, Princeton University Press, 1963, pp. 497-500.

Example Three: Modes of Expression

We now note the *modes* of expression distinct among cultures. In the West, statements have propositional meanings that are eternally set in the logical firmament. It matters little how it is put; it always says the same thing. In China, sentences sparkle alive, rhyming in rhythmic progression. The rhythm throbs, beating its heart into things' *sense* to evoke the readers variously, to open out into various sense-horizons unsuspected and soaring unlimited.

"The substance of the beautiful is a certain rhythm and harmony in motion, as the atoms dance in circles through the void."[13] Thus, China is not rhetorically irresponsible; its heartbeat of sense has its sound base in things' vibrating rhythm, to breed sense dancing as body-rhythm of all existents, to charge vitality to beget life. Life dances to compress into its sense, to compose story that in turn compresses into poetry rhyming in singing rhythm. And then life's sense sings to dance in rhythmic human sentences.

Naturally, rhythm musical in substances of the world thus breeds sense as part of existential rhythms that dance[14] to breed life, and rhythm-sense grows variously all over Mother Nature, and its sense shimmers in breeze this way and that out of the original rhythm, to express in *our* sentences. It stands to reason, then, that missing the sentence-rhythm misses its life-sense.

Let us repeat this crucial point. Rhythm softly "sings" sense in a sentence, and so missing rhythm misses the sense of a sentence. Such sense-evocation is a poetic creation rippling forth variously, calmly in its own dance of life-sense. An example could help. Let us take Confucius' simplest quip so rhythmic (17/2), "Born alike, practiced apart 性相近也, 習相遠也," among all Chinese sentences that are in poetic prose rhymed.[15]

Surprisingly, we would not be surprised if such a simple sigh evoked two later listeners Mencius and Hsün Tzu, to develop into two contrary trends of profound influences in China. Mencius took our "nature" as *good*, and warned us against pulling at our good seedling to "help growth"; he wanted us instead to nourish our innate life-thrust to grow cosmic (2A2). Hsün Tzu in contrast took our "nature" as *bad*, and wanted education to shape our growth, to breed in his students the brutal school of Legalism and Realpolitik of dictatorship.

All such contrary developments originated in the provocative power of poetic resonance in Confucius' single simplest sigh. Such exciting evocative poetry is lost in Lau's "Men are close to one another by nature. They drift apart through behavior that is constantly repeated."

---

[13] George Santayana, "Normal Madness," in *A Treasury of American Poetry* (1999), eds. Allen Mandelbaum & Robert D. Richardson, Jr., NY: Random House, 2003, p. 435.

[14] "BBC-Birds Dance" in http://www.youtube.com/watch?v=IMbDjNDD4cM fascinatingly validates this point. See on the unity of dance and music, Curt Sachs, *World History of the Dance* (1937), NY: W. W. Norton, 1963, Olga Maynard, *Children and Dance and Music*, NY: Charles Scribner's, 1968, and Marion North, *Body Movement for Children*, Boston: Plays, Inc., 1972. Ancient China has all this in its classics shot through with mentions of music and dance (also as reverent ritual 禮). E.g., omitting the "禮" that appears all over, see *Chuang Tzu* (3/2-4, etc.); 樂記 in 禮記 (pp. 513-551, 2004), 樂書 (pp. 1213-1275) and its surrounding chapters in 史記 (2008); 樂府 and 詮賦 (pp. 63-81), 聲律 (pp. 323-329), and 知音 (pp. 465-472) in 文心雕龍 (民83); 大樂, 侈樂, 適音, 古樂 (pp. 208-243), 音律, 音初, 制樂 all preceded by 季夏 in nature and followed by 明理 of nature (pp. 249-295), and 樂成 (pp. 890-899) in 呂氏春秋 (民84), all published by 臺北市三民書局. Cf. "樂" in 詩論分類纂要 (朱任生編著, 臺灣商務印書館, 民60) and 中國美學史資料選編, 上下兩冊, 光美書局 or 輔新書局, no editor, no date, no place. And so on.

[15] In rendering Chinese rhymes into English, interculture happens.

Even Chan's "By nature men are alike. Through practice they have become far apart,"[16] missed Confucius. Why?

The reason is simple. Put this prosaic way, the passage naturally makes us wonder, "Now, who would not have known all this nature-culture sequence? What else is new?" No Mencius or Hsün Tzu would have got excited at such a platitude boringly didactic. No wonder, Hegel the literalist despised Confucius as a tiresome platitude-mouther. Let us see *how* all this loss of sense happens when sentence rhythm is missed.

Sentences in China have no system, no explicit grammar; they exhibit an organic logic of living in historical modulation. Missing this living rhythm *falsifies* the sentences even if they are "accurately" rendered. In fact, it is worse; the accuracy hides how the reader pulls the sentences prosaically translated into the reader's frame.

Literalism is the reader's easy way to pull into reader's frames, to end in "eisegesis." How does the missing happen? Literalism misses the rhythm that is the throbbing sense, thereby to miss the sense. The readers are now those "*Analects* citers, *Analects* miss-ers."[17] "But, now, why does attending to rhythm attend to the sense of a sentence? What makes the rhythm as the sense?"

Rhythm-sense unity is originated in the very existence of things. Existing things sing to vibrate what they mean, to sing their sense rhymed in rhythm to resonate from one thing to another. Naturally poetry, rhymed, sings out the story of the sense of the actual. The story unpacks poetry to tell forth the sense in prose never prosaic, ever in probing sense to draw in people reading it to draw out their creative reactions to it.

How could the rhythm of the prose draw? Its sentences rhyme with the sense of the vibrating actual, to resonate spreading what they tell of to the reader told to. This is how the poetic prose draws in the readers to draw them out. Things' hearts beat their sense to vibrate the readers' spines. So, in short, the rhythm is the sense; missing the rhythm misses the sense.

Here the kid watching joins in the play shouting, tumbling among all kids. The sense is the sentences playing dancing the actual, spreading stomping quite messy. All this is the dynamics of sentences singing; no singing, no sense. And the sense is not actualized until it spreads, and the spreading is vibration that is the sense of the actual. This sentence has just repeated itself, and self-repetition must spread.

This is why the sense cannot help but spread, for the sense is incomplete without the spread. The sense is alive as things are. The sentence raises "one" to have "three" returned; raising one is incomplete without three returning. No wonder, Confucius said, "If raising one and get no three-returns, then not again" (7/8). Literalism kills the spread from "one" to "three." Literalism no-singing *stops* the sense singing together, dancing, stomping their feet together, spreading. Literalism is lethal.

Let us repeat this important point. Sentences in rhythm follow and rhyme with the heartbeat of things happening, all existents being vibrations in co-rhythmic inter-rhyming. Reading and reciting the sentences in rhyme, we are tuned in, to vibrate in their sense, and soon we are drawn into the rhythm to continue, as Mencius and Hsün Tzu did. By the same

---

[16] See D. C. Lau, *Confucius: The Analects*, Hong Kong: Chinese University Press, 1992, p. 171, and Wing-tsit Chan, *A Source Book in Chinese Philosophy*, Princeton University Press, 1963, p. 45.

[17] This is twist—an interpretation—of Japan's "*Analects* read, *Analects* dumb 論語讀みの論語知らず."

token, Mother Teresa tells us this story, so simple and irresistible, being straight from the little child in hunger, intimately "rhymed" with her.[18]

"I picked up a child from the street, and from the face I could see that little child was hungry. I didn't know how many days that little one had not eaten. So I gave her a piece of bead, and the little one took the bread and, crumb by crumb, started eating it. I said to her, 'Eat, eat the bread. You are hungry.' And the little one looked at me and said, 'I am afraid. When the bread will be finished, I will be hungry again.'"

The story abruptly ends here. We are now drawn by these simple words, rhyming with that little missy, into continuing feeding the starving little missy here, then another missy there. That is the irresistible power of sentence-rhythm for us to "rhyme in" nodding to its sense in our living. Literalism loses such drawing-in to draw-us-out.

Literalism flattens to kill Mother Teresa's tacit appeal and Confucius' unstable provocation, of poetic punch that creates novel meanings unimagined before. Hegel sadly missed this power in Confucius and so missed him; literalism misses the life of a sentence rhyming out of life.

Hegel is just one of all Sinologists, including Chinese scholars, as famous Lau and Chan cited above. They missed this poetic thrust in Mother Teresa who spread her charity worldwide, as they missed Confucius who promoted to propagate this poetic thrust throughout Chinese history; this is why Chan said that Confucius single-handedly "shaped" Chinese culture,[19] not knowing how it happened.

In a poem, each word is charged with power to mean more than it says. Once such vibrating power to mean is lost, many words must be used to cover the territory comprehensively, explicitly, and then these words lose their power to mean. The less sense is meant, the more words are needed for more coverage; words are now senseless ciphers. And then all power comes to concentrate in the crowd's brute power, to end in death of people, pan-death in senselessness. Such is the ultimate end of literalism.

If literalism is deadly and kills, poetry is alive and enlivens. The power of poetry is the power of a baby so loud so silent even while crying, for a baby never talks; it just expresses, as nature incarnate. Meanwhile, birds chirp to softly wrap up jagged harsh corners everywhere for them all to *mean*.

In all this, birds are so fragile, and so irresistible in their tender helplessness; their helplessness expresses as the tiny helpless baby does. It is the true power of poetry, as nature is its baby bird power chirping naturing. Tiny red leaves hide behind all green of autumn. Are you so shy as to hide your beauty? Lao Tzu and Chuang Tzu also tirelessly recite tenderness as strength[20] birthing without ceasing 生生不息, and Confucius was so enthralled by nature's silent power that breeds everything with meaning (17/19).

---

[18] *No Greater Love: Mother Teresa* (1995), eds. Becky Benenate & Joseph Durepos, NY: MJF Books, 1997, p. 97. Almost all sentences in the book are like this, so moving, so truncated.

[19] Ibid., p. 14.

[20] The "baby" is one of Lao Tzu's four salient images of the cosmos; the other three are mother, valley, and room. Chuang Tzu constantly referred to the little baby and the little bird as the invincible power of nature constantly erupting life.

In general, the West's mode of expression is mathematical, as Keyser says without explicitly saying so.[21] Explicit exactitude, digital computation, and comprehensive precision feature this Western mode. China's general mode is rhythms rhyming with the way things go, in the Threefold Family of Heaven, Earth, and Humanity developed into history. The rhythm musically dances out the sense in daily living. Following along with subtle discernment, in deep respect of contingent happening, features China's mode of expression.

Of course, mathematics is harmoniously musical, and music is tapped, sung, and danced in mathematical rhythms. Mathematics and rhythm are intimately related. But relation is not identity but backed up by differences. Mathematics differs from rhythm, to interrelate to compose humanity in musical cosmos. Such relational constitution is the principle, praxis, and goal of interculture.

Example Four: Limit

"What about the notion of 'limit'? Limitation is power, we know, but how does limit breed power?" Power is signaled as "limitless 無窮" by taking off from the base of "limit 窮." The base is needed to kick it to launch out forward limitlessly. So far, both the West and China agree; still, China is more intent on the negative thrust of the kick than the West's benign nod to it. In China, the negative *is* the power of the positive; China is forever fascinated with such positive power of the negatives that never overreaches itself.

This negative-positive unity is shown in something interesting in China. Another word, also meaning "limit 極," can mean both "limit," as in "no limit 無極," *and* "no limit," as in "Great Ultimate (Limitless) 太極." Such Yin-Yang inter-involvement of negative (limit) with positive (limitless)—in fact, "limitless" is a double negative, "limit" and "less," turned an enormous positive, "limitless"—is unheard of in the West.

This point has an interesting ethical spin-off in the notion of the "self." Bare selfness, itself blank, can breed unselfishness *and* selfishness, as subjectivity can be soaring authenticity or asphyxiating subjectivism. The task of the self as the base taking off is to steer away from the selfishness of subjectivism self-enclosed, to strive toward opening out into the others as my alter egos, in unselfishness.

One way to do so is to "dialogue" as inter-revolution of frames, at the base of interculture. China is intent on intersubjectivity, for the self—bare limit—to intimately and familiarly breed interpersonal sociality, a community as a reach-out of family-intimacy. Dialogues are one natural way of doing so, in interweaving literature 文 into history 史; China is the culture of literary history and historical literature 文史, and of course history is literature propagating itself in time as meaningful inter-human living.

China naturally takes to dialogue as fish take to water. First, all Chinese sentences tell stories, factual and fictive, and storytelling inherently opens to the story-listeners to persuade them. Such story-persuasion amounts to "arguing" in a most convincing way, as it is our natural

---

[21] Cassius J. Keyser, "The Humanity of Mathematics," *The American Scholar Reader*, eds. Hiram Haydn and Betsy Saunders, NY: Atheneum, 1960, pp. 30-43. By his striking title, Keyser means that Western mathematics molds the way the West views the whole humanity and the world.

mode of dialogical communication. Here storytelling argues, as Ssu-ma Ch'ien did in his monumental *History Records* 史記 to irrevocably indict the power that be that indicted him.

A second spin-off from self-as-limit is listening that harvests an active seeing through of the confessor. As cited before, the great politician Kuan Chung 管仲 greatly appreciated bosom friend Pao-shu Ya 鮑叔牙 for listening so intently to his rhythm of talents in his series of failures, as to recommend him to premiership in Pao-shu's own state, and Pao-shu himself silently retired. Dialogue listens and promotes.

Such heartfelt perception in dialogue takes time; it brews slowly as an art of time. Here we need an art of going slow, of sauntering and goofing around, as haiku poet Basho (Mr. Banana) slowly trudged all over the entire Japan, simply for nothing. It is being laid back, enabled by countryside air, but no one stops us from bringing it into a New York City.

Such is the art of slow living to see into things with leisure. Confucius says (2/4), "Seen-through their wherewith, observed their where-from, and perceived their whereat, how could people be unknown, how could they be hid?"[22] It is Mother Nature; last night it violently rained, and now at dawn tiny flowers are waving at me in soft breeze. Nature does storms in leisure, and our leisureliness joins in. If "make haste, make waste," then making slow, we can make soulful harvest, with heartfelt listening in dialogue. Where is the busy, busy world of Euro-America today?

Example Five: "Precision"

"Precision" in the West differs from "precision" in China: In the West, when "precision" is explicitly mentioned, it predominantly means logical precision that is predominantly mathematical and explicitly exact. This thrust structures philosophy and the entire "sciences natural and empirical" that typify the thrust of the West.

For all that, some discerning master logicians worry about universal mathematical precision. Whitehead blustered as his last public statement, "The precision is a fake," for "1+1=2" does not apply to gunpowder added to a spark, but he did not say what sort of precision is not a fake. Husserl the mathematician toward the end of his life loudly worried about "exactitude in the humanities," also without resolving his worries.[23]

China has a different sort of precision that intimately *fits* actuality, flexuously conforming to the shifting situation. "That was one time; this is one time," said Mencius (2B13). Seeing talent-less-ness lets a gnarled tree survive the axe and cooks a goose that does not cackle, Chuang Tzu smiled and said that the best is to time-harmonize, now dragon-soar, now snake-slither, ever in line with the times (20/1-7). Situational fit, in line, is precision-in-situ.

---

[22] Both Kuan Chung, and Confucius' saying (2/10) have been cited under a different context of psychology above. Now they are cited to explain dialogue. This is one more example of how the same sentences in rhythm intimate variously different implications.

[23] Husserl's worry is proverbial. Whitehead's quip appears, to clinch his "Immortality," *The Philosophy of Alfred North Whitehead*, ed. Paul A. Schilpp, La Salle, IL: Open Court, 1951, pp. 699-700.

China's incredible story, justly well-known, is dubbed "Uncle Fort lost horse."[24] Recently an Uncle above the fort (at town limit), computing fortune well, had a horse lost, gone to the Hu barbarous tribe. Comforted, the "father" asked, "This, how could it not do weal?" Months later, the horse returned with a Hu stallion. Congratulated, the father asked, "This, how could it not do woe?"

Their household was rich with fine horses; his son, fond of horse-ride on that Hu stallion, fell and broke his leg. Comforted, his father asked, "This, how could it not do weal?" A year later, the Hu tribe greatly entered the fort, young folks fought them, to die nine out of ten; the crippled son alone survived. The story abruptly stops here, as Mother Teresa's sentences do, for such stories have no end.

Now, these events were all surprises unpleasant and pleasant. Uncle Fort readied himself for such contingencies, come what may. He kept mumbling questions, "This, how could it not do weal?" and "This, how could it not do woe?" The questions tightened his life ready, flexuously fit to the next *turn* of events, precise without ceasing to fit in contingency alive. This story has no end, for Uncle Fort is ever fit and tight immortal. Such story of immortality in contingency is unheard of in the West.

All such life-stance goes *in line with* Lao Tzu's chant (58), "O woe, where weal leans! O weal, where woe lurks!" Disasters signal hope; things going well counsel caution. "Ever ready" and "in line with" depict China's immortal situational precision. This precision never sits stable but shifts *as* the situation shifts. Life-precision consists in this contingent "as"; we must now consider *contingency*.

Example Six: "Contingency"

Contingency shows culture-differences the most. It is a hardcore scandal to the West,[25] while China cherishes the *actual eternity* of *contingency* that cannot be mocked, in contrast to the eternity of logical necessity cherished by the West. Sadly, obsession with logical necessity commits the West to a contradiction as follows, to result in the West's inability to deal rationally—reasonably—with contingency.

Plato drew a line between rational necessity and uncertain actual happenings, and tried to jump over this unbridgeable ditch he himself created; it is a self-imposed contradiction to draw a line to forbid crossing over, and then tries desperately to cross it over. Hume limited our knowledge to derivation from sensory experience, separating it from pure logical reasoning, and then tried to understand both with his logical rationality.

Kant follows Hume to confine our "knowledge" to our schema of transcendental logic, and then tries to understand sensory experience with rationality, which he had to deck up as "transcendental reason." Such contradiction continues. They separate-create a ditch and then try

---

[24] See 人間訓 in 淮南子 (臺北市三民書局, 民86, p. 965). Again, this story was cited for a similar context of fitting in uncertainties of life, and now for precision-in-situ. The same story shimmers in various implications due to its provocative poetic character in situ.

[25] Contingency as a supreme scandal to Western thinking is well known, and also has been treated in my "Chinese Philosophy and Story-Thinking," *Dao: A Journal of Comparative Philosophy*, Summer 2005, pp. 217-234. So this portion will elaborate on an amazing Chinese treatment of contingency.

to jump over the ditch of their own creation. Similarly, Hegel took logical reason as in motion, and desperately, without justification, identified his moving reason as moving reality he sees.

Lessing boldly proclaimed the "broad ugly ditch" between logical necessity and empirical contingency, being unaware that his rational proclamation affirms the separation (ditch) with reason on one side of the ditch he created, to commit a contradiction. In all, separation and contradictory jump proclaim the inability to touch contingency with the West's rationality.

And the list goes on about the separation and the jumping over at the same time. All their moves continue to register "a series of footnotes to Plato," as Whitehead said, who was conscientious enough to proclaim, "The precision is a fake," to commit the contradiction of bankrupting precision with precision, bankrupting logical rationality by hitting the rock of contingency.

In contrast, China thrives on contingency in its historical reason as its story-thinking. I am lost gazing at the roadside flowers that remind me of my enchanting orchids at home. I am so full, and I am speechless when I am filled—to the sky so vast so deep. Such "things' ideas" as these are alive. I must be dragonflies hovering around to catch delicious bugs of ideas alive hovering around. That is how we live contingency in full, all so unexpected.

O the cloudless autumn sky so high! O the tiny toddler we can never win but are ever won over! We smile at both dwelling in both, so happy and full for no reason but that we live in them. We are so full as long as we dwell in them, and keep them in our spines, the sky with the toddler so fresh! That is contingency alive and life-reasonable. That is China.

Thus contingency is so pivotal both for our actual reasonable living and for cultural differences. Now this subsection on contingency is further elucidated by dividing into four long sub-subsections: contingency as beyond us, as eternal, as factual, and as historical. All this exposition of contingency is extrapolated from China's concrete thinking, i.e., its story-thinking in history-thinking, in contrast to the West's purely logical thinking.[26]

[1] Contingency Is Beyond Us

Contingency is what happens beyond our reason, our expected "natural law." *For us*, contingency is natural happenings beyond our prediction, to make our "miracles," as we are amazed that things happened cannot "un-happen" nor can it be otherwise than as it has happened. Seen *from God*, contingency is grace unexpected by us; it is grace after grace, grace upon grace, and this grace matching that grace[27]; here is God behind our God, God hid in contingencies.

We must invoke God to make sense of living through contingencies, as we confront the eternal God unexpectedly. "[W]hatever God does shall be forever. Nothing can be added . . . nothing taken from it. God does it that men should fear"; "what I have written, I have written," says Pilate for God.[28] Whatever God does and writes is whatever that happens—beyond us. God is eternity, and so we meet eternity in contingency that we live.

---

[26] Of course, many Western poets and novelists soar into actuality as Chinese writers do, but they do so against the background of "purely logical thinking." Chinese writers have no such background, and so their soaring is somehow—extra-logically—different from Western.

[27] "Anti" in John 1:16, "charin anti chariots," carries three meanings—in place of, upon, and matching, says Raymond E. Brown (*The Gospel According to John I-XII*, The Anchor Bible, 1966, p. 16).

[28] Ecclesiastes 3:14, John 19:22, NKJV.

[2] Contingency Is Eternal

All events constantly and continually happen beyond life and death. Now, what is said here is constant, and this constancy dynamics is eternity. This eternity is called by the Christians the divine love that *gives* itself to us unconditionally (John 3:16). As we touch things contingent, we touch divine eternity, and we give thanks. "Why do we have to give thanks for contingency? What do you mean?" Let me explain.

Every thing on earth is so fragile, especially I am so weak and uncertain. Just compare this earthly situation with any other planet, even with the moon. Our earthly conditions are incredibly mild and warmly smiling to anything alive. Still, things perish as soon as slight "irregularities" strike, called "tornadoes," "earthquakes," "floods," "droughts," "heat waves," "freezing cold spells," as if the world is coming to an end.

The point of our living, then, is to live with our fragility. I must admit my self as weak, and begin everything in life here. I must plan on obsolescence, not on eternity as I instinctively do. Live now. Never take advantage of frivolous benefits that come and go. Never look down on others as weak as I am. My petty lording over others will soon boomerang back on me. "Things are to be met, not sought 可遇不可求," says China. So, be *grateful* when met, and let go of chances missed and others unsavory, all beyond me.

"God" is pulled into such contingency because contingency is somehow divinely final as above shown in connection with my fragility. So, remembrance in story-thinking is important; it collects contingencies as the eternity of history. The Bible is a collection of history and contingencies, as China is history-conscious where history is something absolute, equivalent to something divine.

Contingency has unexpected finality that impinges on our life for ever. Whatever happens just happens, no ifs or buts about it. I happen to be no contemporary of Confucius', and as I read this book, I cannot read that book, while birds are chirping now, not yesterday. I can do nothing about all such contingencies.

That is the finality of history beyond expectation, beyond *our* reason. There is no room for argument, no negotiation is possible, and that is that for all eternity. Contingency is set and eternal, quite awesome, for it is eternally determinant of me and all things surrounding.

Moreover, amazingly, the eternity of contingency is itself contingent, i.e., dynamic. Things Yin the negative is involved with things Yang the positive, internecine inter-nascent, in fivefold inter-going of thing-powers 五行. The Yin and the Yang inter-involve threefold (two to the power of three) into Eight Trigrams that are doubled up (two to the power of six) into Sixty-Four Hexagrams. How does all this strange mathematics of actuality *actually* go?

Lao Tzu sighs, "O woe where weal leans! O weal where woe lurks!" (58) Huai Nan Tzu nods with a story of Uncle Fort ever prepared, asking, "This, how could it not do weal?" and "This, how could it not do woe?"[29] That is to partake of the Yin and Yang rolling contingencies throbbing, internecine inter-nascent, ahead into the future.

"How does it work?" It works this way. God the Beyond of the future gives me an occasion to pray for something, to strive after some ideal, thwarted now yet, such as illness to heal, something someone has been failing to do, and some plan yet to fulfill. And then I feel that God shines into my prayer, in my striving; he is already there ahead, beckoning me. That is contingency dynamics beyond that lures me on.

---

[29] See 人間訓 in 淮南子 (臺北市三民書局, 民86, p. 965). It is cited for the third time, now in connection with the Yin-Yang inter-involvement.

In contingency I am not alone, for I am invited into my days going on, and I am in the future yet to come to be. I am privileged to be part of what is coming. That is contingency dynamics. When I see a need, I am invited to join in to "fix it." In fact, any situation is an invitation by the glorious cloudless sky to whose deep blue all trees soar, and the shaded breeze announcing the autumn on its way. I go on into them, as part of contingency dynamics.

All such dynamics works itself out in woe-weal inter-leaning-lurking to inter-birth (Lao Tzu 58). The whole system of *Mo Pien* 墨辯 progressing can also logically retrogress; P implies not-P that implies P in return. Graham's massive study of it[30] misses all this dynamism both logical and contingent, both rational and actual. This is the "logic of contingency" (despised in the West as "the law of the jungle") that defies the linear "law of evolution."

"Now how such logic of factual contingency, distinct from the unidirectional law of logical necessity, relate to *this* logical law, if any?" There must be such relation because both sorts of logic inhabit the same actual world, yet such relation is beyond us to understand.

No wonder, Lessing[31] said that there is an un-jumpable "ugly broad ditch" between them. This Platonic "ditch" ciphers the mystery of the relation between logic and contingency. The West alone raises this problem, however, because it alone draws the unbridgeable line and tries to jump over it. Thanks to such a move, we are made aware of the cohabitation of logic and contingency understanding.

Meanwhile, China realizes in life's spines this dynamic truth of our contingent living. While we keep trying to solve "problems," our life comes to be living *with* problems, managing them. We take advantage of every cluster of problems as they senselessly arise. This is living in contingencies; their joints form and vanish as Bach's piano-works, and our living with problems turns impressively rich as Bach's piano music.

"It is relativism!" Yes! Relativism *here* inter-faces 相對[32] to inter-oppose 相對立, to handshake all around. A handshake requires standing inter-opposite, as interculture confronts opposing cultures. Everyone is alone if not lonely; we can only meet, not seek.[33] Meeting typifies contingency of the fact of life. contingency is relativism of actuality.

When we meet, it is a miracle of the grace of a handshake. We see a world when we *meet* a sand-grain among so many grains. Kids "love trash" on a Sesame Street; kids meet trash with gusto as we meet Bach in awe. To meet is the fact of contingency; it is best if we love it when we meet, come what may.

As Bach is beautiful anywhere we stop listening, so any segment of our living is now full if not fulfilling, as shown in Bach often beginning beautifully and ending clumsily, for it cannot end. That is also how Uncle Fort's story of living through contingencies has no end, for it can end anywhere and we find it so full, full of itself.

"Anywhere" ciphers "no end." This is daily contingent living, and also makes for why "history" has no end, for history is autotelic, an end-in-itself. Any segment of history is final, while it connects itself to any segment before and after it. Inter-connection inter-links into autotelic endlessness of history.

---

[30] A. C. Graham, *Later Mohist Logic, Ethics and Science* (1978), Chinese University of Hong Kong, 2003.

[31] *Lessing's Theological Writings*, ed. & tr. Henry Chadwick, London: Adam & Charles Black, 1956, p. 55. Lessing did not say contingency is eternal, though.

[32] Relativism is 相對主義 in Chinese.

[33] "只可遇, 不可求," says China. This fact typifies contingency.

All this describes the triumph of the logic *of* contingency, forever ending without end. Its end is endless as pragmatist Dewey[34] said of actuality-contingency of praxis, and of course "ends are endless" makes no straight logical sense in the West; thanks to his pragmatism, Dewey is unintelligible in the West. The saying is experientially intelligible alone, in the Chinese logic of historical contingency.

[3] Contingency Is Factual

Contingency is kin to "fact" that has two features. One, fact is fact; whatever happens just happens, however explained. So, fact is brute, final. Two, fact is fact only as recognized as "fact" by us. No human recognition, no fact; falling trees in no-man's land is no fact. So, fact comes loaded with human significance. Our story of fact does not end here, however.

The fact is, humans are so various, varying, and diversified through time, that recognitions of what a fact means are varied. Seemingly final facts are surprisingly various, as any historian tells us. In other words, facts are humanly alive and open far and varied, called "contingent." Thus, fact is contingent and yet it remains final, mysteriously decisive.

All this sounds spooky but it is a simple open-and-shut case, yet it continues to amaze us. "How does a simple fact amaze us?" A day begins to end itself; it is an end in itself. The simple fact is that many ongoing days produce Gregorian chants and medieval carols that cannot be intently listened for tunes and melodies, nor are they yet droning tuneless background music.

Being listened without listened to, these vibrations of beings make up tuneless tunes. Our eyes "freely saunter" in "sidelong glance" (Thoreau), in indirect "relaxed attention" (Wordsworth), for the ripest intuition to *come* to us indolently in wholeness of impression, to spontaneously compose tunes-in-words (Thoreau).[35] And yet, wonder of wonder, such spontaneous coming so indolent is a miracle of all miracles never expected or suspected before.

"What happened to you, pal? You told us not to impose our culture onto others. Here you interpret the West in Chinese terms." A good query you raised, my pal. This is the slippery part of interculture. On one hand, we should not see other cultures in our cultural lens; on the other hand, we must listen and learn from others, and learning cannot happen without "us" learning "in and from our culture."

Their critical difference lies in our attitude in dealing with other cultural-frame. We should never impose our frame; instead we must *let* other frame come in to change ours, to enrich ours while we are in our frame. We must really listen to the other, and never hear our own voice in our listening. In so doing, though, we must watch ourselves never to slip into interpreting others in our terms, nor lose ourselves to slip into "being" others that is actually pretending to be others. Now let us go back to tuneless tunes of being-vibrations.

These natural tuneless tunes, as countless leaves swing shimmering in fugue-breeze, must have originated Bach's piano works, to parallel music in China, as Chuang Tzu noted in nature's "heavenly pipings" belched by Great Clod (2/3-8).[36] In Bach, we hear and see many

---

[34] Here we listen to Western Dewey with Chinese ears, to enrich China. Listening is explained soon.

[35] These phrases are culled from F. O. Mattiessen's slightly verbose *American Renaissance* (Oxford 1941), NY: Barnes & Noble, 2009, p. 98, presenting Thoreau.

[36] "Gregorian Chants for All Seasons," *VoxBox,* 2 CDs, "Medieval Carols," *Naxos,* "Magnum Mysterium, I, II," *Decca,* 4 CDs. Compare "中國傳統樂器: 名家名曲," 鶴鳴唱片 *Her Ming Records,* 10 CDs.

simple events, nothing special in themselves, inter-web to compose Bach-like tapestry of tunes so exquisite, inter-open to open far and wide, coherently and contingently, ever going forward.

Small flowers wave at me, each made of incredibly complex elements that are themselves flowers. Such tiny flowers compose small flower-clusters casually waving at me. They are simple complexity that composes unobtrusive beauty—for not even me have noticed it until now—that is nature. Shifting clouds up there are smiling changing every two minutes, each cluster so beautiful, so spellbinding. All cosmic choruses bring us back home to ourselves, smiling together.

Now, who would dare deny that our daily meals and routines are Gregorian chants in Bach in China and in elsewhere? They are intercultural harmonics of our days. A day goes into another, as summer shades restful to shade into winter sun lovable, and day to day is good day. Peeping far, Basho sees "no one goes down it; this autumn road at dusk,"[37] and then, Basho walks down it, each autumn daybreak.

Basho sounds so poetic, but "no car goes down it" is the common condition for crossing any street. Crossing the street is full of poetic depths all integral. And then I see this wooden old chair, no one sits down it, and this parked car, no one drives down it, and this casual tall tree, no one looks up it. And the world is now sheer poetry. In such a way as this, days are endless ends-in-themselves, inter-weaving Bach's piano, Basho's haiku, and China's music, into rich and beautiful webs. That is fact, and it is contingency final, open, coherent, and beautiful beyond logic.

Let me put it another way, perhaps a bit spread out to come back later. The choice, "to let unknowns be unknown, or not to let," divides China from the West. The West says, "No, we should not let unknown remain unknown," and proudly makes "progress in science our knowledge."

Meanwhile, China silently lets many things be unknown. "Why things happen as they do, why happen at all, why positives and negatives (in whatever senses) inter-involve to inter-birth, etc., all these questions are all beyond us," China says, "So, let us know that unknown is unknown,[38] to let that unknown be unknown; that is to know. We just focus on *how we* can thrive in whatever happens, and let go of 'why'-questions, or even 'what' or 'how' questions." Nescience is part of science. Do we see Buddha nodding here?

"So, we had better just live with these unknowns, to manage them the best we can, one moment at a time, looking ahead." China is thus dubbed "pragmatic," "historical," letting things be, known or not. China follows common sense time-honored that shifts as time goes, never asking why or how the shift happens, or what the shift means. China simply follows along. This is beczause, Chuang Tzu says (3/1), "Our life has limits while knowing has no limit. With limit to pursue no-limit is risky. Knowing so and still make for knowing is nothing but risky indeed."

You would of course say, "My god, this is decadent, stupid withdrawal!" Well, China in all its self-restraint has its eyes wide open, being quick to discern the shifting trend to blend in. Far from stupid, this way of living is prudent, and its prudence makes a sort of knowledge, to "make money," to make a living.

---

[37] "Winter sun lovable 冬日可愛" and "Day to day, it is good day 日日是好日" are Zen sayings. Basho's 芭蕉 poem appears as the second haiku in Robert Hass, ed., *The Essential Haiku*, Hopewell, NJ: The Ecco Press, 1994, p. 11 (modified).

[38] "不知為不知, 是知也," said Confucius (2/17).

"I am not convinced at all yet, my stupid Chinese pal." Look, can you tell me why you make "progress in science"? Isn't it to satisfy our curiosity *to* "live better"? Can you probe further and ask why you want to live better? Does your science pursue *this* query? You obviously have to *stop* somewhere in your relentless pursuit of knowledge, but why do you stop? Isn't all pure theoretical science "human" after all, then? So, how do you differ from me?

Birds come, and then they go, after we feed them as we enjoy them. A deer came, and it went, after we fed it, and now we miss it as we feed birds instead. Isn't it life to see all this coming and this going? Do we want to know the whys of birds and deer? Do we want to know more than what we have found so far? *What* do we want to know? *Why* do we want to know what or why?

However we ask, whatever we think about things, things keep rolling on as they stay with us, for we are rolling on with them. Letting things be, rolling as they do, we roll with them, as we listen to their music rolling. Now, what else is new? What else is needed? All this is China, isn't it? We call all this fact in China, living with contingencies. "Living with contingencies" makes history. In other words, contingency is historical. Hitting this idea hits a whole panorama of history-as-contingency in which we live and have our very being.

[4] Contingency Is Historical

The "eternity" of contingency describes how the really real here now bumps into us, to shape us for good, for good or ill. We call this reality of the contingent, "history." Such realization of the reality of contingent facts, as history, raises the question of what reality is. History challenges us to think on what the "real" means. Let us look at the West first for an answer.

Locke and Hume went wrong—and Western natural science went along—in taking the primary "real" as *only* what we experience in sensory perception now, from which images and feeling are derived, as Plato derived the actual from *the* real, the Forms. This is a typical West, systematizing the diverse actual into a set logical frame. Natural science tries hard to statistically adjust this Procrustean bed of Platonic logical rationality by experiments under logical control.

Naturally, the West's reflections on history are less rich than, say, reflections on language and epistemology. Among many Western history-reflections, Collingwood's is most typical if not essential. Since everyone seems to agree on his definition of history as "reenactment,"[39] despite cacophonies of criticisms. Now here is my Chinese *disagreement* to balance off the record.

I hesitate to adopt Collingwood as *the* definition of history for three reasons. *One*, reenactment is "acting-out again"[40] a set script of drama. The acting [a] assumes that the

---

[39] See R. G. Collingwood, *The Idea of History* (1946), 1993, and *The Principles of History*, 1999, both published by Oxford University Press.

[40] "Collingwood may or may not have meant reenactment as acting-again a drama," you say. Well, if so, give me *what* he means. He wavers between acting out the past again, and repeating the past—as Pythagorean theorem and Roman constitution—and such wavering reveals his thinking of drama at the back of his mind, for he never clearly defined what reenactment is in all his verbose responses to criticisms out of objective scientism of the day. We feel for him, while we lament his unclarity on this key term, tacitly assuming dramatic re-rehearsal that is what dictionary says.

acting follows the script ready at hand, such following is [b] decided by the actors out of their freedom whether to follow or not, and [c] the actors' intention expresses their acting.

Two, in contrast, history is life's "drama" that *lacks* the three features of contrived human dramatic rehearsal, as above described. History has [a] no ready-to-hand script[41] for actors to follow, who [b] never decide to follow history-script nowhere in sight, for actors in history have [c] no conscious "intention to act out history," for acting out history is too histrionic to make sense. *All* persons in history proudly proclaiming to be "historic" have, without exception, turned out quite otherwise than what they intended.

Three, lack of intention to "follow history," whatever it means, is important here. "Following history" is meaningless, for history has [a] no ready-made script to act out on; on the contrary, our activities form and show "script" to later historians. This "later" is history. We have [b] no free decision on history, for we do not choose to partake of or perform history, for we *are* history on the go, in the making, we act [c] without intending to become history.

Thus all our living activities are part of history, later to manifest as such without our knowing it now. History is our total life now acting out on life's own, to manifest itself unawares as part of history later; there is no intention to purposely act out history. Chang said,[42] "The three *Chronicles* speak of no 'chronicle,' as everyone has a self that allows no 'self-ing' of its self." History continues one's self that advertises no self; as the self touted pollutes away the self, so histrionic reenactment misses history.[43]

In all, "reenactment" mis-describes "history." We never "act out history"; we live our own life, and then our living is seen by later historians as part of history without our knowledge, decision, or intention. All this shows how the West tends to directly make explicit whatever it studies as an object of study. China tends to let it be in indirection, hinting subtly, to earn the dubious honor of "the inscrutable Orient." History is *real* beyond our explicit awareness; here in history China's approach is more appropriate than the West's is.

Now, let us go back to considering what "real" is. Actually, "real" is "sensed," to mean meaningful beyond sensory-sensed. The real is an *impact* on me and on us that shapes us all, sensory or not. Some examples here can show us the real as an impact beyond sensory experience now, derived from sensory experience or not.

I have a bad nightmare, I then wake up panting in cold sweat; nightmare *gives* an impact beyond sensory perception now, never derived from it. Died in 1945, now absent for over half a century, "Hitler" is our public nightmare still haunting us now. Our ideals and plans, we imagine in minds, nowhere now yet, excite us now to shape our direction of struggles at the moment here now.

---

[41] Collingwood cited Pythagorus' mathematics and Roman constitution as we today exactly repeat them (*The Idea of History*, op. cit., pp. 217-218). His move can be taken as an exact rehearsal of a dramatic script. But Pythagorus' mathematics and Roman laws are a small part of history, not history itself, as a drama in the theater is not life but a part of life. We would never know how history as such s a whole could be a dramatic script on a par with Pythagorus or the Romans. Citing them as an example of history makes fallacious analogy; Pythagorus or Roman law does not explain history, nor does history explain them.

[42] 「三傳不言傳, 猶人各有我而不容我其我也。」said 章學誠, in 文史通義, 經解上, in 北京中華書局, 2005, p.93.

[43] We can turn "unhistorical" and still turn historical in the end, as we can be unnatural and are still natural; the same can be said, mutatis mutandis, of the self that can go selfish or unselfish. This sort of complications come out of the comprehensive character of "history," "natural," and "self"; the same problem is shown in "all" and "universal." Still, "all" does not demolish distinctions. Being unhistorical remains illegitimate as being unnatural or selfish is unallowable. This is an important point to notice.

By the same token, the past is the milieu for all the above impacts, and it is beyond sensory perception now, yet it is quite real and essential to our living now. Our fore-parents now deceased are actively responsible for our *being* here now, having bequeathed us culture in which we live and have our being.

Culture consists in our mode and frame of thinking, our language, our convention and tradition, including fashions we breathe in to shape our lifestyle. All books written back then are here now for us to consult with, and all information, including information at today's cutting edge newsstand, is also made back then.

We are shaped unawares by all such past legacies called "history." We confront it as we practice living now on the basis of the past legacies, as shift them unawares as we adjust to them. We "improve" on them, "revise" them, and even "revolutionize" them, unawares or not. We cannot help but interact with history as long as we live along, as we engage businesses daily. History is now; it is ourselves we confront, though it is itself invisible and intangible, beyond our sensory experience.

Education brings out all this past-impact, explicitly to our awareness[44]. Being fore-aware is to be forewarned to forearm; this "fore" is education. And, for all its forearming, education is all education in history. All education is history-cultivation of our selves, and all this while history education in person-cultivation forms history, to become part of history continuing. In all this, even kicking history continues history; it is thus that history-now goes toward the future.

History of the past is both now and tomorrow. Confucius loved the ancient to seek it (7/1, 19), dreamed of ancient Duke Chou (7/5), *as* he was awestruck at the young born later (9/23). Confucius was between ancient and future, catalyzing the future by raising past-one to evoke three-to-come in the young (7/8); he loved them all, past, present, and future. All this love makes education. We must be a Confucius to continue his catalyzing middleman-ship in love, education, and this continuation *is* history quite unsuspected by educator and educated.

Now, such amazing unsuspected continuation is *contingent*, being unpredictable, unforeseeable, and uncontrollable. History forms its own laws as rhythms rhyming forward, and we can only retrospectively perceive the rhythm. Retrospection is the power of history, in which we restore to prospect. We live forward, being powered by looking backward, riding on the crest of the contingent rhythm to rhyme on ahead.

Moreover, history pushes each of us differently, as each of us inter-differs, to push all of us ahead. History is our-unknown contingency at work on us in us. Historic life is larger than logic because contingency is. Far from being "without rhyme or reason," contingency in history rhymes alive beyond static reasoning timeless. History beyond our understanding is contemporary with us forwarding us.

Living in history, we are reminded of music. Mozart spins out many melodies, each beautiful alone; his beauty is in each tune so outstandingly melodious.[45] In contrast, Bach's beauty is in the choral networking of many notes that are simple and senseless, "nothing" in

---

[44] Education that brings out our awareness of inheriting the past *differs* from our awareness of our acting out history. The former is needed; the latter is impossible. This is because education is not history but giving past heritage to the young learners, and meanwhile turns into history itself. The distinction is subtle but important, though perhaps few would confuse history with history-education.

[45] Read just the two moving stories, Maynard Solomon, *Mozart*, NY: HarperCollins, 1995, and Stanley Sadie, *Mozart: The Early Years 1756-1781*, NY; W. W. Norton, 2006, Sadie's last book. Neither noted what I found here, however.

themselves, as we realize when listening to his magnificent organ and piano music. Other composers seem to be positioned between these two extreme masters.

Thus Mozart composes many concertos; there the solo performer soars high to which the whole orchestra accompanies. In contrast, even Bach's so called "violin concertos" (not many extant) are choral harmonies with orchestra. "Sonatas and Partitas for Solo Violin" and "Suites for Solo Cello" are choruses of networks spread out into single sustained notes and tunes. Their beauty remains choral.

In Bach's piano music[46], many simple tunes weave into a continuous network so inevitable yet unexpected at each move, making the series fresh and enchanting. Likewise, many simple senseless events happen overlapping into a continuous network of happenings quite inevitable and at the same time quite unpredictable and eye-catching, so much so that fiction-writers flock to make novels out of what have happened.

Both Mozart and Bach express "beauty in harmony," but in different styles. Mozart sings a single hero shaping up the trend of the times; Bach rhymes the trends shaping the hero. Contingency does both, one inciting the other in an unpredictable way, to compose history. Styles of melodious Mozart and choral Bach inter-rhyme to web forth the history-net, throbbing ahead in beauty time-musical, in deep life-significance. So would China say.

And then China would continue. We must be warned here on how easily we can fail contingency in history. On one hand, we should not live irresponsibly, "drunk lived, dreamt dead"; it is quite unhistorical. On the other hand, we cannot try to be consciously histrionic, playing up a dazzling "historic paragon." Confucius and Mencius firmly denied being a "gentlemanly sage 君子," and in their steadfast refusals while living each day on its own, they turned out sagely, despite themselves.

Not to be dissolute, never to play up, and people turn out "historic" and "historical." Being spontaneously themselves, they *are* truly historical. Becoming historical is an art of spontaneity, not sleeping, not trying, but living to the hilt each moment as fully oneself. In the meantime, things shape themselves up into history.

President Ch'en Shui-pien 陳水扁 of Taiwan committed both mistakes of history mentioned here. He was both overzealous about his historic mission of shaping Taiwan, *and* given to dissolute life in petty money-greed. History offered him, in a silver platter of presidency, the historic mission of shaping the new historic Taiwan from scratch, and he failed miserably in the mission in his petty dissolute desire for private wealth.

His failures are dramatic and stunning. He was *the* brightest student in all schooling since kindergarten, the brilliant lawyer having successfully defended so many freedom fighters accused of sedition, the Taipei city mayor who had sent this biggest city in Taiwan on its way to prosperity. He pushes his wife's wheelchair who survived crippled the "truck accident." He won a landslide victory in the nationwide popular election, the first ever democratic election in Chinese history.

---

[46] "J. S. Bach: Solo Keyboard Works," by András Schiff, *Decca*, 12 CDs. Listen also to Bach's "Musical Offering" spun out of a silly concatenation of notes jokingly offered by a duke. Bach's genius pulls off such a musical stunt. China's foreknow-ers 先覺, heroes who shape the times 英雄造時勢 by worrying before the world worries, rejoicing after the world rejoices 先天下之憂而憂, 後天下之樂而樂, come to mind; they are single Mozartian persons at work toward Bach-like choral joys of the world. Of course, the times also shape the heroes 時勢造英雄, and such inter-shaping makes the Bach-like fugue-like history.

Incredibly, however, during his presidency, Taiwan plunged from the pinnacle of economic miracle to the bottom of nationwide poverty. During those dire days he and his family amassed billions of dollars of wealth. He is now in jail on enormous corruption charges. He is a meteor shooting up the sky only to fall down dramatically. Reading his inauguration speech in June 2000 so glorious[47] gives us an unbearable heartache.

Moreover, here is a second surprise. Mr. Ch'en's failures have saved Taiwan from disastrous invasion by its big neighbor bully, the Communist China. Taiwan now enjoys its de facto independence precisely because Ch'en failed in his pledged independence-mission.

Such is dynamic contingency that pulls off its double dialectical tricks so historic to stun us, one, the capable Ch'en pledging and failing in Taiwan independence, *and* two, Taiwan now still independent precisely due to Ch'en's failure in independence. Mr. Ch'en is an amazing contingency incarnate. Woe is indeed where weal leans, Yin and Yang internecine inter-nascent.

He himself has failed, while his ideal belongs to us all. After his failure, his ideal must be shared and striven after by all Taiwan kinsfolk, while we are grateful that his failure saved Taiwan from the brink of disaster, and learn from his historic "failure of success" to be more wary and shrewd in scheming for his ideal of Taiwan independence.

Such is our living, always surprising, now pleasantly, now unpleasantly, often together, always engaging Mozartian in Bach-like rhyme. Such is a Chinese impression of Western Bach echoing Chinese cosmic music—of living. Dull daily routines vibrate together excitingly enough to deserve writing down into "history" so musical so rhythmic, stunningly significant.

Now, what can we say to all this description of history? History is not a simple "now"-extended, nor is it a simple "object" out there, and yet history is also an inner part of us now, and it is also something objective to examine and learn from. So history is a part of us we cherish (without which we would not have existed) yet it is somehow intangible, on one hand, and something objective yet subject to our interpretation in order to exist as something objective to be studied and learned from, on the other.

History is part of our self-examination yet we can do nothing about it, although we have to interpret it, i.e., do something about it. We do something about history (examine and learn) that exists only when we do something about it (interpret it), which yet we can do nothing about (what happened has happened), and yet it exists as beyond our doing anything about (history happened once and for all), yet only as we do something about it (interpret it). Such bewilderingly convoluted complexity is history!

No wonder, history is beyond the West's frame of straight objectivity, and of simple objectivity-subjectivity dichotomy, and of explicit comprehensive clarity, and of analytical precision. History is beyond dichotomy and precision, for history is more complex than dichotomy, more subtle than precision.

Thus history appears as "something" complex and subtle thanks to the West's inability to tackle it *and* thanks to China self-touting as "history culture." History starkly shows itself off as complexly subtle *contingency* that we are, and where/when we live. "What does China do with contingency?" Well, China lives history as contingency.

"How does China live history?" Look. Prayer says what you want to God and does what you want for God, and hears intently what God wants for you and does to you. Prayer is a

---

[47] "陳總統水扁先生就職演說," in 奮鬥月刊五六〇期, 國防部青年日報社, 中華民國八十九年六月一日出版, pp. 4-11.

dialogue in life with God beyond us. In China, "God" is Heaven as the history of the Family of Heaven, Earth, and Humanity. All this is how China lives history to live contingency through life.

In sum, contingency is seen to have four features; it is beyond us, eternal, factual, and historical. These features gather up into something exciting beyond description; we call it the law of contingency, rhymed "without reason" predictable, inevitable and unexpected, for it is exigent and open-ended, forming a horizon of reality continuously shifting from past-scape to future-scape within present-scape.

Let us be concrete. "Now faith is the substance of things hoped for, the evidence of things not seen," says the Book of Hebrews in the Bible (11:1), and cites many sages and prophets of old who are the fore-know 先知 ("prophets" in Chinese), the fore-sense 先覺, and the fore-wise 先哲, being "worried before the world worries, glad after the world is glad," as Fan said. All this is touted as something extra-ordinary. Still, in Uncle Fort's[48] lifestyle, this is a basic daily essential to thriving in contingency, come what may. Ancient sagely life is our daily essential.

This life-essential "law of contingency" is not random or arbitrary yet beyond logical necessity. It is logos alogoi, not "anything goes" yet anything is possible. Thus contingency, free prospectively, inevitable retrospectively, is exciting and adventurous. It makes possible "adventures of ideas (Whitehead)" that is continuous philosophy in the West and wisdom alive in China.[49] Everything is permeated by joyous vitality beyond joy and sorrow, congenial to contingency.

"How are *we* to relate to contingency while living it?" We are being with things without being with them, as Chuang Tzu said (6/62). Birds chirp, insects beep and both sing as I walk on, meeting nameless grass and tiny flowers waving. That's how I partake of contingency, intimately related to it. They have nothing to do with me, as the vast blue sky and tall thin trees soaring, but I feel so good meeting them without meeting them, as I feel deeply thinking of President Ch'en in jail, to feel being with history without being with it, for I am a Taiwanese outside Taiwan.

I look up at the deep blue sky various trees soar up to, thin ones, leafy ones. Simple vapor, with no paintbrush, creates clouds of all sorts in all shapes and floating sizes, and in all colors from brilliant white to deep dark, from dawn yellow to dusk pink, changing shapes and configurations every two minutes, spreading silently!

The sky is alive sparkling, in varied casual beauties, with simple vapors shapeless and colorless. Very few people notice such vast stunning beauties tucked away up there, but Mother Nature does not care. She keeps sprinkling myriad sky-beauties every two minutes of the day, and every moonlit night so shy, so silent.

Such is the usual sky I look up to as I take a deep breath, as I walk daily on. I need not tell of the sky in the rain, or shrouded in fog dreamy, or with stunning double rainbows against the blue so bright high, or stormy lightning, thunderous so scary. My routine sky above my routine walk is enough to enchant me, looking up without ceasing, at every step of my life's way.

---

[48] Hebrews 11:1 is quoted in NRSV. 范仲淹 says, "先天下之憂而憂, 後天下之樂而樂," to conclude his "岳陽樓記." See *古文觀止*, 高雄麗文文化公司, 1995, pp. 819-820. The well-known story of "塞翁失馬" is told in 人間訓 in *淮南子*, 臺北市三民書局, 民86, p. 965, cited for the fourth time here in the context of fore-preparing for the future.

[49] See my *Chinese Wisdom Alive: Vignettes of Life-Thinking*, NY: Nova Science Publishers, 2010.

The sky pulls me up into the vast unknown so familiar, for after all it is my daily sky. I am the kid looking up spellbound. This sky-beauty permeating all above, to spread down all over, is indeed rhythmic musical so vast, so calm. If this is not the sheer beauty of contingency so simple, so subtle, I would not know what is.

Haiku poet Basho peeked at the dusk road of autumn, no one walks down it, and I deeply feel the sentiment different from American Frost walking on the road rarely taken. I thought that was special, but no, I peek at a road no one walks down it, *every* time I go across the street. I had better cherish every happenstance I meet, as beautifully expressed in Chinese as "惜緣 to cherish meetings as karma." Journalism and news information are based on this maxim, that somehow touching on information is itself to be treasured.

Mind you. All these six examples show common sense being different from logic, while common sense is the law of sense shared in common by logic and contingency, a true *ius gentium,* a universally recognized law of thinking and behavior. Still, it remains the fact that common sense easily decides where-when to apply the logical "1+1=2," while its decision is beyond logic to compute.

Now, "where-when to apply" is where contingency is, where common sense is at home. Common *sense is consensus gentium* of the human world, the logic of the globe globalization develops, and it is beyond logic to understand because contingency the home of common sense is beyond logic. It is where China is at home that is not the West, frame-different. Let us push this point a bit further, apropos of globalization pushing itself globally.

"Consensus" the common sense is "a general practice," "a custom."[50] Western philosophy illicitly extrapolated it into *theoretical* "universal." This extrapolation is illicit because, as master logician Whitehead said, common sense relevant to contingent actuality is beyond logical computation—"1+1=2" cannot apply to gunpowder added to a spark; common sense easily knows how it cannot apply, logic does not—and so logical "precision is a fake" to actuality. Such decision of Whitehead's itself is common sense, not logic. Common sense cannot become "logically universal."

I wish Whitehead pushed *his* peculiar argument further, for if he did, he would have realized that his argumentation is commonsense-logical beyond mathematical "logic" cherished by Western philosophy; and *this* "logical argumentation" is what China pursues. But Whitehead did not push his argumentation further, for it was his last public statement.[51] He remains Western; he did not touch China. It is sad that he did not engage China.

Kipling says, "Oh, East is East, and West is West, and never the twain shall meet"[52]; this line now manifests its grain of truth in our new line, "Oh, East is East, and West is West, and the twain should constantly meet" to inter-enrich, facilitated precisely by their frame differences, by "east is east, and west is west."

Kipling did not realize that "meeting" *needs* differences, and we should never let difference lead to "never the twain shall meet." Dialoguing with Kipling, meeting with him, makes us realize this critical truth of humanity. To this crucial theme of "meeting in differences" we now turn.

---

[50] See *Oxford Latin Dictionary* (1996), ed. P. G. W. Glare, 2002, p. 412. .
[51] Whitehead's quip concludes his "Immortality," his last essay in *The Philosophy of Alfred North Whitehead*, ed. Paul A. Schilpp, La Salle, IL: Open Court, 1951, p. 700.
[52] *Rudyard Kipling's Verse: Definitive Edition*, Garden City, NY: Doubleday, 1940, p. 233.

THREE: HOW WE INTER-HANDLE FRAMES

We are all compelled to deal with confrontations of cultural frames in their radical differences such as above described, in our small Global Village today, but we must be cautioned. We have proper ways to handle these radical cultural differences, and improper ways to handle them. Monocultural handling of different cultural frames is improper; intercultural handling of them is proper. Let us consider monocultural handling, "how not to," and then intercultural handling, "how to."

How-not-to: Monoculture

Being in our own comfortable cultural frame, we would naturally take any exotics in our own cultural way, spontaneously in monocultural way. First, we would put "alien cultures" in our frame, almost instinctively. The West naturally understands China in its own logical manner, as the West takes for granted that its logicality is the most "fair and universal" among *all* cultures worldwide.

Here is an obvious fallacy; "universally applicable" slips into "*alone* universally applicable." These mono-cultural sinologists take Western "logic" as *alone* universally valid, and its natural science based on its logic as alone universally applicable, simply because both are universally applicable. The West never realizes that any other frame may *also* be universally applicable.[53]

This Western frame is now the *sole* standard by which all sinologists sift to catalogue all things Chinese; anything Chinese outside this frame is safely brushed aside as ancient, obsolete, and superstitious, unworthy of our decent scholarly attention. They can be safely ignored as museum pieces. Such is the practice of monoculture.

Now my claim above sounds too sweeping as to seem irresponsible, and so I cite here six well-known sinologists to instantiate my point, that sinologists today are monocultural.[54] I cite only Westerners because they are "worshipped" by Chinese sinologists trying "belatedly" to follow them. I omit this latter point for now[55] and focus on these six, Richards, Fingarette, Graham, Harbsmeir, Hansen, and Yearley.[56]

I. A. Richards' *Mencius on the Mind*[57] cites all *logically* possible readings of *Mencius* 4B26 plus 30 odd others, then scrupulously followed through each reading. He never notes

---

[53] I know of only one exception to this universal monoculture-attitude in the West. Paul Feyerabend (*Against Method* [1975, 1988], London: Verso, 1993) vigorously proposed a plurality of "natural sciences" along the line of plurality of cultures, especially taking Chinese science as parallel to Western science. It is a sight to behold, though of course I have my own hesitations on *how* he demonstrates in Western way.

[54] On outrageous flouting of Western monoculture, see *Stones from Other Mountains: Chinese Painting Studies in Postwar America*, ed. Jason C. Kuo, Washington, DC: New Academia, 2009. My review of it is forthcoming from *Journal of Chinese Philosophy*.

[55] I will mention one exception, a military instance below.

[56] I also omit all their brilliant contributions to sinology, and just concentrate on their monoculture, for it is their shared defect, major and quite serious.

[57] I. A. Richards, *Mencius on the Mind: Experiments in Multiple Definition*, Westport, CT: Hyperion Press, 1932. His experiments are purely logical, purely Western.

the "historical possibility" of what possibilities the Chinese interpretive tradition *cuts*, and *why*. His analytical "experiments" and exhaustive "following ups" are Western, not Chinese.

Chinese people do not experiment on all logically possible meanings in a passage; they just live it to taste some of its implications, while being ever open to more possibilities never exhaustible. No Chinese would have dreamed of doing Richards' "outrageously comprehensive" operation on the time-honored texts of *Mencius*.

On *H. Fingarette*'s *The Secular as Sacred*[58] on Confucius, Chinese readers would *feel* "off tune," and its tapestry is felt woven by alien threads of analytical reductionism. To take just one example, "She is silent about it" can mean "It's not in her," or "She assumes it" as emotion-charged Psalms have few emotive words.

To see if silence means absence or assumption, we must look into textual context and its commentaries. Fingarette refused to consult with "later additions" in the *Analects*, and commentators Mencius, Chu Hsi, Wang Yang-ming. For him silence is just absence, logically, straightly, one-dimensionally.

Warm reverent *li*-rite 禮 is simple social convention with an inexplicable "magic" to draw people (chs. 1, 5). Confucius' respect of history (as a matrix of desirables) is his "strategic maneuver" to sway people to local Lu culture (ch. 4), Tao is a "social convention" to shape us, minus the vast Heaven-Earth context (ch. 2), and *jen*-personality 仁 is response to interhuman sociality, minus unperturbed personal integrity, and private-personal distinction vanishes in an inner-outer separation (ch. 3). Such one-dimensional monotony!

A. C. Graham with all other sinologists take *Mo Pien* 墨辯 and Name Scholars 名家 to be straight logicians in the West's sense, purely scrutinizing the logical coherence of saying anything. But Name Scholars are intent on *pragmatic* "righting names 正名" where names are what we profess. "Right names" has at least two senses.

Confucius' "righting-names" stresses the professing-*praxis* match; Name Scholars' "righting-names" stresses professing-*actuality* match.[59] This is the whole point of the poetic punch, "white horse, no-horse," etc., sounding paradoxical to jolt us to be careful on how and what we *say* about things *actual*. Graham and all sinologists bark up the wrong tree. Graham's gigantic volume on *Mo Pien*[60] is a gigantic mistake.

C. Harbsmeir in two places[61] simply interprets *all* "philosophical" passages in China only from his narrow logical point of view à la Aristotle and Tarski.[62] It is naked logical thinking of the West proudly imposed on Chinese, completely ignoring *how* Chinese sentences

---

[58] Herbert Fingarette, *Confucius: The Secular as Sacred*, HarperSanFrancisco, 1972.

[59] All extant books by Name Scholars begin by declaring their purpose as "righting names." See 公孫龍子(2004, p. 2), 鄧析子 (民86, p. 7), and 尹文子 (民85, p. 2), all published by 臺北市三民書局. Chuang Tzu joins the Confucian name-praxis match to the Name-scholarly name-actuality match, by making name scrutiny bitingly relevant to actuality that constantly shifts; the shift is a headache of "contingency" to Western science (i.e., knowledge), while Lao Tzu (58) and Huai Nan Tzu (in "Uncle Fort Lost Horse") above cited freely thrive on it.

[60] A. C. Graham, *Later Mohist Logic, Ethics and Science* (1978), Chinese University of Hong Kong, 2003. All his other volumes take for granted "thinking" in China as logical in Western sense.

[61] Christoph Harbsmeier, "Marginalia Sino-logica" in *Understanding the Chinese Mind*, ed. Robert E. Allinson, Oxford University Press, 1989, pp. 125-166. *Language and Logic in Traditional China: Science and Civilization 7/1*, Cambridge University Press, 1998. In both cases, Western "logic" is solely central.

[62] *Chinese Mind*, op. cit., p. 126.

proceed. In addition, he is woefully ignorant of how dated *his* "logic" is even in the West, where postmodernism has bracketed and deconstructed exact logical analysis of logocentrism.

C. *Hansen* is today's Richards, naively assuming Western "analytical logic" as universally applicable,[63] confidently pushing his analytical "unified interpretation" all through Chinese history,[64] subtitled, "Philosophical Interpretation" where "philosophy" *is* Western analysis of Dennett, Nozick, Kripke, Parfit, Quine, Rawls, and Rorty.

Hansen does not even notice John L. Austin that A. C. Graham espouses.[65] It never occurs to Hansen that reasonableness is wider than analysis, as life is bigger than logic; he never realizes that China has been proposing and practicing life-reason that includes logic but different from it. He is worse than Graham who recognizes non-analytical *spontaneity* in China, and less sensitive than Arthur Wright who takes Chinese *thought* to be between "philosophy" (Stanford analyticity) and commonsense convention.

In his historical rehearsal of Chinese schools, Hansen treats *all* schools of thought on the *same* analytical plane.[66] He never asks *why* all schools except Confucianism fell by the wayside of official thought; he assumes that these schools fell by extra-logical accident, none of his concern. His analytically coherent view of Chinese thinking comes off so palatable to today's Western thinking trend that he is quite popular.

Hansen peeps into China through a tiny keyhole of analytical logic, blind as Harbsmeir to indirection, humor, irony, non-sequitur, contradiction, storytelling, and laughter, all so Chinese, especially typical of Chuang Tzu. Hansen touts his blindness in his title, "Daoist theory," proud of being a "daoist," a "reincarnation of Zhuanzi."[67] Such odd irony makes us able neither to laugh nor to shed tears.

L. H. Yearley[68] constructed a tripartite frame as a Procrustean bed to fit in Mencius. He pulls out concepts and theories from Mencius' ad hoc stories, provoked forth from shifting situations, and then reprocesses Mencius' story-persuasions in situ into eternal logical arguments. Mencius was playing with arguments[69] to persuade, saying (2B13), "That was one time, this is one time," wholly devoid of *explicit* consistent line of argumentation assumed by Western Yearley.

Yearley completely bypassed this Mencius-in-situ in the fiery thick of the controversy. To someone who said he loved to argue, Mencius quipped impatiently (3B9), "How could I

---

[63] Victor H. Mair, ed., *Experimental Essays on Chuang-tzu*, Honolulu: University of Hawaii Press, 1983, pp. 24-26. Mair has enough sense to take these essays as "essays," intellectual *trials* that Watson hesitates on (p. xv); Hansen has none of such hesitation. Clever fools rush in where perceptive angels fear to tread.

[64] Chad Hansen, *A Daoist Theory of Chinese Thought: A Philosophical Interpretation*, Oxford, 1992, where "Dao" is logical analysis for Hansen.

[65] Hansen rejects Graham's reading of China (ibid., pp. 1-2).

[66] Revealing is the sentence with which his volume begins: "A missing text is always an exciting discovery." *Causes* for the missing are never examined. He just digs up "obscure" schools of thought, treats them, in his way, on a par with prominent schools, and then turns around to disparage their prominence. Such roughshod ride is so insensitive to China!

[67] See his Acknowledgement. He did treat "paradox" but always from the West's logical point of view, never from Chuang Tzu's angle. Why he claims kinship to "Daoist" or "Zhuanzi" is anyone's guess. Is it because Taoism tickles his logical palate, more than dull authoritative Confucianism?

[68] Lee H. Yearley, *Mencius and Aquinas: Theories of Virtue and Conceptions of Courage*, Albany, NY: State University of New York Press, 1990. "Theories" and "conceptions" are completely in line with Aquinas' frame.

[69] On playing with arguments, see Kuang-ming Wu's *On the "Logic" of Togetherness*, Leiden, Brill, 1998, pp. 150-215.

love arguing? I just cannot help it!" His heat Wang Ch'ung in later days caught,[70] but Yearley never did.

Yearley just processed the fiery Mencius into another Western theoretician quietly spinning out theories and concepts. Yearley barked up his wrong Western tree, taking it identical to Aquinas *and* Mencius. Comparison is *frame*-comparison; claiming to "compare," he never did.

Yearley's conceptual extrapolation from Mencius into Aquinas' frame shows Yearley's assumption that all thinking is Aquinas' conceptualization *alone*, to make a monocultural imposition, blind to another frame that is *also* thinking, Mencius' *as* heated advocacy of his life-vision. This passionate unity of vision and its thoughtful living is Mencius' style of thinking. Yearley's Thomistic theoretical frame misses this alternative frame of thinking-as-living.

In sum, thus it is that the Western sinologists today (actual Chinese people and non-Chinese) have been using exotic Chinese vocabulary to converse in Western grammar, syntax, and logic. They discuss in Western language with Chinese words, engaging in the West's monologue in the West's thinking frame. It is all Western; no China is here.

Today, China at the cutting edge of racing to modernize military weaponry is so tragic, in that China has bought in the West's frame of international cutthroat contest. Here is no Grand Historian to judge as in the ancient days of *Tso Chuan* 左傳 and *Shih Chi* 史記. Instead, China is here today joining in the naked brutal global monoculture. Another form of China's world dominance *in Western style* is in economic wars; so many products worldwide are stamped "Made in China."

"But then, where is China's cherished frame, 'Within Four Seas are all brethren' to shake hands with the Greek sophists' cosmopolitanism?[71]" Perhaps one hopeful sign is Chinese cuisine.[72] Chinese food is feeding the world; even Greenland has some Chinese restaurants, and best foods are served in Chinese restaurants in Leiden in the Netherlands. We would fervently wish that China's humanized pan-family thinking deliciously feed and nourish the world. Let me go over my impressions on Chinese scholarship on China.

Beautifully vigorous and profound are Chu Tzu-ch'ing 朱自清, Wen I-to 聞一多, and Lu Hsün 魯迅; I learned much from these three giants. The so-called Eight Greats—four in China, four in Taiwan—disappoint me, filled with jargon and platitudes, wilting, empty. Wing-tsit Chan 陳榮捷 is balanced, comprehensive, over-simple, and insensitive to China's distinctive nuances and subtlety.

D. C. Lau 劉殿爵 explains China away in platitudes to cater to Western taste, as Chang Chung-yuan 張鍾源 explains Lao Tzu away with Heidegger, insinuating how today's deep Heidegger has replaced dated obscure Lao Tzu.[73] An eye-opening panorama of refreshing China and refreshing West is yet to emerge in the future horizon.

---

[70] Wang Ch'ung 王充 said that this Mencius' burning zeal was responsible for Wang's writing of the massive *Balanced Critiques* 論衡, in 對作篇, 臺北市三民書局, 民86, p. 1469.

[71] *Analects* 12/5. On Greek sophists' cosmopolitan "unity of mankind," see W. K. W. Guthrie, *The Sophists*, Cambridge University Press, 1971, pp. 11 (note 2), 24, 44, 153, and 160-163.

[72] So many pages are devoted to Chinese cuisine in Lin Yutang's *My Country and My People* (1935) and *The Importance of Living* (1937), both published by NY: The John Day Company.

[73] Chang Chung-yuan, *Tao: A New Way of Thinking*, NY: Harper & Row, 1975.

How-to: Interculture

Now, in view of all this how not-to-do, how to *properly* do interculture can easily be extrapolated. It is that we should never appropriate Chinese into the West's frame. Instead, we must *mutually* learn of the basic cultural thinking modes; it amounts to a dialogue in a radical frame-revolution on all dialogue partners.

Meanwhile, many Chinese scholars, at home in English, enthusiastically embrace the above Western interpretations as the unsuspected *authentic* Chinese thinking, hidden behind their moldy age-old classics.[74] They can turn this sentiment to good account. Concretely, Chinese scholars must go through the fire of Western logic to cultivate logical *sensitivity*[75] so as to appreciate afresh the distinct features of *their* Chinese thinking mode.

As it finds its own genius, China can now be enabled to set Western "precision" free from *its* set rigid logical frame. All this while, China must use its own story-thinking[76] to better its history-thinking, to turn relevant to "today," out of its traditionalism-rut, by turning more self-reflective (as history-thinking is), self-examining and self-aware, as Socrates urges us all with his life, culminated in the critical moment of the unity of ideal with life-practice.[77]

The West, on its part, should *stop* taking for granted its own frame of thinking as non-cultural and universal; we are all humans, we can never get out of our own culture our own skin. The West should instead sensitively gaze at how China thinks, how it thinks with poetic perception that parallels nature-poets such as Robert Frost.[78]

Subtle flexuous precision to actuality in constant changes can result, to please Husserl (human exactitude), Whitehead (actual precision a fake no more), and Wittgenstein (logic as game, notions as fibers) to enrich the West, as it learns from China's story-thinking and history-awareness. Quotations from the West are made above to try out this route of finding surprising depths and riches in the West, in Chinese gaze.

Some philosophers bubble up with new thoughts, with no time to bind them into bundles of system. That is why they are aphoristic, jumping fresh without rhyme or reason, to point to life with rhyme and reason beyond philosophy. French thinkers are typical, but Nietzsche is also, and in fact all thinkers worth their salt are at heart aphoristic; they just pretend being systematic. Postmodernism finally punctured their pretension, in line with logician Whitehead who blustered, "The precision is a fake."

---

[74] Exceptions are the three giants mentioned above, Chu Tzu-ch'ing, Wen I-to, and Lu Hsün. They all used the logical sensitivity cultivated by going through the Western fire of logic to display China's genius.

[75] See my "'Let Chinese Thinking Be Chinese, not Western': Sine Qua Non to Globalization," *Dao: A Journal of Comparative Philosophy*, 2010, pp. 200-202, and refurbished as the last chapter in my *Chinese Wisdom Alive: Vignettes of Life-Thinking*, NY: Nova Science Publishers, 2010, pp. pp. 451-484.

[76] On Chinese story-thinking, see my *Story-Thinking: Cultural Meditations*, NY: Nova Science Publishers, 2011, "Distinctive Features of Chinese Hermeneutics," *Taiwan Journal of East Asian Studies*, June 2004, pp. 233-247, and "Chinese Philosophy and Story-Thinking," *Dao: A Journal of Comparative Philosophy*, Summer 2005, pp. 217-234.

[77] This unity was achieved at the rare high moment in human history of thinking, in Socrates' self-defense, the *Apology*. For more on cultural inter-learning, see my "World Interculturalism: China Written in English," *Taiwan Journal of East Asian Studies*, June 2005, pp. 1-42.

[78] Many refreshing prose essays and eye-opening speeches in *Robert Frost: Collected Poems, Prose, & Plays*, NY: The Library of America, 1995, deserve pondering in our intercultural context. "To the Poets of Japan" (p. 817) and "To the Poets of Korea" (p. 840) are worth reading; they are brief and punchy.

In short, the West has no choice but to go *out* of its frame to learn, learn, and learn from life to revolutionize itself into its rebirth! So has China been learning from life out of living, in history, in story-thinking. Such learning is good for the West and good for China, inter-enriching-deepening to enrich our lifeworld.

"Now you told us not to see other cultures in our own cultural lens our frame, but culture-contact involves looking at others in our lens. You want to eat the frame-cake and have it." This is a good objection. My grateful response is that the look itself changes in its intent looking, and the frames inter-learn to inter-change as they meet. A concrete example should clarify this important point. Let us take a critical one, Western "psychology" as "science."

Let us note, in connection with psychology, that not scientism of objectivity, but observant empathy in inter-listening, makes for genuine understanding, in inter-human undergoing. My son John told me of himself pricked as his Baby David was pricked, crying, for blood-test. I was in tears as I heard it. Standing-under the roofs of each other's homes undergoes heartfelt their joys and sorrows that under-go my skin. Inter-undergoing understands. Here I body-listen, body-feel, and body-understand.

It is this undergoing understanding that is psychology the science beyond science of scientism, our human body-knowledge that breeds objective knowledge, in objectivity appropriate to the nature of each object. It is not extravagant to claim that such empathic knowledge, psychology, is the home of all sciences, their root. This is because all sciences are human-based; all sciences are thus human sciences, which psychology peculiarly *is*, at the root of all sciences.

Something as above is what China would say as it intently listens—listening is psychology[79]—to the West's psychology today. Such realization of what "psychology" really means is fleshed out by China body-listening to the West to benefit the West, thereby enriches China that has no "science" of psychology. Now, what we have just learned about the West's psychology is what interculture inter-learns in *all* life-pursuits.

FOUR: *THIS* ESSAY URGES INTERCULTURE

Confession in self-examination is good for the soul of writing, as both Socrates and Confucius urged us. Thus, this penultimate section examines this essay, by responding to a query on where this essay itself is situated, if culture is the basic frame of thinking and this essay wants West-China to interculture, as it considers both cultures in one of their languages, English. "Doesn't this essay fall into a bottomless quagmire of considering a matter with the matter itself, as investigating eyes with eyes?"

My response is that this essay does not duplicate China or the West. The essay is neither totally Chinese nor totally Western, and therefore it is congenial in both milieus, though this essay is not quite either China or the West. The essay is congenial to both yet provocative to both.

To begin, China does not define and argue as this essay does; nor does the West see anything like this essay that "argues concretely" in this story-way. At the same time, China finds this essay's story-thinking familiar, and the West finds its argumentation congenial. The upshot is that this essay serves as a friendly invitation, an inviting catalyst, for both to come

---

[79] See Erich Fromm's posthumous *The Art of Listening*, NY: Continuum, 1994.

together, shaking hands from opposite ends, dialoguing to learn from one another in mutual appealing provocation among different frames of thinking.

Moreover, far from logically empty, "tautology" among actual *existents* is inter-involving, inevitable and enriching.[80] To be oneself as oneself (A is A), as one stands-out (exists) against the others different (not non-A), is one's existential exercise to authenticate oneself.

Interculture is an exercise in cultural tautology, and so it comes quite natural. Naturally, this essay is an extension of what I have been doing ever since I saw "Chuang Tzu as world philosopher at play" in 1982 (Crossroads). Since then I have been reveling among our spines that vibrate China and the West inter-resonating. How do I do it?

With the Chinese eye I learn from the West, as I learn from China with the Western eye, in all their inter-rhythms, never simply fitting the other culture into the lens of any one culture. These "eyes" are logical sensitivity (not logic) in analytical perceptiveness (not analysis), gained by China's sensitivity gone *through* the fire of the West's logical exactitude.

All pages above and below are refreshing harvests of such *fresh* learning of China in the West and of the West in China. These eyes seeing and learning do not fit the West into China's frame, much less fitting China into the West's frame, but allowing China and the West to gaze *at* each other in amazement, sensitive and perceptive, to redound to deepen their respective selves.

Now, Confucius is no tiresome teacher of tired platitudes but an insistent man on life's way, ever yearning after the spontaneity of joyous humanity in love with fresh daily evocation from history, from friends, and from Heaven and Earth. Chuang Tzu is no longer a timid reclusive relativist; he is shown to lustily play with profundity, persistently blazing irresistible vitality, soaring into actuality self-forgetting.

At the same time, seen from China, Plato is no longer a pattern-setter but an avid initiator of passionate vision. No wonder everyone ever since has been following suit, to form a "series of footnotes" to him. Aristotle his student is less a meticulous cataloguer than an eye-opening synthesizer. Kant opens my eyes to concrete "critical Socratism" of drama-sensitive Gabriel Marcel. And the list goes on. Everyone comes out *alive*.

In such existentially tautological manner, the West comes alive *as itself* in China, as the West etches forth China *as China* so distinctive; both China and the West shake hands by standing inter-opposite, smiling heartfelt, inter-fulfilled. Thanks to their radical frame-differences, our routine actual world sparkles in shimmering mystery in daily lure of deeper living ahead, self-bettering together. Our shared joy makes us cherish our frame-differences all the more, to inter-learn to inter-deepen each other.

FIVE: OUR GOAL IS NOT MONOCULTURE BUT INTERCULTURE

What is said above on frames inter-learning is not an idle pie in the theoretical sky. Interculture is forced on us living in our world-cultural Global Village today. We must deal with pesky cultural differences somehow, in our daily intercourse journalistic, economic, sociopolitical, and inter-continental.

---

[80] The reader can see that our consideration of the law of identity as this essay began, and repeated in the middle, is rehashed afresh here.

Our world today *is* a multicultural world, whether we like it or not. Our US markets are flooded with products made in China, in Thailand, in Venezuela, in almost anywhere except in USA. We simply must deal with so many cultures rushing into our daily lives in *our* neighborhood.

"How do we deal with these bewildering 'alien cultures'?" Let us respond to this crucial question. We have two ways of dealing with the world's many cultures, monoculture easy and lethal, and interculture natural and nourishing. Let us consider *monoculture*, then interculture.

Monoculture

We would instinctively lord over alien others with our own frame—"Where are you from?" we proudly ask—to glorify in *our* Pax Americana, identifying modernity as unilaterally Western if not American. That is an easy way out, and a sure way to world domination into world collapse, perishing in isolation, even in isolation in monocultural world dominance, to perish in isolation together, to die an odd death of the lonely crowd.

In fact, our world today is actually dying of odd monoculture-death. "Is monoculture so deadly?" Let me explain. We know monoculture has three varieties, ethnocentrism, appropriation, and universalism. In ancient days, *ethnocentrism* was the rule. "Central Kingdom 中國" was China; "the Root of the Sun 日本" was transliterated as Japan. The sun never set on the United Kingdom; exotics were "barbarous" to the civilized Greeks and Jews.

Such ethnocentrism often despised and rejected other cultures. Wars often broke out of this frame; wars have been our favorite ploy to smash others different. Wars continue even today as in Palestine. God forbid if the State of Israel was built on this base of hatred.[81] God forbid if the Communist China today flourished militarily in xenophobia to wash its historical shame of invasions in the recent Ch'ing Dynasty.

After ethnocentrism come today's two monocultural varieties, appropriation and universalism. Things culturally different from our familiars are understood in our terms, interpreted in our frame, and what cannot be thus *appropriated* are neglected, or thrown into the museum-basket of "ancient obsolete superstition." To compound the woes of appropriation, the appropriated cultures often admire the strong appropriating culture as their authentic selves so modern today.

All agree that these alien exotics are to be substituted with *today's* analytical logic and natural science universally applicable. Such *universalism* is the third variety of monoculture. It is of course Western; the Euro-America is modernized civilization, one and only. Modernity in fashion today is Western logic and Western science; there exists no other sort of logic or science.

Why? Simple; it is because *all* things are handle-able by the West's analytical objectivism, and so all things are *nothing but* objects of analysis. Is it a fallacy of distribution, or of misplaced totality? It is clearly a fallacy of universalism so slippery that it has various heads. Such simple fallacy of universalism is committed by monoculture to bulldoze over nature into eco-disasters; it is monoculture come of age, universalism in other-appropriation, ever blind to its tacit assumption of ethnocentrism.

---

[81] "United States" and "European Union" escape connotations of ethnocentric monoculture, though I wish they had names less ambiguous, e.g., "Federated States" or "Federated Europe," or "league," or "pact."

"All this Western stuff is good for you and for us all"; such a "good will" paves the way to hell of perdition. It is because monoculture perilously performs "ethnic cleansing" for cultural purity more extensive than military Hitler's and brutal Milosevic's put together. It spells death to various human races and cultures, killing their futuristic fertility. Eco-disasters physical and cultural under unilateral "natural science" are the result. Monoculture is the lethal crime against humanity.

Interculture

Now, the alternative to deadly monoculture is naturally "interculture" in which all cultures thrive into their respective selves under Mother Nature inside us and around, birthing without ceasing, as both Greek *phusis* and Chinese 生生不息 (birthing, birthing, without ceasing) amply indicate. *Interculture* is the only way to our thriving together, all of us, and this way goes inter-framing. Interculture is, however, easily confused with two pursuits unrelated to it.

One, because interculture stresses letting China be China, not Western, and letting the West be Western, not universal,[82] it can be taken as another parochial patriotism, "*our* nation good or not!" we shout.[83] But interculture is inter-learning among *many* different cultures, not parochialism self-sealed in obsolescent rural tibalism.

Two, because interculture is global, it is taken as a bland universal culture beyond local ones, but interculture is interaction among *local* cultures. As patriotism is ethnocentric monoculture, so world culture is universalistic monoculture, a Platonism. Interculture has nothing to do with either sort of monoculture universalized.

Let me be specific. Interculture inter-changes all parties involved, while monoculture changes not itself, just others. Monoculture absorbs another culture into ours, taking it as just a part of our own. Our culture is *the* universal frame that interprets everything under our sun. Nothing here changes to change everything there into here.

Interculture in contrast inter-listens to mutual frame-differences to inter-learn, to inter-change to inter-enrich respective integrities of all cultures. Each frame warms up the novel other to renovate and deepen its own familiar frame. Here happens a continuing dialogue to inter-evoke for each to grow, i.e., to change into each richer deeper self, as it is provoked by the other to listen to the other and learn from it.

Thus monoculture changes the other into our own unchanging frame, to destroy the *other* culture-frame in meticulous suffocation, in euthanasia all around, where the dominating culture perishes by no longer standing-out (literally ex-isting) against the dominated now vanished. Interculture in contrast changes *both* culture-frames, ours and yours, and we grow into us as you grow into you.

---

[82] See my "'Let Chinese Thinking Be Chinese, Not Western': Sine Qua Non to Globalization," *Dao: A Journal of Comparative Philosophy*, 2010, pp. 192-209, refurbished into the last chapter of my *Chinese Wisdom Alive*, NY: Nova Science Publishers, 2010, pp. 451-484.

[83] E.g., patriotism in vogue in China in the early 20th century comes to mind; see an important document on the fierce patriotic debates then on how to deal with foreign cultures, 翼教叢編, 楊菁點校, 臺北中央研究院中國文哲研究所, 民94.

To have interculture, we must see how many frames of thinking our world has. Our shared world has at least three different frames. At the base of the [a] West's logic and [b] China's story-thinking, things are vibrating in [c] music-rhythm that resonates with all our thinking.

All things shake syn-chronically sym-spatially, all sym-pathetically. Western theoretical physics tells us so, to join China's Yin-Yang inter-resonance among contraries in Heaven and Earth among myriads of things,[84] waiting to be clarified by the West's logical precision. It is vibration *together* among *different* tunes of rhythm.

Such vibration is in rhythm among different tunes; it is music of all varied things, the music of many spheres *of* this world actual and concrete. Perhaps logic-thinking and story-thinking, so inter-different, would naturally gather, and should gather, to vibrate in musical rhythm together into "nature-thinking," made possible only in interculture.

"Now, *how* do we gather to interculture into such world nature-thinking?" This is a critical question, isn't it? It is differences that gather, and difference is alien, and we instinctively shrink from alien difference outside us, but shaking hands requires standing mutually opposite; we cannot shake hands standing on the same side, one single side.

"But how can we shake hands standing opposite to each other?" Confucius says of the necessity of warming up the old to know the new (2/11). We on our part insist, "We must warm up the alien new to know our old, before we can each warm up our respective old frames *afresh* to know the new outside us."[85]

Here, learning heartfelt, to realize that the other so irritatingly alien is after all my alter ego, is a necessary precondition for body-knowing "oneself as another" that Ricoeur facilely rehearsed.[86] Such inter-learning happens in intercultural gathering; it is so inter-revolutionary as to shake us up *out* of our respective cozy frames, to com-pose our global kaleidoscope of families. Different members make up a family of differences that makes for family "concord," literally "together-heartfelt," inter-hearted.

The family of differences in the actual world is much more complex than we suspect. Our thinking, words, and actuality never fit well, and one always distorts the others. Poetry shows such deranged distortion as in Kung-sun Lung's punch, "White horse, not a horse." It is a distorted relation as Chuang Tzu's "myriad things and I make one" (2/52-53) is. Both distorted relations are poetic, rhythmic, and logical, to wit, reasonable and world-singing.

We say "these sayings" are wrong; they smile and point at us, saying, *we* are in "illusion of consistency" among thinking, words, and actuality. A dramatic example of our misfit with actuality is how we relate to the child. The child is starkly with us for us to care for, yet the artists have to "imagine the childhood."[87] Those painters are of course adults, worlds apart from the child, and what they imagine and express in words of paintings are so "ugly," distorted away from the innocent beauty of the spontaneous child.

These painters try through the ages, of course, and their very *trying* to go close to the child drives them away from the actual child. The more they try, the farther away they are

---

[84] Egypt, Greece, Rome, India, and Tibet all knew that rhythmic vibration is the basic force in the universe. See an all-sweeping volume by Jonathan Goldman, *Healing Sounds: The Power of Harmonics*, Shaftesbury, Dorset, UK: Element, 1992.

[85] My *On Metaphoring: A Cultural Hermeneutic*, Leiden: Brill, 2001, is built on this insistence.

[86] Paul Ricoeur, *Oneself as Another*, University of Chicago Press, 1992.

[87] See a historical collection of childhood-paintings by Erika Langmuir, *Imagining Childhood*, Yale University Press, 2006.

from the simple child. They try to depict adult treatment of the child more than presenting the subtle depth and disarming sublimity of the child itself.

The "childhood" they "imagine" is their adult childhood, a contradiction, a distorted relation to the child. Mencius sighs that the great adults lose none of their baby heart (4B12). These painters have lost their baby-heart at their core, for they *are* adults "imagining childhood" that has nothing to do with the actual child. But the child does not paint-well, and its relied-on painters and the child together make up the paintings of the child so imperfect, so unlike the child.

Such lack of perfect fit pushes life forward as the child does us. Imperfection (child) in de-ranged distortion (adult paintings) is the dynamo of living-on. Distortion is life that abhors it; de-ranged distortion mothers medicine to put us together healthy, and such continual putting-together, never complete, makes life alive if not worth living.

Name scholars and Chuang Tzu in ancient China present the realm of such unity of radical differences in frame-deepening and frame-de-ranging, and this "and" makes the cosmic Yin-Yang dynamics of poetic logic of things logically poetic. This move expresses the "righting" of "righting names." To say all this in itself, as we have it here, cannot thus be straightly logical but makes a collection that is logically poetic; it is a celebration of de-ranged cosmos alive, where world dissonance makes world harmonics. It is globalization in localization.[88]

Imperfection depicts misfits and distortions that are forwarding life without ceasing, ever de-ranged, ever growing to arrange itself repeatedly, to align itself with actuality, to express in language, and all this comes out in poetry as vignettes of living-logic. Such is the Music of the Spheres in us *and* around, and this "and" is ever dissonant rhythmic, throbbing alive, in globalization.

Such is the poetry of world logic, the world-prose in human words dissonant and rhythmic, throbbing as the world irresolutely actual, in life-seasons beginning at the child ever beginning, wobbly alive. Children have no logic but poetry the life-logic disarming beyond us. Kids need no license to drive tricycles, and they give their hatred to Mother Nature. "Mom, I hate Charlie; I want to kill him." Mom says, "Ok, you can kill him tomorrow. Now, come eat, dear." "Ok, mom," and all hatred is forgotten, no-do, in Mother Nature.

Once I asked a little missy, "Do you like to be pretty?" She softly nodded, to move me deeply. So I said, "I like to be pretty, too," and we parted good pals. I thought of why she moved me so deeply, and I nodded to myself. It was when her child-heart touched my deep heart quite genuine, beyond all pretension, conscious or unconscious. Such child-heart is the root of all scholarship, Li Chih said.[89]

To stop such thoughts on child-living from wandering into reveries, let us think of time lived into history. I live on as my moment flows from this one to the next. All this while, I recognize the continuation of this moment from that moment, and all this continuation I recognize as mine. This recognition of mine composes and constitutes my self, my identity. This re-cognition is my con-sciousness, my self-consciousness, as my I-identity, to distinguish me from mere animal living immediate, non-self-aware.

---

[88] Essays by Drs. Chang and Sun in our volume above detail these points, but in their distinct ways.

[89] "童心說" in 李贄文集, 北京社會科學文獻出版社, 2000, I:91-93.

To lose such self-composing con-sciousness loses the self, says neuropsychologist Sacks.[90] Such immediate self-consciousness—childlike—from one moment to the next is "history." So history is my self-composition. History is my immediate self continuing. Observing the self-composing process composes history. History is the originative-knowledge most intimate, the originative-science most basic. History is my today; I am history as I continue to live on.

The science of history differs from, to originate, the usual knowledge, *usual* science, of sensory experience and experience of thinking, of ideation. The West has been keen on the usual sciences of objective experience, not experience itself. China has been living in history to express history in narrative literature. Such history is the originative natural science of—knowledge of—history. It is about time—the world history is ripe now—for the West and China to join to develop a "science of history."

The science of history is not history but history made self-conscious as sublimated "scientific objectivity" of the West, self-consciousness (history) through the ages made self-conscious (science of history) today, to develop further as such. This science of all sciences is incorruptible while a series of dying continues through time. The science of history is the fruit of interculture globalizing.[91]

Finally, allow me to divulge this fascinating scene to you. Wittgenstein's notional fibers crisscrossing[92] parallel Bach's fugue-network of notes crisscrossing to enrich one another; remember music-thinking that vibrates with things vibrating in musical rhythm? Such thing-music is life-inevitable, and forever fresh and unexpected. Do we hear naughty Tommy shouting, "I just wanna!"? He always initiates a refreshing music of life!

This cosmic music is so stable and fresh that it can be stopped listening any moment, and we feel we are fulfilled right there, not cut off in the middle of nowhere. Such is Bach's piano-works; they resonate with webs of traffic on life's way Lao Tzu calls "heaven net" (73), among all existents vibrating in musical rhythm at their bones.

Lao Tzu is a Bach with natural heaven's web of contingent events, constantly crisscrossing to weave out one tapestry after another of woe in weal, weal in woe, and the Uncle Fort is the hero who rides on the crest of such inter-involved web-waves of contrary contingencies. This network is fugue-like (Bach), notional (Wittgenstein), and event-full (Lao Tzu, Huai Nan Tzu), all at once. Now, have you seen interculture at work here? Isn't globalization going on here?

Here, each element, each event, must refer to all others to understand itself and others, *and* thereby the whole network. Hofstadter[93] tried something similar among Gödel, Escher, and Bach, and fell far short of their triune *inter*-involvements on all three levels, musical, notional, and event-full, all intercultural, spreading through the cosmos globalizing world without end.

Now, have you noticed it? Our very *saying* all this amounts to calling out attention to *begin* to net these networks. Such netting the nets is "interculture," isn't it? And *we* ourselves must net the nets. Being in this world-cultural Global Village, we have a job to do on this

---

[90] See "Mr. Thompson" in Oliver Sacks, *The Man Who Mistook His Wife for a Hat*, Touchstone, 1998.

[91] Dr. Tang's essay on "history in globalization" develops this theme, but in his distinctive way.

[92] Ludwig Wittgenstein, *Philosophical Investigations* (1953), NY: Macmillan, 1968, §§66-67, p. 32^e. He was a musician, and the image here must have been inspired by musical intertwining of notes.

[93] Douglas R. Hofstadter, *Gödel, Escher, Bach: An Eternal Golden Braid*, NY: Random House, 1980.

Village, to wit, to turn it into such grand nature-network of grand globalization that begins at this tiny saying.

Interculture heads to inter-species inter-being all in Mother Nature. As flowers and bees compose life-concord, all beings come alive by inter-species, which is the origin of interculture. Interculture is an absolute must for each culture to engage to come alive as itself. Here everyone is a winner, even among species. Globalization wins everyone.

A beautiful deer with young prim horns wandered into my neighbor Clark's yard. He proudly proclaimed, "That deer slept in *my* yard!" "It did not sleep in mine," I timidly admitted, and then asked, "Did he eat your flowers?" He grinned, "He ate my crabapples," as he brought out a pail of water; the deer drank from it. Then, mumbling, "He will grow big yet," he picked some fruit from branches too high for deer to reach, leaving some for the birds. We are all excited. I even dreamed that deer that night.

"Our deer" is Nature's outrageously free gift of joy to us all. I am sure the deer pleases us more than he is fed. Life is now so full, with joys and privileges of inter-species in our eco-family all the time, all so softly hushed, for we do not want to disturb the deer. We call it feeding deer; kids call it fun playing. And then, some days later, the deer left us. We now feed so many birds so different from us, again. We still miss that deer, as Clark mumbles, "He may come back…" We nodded in silence.

The fun is in feeding deer so new and different from birds. To feed is to play, for play feeds, and new play is new dawn. Every day dawns a kid to join other kids to shout and play. A kid watching beside soon joins in. We kids at dawn relish jumping into our frame-games. Kids call the relishing, "play," play learning from deer and birds on how to feed them. Learning is playing, isn't it? Such inter-learning is interculture, isn't it?

We have so many kids of deer and birds to learn from to feed them *their* ways, to play games of life together. Adults call kids' play-together "inter-handling thinking-frames." Whatever we call it, it is awesomely *fun*, as things keep changing and we keep playing new games of new thinking, new cultures in new species-frames, to feed one another. We have watched such life-playing of globalization long enough. Shall we join in? Thanks for the fun, folks.

CODA: DAWN, POETRY, MUSIC

Seven is a lucky number to chant globalization in Dawn, Poetry, and Music. Here are the seven stanzas of the chant.

1. The future is the dawn singing inevitable coherence that is what things are all over. The dawn is moving, here not here, now turning, on the go out into morning.

2. Globalization is such Dawn, and such Dawn into the future is globalization. What is globalization? Such Dawn is. What is the dawn coming out together? It is globalization. Dawn, Poetry, and Music form a dynamic synonymy to compose globalization on and on.

3. No one minds such synonymy on the dawning. It is not an It but a milieu in which we live and move alive, and the milieu is itself Mother Nature alive moving on. Dawn in Poetry of Music gives smiles, so globalization gives the joy of spring breeze birthing.

4. Globalization as Dawn, Poetry, and Music gives joy to demand joy. Globalization requires us to create joy of Dawn in poetic Music. We must create joy, as we are demanded by joy of Dawn, Poetry, and Music. Dawn chants Music in rhythm of Poetry of sense in rhyme. We must join, with hands and hearts, into cosmopolitan togetherness. Our joyous struggles toward such joy are themselves Dawn in Poetry of Music global. Our struggles are globalization of joy in the making.

5. Dawn is silent, while Poetry and Music silently intone Dawn-silence. Silence ciphers our tacit nature, our ordinary routines in daily Mother Nature. We must silently live out Dawn in Poetry of Music as if nothing is the matter.

6. Dawn, Poetry, and Music can be dotted with kicks and jolts, shocks and scares. Dawn, Poetry, and Music go on in bumps, to wail sometimes, to shout in elation some other times. Dawn-silence reigns over all such jolts and joys into Poetry and Music. All this is the stunt globalization pulls on us. We ride on its crest of the waves, come what may, into Dawn, Poetry, and Music deepened by such bumps.

7. Universal is inter-versal to inter-shuttle in dialogues among local cultures, into Dawn of Poetry and Music of globalization. We are here now invisible in its midst, to serve as its Workers

INDEX

A

Abraham, 5, 247
abstraction, 162
abuse, xiv, 235
access, 5, 17, 19, 20, 21, 26, 28, 29, 30, 32, 37, 38, 90
accessibility, 77
accommodation, 61, 64, 65, 66, 67
accountability, 38, 42, 46, 48, 49, 50, 51, 52
accounting, 28
acculturation, 76
acid, 142
acidic, 222
actual output, 47
actuality, viii, xxiii, xxvii, xxix, 95, 96, 108, 110, 111, 112, 113, 114, 162, 163, 178, 180, 185, 186, 191, 202, 208, 209, 211, 212, 242, 243, 245, 252, 257, 262, 265, 266, 268, 269, 270, 271, 300, 302, 303, 304, 305, 313, 315, 318, 320, 323, 324
acupuncture, 143, 145
AD, 56, 57
adaptation, 20, 152, 191
adaptations, 191
adequate housing, 5
adjustment, 77, 295
administrators, 46
adolescents, 67, 246
adults, xviii, 67, 161, 163, 235, 269, 281, 323, 324
advocacy, xxvi, 41, 317
aesthetic, 286
affirming, 290
Africa, vii, xxviii, xxix, 1, 3, 6, 7, 15, 17, 18, 19, 20, 21, 22, 23, 24, 26, 27, 28, 29, 30, 31, 33, 34, 45, 198, 290
age, xx, 7, 15, 54, 136, 164, 294, 318, 321
agencies, 10, 20, 29, 36, 38, 39, 41, 46, 47, 48, 50, 51
agricultural sector, 37

Algeria, 29, 30, 31
ambassadors, 253
American culture, 59, 198
American Psychiatric Association, 56, 67
American Psychological Association, 68
amphibians, xxx
ancient world, 225
anger, 138, 220
anthropologists, 56
anthropology, 51, 56, 76
antithesis, 108, 109
anxiety, vii, xxviii, 1, 46, 55, 56, 57, 58, 59, 61, 65, 67, 68, 69, 138
anxiety disorder, 56, 57, 59, 67, 68, 69
apples, 95
architects, 81
Argentina, 3
Aristotle, xxix, 109, 111, 242, 294, 315, 320
arson, 56, 57
articulation, 90
Asia, 5, 23, 27, 28, 29, 33, 37, 50, 51, 52, 53, 120, 203, 274
Asian countries, 78
aspiration, 95
assessment, 48, 53, 57, 58
assets, 9, 42
asymmetry, 42
atmosphere, 185, 224
atoms, 155, 296
atrocities, 203, 206, 220, 282
attachment, 68
attitudes, 39, 41, 49, 58, 59, 66, 68, 74
authenticity, xv, xix, 299
authority, 42, 51, 75
autonomic nervous system, 142
autonomy, 46, 47
avoidance, 12, 56, 67
avoidance behavior, 67

awareness, 48, 88, 182, 219, 226, 234, 278, 286, 292, 308, 309

B

background information, 77, 180
background noise, 121, 126
bacteria, 217
bail, 10, 13
bandwidth, 26, 28, 29, 30
Bangladesh, vii, xxviii, xxix, 1, 35, 38, 39, 40, 41, 42, 43, 44, 45, 46, 47, 49, 50, 51, 52, 53, 54, 100, 285
bankers, 95
banking, 13
bankruptcy, 37
banks, 6, 10, 11, 42
barriers, 26, 45, 47
base, x, xvii, xix, 19, 29, 32, 38, 41, 51, 110, 113, 149, 157, 159, 160, 163, 201, 238, 239, 248, 296, 299, 321, 323
basic education, 53
behavior therapy, 57, 58, 67
behavioral problems, 57
behaviorism, 61, 66
Behaviorism, 57
behaviors, 57, 60, 61, 65, 67, 72, 73, 78, 108, 294, 295
belief systems, 38
beneficiaries, 42, 51, 52
benefits, vii, xxx, 4, 8, 13, 14, 15, 18, 31, 37, 41, 45, 67, 74, 81, 92, 110, 164, 171, 175, 178, 180, 205, 215, 230, 303
benign, 299
Bhutan, 100
bias, 39, 71, 72, 74
bible, 80
Bible, xxv, 180, 212, 302, 303, 312
bilingualism, 72
birds, xxiii, xxvii, 99, 100, 139, 156, 185, 186, 208, 262, 287, 289, 298, 303, 307, 326
birth control, 14
births, xx, 160, 226, 283
black hole, 63
blame, 185
blends, 232
blindness, 219, 294, 316
blogs, 73
blood, x, 15, 63, 165, 209, 241, 282, 319
blood pressure, 63, 241
body fat, 67
bone, xix, xxiii, 162, 216, 222, 282
bones, xix, xxiii, 162, 216, 222, 261, 282, 325

boreholes, 7
Botswana, 19, 26, 30, 31
boxing, 64
brain, 164
brainwashing, 80
Brazil, 3, 100
breathing, 16, 99, 122, 123, 126, 140, 142, 150, 166, 189, 190
bribes, 46
Britain, 15, 16
Broadband, 28, 32
brothers, 178
brutality, xxiii, xxvii, 64, 203, 232
Buddhism, 60, 113, 120, 122, 132, 255, 269
budding, xi, 79
Burma, 100
Burundi, 31
Bush, George W., xxx
business ethics, 231
businesses, x, 13, 190, 217, 231, 309
Butcher, 56, 57, 68

C

cable system, 27
cables, 19
Cameroon, 9
campaigns, 111
cancer, 63, 202
capacity building, 50
capitalism, 91
capsule, 179
Caribbean, 23
Carter, Jimmy, 9
cartoon, 281
case studies, 39
case study, 39, 52, 53
cash, 6, 210
cash crops, 6
catalysis, 242
catalyst, xxiii, xxv, 172, 173, 187, 270, 289, 291, 319
categorization, 177
causality, 225
CERN, 31
certificate, 43
Chad, 272, 281, 316
challenges, 21, 38, 39, 44, 48, 52, 53, 72, 73, 74, 76, 77, 81, 159, 164, 207, 245, 246, 307
chaos, 63, 88, 89, 114, 116, 117, 126, 255, 277
charities, 11
chat rooms, 77
chemical, 62, 80
Chicago, 28, 33, 172, 191, 202, 262, 273, 290, 323

chicken, 274
child mortality, 7
childhood, 67, 323, 324
children, xix, 5, 7, 9, 10, 15, 19, 67, 77, 120, 161, 163, 178, 183, 216, 220, 226, 230, 257, 258, 295
Chile, 26
Chinese medicine, 111, 135, 136, 142, 144, 145, 146, 149, 150, 152
chopping, 236
Christianity, xxii, 178, 179, 209, 267, 282
Christians, 303
Chuang Tzu, xx, xxxi, 55, 59, 64, 68, 69, 120, 121, 124, 128, 131, 132, 133, 173, 175, 177, 178, 180, 185, 186, 187, 189, 191, 192, 222, 246, 247, 250, 258, 260, 265, 267, 276, 284, 295, 296, 298, 300, 305, 306, 312, 315, 316, 320, 323, 324
citizens, 206, 207
citizenship, 43, 53
City, 156, 300, 313
civil society, 9, 36, 44, 45, 48, 49, 52
civilization, 12, 89, 97, 98, 99, 121, 183, 321
clarity, 125, 126, 129, 130, 158, 162, 163, 164, 311
classes, 245
classical conditioning, 57
classification, 132
classroom, 76
cleaning, 10, 219
clients, 57, 58, 59, 61, 62, 63, 65, 66, 250
climate, x, xviii, xxvi, xxvii
clinical symptoms, 57
closure, 222, 250
clothing, 279
clustering, 51
clusters, xxvii, 306
coercion, viii, 274
coffee, 6
cognition, 61, 140, 141, 324
cognitive function, 141
cognitive therapists, 59
cognitive therapy, 57, 58, 59, 60, 61, 63, 64, 65, 66, 67, 68
coherence, viii, ix, xxii, 160, 183, 200, 201, 209, 210, 211, 232, 233, 239, 244, 255, 286, 315, 326
cold war, 45, 51
collaboration, 28, 29, 77
collateral, 42
colonization, 46, 92
commerce, 18, 106, 108
commercial, 10, 11, 38, 42, 45, 91, 105, 156, 208, 218
commercial bank, 42
commodity, 41

common sense, vii, xv, 109, 158, 160, 164, 191, 208, 219, 238, 241, 261, 275, 291, 294, 306, 313
communication, xxviii, 19, 31, 32, 36, 44, 89, 90, 92, 93, 254, 271, 284, 300
communication technologies, 89
communism, 183
communities, 4, 37, 38, 39, 40, 44, 46, 47, 49, 53, 93, 107, 198, 206
community, 4, 9, 12, 15, 28, 39, 40, 41, 43, 44, 45, 46, 47, 48, 49, 52, 53, 71, 72, 79, 104, 105, 156, 197, 199, 200, 240, 242, 243, 258, 262, 274, 276, 280, 290, 291, 295, 299
community support, 49
compassion, 127, 231, 269
competition, x, 13, 22, 41, 48, 113, 229, 232, 235
competitive advantage, 17
competitiveness, 34
competitors, 229
complement, xv, 112, 159, 162, 166, 240, 293
complexity, 52, 183, 306, 311
compliance, 138
complications, 185, 308
composers, xix, xx, 188, 234, 253, 277, 310
composites, 243, 252
composition, xv, xix, 184, 188, 198, 202, 242, 283, 286, 325
comprehension, 150, 268, 278
computation, 31, 293, 299, 313
computer, 90, 284
computing, viii, 157, 225, 301
conception, 135, 136, 137, 139, 149, 152
conceptualization, 317
Concise, 175
concrete thinking, 157, 158, 161, 162, 163, 165, 208, 302
conditioning, 57, 124
conductors, xv
conference, 16, 75, 230
confession, 186, 211, 246, 278
confinement, 112
conflict, xiv, 45, 51, 57, 60, 61, 71, 113, 159, 235, 280
conflict resolution, 71
conformity, 47, 136, 281
confrontation, xv, 116, 159, 167, 280, 293
Confucianism, xxvi, 55, 111, 127, 132, 187, 188, 192, 274, 285, 316
Confucius, xxix, 4, 64, 88, 99, 122, 165, 166, 173, 178, 180, 183, 186, 187, 189, 192, 247, 266, 274, 275, 284, 294, 295, 296, 297, 298, 300, 303, 306, 309, 310, 315, 319, 320, 323
Congress, 274
congruence, 65

connectivity, 25, 26, 29, 30
conscious knowledge, 190
consciousness, 52, 88, 89, 140, 141, 142, 182, 294, 324, 325
consensus, 115, 117, 313
consent, xxv
conspiracy, 10
constituents, 42, 135, 136
construction, 210
consulting, 71, 207
consumers, 28, 29
consumption, 178, 245
contingency, xxiii, 156, 157, 200, 229, 265, 267, 293, 301, 302, 303, 304, 305, 306, 307, 309, 310, 311, 312, 313, 315
contour, 162
contradiction, 97, 110, 157, 161, 248, 301, 302
control group, 58
controversial, 41, 62
controversies, 178, 181, 244
convention, 105, 291, 309, 315, 316
conviction, 148, 267
cooking, 12
cooperation, 18, 29, 38, 61, 216
coordination, 80, 98
correlation, 22
corrupt governments, 3, 6
corruption, 8, 9, 46, 48, 49, 95, 311
cosmopolitanism, xi, 98, 206, 207, 257, 271, 272, 317
cosmos, xxvi, 151, 160, 182, 185, 224, 225, 229, 233, 252, 255, 258, 260, 267, 273, 275, 277, 283, 285, 286, 295, 298, 299, 324, 325
cost, 15, 19, 26, 28, 32, 41, 47, 100, 215
cotton, 6
counsel, 301
counseling, vii, xxviii, 1, 61, 62, 68, 71, 72, 73, 74, 75, 76, 77, 78, 79, 80, 81, 250, 294
counseling psychology, 71, 72, 73, 74, 75, 76, 78, 81
country music, 224
covering, xxix, 26, 27
creativity, 115, 179
crimes, 10, 206
criminality, 230
criminals, 95, 247
crises, 10, 191
criticism, 147, 192, 209, 220
Croatia, 53
crops, 6
cross-fertilization, 190
crossing over, 301
CT, 54
cues, 73

cultivation, 128, 140, 141, 142, 189, 231, 285, 295, 309
cultural conditions, 36, 48
cultural differences, 56, 175, 179, 289, 291, 293, 302, 314, 320
cultural heritage, 182, 183, 201, 204
cultural norms, 46
cultural tradition, 41, 74, 192
cultural values, 78
cure, xxx, 14, 15, 16, 56, 71, 79, 80, 98, 99, 112, 136, 148, 150, 203
cures, 16, 80
currency, 6, 85
current account, 43
cycles, 229
cyclones, 182, 255

D

daily living, xxvii, 105, 204, 228, 229, 243, 299
dance, 234, 255, 273, 296
dancers, 277
dances, 296, 299
danger, xviii, 37, 79, 80, 110
data collection, 39
data transfer, 31
database, 19, 32
deaths, 226, 271
debt service, 7
debts, 6, 7, 16, 285
decentralization, 43
deconstruction, 127
decoration, xxiii, 124
deduction, 199, 210
defects, 181
defense mechanisms, 57
deforestation, 218
democracy, vii, xxvii, 37, 53, 189, 207, 240, 247, 290
demography, 90
Denmark, 10
deposits, 10, 46
depression, 63, 67
depth, 35, 39, 87, 90, 140, 141, 150, 206, 212, 254, 258, 262, 324
desensitization, 57, 58, 64
desiccation, 137, 138
despair, 4
destiny, 86
destruction, xvi, 53, 93, 112, 121, 222
detachment, 75
determinism, 210, 225
devaluation, 36

developed countries, 9, 10, 18, 21, 32, 46, 48, 90
developed nations, 90, 91
developing countries, 5, 6, 10, 19, 20, 34, 36, 37, 42
developing nations, vii, xxviii, 1, 3, 43, 81, 285
devolution, 48
diabetes, 241
dialogues, vii, xiii, xiv, xxviii, 83, 104, 106, 114, 117, 159, 163, 164, 166, 186, 189, 192, 196, 197, 198, 199, 201, 208, 209, 210, 237, 239, 244, 247, 261, 265, 269, 278, 279, 293, 327
dichotomy, 311
diet, 138
digestion, 147
digital divide, 26, 27, 29, 33
dignity, 201, 202, 225, 256
direct investment, 18
disaster, 9, 12, 13, 48, 80, 92, 93, 96, 97, 98, 99, 203, 206, 207, 215, 218, 222, 225, 226, 229, 230, 234, 256, 261, 286, 287, 311
disclosure, 10
diseases, 5, 15, 80, 135, 136, 138, 143, 144, 146, 148, 149, 150, 276
disorder, 56, 57, 67, 68, 69, 146, 277
disposition, 73
dissonance, 177, 185, 232, 241, 243, 244, 252, 255, 324
distinctness, 243, 271, 289
distortions, 97, 174, 324
distress, 57, 138
distribution, 19, 29, 42, 321
divergence, 294
diversification, 92
diversity, 74, 76, 92, 93, 98, 100, 101, 200, 249
divorce rates, 232
DNA, 136, 149
doctors, xxv, 148, 149, 185, 225, 250
DOI, 25, 33
dominance, vii, x, xiv, xxviii, 83, 86, 164, 190, 240, 272, 290, 293, 317, 321
donations, 41
donors, 19, 38, 41, 42, 43, 44, 45, 46, 47, 49, 51
drawing, xxiii, 125, 192, 193, 199, 206, 227, 254, 298
dream, x, xi, xvi, xxiv, xxv, xxvii, xxix, xxx, 94, 95, 97, 99, 107, 121, 208, 231, 236, 272, 282
dreaming, 97, 268, 278
drugs, 146
drying, 287
dynamic factors, 73
dynamism, 304
dyspepsia, 136

E

earnings, 45
earthquakes, 206, 303
East Asia, 5, 120, 128, 132, 269, 318
echoing, 275, 277, 311
ecology, xvii, xxviii, xxix, xxx, 193, 215, 216, 217, 218, 219, 220, 221, 222, 223, 224, 225, 226, 227, 228, 229, 230, 231, 233, 234, 236, 262, 286
economic change, 15, 39
economic development, 47
economic disparity, 12
economic empowerment, 40
economic growth, 17, 19, 32, 33, 37, 38
economic integration, 31
economic problem, vii, xxviii, 1
economic progress, 17, 18, 19, 21, 31
economic relations, 36
economics, vii, xxviii, 1, 53, 90, 98, 215
Edgar Allen Poe, 126
education, xxx, 6, 7, 15, 16, 17, 18, 19, 21, 22, 23, 28, 29, 30, 31, 32, 33, 34, 41, 42, 52, 53, 78, 105, 115, 182, 183, 188, 189, 196, 290, 296, 309
educational institutions, 24, 25
educational services, 71
educational system, 73
educators, 72, 73, 76, 78
egg, 231, 274
egoism, 59
Egypt, 4, 26, 29, 30, 31, 228, 323
elaboration, 56, 67, 164, 180, 184
election, 310
electricity, 43
electrons, 155
e-mail, 73, 77
emergency, 15, 62, 145
emotion, 68, 315
empathy, 184, 319
employment, 37, 40, 49, 144
empowerment, 40, 42, 43, 49, 51, 52
encouragement, 244
enemies, xiv, 11, 206, 207, 209, 215, 227, 228, 232, 248
energy, 123
enforcement, 10, 11
engineering, 33
England, xxviii, 13, 16, 35, 52, 67, 68, 99, 209, 273
enrollment, 7
entrepreneurs, 42
entrepreneurship, 53
entropy, 275
environment, 20, 64, 105, 108, 112, 138, 219, 249, 276

environmental change, 33
environmental conditions, 57
environmental crisis, 49, 53
environments, 57, 104
epistemology, 307
EPR, 50
equal opportunity, 19
equality, 240, 278
equilibrium, 125
equipment, 31, 48
eros, 282
ethical issues, 40
ethics, 13, 219, 224, 230, 231
ethnocentrism, xxv, 281, 321
etiology, 57
EU, 29, 206
Eurasia, 29
Europe, 10, 14, 23, 28, 29, 30, 32, 86, 260, 290, 321
European Commission, 32, 50
European Union, 3, 321
euthanasia, 322
evidence, 48, 50, 53, 120, 253, 312
evil, xii, 12, 130, 291
evolution, 89, 186, 201, 216, 304
examinations, 148
exclusion, 40, 45, 49
excretion, 149
exercise, 36, 43, 101, 142, 268, 320
expenditures, 22, 23
expertise, 111, 119, 294
exploitation, xiv, xv, 49, 218
exposure, xxv, 10, 11, 57, 58, 106, 162, 203
extinction, vii, 92, 98, 104, 217, 218, 271

F

fabrication, xix
faith, 4, 45, 46, 209, 212, 312
families, 12, 67, 323
family life, 216, 225
family members, 160, 216, 220, 229, 231, 232, 233, 250
fat, 67
FDI, 18
fear, xvi, 58, 112, 135, 138, 204, 241, 302, 316
feces, 5
feelings, 48, 56, 57, 59, 65, 79, 97, 130, 138, 192, 228, 276
fertility, 322
fertilization, 190
fever, 63
fiber, 19, 27
fibers, 318, 325

fidelity, 177
fights, 223, 249
financial, 4, 6, 9, 10, 11, 13, 15, 18, 36, 37, 41, 45, 48, 60, 91, 270, 282
financial condition, 10
financial XE "financial" crisis, 37
financial XE "financial" institutions, 4, 9, 13
financial institutions, 6
financial institutions, 91
financial institutions, 282
financial resources, 37
financial support, 45
fine arts, 142
fish, ix, 60, 130, 177, 192, 228, 241, 299
fitness, 139, 192, 245
flavor, 105
flex, 111, 181
flexibility, 48, 104
flights, 156, 218
floaters, 64
flooding, 274
floods, 303
flowers, xxxi, 99, 100, 110, 156, 217, 274, 283, 287, 288, 300, 302, 306, 312, 326
fluid, 104, 117
folklore, 76
food, xxix, 14, 37, 141, 317
food security, xxix, 37
force, 10, 14, 16, 18, 43, 245, 323
foreign aid, vii, xxviii, 1, 47
foreign assistance, 43
foreign direct investment, 18
foreign policy, 90
forest fire, 218
formal education, 42
formation, 148
formula, 144
foundations, 11, 57, 247
fragility, xx, xxi, 303
fragments, 121, 145
framing, 55, 202, 291, 322
France, xxvi, 3, 27, 31, 178, 189
free trade, 36
freedom, 37, 60, 107, 108, 109, 110, 112, 113, 208, 308, 310
freezing, 303
Freud, 160, 198, 294
friction, 51, 279, 280
friendship, xxiv, xxv, xxvi, xxviii, 227, 250
fugue, 305, 310, 325
funding, 38, 41, 44, 47, 48
funds, 7, 9, 16, 38, 44, 47

G

generalized anxiety disorder, 57, 67, 68
Generalized Anxiety Disorder, 57
genes, 7
genre, 187, 188
geography, 90
George Berkeley, 286
Germany, 3, 16, 99, 109, 253
Gestalt, 291
global competition, 22, 41
global economy, 91
global leaders, 5
global management, 230
global prosperity, 12, 13
global scale, 18, 219
global trade, 11
global village, 73, 92
Global Village, x, xii, xxiv, xxvii, xxviii, xxx, 13, 100, 159, 164, 166, 167, 217, 219, 239, 245, 262, 279, 283, 284, 314, 320, 325
global warming, 271
glue, 173, 186, 187
God, xxvii, 5, 60, 165, 173, 208, 209, 228, 236, 246, 248, 256, 287, 302, 303, 311, 321
good deed, 220
goods and services, 18, 31, 91
goose, 300
governance, xxvii, 53, 54, 207, 282
government policy, 26
governments, 3, 6, 36, 46
governor, 111
grants, 7, 42
graph, 129
grass, x, xxiii, 15, 47, 182, 217, 221, 223, 260, 287, 312
grassroots, 13, 43
grazing, 219
Greece, xxv, 99, 144, 173, 273, 323
greed, xx, 10, 11, 12, 231, 310
Greeks, 89, 96, 273, 321
Green Revolution, 14
group therapy, 58
growth, 10, 17, 19, 32, 33, 37, 38, 52, 53, 95, 112, 116, 162, 241, 243, 245, 246, 256, 259, 263, 268, 290, 296
guardian, 16
guidance, 158
guidelines, 39
guilt, 64
guilty, 12
gunpowder, 164, 300, 313

H

halos, 228
Han dynasty, 143, 144
happiness, xii, xxi, 59, 100, 215, 216, 230
harmonization, 124, 125
harmony, 40, 135, 136, 137, 138, 139, 142, 143, 144, 146, 147, 149, 150, 151, 152, 186, 232, 243, 244, 252, 260, 275, 296, 310
harvesting, xxvii
Hawaii, 68, 120, 125, 132, 316
Hawking, Stephen, 267, 275
headache, 157, 315
healing, 59, 61, 62, 63, 80, 111, 142, 148, 149, 150, 151, 206, 222, 253, 286
health, ix, xxx, 6, 7, 8, 10, 16, 19, 20, 59, 61, 63, 68, 71, 72, 75, 76, 78, 81, 100, 135, 139, 151, 207, 220, 241, 253, 286
health care, 7, 68, 139
health services, 10
hegemony, 91, 98, 99
height, 4
helplessness, 222, 298
hermeneutics, 119
HHS, 120, 128, 129
higher education, 17, 18, 19, 21, 22, 23, 28, 29, 31, 32, 33, 34
historical reason, 302
holism, 101, 152
homeostasis, 116, 268
homes, 29, 181, 319
Honduras, 7, 9
honesty, 285
Hong Kong, 124, 132, 180, 297, 304, 315
horses, 301
host, 76
House, 32, 120, 123, 131, 241, 256, 296, 325
housing, 5
hub, 63, 172
Hui Tzu, 178, 187, 192
human actions, 108
human behavior, 78, 108
human body, 94, 157, 158, 159, 160, 257, 319
human capital, 17, 18
human development, 18, 105
human experience, 85, 86, 87, 89, 92, 101, 175
human health, 151
human nature, 68, 79, 274
human right, 4
human sciences, 319
human security, 53
humanism, 62, 66, 240
humidity, 137, 138

Hunter, 40, 51
hunting, 141
husband, 295
hydrogen, 156
hypnosis, 58, 68

I

ideal, xxix, xxx, 61, 79, 86, 97, 98, 100, 107, 165, 171, 172, 176, 208, 240, 257, 290, 303, 311, 318
ideals, 98, 111, 117, 308
identification, 58, 98
identity, 104, 105, 106, 110, 115, 122, 190, 201, 202, 244, 256, 289, 290, 291, 292, 299, 320, 324
ideology, 36, 37, 48, 203
illicit money flow, 3, 9, 11
illumination, 125, 128, 129, 130
illusion, xvii, 204, 323
image, 46, 126, 222, 281, 325
images, 298, 307
imagination, xi, xxiv, xxv, 100, 162, 201, 208, 236, 268, 285, 286
IMF, 5, 6, 7, 37, 91
imitation, 184
Immanuel Kant, 208
immortality, 122, 254, 301
immunization, 58
imperialism, 37
improvements, 9, 98
impulses, 57, 108
inadmissible, 281
inauguration, 311
incidence, 38
income, 5, 7, 13, 14, 20
independence, 15, 48, 107, 109, 112, 113, 197, 311
India, xxv, 3, 15, 27, 28, 99, 198, 203, 273, 323
Indians, 278
indirection, 308, 316
individualism, 46, 74, 110
individuality, 109, 112, 114
individuals, xiv, 4, 5, 46, 74, 77, 93, 104, 109, 111, 116, 182, 221, 273, 274, 283, 295
indolent, 305
Indonesia, 3, 52
induction, 156, 199, 210
industries, 6, 24, 40, 91, 92
industry, 8, 46, 115
inequality, x, 37, 44, 91
inevitability, 107, 160
infants, 230
infrastructure, 17, 18, 19, 25, 26, 27, 28, 29, 30, 31, 32, 33, 180
ingredients, 17, 87, 156

inheritance, 144
injure, 141
injury, 230
insane, 60, 62, 64, 80, 203, 249, 282
insanity, xx, 100, 262
insects, xx, 283, 312
insecurity, 37
instinct, 223, 230
institutions, 4, 6, 7, 9, 11, 13, 18, 19, 20, 21, 23, 24, 25, 28, 29, 30, 32, 33, 37, 42, 44, 53, 91, 282
insulation, 48
insulin, 142
integration, 18, 36, 37, 40, 55, 56, 65, 66, 73, 91, 138
integrity, xv, xvi, xxii, 158, 162, 175, 188, 195, 282, 290, 315
intellectual capital, 17, 18, 19, 21, 32, 33
intellectual property, 21, 23
intellectual property rights, 23
intelligence, 160
Inter-American Development Bank, 50
intercourse, vii, x, xxviii, 83, 280, 320
interdependence, 78, 112, 113, 213
interest rates, 6
international financial institutions, 6, 91
international law, 106, 218
International Monetary Fund, 5, 6, 7, 37, 91
internationalization, 22, 76
internship, 72
interpersonal relations, 68
intervention, 63, 64
intestine, 202
intimacy, 90, 278, 280, 299
introspection, 141
invasions, 321
investment, xxv, 7, 18, 21, 22, 50, 91, 100
investments, 25, 42, 48
investors, 6
IPO, 34
iron, 156, 160
irony, 137, 178, 316
irritability, 57
Islam, vii, xxviii, 1, 35, 37, 44, 46, 51, 285
isolation, 28, 40, 49, 103, 104, 106, 109, 110, 112, 114, 115, 116, 117, 157, 158, 161, 163, 245, 321
Israel, 81, 321
issues, xxix, 19, 21, 31, 36, 40, 42, 46, 47, 50, 53, 73, 75, 76, 77, 78, 92, 95, 103, 104, 114, 116, 128
Italy, xxv, 3, 99

J

Japan, xxv, 3, 10, 24, 99, 135, 136, 137, 142, 143, 145, 146, 147, 149, 150, 151, 152, 177, 178, 198,

203, 206, 209, 211, 228, 237, 269, 270, 274, 297, 300, 318, 321
Jews, 178, 250, 321
joints, 304
journalists, xxvii, 10, 115, 204, 205, 207
jumping, 66, 165, 177, 180, 217, 235, 236, 251, 254, 275, 302, 318, 326
jurisdiction, 11
justification, 61, 285, 286, 302

K

Kenya, 26, 27, 30, 31
Keynesian, 48
kicks, 327
kidney, 185
kill, 114, 115, 180, 203, 231, 232, 298, 324
kindergarten, 80, 200, 310
kinship, 250, 316
knowledge economy, 19, 33
knowledge-based economy, 17, 18, 19, 21, 24
Korea, 3, 24, 127, 132, 145, 274, 318

L

labeling, 65
laboratory studies, 77
lack of confidence, 41
lakes, 275
landlocked countries, 37
landscape, 22, 33, 73
languages, 36, 41, 71, 76, 127, 175, 182, 270, 319
Lao Tzu, xxii, 68, 128, 172, 173, 174, 178, 179, 180, 187, 224, 229, 235, 247, 288, 293, 295, 298, 301, 303, 304, 315, 317, 325
Large Hadron Collider, 31
Latin America, 7, 23, 24, 29
law enforcement, 11
laws, 11, 60, 106, 156, 171, 172, 184, 201, 218, 225, 277, 292, 308, 309
LDCs, 19, 21
lead, xv, 93, 113, 131, 143, 173, 183, 223, 289, 291, 313
leadership, 44, 45, 51
leadership development, 51
leaks, 60
learners, 309
learning, 18, 21, 28, 29, 30, 42, 48, 71, 72, 76, 80, 98, 111, 129, 160, 161, 163, 164, 167, 172, 183, 190, 204, 206, 223, 235, 244, 247, 254, 279, 292, 295, 305, 318, 319, 320, 322, 323, 326
legal protection, 12
Legalism, xxvi, 296

legend, 120, 165, 201, 243
legislation, 108
legs, 145
leisure, 8, 192, 265, 300
lens, 292, 305, 319, 320
lethargy, 219
liberalisation, 53
liberty, 240
life expectancy, 19
life-thinking, 81, 188
lifetime, 165, 220
light, xviii, 18, 24, 31, 104, 113, 123, 124, 129, 164, 205, 260, 276, 280, 290
Lincoln, Abraham, 247
loans, 6, 40, 42, 45, 48, 285
local community, 47
local conditions, 47
local government, 4, 9
localization, vii, xiv, xxviii, 83, 85, 86, 87, 89, 90, 91, 92, 93, 94, 95, 96, 98, 99, 100, 101, 260, 324
logical implications, 110
logical reasoning, 301
loneliness, 78, 222, 248, 260
longevity, 135, 136, 137, 138, 143, 149, 253, 283
love, xxi, xxii, xxiii, xxiv, 88, 95, 99, 165, 175, 216, 218, 222, 228, 235, 236, 248, 249, 253, 258, 280, 281, 285, 303, 304, 309, 317, 320
loyalty, xxvii, xxviii, 127, 269, 285
luminosity, 128
lying, 186

M

magnitude, 21
majority, 5, 13, 37, 41, 46, 62
man, xxiii, xxiv, 62, 64, 126, 127, 128, 160, 192, 198, 201, 272, 286, 305, 320
management, xvii, xxi, xxiii, 6, 9, 13, 47, 48, 49, 52, 57, 58, 67, 68, 69, 158, 215, 216, 217, 219, 220, 222, 223, 225, 230, 234, 236, 241, 262, 285
Mandarin, 275
manipulation, 158
manufactured goods, 208
mapping, 39
marginalization, 52
market economy, 91
marrow, 222
marsh, 60
martial art, 142
Martin Heidegger, 125, 128, 129, 131, 268, 277, 290
Marx, xxvi, 8, 38, 52, 86, 178, 272
mass, 10, 16, 37, 115
materials, 76

mathematics, 156, 164, 186, 299, 303, 308
matrix, 315
matter, xiv, xxiii, xxix, xxxi, 4, 10, 12, 16, 46, 56, 79, 87, 104, 115, 122, 146, 148, 151, 158, 165, 184, 206, 207, 212, 218, 219, 221, 225, 239, 244, 253, 262, 271, 282, 286, 319, 327
measurement, 51
meat, 187, 282
media, 77, 93
mediation, 139, 142
medical, xxviii, xxix, xxx, 12, 15, 32, 57, 62, 76, 80, 136, 142, 146, 147, 148, 149, 150, 151, 161, 185, 218, 225, 294
medical science, 147
medication, 68
medicine, xxix, xxx, 37, 111, 135, 136, 137, 138, 139, 142, 144, 145, 146, 147, 148, 149, 150, 151, 152, 202, 250, 324
Mediterranean, 29
melody, 174, 255, 295
melt, 97, 161, 287
melting, xxiii, 167, 200, 271, 282
melts, 235
membership, 44, 46
Mencius, 12, 124, 127, 163, 164, 173, 175, 177, 178, 180, 181, 188, 189, 192, 219, 231, 239, 250, 266, 271, 285, 296, 297, 300, 310, 314, 315, 316, 317, 324
mental disorder, 56, 67
mental health, 71, 75, 76, 78
mental illness, 55, 56, 201
mentor, 76
merchandise, 230
Merleau-Ponty, 119, 120, 121, 125, 126, 127, 131, 132
metaphor, 111
meteor, 311
meter, 255
methodological implications, 61
methodology, xviii, 52, 61, 62, 71, 78, 79, 81
Mexico, 3, 6
microcosms, 265, 269, 275, 276, 277
Middle East, 23, 29
migration, 36
military, 12, 111, 159, 183, 206, 209, 314, 317, 322
mind-body, 135, 136, 139
Minneapolis, 50
mission, 75, 78, 282, 310, 311
missions, 38
misunderstanding, 113, 114, 115, 117, 174, 280
misuse, 49
mixing, 100
models, 36, 37, 71, 72, 91, 235, 236

modernism, 53
modernity, xviii, 103, 104, 114, 203, 240, 321
modus operandi, xiv, xxix, 104, 109, 111, 117, 161, 165, 168, 182, 186, 195, 198, 204, 253, 272, 278, 279
mold, 274
molecules, 155
momentum, 30, 32, 89
money laundering, 11, 41, 49
monopoly, 98
morality, 106, 108
Morocco, 29, 30, 31
mortality, 7, 14
mosquitoes, 218
Mozambique, 7, 30, 31
multidimensional, 167
multinational corporations, 10, 11
muscles, 207
museums, 216
musicians, ix
mutuality, 112, 114, 159, 267, 274, 290
myopia, 109
mythology, 96

N

Namibia, 31
naming, 123, 129, 167, 190, 240, 248
nation states, 92, 93
national borders, 18, 31, 71
national debt, 285
NATO, 206, 285
natural disaster, 38, 48, 206
natural laws, 156, 201, 292
natural resources, xvii, 18
natural science, 201, 241, 262, 267, 273, 307, 314, 321, 322, 325
natural sciences, 201, 314
negative consequences, 92
negative emotions, 66
negativity, 121
neglect, 195, 203
negotiating, 286
negotiation, 38
nervous system, 142
Netherlands, 317
networking, 29, 33, 309
neutral, 43, 115
New South Wales, 50, 51
New Zealand, 48, 52, 54, 167
next generation, xx, 275
NGOs, 35, 36, 38, 39, 40, 41, 42, 43, 44, 45, 46, 47, 48, 49, 50, 51, 54

Nicaragua, 9
Nietzsche, 318
Nigeria, 9, 26, 27
Nixon, Richard, 10
nonprofit organizations, 9
North Africa, 29, 30
North America, 23, 28
North Sea, 131
Norway, 10

O

obedience, 218
objectivity, 74, 262, 311, 319, 325
obstacles, 175, 253
oceans, 218, 223, 227, 273
OECD, 22, 23, 33, 34, 46, 53
officials, 46
oil, 6, 218
old age, 294
one dimension, 195
opacity, 10
open heart surgery, 185, 248
open-mindedness, 80, 115
openness, viii, 73, 78, 253
operations, 10, 47, 80, 229
opportunities, 37, 39, 44, 52, 73
oppression, 178
organ, 158, 310
organism, 156
Organization for Economic Cooperation and Development, 53
organize, 56, 76
otherness, 292
outreach, 53
outsourcing, 13
overlap, 155, 157, 270
overpopulation, 277
oversight, 9
ownership, 11, 49
oxygen, 126, 156

P

Pacific, 23, 29
pain, viii, xxi, xxv, xxx, 4, 6, 11, 12, 56, 63, 71, 80, 96, 110, 116, 159, 168, 185, 201, 203, 207, 209, 216, 218, 222, 231, 234, 235, 236, 244, 245, 246, 247, 248, 249, 250, 258, 260, 261, 277, 278, 280, 281, 287
painters, 323, 324
pairing, 211, 247
palate, 164, 316

pancreas, 142
panic disorder, 68
parallel, 58, 121, 125, 190, 200, 231, 247, 269, 305, 314, 325
parental care, 269
parents, xv, xvi, xix, xxiii, xxv, 12, 67, 161, 175, 182, 192, 198, 202, 203, 216, 223, 235, 236, 257, 258, 285, 293, 295, 309
participant observation, 39
participants, 76, 78
particle physics, 31
patents, 21, 23
pathology, 136, 138, 149
patriotism, 322
PCT, 23, 24, 25, 34
peace, xxvii, 99, 165, 226, 227, 286
pectoralis major, 142
pedagogy, 274
peer review, 20
perfectionism, 97
performers, xv, xix, 184, 185, 188, 253, 277
perpetration, 12, 192
perseverance, 77
personal life, 188, 225
personal relations, 44
personal relationship, 44
personality, 315
personhood, 295
persuasion, 15, 299
Perth, 50
pharmaceutical, 144
pharmaceutics, 144, 147
pharmacological treatment, 57, 67
pharmacology, 147
pharmacotherapy, 57
phenomenology, 119, 120, 295
Philadelphia, 231
phobia, 68
physical health, 63
physical laws, 225
physics, 31, 267, 323
physiological mechanisms, 62
physiology, 79, 294
piano, 228, 304, 305, 306, 310, 325
Picasso, 62
pigs, 98
pipeline, 29
pitch, 220, 221
plants, xxiv, 186, 218
platform, 90, 92, 123
Plato, xxix, 86, 94, 95, 126, 180, 186, 257, 261, 272, 276, 277, 294, 301, 302, 307, 320
plausibility, 241

340 Index

playing, xv, xix, xxiii, 19, 44, 64, 171, 177, 235, 240, 241, 268, 297, 310, 316, 326
poetry, ix, xiii, xxix, 129, 161, 181, 184, 205, 223, 237, 239, 249, 253, 254, 255, 256, 268, 284, 286, 288, 292, 296, 297, 298, 306, 324
poison, 148, 149, 218, 272, 276
policy, 26, 30, 32, 36, 39, 41, 45, 47, 48, 49, 50, 90
policy choice, 47
policy issues, 36
policy makers, 48
political enemies, 209
political ideologies, 46
political instability, 38
political party, 46
political power, 43
political problems, 48
political system, 43
politics, 36, 43, 44, 50, 51, 90, 98, 105, 106, 108, 189, 290
pollution, 91, 215
ponds, 221, 275, 276
pools, 124
poor performance, 24
population, 3, 5, 14, 23, 28, 38, 40, 72
population control, 14
population density, 38
populism, xxvii
Portugal, 27
post-industrial society, 36
postmodernism, 316
potential benefits, 74
poverty, x, xxi, 3, 4, 5, 6, 7, 8, 9, 10, 13, 14, 15, 16, 18, 19, 32, 37, 38, 39, 41, 42, 47, 51, 52, 53, 54, 91, 92, 98, 172, 220, 282, 311
poverty alleviation, 10
poverty reduction, 18, 32, 37
power relations, 41, 46
practical knowledge, 42
pragmatism, 189, 305
praxis, 149, 151, 189, 211, 212, 215, 266, 270, 271, 299, 305, 315
prayer, 303
precedents, 206, 240, 290
pregnancy, 67
preparation, 40
preservation, xvii, 223
presidency, 115, 310, 311
President, 310, 312
prestige, 15, 74, 96
prevention, 58, 59
primacy, 87, 88
primary school, 7
principles, 74, 107, 161, 162

private banks, 42
private sector, 10, 48
privatization, 6, 51, 230
probability, 156
probe, 177, 242, 244, 307
problem-solving, 104
producers, 40, 41, 42, 44, 45, 47, 48
professionals, xxx, 72, 76, 78, 80
profit, xv, 42, 91, 122, 137, 179, 230
profiteering, xiv, 215
prognosis, 19
project, 26, 27, 30, 41, 48, 54, 59, 77, 128, 205, 221, 225, 226
proliferation, 284
propagation, 11, 12
property rights, 23
prosperity, x, xix, xxviii, 4, 9, 12, 13, 14, 15, 159, 211, 218, 282, 295, 310
protection, xvi, 12, 53
psychoanalysis, 66, 68, 198
psychological problems, 60
psychologist, 60, 62, 63, 66, 74
psychology, 50, 60, 61, 62, 64, 66, 68, 69, 71, 72, 73, 74, 75, 76, 78, 79, 81, 198, 293, 294, 295, 300, 319
psychopharmacology, 80, 294
psychoses, 61
psychotherapy, 57, 59, 60, 61, 62, 66, 67, 68, 69, 80
public administration, 48
public goods, 37
public health, 8
public interest, 51
public opinion, xxvi, 205
public service, 48
publishing, 20, 181
punishment, 269
purity, 163, 235, 322

Q

qualitative research, 77
quality of life, 37, 115
quantification, 74, 294
query, 178, 305, 307, 319
questioning, 125, 166, 183, 207, 209, 210
quotas, 42

R

race, 207
racing, 141, 317
racism, 220, 249
radar, 26

radiation, 206
radio, 201
rash, 304
rationality, 60, 88, 107, 121, 301, 302, 307
reactions, xxv, 46, 297
reading, xx, xxiv, xxix, 76, 90, 173, 183, 201, 297, 314, 316, 318
real time, 89, 90
real wage, 37
reality, xxvii, 37, 65, 66, 74, 75, 81, 86, 88, 90, 91, 92, 122, 139, 187, 197, 262, 302, 307, 312
reasoning, 66, 113, 204, 234, 241, 301, 309
recall, 294
reciprocity, 15, 164, 210, 279, 280
recognition, xxx, 18, 31, 38, 98, 208, 209, 305, 324
recommendations, 81
reconstruction, 9, 15, 164
recycling, xxii
Red Sea, 259
redistribution, 41
reductionism, 315
reflectivity, 248
reflexivity, 248
reform, 37, 39, 47, 50
reforms, 48
regionalism, 206
rehabilitation, 59
rehearsing, 210, 247
reinforcement, 144
rejection, 66, 113, 114, 185, 230
relativity, 140, 141, 292
relaxation, 57, 58
relevance, 74, 77, 199
reliability, 39, 77
relief, 5, 7, 8, 9, 15, 165
religion, xxv, 88, 105, 108, 267, 269
renaissance, 274
rent, 43
repair, 97, 181, 225
replication, 40, 184
reputation, 9
requirements, 55, 77, 262
research institutions, 29
researchers, 22, 28, 31, 59, 77, 78
resistance, 52
resolution, 71, 114, 207
resources, xvii, 11, 13, 18, 19, 20, 21, 22, 29, 32, 37, 38, 41, 43, 44, 77, 111, 182, 206, 207, 219, 293
respiration, 140, 142, 150
response, 16, 36, 45, 72, 74, 121, 161, 191, 192, 315, 319
restaurants, 76, 271, 277, 317
restructuring, 8, 58

revenue, 10, 43
rhythm, xxii, 174, 177, 184, 189, 192, 232, 233, 253, 254, 255, 284, 286, 296, 297, 298, 299, 300, 309, 323, 325, 327
righting, 167, 266, 315, 324
rights, 4, 23, 37, 249
risk, 48, 79, 96, 176, 202, 227, 290
risks, 72, 74, 75, 79, 106, 174, 175, 271
root, 14, 16, 99, 138, 163, 203, 215, 216, 219, 226, 231, 246, 247, 276, 279, 319, 324
roots, 15, 47, 74
routes, 9, 245
routines, 201, 235, 273, 306, 311, 327
rowing, 259
rules, xxiii, 104, 116
Russia, 3, 99
Rwanda, 30, 31

S

safety, 46
sanctions, 295
SAP, 6
Saudi Arabia, 3
savings, 46
scaling, 39
schema, 301
scholarship, 94, 130, 136, 317, 324
school, xxvi, 7, 15, 18, 19, 61, 67, 111, 147, 149, 210, 296, 316
school enrollment, 7
schooling, 7, 310
science, xxiii, 17, 18, 20, 22, 62, 74, 75, 80, 94, 108, 111, 136, 147, 149, 157, 186, 191, 229, 241, 262, 267, 271, 273, 292, 294, 295, 306, 307, 314, 315, 319, 321, 322, 325
scientific publications, 21, 22, 25
secretion, 142
security, xxix, xxx, 37, 53, 232
seed, xv, 15, 182, 246, 259
seedlings, 79, 182, 218
self-assessment, 48
self-awareness, 292
self-consciousness, 324, 325
self-destruction, 112, 222
self-identity, 201, 244, 256
self-interest, 43
self-reflection, 66, 292
self-repair, 225, 226
self-sufficiency, 107, 109, 110, 112, 113
self-understanding, 61
seller, 19
sellers, xxv, 230

semiconductors, 33
senses, xxii, xxix, 65, 88, 106, 108, 177, 178, 241, 242, 259, 267, 306, 315
sensing, 255
sensitivity, 12, 79, 80, 165, 175, 179, 185, 189, 280, 286, 318, 320
sensory experience, 301, 308, 309, 325
service provider, 28
services, 6, 7, 9, 10, 14, 18, 28, 29, 31, 38, 40, 41, 47, 48, 49, 71, 91, 218, 220
sex, xix, xxi, xxiii, 216, 280
shade, 306
shame, xiv, 260, 321
shape, 4, 5, 104, 105, 116, 121, 123, 126, 129, 131, 189, 196, 197, 199, 201, 203, 210, 232, 252, 273, 274, 289, 291, 295, 296, 307, 308, 309, 310, 315
sheep, 7
shock, 52, 105, 178, 228, 256, 278, 286
shores, 64
shortage, 14, 143
showing, viii, xxix, 25, 95, 173, 193, 200, 209, 211, 230, 239, 280
sibling, 207
siblings, xix, 67, 223, 228
signs, 156
silver, xxiii, 95, 206, 248, 310
skeleton, 165
skin, 7, 79, 266, 279, 318, 319
slavery, 92, 115
sludge, xxiii, 234, 268, 277
smoking, 115, 219
social capital, 43, 45, 50, 51, 52, 53
social change, 37, 45, 49, 53, 78
social consequences, 33
social development, 45, 47, 49
social exclusion, 40
social injustices, 205
social integration, 40
social justice, 81
social life, 49
social movements, 54
social network, 43, 53
social norms, 294
social order, 122
social participation, 40
social phobia, 68
social policy, 50
social problems, 92
social psychology, 50
social relations, 36
social security, xxix
social welfare, 37
social workers, 43, 225

socialism, 91
socialization, xxx, 105
society, 4, 9, 15, 20, 36, 44, 45, 48, 49, 52, 63, 105, 107, 148, 156, 172, 205, 267, 285
sociology, 33, 294
Socrates, x, xxix, 4, 88, 96, 99, 161, 164, 165, 166, 247, 248, 276, 285, 318, 319
solution, vii, xxviii, 4, 5, 6, 8, 14, 15, 16, 28, 83, 89, 93, 95, 103, 104, 106, 113, 114, 127
Somalia, 31
somatic nervous system, 142
South Africa, 3, 19, 21, 26, 27, 29, 30, 31, 33, 81
South America, 26, 28
South Asia, 27, 33, 37, 50, 51, 52
South Korea, 3
Southeast Asia, 203, 274
sovereignty, 37
soy bean, 14
space-time, 89, 92
Spain, 49
specialization, 36, 74
species, 162, 192, 217, 225, 289, 326
specific thinking, 157, 175
speculation, 172, 265, 269
speech, 53, 128, 311
spending, 7, 16
spin, 228, 234, 272, 299, 300
spine, 222
spontaneity, 63, 65, 310, 316, 320
Spring, xx, 4, 12, 91, 122
sprouting, xxii, 287
stability, 253
staff members, 39, 40, 41, 44, 45, 47, 48
stakeholders, 38, 39
stallion, 301
standardization, 114
stars, 95, 157, 228
starvation, xxi, 14, 277
state, 18, 21, 22, 29, 30, 36, 38, 43, 48, 51, 90, 107, 108, 123, 160, 223, 274, 300
states, 20, 37, 48, 51, 52, 90, 92, 93, 111, 128
statistics, 220
statutes, 129
stock, 6
stomach, 140, 141, 142, 150, 250
storms, 217, 221, 283, 300
story-hearing, 196, 200, 202
story-notions, ix
storytelling, ix, xviii, 160, 187, 195, 196, 197, 199, 200, 201, 202, 257, 261, 283, 299, 316
story-thinking, ix, 157, 158, 160, 162, 238, 302, 303, 318, 319, 323
stress, 59, 101, 150, 195, 204, 246, 291

stressors, 67
stretching, 114, 260
stroke, 159
structure, xvi, xxi, xxii, 11, 43, 44, 51, 59, 62, 73, 88, 94, 161, 162, 180, 201, 220, 291
style, ix, 56, 79, 121, 125, 129, 149, 151, 152, 157, 174, 184, 188, 237, 238, 295, 317
Styles, 157, 159, 310
subjectivity, 113, 188, 295, 299, 311
sub-Saharan Africa, 19, 21, 28, 30
subscribers, 28
Sudan, 3, 27, 30, 31
suicide, 96, 164, 202, 203, 212, 222, 245, 249, 254, 262, 292, 293
Sun, vii, xxviii, 83, 94, 95, 103, 111, 227, 282, 321, 324
supervision, 129, 132
surplus, 143
survival, vii, 60, 106, 195, 203, 207, 218, 219, 225, 249, 269, 289
sustainability, 40, 46, 47, 50, 51, 52, 54
sustainable development, 42, 44
sweat, 218, 308
Switzerland, 10, 12, 32, 34
sympathy, 246
symptoms, 57, 58, 61, 143, 148, 149
synthesis, 108, 109, 110, 136, 137, 139, 144, 147, 149, 150, 151, 159, 163, 164, 257
systematic desensitization, 57

T

tactics, 15
Taiwan, xxviii, 3, 78, 103, 137, 171, 195, 203, 215, 231, 237, 258, 265, 269, 274, 289, 290, 310, 311, 312, 317, 318
talent, 300
Tanzania, 7, 9, 30, 31
target, 40, 41, 48, 78, 172
tax evasion, 10, 12
tax system, 11
taxation, 218
taxes, 11
taxpayers, 13
teachers, xxv, 7, 43, 49, 183
teams, 31
techniques, 11, 48, 57, 61, 64, 65, 66, 105, 108, 136, 148, 149, 223, 294
technologies, 74, 89, 90, 91, 92, 148, 202, 206
technology, x, 18, 19, 20, 21, 22, 27, 34, 36, 41, 46, 48, 51, 73, 91, 92, 95, 98, 108, 111, 114, 115, 116, 136, 145, 147, 190, 227, 271
temperature, 156

tension, 57, 103, 128, 155, 156, 159, 163, 165, 242, 243, 245, 248, 251
tensions, 47, 164
territory, 79, 131, 298
terrorists, 12, 282
tertiary education, 19, 30
testing, 31, 66
textbook, 80
textiles, 92
Thailand, 321
therapeutic approaches, 59, 67
therapeutic change, 63
therapeutics, 146
therapist, 61
therapy, vii, xxviii, 1, 57, 58, 59, 60, 61, 62, 63, 64, 65, 66, 67, 68, 69, 97
Third World, 6
Thomas Kuhn, 202, 262
thoughts, viii, 55, 56, 61, 65, 129, 145, 147, 180, 183, 227, 237, 240, 318, 324
threats, 47, 48, 103, 104, 106, 113, 114, 117, 206, 245
Tibet, 323
time frame, 41, 89
tobacco, 8, 115, 219
toddlers, 212
tones, 141, 156
tonic, 232, 244
tooth, 250
topology, 29
tornadoes, 303
toxicity, 144
toxin, 219
toys, 95, 200, 223, 230, 252
trade, x, 11, 13, 18, 36, 37, 43, 47, 91, 107, 231
trade agreement, 47
traditionalism, 318
traditions, 41, 74, 75, 105, 119
trafficking, 196, 270
trainees, 76
training, 41, 45, 48, 68, 72, 73, 74, 76, 77, 140, 142, 149, 150, 151, 210
training programs, 72, 74, 76, 77
transaction costs, 38
transactions, 78, 107, 230
transcendence, 112, 113, 211, 212, 267, 268
transfer of money, 9
transference, 172, 173, 182, 183, 184, 188, 190
transformation, 36, 42, 52, 113, 116, 295
transformations, 229, 274
translation, xxviii, xxix, 64, 78, 81, 106, 124, 125, 128, 129, 130, 131, 171, 172, 173, 174, 175, 176,

177, 178, 179, 180, 182, 183, 184, 185, 186, 187, 188, 189, 190, 191, 192, 286
transmission, 136, 182, 183, 188
transnational corporations, 18, 23
transparency, 9, 10, 11
transportation, 92
Treasury, 296
treaties, 107
treatment, 8, 55, 56, 57, 58, 59, 61, 65, 67, 68, 69, 234, 301, 324
trial, 179, 203, 256, 266
triangulation, 39
triceps, 142
Tse-tung, Mao, 178
Turkey, 3, 10
turtle, 220
twist, 96, 97, 127, 175, 176, 248, 297

U

UK, viii, 10, 27, 32, 48, 50, 51, 52, 53, 323
UN, 19, 20, 31, 206, 285
UNDP, 19
UNESCO, 35, 50
unhappiness, 97
unification, 269
uniform, 90, 92, 96, 97, 101, 115, 117
unique features, 78
United, 3, 5, 9, 11, 19, 20, 21, 34, 47, 50, 52, 54, 55, 71, 72, 73, 75, 76, 81, 86, 181, 240, 321
United Kingdom, 3, 47, 321
United Nations, 5, 9, 20, 21, 34, 50, 52, 54
United Nations XE "United Nations" Development Program, 5
United States, 3, 11, 21, 55, 71, 72, 73, 75, 76, 81, 86, 181, 240, 321
universality, vii, x, xviii, xxv, 87, 93, 94, 96, 109, 111, 157, 158, 159, 162, 165, 199, 200, 239, 240, 252, 257, 281, 286, 293
universe, 58, 121, 126, 135, 136, 139, 142, 149, 163, 185, 189, 292, 323
universities, 17, 18, 19, 23, 24, 25, 29, 31, 34, 77
urban, 39, 40, 218
USA, x, xxvi, xxviii, xxx, 3, 6, 7, 9, 10, 13, 17, 51, 55, 71, 74, 76, 77, 78, 80, 85, 171, 178, 183, 208, 209, 253, 258, 274, 278, 279, 294, 321

V

vaccinations, 7
vacuum, 103
vapor, 124, 312
variations, 275, 284

varieties, xiv, 100, 188, 321
vehicles, 39
vein, 294
Venezuela, 321
vibration, 252, 253, 255, 297, 323
violence, 178, 206, 269, 278
viscera, 231
vision, xxx, 62, 74, 81, 89, 90, 91, 92, 93, 99, 107, 121, 157, 162, 181, 208, 262, 268, 286, 317, 320
visions, 90, 91
visualization, 28
vocabulary, 282, 317
voting, 44

W

wages, xxvii, 37
Wales, 50, 51
walking, 115, 217, 224, 228, 278, 313
war, xxvii, 7, 38, 45, 51, 111, 165, 227
warts, xxv
Washington, 67, 68, 247, 253, 314
Washington, George, 247
waste, 91, 235, 282, 300
water, ix, xxx, 5, 7, 29, 62, 100, 122, 126, 129, 156, 161, 172, 223, 233, 235, 241, 267, 277, 299, 326
weakness, 42
wealth, 14, 92, 100, 310, 311
wear, 99
web, 19, 28, 306, 310, 325
welfare, 5, 9, 11, 16, 37, 48, 50, 216
welfare state, 48
wells, 261
West Africa, 27
Western countries, 38
whales, 271
wheezing, 255, 276, 291
whistle blower, 12
WHO, 20
wholesale, xv, 39
wilderness, 217, 219, 233
windows, 226, 286
withdrawal, 142, 241, 306
witnesses, 43
wood, 128, 294
workers, xxvi, 8, 43, 47, 49, 178, 225
workforce, 17, 19, 31
World Bank, 6, 7, 9, 39, 54, 91
World Health Organization, 34
world order, 91
World Trade Organization, 37
worldview, 73, 136, 291

worldwide, x, xi, xii, xiii, xiv, xvi, xviii, xix, xx, xxvi, xxxi, 5, 8, 9, 10, 11, 12, 13, 14, 16, 18, 23, 88, 89, 91, 93, 97, 98, 99, 100, 107, 113, 115, 165, 198, 199, 200, 203, 204, 205, 206, 207, 210, 212, 219, 220, 223, 233, 238, 239, 243, 257, 258, 260, 270, 288, 298, 314, 317
worry, 56, 57, 271, 285, 300
WTO, 37

Y

Yale University, 20, 32, 54, 222, 240, 250, 267, 323
yang, 86, 123, 126, 131, 143, 144, 146, 150
yarn, 201
yield, viii, xxi, xxv, 13, 112, 143
yin, 86, 123, 126, 131, 143, 144, 146, 147, 148, 149
yin-yang, 143, 146, 149
yuan, 128, 131, 143, 179, 317

Z

Zimbabwe, 30, 31
Zulu, 19, 34, 221